JewishGen and the Yizkor Books in Print Project

This book has been published by the **Yizkor Books in Print Project,** as part of the **Yizkor Book Project** of **JewishGen, Inc.**

    JewishGen, Inc. is a non-profit organization founded in 1987 as a resource for Jewish genealogy. Its website (www.jewishgen.org) serves as an international clearing house and resource center to assist individuals who are researching the history of their Jewish families and the places where they lived. JewishGen provides databases, facilitates discussion groups, and coordinates projects relating to Jewish genealogy and the history of the Jewish people. In 2003, JewishGen became an affiliate of the **Museum of Jewish Heritage - A Living Memorial to the Holocaust** in New York.

    The **JewishGen Yizkor Book Project** was organized to make more widely known the existence of Yizkor (Memorial) Books written by survivors and former residents of various Jewish communities throughout the world. Later, volunteers connected to the different destroyed communities began cooperating to have these books translated from the original language—usually Hebrew or Yiddish—into English, thus enabling a wider audience to have access to the valuable information contained within them. As each chapter of these books was translated, it was posted on the JewishGen website and made available to the general public.

    The **Yizkor Books in Print Project** began in 2011 as an initiative to print and publish Yizkor Books that had been fully translated, so that hard copies would be available for purchase by the descendants of these communities and also by scholars, universities, synagogues, libraries, and museums.

    These Yizkor books have been produced almost entirely through the volunteer effort of researchers from around the world, assisted by donations from private individuals. The books are printed and sold at near cost, so as to make them as affordable as possible. Our goal is to make this important genre of Jewish literature and history available in English in book form, so that people can have the personal histories of their ancestral towns on their bookshelves for themselves and for their children and grandchildren.

Lance Ackerfeld, Yizkor Book Project Manager
Joel Alpert, Yizkor Books in Print Project Coordinator

BRZEZIN
BRZEZINY

Our Shul

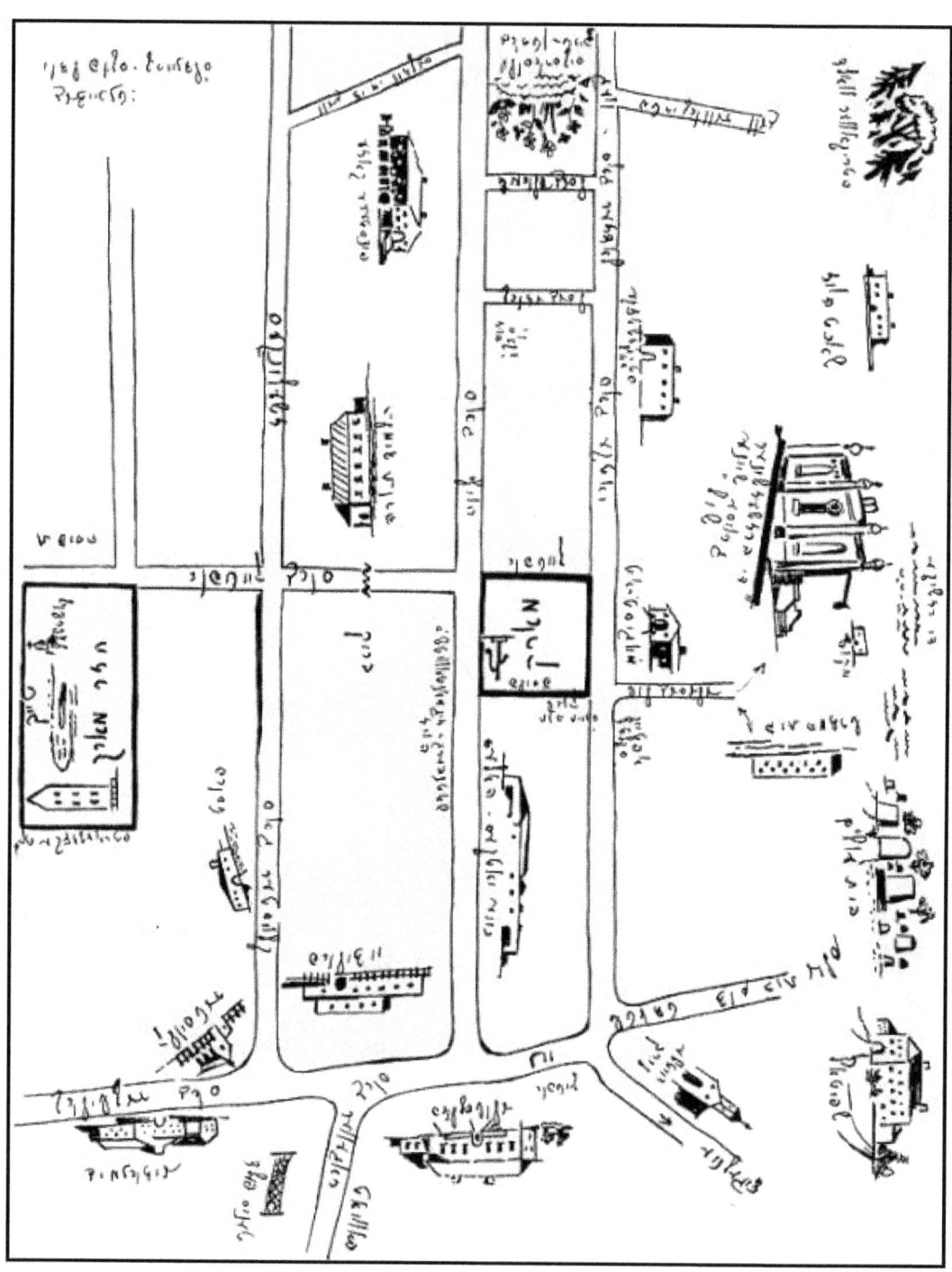

Map of Brzezin

BRZEZIN
Memorial Book

Edited by A. Alperin and N. Summer

Translated from the Yiddish by Renee Miller

English Edition Coordinated and Edited by Fay Vogel Bussgang

Published by JewishGen, Inc., New York, NY
An Affiliate of
The Museum of Jewish Heritage - A Living Memorial to the Holocaust

*This translation is dedicated to Fay's father, Joseph Herschel Vogel,
born in Brzeziny in 1890 as Hersz Bursztajn*

Brzezin Memorial Book

English Translation copyright © 2012 by JewishGen, Inc.

All rights reserved. This book may not be reproduced, in whole or in part, including illustrations in any form (beyond that copying permitted by Sections 107 and 108 of the U.S. Copyright Law and except by reviewers for public press), without written permission from the publisher.

First Printing: February 2012

JewishGen, Inc.
An Affiliate of the Museum of Jewish Heritage
A Living Memorial to the Holocaust
36 Battery Place
New York, NY 10280

JewishGen, Inc. is not responsible for inaccuracies or omissions in the original work and makes no representations regarding the accuracy of this translation. Digital images of the original book's contents can be seen online at the New York Public Library Web site.

Printed in the United States of America by Lightning Source, Inc.

Library of Congress Control Number (LCCN): 2012930457

ISBN: 0-978-0-9764759-4-1 (hard cover: 466 pages, alk. paper)

**Originally published in Yiddish by the
BRZEZINER BOOK COMMITTEE**
NEW YORK — ISRAEL
1961

New York

Jacob D. Berg, chairman
Joseph Shaw (Shaibowicz), secretary
Abraham Rozenberg
Fishel Maliniak
S. Sobowinsky
Sam Fox
Jehuda Fuks
Louis Hauser
Ruth Hauser
Melech Herszenberg
Izzy Rozenblum*
Nachum (Nathan) Summer**

California

Joseph Diamond
Roda Chernick
Willi Newman
Max Segal

Chicago

Louis Sanberg

Israel

David Lencicki*
Aron Mendlewicz
Mojsze Har-Jaffe (Szajnberg)
David Poliwoda
J. Erlich
Monisz Gutkind
Szlama Pinczewski
Fiszel Benkel
A. Fogel**

Canada

Abraham Abramowicz

Paris

Bernard Kujawski

Australia

Fela Tushinsky

Originally printed in the United States by
SHULSINGER BROS. LINOTYPING & PUBLISHING CO.
21 East 4th Street, New York 3, N.Y.

---

* Deceased at time of original publication.
**Name included in the English page of the Book Committee in the back of the book.

Book Committee Seated in the front row from right to left: Abraham Rozenberg, Fishel Maliniak, J. D. Berg, A. Alperin (editor), Nachum Summer (associate editor), Standing from the right: Joseph Shaibowicz (Shaw), S. Sobowinsky, Sam Fox, Jehuda Fuks, Ruth Hauser, Louis Hauser, Joseph Diamond, A. Rozenblum, Melech Herszenberg

TABLE OF CONTENTS

INTRODUCTION

	Original page #	English page #
Acknowledgments for the English Edition		xiii
Fay Vogel Bussgang: Foreword to the English Edition		xv
Jacob David Berg: Our Book	xi	xvii
A. Alperin: *Sefer Brzezin* (A Short Introduction)	xiii	xix
Jacob Pat: About *Sefer Brzezin* and the Destroyed Town of Brzezin	xvii	xxiii

PART ONE: BRZEZIN AND BRZEZINER JEWS

	Original page #	English page #
Joseph Shaibowicz: Brzeziny in History	3	3
Aron Fogel: Past Generations	21	32
Jechiel Erlich: The Last Kadesh	31	47
David Lencicki: Brzeziner Tailors	40	61
S. Pinczewski: Brzeziner Rabbis and Hasidim	44	67
Jacob David Berg: The Jews of My Generation	46	70
Jacob David Berg: Our *Melamdim* [Teachers]	56	84
Melech Herszenberg: Benjamin Melamed	59	89
Aron Mendlewicz: Two *Mishpokhes* [Families]	61	92
Mojsze Frank: A Bundle of Memories	69	104
Izrael Kahn: A Brzeziner Jew—A Grand-Vizier in Turkey	72	109
List of Brzeziner Jews Who Were Contributors to Keren Kayemeth in 1913	75	113
Joseph Shaibowicz: Toward a History of the Brzeziner *Kehile* [Community]	78	118
The Great Synagogue in Brzezin	84	127

PART TWO: BETWEEN PROSPERITY AND DESTRUCTION

	Original page #	English page #
Fiszel Maliniak: Brzezin Between Two World Wars	87	131
Fiszel Maliniak: Election of Rabbis in Brzezin	97	146
Abraham Rozenberg: Brzezin's Way of Life	98	148
Abraham Abramowicz: The Workers Movement in Brzezin	104	157
Jechiel Erlich: A Stroll Through Our Shtetl	108	163
Icchak Janasowicz: My Gate to the Great World	109	165
Welwel Rozenblum: Two Victims: Memories of the First World War	112	169
Left Poale Zion in Brzezin in 1931	115	174
Herzl Society in Brzezin	116	175
Chaim-Icek Grynfeld, *z"l*	117	178
Abraham Rozenberg: Jewish Sports in Brzezin	118	179
Welwel Rozenblum: Icchak Kacenelson in Brzezin	122	184
Malka Rose (Rozenblum): Yiddish Theater in Our Shtetl	124	187
Nachum Summer: Poems	126	190
My Shtetl Brzezin, Our *Besmedresh*, A Tribute to Judel the Watercarrier, The *Oyel* of Reb Szymon Bal-Rakhmones		
Nachum Jud: *Shnayder-Yinglekh* [Tailor Apprentices]	130	198

PART THREE: ON THE RUINS OF OUR SHTETL

The First Victim	133	201
Aron Fogel: The First Shocking Encounter	134	202
Dr. S[tanisław] Warhaft: I Saw the Destruction of Our Shtetl	135	204
Abraham Blankiet-Sulkowicz: Destruction of Brzezin	140	212
David Tuszyński: There Once Was a Jewish Shtetl Brzezin	144	218
Dora Zagon-Winer: I Saw the *Khurbn* [Destruction]	147	223
Chaim-Lajb Fuks: Our Two Writer-Martyrs	149	226
1) Jacob-Ber Gips	149	226
2) Melech Fogel	152	230
Genia Brandschaft: The Wretched Cry	154	233
Rywka Tajczer: In the Tragic Years	154	234
Matseyve [Gravestone] in Bergen-Belsen	155	235
Rywka Hendler-Gocial: The Brzeziner Jewish Community During the Time of the Ghetto	156	236
Rhoda Hendrik-Karpatkin: Visiting Ancestors' Graves in Brzezin in 1960	157	238
Jehuda Fuks: Brzeziner Jews in the Wide World	160	242
Jews in Brzezin Before and After the Destruction	162	245

PART FOUR: BRZEZINERS IN AMERICA

Nachum Summer: Our *Landsmanshaft* [Society of Fellow Townspeople]	165	249
Nachum Summer and Fiszel Maliniak: Relief Work and *Shikkun Brzezin* [Brzezin Housing Project] in Israel	182	275
Brzeziners and Lodzers in California	193	289
Lajbuś Lehrer: Jankiel Chaim-Icek's	195	292
Mordke Dantsis: Nachum Summer, the Brzeziner	196	294
Aszer Grossman: A Letter From a Landsman	197	296

PART FIVE: BRZEZINERS IN ISRAEL

Mojsze Har-Jaffe (Szajnberg): The First Brzeziner *Chalutzim* [Pioneers]	201	301
David Poliwoda: Our *Landslayt* in the *Yidisher Medine* [Jewish State]	203	304
How the *Shikkun Brzezin* was Built	207	310
Fallen in the Defense of Israel	213	316
G. Waldman: David Lencicki, *z"l*	216	320
The *Matseyve* [Tombstone] on Mt. Zion	217	322
Our Leaders in Israel	219	325
Photographs of Brzeziner Jews in Paris	222	330
Heartfelt Thanks	226	335
Jacob David Berg: My Father, Chaim-Icek Ajnbinder (Nisenberg)	227	336

PART SIX: YIZKOR [MEMORIAL] SECTION

Z. Segalowicz: Don't Forget My Soul	229	341
Alphabetical List of Martyrs	231	344
Pictures and Memorials	241	361

Monument erected at the cemetery of the New York *landslayt* as a memorial to the martyrs

Acknowledgments for the English Edition

This English translation of the original Brzeziny Yizkor Book has been a labor of love for both the coordinator-editor, Fay Bussgang, and the translator, Renee Miller. Fay, whose father was born in Brzeziny, wished to make the Brzeziny Yizkor book accessible to younger generations who did not know Yiddish, the language in which the book was written. As an avid genealogist, she was eager to know more about the world from which her father came and anxious to share that knowledge with others interested in Brzeziny. Renee was prompted to join this undertaking by a love of the Yiddish language, which she first learned as a child and then studied as an adult. She had no connection to Brzeziny but was motivated by a desire to use her growing knowledge of the Yiddish language for a worthwhile project. Though strangers until brought together by JewishGen's former Yizkor Book Coordinator, Joyce Field, we worked extremely well together as a team, entirely as volunteers.

Renee translated the text from Yiddish into English. When passages in the book were obscure, she was helped by her colleagues at the YIVO Jewish Institute of Research in New York, where she was a volunteer. Fay made sure that the narrative was clearly presented and flowed smoothly. She used numerous resources in print and on the Internet to verify facts and spellings of names, places, and organizations and added explanatory footnotes. She also compiled an index of the names that appear in the book, so that future generations could find relatives without difficulty. Fay's Polish-born husband, Julian, translated Polish words and checked the text for clarity; Tamar Duke-Cohen carefully read the manuscript and made many good suggestions. Later, when publication as a book became a possibility, all the photographs were scanned, and Osnat Ramaty painstakingly enhanced them digitally. Fay then formatted the text, pictures, and captions, and Bernard Jacobson did the final proofreading. The cover was designed by Nili Goldman.

This whole undertaking would not have been possible without the vision of the staff of JewishGen, which created the Yizkor Book Project, ably managed first by Joyce Field and then by Lance Ackerfeld. The Yizkor Book Project has encouraged the translation of countless memorial books from destroyed communities and offers a means for the public to have access to these translations by posting them on the JewishGen Web site. JewishGen's new initiative, Yizkor Books in Print, headed by Joel Alpert, aims to facilitate the publication of fully translated books and is a significant addition to the Yizkor Book Project's initial mission.

We have thoroughly enjoyed working on this project, and we sincerely hope that this translation, which provides a vivid glimpse of prewar small-town Jewish Poland, will be as meaningful to others as it has been to us.

Fay Vogel Bussgang
Coordinator-Editor of English Edition

Foreword to the English Edition
Fay Vogel Bussgang

It should be noted that this published version of the Brzeziny Yizkor Book is not identical to the translation that was posted previously on the JewishGen Web site. Some changes in spelling have been made to assure internal consistency, and certain editorial changes have been made to conform with current publishing guidelines.

It should also be noted that the word Holocaust is not used anywhere in this book to describe the tragedy that befell the Jewish people of Europe, because this term did not come into common usage until after the original Yizkor book was written.

All Polish or Russian words that appeared in the original text, as well as many familiar Yiddish words, have been retained to give a flavor of the language used by the Jews of Brzeziny. The spelling of Yiddish words used is, in general, that recommended by YIVO Jewish Institute of Research. Words that appear in parentheses are part of the original text, while translations or explanations that have been added by the translator or editor are placed in square brackets. If a word is familiar or used frequently, the translation is given only the first time it appears in a section.

Throughout the book, the town is referred to by its Yiddish name, Brzezin, except in the chapter about the general history of the town, where its Polish name, Brzeziny, seemed more appropriate.

Transliterating names and surnames from one language to another is a difficult task, and, in the case of Jews from Poland, the names have passed through several language changes over time. Thus, it is difficult to ascertain which is the "right" spelling—if one exists. For the most part, names in this translation have been spelled as they most probably were in prewar Poland. This was done in order to make it easier for researchers to trace their ancestors back to Poland and find official records there. As is the custom in Poland, the feminine surname endings "cka" and "ska" have been used for women (Sawicka, Kowalska) rather than the masculine surname endings "cki" and "ski" (Sawicki, Kowalski).

For people whose names appeared only in the section written about Brzeziners in the United States, the names were spelled as they were used in the United States if this could be determined through publications of the Brzeziner Society. However, names beginning with "R-O-Z," such as Rozen and Rozman were kept in their original spelling to be consistent, even though in America some of them may have been written as Rosen or Rosman. Some examples of alternate spellings of surnames used in America are described in a footnote on page 250 in the chapter "Our Landsmanshaft" by Nachum Summer.

When looking for names of relatives, it should be kept in mind that people may have been referred to in several ways: by their given name plus their legal surname, by their given name plus their profession, by a nickname, or as the son or daughter of someone. Thus the same person may appear in the book under different names.

A simplified key to the pronunciation of Polish names is displayed on the following page; an Index of the people mentioned in the book is included at the end of the volume.

We apologize in advance for any inadvertant errors.

Simplified Key to Pronunciation:

Most letters in Polish are pronounced similarly to their English equivalents except for the following whose approximate English equivalents are given:

ą = on [nasalized] (om before b/p)	w = v
ę = en [nasalized] (em before b/p)	y = i as in fit
c = ts	ch, h = h as in Helen
i = ee	ć, ci, cz = ch
j = y	ś, si, sz = sh
ł = w	ź, zi, ż, rz = zh
ń = n as in onion	prz = psh
ó = oo/u	trz = tsh

Our Book (pp. xi–xii)

Jacob David Berg

It is a custom that a collection by a number of authors, especially a book that is dedicated to the memory of a *rebbe* [Hasidic rabbi] should have a foreword. Let me say here a few words about the history of this *yizkor* [memorial] book, which ought to be a kind of *matseyve* [gravestone] for my, your, our *shtetl*, Brzezin.

It was in the year 1950. At that time, I had traveled to Israel as the chief representative of the Benevolent Society of the Brzeziner Landslayt in America, and, as their chairman, I had the mandate to find out what would be the best way to help our brothers and sisters, the survivors who were rescued from the camps. I found out, alas, that their situation was a difficult one. Most of them lived in temporary housing, in tents, from which they had to be gotten out as fast as possible. I had a talk with some of the leaders of the *landslayt* [fellow townspeople], and it was decided that first of all, the needy—approximately forty *mishpokhes* [families]—had to be provided with a roof over their heads. A project arose to build an apartment building in Kfar-Ono and establish a community center nearby, a cultural center, for the intellectual satisfaction of the *landslayt*. The plan was that the building should carry the name of our *shtetl*, Brzezin.

The project inspired me deeply. And although I saw before me the financial difficulties, I also knew that with deep conviction, strong will, and with the first ten thousand dollars that our treasury possessed, we could begin the holy work at once. I also knew that our Brzeziner *landslayt* in America and in other lands, although most of them were not rich people, have warm hearts and brotherly feelings for all those who need help.

And with that plan I prepared to return home and influence our *landsmen* [fellow townspeople] to begin as soon as possible the great work of building. But just before my leave-taking from our *landsmen* in Israel, an additional project was born that was no less important than the apartment building or the plan for a community center. I recall how our beloved David Lencicki—who is, alas, no longer among the living—turned to me at a gathering with tears in his eyes:

> Friend Jacob, you came here as the messenger from our *landslayt* in America, and you have undertaken to fulfill a great assignment to create apartments for our brothers and a cultural center for holidays and days of mourning; but it is no small thing to create a *sefer hazikaron* [memorial book] for our Brzezin, where our parents and the generations before them lived. Brzezin, which was known as a *shnayder-shtetl* [tailoring town], had also created precious, sincere, God-fearing, virtuous Jews, scholars in Torah and in worldly learning. Let us set them a worthy monument through a *sefer*!

And when I saw that the great audience at the gathering had displayed enthusiasm and had applauded these words, I returned home to our leaders in America with the three-part plan: to build an apartment building and a community center in Israel and to begin preparing a *yizkor* book.

After a time of difficult, intense (often, alas, thankless) work, the first two, with *mazl* [luck], were completed; the apartments and the community center were built for the

Brzezin *landsmen*—buildings that were very useful for all who were in them and *nakhes* [pleasure] for those who visit Israel and meet with our *landsmen* in the apartment building.

And it may sound a little strange, but building the houses of stone and cement was easier than creating the monument on paper, the *yizkor* book. Yes, there were all kinds of difficulties on the way—material, technical. Let us forget all the difficulties today, when before us open the pages of our modest history, when we get down to reading and remembering everything and everyone that are for us loved and dear—the individuals who are with us and those who are no longer with us, above all the *kedoyshim-otehoyrim* [sainted martyrs] who have vanished with the annihilated portion of the Jewish people.

It was, as it is said, difficult work, but divine inspiration overtook all who one way or another lent a hand. *Landsmen* from all parts of the world responded with help, from Africa and Brazil, from Australia, Argentina, and Canada, from a number of cities in America, and from the land of Israel. Everyone did something for the book according to his or her means and ability. Let here, in the first rank, be remembered with *koved* [honor] and thanks our friends Nachum Summer and Joseph Shaibowicz. They worked in libraries and archives and collected information, pictures, and documents about Brzezin; they corresponded with the Jewish Historical Institute in Warsaw and researched material from the YIVO Institute for Jewish Research in New York; and they gave up their hours of rest after daily toil—all with the aim that our *Sefer Brzezin* should become something substantial, a creditable monument for our generation and the generations to come.

It should be understood that our friends and active leaders in Israel were equal partners in the holy work. They worked by researching the necessary material and information; they were with us as equals, concerned that the book should be both detailed and of the highest quality. Let us remember all the coworkers and creators of the *Sefer Brzezin*: Aron Alperin, the distinguished writer, and *landsman* Nachum Summer, who edited the *yizkor* book; the members of the Book Committee in Israel—Manny Gutkind, Mojsze Har-Jaffe, David Lencicki, of blessed memory, Jechiel Erlich, Aron Fogel, Szlama Pinczewski, and David Poliwoda. In America—Joseph Diamond, Louis Hauser, Melech Hirsh [Herszenberg], Fishel Maliniak, Nachum Summer, Abraham Rozenberg, Julius Fox, Sam Fox, and Joseph Shaibowicz.

And above all—the ten score brother and sister *landsmen* all over the world, all those who donated and contributed in advance to the *yizkor* book, thereby providing the foundation for the publishing of *Sefer Brzezin*.

To all these—a heartfelt *yasher-koyech*! [Well done!]

Jacob David Berg

Sefer Brzezin: A Short Introduction (pp. xiii–xvi)

A. Alperin

Along the dirt roads of Crown Poland [Kingdom of Poland] lies a *shtetl*, not far from Łódź [pronounced Woodge in Polish], not far from Piotrków, to the side of the railroad line. The town is Brzezin. Among *landslayt*, there is a disagreement concerning how the *shtetl* should be recorded in history. Should this *shtetl* be called Brezin, Brzezin, or Brzeziny, the way it was, or the way it certainly is now, by its Polish name?

The debate is certainly not more than for the sake of history and—to erect a *matseyve* [gravestone]. Because the *shtetl* is no more, let it be called whatever it is called now. No longer is there a Jewish Brzezin. It was erased from the Jewish map of the world, together with hundreds and thousands of *kehiles kdushes* [sacred communities] of Jews who once lived, once struggled, once created, once helped carry the golden chain of eternal Israel— and perished a violent death.

We don't even stand today at their *kvorim* [graves]. Maybe there are some graves still left, and perhaps they also have already been obliterated from the earth. The destruction is total, in the same way as the war of the Nazi murderers against the Jews was total. Today we place a collective gravestone for that which once was the Jewish *shtetl* Brzezin. Our collective gravestone is this very *sefer* [book], which will remain a memorial and which will be read by the children and grandchildren of our survivors.

We wish to announce and relate that there was in the *shtetl* of our ancestors in Brzezin a fine, genteel Jewish community. When there was a Jewish tribe in Poland of more than three million souls with their great *yikhes* [distinguished lineage]; with their rich culture; with their yeshivas [schools of advanced religious instruction] and modern schools; with their rabbis and writers; with their businesses and political leaders; with their great economic standing and deep spiritual foundations—this *shtetl* Brzezin also sparkled with Jewish life, with achievements and accomplishments for *klal yisroel* [the Jewish people].

The *shtetl* developed its own image and took on its own color in the Jewish reality in former Poland. In the beginning of the present century, you could ask all over Poland, Lithuania, and Russia about the *shtetl* Brzezin, and you would promptly receive a reply. The *shtetl* was known all over; everyone knew about the *shtetl* Brzezin. Who had created such a great and good name for this small *shtetl*? Jews and only Jews—the *tates un zeydes* [fathers and grandfathers] of the present survivors, who are widely scattered over the entire world and from whom no one is left in Brzezin itself.

The fathers and grandfathers built the Jewish *shnayder-shtetl* [tailoring town] Brzezin. The name of the *shnayder-shtetl* was carried far and wide over old Eastern Europe. Brzezin was a part of the social history of Eastern Europe, the history of industrial development and its processes. Jewish tailors maintained the economic standing and the entire importance of the *shtetl*—until the dreadful, total destruction of the Jewish *kehile* [community] and of Jewish life in Brzezin. And without the Jewish tailors there is no Brzezin, not the world famous Brzezin of many generations past—let the *shtetl* now be whatever it is.

The *tates un zeydes* from the widely scattered Jewish survivors of Brzezin—the tailors, the machinists, the merchants, the agents on commission—elevated their craft and business trade to great heights. The older generation of Brzezin tailors were genteel, Hasidic Jews who united Torah and craft into one. The younger generation joined the *maskilim* [supporters of the Enlightenment], the Zionist movement, and the national freedom organizations in Jewish society and proudly carried the name "Jew." Jewish communal life was carried out with great attention, and just as in their business life, Brzeziner Jews went beyond the borders of their *shtetl*. Brzeziner supply depots, with their connections, extended deep into Russia, to white Siberia, from where the merchants, the *kuptches,* used to come down to buy finished clothing from Brzezin. And in exactly that way, Brzezin Jewish businesses, party representatives, and cultural leaders were connected with the world leaders of the Jewish people, with the leaders of the time—with the leaders of Zionism, with the builders of the old-new Jewish homeland, with the pioneers of the Jewish *yishuvim* [settlements] in the new world and, above all, in the United States.

As luck would have it, when the terrible destruction of their old home *shtetl* came, the survivors from Brzezin, during their wanderings, received a great deal of help from *landslayt* who had built new homes and built themselves a secure existence in free America. Also Brzezin *landslayt* from Eretz Yisroel [land of Israel], immigrants from before the war who were among the builders of the Jewish homeland, hastened to help those from the *shtetl* who had been rescued. Also *landslayt* in Canada, in South America, in distant Australia responded to the call for help. Those *mishpokhes* from the *shtetl* who remained alive, the community of Jews remaining from Brzezin, worked together in the holy fraternal rescue work.

Together with the fact that Brzeziner children have made the greatest sacrifice on earth for the Jewish homeland and gave their young lives when the hour struck to free the Jewish homeland, also Brzeziner *landslayt* in America made a great effort—although it certainly cannot be compared with that of the fallen fighters—and did constructive work in the rebirth of the homeland. Brzeziner *landslayt* in America built the Brzezin apartment building, not far from Tel Aviv, where families from the survivors settled down in *heymish* [homey] surroundings, with the memories of the saintly ones lost in the complete destruction of their old home *shtetl*.

A memorial for Brzezin was erected in the Jewish homeland for generations to come. Our hope is that this memorial will be cherished in the Brzezin apartment building, together with the traditions of the martyred community of the *shtetl*. We are strong in our faith that the coming generations, the children and descendants of the survivors of the Brzezin community will retain in their memory the good name of the *kehile kdushe* of their ancestors.

* * *

We write about them all in this Brzezin book, which is now presented to the *landslayt* for all time and to the coming generations. It is a *yizkor* book and a history book. The entire life of the Brzezin *kehile* flows by in the book—from the earliest time to our days of terrible destruction; the path of ascent, development, blossoming until the decline and the completely annihilating doom; the path from the pangs of childbirth until the *umkum* [total destruction]. It is seen in the research, essays, and memoirs, written and immortalized by our own *landslayt* and passed on to the coming generations, the descendants of Brzeziner Jews, and to future historians of eradicated Polish Jewry.

It is a modest book. It does not claim to enter the sanctuary of fine literature. This was also not the assignment of the participants in the book and certainly does not have to be the aim of any publisher, nor of any author of a *yizkor* book. The publication of *Sefer Brzezin* comes from a deep inner striving of a group of *landslayt* in America and in Israel to keep alive the spiritual heritage of their destroyed former home *shtetl*. And with the publication of this book, the group of *landslayt* wanted to fulfill their sacred duty to entrust the heritage of the ancestors of the *kehile kdushe* [sacred community] *fun dor tsu dor* [from generation to generation].

We fulfilled the duty within the framework of our modest strength.

* * *

What is a *yizkor* book? It is a part of our collective effort and care to maintain the continuity, to give to the coming generations the heritage that we alone took over from our beloved *tates un zeydes*.

Only a people who have a memory have a future. It is so also with a *mishpokhe* and with the survivors of our destroyed *kehile* [community] from our old hometown.

In the memoirs, discussions, stories, and family chronicles, the readers—and we mean principally the *landslayt*—will still find in this *yizkor* book the *kehile* of Brzezin. They will remember hundreds and hundreds of names of their own friends and relatives who once created a Jewish life, carried out their part in the eternal spiritual existence of our people—and are here no longer. Many of them, the majority, were struck down before their time by the Nazi murderers, killed among the six million of our martyrs in Europe.

Their holy memory continues to live in this very book, in this very modest *matseyve* that *landslayt* alone have erected for them in the remembrances and writings in this *yizkor* book.

The memory of those who were murdered lives on in the hearts and minds of the remaining Jews of the *shtetl* on both sides of the ocean, in America and in the land of Israel—the *landslayt* who recorded their inner thoughts in eternal memory here in this modest book. And thus did they record and publish this very book—also so that the future generations, the children, the grandchildren, the great-grandchildren, and to the end of generations shall again extend the golden chain of the memory of the *kehile* from which their ancestors came. In years and years to come, we shall remember the names of our own and our dear ones who were recorded in eternal memory here and there in this *yizkor* book.

We know that our ancestors live in us. Evidence of that is this very book, written not by any professional writer, but by ordinary Jews, *landslayt*, who tell about their *shtetl* and about Jews from their *shtetl*. Our goal is that our ancestors, the holy Jews from our annihilated community, should live in the hearts and in the memory of future generations. This was our aim, and it was also our duty. This book is the result of our concern and effort. We publish this book with the hope that the coming generations will value the great concern and effort and—remember where they came from and know the responsibility that lies with them to maintain and hold dear the heritage that they have received.

* * *

The *landslayt* who recorded their memories that were published in this book wrote them down with great respect. They have done so to the best of their recollection, the way they understand and evaluate the destroyed life of their home *shtetl*. For the most part they are family chronicles, but all together they make up the history and the picture of the one great family of the annihilated Jewish community of Brzezin.

And, as family chronicles, the writings in this book are mostly personal, *heymish*. In this lies the special significance of each *yizkor* book, both for the history of the *shtetl* and also for the general history of the murdered Jewish people in Poland. But as in family chronicles, here and there, family considerations slip in that have a smaller relevance to the public and possibly also certain inaccuracies. Therefore, the authors of the various works in the Brzezin memorial book bear the full responsibility themselves for their published descriptions, conclusions, and evaluations. The editors of the *yizkor* book deem it necessary to explain this with great emphasis and determination. And although the family chronicles and other works in this *yizkor* book are written by non-professional writers, we are sure that they will enter our rich literature and folk memoirs that are being so strongly and warmly evaluated and which are such a great treasure for our historians for their scholarly work.

All the *landslayt* who in this book published their remembrances are very knowledgeable about the life that once existed in their home *shtetl*. They are still steeped in the intellectual roots, in the surroundings of the *shtetl* from which they came. They still spiritually breathe the Jewish heritage of the *shtetl*. And they have made the greatest and sincerest effort to express their feelings about their near and dear ones from the former community in the Brzezin that was annihilated. They have given the greatest and sincerest effort to bring to life their destroyed Jewish *shtetl* in reminisces that they have faithfully, in a *heymish*, familiar language, recorded in the *yizkor* book. And their compositions are truly folk memoirs—in the best meaning of the word.

And therefore—we believe that this *yizkor* book of the annihilated Jewish community of Brzezin is not only a *sefer hzikhroynes* [book of memoirs] that is bequeathed to the coming generations of *landslayt*. *Sefer Brzezin* is also—according to our modest interpretation—an important contribution to the general history of the Jewish total destruction in Poland, and not only for the lament after the destruction—which must be written down and cared about for generations to come—but also for the research for the "book of chronicles" of the thousand-year past of the Jewish people in Poland, which had in the course of long generations spiritually nourished and maintained our widely scattered Jewish people over the entire world.

The Hasidic *shnayder-shtetl* Brzezin—which is portrayed in this *yizkor* book—is a ring in the golden chain of annihilated Polish Jewry. Because of the good deeds and sacred heritage of its inhabitants, the memory of this town will live in our present generation and will continue to live for many, many generations.

About *Sefer Brzezin* and the Destroyed Town of Brzezin
(pp. xvii–xx)
Jacob Pat

If only real Brzeziners who were born in Brzezin were allowed to write in *Sefer Brzezin*, I would not have that right, since I am a Bialystoker-Warszawer, where I often heard about Brzezin. I knew that the Białystok looms, which were humming days on end, also produced goods for Brzezin. Later I was a *ben-bayes* [member of the household] in Brzezin, coming there for evenings, meetings, holding lectures, walking its streets. I knew it well, sat on the benches near the houses with a bunch of writers, dressmakers, and enjoyed myself well into the summer nights, spoke to hundreds, thousands of Brzeziner Jews—all remain continuously alive before my eyes. As my old good friend, the real kosher Brzeziner, Jacob David Berg—with Brzezin dear to his heart—asked me to write something for *Sefer Brzezin*, once and for all I felt that I should do it.

I have certainly seen Brzezin in its time of intense growth between the world wars. I have certainly seen Brzezin in its total destruction after World War II. I certainly see now before my eyes, in my imagination, the Brzeziner Jews. I see them in the large well-packed Firemen's Hall. I see the enthusiastic, carried-away young brothers. I see the way they pay attention with open mouths, devouring every word, and see, see in their enthusiastic, spellbound state that they are ready to spring up from their seats and set out to conquer the world.

Brothers, friends from Brzezin, I will also take part in writing about you in *Sefer Brzezin!*

I did not want to rely only on my memories. Before writing these lines, I read through all the articles that are a part of *Sefer Brzezin*—a great deal of historically important material. It is a true *Megile Brzezin* [complete story of Brzezin]. It is certainly the holiest *matseyve* that the idealistic Brzezin survivors could have raised for their town.

First of all, let me make a few general observations about the archives that are included in the *Sefer*. By now, hundreds of books have already been published about the hundreds of destroyed Jewish *shtet un shtetlekh* [towns and villages], about the millions of Jews who became holy martyrs. The Brzeziner *sefer* is certainly an exception; it is a completely unique *sefer*.

It is important in the distinct character and weight of the writings that are included in it. There is no nonsense, no florid language. No, the articles are charged with facts, with important material, with *shtiker lebn* [pieces of life]. In them are recorded for generations to come hundreds of Jews of all kinds, *frum un fray* [observant and non-observant], teachers and tailors, Hasidim and socialists—all those who built an honest life of hard work, built a unique industry. I read in them the history of generations and generations in the town, of the Jewish community, of its *khevres* [societies] and institutions. Jews come to life before one's imagination who were Hasidim, Jews who were *mayminim* [believers], Jews who were fighters, Jews who were strikers, Jews who went to Siberia, went to prison in a procession of convicts. It is a collection of historical material that must now be used by writers and artists so that they may create works of art from this material. There were so many full-of-life, energetic, creative, dynamic Jews, master builders of a virtuous, creative life.

In the simple day-to-day tales, in the chronicle of years, in the hundred facts of life that tell about the days and nights, the weekdays and *shabesdike* [Sabbath days] that were filled with activity, with deeds, with worrying about particular details and the community at large—in all these lie the solution to the mystery of the wonder of Jewish folk life, also the greater mystery of the unbelievable saintliness during the ghetto years, in the years of the downfall at the hands of the butchers.

* * *

I move on to the years when the *kehile kdushe* [sacred community] Brzezin still lived. Twenty-one kilometers from Łódź and 101 kilometers from Warsaw lay Brzezin, to which, in the years between the world wars, either the train brought me or, most often, the bus. I see now a picture swimming by from that time—a host of young people, boys and girls, also middle-aged craftsmen who waited for the bus in the marketplace—a circular plaza, cobblestoned, shops all around, small businesses, open stalls. But one sees only the local people who occupy themselves by chatting, giving *sholem aleykhem*s [greetings]. I come out of the railroad car and fall into tens, hundreds of *sholem aleykhem*s. Their *tates un zeydes* also did the same when they welcomed a *rebbe* who came to them. The same from generation to generation, one generation taken over by the next. Not now and not then was there such a tumultuous ardor, such a cordiality, as with Hasidim when they would entertain their *rebbe*. There is no translation for it—it was *simkhe-vesosn* [holiday joy], a true cordiality, a bliss, a *mitsve-freyd* [joyful deed] when Hasidim welcomed their *rebbe*. There was a mix of the world to come and the pleasures of this world. It also overtook the younger generation—call it by any name you want, basically it is the same. Soon people will empty into the street, in a group. Jews will come out of their doors, remain standing on the cobblestone pavement. Youngsters will run closer, "*Sholem aleykhem, khaver* [Greetings, comrade]. "*Sholem aleykhem.*"

The town sees, the town knows that "the speaker has come." He is already here; there he goes with his friends. Hasidim were displeased with this; older Jews were upset. The speaker will lead the children astray from the straight path. . . . But one can do nothing; no one can help. It is such a time, a new time.

Later, we will be together in the large Firemen's Hall. "They are looking for trouble," a blunt Hasid says to himself, a stubborn person. They go to the "lecture." No, don't call it a lecture; it is something different. It is something more. It is magic. They will hear what's going on in the wide world, in Warsaw and in Paris, in Vilna and in Moscow. They will hear about the Jewish workers, about their fight, about their great hope, and at the end, with all their strength, they will sing, enflamed, the strange, delicious Yiddish socialist songs.

At that time, this was not just an ordinary little town in Poland. No, it was Brzezin, the town of work, the town of factories, of tailor workshops, of the Jewish proletariat. Indeed, it was from here that they sent the fanciest clothing out into the great world, into the warehouses; surely we clothed an entire world!

In my head, in my imagination, are mixed together my own memories and pictures of Brzezin with the descriptions that were prepared so loyally and honestly by the

ABOUT SEFER BRZEZIN

Brzeziners who have written in such a genuine manner for *Sefer Brzezin*. Here I see again, as before, the hundreds of sewing machines and the great Brzezin tailor workshops. I see the Jews who work with all their strength; I see them heating the irons; I see, as I once saw, the way they pack the Brzeziner bundles of clothing, stuff the transport crates with the blue inscriptions on the large boards. There the wagon drivers crack their long whips at the harnessed horses, and the wagons, with the wooden slats on the sides, loaded high with crates of goods, go off with the crates and with the wagon drivers. They go off to the train, to the railway station; they go into the wide world.

Respect, brothers! There are no loafers; ordinary Brzeziners, shears and irons, provide an entire world with garments. They clothe the naked. There are no cane twirlers there, no idlers. The translation of Brzezin is work. Brzezin means toil, means well-made, quickly made; the merchandise has to go all the way to Siberia, to China, Australia. Brzezin means ideas, means industry—it is certainly a new and great expression, "the clothing industry." Brzezin means a new world.

Memories come. We used to sit in Brzezin on the benches half the night, and with us were the Brzezin Jews who were knowledgeable, who had read a book, had delved into Brzezin history. Sitting there were Jews who remembered the stories of their *zeydes* from the old men in the *besmedresh* [prayer house]. They say that Brzezin is called Brzezin because, at one time, a great birch forest stood there [*brzoza* = birch], that the landowners used to go hunting in the forest.

In 1366 King Casimir the Great gave Brzezin the status of a town with the right to hold fairs.

Years and years later, the forest was hacked down, and houses were built. Breweries were built; a town was built. Later Jews came, built workshops, built factories, made contracts with Łódź and Białystok.

A Talmudist and dreamer sits with me. Once again I see before my eyes that Jew who remained in his old age a Brzezin patriot and could, by no means, ever forgive Łódź, which had so outgrown Brzezin—which in the 1900s still had a great deal more people than Łódź.

Who knows why that happened. Each town also has its *mazl* [luck]. Who knows why in Kutno they dealt in cattle and in Żelichów they made boots; who knows why in Krynki they worked with leather and in Brzezin they made trousers and coats and clothed a world of *goyim* [non-Jews] all the way to Siberia. Hard to have answers. A thousand reasons contributed. Why does it turn out to be the destiny of a ninety-six-year-old Brzeziner tailor—who, well into his very old age sewed with a needle even without an eyeglass—to be the founder of the Brzezin tailors union? It was a kind of *mazl*.

I mix together all that I remember, that I have heard and seen in Brzezin, also what has now been written by the Brzeziner writers for *Sefer Brzezin*, and again there emerge before me the shapes of those who built Jewish Brzezin, who organized the tailors, fought there for a better life, together with those who had the initiative, were bright and capable, had a wanderlust, picked themselves up, left Brzezin, and built new homes in America and in Eretz Yisroel.

Such were the Brzezin Jews, deeply-rooted oaks with long branches, craftsmen Jews, Jews who fulfilled the commandments, who were God-fearing Jewish tailors, who fulfilled the *mitsve* [commandment] "with the sweat of your brow shall you earn your bread" (Genesis 3:19). They cut the manufactured fabric from Łódź and Białystok, sewed, stitched, pressed, and sent their completed garments into the wide world.

* * *

I simply could not pry myself loose from reading and re-reading the writings in *Sefer Brzezin*—the stories about the agents on commission and traveling salesmen, about the employers and employees, the stories about the Hasidic sons and sons-in-law who got into textiles, into manufacturing, the stories about the former young men of the *besmedresh*, former yeshiva students who built the great clothing industry with zest and imagination.

I leaf through the galleys and read about the socialist work that began and grew in Brzezin—it began from the depths and the gloom of the workrooms. I myself did not see the beginning, but I did see its continuation, heard their speeches, their sharp senses and wisdom, and was a witness to the new winds that blew there. Indeed, there was once ardor, indeed, there were once Hasidim, rabbis, but a new fervor came, with momentum, a new fervor, new Hasidim, and new *rabonim* [teachers].

Let us again remember how a young Brzeziner, a yeshiva *bokher* [student], came back from Vilna to Brzezin. He did not come of his own free will; he was brought there in a procession of convicts, brought by White Russian policemen. He was deported from Vilna for underground socialist work; he had in his pocket a card from the Bund [Jewish Socialist Party]. He was the son of an old Hasid from Warka, Reb [title of respect] Chaim-Icek. He is today Jacob David Berg, the chairman of the Sholem Aleichem Institute in New York, who plays an important role in Yiddish cultural work in America. He is the one who recently persuaded me that I should write something for *Sefer Brzezin*.

I write and see at the same time public gatherings in Brzezin. There will not be such meetings again in the entire world. The meeting is in the *shul* [synagogue]. It is already evening in the town and evening in the heavens. Not only had almost a thousand passionate Hasidim come down in the darkness, but also generations came down with them. We were all together then in a higher world, a brightly lit one, as if the echo from the noise of the sewing machines would unexpectedly sound in the hollow of the great *shul*, the exclamation "*Khaverim un khavertes!*" [Male comrades and female comrades] floats down, and they marshal themselves with a passionate dream of a new world, of new people, new Jews for a greater freedom that will come. Whoever was worthy of having the honor of seeing the way the poor young tailors from Brzezin dreamed, they would at that time have been able to conquer the world. The world would be good and beautiful, the people would be good, there would be freedom and peace, the Jews would be!

An image comes to me about what they told me in those distant years in Brzezin. A tailor there has been called for a long time Shirhamayles [songs of praise]. Why such a name? When he did not have any work, he could not sit idle; he used to fill up his days reciting from the Book of Psalms. Thus they gave him the name Shirhamayles.

Mixed up in my mind are the Brzezin Jews I had seen with my own eyes—with whom I had chatted in Brzezin, about whom I had spoken at the Brzezin meetings, may they rest in peace—with the images and types from the memorial book [*Sefer Brzezin*]. At the same time, the songs the Brzezin workers sang by the sewing machines ring out. I hear the song they sang then with such gusto, "By the Pyramids." The songs of the theater also emerge—"Come Home, Isroelik"—and the songs that ridiculed "Fonien," who uselessly toiled so that Manchuria could remain.

Surrounding me are the Brzezin scholars, cantors, singers. The Jews with the outlandish names emerge, nicknames—Herszel Korekh, Abraham Korekh, Abraham Czumski, whose coaches carried passengers to Kaluszyn. The Jews who made a pilgrimage to Palestine, to Eretz Yisroel, emerge; the Brezeziners emerge who were untimely dispersed to the ends of the earth.

Through generations, over the years, traditions and experiences were established, and there evolved an educational system for children; old teachers came, *rosheshive* [board of a yeshiva], and new teachers and female teachers. To this place came Jankiele Melamed, Abraham Mojsze Melamed, Szlama Perec, Herszel Litvak, Icze Majer Melamed, Henoch Melamed, Gimpele Melamed, Abraham Kaluszyner, Mojsze Pabianicer.

The correction sheets from the *sefer*, the galleys, as I already said, do not let me go. There were certainly not only tailors in Brzezin; the scenes of the life there unwind as if in a panorama and wrap around you. Those who remembered them wrote about them for future generations.

Let us also not be embarrassed; let us remember a Brzezin market fair on a Thursday. Let us not believe that in Brzezin there were only tailors and teachers. The authors of the memorial book also brought to life, as if called up from the other world, the market place with its merchants, male and female, the baker and the jugglers, the organ grinders with the parrots. Also came the beggars, the cripples, who sat on the ground and sang heartrending "moralizing" songs.

The horse traders also appear at the pig market, the husky butchers and animal handlers, who with great strength make the blood spurt from the necks. See, there is a big fair. They clasp hands together. After the fair they sit in the taverns and allow themselves a fling with roasted goose, chicken livers and gizzards, marinated herring, sour pickles, and foamy beer. All kinds of liquor is drunk—from aqua vitae to 90 percent alcohol; after a strong drink one eats a hard, salty cheese.

I would like to repeat a few lines about the fact that Brzezin grew along with the greatest centers of the ready-made clothing industry, that the extremely energetic, the boldest, came from the "extreme depths of Brzezin poverty." It is surely something to marvel at, as it is told in *Sefer Brzezin*:

"Without worldly education, with scant contact with the surrounding world that lay outside the narrow confines of their isolated *shtetl*, they, the Brzeziner Jews, reached into the most remote corners of European and Asiatic Russia until their export amounted to the sum of eight million rubles."

Brzezin and eight million rubles—would you believe that?!

The Jewish worker organization in Brzezin, the Zionist organizations in Brzezin, the May demonstrations, the needleworkers union, the Jewish library loaded with Yiddish books, the hungry book-readers.

They come to read in Brzezin, writers come, the poet Icchak Kacenelson. Readings take place in the great Firemen's Hall, in the Hall of Life. Brzezin has plays in the theater—they play *Shma Yisroel* by Osip Dimov, *With the Tide* by Sholem Asch, *The Jewish King Lear* by Jacob Gordin, *People* by Sholem Aleichem, *The Eternal Song* by Mark Orenstein.

What did they do in Brzezin after a theater performance? They used to carry the benches out of the hall into the courtyard, the Brzezin *klezmer* [musicians] played one dance after the other, and the people together with the actors danced until daybreak.

I look at a picture published on page 158 of the book. It is a gruesome picture. It grieves the heart. It is a picture of a heap that is left of Brzezin—a heap like a mass grave. Under the picture is printed:

> This once was the Jewish cemetery of Brzezin. The little mountain that you see in the picture is the mass grave of the collected skulls that were found after the great destruction. This picture was taken in 1960 by the writer, a grandchild of Lajbl Hendrykowski and the daughter of Jechiel Hendrykowski.

Mrs. Rhoda Hendrik-Karpatkin speaks to us this way in *Sefer Brzezin*, "The Jewish population gave Brzezin life, zest, culture. With their diligence, hard work, and enterprise, the Jews made the town famous...."

Now there is almost no one left. That Brzezin is gone forever, but a rich heritage is left.... "The children and grandchildren of the Brzezin Jews brought the same spiritual legacy to America and Israel and everywhere else. The publication of this monumental *sefer*, in which have been immortalized our most loved and dearest ones, is yet another small ring in the golden chain that gives honor to all the generations of Brzezin Jews."

* * *

Here I pause. I wanted somehow, to at least do my part for the truly historic, important work to immortalize our wonderful past as it is in *Sefer Brzezin*.

Part One

Brzezin and Brzeziner Jews

Brzeziny in History (pp. 3–20)

Joseph Shaibowicz

FORWARD

Information about the modern history of Brzeziny[1] [pronounced Bzhezhiny] and its Jews was burned with our holy community and mixed in with the ashes of the millions of our people who were martyred. What's more, until now, no history or monograph about Brzeziny has been written. Therefore, my task has involved great difficulties. Not only did the historical materials have to be analyzed; they first had to be found and assembled. This is, therefore, a pioneering work. Naturally, this is not a full history of our town. There are still scattered treasures with documents in different archives and museums throughout the world that are waiting to be used and still need to be examined. Today, after Hitler's plague, when our *shtetl* lies in ruins together with Polish Jewry, this work is a modest contribution to the memory of the thousands of our people, who, with their hard work and virtuous, toiling lives made it possible for our *shtetl* Brzezin to become known throughout the world.

I use this opportunity to thank the Jewish Historical Institute in Warsaw, the YIVO Institute for Jewish Research in New York, and, most particularly, the entire staff of the Kurski Archive in New York for their useful advice and much-needed friendly help.

J.B.S.

I TOWARD A HISTORY OF BRZEZINY

The town Brzeziny is in the Łódź province by the Mrożyca River, a *powiat* town [county seat], seven kilometers away from the Koluszki train station, twenty-one kilometers from the city of Łódź, and 101 kilometers from Warsaw.

The history of the town is long and consists of several stages. The first one cannot be determined; it is wrapped in a thick haze. The town's beginnings reach back to the early epoch of the rise of the first towns in Poland, approximately over nine hundred years ago. There are documents as early as the fourteenth century, for example, showing the privilege granted by King Casimir [Kazimierz] the Great with a right to hold fairs. Two hundred years later (1566), this privilege was reaffirmed by King Sigismund Augustus [Zygmunt August]. Because of the lack of written documents before the fourteenth century, we must examine the earlier centuries of Brzeziny through the architectural form of the churches. Their style bears witness to the beginnings of Brzeziny.

---

[1] In most chapters of the English translation of the Brzeziny Yizkor Book, we have used the town's Yiddish name, Brzezin, as that was how it was known among Jews. However, since this chapter is a history of the town as a whole, the Polish name, Brzeziny, is used.

A legend recounts that in distant times, the town was spread out, and it was called Krakowek. However, due to a punishment by God, it collapsed. There is also a story that because of an epidemic, the entire population died out.

The legendary tale relies on the fact that even now one can find, in the fields and meadows in and around the town, signs of stone foundations and cobblestone streets. The legend seems to relate that, for extraordinary reasons, on the spot of the former Krakowek, there grew a forest of birches [*brzozy*]. From that comes the name of the newly-risen town: Brzeziny.

Brzeziny, over a long period of time, became famous in the market places all over Poland for its crafts. Initially, during the time of the Swedish wars with Poland (1621–26), sharing the fate of many other towns, it was destroyed. This was followed by an infectious disease that had been raging through Western Europe and in Poland. Inscriptions on *matseyves* from the year 1629—still visible in the town cemetery—show evidence of the epidemic.[1]

In the course of time a new town arose on the ruins of the former great Brzeziny. A bourgeois element arrived that did not know its past. People often encountered caves and ruins in the earth and, unable to understand them, attached a supernatural motif, thus creating the legends. The first historical documents that we have are from the fourteenth century.

A. Szelewski, in a "historical-archeological" account about the parish church and other monuments in Brzeziny, based on a statistical description of the town, states:

> The town Brzeziny had a glorious beginning—it was called Krakowek (little Kraków)—and it must have covered a wide area, judging from the ruins of collapsed houses that remain and from the paved paths around them. The history writers also confirm this.[2]

And Wajer states that the Swedes assaulted the Lasocki Castle.[3] Various stories circulate about the Swedes. Surowiecki indicates that, in general, the town's fall was apparent in the following ways:

> The glorious state of these towns and their inhabitants disappeared in Poland. Only sad memories and feeble shadows remind us of them. There, where monarchs with their numerous courts used to reside, there, where beleaguered people found refuge with the citizens, now the few families passing through cannot find any place even for one night. In Wiślica, Kętrzyn, Warta, Radom, Opatów, Koło, Chojna, Nowe Miasto, Brześć-Kujawski, etc., where once Sejms [Polish parliaments] and land councils met, where royal assemblies and landowners meetings were held, now you cannot find three decent houses for travelers in these places. Streets, suburbs, little palaces, beautiful community houses of once great Sandomierz, Lublin, Gniezno, Rajgród, Drohiczyn, Bydgoszcz, and many other places lie buried in gardens, in fields, in ruins. Only accidentally discovered caves, cellars, and streets found here and there bear witness to their former greatness.

In his remarks he adds:

---

[1] There are no longer any gravestones in the Brzeziny Jewish Cemetery.
[2] *Pamiętnik religyjne-moralny* [Religious-moral memoir] (1851), 20:12. (Author's note)
[3] *Pamiętnik religyjne-moralny* [Religious-moral memoir] (1851), 20:14. (Author's note)

Minister Lubieński, going once outside Brzeziny, found between gardens and wildernesses a significant water source and also mud, because of which, he was forced, with difficulty, to leave the place. Upon returning there after a time, he observed that the water and the dirt had disappeared. Astonished by this unexpected happening, he began to dig in the earth, and here and there he found cellars and signs of precious town walls that in the past had once been incomparably larger.

In order to better understand contemporary Brzeziny, it is necessary to have some concept of ancient Poland.

In the year 960 in Poland, there arose the first royal dynasty with the legendary Mieszko, who married a Czech princess and accepted the Christian faith.

(There is a legend that the first Polish king was a Jew by the name of Abraham Prachownik. The peasants, unable to decide who should become their king, decided to place a guard on the bridge to Kraśnik or Kraśniewicz, and the one who appeared first on the bridge would become king. At dawn the first person to appear was the Jew Abraham Prachownik, and the peasants crowned him king. The Jew hid himself as he did not want to be their king. On the third day, Mieszko collected a multitude of peasants and, with sticks, stormed Abraham Prachownik's house. The Jew, pointing at him, told the peasants that this Mieszko should become the king as he was strong and had courage, and Mieszko became king.)

This was the beginning of the Piast Dynasty, which ruled for five hundred years. At that time in the Brzeziny vicinity lived the Mazovian tribe, which had spread to Sieradz and Łęczyca, the boundary of the Polanian tribe. The Polanian tribe occupied the area of Poznań, Gniezno, and Kalisz and was the largest and most important among the many tribes in Poland. The entire land was later named after the Polanian tribe—Polonia, Polska—*pola* (field). The names of the other tribes quickly disappeared. The Piast Dynasty united numerous tribes between the Odra and Bug Rivers and created one kingdom.[1]

This was also the time when Poland adopted Christianity (963). Until that time the tribes were pagans; they believed in the cult of the dead, in fire, in the sun, etc. Even until as late as the twelfth century, idolatry was widespread. Names that were given to people and places are reminders of this.

In the eleventh century there was already a settlement in Brzeziny. In 1099 the building of the parish church, Święta Anna [Saint Anna], began. In honor of the completion of the church, the year 1123 was engraved on the bell.[2] Brzeziny became the most important place in the area. Hundreds of years later the church was rebuilt (1710). From the parish church, underground, ran a cave and a stone canal in an obscure direction. There is a hypothesis that the passage was built during the time of the Tartar invasion or the Swedish wars. These are only theories.

---

[1] The tribes always fought and attacked one another. The major tribes that occupied Poland were Polanian—Poznań region, Silesian—Wrocław, Vislanian—Kraków, Mazovian—Płock, formerly the Lechites, Abodrites, and Wilzi, etc. Their major employment was hunting and agriculture. (Author's note)

[2] *Słownik Geograficzny Królestwa Polskiego* [Geographical Dictionary of the Kingdom of Poland], 761. (Author's note)

In a geographic dictionary, we read:

> The date of the establishment of Brzeziny is unknown. The authenticity of the privileges that King Casimir the Great gave in 1366 and that were confirmed through Sigismund Augustus in 1566 is doubtful. In the fifteenth century, it must have been a well-populated town, since for the Prussian war, the town provided thirteen armed men at one time, while other towns from the Łęczyca voivoidship [province], to which Brzeziny belonged at that time, supplied only two. . . .

This war of the Teutonic Order of the Knights of the Cross, which often attacked Poland and other Slavic lands, forced the Poles to marshal all their strength in the fight against the Order—which ranked as a most treacherous and aggressive arm of Prussian feudalism. In 1410 the Poles succeeded in defeating them in a historic victory at Grunwald. The Poles, Czechs, Lithuanians, and Russians had joined together in the bitter fight against hatred of Slavs. The war of the united army against the Knights of the Cross was financed to a significant degree by Jews.[1] The victory over the Order was not complete because of intrigues and the intense opposition of the Vatican—since the Knights of the Cross had carried out the wars ostensibly against pagans, in order to turn them toward Christianity.

Only in the time of Casimir IV Jagiello [Kazimierz Jagiellończyk] (1427–92) did Poland finally liquidate the political power of the Knights of the Cross and regain access to the Baltic Sea. At that time Brzeziny was among the most significant towns in Poland. After the controversy over Prussia and the expansionism of the Prussian feudal lords, Poland moved into the first rank of the advanced monarchies in Europe.[2] After making peace on 9 October 1466 in Toruń, Poland got back the territories of East Pomerania [Pomorze] and Michałowska [now part of Chełmno] and also Marlborg [Malbork], Elbląg, Sztum, and Warmia. Prussia came under Poland's control.

In a second place we read that in 1585 the town of Brzeziny was a very large town in which fine artisans lived.[3] The town belonged to a landowning family, the Lasockis. The Swedish wars reduced the population and impoverished the inhabitants. As a result, Antoni Lasocki, *kasztelan (starosta)*[4] of Gostynin, striving to improve the lot of the town, went to King Sigismund Augustus[5] in 1577 and asked him for a permit for three annual market fairs in the following order—on the morning after New Year, on the Monday after Boże Ciało [Corpus Christi], and on the morning after St. Bartholomew's Day.

Only in the fifteenth and sixteenth centuries do we have actual information about the economic condition of the town. From it we see that both in terms of the population and the craftsmanship, Brzeziny could be considered to rank among the most important towns in Poland. Clothing articles produced in Brzeziny were distributed in the markets of Greater Poland [Wielkopolska] and also in the east, where there was a great demand for them.

---

[1] Zakon Krzyżacki [Order of the Knights of the Cross]. (Author's note)
[2] Ber Mark, *History of Jews in Poland*. (Author's note)
[3] See material found in the Archive of the Finance Ministry, 13:46. (Author's note)
[4] At that time, the local administrator had the title of *kasztelan*; after 1918, when Poland became a republic, the local administrator was referred to as a *starosta*.
[5] In the actual text, the author mistakenly wrote "Stanisław Augustus," a ruler in the 1700s.

There are two versions as to when Brzeziny became a town, both from the fourteenth century.

The first version is from 1315. At that time Brzeziny became a town and began to have market fairs. In the Middle Ages only a town had the right to have fairs. The status of town also meant a guarantee of protection for the inhabitants.[1] Because of this important event, a new stone church was erected in the Gothic style; the date 1315 is visible on the iron doors. The Gothic style is completely in accord with the architecture of that time. The decor of the church was famous in all of Poland. In the course of the century, the artistry lost its luster. The superb paintings that made it famous in Poland were dirty by then and were often stuck together. The wooden roof was repaired endlessly.

An old church that was later renovated

On the great altar was kept an exquisite picture of the Lord's Resurrection [*Zmartwychwstanie Pańskie*] painted on wood. In the shrine was the major painting of Christ's coronation [*Ukorowanie Chrystusa*], also painted on wood, with a gypsum undercoat. The extremely large altar and the exquisite paintings are an incomparable reminder of the Polish-Czech art of the fourteenth and fifteenth centuries, which was strongly influenced by the Prussian art of the Middle Ages. Later the church collapsed, and only in the middle of the nineteenth century was a new church built on its ruins (1856).

The second version [of the beginnings of Brzeziny] is finally a documented one. In 1366 King Casimir the Great gave Brzeziny the privilege of becoming a town and holding periodic fairs. King Sigismund Augustus reaffirmed this privilege in 1566. Not all historians are in agreement about the authenticity of this privilege. It is presumed that the first version is the correct one. In honor of the privilege given by Casimir the Great, the Church of the Holy Cross [*Święty Krzyż*] was erected.

In the fifteenth century, after the town grew, the Church of the Holy Spirit [*Święty Ducha*] was built, together with a hospital.

Josef Lasocki, who was also the *kasztelan (starosta)* of Gostynin, erected a new church in 1737.

In 1860 Prince Ignacy Polkowski rebuilt the church. In 1627 the landowner Kasper Lasocki erected a Reformed Church in the Baroque style. Twelve years later (1639), a small chapel was added to it. In 1700 Adam Lasocki, who later became the *kasztelan* in

---

[1] Dr. Jacob Shatzky, *History of Warsaw*, 11. (Author's note)

Sochaczew, built a church. In 1719 the Brzeziny burgher Stanisław Bojakiewicz erected a wooden church.

A well-known traveler by the name of Verdum visited Brzeziny in 1690, and he describes it as a superb, large town with pretty houses. In particular, he remembers the churches from the fourteenth century in the Gothic style and also a castle where the *kasztelan,* who was a member of the Senate, lived.

In 1457 Piotr Lelewicz from the Brzeziny area was appointed *kasztelan* in Inowrocław and later became an advisor to the king's court.[1] His name, or his father's name, appears as a signatory on the treaty at Brześć [Brześć Kujawski] with the Knights of the Cross in 1436.

The economic development of Brzeziny corresponded to the development of other towns; this is thought to be of great significance.

Sarnicki wrote that in 1585 there were "select, skilled craftsmen" in Brzeziny, that the clothing industry was highly developed, and, at the Poznań market, textiles from various towns and *shtetl*s were found—from Kutno, Grójec, Leszno, Brzeziny, Płock, Sierpc, Łowicz, Łęczyca, Koło, Inowrocław, Łomża, Rychwał, Płońsk, and Sieradz.[2] From there they were transported in the direction of Vilna and Minsk, and in a second direction, to the west, where it is possible they were brought as unfinished goods that were later reworked as finer cloth.

In the sixteenth century the economic condition of the town was very good. In 1576 the earnings in Brzeziny surpassed the earnings of the provincial town of Łęczyca. Here are a few figures from the town taxes:

>from the roads–76 *grzywny* [old Polish coins]
>from 40 kegs of hard liquor–24 *grzywny* a piece
>from 35 vagabonds–12 *grzywny* each
>from 30 artisans–4 *grzywny* each
>from 50 tenants–12 *grzywny* each
>from 12 women–6 *grzywny* each
>from 10 women–6 *grzywny* each
>from 3 women–9 *grzywny* each
>from 3 women–8 *grzywny* each
>from 2 women–4 *grzywny* each
>from journeymen artisans–8 to 11 *grzywny* each
>from 23 bakers–4 *grzywny* each
>from 29 innkeepers–12 *grzywny* each
>from 9 coachmen–12 *grzywny* each

---

[1] Piotr Lelewicz later changed his name to Strykowski. It is possible that he came from Stryków, several kilometers from Brzeziny. (Author's note)

[2] Ignacy Baranowski, *Przemysł Polski w XVI wieku* [Polish industry in the 16th centruty], 152, 154 and J. Kołaczkowski—in the work *Wiadomości o fabrykach i rękodziełach w dawnej Polsce* [Information about factories and handcrafts in Old Poland]—stated that among other things woolen cloth was produced in the eighteenth century in Brzeziny, Biała, Bielska, Błaszki, and Ciechanowiec, etc. (Author's note)

from 10 butchers–12 *grzywny* each
from 3 cloth makers–12 *grzywny*
from 7 petty merchants–12 *grzywny* each
from 79 1/2 *łan* [about 3300 acres] of land–20 *grzywny* each

Altogether the town paid 271 florin, 11 *grzywny*, and 4 *denars*.[1] At that time, Jews played an active role in the economic life.

Stryków, which in the past also had large markets, only paid 61 florin.

The economic life in Brzeziny, as everywhere during the Middle Ages, was entirely regulated by the church. The priest blessed the merchants on the day of the fair and had authority over the life of each individual from birth to death. The Roman Catholic Church considered itself the guardian of religion—which was not yet firmly established in the hearts and minds of the inhabitants. In general, Brzeziny was one of the first places where Christianity was widespread. As early as 1180, in the provincial town Łęczyca, a convocation of the Christian Synod took place where certain restrictions against Jews were established. Participating in the assembly, apart from a large number of clergymen, were Bolesław, the Prince of Silesia in Wrocław, Leszek, the Masovian, and Otto, from Poznań.

In the eighteenth century a clear decline became apparent in Brzeziny due to the frequent wars and internal discord in Poland. In 1772 Prussia took over the most Polish[2] areas of the Polish state—the provinces of Pomorze (Pomerania), Malbork, and Chełmno—with the exception of the cities of Gdańsk [Danzig] and Toruń [Thorn]. Twenty years later, Prussia seized Gdańsk and Toruń, the provinces of Poznań, Gniezno, Inowrocław, all of Kalisz, Brześć, Kujawa, sections of Sieradz, Wieluń, Łęczyca, Płock, and parts of Rawa and Mazowsze [Mazovia], with a total population of 1,200,000 souls. At that time, Brzeziny was included under Prussian rule and became the seat of the district council [Landrat] under the name of South Prussia. (In this period, according to an imperial decree from 17 April 1797, it was required that every Jew add to his Jewish name a surname, which he could choose himself.) This lasted fourteen years, from 1792 until 1806. In this period, a large German immigration to Brzeziny began. Also, the then small *shtetl* Łódź belonged to the *powiat* of Brzeziny.

At the end of the eighteenth century, the Prussian kaiser visited Brzeziny during his extensive travels over the recently captured Polish territories. The kaiser remained a little longer in Ujazd, a small town near Brzeziny.

The third and last partition of Poland (following the heroic Kościuszko uprising in 1795), which was ratified in St. Petersburg on 26 January 1797, gave Prussia the remainder of the Rawa and Mazowsze provinces, with Warsaw as the capital, and named it "New East Prussia."

From 1807 until 1815, in accordance with the boundaries established by Napoleon, Brzeziny came under the control of the Duchy of Warsaw.

---

[1] A florin is a gold coin worth today [1961] approximately 2/3 of a dollar. A *grzywna* is 48 *groszy* (the *grosz* had a high value). *Złoty* and *denar*s were small change. (Author's note)

[2] The author must have meant the "most Germanic areas of the Polish state" rather than the "most Polish areas of the Polish state."

According to the resolution at the famous Congress of Vienna (1815)—where those at the very peak of reactionary Europe of the time convened, with Metternich at the head—Brzeziny, together with Congress Poland, passed under the protection of Czarist Russia and belonged to it until 1914. Afterward, Czar Alexander I visited the most important towns in Poland, among them also Brzeziny and the small town of Łódź (1825). At the beginning of the nineteenth century, Brzeziny had four times as many people as Łódź. Brzeziny received a commendation from the Czar.

During World War I, Brzeziny was occupied by Germany from 1914 until the proclamation of Poland's independence in 1918.

The modern Brzeziny that we knew arose and developed without any tradition; it moved ahead only as an outgrowth of the industrial development in all of Poland in the nineteenth century and in very close connection with the tumultuous industrial growth of Łódź and vicinity. Consequently, we have to think about the Brzeziny of the nineteenth and twentieth centuries independent of the previous centuries, that is, before the 1793 division of Poland.

A street in Brzeziny at the intersection of Traugutta and Nowe Miasto [New Town] Streets. On the right is the house where Dr. Stodółkiewicz lived, and on the left is the house of Arje Dawid Perlmuter.

II THE TEXTILE INDUSTRY AND TAILORING IN BRZEZINY

A.

The development of tailoring in Brzeziny came about after other forms of production had blossomed all over Poland.

At the end of the eighteenth century there arose among the prosperous Polish population a new awareness and the sense of a need to industrialize the country. Also, the owner of Brzeziny, the landowner Lasocki, wanting to elevate the town from its lowered status, had begun to bring from afar German weavers from Prussia to produce goods. He gave them various privileges. They were also given the northeast part of the town (Nowe Miasto) so they could build homes for themselves there. In 1801 a certain Johann Freilich settled there. In 1802 his brother, Christian, came, as did Samuel Arnold. In 1804 Samuel obtained Polish citizenship.

After the Congress of Vienna (1815), when Poland was ultimately divided between Prussia, Russia, and Austria, many Germans streamed into Brzeziny. Later, with the great capitalistic development of Łódź, many of them left Brzeziny and settled in Łódź and surrounding small towns. Izabela Lasocka, who came from the well-known aristocratic Ogiński family, took a special interest in the German artisans in Brzeziny. She helped the newcomers to establish and develop cloth production. A. Szelewski wrote in 1851, "The

Lasocin part of town (called after the owner, landowner Lasocki) is inhabited throughout with experienced artisans."

The great influx of colonizers in such a short time changed the appearance of the town. Brzeziny, as early as the year 1795, just after the fall of Poland, had numbered two hundred fifty families, even counting the Jews, and barely five brick dwellings and 184 wooden ones. Nevertheless, in the time of the Prussian reign, Brzeziny became the seat of the land council. (Brzeziny and its vicinity fell to the Prussian kaiser in the year 1793.)

In a short time, the work of industrializing the town, then a part of Congress Poland, bore fruit. In 1818 there were already eighty cloth producers in Brzeziny. Each workshop employed hired helpers; there were workshops that employed as many as seventy men and women workers. In 1824 there were already 194 masters employed in weaving cloth. Navy blue cloth was manufactured for the military.

The development of the cloth industry significantly influenced the increase in the town's population. By 1827 the population already numbered 3,492 residents. At that time, Jews amounted to 27.1 percent. There were already 299 dwellings.

In 1831 town boundaries were established. We have little information with which to evaluate how the established borders affected the future development of the town. However, it happened that textile manufacturing mainly sought the domestic market. No great economic changes were evident. In 1839 Lasocin (the part that had belonged to the landowner Lasocki) was turned over to the state. In 1851 there were 4,783 residents, excluding the military. The number of permanent residents there was much greater than in the *powiat* town of Rawa, to which Brzeziny belonged at that time. In that number are included 2,404 Roman Catholics, 1,887 Jews, and 587 Evangelical Christians [Protestants].

Although the establishment of a number of borders between Congress Poland and Czarist Russia did not bring about any great change in the textile industry, what did matter is the development of the Łódź textile industry—especially the introduction of steam-run machines and mechanical improvements. This development created a world-class, powerful competition for Brzeziny manufacturers and also for the cloth weavers in the surrounding *shtetl*s. Cheap Łódź products dominated the domestic market and also found a larger market in Russia. The great demand for Łódź goods influenced the growth of the Łódź textile production, and simultaneously, Brzeziny textile production fell.

Szelewski writes:

> In this town, from as far back as one can remember, cloth manufacturing flourished and continues to this day, but now only less fancy kinds are manufactured. There are 16 such manufacturers of medium quality cloth, of *baja* [thick flannel], *dery* [saddle cloths], *szale* [shawls], etc. *Dery* from Brzeziny are particularly elegant and sought after in Warsaw. There are 74 manufacturers of what is known as homespun cloth. There are also 2 dye works, 2 stocking factories, and 1 oil factory. There are 277 artisans, 77 shoemakers, 67 tailors, and 19 bakers. They come for bazaars and fairs, especially for grain and cattle, horses, and everything for which one does not have to pay *rogatka* [a toll]—various textile products of cotton, linen, footwear, attire, and so forth. The shoemakers and tailors carry their products to other towns, and the customers clamor for Brzeziny articles. Fairs in Brzeziny occur fourteen times a year.

Counting the "producers and traders," Szelewski includes under that name all sorts of products and trade that were brought to the bazaars and market fairs in Brzeziny. At that time, shops were uncommon. The trading took place in the town marketplace on market days.

> Additional producers and merchants in Brzeziny were 3 town merchants, 23 stall keepers, 3 wine dealers, 1 aquavit dealer, 13 butchers, 10 wagon drivers, 4 harness makers, 8 cotton manufacturers, 11 cloth merchants, 6 iron merchants, 15 grain dealers, 25 salt merchants, 3 glaziers, 15 wood merchants, 15 pot merchants, 1 chimney cleaner, 5 leather merchants, 9 wool merchants, 14 herring merchants, 15 flour dealers, 1 musician, 3 gardeners, 8 producers and sellers of candles and salt, 3 of vinegar, 5 of oil, 4 of paper, 18 miscellaneous, 4 dealers in used clothing, and 2 guest houses or hotels.

The manufacturers produced 37,800 *arshin* [Russian measure equal to 28 inches] of a middle quality textile, 27,880 *arshin* of coarse quality cloth. The value of the machines and accessories was 4,575 rubles. Besides that, everyone had a bit of land. If one did not succeed in his specialty, the parcel of land helped him.

There were six guilds—textile workers (cloth weavers), potters, bakers, tailors, shoemakers, and a separate German guild. The town paid 2,737 rubles and 8 kopeks in taxes, weight and land fees.

According to Szelewski's description, everything ran its natural course. The manufacturers were the owners of the weaving workshops and worked for themselves at home, often with the help of one or several artisan workshops; they worked with their family and hired helpers. To a certain extent, the artisans were independent both in work and also in their production methods. In the course of events, in the struggle with machine production, the working classes lost their independent role, and the great majority became proletarians. Others became *chałupnicy* [cottage workers].

Below is a table of independent textile manufacturers and their gradual disappearance during the period of one hundred years. We will look at the time period 1801 to 1901.

Table 1

Year	Number of Masters	Number of Workers	Production in *Arshins*	Production in *Rubles*
1801	1		--	--
1818[a,b]	80[a]	114	--	--
1824	194	612	--	--
1851	90	--	65,680	27,607
1880[b]	25[b]	--	--	158,800
1886	19	25	--	4,110
1892	13	15	8,690	--
1893	14	15	--	9,600
1899	6	11	--	2,100
1900	3	10	--	2,000
1901	5	10	--	2,280

a. According to information from Vice Mayor Bojakiewicz. (Author's note)
b. Samuel Orgelbrand, *Encyklopedia Powszechna* [Universal Encyclopedia]. (Author's note)

Table 1 shows the rapid growth of textile manufacturing until 1840. In the subsequent fifty years, the Brzeziny textile manufacturers struggled against the Łódź textile industry. The rivalry could not last, and over time, almost all the individual workshops closed. The kind of influence that the textile industry had on the general evolution of the town and its inhabitants, as well as the development of the town, is demonstrated in Table 2.

Table 2

Year	Inhabitants	Catholics	Jews	Protestants	Houses
1827[a]	3,492	--	27.0 %	--	299[b]
1859[c]	5,185	40.0 %	47.0 %	13.0 %	459
1886	7,420	--	--	--	538[d]
1890	7,980	41.2 %	47.2 %[e]	11.5 %	558
1893[f]	8,794	38.9 %	49.9 %	11.1 %	682
1900	9,641	--	--	--	--
1903[g]	9,181	--	--	--	--
1905	--	--	--	--	--
1907	16,920	40.0 %	--	--	--
1910[h]	15,581	--	--	--	--
1913	17,108	--	54.4 %	--	--

a. P. Radecki. (Author's note)
b. P. Radecki. (Author's note)
c. Samuel Orgelbrand, *Encyklopedia Powszechna* [Universal Encyclopedia]. (Author's note)
d. *Obozy Piotrkowskiej Gubernii* [Camps of the Piotrków Gubernia]. (Author's note)
e. Orgelbrand, *Encyklopedia Powszechna*. (Author's note)
f. Strasburger and Grobski. (Author's note)
g. *Tydzień Piotrkowski* [Piotrków Week]. (Author's note)
h. *Rocznik Statystyczny* [Statistical Yearbook]. (Author's note)

B. TAILORING

The beginning of home tailoring in Brzeziny came about in the year 1886. Before that there were tailors in the town, Christians and Jews, who worked for local markets. The Christians—some of them also owners of land—produced "white fabric" from clean white wool. They sewed thick white coats for peasants from the principality of Łowicz. They distributed them through markets in Łowicz, Piątek, Żychlin, and other places. These industries, comparable in size to the Łódź cotton thread production, were so large that they overwhelmed the surrounding markets. Gradually the demand fell, and finally, in the last twenty years, only two tailors (Budrzewski and Bojakiewicz) were left.

In 1886 several Jewish tailors began sewing suits of clothing of so-called *pilka* [coarse cloth]. They took them to Warsaw for sale. At the beginning, they had been only occupied with sewing trousers, which the tailors Winter, Dymant, and Rozen made. Later, they also made vests and then men's jackets, taking all of them to Warsaw on consignment, where Russian agents on commission came to purchase the suits to take to Russia.

From this modest beginning sprang up Dymant's first shop. According to what the organizers said, "You could put the entire shop on one table." The contract workers worked together with the journeymen in one room. Others got wind of the cooperative, and, unable to join it, decided to create for themselves a second cooperative, into which entered Najman, Majer Horn, and Hil Rozenstrauch.[1] The first two sewed men's jackets, and the third, sets of trousers and vests.

As we see, shortly after the first phase of tailoring in Brzeziny, a division of labor was introduced. Everyone specialized in one part of the suit. Later, production was divided up even more. Other towns also adopted the Brzeziny system of work.

When the tailors got wind of the fact that the men's clothing they produced was bought in Warsaw and traveled all the way from Warsaw to Russia, they began making direct contact with Russian firms. In 1892 newcomers from Kishinev assisted Aron Lechtreger, who was literally ruined during a pogrom in Russia, in this. Being himself an agent on commission and knowing the Russian market, he sent samples of Brzeziny production to Russian merchants. Small shipments of suits of clothing to Russia began at once. He was also one of the first to pay for merchandise with a promissory note, which gave impetus to increased production.

The characteristic feature of tailoring in that epoch was the origin and the far-reaching development of the so-called magazine,[2] whose owners had committed a certain capital and worked in the magazine, worked alone, and also parceled out work to tailors to do at home.

In 1892 the *Tydzień Piotrkowski* [Piotrków weekly newspaper] mentioned that in Brzeziny there was a workshop for men's attire as well as a storehouse for petroleum. In 1894 there were already a number of magazines with an annual volume of 79,000 rubles.[3]

The year 1893 saw an increased number of significant bankruptcies for the newly arisen tailoring trade; almost all the magazine owners had failed to pay regularly. The only exception was Szotenberg and Zygmuntowicz, one of the largest firms in Brzeziny. Having a solid financial base and organized bookkeeping, they demonstrated not only an ability to survive the difficulties of establishing workshops but even showed growth, and in 1908 they established their own bank. The numerous bankruptcies indicated the speculative character of tailoring at the time of the establishment of the magazines. The arriving Russian element had not thought how to develop tailoring, only how to become rich. A repercussion of the occurrences of bankruptcy also found a place in the press, where we find the following notice concerning Brzeziny:

> Manufacturers from Łódź suffer from the bankruptcies in Tomaszów, Zgierz, and Białystok, as do a great number of poor tailors in Brzeziny, who, together with their families, have invested weeks and months of work and also their savings and

---

[1] After World War I, Najman and Horn were owners of magazines and gave work to cottage workers, and Rozenstrauch died from hunger in wartime. (Author's note)

[2] The word magazine, originally meaning a warehouse, came to signify in Brzeziny a small clothing enterprise. There, clothing was designed, and material was cut and parceled out to cottage workers to be sewn. The finished clothing was then brought back to the shop where it was sorted, bundled, and stored until shipped to Russia or other markets.

[3] *Obozy Piotrowskiej Gubernii* [Camps of the Piotrków Gubernia]. (Author's note)

uncollected promissory notes. A definite stagnation has occurred, and thousands of machines stand idle.

In 1894 the situation improved; three million rubles worth of suits of clothing were sold. A number of the bankrupted firms were working again, after they came to an agreement paying off twenty to forty percent on their debt.

In general, one must stress that since the rise of tailoring in Brzeziny, there were favorable and unfavorable cyclical circumstances in trade—good times and deep crises. The crises provoked bankruptcies, and many people fled to foreign countries. When times improved, the debt was reduced, and production started again. As an illustration, we will take the years 1894 to 1896, inclusive.

In the beginning of 1894 there was a standstill, but soon there was a lot of work. 1895 was an exceptionally good year; tailors could not keep up with the orders from Russia, and Brzeziny experienced a time of prosperity. In 1896 a crisis came—little work and a great number of bankruptcies.[1] Consequently, we see that every year artisans experienced different times depending on the demand for their products. There was a constant uncertainty that was closely linked with the production of stock.

As we see, the creators and organizers of the inventory system were Jews who came from Russia. The Russian-Jewish immigrants encouraged the creation of workers' cadres—masters and journeymen. This phenomenon appears particularly clear in the mobility of the population—the permanent and temporary residents of Brzeziny—and especially in the rapid growth of the town.

To illustrate this, we cite here the growth of some towns in the period 1860–1921 according to Weinfeld.

An increase in the population took place over time. After the war, the decrease of the Brzeziny population was significant. Professor Buzka states that the population of Congress Poland grew 35 percent in the years 1819 to 1858. In the period from 1823 to 1853, Brzeziny grew 68 percent. From 1858 to 1910 the population in Congress Poland grew 167 percent, and for the same time period, Brzeziny grew almost twice as much— 300 percent.

The listed numbers show two important periods: first, the years 1890–96, when Russian-Jewish immigrants came to Brzeziny in large numbers and established tailoring enterprises; and second, the years 1905–14, the time of the renewed Russian-Jewish immigration under the influence of the revolution (1905) and the pogroms in Ukraine.

In 1907 thirty-five hundred souls came to Brzeziny, which amounted to 21 percent of the population of the town at that time. In fact, the Jewish population in 1903 amounted to 55 percent of the entire population. In later years, the percentage dropped somewhat.

Because of the rapid growth of the population, there was a severe housing shortage and an extremely acute shortage of space for workshops. There was a great deal of construction activity. Many houses were built. The majority were brick houses, which in 1859 had amounted to barely two percent; in 1904 [brick houses] surpassed 23 percent. Brick houses also improved fire safety.[2]

---

[1] See *Tydzień*, no 7, 1895–96. (Author's note)
[2] In earlier times the houses were firetraps. In 1875, sixty-nine wooden houses burned down; in 1881, eleven; in 1884, six; and in 1886, sixty-four. (Author's note)

ENTERPRISE OWNERS, MASTERS, AND JOURNEYMEN

In the tailoring profession there were three main levels—magazine owners, masters, and journeymen (apprentices and female hand stitchers belonged to the journeymen category). In addition to the three main levels, there was a group of independent artisans who were totally independent economically in their tailoring work. These were makers of padding, buttonhole makers, and one can include bookkeepers and magazine employees in this group. The following table from 1921 shows the increase in number of souls in Brzeziny and other towns.[1]

Growth in Percentage

Town	1800–1810	1910–1921	1800–1921
Warsaw	+485.1	+119.2	+578.4
Łódź	+1473.6	-94.0	+1385.9
Częstochowa	+806.7	+112.7	+900.9
Brzeziny	+300.4	-68.4	+207.8

Population in Thousands

Town	1860	1870	1880	1890	1900	1910	1913	1921
Warsaw	161.0	297.0	383.0	523.1	686.0	781.0	845.1	931.2
Łódź	32.6	39.0	45.2	136.1	288.1	480.3	450.3	451.8
Częstochowa	9.0	14.8	21.2	28.7	47.6	72.6	89.6	89.6
Brzeziny	5.1		6.3	7.9	15.5	15.5	17.1	10.5

Number of Souls Who Make a Living from Tailoring (Totals)*

Shopkeepers	50	174
Cutters	9	35
Bookkeepers	5	22
Padding makers	12	52
Padding workers	22	80
Master Tailors	308	1396
TOTAL	406	1759
Journeymen	450	622
Apprentices	255	125
Hand stitchers (female)	248	200
Masters, women	27	60
Buttonhole makers	10	65
TOTAL	990	1072
GRAND TOTAL		2831

* Meaning of this column not clear. (Editor's Note)

---

[1] Although 1921, when the survey was administered, was the period when postwar tailoring was on the verge of reorganizing, I still contend figures are far from reliable. The Needleworkers Union gave me the information that the number of workers was significantly greater than stated here. (Author's note)

The workshops in Brzeziny were generally in the kitchen, even if the master had one or two other rooms. In each workshop there were one or more machines, mostly two or three. The Singer Sewing Machine Company had a franchise in the town. Before World War I, there was a Singer representative who sold machines on strict terms. After the war, the terms changed radically. Those who sold their machines during wartime bought them back later or bought other used, repaired machines.

Every entrepreneur employed several masters. The work was done in the masters' workshops. A master worked for several magazine owners. The work was executed by the master and his family (wife and children) with the help of one or more journeymen, a female hand stitcher, and an apprentice. There were different grades of journeymen; they were paid by the week and had to complete a specified amount of work. Apprentices were hired for a specified time (from Pesakh [Passover] to Sukes [Feast of Tabernacles] or from Sukes to Pesakh), for room and board and sometimes also given a minimum of pocket money. The apprenticeship lasted, before the war, from two to four years; after the war, from one to three years. By the end of the war, apprentices were already being paid by the week.

The following table shows the large number of family members that the masters employed.[1]

	Total	Working for the father	Working for strangers
Journeymen	352	241	111
Hand stitchers (female)	136	123	13
Apprentices	55	22	33
TOTALS	543	386	157

Before World War I, the owners were organized into an association under the name "Producers Association of Ready-Made Clothing." There were ninety members. The war caused their flight to Russia, together with the reserves of finished clothing. After the war, the majority of those who were left alive came back and renewed their economic activity.

AFTER THE WAR

World War I completely ruined the tailoring trade in Brzeziny. When the war broke out, the magazine owners ran away to Russia, mainly to Yekaterinaslav. Szotenberg and Zygmuntowicz established large magazines there, making very good deals. After the war, fearing the Bolshevik Revolution, they hurried home, but they were murdered on the way. Some others met a similar fate. In 1918 a number of tailors that the war had driven out and ruined returned to Brzeziny. During the war years, many occupied themselves with smuggling food to Łódź and the surrounding *shtetl*s.

---

[1] The survey was taken of a portion of each category of tailors. There were four kinds of master tailors—the first kind were the extremely good ones, the second kind were at a slightly lower level, the third kind were middle level, and the fourth kind, the lowest. Also the pay for each group was different. (Author's note)

The situation changed with the rise of the Polish state. In Brzeziny in the beginning of 1919, the government ordered larger amounts of merchandise for the army. A distinguished Łódź manufacturer came to Brzeziny to see if the Brzeziny tailors were capable of fulfilling the military's order. There were many obstacles to overcome. Among others there were simply no sewing machines, since during wartime the tailors had sold the machines to alleviate hunger. Ten masters joined together with Mordechai Winter at their head. They decided to try to fulfill a three-month military contract. They barely found one hundred sewing machines in the town. They divided the tailors into groups of six. Each group received only two machines. Of the thirty-two groups, one part sewed pants, others, uniforms. Those who did not sew occupied themselves with other tasks. The army contract ended in October 1919. A group of disgruntled tailors left for Łódź.

A bit of revival came with the return of Sułkowicz, who before the war worked for Szotenberg and Zygmuntowicz and during the war became well-to-do. Sułkowicz, in partnership with two other tailors, established the first magazine. Right after that sprang up a second magazine. The two enterprises began giving out work to tailors, and others followed. In 1920 there were ties linking them to all of Poland, and in the forefront was Galicia, from which major merchants began to come, mainly from Lemberg [Lwów] and Kraków.

In 1921 a two-week-long strike broke out because of a rise in prices. Groups of up to three tailors began to buy a bolt of cloth and even half a bolt of cloth. They made garments and prepared them for the coming season. They advertised them well in the press. Within a short time, merchants came from different towns to buy directly from the tailors. It may be that the tailors had as their goal to free themselves economically from the magazine owners and take their fate into their own hands, but at the end of 1921, a crisis in the tailoring trade broke out. This compelled the economically weaker masters to surrender and again accept work from the magazine owners. A number of persistent master tailors held out, however, and became independent. Especially successful were those who received help from American relatives in higher-value foreign currency. Later, they themselves parceled out home work to other tailors.

SALES MARKETS

Before the war most of the Brzeziny production went to Russia. Brzeziny suits of clothing were also sold in Warsaw and other Polish cities, since they were able to compete with the local production due to a low price. Sizable shipments were sent to Little Russia (Odessa), the Siberian markets (Yakutsk, Khabarovsk, Vladivostok), to Kavkaz, Donetsk (Ekaterinaslav [Dnepropetrovsk], Rostov) to Turkestan, to Vilna, Moscow, and even to China. These enumerated markets give us a picture of the resourcefulness of the Brzeziny magazine owners.

Although the following table is incomplete, it certainly gives a good idea of the train shipments of Brzeziny work that traveled to Russian markets.

Dispatched From Station					Amount in *Pood* (40 Russian pounds)*				
From:	1890	1891	1897	1899	1900	1901	1905	1909	1912
1) Rogów to Russia	734	4,968	25,732	22,235	42,556	40,704	49,960	12,594	--
Russia to**	--	--	--	1,926	3,080	3,379	1,774	--	--
Baku	--	--	--	1,555	3,295	1,993	2,485	--	--
Bakhmut	--	--	--	1,199	--	--	--	--	--
Vladikavkaz	--	--	--	1,717	2,749	--	--	--	--
Rostov	--	--	--	1,344	--	--	--	--	--
Petersburg	--	--	--	1,752	--	--	--	--	--
Lugansk	--	--	--	1,024	10,532	6,946	11,753	--	--
Odessa	--	--	1105	--	--	--	1,096	--	--
Kharkov	--	--	--	--	--	--	1,044	--	--
Elizavetgrad [Kirovograd]	--	--	--	--	--	--	--	--	--
2) Koluszki	12	--	31	--	--	--	--	--	--
3) Łódź Fabryczna	9,256	10,015	11,761	20,309	--	--	--	--	--
through Koluszki	--	701	--	--	18,029	17,700	81,360	254,177	240,528
	--	--	--	--	30,352	64,321	--	60,170	61,888
4) Częstochowa	115	781	2,428	--	1,331	1,531	--	193,977	177,993
5) Ruda Guzowska	560	4,627	21,440	36,300	4,714	60	14,841	4,958	--
Żyrardów	--	--	--	--	--	--	--	10,281	45,582
6) Zawiercie	--	--	--	--	--	--	--	--	25,583

* Relying on the Brzeziny method of calculating that eight suits of clothing weigh one *pood*, we come to the following approximate number of suits of clothing dispatched—in 1800, 5600 *pood*; in 1891, 32,200; in 1897, 200,000; in 1899, 176,000; in 1900, 480,000; in 1901, 464,000; in 1905, 400,000; in 1909, 576,000, and in 1912, 592,000. (Author's note)

**This table is translated as it appears in the book. However, it may have been incorrectly transcribed for the original publication. It is possible that all the numerical entries in this section should be pushed down one row so that there would be no entry in this row and there would then be an entry in the Elizavetgrad row. (Editor's Note)

NEGOTIATIONS BETWEEN LABOR AND CAPITAL

Before the war, due to the fact that the workers were not well organized, negotiations between labor and capital [owners of enterprises] never led to a strike. After the war, the newly arisen profession-based unions, following the example of other industrial centers, began strike actions to compel employers to comply with their demands. In the beginning, this was not a simple problem. The organizers did not know what sort of situation such an unplanned strike might bring about. They had not properly estimated the appropriateness of the moment for confrontation and whether or not the contractors would be concerned enough to comply with their demands. Time taught them to select strike action at the time when there was a need for their work.

Taking into account that after the war Polish money and the [German] mark fell in value by the hour, striking was the only effective means to improve the wretched condition of the tailors. On the other hand, the frequent conflicts caused the magazine owners to pay starvation wages when work was scarce in bad times, and the starving artisans needed something to give them earnings. Because of this, the tailors worked and suffered, waiting for better times that seldom came. To show the result of calling strikes at an inopportune time, it is enough to mention the frequent "lockouts" proclaimed by the magazine owners. For long weeks they indulged themselves by not giving out work to the tailors.[1]

In order to characterize the distribution of work time just after the war, we present the following table by year and month from 1919 to 1922:

Year	Month	Pattern of work
1919	From January to March	Worked part time to execute military work on trial.
	From April to September	Worked to carry out military contracts.
	From October to December	Did not work when the magazines were closed because of speculation and usury.
1920	From January to December	Began going back to work.
1921	From January to May	Three-week strike of master tailors because of the fall of the mark. It ended with a small salary increase.
	June	Worked, a short work-strike for an eight-hour workday. Ended without result.
	July-August	Worked without interruption.
	September	Four-week strike of master tailors—without result.
	From October to November	There was no work.
	December	A lot of work; the price was raised 100%.
1922	From January to May	Worked a little.
	From June to July	A workers' strike that ended with a salary increase.
	From July to October	Little work; worked with pauses.

From this data we see that out of forty-six months, the tailors worked only twenty-five, including even a few months with little or part-time work. During this time, the magazines were closed for fifteen months by the government bureau that combated usury

---

[1] Because of a shortage of work and great poverty in the town, JOINT [American Jewish Joint Distribution Committee] ran a help and rescue program. CENTOS [Headquarters of Societies Caring for Orphans and Abandoned Children] (supported by JOINT) was especially interested in helping children. Sick children were sent to summer and winter colonies. CENTOS was concerned with their vocational training, helped them with daycare, and provided meals. Those who went to school spent time in the home after school. CENTOS was popular in Brzeziny even among middle-class people, and it gladly received community help of a ten *groszy* (two cents) weekly contribution. Also, the government and the town council recognized its important work and gave it fixed subsidies. In Brzeziny in 1937 there were 210 abandoned or neglected children—77 girls and 133 boys—who benefited from the help. In 1926, Sejm member Dr. Icchak [Ignacy] Schiper and the well-known writer J. J. Singer came to Brzeziny to arrange a great rescue undertaking, which was needed by the large working class. Since the workers organizations refused to work together with the general committee, two rescue committees were formed, one for community elements and the other, for workers. (Author's note)

and speculation. It shows, however, that there were strikes for three months, apart from a series of smaller strikes that were not taken into account here. All the strikes were for a salary increase or a shorter workday. Only in 1922 was a small improvement noticeable. In later years, after the stabilization of the Polish *złoty*, the situation improved a little— but really only a little, not more.

In the earliest postwar period of Brzeziny tailoring, the scourge of the economic policy by the government authorities, especially the office for combating usury and speculation, was also added. At the end of 1919 the government sealed up all the magazines. The intervention of the town government to advocate for their opening did not help. Extensive correspondence with clarifications from the town council was carried out with the higher financial authorities in Warsaw, but all to no avail.[1] The road to building themselves back up was a difficult one. In 1920 many magazine owners and tailors left Brzeziny and went abroad. At the same time, others sought new paths and markets for Brzeziny production. In 1922, because of the rapid rise of the pound sterling and the dollar, efforts were made to take Brzeziny tailored goods by way of Danzig to England and the United States, where the Brzeziny merchandise could easily compete with the local market.

A great obstacle in the development of postwar tailoring was the lack of credit because of the low value of the mark. After the stabilization of the *złoty*, the financial world also became interested in Brzeziny. In the beginning of 1923 banks and credit institutions were established—a local Cooperative Bank and the Jewish Savings and Loan Society. The Warsaw Credit Bank also opened a branch in Brzeziny. The banks stimulated business but also rekindled the earlier woes of promissory notes, wherein 12 percent was deducted [by the bank upon redemption] from the half-year IOU's that the tailors got for their work. In later years the IOU's and the percentage deducted were the main causes of conflicts between labor and capital.

III BRZEZINY POWIAT

The Brzeziny *powiat* [county] in the Łódź *województwo* [province] was created from half of the Rawa *powiat* and parts of Łęczyca. Brzeziny's borders were with Rawa and Skierniewice to the east, with Łowicz and Łęczyca to the north, with Łódź to the west, and with Piotrków to the south. When Piotrków became a province from parts of the Kalisz, Łęczyca, and Kielce provinces, the Brzeziny *powiat* was assigned to Piotrków.

---

[1] According to a decree of the Łódź county office in the fight against usury and speculation, the contractors had to post signs in the most visible place in the magazine with the price lists for each article. The signature of the owner and the date he had posted it had to be on each list. Every two weeks, one had to report to the financial office. Failure to comply promptly with the decree involved severe penalty. I cannot bring here all the correspondence of the Brzeziny town hall and town council with the Warsaw and Łódź government organs, where it is shown that the town was literally ruined by these draconian decrees. It is enough that on 11 September 1920 the Ministry for Provisions notified the town council in Brzeziny that the merchants Jechiel Mojsze Gotlib, Dawid Ikka, Mordechai Ikka, and Mojsze Zyndel were entitled to get back their confiscated ready-made garments. (Author's note)

Its surface occupies 20.28 square miles of essentially flat land. Until not long ago, it was still covered with forests and marshes, as evidenced by the numerous names of the towns and villages—Brzeziny [*brzozy* = birch], Lipiny [*lipa* = linden], Leszczyny [hazel], Osiny [aspen], Rokociny [creeping willow], etc. There were also numerous small brooks and streams. The southern body of water that is part of the *powiat*—the Czarna Wolborka River—flows into the Pilica, forming the border of the *powiat* for a couple of miles. A watery dividing line runs through the environs of the Brzeziny *powiat* between the town of Brzeziny and the villages of Grzmiąca, Lipiny, and Małczew, where the highest mountains are found. These mountains reach 122.8 *sążni*[1] near Lipiny and Teolin, on the right of the highway between Brzeziny and Łódź, and 104 to 108 *sążni* near Małczew and Grzmiąca. To the north of these mountains, the water flows from the river Mroga into the Bzura. The Warsaw-Vienna Railroad, cutting through the length of the Brzeziny *powiat*, fostered the development of the manufacturing industry in Tomaszów. Tomaszów's location on the southern border also fostered a strong growth of agriculture, although the soil there was of mediocre quality.

The numerous roads that cut through the *powiat* in various directions linked the most important towns and villages. The railroad from Koluszki to Łódź made this line well suited to the development of agriculture and industry. With the building of the railroad and roadways, the forests disappeared. Only near Ujazd were there still large tracts of forest, which were also disappearing because of the development of the Tomaszów textile industry.

In 1890 there were six cotton mills in the *powiat*, a mere 2000 weaving workshops, 525 cloth workshops, 14 distilleries, 2 beer breweries, 1 distillation factory, 1 paper factory, 1 steam mill and 88 ordinary mills, 1 lime factory, 10 brickyards, and 3 iron works.

As to the organization of its judiciary, the Brzeziny *powiat* was divided into four district courts—Wola Cyrusowa, Galków, Ujazd, and Stryków, and into one lower court for Brzeziny and Tomaszów.

As for administration, the Brzeziny *powiat* was divided into fifteen *gminy* [administrative districts]—Będków, Bratoszewice, Biała, Ciosny, Długie, Dmosin, Dobra, Lipiny, Łaznów, Łazisko, Mroga Dolna, Mikołajew, Niesułków, Popień (Jeżów), and Osada. Those without town status were Głowno, Stryków, Jeżów, and Ujazd. The two largest towns were Tomaszów and Brzeziny.

In 1890 the population of the Brzeziny *powiat* numbered 93,778 souls. This number included 18,393 Evangelical Christians, 15,528 Jews, and 120 Greek Orthodox; the rest were Roman Catholics.

TOWNS AND SHTETLS AROUND BRZEZINY

Ujazd

Ujazd was a *shtetl* in the Brzeziny *powiat*. At the beginning of the fifteenth century, Piotr Tolk from Stryków proposed building a town on the newly cleared forest land. The village Jews were given a twenty-year exemption from taxes. The founder of the town

---

[1] A *sążeń* [pl. *sążni*] is close to 3 ells long [approximately six feet]. (Author's note)

received from the king the privilege of holding two annual market fairs in addition to the weekly markets. In 1485 the various privileges were renewed for the new owner of the town, Piotr Dunin. When Dunin's grandson married off his only daughter, Anna, Dunin gave her the town of Ujazd as a dowry. In 1594 her husband became *kasztelan (starosta)* [local administrator] of Sochaczew and later of Brzeziny.

In 1616 Kasper Denhopf obtained from the Sieradz province an estate and palace in Ujazd for his wife and daughter. In 1786 the palace was repaired. The Prussian kaiser stopped there at the end of the eighteenth century when he visited the newly captured provinces. He stayed at the palace in Ujazd.

When in 1584 Ujazd went to the Ossoliński Family, Krzysztof Ossoliński built there, on the very top of the mountain, a castle in the Italian style. On the entry tower (built in 1631) was a large stone cross. A defensive wall ringed the palace. The castle was very well known in Poland. The structure incorporated—based on the time periods of the year—four spires, as in the four seasons of the year, twelve halls, as in the twelve months, fifty-two rooms for each week, and three hundred sixty-five windows for each day. There was a glass roof with water where there were goldfish. On the walls between the windows were engraved the names of their ancestors in their own signatures.

There were superb gardens there. Eleven years later, the Swedes surrounded and destroyed the castle. Until shortly before the end of the nineteenth century, there were still remarkable remains of the castle.

Ujazd was also famous for its traditional Jewish life. A son-in-law of the famous *rebbe*, Fiszele Strykower, was *rebbe* there. After World War I, national cultural Jewish youth organizations were created there, which carried out widespread enlightenment activities. With the exception of a small number of rescued Jewish survivors, Jewish Ujazd, along with the six million holy martyrs in Europe, was completely destroyed.

Głowno

Głowno was a *shtetl* in the Brzeziny *powiat*, already known in 1427. It was established by a Mazovian prince. In 1522 King Sigismund I approved municipal privileges. In the seventeenth century the town belonged to the famous landowning family the Czarneckis. In 1827 there were seventy-six houses there and 972 inhabitants. Norblin's silver factory in Głowno was very well known in Poland.

Tomaszów

Also known as Tomaszów Mazowiecki or Tomaszów Fabryczny, Tomaszów was the biggest town in the Brzeziny *powiat* by the Wolborka River, which converges beyond the town with the Pilica and Czarna Rivers.

More that two hundred years ago, this was a site of forests and swamps, and it belonged to the landowner Ostrowski, who was at that time chairman of the Senate.

Tomaszów began developing only one hundred fifty years later, after the Congress of Vienna, when Poland was given to Czarist Russia, and, in the last third of the nineteenth century, it made rapid progress. In 1879 there were twelve thousand residents with twenty-two enterprises powered by steam. As early as 1886 the town produced textiles and hardware worth seven million rubles and employed eight thousand workers.

The town and surrounding area had superb, beautiful scenery and had a large number of people engaged in trades.

Because of its own importance and stature and above all because of the fact that Tomaszów itself is ready to publish a big *yizkor* book, we are only mentioning it as a town in the Brzeziny *powiat*.

Jeżów

Very long ago this was a village with the name of a Mazovian prince. The town's name Jeżów derived from that. Konrad I, a Mazovian prince and clergyman, gave it away as a gift early in the first years of his reign. Bolesław, a Mazovian prince, elevated Jeżów to the status of a town with privileges beginning in 1272. Later, at the request of a Lublin senior cleric, the Mazovian princes, and the Polish kings, other privileges were added. King Sigismund I twice, in 1519 and in 1537, freed the citizens of the town forever from the obligation of providing horse-drawn wagons for military use.

In Jeżów in the sixteenth century, there were blacksmith, wheelwright, and shoemaker guilds. In 1778 King Stanisław August renewed the privileges of holding the already established market fairs and added four new ones.

In the local church, there were stands from the distant Middle Ages that were almost a thousand years old. Later, Jeżów became less important, but its market fairs were renowned in the entire area.

There was a significant Jewish settlement there, hundreds of bright people and a progressive, religious, and secular youth organized into clubs, unions, and societies. The well-known Jewish writer Icchak Janasowicz came from Jeżów.

With few exceptions, all the Jews perished in Hitler's death camps.

Stryków

Stryków was a *shtetl* eleven kilometers from Brzeziny—called Strikkov until the sixteenth century. Paprocki calls it Streijków. It is situated by the Moszczenice River, which flows into the Bzura.

Stryków is among the oldest settlements in the Brzeziny area. Very long ago, it was the stopping place between the provincial towns of Łęczyca and Rawa. Already as early as 1394 Stryków was a town, and Władysław Jagiełło decreed in Brzeziny that Stryków should pay taxes on wagons, horses, and cattle.

The Stryków landowner, Piotr Strykowski, became *kasztelan (starosta)* in Inowrocław in 1457. He also served as advisor to the imperial court for an extended period. His or his father's name was signed on the famous treaty with the Teutonic Knights of the Cross in Brześć [Brześć Kujawski] in 1436. This family, Strykowski, after whom the present-day town is most likely named, dispersed to different lands after accumulating a large estate.

In the fifteenth century Stryków went to Mikołaj of Kurozwęki, whose underage heir, after the death of his father, was under the guardianship of Jan Łaski, the Archbishop of Gniezno, and his brother, Jarosław. In the sixteenth century Stryków belonged to landowner Jarosław Łaski. He received Stryków as a dowry from the Kurozwękis when the Kurozwękis divided their estates (1531) with their brother Stanisław in Kraków.

Stanisław gave Stryków to Łaski. From the Łaskis, Stryków went to the Moskowskis. In the middle of the seventeenth century Stryków passed over to the Malińskis, and in the eighteenth century, to the Czarneckis.

In 1459 Stryków provided six foot soldiers to the Prussian government, which shows that it was a significant *shtetl*, while other towns provided only up to two soldiers.

After a fire destroyed the town, Sigismund I freed the town from various taxes for fifteen years (1520). In 1525 market fairs were added, and in 1543 Stryków was again freed from the burden of taxes. In 1576 five *grzywny*, eight florin, and twenty-four *groszy* were collected.

By the end of the sixteenth century there were the following artisans: 5 fishermen, 6 shoemakers, 6 tailors, 3 blacksmiths, 13 bakers, 2 potters, 5 furriers, and 2 barrel makers. They paid [as taxes] between 5 kegs of *mashke* [liquor] up to 24 *grzywny*. The three butchers paid up to 12 *grzywny*. Altogether the town paid 59 florin and 18 *groszy*.

In 1827 there were 141 houses with 2,022 inhabitants, of which 1,332 were Jews. In 1858 there were already 171 houses, 4 of them brick, with 2,613 inhabitants, of which there were 1,744 Jews and 88 Germans; the rest were Roman Catholics.

In the eighteenth century there was a large Jewish population in Stryków, twice as large as in Brzeziny, with well-known rabbis. Rebbe Fiszele was famous in all of Poland as a miracle worker. Twenty-nine villages belonged to the Stryków *kehile* [Jewish community]. Zgierz, then a village of nine Jews, also belonged to Stryków. The first Jews who died in the village of Łódź were buried in Stryków.

After the Nazi destruction there were no more Jews in Stryków.

Koluszki

Koluszki, a small town six kilometers from Brzeziny, was a significant railroad junction on the Warsaw-Vienna and Warsaw-Łódź lines. The majority of Brzeziny goods went through Koluszki.

In 1764 there were already eight Jews living there who paid their taxes to the Brzeziny *kehile*. Until the war, ten Jewish families, who later shared the fate of all the Jews of Poland, lived there. Few saved themselves.

Rogów

Rogów was a *shtetele* [very small town] near Brzeziny, near the river Mroga, belonging to the *gmina* [administrative district] of Mroga Dolna. Its small railroad station, eight kilometers from Brzeziny, lay halfway between Brzeziny and Jeżów. In the beginning of the sixteenth century, Rogów paid a tithe from numerous estates to the ecclesiastical representative of Jeżów.

There were ten well-to-do Jewish families. Almost all of them perished.

IV ORGANIZATIONS

As we have already seen above, the war [World War I] seriously reduced and impoverished the population. It suffered seriously economically and could no longer maintain its prewar status. As a result, a communal social movement sprang up. After the rise of the Polish state, a multi-branched communal life began. It was as if all the sluice gates were inoperable and the streams overflowed all the banks. Ideas that formerly remained underground suddenly became winged with enthusiasm and emerged on the surface of Jewish life. Social, economic, cultural, sport, and youth organizations of all types feverishly developed their activities in all directions. A number of the organizations were of lasting value, while others were not. There were those that existed sporadically. I will here describe only some organizations that were active over a longer time period and left their mark on the town.

The Master Tailors Union

The Master Tailors Union was founded in 1909 and played a very important role, not only among tailors, but also in town life in general. The founders were Szlama Gelb (Szlama the lame), Mordechai Winter, Uri Szajbowicz, Abraham Frajnd, and two others whose names I do not know. The first founding meeting took place in Uri Szajbowicz' house (Uri Glazer's). During the next several weeks, four more meetings took place, where they talked about the miserable conditions of the tailors. An organizer, who came especially from Łódź, proposed to organize the union.[1] The plan was very characteristic of that time, in which the "Black Hundred," a reactionary league in Russia sent by Czarist petty tyrants, suppressed every free thought. A trade union was heretical; therefore, they agreed to form a mutual aid society. The statutes had the following goals:

1. To have a *shul* in which the members could *daven* [pray].
2. To write their own *seyfer-toyre* [Torah scroll].
3. To help downtrodden members.
4. To have the right to assemble twice a day.[2]
5. To have the right for someone to attend the sick.

A delegation went to the governor in Piotrków to have the statutes legalized. The governor, a great enemy of workers and an even greater hater of Jews, turned them down. They waited there until the governor traveled out of town, and with the help of a twenty-five ruble piece, the assistant governor legalized the statutes—along with the instruction that pictures of Czar Nicholas and his wife must hang in the union's headquarters.

The meetings took place after *minkhe* [afternoon prayer]. The tables and chairs were arranged in the back of the synagogue lectern, and the speaker at the lectern was always referred to as the cantor. Gradually the union developed. The main activity was the mutual assistance of its members.

After the war, the union grew greatly; it played an important role in the economic and social life of the town. During the local and national elections, all the political parties took pains to get support from the Master Tailors Union. The Master Tailors Union always had their elected members on the town council, the *kehile* [Jewish community council], and the *krankn-kase* [fund for the sick]. The important leaders were: Abraham

---

[1] Mojsze Korpel, a gifted leader of the meat workers in Łódź, organized the Meat Masters Union. He also organized the Meat Workers Union in Warsaw, Kielce, Radom, and Kalisz. He is now a Histadrut [Workers Union] leader in Israel. (Author's note)

[2] At that time more than three people could not assemble without a permit. (Author's note)

Frajnd, Mojsze Działoszyński, Pejsach Grynszpan, Lajbl Szajbowicz (Lajbl Byk), Herszel Szmulewicz, Majer Kozak, and Mojsze Berber.

In 1927 the Polish government implemented a trade guild statute that renewed the old privileges of the guilds, with the intention of restricting Jewish access to work. According to the statute, the guilds had to issue master certificates, without which one could not operate a workshop. The Master Tailors Union carried out an intense battle to weaken the effect of the evil decree. Thanks to the strong protest movement, organized jointly with the Socialist Artisans Union, the so-called tailor *chałupnicy* [cottage workers] succeeded in getting the evil decree repealed.[1] But this did not last long. In 1935 the anti-Semites achieved their aim. It did not help to argue that modern economic life demanded freedom of work and employment. By means of examinations, guilds, and closed groups, Jewish artisans were threatened, and, even worse, these actions brought about unemployment and poverty.

The Master Tailors Union separated itself from public political influence and thus managed to pull through all the storms and political changes in Poland.

The Clothing Workers Union

The trade movement grew up in an atmosphere of revolutionary political struggle. Under the influence of the violence of 1905–6, Brzeziny, like the majority of the cities in Russia and Poland, organized itself for a decisive battle. Proclamations, strikes, arrests, and banishments to Siberia—all these helped the workers become aware of their need to be organized according to their status in an organized workers society. Before the war, the political workers parties conducted direct economic battles for the workers. After the war, the Needleworkers Union [presumably part of the Clothing Workers Union] was organized. The organizers were Szaja Bocian, Majer Szwarc, and Lustig. From time to time the Needleworkers Union would abruptly change, not always for the best, depending upon which political movement had influence over it. There were also objective causes for its instability. A journeyman who joined the [Clothing] Workers Union, in the course of time, would become a master himself. He would then of necessity become a member of the Master Tailors Union and employ other workers. This was a mass phenomenon.

The large worker emigration and the high percentage of workers who worked for their own parents weakened the union. Certainly, disregarding all the difficulties, the Workers Union achieved important gains for workers. At the initiative of the Workers Union and with the help of inspectors of workplaces and of the town hall, a conference took place on the strict observance of the eight-hour workday, which in truth had never been put into practice. In 1926–27 factions from Poale Zion [Zionist Labor Party], Royte [Reds–Communists], and the Bund [Jewish Socialist Party] existed within the union. There were approximately seven hundred members. The union had a beautiful library and a good drama club, with a part-time director who periodically staged works from the Yiddish repertoire and from workers' lives.

---

[1] The *chałupnicy* [cottage workers] were a split-off section of the Master Tailors Union. They joined together in the Socialist Artisans Central. They worked with only one apprentice. Their representatives were Hersz Finger, Abraham Opatowski, and Lajbl Sender. (Author's note)

A First of May demonstration was organized in 1927, which Brzeziny had never seen before then. The streets lost their normal appearance. One did not hear the hum of the machines. All the workers dressed as for a holiday. Activity stopped. The closer to the gathering place near the Workers Union, the more evident was the scope of the united workers' strength. All the political workers parties hurried with their red flags to their designated places. At the head went the representative of the Clothing Workers Union, the mayor, and a representative of PPS [Polish Socialist Party]. With banners and slogans for an eight-hour workday and higher wages, the battle against Fascism, child labor, and the persecution of the Yiddish language and culture and for a workers government—the demonstrators marched through the main streets of the town, and a large orchestra played songs about work and battle. Hundreds of workers participated in the joint march. Three-quarters of them were Jewish workers.

A scene in a tailor workshop in Brzeziny—Ezekiel Niewodowicz with his daughters and hired hand stitchers.

The Commercial Employees Union

The Commercial Employees Union, which took no part in any economic action, was organized in 1926. Its main activity was a social one. The membership was entirely Jewish.

The Transportation Union

The Transportation Union was organized in 1929. It mainly organized the street porters and the porters from businesses and warehouses. The main organizers were Rywen Blat (Rywen Ciołek), Zelig Hauzner, and M. Rozenstrauch. The union began with thirty members and did well.[1]

The Left-Wing Poale Zion, the Bund, and the "Reds"

A.

The Poale Zion [Zionist Labor] movement, from the time of its foundation in 1906, represented a strictly Marxist point of view toward all the problems of Jewish working

---

[1] In a letter to *Arbeter Tsaytung* [Worker Newspaper], number 33 (1929), we read that the Transportation Union had demanded a wage increase from the master bakers and flour merchants. The action succeeded. They also planned to work on a communal basis. (Author's note)

life. It was predestined to play a leading role in the political education of the Jewish worker. After the resolution of national boundaries in 1920, the Brzezin organization went completely over to Left Poale Zion. For legal reasons, Poale Zion joined "The Society for Workers Evening Courses" in 1923 and carried out broader work with the masses. Among the young and old, the significance of "Marxist Borochovism" [Marxist-Zionist views of Ber Borochov] and "Proletariat Palestinism" was very clear. They [Poale Zion] helped organize trade unions. They had the most widely-read library, a drama club, and frequent lectures and reading of papers—with lecturers from Warsaw. The most important leaders of the movement came—Zerubawel, N. Buxbaum, Federzajl, Ringelblum, Loew, Josef Rozen, Dr. Rafał Mahler, and others. Local teachers and leaders taught literature, political economics, and historical materialism.

In 1925 a rift took place. A significant group of important leaders went over to the Communists; others went to the right and to the Bund [Jewish Socialist Party]. In subsequent years, the organization made an effort to make up for the loss from this split. In the later 1920s they won three seats on the town council, which at that time was regarded as a significant victory. For the first time, a female worker, Ester Winter, was among those newly elected to the council. A different impression was created in the town council by the resignation of Comrade Mordechai Dawid Biedak. At the first meeting of the newly elected town council in the large Firemen's Hall, he seceded from the organization in the name of the Poale Zionist town council faction, with a militant twenty-minute speech in Yiddish, in which he demanded equal rights of life, work, and culture for the Jewish masses. The anti-Semitic Endeks [National Democratic Party] gnashed their teeth and formed their own groups. The secession signaled the awakening of the Jewish worker between the two world wars. There was enthusiasm, boldness, and dynamism and especially an awareness of the goal. They knew and understood what they wished to achieve. In later years, they suffered from police persecution; they became partly illegal.[1] In 1939, just before the great destruction, Poale Zion, in a united front with the Bund and other worker parties, was still able to win six seats on the town council.

The most important leaders in the establishment of the Society for Workers Evening Courses were Mojsze-Icek Ginsberg, Josef Baruch Szajbowicz, Mordechai Dawid Biedak, Lajb Sieradzki, and Jankiel Dawidowicz.

B.

Before World War I, the Bund [Jewish Socialist Party], above all, encouraged the workers in the fight against capitalism and exploitation. The proclamations, the revolutionary songs, the harsh political action against the Czarist decrees, the organizing of workers circles—all these greatly helped to open the world for the oppressed Jewish working masses. They become permeated with the consciousness of their human worth. "The [working] class does not deserve freedom if they cannot fight for it," L. Martov said.

At the beginning of the century, under pressure from the Bund, Jewish workers broke with the old leaders and antiquated traditional patterns and carried out a *coup d'etat* in

---

[1] The police closed the organization Society for Workers Evening Courses in 1934. (Author's note)

Jewish life. In 1905 the Bund organized strikes and street fights in Brzeziny.[1] There were arrests, banishments to Siberia, and so forth. After the war the Bundist influence was limited, though still significant.[2] In the thirties the organization became stronger and expanded its influence into broader worker and intellectual strata. The Bund controlled the Socialist Artisans Union. In the town council election in 1939, they gained five seats—the largest Jewish worker faction in the town council. The most important leaders were Szmul Akerman, Abraham Opatowski, Hersz Finger, and Lajzer Jakubowicz.

In the time of the Nazi destruction, the Bundist party leaders were active in Brzeziny. After the transfer of the Brzeziny ghetto inhabitants to Łódź, Abraham Opatowski, a former Bundist councilman in the Brzeziny Town Council, was co-opted by the Łódź resistance group to direct self-help work in the ghetto.[3] The Bundist group in the ghetto numbered fifteen men.

C.

The "Royte" [Reds (Communist)] organization in Brzeziny came into being in 1923. Its founders were mostly middle-class and half-assimilated elements. Because of the fact that the party was illegal, its members, in a conspiratorial manner, worked through the legal organizations, mainly the trade unions and workers parties, where they created Communist factions that led to divisiveness. In a short time, they became the dominant strength in the trade unions. They also exercised a great influence over students and youth from middle-class organizations. They created a militant fighting spirit among the workers; they especially fought for a shorter workday.

With the free time that they won, the workers developed an interest in communal problems, and this also awakened them to life around them. A striving for education, reading books, sprang up. The rise of culture came with the growing fighting spirit. Every Shabes [Sabbath], get-togethers and lectures took place on current themes. The Workers Council Hall, which could hold several hundred people, was always packed to the rafters. Later, the Polish Union of Construction Workers and the Workers Cooperative came under their influence. Earlier, the Construction Union and the Cooperative were under the influence of the Polish Socialist Party [PPS]. The Communists took them in under the leftist PPS that was their affiliate. During the Spanish Civil War, a small group went to

---

[1] The Piotrków governor wrote in his journal of 12 April 1902, number 227, "The socialist movement has already given birth to a separate Jewish party, the 'Bund,' that according to news from the police is growing more than all other parties. At their convention, it was decided to use all their efforts for full equality for Jews. Jews should have full civil and political rights along with other nationalities." (Author's note)

[2] In *Lodzer Veker* [Łódź Awake] of 12 May and 1 June 1928, we read that in the current year there was a united First of May celebration jointly conducted by the Polish Socialist Party (PPS), Royte [Communists], the Bund, and Poale Zion; that the Bund and Tsukunft [youth group] in Brzeziny had over one hundred members; and that at the Łódź regional conference of Bund youth (Tsukunft), the Brzeziny delegate reported on widespread Bundist activity. Forty copies of *Folkstsaytung* [People's Newspaper] and a great number of *Yungt Veker* [Youth Awake] and *Lodzer Veker* were distributed. (Author's note)

[3] See the article by Jakub Nirenberg, secretary of the Łódź committee of the Bund, in *The Years of Jewish Destruction*, 1946 (the voice of the underground Bund). (Author's note)

Spain to fight. There was even a courageous fighter, a leader of a brigade, who fell heroically in battle. The Communists also popularized support for those who were arrested. The entire spectrum of the workers parties had MOPR[1] books to sell and, with this, assisted the local people who were arrested for political reasons.

In the course of time, under the extraordinary political persecutions, emigration, and personal disappointments, the movement declined drastically. The most important leaders, if they were not sitting in prison, had dispersed to other cities. Many of them went to South America, Western Europe, and Russia.

FINAL OBSERVATIONS

Writing about the workers' Brzeziny, the workers' parties, and the trade union movement, I have deliberately avoided the class struggle between workers and capital, although without a doubt it existed, and, very often, in a passionate and intense form. Today, after the Nazi murderous plagues, when our sacred Jewish community has been annihilated along with all Polish Jewry, that other struggle no longer has any significance for us.

---

[1] International organization to support the politically persecuted. (Author's note)
 MOPR [Mezhdunarodnoye Obshtchestvo Pomoshtchi Revolutzioneram—International Society for the Aid of Revolutionaries].

Past Generations (pp. 21–30)

Aron Fogel (Tel-Adoshim)

A SHORT FOREWORD

In memory of our beloved *shtetl* Brzezin, I will try to put down on paper the recollections and material that I have gathered over the years.

During the '60s and '70s of the nineteenth century, there was a Jewish tailor (a Cantonist)[1] in our *shtetl* by the name of Kozele Sznajder. This simple Jew understood that it was hard to live from the work of one's own ten fingers, and he began to urge two of his Jewish acquaintances who were like him to make a business from their children. Teach them a trade so that they would be able to support the family.

They gave him their children, who worked just for meals for several years, and he made tailors out of them. It never occurred to the Jew that the young men would later grow up to be big industrialists, who would create a worldwide name for their town and produce millions of rubles in volume. The beginnings were not so easy.

Sunday, very early, scarcely having time to finish *davening* [praying], our young men, the tailors, girded themselves, assembling everything they would need. They took a small sack and, first of all, put in a *talis* [prayer shawl], *tfilen* [phylacteries], a *sidurl* [small daily prayer book], and then the more profane items—a needle, a thimble, and a piece of wax—and got underway. All the way they prayed to God that he would protect them from bad dogs and he would give them a good beginning. With great dread and faith, they came into the village. Until they found the house the tailor had assigned to them, they almost died. They entered the house half dead but took courage and proceeded to do what they had to do. And that is the way they worked from Sunday to Friday. Friday, they raced home to wife and children for Shabes.

They might have worked like that forever had it not been that, first of all, the families began getting bigger, and second, Kozele began sending out new tailors. The village began to be too crowded to be able to support such a large number of tailors. They had to look for a solution. They called together all the tailors, who had in spite of the circumstances actually saved a few rubles, held a meeting, and made a resolution.

This resolution takes us to the second stage of the development of our industry.

BACK FROM THE VILLAGE TO THE TOWN

At the meeting, it was resolved that they would travel by themselves to the then nearest weaving town, Zgierz, buy some material and, on their own, sew it and then take it to Warsaw to sell.

---

[1] A Cantonist was someone who, as a youngster, had been pressed into long years of military service during the reign of Czar Nicholas I, 1825–55, and therefore had little chance for education.

At that time, something began happening in Greater Russia. The Russian peasant began demanding the most primitive thing—a pair of pants on his body. Jewish merchants from Ukraine and Greater Russia used to come to Warsaw to buy the tailors' private work. In Warsaw there was a shortage of hand workers. They actually received our Brzeziner tailor-merchants with open arms, as esteemed guests.

So began the second stage of the creation of our manufacturing—through the connection of our small Brzezin with big Warsaw, as middlemen to the Russian market. And even though now making a living was still not very easy—since the long trip was not by car, not even by railroad, but simply by horse and wagon, and the trip to Warsaw took two full days—they were nevertheless satisfied.

The way it was recounted to me by the pioneers of that time, Reb [title of respect] Szlama Josef Ikka, *z"l* [*zal*—of blessed memory], Reb Herszel Rozen Korekh, *z"l*, Raszewski, *z"l*, Frankensztajn, Magnes, *z"l*, and many others, that was the happiest time of their lives. They carried on with might and main and, because of it, saw a new world unfold before their eyes, and second, who can imagine how we enjoyed ourselves on the journey—so the old foxes told me.

[He told me this] when he was already a Jew in his eightieth year, a fine, esteemed man of stature in town. But our people were growing older, and the difficult trips began to bother them.

Izrael Mojsze Warszawski, the oldest tailor in Brzezin, was ninety-six years old when this picture was taken, and he worked without eyeglasses.

In the meanwhile another situation was occurring in Russia. As they looked around they saw that the textile industry was almost entirely undeveloped. Everything had to be brought in from foreign countries. Within the country itself, there were no professionals, so the government turned to the nearest neighbors—the German weavers. The government promised the German master weavers various benefits. They were given free land and loans to build homes; they were given long-term credit in order to settle their affairs. In this way, they were assured that they would not be cut off from their previous homes, that is, if they were not happy, they could easily return to them. To this end, the small *shtetl* Łódź was selected, located on the Łódka, as the little stream that flowed through the town was called. And they, the Germans, actually began building the future great textile industry in the Russian Poland of that time.

Łódź is located just twenty kilometers from our Brzezin. The closeness greatly aided the development of our tailoring industry. When the Łódź weavers began to sell their goods, they had to send them to the Russian markets. The Lithuanian, Ukrainian, and Russian Jews took note of this. They were good merchants, and they seized this opportunity for business. They became the middlemen between the new Polish industry and the Russian markets. These Jews had heard of the Brzezin tailors who were selling their goods in Warsaw.

A Jewish agent on commission from Russia named Berman settled in Brzezin and began to bring customers from afar, directly from Russia to Brzezin. Soon, more agents began arriving from Bessarabia and the Ukraine, and each one brought with him a few customers, so that in a short time, they began to experience a shortage of workers. The demand for finished garments became stronger and stronger day by day.

WORK GIVERS AND WORK TAKERS

Eventually, three categories of tailors were created in our town: 1) work givers, 2) work takers—that is, those who received some cut material to work on at home, and 3) journeymen and apprentices who worked in the small workshops.

In the beginning, the work givers and the work takers lived together like brothers. They were like one *mishpokhe*.

At that time, a Hasidic family named Jakubowicz came to our town. The head of the family, Reb Herszel from Wały, *z"l*, was a large landowner. The village Wały lies not far from Brzezin. This wealthy Jew had liquidated his village holdings and come to live in town among other Jews. The son of Reb Herszel of Wały, Reb Perec Jakubowicz, *z"l*, became a *magaziner* [owner of a clothing enterprise]. This is the new name that originated in our town, with the entry of a stranger, not a tailor, in that level of business. Reb Perec, not a tailor himself, brought into his magazine a couple of tailors who did the professional work for him. This was also the first contact between the Hasidic Jews and the tailors.

Imitating Perec Jakubowicz, other magazine owners came into being who eventually brought bookkeepers and assistant bookkeepers from Russia.

I remember one of them—Wasilkowski. He had brought with him a beautiful Hebrew library. A second Jew, Baruk, belonged to the Russian Social Democratic Party. Our merchants immediately sensed that the new element brought change. First, they did not want to work long hours; they began to talk about a ten-hour workday. Our people did not easily agree to such an upheaval. They began to search for means of avoiding being completely gobbled up by the "Litvaks" [nickname for Russian Jews]. And the house of Jakubowicz came to their aid again. Reb Perec had three sons—Reb Szymon, Reb Abraham, and Reb Pinkus. All three were religious scholars. They went into the business, which actually eventually became the House of Perec Jakubowicz and Sons. Other magazine owners imitated him and brought their children into the business.

This resulted in a serious crisis; the Grodzisk Hasid, Reb Josef Machel's, became connected by marriage with the pioneer of our industry, Reb Szlama Fuksel. This was almost like a revolution, that a simple tailor should marry the daughter of a Talmudic scholar.

The barrier was broken, and Hasidic young men entered the tailoring business. Such a gentle young man—a great Talmudic scholar and Hasid—as Reb Hersz Mendel Pinczewski, *z"l*, was the first to bring tailoring accessories for the magazine owners from Łódź to Brzezin. He was very successful, and his home became the center where the magazine owners used to gather to receive the material from Łódź. It is worth noting that the children of Reb Hersz Mendel were ultimately among the biggest manufacturers in the Polish Manchester, that is, in Łódź.

Old gate of Brzezin cemetery

New winds began to blow in Russia in general, and they also brought new ideas to our *shtetl*. We ourselves still did not know what we wanted and to what we aspired. But everyone understood that things could not remain as they were. Generally, this came from the working intelligentsia. They brought various pamphlets—pamphlets that urged one toward a more humane life. In these booklets, it was written that the worker is exactly equal to the work giver. They started to complain that the air was stifling, and, remarkably, everyone eagerly embraced the "new winds"—from apprentices, journeymen, and masters up to the *besmedresh bokher* [prayer house young man].

In our town there was a Jew, a wealthy man. All his life he was a leader in the town. He paid for the writing of a Torah scroll and gave it to the *kehile* [Jewish community] as a gift. He also gave land for the cemetery as a gift. This Jew was called Reb Szlama Silski, *z"l*. He brought [to Brzezin] a son-in-law for his only daughter, a fine person, a great scholar and man of distinguished lineage, Reb Arje Dawid Perlmuter, *z"l*, a son of the Radom *rebbe*. The oldest son of Reb Arje Dawid, Reb Mojsze Eliezer, *z"l*, was also brought up in the spirit of his elders—in the Hasidic movement and education. It was this very young man who took upon himself to break away from the narrow confines. Obviously, the chance circumstance that he had lost his mother in his youth helped, as when his father brought a second wife into the house, his grandfather gave him a room in his home. That is how he got the opportunity to browse through religious books undisturbed, which for young men of his station was forbidden.

The young man became a *maskil* [follower of Haskalah—Enlightenment] and created a circle of modern Hebrew students in his home. He assembled a small group of students for whom the [Hebrew] language was not strange. Most of the students were *besmedresh bokhoyrim* [young men from the Orthodox prayer house]. In that way they also began studying and reading modern literature. As chance would have it, a Jewish part-time pharmacist named Wolman had an apartment in the same house. This was a novelty. Generally, at that time, Jews thought of pharmacists as intelligentsia. He also had a wife, an intelligent, nationalistic Jewish woman. She knew modern Jewish literature well, and she was also a strong supporter of Dr. Herzl's Zionism.

Our young Perlmuter, having become acquainted with the woman, began, under her influence, to spread Zionism in our town. They began buying illegal goods—that is, *shekels*[1]—and participated in the elections to the Zionist Congress. The young Perlmuter was not afraid of the Hasidim, having Arje Dawid for his father. He also was not afraid of the police, because his grandfather was Reb Szlama Silski, the community leader. Nonetheless, it happened that "good Jews" could no longer keep silent and sent the police into his *shtibl* [small Hasidic house of prayer] on an inspection. They actually found that

---

[1] Buying *shekel*s was a means of contributing to the World Zionist Organization.

not everything there was entirely kosher, and he took all the responsibility for it himself. The prestige of his family really helped, and all ended peacefully.

When Reb Mojsze Eliezer, *z"l,* left Brzezin, his mission was already in safe hands. His students continued his work and became in time the Zionist leaders in Brzezin.

At the head of the activities for young men were Reb Chaim Baruch Szulzinger, *z"l,* the *shoykhet*'s [ritual slaughterer's] son, and Reb Aron Mendlewicz, son of an esteemed Hasidic and wealthy family. Reb Aron Mendlewicz is actually in Israel now. Reb Mojsze Fogel, *z"l,* also worked with him. Young tailors were also enlisted in the Zionist movement. Among the buyers of *shekel*s was Reb Mojsze Złotnicki, a tailor who lives in Israel today.

On the other hand, on the tailors' street, the opportunity for [Zionist] activity was much more open. The reasons? One did not have to search for them. They began with the apprentice who was badly exploited by his master. Instead of learning the trade, first of all, he had to wait on the *baleboste* [homemaker]—help her rock the child to sleep and run errands. Also, the journeymen had to work long hours for a small salary, and even the master, who was exploited by the magazine owner, felt badly abused and began saying that something had to be changed.

A little bit of enlightenment was enough to wake them up to the accumulated bitterness and turn them toward action.

The covert enlightenment work was in the hands of outsider intelligentsia, and they carried it out thoroughly. They were, however, careful enough not to reveal themselves. They entrusted the work to others. In the meantime, they defended the child workers. At that time, the Haskalah had already deeply penetrated into Brzezin. There were actually among the tailors of distinguished lineage, such as the children of Reb Lajbele Żychliński, *z"l,* those who were *Hatsefirah* [The Dawn][1] readers. The *maskil* [follower of Haskalah—Enlightenment] did not make *besmedresh bokhoyrim* [scholars] of his children—only simple tailors. And so also Hendrykowski's children, Syna Goldkranc, *z"l,* a brother of Mordkele, the *gabe* [synagogue treasurer/warden], *z"l,* Reb Jakub Josef's grandchild, and Reb Josef Aszer's children. These very children of Hasidic and well-to-do families were tailors. And when such an element was found among the tailors, the others listened to their words. There actually arose a long line of Brzezin children of tailors, who were completely organized by the movement that later took on the character of a revolutionary freedom movement.

At this point, I want to remember several names: Hersz-Iser Rozenblum—the martyr from Brzezin—son of buttonhole maker Reb Mojsze-Jojne, *z"l.* Incidentally, at that time the buttonhole-making trade grew a great deal in the town with the growth of our industry, and it was thought to be as honorable a trade as tailoring. One did not have to undergo such a difficult apprenticeship. This trade actually began to employ Hasidic Jews such as Reb Natan Łęczycki, *z"l,* Icek Majer Łęczycki, Reb Dawid Bajbke's grandchild, Reb Aron Grynbaum, a son-in-law of Reb Herszel of Wały, and Mojsze-Jojne, mentioned above.

Hersz-Iser Rozenblum was the first Bundist [Jewish socialist] in our town and also the first victim who was banished to Siberia. He organized a small Bundist group in our

---

[1] *Hatsefirah* was a Hebrew language newspaper in Warsaw.

town. In the initial group he enlisted his brother, Jakub Eli Rozenblum, Mendel Chana's son, and also Icek Kersz and Jakub Dawid, Reb Chaim-Icek's son. Jakub Dawid, a yeshiva student, came back from Vilna in a procession of convicts led by the Russian police. He was banished from Vilna for underground activity, and he brought with him an identity card from the Bund (he is now the well-known Brzezin community leader Jacob David Berg). Also belonging to the group were Jakub-Ber Gips—son of Reb Abraham Gips, z"l, and grandson of Reb Nachman Łęczycki—Menachem Budnik, and Berysz Jarnower.

They were quietly organized by Hersz-Iser Rozenblum and the Lithuanian bookkeepers in our town. They began to organize the Brzeziner poor. They began reading various pamphlets to enlighten and prepare for the "day that must come." Their work was carried out strictly undercover, but quickly the secret permeated every home. It even got to the young *kheyder* [Jewish elementary school] students. They also began talking about organizing, not understanding the significance of the word.

The pioneers held their own in a tremendously difficult endeavor. Meanwhile, they themselves sat at machines until late into the night, because first of all, they had to pay the big *bal-khuv* [taskmaster]—the stomach. They themselves had to prepare to be able to persuade others. Then they had to find time for the work of persuasion. They had to sort it all out in such a way that they were prepared for problems. They could not forget that there were people who could cause trouble and report the secret to the police. This evoked fears of Siberia. For that reason, they used the holy Sabbath. On Shabes, from early in the morning, we would see our toil-weary workers going on foot. They no longer went through Koza Lane to the meadows but went in groups of three or four up through the main street. There, beyond the engineer's house, there were no eyes or noses that could find out what was going on there. On Saturdays, the street that went out of town was teeming and full of apprentices. At that time, Brzezin numbered about two thousand workers.

What was going on there on the main street? This, no one knew. It certainly did not interest our magazine owners that the youngsters played there, as long as they did the work. The youngsters might have played a few hours, but soon they would make *Havdole* [ceremony at close of the Sabbath], and the machines would draw them back to the 108 hours of work. They joked with them, "Say, youngster, were you just at the *birzhe* [office]?" That is how they got the nickname the "*Birzhaner*." The youngsters were silent and did not answer one word. They responded with serious faces—but secret glances—to the questions and went quietly back to their work.

Suddenly, they learned of a new secret, that far away, beyond the town, there would be a meeting on Shabes. This was certainly a bit more serious. This smelled already of committing a violation of the laws of the state.

The magazine owners joked around again. "*Nu, gib a kuk* [Well, take a look]," they said. "They are going to overthrow Czar Nicholas, and they claim that Gimpele Melamed's daughter actually said that she will live to see the day when Nicholas will no longer be Czar." It did not occur to our magazine owners that there at the meeting they talked more about the magazine owners themselves than they spoke about Czar Nicholas. But the magazine owners had their own worries that they had to attend to before they looked into the activities of the youngsters.

Our magazine owners had their concerns—how to gain even more sales markets in great Russia. The various traveling salesmen actually began to penetrate the furthest corners of the land. New names of cities floated by every day. In Brzezin we were almost up to Tobolsk, Irkutsk, and other cities. It is understandable that such distant areas as Siberia created new problems for our tailors of that time. Because of poor transportation connections in Russia at that time, shipments from Brzezin to Siberia took six months until the merchandise reached the merchant. The customer did not want to pay money six months before he received the goods. They had to find a way to adjust to the new conditions. In that way, a paper bridge was created in the form of *nokhnames* [cash on delivery], that is, the customer would pay for the goods when they arrived at his train station.

They began giving other merchants credit on promissory notes. Here our "merchants" entered a new line of business about which they had never before dreamed. They had to create a place where "paper" would be exchanged for real money. To that end, they had to create either credit or deduct a collection fee. They developed a tie to banks, which deducted a small collection fee. In that way, they became involved in a line of business called "banking." There was even a firm in Brzezin of former tailors that already took care of "business matters." These were the biggest magazine owners—Szotenberg and Zygmuntowicz. They were already merchants of top rank, and they had reached such a level that for them there was no Pale of Settlement in Russia, as there was for other Jews. They used to travel freely even to Moscow or St. Petersburg. They were actually the first to open a banking house in Brzezin.

In time, the apprentices from little Koza Lane proceeded to form their own bank, and they gave the bank the name *Wzajemny Kredit* [Credit Cooperative]. They developed ties with big banks. We had already advanced so far with our merchants that many of them became shareholders themselves in their own banks.

Employed in tailoring. In the picture we see Abraham Frajnd, chairman of the Tailors Union, who was killed in the Nazi death camps

The name Brzezin became better and better known from one corner of Russia to the other. This was another reason why the magazine owners did not notice what the youngsters were doing and with what they were occupying themselves. They themselves were occupied with increasing their business, with spreading their merchandise, and making the name of the town well known.

But the youngsters at the central office also did not rest.

The day came one Sunday morning. Everything was ready for work. The charcoal lay near the iron and only waited for the apprentice to come and set fire to it. The machines had been cleaned and oiled; the master had already evenly counted out the work and laid out the packets for the machine workers. The clock stood at six in the morning. The workers did not appear. The master wandered about upset and was already figuring out what sort of deduction to give the journeymen for being late. And the apprentice? He would take full revenge on him! Him, he would completely throw him out! Such *khutspe* [nerve]!

Time did not stand still; he became restless. Probably something happened. Maybe one should take a look at the neighbor's place, see what was going on over there, talk it over with him. He opened the door to go into his neighbor's place, and there stood the neighbor at the door, and they both looked at each other silently. Their expression spoke. "What? By you, too? What happened? Who knows what calamity has befallen us?" And they blurted out, the way they would in the middle of a conversation, "Didn't we know that nothing good could come from their meetings? But why didn't they come? Don't we definitely have a right to know what they want? No one has ever heard of such nerve!! And just this week I took on work from another magazine owner—I meant to kill two birds—grabbing another few hours of work to earn another few guilder. Alas, what have we from all our work?" And continuing, "Does it pay to use up your life? What do we have altogether from our drudgery? Working day and night, and how does the Brzezin proverb go? 'The tailor sews all week and earns a *dreier* [a three cent piece].'"

That is how the time passed. It was already almost seven in the morning and no sign of anyone.

Then one of the neighbors called out, "Maybe it's a good idea to find out what is going on with the others? Maybe it's a good idea to see what is going on in the marketplace?" Both went into their homes, got dressed, and went out. An ordinary day, not a Saturday, not a holiday, not, God forbid, any funeral—and suddenly one had time to go into the marketplace! There in the marketplace ten master tailors were already gathered; they stood about, and on their faces was a question mark—what happened?

Standing like that, one called out, "A fine thing we have, that we don't have any place to exchange a word. What dog doesn't have a dog house?"

Meanwhile, it was agreed to go into Chana-Chaja's tavern to grab something to eat and contemplate some sort of plan. "In the meantime, maybe they would come; we would hear what they want." Not thinking about it too long, they quickly went into the tavern.

What they said there no one knows, since they all talked at once—and in fact, did not talk, only yelled. One did not hear the other until Mordechai Winter stood up, or Szlama Gelb, and banged on the table exactly the way the *shames* [sexton] starts the Hallel [hymn of praise] in *shul*. It became quiet. He said, "Children, I myself don't know what we are going to do, but we have to rent a house. In the house, we will be able to talk among ourselves, and no strange ears will overhear."

Then, such a house was rented, and after a while, the organization that was called Professional Master Tailors Union was formed there. There, one always drank a few kegs of beer in memory of the first meeting in the tavern, since without a little *mashke* [liquor], the meeting was worth nothing at all. Actually, later, all the issues between masters and journeymen, between magazine owners and masters, were settled in this house.

Meanwhile, on that first Sunday, they went home with nothing. As the clock stood at eight, all the apprentices and journeymen came to work. They came in a little embarrassed, but with a resolve that they would begin working from eight in the morning until eight at night and no longer. Such a "revolution" our tailors had not anticipated.

THE FIRST CLASH BETWEEN WORKERS

Suddenly the entire line of reasoning fell apart. How would they manage with twelve hours of work? With sixteen hours they could not make a living. They were not bold enough to request an improvement, demand a raise in pay from the magazine owners. As a matter of fact, they were afraid of the magazine owners—in case, God forbid, they should shut down and give them no work at all.

First of all, they [the master tailors] tried to talk to the workers, threatening them that if they did not go to work as usual, they would throw them out and bring others in their place. This method partially saved the day. There were those workers who became frightened. This method fell through mainly with the apprentices and foreign workers. Most of the foreign workers ate and slept at the master's place, so they were able to work a little longer at night. In the morning they got up a little earlier, and in that way, they were able to violate the resolution concerning the new working hours. But soon the "secret hand" that directed the campaign came. In the workshops where they had forced the workers to work overtime, work was completely shut down. This was called a "strike."

The apprentices or journeymen who resisted were thoroughly beaten, and that is how the first conflict of workers against workers happened, that is, between master tailors and journeymen.

The magazine owners joked constantly. "How are the striking youngsters?" they asked. From week to week the situation became more tense. There were many cases where the workers did not want to submit to the orders of the campaign leader, because the magazine owners were secretly resorting to all kinds of tricks. They promised them an additional guilder a week. In such a case, the workers used to fight each other. In the middle of the day, a few workers used to come into the workshop, and in the name of unity, they would stop the work and take the workers into the street. Judgments or trials took place against the strikebreakers and discipline breakers. At that time, our group got the name Akhdes Yungen [United Youth].

However, the masters could not remain indifferent to all of this, since they were unable to carry out the work of the journeymen by themselves. Since a twelve-hour day did not provide a living wage, they had to comply with the demand of the aforementioned Mordechai Winter and rent a place where they could meet and talk over what to do.

To take such a big house where a few hundred people could gather was not kosher according to the Russian laws. The name had to be changed. The house actually got the name Shnayder Minyen [prayer house for tailors]. They actually said prayers there and, at the same time, talked together about how they could adapt to the new situation. There was no other choice but to come to the magazine owner and ask if he would supplement the payments a little so they could survive.

THE SOCIAL AND POLITICAL INSTITUTIONS

Our magazine owners did not want to supplement the payments, that is, add money from their own pocket. Incidentally, they did not want to give the workers the opportunity for fresh demands. Thus, the magazine owners also began to organize and created their own union in order to weaken the workers' demands with united strength.

The government quickly legalized the magazine owners union. That was the way social life in Brzezin was structured as the professional institutions were arising. The magazine owners union operated entirely legally, the Master Tailors Union was hidden under the cloak of a *shul*, and the third, the union of the proletariat, was entirely without a home and without a name.

A wave of strikes broke out in our town. Our proletarians made new demands. Now they asked for higher wages and also humane treatment of journeymen and even of apprentices. And if they still did not accede to their demands, the workers struck. The machines didn't operate; the *khazonishe nigunim* [cantorial melodies] emanating from the workshops stopped. It became more lively outdoors. As they disappeared entirely from the town, the town took on the look of a cemetery. Where did they vanish? One knew and did not know. One knew, for example, that the disappearance was connected with meetings that took place somewhere, but where? And who was leading the campaign? That was a secret.

Since the youngsters struck, our masters had to get together in their *shul* and think about what else to do. Until they came to an agreement, they made common cause with the strikers and passed on the demands to the magazine owners. This caused another meeting of the magazine owners, and there, finally, the matter was considered from the business standpoint. If the strike broke out during the season when the merchants badly needed the work, they negotiated. They complied a little bit and saw to it that the strike was not protracted. If they encountered the strikers during the slow season, then our merchants declared a "lockout," and then the strike failed. In the meantime, it did not come to drastic measures. No policemen were used yet, and certainly not any tough guys. The latter had already lost ground. On one side, people were ashamed of them, and on the other side, they represented an organized force that everyone was afraid to tackle.

In this way our small *shtetl* progressed, and it was recognized everywhere one turned.

Life began to be a little easier. The new era was felt in town. A building campaign began in the town. The wooden houses were taken down, and in their place came two to three story brick houses. They felt it was too crowded to live eight to ten people in one apartment, so they actually changed to two apartments, two apartments with a kitchen. In addition to this, they felt more generous with money. Among our tailors, finally, a few extra rubles clinked against each other, so that they themselves became magazine owners, which was the aspiration of every tailor. In truth, this was not enough, but to allow money without good reason to lie around unused was also not practical. At that time, several Hasidic, observant Jews came to the help of the town, sincere people who were concerned only with the public good.

They were Reb Arje Dawid Perlmuter, *z"l*, Reb Dawid-Lajb Halbersztadt, *z"l*, and the grandchild of a wealthy grandfather, Reb Mojsze Zyndel Goldberg. The families Halbersztadt and Mendlewicz were wealthy Hasidic families who lived apart from the tailors. But in such projects for the public good, they put their shoulder to the plow. As good as Reb Aron Mendlewicz was in Zionist work, so also was Halbersztadt in the new economic activity. Reb Jecheskiel Najman, who was also among the active leaders, should also be remembered.

This group began to establish in Brzezin the first savings and loan bank—the cornerstone for the later cooperative bank in town. The bank had a two-fold purpose. First, people deposited their hard-earned *groszy* there, which earned a few percent a year. Second, the money served as principal in order to make it possible to give small loans at a low percent to Jews—who ran around all year searching for a loan without interest and a tailor's promissory note at a reasonable rate.

This was one of the nicest institutions created in Brzezin at that time. Confidence in this institution grew from day to day. There was hardly a single Jewish house in which you did not find a savings book.

From *groszy* Jews compiled dowries for their daughters. They carried the money to the savings and loan bank. Meanwhile, young men saved a few rubles there. In a word, the institution was such a part of life that one could not understand how it could have been different.

Then a second group of Jews, with Reb Abraham Gips, *z"l*, Reb Herszel Kranc, *z"l*, Reb Jakub Szlama Fogel, *z"l*, and Reb Alter Zagon, *z"l*, created the first philanthropic institution in town by the name of Lines Hatsedek. Its purpose was noble—to bring help to all the sick without regard to their ability to pay, to bring them comfort during the night.

The kind of importance such work had in that time and how much the Lines Hatsedek helped alleviate the needs of sick and helpless Jews, only those who lived in the *shtetl* at that time can understand.

EDUCATION AND CULTURE

Many of the children of the magazine owners went to other cities to study. Originally it was because of business—that is, in order to help the parents read a letter from a Russian merchant and also to overcome the confusion with numbers. But, after a time, one started to see among us locals some boys with different clothing, with shiny buttons. These were the *gimnazjum* [secular secondary school] students. One already saw in the future our own doctors and lawyers. Also, in the field of Jewish education, there was great progress. Now one actually learned Hebrew, not in Reb Eliezer Perlmuter's garret, *z"l*, but in a modern school that was called Kheyder Mtukn.

After several failures by Russian Jews to introduce such a *kheyder*, finally a Jew, a stubborn man by the name of Mirkin, came and opened such a school at Perlmuter's, in his courtyard. For a while, it was for girls. And a remarkable thing happened—even though they had to pay for the schooling, nevertheless, there were enough girls. The school did not get any subsidy from anyone. Another chance occurrence helped Mirkin to maintain the school.

At that time, an evil decree was issued that all Jewish children had to attend a non-Jewish school a few hours a week and learn Russian. The Jews did everything to stave off the decree, since how could Jews send their children to a *Bikel*?—that's what they called the Russian teacher. And since prayers and bribery did not help, it was simply a God-sent miracle that the Hebrew school existed. The teacher had a permit for the school. In it on the wall hung a picture of Czar Nicholas. For a while, they sent the youngsters to Mirkin for only a few hours a week, until the evil decree was rescinded.

There they were doubly successful. The children learned with their heads covered—not the way it was with the Russian teacher where one had to sit a few hours bareheaded—and also, the Jew made a living. In the meantime, young men began to visit the Mirkin school, partly to learn Hebrew and, at the same time, partly to be near the girls.

The school continued to operate in Brzezin. It only changed its name; instead of Mirkin, later, a Jew named Polański came. This Jew already had a school for boys and girls together, and he had evening classes for grown-ups.

Almost at the same time, a new cultural institution opened. One of Lajbele Żychliński,'s sons, Syna Żychliński, himself also a tailor, but a tailor who read *Hatsefirah* [The Dawn], opened up a small Jewish library. It was a small one, because, first, he did not have the financial resources for a large library, and second, there were not a great number of readers in the town.

As for the work of the community, as in a great number of other small towns, one person carried it out. All his [adult] life, Reb Szlama Silski, z"l, was the *dozor* [Jewish community official] for the town. He even had another *dozor* working with him, but he had the authority, not the other one. After his death, it changed a little. They elected three overseers to manage community life. Besides them, there also was a secondary board of seven people that was called Shiveh Tuveh Hoyer [Town's Seven Best]. They only had an advisory role, but the one-person rule had ended. The new *dozor*s were not actually elected in accordance with all democratic rules, not through general elections as we remember in the last years. Then, only those who paid a large *etat* [Jewish community assessment based on financial standing] had voting rights. The *meyukhsim* [men of stature], the privileged men, were actually the ones who were elected, but certainly there was already contact between ordinary Jews and the elected officials. A small reform, but still a reform.

The year of the first Russian Revolution, in 1905, approached, and after the failure of the revolution came the pogroms against Jews in a string of cities.

As in other cities, the Jewish workers, the socialists among us in Brzezin, began to promote fighting gangs, which had to be the protection brigade for Jews, to help when needed to repulse attacks by hooligans. At that time, our town heroes were truly not just accepted but esteemed. One saw in them persons who were ready to sacrifice themselves for the Jewish people. It was said that "they" even taught themselves how to shoot.

New faces began appearing in the streets. The ordinary workers became bolder and no longer kept their demands a secret. They spoke openly about shortening the work hours, about regulating payment for work, about better relations between masters and journeymen. In order to show their strength, demonstrators came out into the Brzezin streets in black shirts and turned-up little collars and with belts worn on the hips. A journeyman-tailor who had already worked in Brzezin several years was the head of the gang. This was the blind Chune. Poor thing, he didn't know anything about what was going on. He knew only what they wanted him to know, as much as Szlama Strykower and others wanted him to know, but he had "rank," and one had to be afraid of him. In his name, work was suspended.

To resolve various conflicts, they brought in a very strong person—one who came to the town for a short time but took the entire town into his hands—and everything moved as if on wheels. Nobody knew the secret, who he was and where he was from. Everyone tried to guess. One said he was a Valozhyn yeshiva student. Was it not so? One saw surely a *gemore-kop* [one with a head used to studying the subtleties of Gemore].[1] The second one guessed a graduated attorney, and maybe even a *lamed-vovnik* [one of the thirty-six mythical good men]. Who knew? What was a fact was that they now turned to him not only in tailoring matters but also, for example, regarding a feud between the orphans of Reb Szymszon Erlich, z"l, and the orphans of Szymon Krawiecki, z"l, over a soda-water factory that both fathers had in partnership. The children of both families could in no way come to an agreement as to how the inheritance should be divided. Who had not already tried to straighten out this conflict? So they turned to this person. The "trial" lasted two days, and on the third day, there was peace between the two families until their last years.

A tailor in Brzezin. The boss is very busy, but from the expression on his face, one sees he does not belong to the wealthy class.

Generally, our magazine owners did not have such a good life under the domination of this person, but they also had to keep silent and put up with the *din* [Jewish religious law]. It began to reek of deadly danger. They had begun talking about hitting, stabbing, and even shooting. And at that time, a magazine owner was actually beaten. However, they bit their lips and waited patiently. They were sure that their time would come, but Nicholas was not yet through being Czar.

For the time being, the power in the town was completely with the Akhdes Yungen [United Youth]. People whispered to each other that not only did they not care about the rules of those in power, but also they started rebelling at *yidishkeyt* [Jewish customs]. They did not *daven* [pray] any more, r"l [may God protect us], and smoked cigarettes even on Shabes. This last act nobody had actually seen, but, how do we say it—"Walls have ears."

Once I actually had the opportunity to attend one of their gatherings. How did I, a minor, come to such grandeur? I was then a small boy of eleven. Once, on Tisha B'Av [day commemorating the destruction of the Temple], I and a lot of other children my age, together with older Jews, went to the cemetery, as was the custom, to remember the destruction of the Temple and to pray.

---

[1] The Talmud, a collection of Jewish laws and traditions, is made up of two parts: the Mishne, or code of law, and the Gemore, which contains commentaries on the Mishne.

Suddenly, as we stood and prayed, our Akhdes Yungen showed up. A shudder went through our bones. What do they want from the dead? We understood that this smelled of something not good, so all of us, young and old, began to rush toward the exit to get home faster.

We recall the *Groyse Fenster* [High Society] in those days in our town Brzezin. So as not to give an *ayen-hore* [evil eye], they sent a hundred soldiers with guns to help Pieczana tame the wild ones. *Nu* [well], would one want to contend with the Russians?

As we were actually approaching the exit of the cemetery, there stood Reb Menachem Budnik with his black shirt and his belt on his hips. He curtly said, "Back! Nobody goes out now!" It was very bitter. We went back, I am sorry to say. We could no longer go wherever we wanted. They led us on to the knoll of the old cemetery, and there we really saw for the first time Comrade Baruk, Szotenberg's bookkeeper, and two other comrades standing and giving speeches. They talked about the Czar and about the yellow [yellow-haired] Abraham Mojsze, *e"h* [*olev hasholem*–may he rest in peace], about the Marikover master tailor and about Chaim-Ber Fanya Dymant, *e"h*, the magazine owner. That time is fixed in my memory as one of the orators spoke the following words:

> Comrades, you see here all the *matseves* [gravestones]; they who lie there under the stones, they were once people like all of us. Now nothing of them remains but the stone. Be assured that in our time the same thing will happen to the Russian bureaucracy—with one difference—that from them not even a stone will remain.

We remained standing with clenched teeth. Was it possible? Was there truly nothing left of these people? And the childish head wondered—and where are the bones that will stand up again for the resurrection of the dead?—and other such questions.

It is possible that "he" would have said more, but then they gave a sign—the police. Our comrades went over the fence and disappeared. We dashed to the door and ran home across the meadows at full speed.

At home I breathed easier and was proud of two things. First, I had been at a gathering, and second, I had become a comrade of the bookkeeper Baruk.

As our heroes had sensed that Nicholas had backed down a little and finally decreed elections to the Duma [Russian parliament], they came out into the open. Thus we were witnesses to demonstrations with red flags in the streets. In front went the blind Chune with his gang, four in a row, separating the sacred from the profane, like soldiers. Next came the working intelligentsia, such as bookkeepers and sales clerks, and then the rank-and-file. All walked in a marvelous configuration and sang revolutionary songs, and Pieczana, the policeman, stood at attention for the red flag. He believed—as did a lot of his kind—as did our heroes, that the time of the revolution had truly come. They unfortunately did not know that its days were numbered.

In the meanwhile, our people became more self-confident. At that time in Brzezin, a closer contact developed between workers and masters. The masters had learned a lot, and they themselves were well organized. The masters carefully thought over every worker demand in their *besmedroshl* [small prayer house], and, if it was accepted, they turned to the magazine owners with new demands. When the magazine owners tried to take a stand against them, they turned the problem over to someone else to handle for them. Suddenly, one heard that the magazine owner Majer Horn, *e"h*, stabbed the tall

Emanuel Zygmuntowicz, *e"h*. In that way, methods of physical violence were introduced into the economic fight. The contact between masters and journeymen all the time became closer, and they began to understand, after all, that they were bound by the same interests. They, the bread-givers, clearly noted the situation privately, but in the meantime, they were silent and waited.

They did not have long to wait. The whole business lasted a few months. The tide had turned. The elected Duma in St. Petersburg was torn apart. The reaction intensified in the entire land. The military was sent to cities and towns to establish "order."

To Łódź, which at that time already had ten thousand workers, came a general with the name of Koznakov, with a hundred Cossacks. Foot soldiers and Cossacks came to Brzezin and started up with the workers of the town.

As it happened, I was not in Brzezin at that time. I was in Ger [Góra Kalwaria], in the yeshiva. But Hasidim who came to the *rebbe* told us what was going on in the town. They said it was disheartening. The military and the police, together with certain magazine owners, worked hand in hand. They began to "cleanse" the town. I remember that on the eve of Shavuos [holiday commemorating the giving of the Ten Commandments], Szymon Jakubowicz came to Ger and spoke these words, "I ran away from the town barely alive. It is darkness. Jews are attacking Jews. My eyes should never see again what I saw, what they did to the Akhdes Yungen."

He said that the soldiers found the "hunchback" at the home of Reb Herszel Strzyszewski, *z"l*, in the Orthodox *shul* in the garret. They did not simply arrest him; first they mercilessly tormented him.

After *yontov* [holiday, in this case, Shavuos], when I came home, it was already quiet in the town. I only heard that they had taken all the overseers of the synagogue from the tailors *besmedresh*, such as Mordechai Winter, *e"h*, Szlama Gelb, *e"h*, the yellow Abraham Mojsze, *e"h*, Natan Wald, *e"h*, and others, and they sent them away to Piotrków to prison, where they remained for six months.

The events really upset the entire town. But people soon calmed down. After a time the two sides made up, and they all began to work together again—the magazine owners by spreading the name of Brzezin to all corners of great Russia, and the tailors by improving the quality of the work—not lessening the tempo, in order to be able to compete with those who wanted to try to imitate Brzezin.

That is how the Brzeziner industry was created by means of one hundred percent Jewish effort and difficulties, bitter struggle, and with countless obstacles that stood in the way.

This is how Brzezin developed and how our *shtetl* grew. This was the situation in Brzezin in 1906, with which I end my *zikhroynes* [recollections] of our *shtetl*.

The Last Kadesh (pp. 31–39)

Jechiel Erlich (Kfar Saba)

Whosoever was once of the opinion—and some are still today—that no great Jews of stature ever came from Brzezin, he is mistaken. Historical facts will show that the opposite of this is true.

In the year 1768, approximately, when Gonta, the successor to Chmielnicki, had destroyed entire Jewish communities in the Ukraine with his murderous army, the Balter *rov* [official town rabbi from Balta] Reb Josef Jehuda Szpiro, with his four children, was rescued from the butchers, and one of the four sons, Reb Fiszele Szpiro, was brought up in our *shtetl* Brzezin.

Reb Fiszele married Laja, the daughter of a rich wine merchant in Brzezin. He received *kest* [room and board given as part of marriage agreement] from his father-in-law for a few years.

Reb Fiszele devoted himself to Torah during his *kest* years. He was one of the founders of the Hasidic movement. The Hasid Abraham, the old Tchekhanover [Ciechanów] *rebbe*, and also Reb Levi Yitzhok of Berdichev, the saintly Levi, Reb Henoch of Aleksandrów, and the *rebbe* Reb Bunim of Pshischa [Przysucha] were his Hasidim. The great virtue of love of the Jewish people that was found in Reb Levi Yitzhok of Berdichev he derived from Reb Fiszele Szpiro, who later moved to the nearby town of Stryków, twenty kilometers from Brzezin. Reb Abraham from Ciechanów also traveled to the *rebbe* Reb Fiszele Szpiro (*Hevrit Os* [Hebrew Encyclopedia]). The *rebbe* Reb Fiszele Szpiro was crowned the "Rebbe ben Yokhai" [founder of *kabole*—Jewish mysticism] of his generation. He never understood how one could sacrifice eternal life for material pleasure.

Legend tells us that after he had *kest* for a few years, his wife, the rich wine merchant's daughter, began to demand that he make a living. Reb Fiszele was so steeped in the Hasidic movement and *kabole* that he was not at all able to understand that such a thing existed in life. Every time she demanded that he earn a living, he told her that it would all be fine. . . . God would help. Once coming from the *besmedresh*, he noticed a Jew selling bagels. He asked the Jew how he was making a living. He went home delighted and told his wife, the rich wine merchant's daughter, that she should stand in the street and sell bagels—then she would make a living.

At the grave of Reb Szymon Bal-Rakhmones, the only tomb that remains in the old Brzeziner cemetery.

One can imagine what kind of impression that made on his wife and what kind of day of material pleasure he had.

A powerful mystery of our town also has to be explained—where did the tomb in the Brzezin cemetery of Reb Szymon Bal-Rakhmones [man of compassion], the father of Reb Icchak of Warka, come from? It is possible that he also was one of Reb Fiszele Szpiro's Hasids, as he remained in Brzezin and died in Brzezin? Incidentally, it is worthwhile to remember that after the tragic destruction of Brzezin, whereas Hitler's beasts defiled the Brzezin cemetery, the grave of Reb Szymon Bal-Rakhmones was the only grave that they could not tear apart; until today the grave of Reb Szymon Bal-Rakhmones remains untouched.

Rebbe Reb Fiszele's children and grandchildren remained in Brzezin—a large family with many branches. They lived in Brzezin until the tragic end.

The only son of Reb Fiszele, Reb Jankiel Szpiro, lived his entire life in Brzezin, in Nowe Miasto [New Town]. Like his father, he was completely devoted to God. The *shtetl* called him Jankiele Reb Fiszele's [Jankiele, son of Reb Fiszele]. Reb Jankiele had two sons in Brzezin—Reb Mojsze and Reb Szymon Josef. All his life Reb Mojsze was a devoted worker for the community, a leader in the town. As early as those years, he managed a large business in partnership with his father, Reb Jankiele. Reb Jankiele devoted himself to Torah and the Hasidic movement, and Reb Mojsze managed the business. He would take the goods that the first Germans who had settled in Brzezin had manufactured. Then he would sell them in Warsaw. Reb Jankiele himself did not want to carry out any of the offices of rabbi, and all his life he spent fasting. Reb Mojsze's brother, Reb Szymon Josef, was also devoted completely to God, like his father, Reb Jankiele, and was not concerned with material pleasure.

The Froman families in Brzezin and the Erlich Family came from Reb Mojsze; from Reb Szymon Josef came the Holcberg families. Reb Aron, father of Hillel, the *shames* [synagogue caretaker], was Reb Szymon Josef's son-in-law. Reb Abraham Froman, whom the town called Reb Abraham Warszawer [man from Warsaw], the father of Reb Icek Froman and Małka Chana Erlich, was Reb Mojsze's son-in-law.

When the first German Futterliebs and Ninenbergs immigrated from Germany, they also settled in Nowe Miasto. Because of the language, they could not communicate with any of their Polish neighbors, only with Jews. Therefore, they had to approach Jewish merchants to sell their wares, since they could easily talk together with them.[1] Living in Nowe Miasto, Reb Mojsze Szpiro therefore became the main recipient of German merchandise.

In those days they took Jews as soldiers for Nicholas I, and they had to serve twenty-five years. Reb Mojsze at that time freed as many Jews as he could from the *prisutstvie* [recruitment office].

The old Reb Chaim-Icek, Jacob Berg's father, once told me that as he was facing the drawing of lots, everyone at the recruitment office positively wanted to pull him into the Russian army for twenty-five years. In those years, this was simply to ruin your life. Reb Mojsze stood up and, as a protest, wanted to leave the meeting, because they did not want

---

[1] The Yiddish language uses Hebrew letters in writing, but the spoken language is similar to German.

to free Reb Chaim-Icek, the Hasid from Warka. They soon all agreed with Reb Mojsze, and that is how Reb Chaim-Icek had a narrow escape.

Reb Mojsze had several daughters, for whom he made world-class *shidukhim* [matches]. Reb Azriel Lewi, the old Strykover *rov*, was a son-in-law; Reb Abraham Froman was a second son-in-law. Reb Syna Sapir, the Brzeziner *rov*, was also a son-in-law. Just as Reb Icek Froman was devoted to the community in Brzezin all his life, so also was Reb Jankiel Lewi a leader in Łódź and devoted to his community all his life. Reb Issachar Lewi's children were all *askonim* [workers for the community], leaders in society, and distinguished Jews, scholarly Hasidic Jews, until the tragic downfall.

Reb Lajbele Żychliński, an old, handsome Brzeziner leading figure, once told the story that at the same time that Reb Syna Sapir, *z"l*, became a widower, Elke, the *rebetsn* [rabbi's wife] of Reb Azriel Halewi, the Strykover *rov,* also became a widow. After a time, Reb Syna sent matchmakers to Elke, the *rebetsn*, daughter of Reb Mojsze Szpiro, to say that he wanted to take her for his wife. Reb Azriel was a Kotsker [from Kock] Hasid, Reb Syna was a *misnaged* [opponent of Hasidism], and therefore the widow would not agree. Reb Syna called the top leaders of the town, and among them the teller of this story, to consult with them, and he also asked Elke, "Elke, why don't you want me?"—of course, Elke could not decline and accepted.

In his time, Reb Syna was one of the greatest and most renowned of the group of rabbis in Russia and Poland. The other two were Reb Icchak Elchanon Spektor, the Kovner [Kowno] *rov,* and Reb Eliahu Chaim Meisels, the Lodzer *rov*. Reb Syna must certainly have been a great personality, since the Brzeziner Jews had taken him, a *misnaged*, many years earlier as their rabbi. The entire *kehile* [Jewish community] in Brzezin was, at that time, in the hands of the Hasidim—Vorker [from Warka] and Kotsker Hasidim. When one leafs a bit through Reb Syna's books, one immediately sees his greatness.

I would have to take up too much space if I were to include excerpts from our contemporary grandfathers and great-grandfathers on his moralizing. Merely that in the *parshe* [Torah section] from Shabes Hagodl [Shabes before Pesakh], he would say with unquestioning faith in God, "Have you already taken care of the true Jews, that they should have what they need for Pesakh? Oy, my *shtetl* Brzezin, we lock the doors and then we call out, 'All who are hungry come and eat.'"

I did not know Reb Syna. He died more than ninety years ago. But I knew his grave that was destroyed together with the entire Brzezin cemetery. Reb Syna's gravestone in the Brzeziner cemetery was an *oyel* [structure over the grave]; half-round, it had on the top a four-cornered opening for placing *kvitlekh* [notes of supplication]. They used to pray, and the broken-spirited shed tears.

When Reb Syna died, all the Brzeziner leaders who had sons born that year gave them the name Syna. I will list all the Synas I can recall—Syna Sapir, Eliezer Melekh's son; Reb Syna's grandchild, Syna Mojsze Kopel's; Syna Szeps, Reb Eliezer Szeps's grandchild; Syna Reb Hersz Krauze; Syna the little Korekh's son; Syna Żychliński; Reb Lajbl's son, Syna Klianket [Blianket?]; Syna Kolewiziner's son with the little rings; Syna Reb Icze Ber Dymant's son; Syna, Eliezer Map's brother, and Syna Herszel Bercholc.

This is the way the Brzeziner leaders showed their respect to the memory of their *rov* [official town rabbi] so that he would not be forgotten.

Reb Szymon Josef Szpiro took as a son-in-law for his daughter Perla, Reb Aron, the *shoykhet* in Brzezin. From him developed the great family Holcberg. A sister of Fiszel Holcberg, Laja, married the Zhychliner [from Żychlin] *shoykhet*, Reb Mendel Majer Rozenblum. One of their sisters married Berl Blat, the *shoykhet* from Kalisz, Many, the *nafta* [kerosene] dealer's [son]. From all these branched out great families. A son of Reb Berl, Mojsze Blat, was killed in Israel in the fight with the Arabs, during the time of the British Mandate government. Perla, *e"h* [may she rest in peace], was the second wife of Reb Aron, the *shoykhet*. Reb Hillel, the *shames*, Reb Jojne, and Szyfra, the iron merchant—Aron Fogel's grandmother—were from the first wife. Many victims of the destruction came from these families.

Reb Mendel Majer Rozenblum, the Zhychliner *shoykhet*, Perla's older son-in-law, was a great scholar and a leader of Mizrachi [Orthodox Zionist Party]. At that time, because of this, he was greatly persecuted until he left Żychlin to go to Israel. Reb Mojsze Kalmus, member of the Knesset, was a pupil of Reb Fiszele Szpiro—or as Reb Fiszele from Stryków was called—the Rov.

Rabbi Abraham Joszua Borensztajn in Brzezin was, at the same time, well-known among brilliant men in Poland and the author of *Sanhedrin Ktane* [Lesser Sanhedrin/religious court]. He was *moyre tsedek* [a guide to justice] in Brzezin. His son, Reb Zalman Jekutiel, became the official rabbi in Brzezin after Rabbi Reb Izrael Dwarter.

* * *

I remember the small building that stood in the marketplace. It was Josef Aszer's little building. Later, in the same place stood Mordechai Ikka's large building. The small building is so engraved in my memory because the Aleksander *shtibl* [house of prayer of Hasids from Aleksander] was there. Reb Szlama Icek, whom the town called the *lomer* [lame] Szlama, his small store was also in that little building. Reb Szlama, like his father, Reb Icek, was from the esteemed Kotsker Hasidim—a handsome Jew with a stately appearance. The town leaders would buy from him in order that Reb Szlama would be able to support his son-in-law, so he could study. They all came from Brzeziners devoted to piety. His two even *peos* [long side curls] added charm to his beautiful Hasidic face. From birth, one foot was a little shorter that the other.

I spent most of my childhood years in the Aleksander *shtibl* located in the courtyard. There, Hasidim sat until twelve o'clock and, often, actually all day. Devoted to Torah prayers, they took meals and drink there. Aleksander Hasidim were famous for that.

Everyone contributed a *grosz* or two. Reb Danielekhl Pajczer, a small, charming *yidele* [little Jew], used to gather the *groszy* with great eagerness—it was the estimated cost of a small flask—and he ran quickly to the Russian liquor monopoly that was located at the tavern in Opteyk-Gas [Apothecary Street]. Cutting a herring into fifteen pieces, Reb Danielekhl, the continuous provider of alcoholic drinks for the Aleksander *shtibl*, gave everyone a very small amount of drink and herring, and the exchanging of good wishes with one another began.

A long time ago, Brzeziner Jews contributed, despite their considerable poverty, to build a temple synagogue building with a magnificent appearance. The synagogue was unique among hundreds of synagogues in Poland. A rich woman by the name of Perla, the widow of Mojsze-Zyndel Goldberg, contributed several thousand rubles at that time for the Holy Ark. Indeed, it was artistically carved with all the musicians from the Temple in Jerusalem and with an eagle [Polish national symbol]. And how artistically the eastern wall of the synagogue [where the most highly privileged sat] was carved! The fiddlers and all the other music makers made an unforgettable impression.

There was an old Jew in the town, Reb Chaim-Lajbele Kotsker. An Aleksander Hasid, he used to come summer and winter to *daven* in *shul*. All alone he used to move about in the great synagogue, praying out loud, using the Aleksander intonation, as I, from outside, would always listen to his sweet prayers. Reb Chaim-Lajbele's prayers still ring in my ears today.

In the small Orthodox [not Hasidic] synagogue were to be found prayer books, copies of the Talmud, and post-Talmudic commentaries—on tables made from thick wood, so they could survive the hefty Rambam's Mishne Torah that diligent people over generations had used to study from and sing from in chorus.

Hard working artisans also prayed in the *besmedresh* [Orthodox house of prayer]— tailors, shoemakers, butchers, water carriers, turners [of lathes], and bread bakers. The *besmedresh* was fuller in wintertime, because a very hot fire was kept burning. Early Shabes morning, Szmytke, the Shabes *goy* [non-Jew, who could work on Shabes], used to light the two large stoves. At the crack of dawn on Shabes, the Book of Psalms readers already had hot tea, and therefore, in winter, they used to sit there more than in the synagogue.

In addition to the *besmedresh*, there were also scholarly Jews, handsome Jews, in separate small Hasidic houses of prayer, such as the Ger [Góra Kalwaria] *shtibl*, the Aleksander *shtibl*, the Ostrowiec, the Grodzisk, the Skierniewice, the Rozprza. In addition, there were various *khevres* [societies]—Khevre Tilim [Society for the Reading of the Book of Psalms], Khevre Eyn-Yankev ["Jacob's Spring" Society], Khevre Kedishe [Burial Society], Khevre Lines Hatsedek [Society to Care for the Sick], and Khevre Khayotim [Tailors Society].

The Hasidic *shtiblekh* [small houses of prayer] were almost overflowing with young *kest-eser* [young men supported by in-laws so they could study Torah], and the Torah roused them from a quiet provincial life. They were not engrossed only with Torah study; they were always concerned about the poor Hasidim of the *shtibl*.

The *shtibl* used to furnish dowries and trousseaux for young women, also pay wedding expenses. The entire burden of an impoverished comrade fell upon the *shtibl*. Everything was done without clamor, without commotion, with charity given anonymously, so as not to shame the recipient.

From the *besmedresh bokhoyrim* [prayerhouse young men], from the *kest-eser*, came well-known scholars. I still remember from my time Reb Abraham-Icek Gutkind, Reb Nachman Gutkind's brother, whom the Brzeziner *rov*, Reb Izrael Dwarter, took for a son-in-law. Later, he became the Brzeziner rabbi who could answer religious questions and the author of books on *pilpul* [subtle argumentation on Talmudic texts]. Yekl Rozen, Yekl Tyla Aba Hersz's—as they called him—was a great scholar, with a name known throughout all Poland.

Reb Szlama Szufleder became renowned among the rabbis in Łódź as one of the best Łódź arbitrators.

As for the small Jankiele Zadów's, his brother, Berl, later became a *khazn-shoykhet* [cantor-ritual slaughterer] in America.

Reb Szlama Holcberg, Szmul Hillel's son, became known in Warsaw as a great child prodigy. Reb Mordechai Kochman, Reb Mojszele Tornhajm, and other great scholars also became well known.

Also several distinguished *maskilim* [followers of Enlightenment] came from the *besmedresh*, such as Reb Chaim-Icek Grynfeld, Reb Nachman Gutkind, Reb Szymele Krongrad, as well as Reb Herszel Lachman, who helped spread the concept of Mizrachi.

* * *

There were Jews to whom the town gave various nicknames. As we know, almost all the small *shtetlekh* had this custom.

There was a Jew, Reb Mojsze Rozenberg, who while he was looking at something would wrinkle the eyebrow of one eye—therefore, the town gave him the name *kuker* [looker]. If you did not mention the word *kuker*, only his family name, no one knew whom you meant. Reb Mojszele Kuker—that's what he was called. His brother, a good man, a tailor, was missing an eye; all his life, he was called the blind Michał. Even the children inherited the parents' nicknames. They were called Josel the blind Michał's son, or Icze Mojszele Kuker's, Mojsze Hon Dark Chana's, or son of Icze Ber the Nosher.

Icze Ber was a handsome man of stature, a well-to-do person. He used to deal in horses. During business he used to drink liquor and nibble on a piece of roast meat—so they called him Natchel [nibbler/*nosher*]. There was another handsome town leader with a spirited business head—Reb Michał-Lajb Bernholc [Bercholc]'s son, Herszel. If they did not say Herszel Shakher [chess player?], no one knew whom you meant. They even called the children Herszel Shakher's or Reb Michał-Lajb Herszel Shakher's.

Reb Jecheskiel Roda Laja's Najman once had a tavern in the center of the marketplace. Therefore, he was called Reb Jecheskiel Shenker [*shenk* = tavern].

Mordechai Łęczycki, a friend of mine, liked a *shtikl* [piece] of fish. *Shtikl* became *Pikl* and *Pikl* became *Pakel*. That is exactly what they called him—Mordechai Pakel. Reb Mojsze Yak's father, Reb Mendel, came from Germany, that is, he was a *yekl* [German Jew], and so all his life they actually called his son Mojsze Yak.

Reb Herszel Rozen, a handsome man of stature, was, for that time, very rich—they called him Herszel Korekh [a rich man in the Bible]. All his children and even his grandchildren inherited that name while he was still alive.

Reb Szymon Nowak was never called anything but Szymon Kolabik. Why? I don't know.

All those Jews with such names that were not entirely nice could, however, perform good deeds when Russian Cossacks were fighting with Jews—the strong, young Jews of that time, one of whom was Jankiele, the blind Kokis. He made a stand against the rioters and struck one of them in the face with a brick, knocking out an eye. The rest of the Cossacks were frightened and ran away.

With a small Jewish hat on the top of his head, Towie Haljas, Szlama Gelb's brother, once, when the Polish recruits wanted to make merry in Brzezin and began to pick quarrels with Jews, risked his life and got even with one of them by himself. From that time on it was quiet, and the *goyishe* [non-Jewish] recruits no longer wandered about bothering Jews.

* * *

Brzezin also had a poorhouse. Brzeziner Jews took care of the poor vagabonds who used to wander over Poland's roads. At that time they used to be called *medine-geyers* [country wanderers]. For those Jews there were several huts fixed up with berths for them to sleep in at night in Hercke Katsev's [the butcher's] courtyard. By day, the *talmetoyre* [free elementary school] for poor children of the town was there, with a permanent paid teacher. Reb Dawid Melamed [teacher] taught these poor Brzeziner children.

On Shabes, hundreds of guests used to come to the *shul*, the *besmedresh,* and the Hasidim *shtiblekh*. The *gaboim* [wardens of the synagogue] would put them up at the homes of Brzeziner Jews to eat on Shabes. In a number of homes, two to three guests would sit at the tables set for Shabes. Many did not feel comfortable at dinner if they did not have any guests. They all had a place in the poorhouse. Therefore, they made up the saying—"*kest* [board] in homes and *dires* [housing] in the poorhouse."

In addition to the poor guests, messengers from yeshivas and ordinary preachers also used to come to Brzezin. All guests used to leave the town pleased, with a few *groszy* in their pockets that the Brzeziner Jews gave them.

The Khevre Khayotim [Tailors Society] used to sew shrouds for the dead. Khevre Tilim used to recite Psalms for them. Reb Abraham Gips, *e"h* [may he rest in peace], was the *rebbe* for the Khevre Tilim and used to deliver sermons for people.

In Brzezin, *melamdes* [teaching] was also an occupation among others. We had *dardeke-melamdim* [teachers of the youngest], who used to study with the little children beginning with *alef-bes* [the alphabet] and ending with Khumesh un Rashi [Torah and Rashi commentaries], and Gemore *melamdim* [teachers of commentaries on the Mishne], beginning with Shas [the Talmud] and *poskim* [post-Talmudic commentaries] and ending with the *hoyroe rabones* [learning at the level of rabbi], the time to learn by oneself in the *besmedresh*.

My first *rebbe* was Reb Jankiele Melamed. He was called the blind Jankiele because he always kept one eye closed. He was a small charming *yidele* with a big wooden pointer. His assistant (*belfer*) at that time was Reb Jankiel Rochwerg. Reb Jankiele had also been my mother's *rebbe*. It seems that Reb Jankiele was not a perfectionist or an angry person, because if he had been, he would not have lasted so long in the teaching profession.

Just as the artisans were not able to support a family from their trade alone, so also the teachers did not make a living solely from teaching. They had to have a side line. Therefore, the *rebetsn* Libele had to sell a few vegetables. She used to stand in the market with her little stall—with parsley, small carrots, and potatoes.

In wintertime, during the great frosts, the *rebetsn* Libele used to make a fire in a fire pot. When the *rebetsn* put coals into the iron cooking pot, before they began to burn, the entire *kheyder* would fill with smoke. We children helped the *rebetsn* blow into the fire pot so that it would burn quickly.

Therefore, when dusk came on Thursday, when the *rebetsn* used to peel the frozen, small field apples for *tsimmes* [stewed fruits and/or vegetables] for Shabes, we children used to sit around, and the *rebetsn* would divide the parings among the children. We used to nibble the little frozen pieces. If a thicker piece of paring came her way, she used to give it to me, since I was the best blower into the fire pot.

Besides Reb Jankiele, *e"h*, there were other teachers—Reb Abraham-Mojsze, Reb Eliezer, Reb Szlama Perec. Then there were the Khumesh-Rashi teachers—Reb Pinkus (we called him Pinyele) and the Glovner [from Głowno] teacher. Both of them lived in Dwojra-Laja's building behind the *besmedresh*. I began studying Khumesh-Rashi with Pinyele. The *rebbe* used to beat us children without mercy. We used to quake if he just looked at us. Then there were Reb Nechemia, whom we called the *zvorny*,[1] Reb Szmul Mojsze, the Radzyner teacher, Reb Judel Soyfer's [the scribe's] son-in-law, who was already a Gemore teacher, and the Skierniewice teacher. I studied with all of these. The last one lived at the home of Reb Lajbel Shenker in the garret room. I also remember Reb Melamed Josef and Reb Chaim Mojsze.

A *kheyder*—the *rebbe* and his students, photographed by the art photographer, A. (Alter) Kacyzne, for the New York *Forverts* [Forward]. The photo was taken in Brzezin.

My last teacher was Reb Chaim Mojsze—a little sallow, with a pallid face, and with two long side curls. He was a God-fearing Jew, a great scholar. He was a sub-tenant of Reb Gecel, the *matse-shmure* [strictly supervised *matse*] dealer, who lived in the building of Majerke Shuster in Nowe Miasto, opposite Reb Icek Froman.

Reb Chaim Mojsze, my last *rebbe*, used to go to Rabbi Izrael Dwarter to chat and to study. Meanwhile, we, the already grown children, used to help shake the large sieve that was held up by two sticks over stools. That is how the matzo meal was sifted. Just as we used to get black faces at Reb Jankiele's from the smoke from his wife's fire pot, so we also used to become white as millers at Reb Gecele's from sifting the meal. Only six students studied with Reb Chaim Mojsze Melamed—Izraelik Perlmuter, Jankiel Strzyzewski, Eliezer Ledershniter's [leather cutter's] son, Elimelech Jecheskiel Roda Laja's, I, and one other whose name I do not recall.

Besides the teachers there were scribes, calligraphers, *seyfrim-stam* (scribes who wrote Torahs, *tfilen* [philacteries], and *mezuze*s [small tubes attached to doorpost, which contain inscribed parchment])—Reb Juda Soyfer [scribe], Reb Dawidl Soyfer, Reb Josef Soyfer, the hoarse Reb Szaja's son, Reb Benjamin Josef, Machel's son-in-law. The *seyfrim-stam* also could not manage with their earnings and had to find another source of income. So I remember that Reb Juda Soyfer, *e"h*, all his life engraved *matseyves* [gravestones].

---

[1] Possibly misspelling of *vzvodny* [platoon commander in Russian].

Reb Dawidl's wife carried around raisin wine for making *kidesh* [benediction over wine] from home to home.

The unfortunate wife of Reb Josef (the hoarse Reb Szaja's son) could not work, so he had to go somewhat hungry a fair amount of the time.

* * *

In our town, we had *goyim* who could speak Yiddish very well. I see them pass by now in my memory.

I remember the brothers Chroziemski, one, a shoemaker and the second, a bricklayer with a beard who always served as a fireman in addition to his bricklaying work.

Roman, the mail carrier, also used to speak Yiddish and was considered a friend of the Jews. He used to stuff himself with Jewish fish and fill his pocketbook with Jewish money. The Jews always gave him gifts; if not, their incoming letters would have become moldy . . . that is how the Brzeziner mail seemed at that time. He called every Jew "Rebbe." "Rebbe Reb Jankiel, I have a nice little letter for you," he used to say. He knew for a nice little letter he would surely see a nice little coin.

We had in town a tall Pole with a black beard—the chief of the first fire department in Brzezin—named Aksler. He spoke Yiddish well.

There was another, a short, thin Russian, a plain policeman in the Russian police of that time in Brzezin; Pieczana was his name—with a long two-pronged mustache and sharp jaws. He was a small person. His smallness was offset by how stiff and erect he always appeared. In his time, he instilled terror in all Brzeziner inhabitants. He wore epaulets, as all the Russian police did, of twisted red thread like Fajgele's little braids (the sister of Iczele Mydlak). On the twisted red threads, three brass rings were drawn up, like tailor's thimbles, so that the rings would add Russian police charm. This Pieczana, like Aksler, spoke Yiddish, ate fish at respectable businessmen's, and filled his purse with money from Brzeziner Jews. He was a partner in all large and small thefts. After almost every successful theft, Pieczana would search at the home of the honest businessmen, the rabbi, the bathhouse attendant, the *shoykhet,* and even the sacred priest (only at the real thieves' did he not search). He even hauled them off to jail. He would make noise that he would uncover the theft. He would also search at Bobes' the gravedigger's, or at Elija Mojsze's, the gravedigger's assistant, whom the town called Koyke [berth]. But he did not search at the homes of the real thieves.

I remember that when Bobes and his assistant, Koyke, would just appear in the market square, Brzeziner Jews would begin to cry, not yet knowing who had died. Elija Mojsze's income was not only from victims. He used to go every Thursday door to door begging for *groszy*. Often Pieczana's partners had a hiding place with him.

When the freedom movement began in our town, Pieczana took revenge on the leaders. His name remained infamous among all Brzeziner Jews and Christians.

I remember once when a meeting of artisans took place in the *besmedresh* in Brzezin. While the speaker stood on the platform and was making a blazing, fiery speech about the oppressors of the freedom fight, one of those present suddenly cried out, "Pieczana is coming!" The people began to jump out of the windows. Such terror Pieczana instilled over all Brzezin.

* * *

When tailoring had fully developed in Brzezin, the town got a whole new look. The narrow provinciality began to disappear. They got big city desires. Counting houses opened, where merchandise was handled as in the great cities in faraway places.

A Russian Jew by the name of Gracz opened the first counting house. He had a large-wheeled wagon with a nice white horse that would go around all day gathering purchased goods to take to his counting house on Rogover Street. The merchandise was packed in cases. One began to see Reb Icek Tuszyński's wagons loaded with cases of goods on the cobblestone-paved streets, as Emanuel Dymant's wagons were also. They used to travel to the railroad stations in Rogów and Koluszki. From there the merchandise was shipped away to all corners of Russia. Magazines multiplied from day to day. New businesses arose, such as tailoring accessories, button dealers, and *katazir* [fabric finishing] factories, and new ways of earning a living began, such as producing cotton-padding and making buttonholes. The biggest magazine owners were Mojsze Aron Szotenberg, Reb Emanuel Zygmuntowicz, Reb Perec Jakubowicz with his children, Reb Chaim Ber Dymant with his children, Reb Emanuel Grosman, Roman Winter, Reb Lajbuś-Mendel Winter, Majer Dymant with his children, Reb Herszel Korekh, Reb Jankiel Herszberg, Reb Lajbl Gotlib, Reb Jechiel Mojsze Gotlib, and Reb Szymon Gotlib.

The first accessories dealers were Reb Hersz Mendel Pinczewski, Reb Nachman Gutkind, Reb Szymon Krongrad, Reb Eliezer Apelson, and others.

Reb Icze-Majer Berger had established, in partnership with Mojsze-Pinkus Zelig, a *katazir* factory, as had Reb Aron Aszer's Szymonowicz with Reb Dawid Mendel Michrowski. Reb Aron Aszer's and Reb Dawid Mendel made their *katazir* factory in the basement apartment of Reb Aszer'l Groman's building that stood in the marketplace, at the corner of Synagogue Lane. The *katazir* factories used to steam press [for shrinkage control] the Białystok, Zgierz, and Tomaszów fabric from which were sewn suits, pants, and vests. By day and by night, the foul odor was carried out with the *katazir* steam from their small factories.

Tomaszów and Białystok factories delivered hundreds of bolts of fabric to Brzezin. All this passed through their small factories.

Ten small factories for cotton padding were established and about twenty buttonhole making establishments. The development of the tailoring trade grew from day to day. Day and night the banging of the sewing machines was heard. A specific rattling drifted from the buttonhole sewing machines. The neighbors who lived next door to them were not to be envied, and they themselves were also not so happy.

At that time no one knew anything about a noontime break. Only that you ate quickly and sewed again. At that time, the workers were seriously exploited. Therefore the Bund found a broad opportunity for their activities when it appeared on the Brzeziner horizon.

The freedom movement in Brzezin had nothing of which to be ashamed. At that time we already had worker leaders who were aware of their status, such as Jankiel Staszewer, the blind Chune, and the hunchback, who the town said could speak seven languages. About the blind Chune, they also said that he was the leader of the *bojówka* [fighting squadron].

At that time, the liquidation of the *voyle yungen* [tough youth] began in town. I still remember the names of some of them—Fiszele Wika, Abrahamele Bobes, Dawid Wald, Aron Brilliant, Szaja Lerer, Eliezer Moyfes [magical sign], Szymon Katsev [butcher], Josef Budnik, Eliezer Paker, Majer Bunim Szpicer. Most of them were born in Brzezin.

When new young people arrived in town, they had to give *aynkoyf-gelt* [an initiation fee], that is what the law [custom] was. . . . Reb Szymon Krawiecki's wife, Chana Chaja, had a beer tavern, and indeed at her place, they did this by drinking *lechayim* [to life!] and afterward eating a piece of roasted goose. This lasted until the freedom movement took on real character.

All these *voyle yungen* later became fine, respectable, important, and esteemed men of stature in the town—with the exception of one of the last *voyle yungen* who did not part with his tough guy behavior until the liquidation of the Jews by the Nazis.

A group of apprentices in town were known for their carryings-on at weddings. I still remember the preparations for a Jewish wedding in town, which began weeks ahead. All of Brzezin also prepared. Reb Fajwel Majer was giving in marriage . . . Reb Kalman Hoyker [the hunchback] was giving in marriage . . . Reb Hersz Icze was giving in marriage . . . If Kalman Hoyker's son was getting married, or Tamar, Hersz Icze's daughter, was getting married, or Frajde, Szlama the Hasid's daughter, was getting married . . . they, *kholile* [God forbid!], never spoke of it. It was only said that papa and mama were marrying off their child.

And now, especially, the *klezmorim* [musicians]—Jankiele Kordelas, who once played for the Polish Uprising in 1863, Reb Mojsze with his little fiddle, Fiszel with the trumpet, Wachler, Nechemia's uncle, with the big bass fiddle.

They prepared doubly. I can see the beautiful *besmedresh bokhoyrim* walking alongside the *khosen* [groom], the groom standing in front of the *khupe* [wedding canopy], the reception for the groom by the finest leaders of the town dressed in *shabesdike* [fit for the Sabbath] velvet caps, with satin and silk caftans. They are seated at long tables covered with gleaming white table cloths, decorated with silver candlesticks holding large flickering candles. The smoke of the shared cigarettes given by the groom, with the scent of Aquavit and fresh cake, fill the rooms where the recliners sit—a little tired, with their heads resting on the side, after the drinking and smoking.

The interpretation of some passage by the groom, an exhibition by the jester, his calling out, "Groom, today is your Day of Judgment!" The way the groom puts on the *kitl* [white robe worn during the ceremony] and puts a pocket handkerchief to his eyes. He remembers the *yom hamise* [day of death] . . . he wipes off the tears with his cloth. "To remember!" cries out the jester. Then the bringing to the *khupe*.

Most often it was at the *shul*. Half a town of Jews awaited the *khupe*—young, old—wanting to see the way the groom cried, the way the bride walked, the way they stood under the *khupe*. A trifle? A *khupe*, a *khasene* [wedding] . . .

After the holy prayer, after the singing of the cantor, after Aron the *shames*'s carrying-on, the *klezmorim* used to strike up a cheerful tune. Only then began the childish antics of the apprentices, who inherited the mischievousness of the former *voyle yungen*.

They used to smear their caps in the bake ovens of Zysman Beker [baker] or Smoluch Beker. Later, full of soot, they used to smear the faces of other girls and boys. Only then did the real merrymaking begin. They began to pelt each other with pebbles and lime.

I still remember at Kalman Hoykers child's wedding in the courtyard, Eliasz Łęczycki, the yellow-haired Icze-Majer's son, was hit by a piece of lime in his eye and became blind forever after.

* * *

The rapid development of the tailoring industry in Brzezin brought about a great change in the entire small-town appearance of Brzezin. The glory of the esteemed custom tailor—such as Reb Josel Rogodziński (Reb Josel Warszawer [from Warsaw]), Reb Jecheskiel Szmul Bendkower [from Będków] Blianket, his brother Syna Blianket, and the brothers Sosek—was diminished, and also that of the slightly less important ones—Reb Jerachmiel Tuszyński, Shirhamayles, and others. While it may have taken them a week to sew up a suit or a short jacket, people wore them so long that the fabric fell apart, but their workmanship remained.

The fence around the Brzezin cemetery that the hooligans destroyed.

The modern tailors had the work done in one day. Their speed made the Brzeziner entrepreneur capable of competing with many other manufacturing places in Poland and in Russia. But the custom tailors lost their means of making a living. Those who had no earnings on the side could not manage just on their hard work.

Josel Rogodziński fell into the same situation—or as we called him, Josel Warszawer, a Jew, not a tall one, with a bit of a stomach and a graying beard combed into two points, similar to a Russian general. His clients, the Russian bureaucrats, permitted Reb Josele to sew their custom-made uniforms. Therefore, Reb Josel was quite well acquainted with the Brzeziner district chief, Bazilewski, since Bazilewski, a former colonel, was also one of Josele's frequent clients. When Jewish *tates* [fathers] found themselves in trouble—a son was about to be conscripted by the Russians—Reb Josel was the only one with influence with Bazilewski. Reb Mojsze Aron Szotenberg, the town millionaire, the "champion" of the modern tailoring industry, was taking lessons from Reb Josele.

Since I recalled the name Bazilewski, I will also recall Chana-Golda, wife of Reb Abraham-Pejsach, the *gabe* [trustee] of the Khevre Kedishe. She was the daughter of Reb Fiszel Shoykhet and the sister of Reb Lajbele Żychliński. Since Reb Abraham Pejsach had a nice haberdashery, and he himself had no time for the business—since he had to sit in his *shtibl* and practice Hasidism and bury the dead—his wife, Chana-Golda, was the merchant. The wife of Bazilewski needed everything, and she was a customer of Chana-Golda. That is how she became acquainted with her husband. Reb Abraham Jubiler also used to prevail upon Bazilewski for everything.

At that time the woman Tyla from the dry goods store was a respected woman. As I already said, the Bazilewskis were customers for everything, so they also bought from Tyla. So Tyla actually came to the rescue in an urgent situation.

Reb Jerachmiel Tuszyński was a custom tailor. He used to do alterations, that is, make something from an old garment, from an older brother's garment, for a younger one. The important Parisian artist, the painter Tuszyński, was a son of the deaf Icek, Reb Jerachmiel Tuszyński's grandchild, who was born in Brzezin.

Another well-known tailor with the name Shirhamayles [songs of praise] was very popular in Brzezin. They called him by this nickname because he was truly similar to the other psalm reciter. Shirhamayles was a God-fearing Jew. When he was short two or three day's work in a week, he finished it up with reciting psalms. That's why the town called him Shirhamayles.

* * *

There also were other miserable ways of making a living, occupations such as wagon drivers, water carriers, used clothing dealers, shoemakers, wagon drivers to Łódź, day laborers, and porters who would *shlep* [carry] large packages bound one to the other with thick rope. For this type of *shlepping* the porters used to earn enough to buy themselves a portion of herring for a *grosz* from Etja, the herring vendor in Court Street. It also seemed that Reb Fajwel Wyrobnik's [worker's] son, for dragging two youngsters to *kheyder*, used to get enough to buy himself a portion of cheese from Dark Chana, for a *grosz*, and a *rogalik* [crescent-shaped roll], for one and a half *groszy*.

Dark Hana, also a Brzeziner merchant of that time, used to stand with her store near Lajbele Hendrykowski's beer tavern. Her "store" consisted of a basket of baked goods—rolls, kaiser rolls, bagels, and *rogalki* [pl. of *rogalik*]. On the basket lay a board and on the board, cut portions of cheese, a *grosz* a portion.

The water carriers, with Jankiele Brasz, used to carry two pails of water, hanging on strong oak pieces of timber strengthened with iron, cut out in the center for the carrier's neck. For ten pails of water, they would get ten *groszy* of pocket money. The pails with the pieces of timber were so strongly made that they remained an inheritance for children and grandchildren, since the water carriers had no other inheritance to leave but the pails, just as the porter had his rope.

The earnings of the wagon drivers came to a bit more. They used to take the town merchant—on top of fully-packed wagons—to purchase goods in Łódź. On the way back on the highway, with packed merchandise, they used to pile on passengers, and for three hours dragged themselves home that way. The Łódź wagon drivers were Reb Abraham Mojsze Tsze's, Reb Icek Masza's, Mendel Zomb's brother-in-law, Zelig Reb Icek Masza's, Reb Joel Majer Beker's, Reb Lajb Izrael Kashamakher's [kasha maker], Make, Reb Icek Nuta's brother.

Koluszki wagon drivers belonged to a higher category than the Łódź ones. These were wagon drivers who drove coaches, and they took well-to-do passengers to the train. The coach drivers were Reb Icek Nuta's, Reb Lemel Byk, Reb Abramele Tuszyński, his son Icek Tuszyński, Szymszon Tuszyński, Emanuel Dymant, and Reb Zalmele.

Earning a living became easier when a highway to Łódź was built. The contract to make the highway was undertaken by Szlama Silski, *e"h*. He became rich from it. Reb

Szlama became connected by marriage to the Radomer *rov* when he took his son, Reb Arje Dawid, as his son-in-law. He [Reb Szlama] actually gave him the contract, and in that way Reb Arje Perlmuter also became rich.

The seven members of the Jewish community council made Szlama Silski a *dozor* [community official/overseer], since at that time no elections took place. Reb Szlama died while he was still a *dozor*.

The oppressive economic situation caused a large part of the Jewish youth of Brzezin to emigrate to America. Reb Chaim-Icek's son, our Professor Berg also did the same.

Professor Berg's father, Reb Chaim-Icek, *e"h*, was an old Vorker Hasid. Afterward he became an Aleksander Hasid. Reb Chaim-Icek was also a fine merchant, had a paper store with writing materials and schoolbooks. He had, *keyn ayen hore* [no evil eye should harm them], a houseful of children. He even owned a *britchke* [small half-covered carriage] with a horse, which he used to travel to the German colonies around Brzezin to supply them with schoolbooks. But a considerable amount was lacking from making a living. . . . Friend Berg deliberated for a while, left the provincial happiness, and emigrated to America.

And when you talk about Professor Berg, you must also remember his brother, Issachar, known by the entire town.

The stream of emigration created an oppressive mood among the older religious people. Observant Jews in Poland at that time wanted very much for their children not to go to America, but they had no words of advice. They had to make peace with their fate. Resisting the stream made no sense, and thanks to the farsightedness of the youth of that time, today we have a large Brzeziner Society in America. Today Brzeziner Jews are scattered and spread all over the world.

A Group of Zionists and Intelligentsia of the Town.

Seated from the right: Adele Gotlib, S. Sułkowicz, E. Gotlib.
Standing from the right: Kujawski, Szulzinger, A. B. Gips, Waldman.

Brzeziner Tailors (pp. 40–43)

David Lencicki (Tel Aviv)

Aksler's house [building], which was built in the summer of 1902, was then the first and largest tailors' blockhouse. Mojsze Kopel's house was ready a year and a half later. The place where Stawian's great house later stood was then Emanuel Winter's (Mshumak) lumberyard, and a circus also played there.

Of the fifteen tenants who lived in Aksler's house, twelve were tailors. I would like to recall here the inhabitants of the first tailors' blockhouse in Brzezin.

Reb Eliezer Rajchman (the ample Luzer) was a virtuous, observant Jew, a Grodzisker Hasid. He fastidiously fulfilled the custom of praying with his whole being. He actually danced while *davening*. He had a right to say *zkhoyr bris* [remember the covenant], recited in *shul* on Rosheshone [Rosh Hashanah–New Year] eve. Right after praying, he would travel for the Days of Awe [between Rosh Hashanah and Yom Kippur] to Grodzisk, where he was in charge of the morning prayer. On the morning after Yonkiper [Yom Kippur], he would return home and attend to the *suke* [ceremonial booth erected for Sukes, the Feast of Tabernacles].

Although the *suke* was a usual one, and fourteen families ate in it, Reb Eliezer, with great fervor and with his Hasidic generosity, almost single-handedly took on himself the obligation of the *mitsve* [commandment]. His *kidesh* [benediction over wine], his *zmires* [Shabes songs], and his Hasidic stories had us young people occupied in the *suke* for hours.

The *simkhes* [joyful celebrations] that were held when he married off a daughter, the singing, the dancing, the *sheve brokhes* [seven blessings given at a wedding], deafened the entire town. One has to add that the generosity was Hasidic, not that of a rich man, since, in sum, he was a Jew, a poor man, and maybe that explains the great celebration when he married off a daughter. He died in 1915 at a very advanced age.

The second tenant—Jankiel Zapałki-makher (Zajde) [maker of matches]—lived on the second side of the ground floor; Reb Natan Łęczycki and Abraham Aronowicz (Aron Shuster's), on the first floor. Aron Waldman (Pajger), A. Liskiewiczer (later left for America), Henoch Meilich, a brother of Wolf Ikka, Mojsze Dawid Hasid, a son of Pinkus Job (left for America), and the yellow-haired Abraham Mojsze (Hochspiegel)—were in Brzezin until the end. On the second floor—Josef Gotek (Krell), a son-in-law of Perec Piotrkowski; Lajbuś Hentshke-makher [glove maker] (Borkowski), a brother-in-law of Perec Piotrkowski (left for America), and Szmul Rabinowicz, a Poddenbicer [from Poddębice].

Incidentally, Reb Mojszl Khazn came to Brzezin from Poddębice, where he had been a *khazn* and *shoykhet*. In an annex in the courtyard lived the knife sharpener and the deaf Mojsze, son-in-law of old Pinele.

A group of members of Poale Zion from Brzezin at a meeting.

The apartments in Aksler's house consisted of two rooms, both of equal size, approximately four by four [meters]. The first room, where there was a walled-in stove, was a workshop room that had kitchen fixtures. Two to three large machines stood there—to make the work easier and to iron—also a small table for the hand stitchers and a half dozen stools.

The "living inventory" in the room consisted, most of the time, of ten persons—the master, the master's wife, a journeyman, a seasoned apprentice, a female hand stitcher, a new apprentice or two, and the children of the family. The second room consisted of two beds, a wardrobe or two, a table and stools, a sofa, and packets of cut work—as well as a little work, already pressed, that waited in the cradle until delivery. The cradle itself actually did not have a set place. It depended on the child. If it was a quiet child, it lay in the room. However, if it was a crier or a screamer, the apprentice, who had not yet had his *bar mitsve*, took the child into the kitchen, that is, into the workshop, and rocked the child, placing one foot on the runner. Meanwhile, with his hands, he withdrew the basting stitches in order to give the presser a clean *marynarka* [man's jacket].

Generally, the apprentice was between hammer and anvil, that is, between the journeymen and the master's wife. The master's wife did not do it from meanness, but only because the work was beyond her strength. She needed someone to help her and actually someone onto whom she could unload her bitter heart.

And what is the wonder? Among these ten persons was the first hand stitcher, who contracted herself out without food, since hand stitchers were mostly young girls who ate and slept at their parents' home. For the others, one needed to cook pots of food twice a day. They wanted to keep the workshop operating, so the food had to be tasty and plentiful.

The lodgers in Aksler's house were young people, grown children not yet with families. The work of the master's wife was hard. She had to stand on her feet from six in the morning until eleven to twelve o'clock at night. She had to buy food for the meals, cook, worry about cleanliness, and carry out all women's functions—such as pregnancy and having and raising children in crowded quarters. In summer, the flies burrowed, and in winter, there was smoke from the press irons—one had to seriously worry about cleanliness. It must be said to their credit that all the tailors' wives from Aksler's house in the years 1902–5 were great homemakers. You have to add that the wives also often had to go to the *magaziner*s late at night, after the hand stitchers had left, to do a little hand sewing in order for the journeymen and the assistant machine workers to have something to do in the morning.

The work consisted of padded winter jackets and overcoats, suits of clothing, and separate pants. Preparation for the winter season lasted approximately seven months—from Purim [in early spring] until after Sukes [in autumn]. The winter season was strong, since ninety percent of the production went to the Russian market, as far as Irkutsk, Vladivostok, and Arkhangelsk. Transportation was very primitive. It took three months before the merchandise arrived at its destination. The merchants came after Shavuos [in late spring], when they bought merchandise in stock and ordered merchandise that was to be sent later by a set deadline.

The workers were generally divided into three groups. The third group participated in the winter work. There was a significant group of tailors who did not participate just in the winter work; they worked the entire year, making men's jackets and sets (pants-vests). These were of the highest rank. They were called the "silken fingers." I will mention some highly skilled workers in this category—Mordechai Winter, Godel Grajcer, Abraham Jonas (Opoczyński), Mojsze Aron Shuster's (Aronowicz), Abraham Pakrels, and Fiszel Eksztajn. From the best tailors of sets (pants-vests)—Aszer Fryde, Szlama Lajb Krulik (Kalisz), Pine Tauba's (Fuks), Jekiel Dawid Dzik (Dymant) and Lajbel Lichtel (Rozenblat). Good vest sewers—Chaim Ber Pytel and Hersz Wolf Celcer. Of the good pants sewers, I mention only one—Eli Ber Miller.

I do not want to shame those in the third category, and I mention several of them—sewers of jackets of lesser quality—Mojsze Moc [strong], Abraham Aronowicz, Natan Radoszycer, Josef Rywen Fabisiak with his son, Mordechai Icek. The ordinary sets (pants-vests) sewers were Eli Szajber (Goldberg), Chaiml Zgiwer, Chanina Cwern and Jankiel Zapałki (Zajde). Aksler's house had the honor of having two from the top category—Abraham Mojsze Hochspiegel and Szmul Rabinowicz.

Crowding was not as great at the better tailors. As one could notice, two sacks of charcoal stood in the corner of the home the entire year, an iron cot, two heated pressing irons, and still other things that did not have a set place. During the summer, two stacks of black cotton were also brought to the workshop. There also were tailors who used white cotton, such as Reb Majer Poliwoda, Berl Szaferman, Mojsze Josel Tryber, and Natan Wald, but they did not live in Aksler's house. The cotton blocked the windows of the house through which could have come a little air in the hot summer months. Therefore, when [work for] the winter season ended, and they took out the goat, one breathed freer.

The work-times? In general, it is hard to write definitively about it, and, in particular, because the organization of the workshop played a role. First of all, it required that the master should be fast so that the chief journeymen should not have to help him with his work. Mainly, it was necessary for the workshop to be well organized. This required taking a lot of time so that the workshop could be correctly organized when the apprentice became a journeyman—and this took several years. I will try to describe the development of the tailor workshops in the years 1900–1905.

It has to be said that regardless of the self-enslavement and the self-exploitation of the Brzeziner master tailors, whose working hours had reached in those days eighteen to twenty hours in a twenty-four hour period, they introduced a nice custom—the intersession (maybe they got it from the teachers?). Although both Pesakh and Sukes were the busiest season, they indulged in a two-week break from work. They had to make arrangements with the magazine owners, deliver the machines to the machine operators, and mainly add people to do the work.

Immediately, on the first day of the period between the first and last two days of Pesakh and Sukes, boys between eleven and thirteen arrived—some with parents, some without. The bolder ones came alone from the surrounding cities and towns—Stryków, Głowno, Jeżów, Rawa, Neustadtel, Skierniewice, Ujazd, Tomaszów, Łaskowice, Łowicz, Sulejów, Bielawy, Sobota, Piątek, and so forth.

The apprentice who had finished his apprenticeship in these towns contracted himself for a year or for a specified time. A small number of qualified workers who worked for the made-to-order tailors in their town also did this.

The masters came to the market dressed up with new black hats on their heads, their *żupica* [caftan] unbuttoned, from which a little watch with a watch chain could be seen in the vest pocket, and usually carrying a special small cane. They would begin looking over the apprentices and qualified workers who had come. Of course, the older and more physically developed were grabbed up. This may have played a bigger role for the master's wife, since the youth had to bring up as many as two buckets of water at a time and pour out the wastewater. Once a month, they took in a washerwoman, and water had to be brought in continuously. Afterward, they had to help carry the wash to the attic [to hang to dry], later help turn the mangle [device that pressed fabric by passing it through heated rollers], go on an errand for the master's wife, who remembered something else every time, and pick up the child who was bellowing—having gotten under the treadle of the machines and hurt itself.

And the master? He certainly had something to say! The work had to be brought from the magazine owner and carried back to him; he had to go to the buttonhole maker and to the accessories store to bring cotton wadding. This reminds me of the two-meter pack of wadding that was so large that the little porters disappeared under the mass. Is it any wonder that they looked for a youth who would be physically fit for such a heavy task? Many masters really did not leave things to miracles and immediately took two apprentices who could divide the side work and have time to learn the trade.

As a rule, a youth was taken on for two or three years, with eating and sleeping, a suit of clothes for Pesakh, and twenty-five rubles when the apprenticeship was over. But the apprenticeship rarely ended in a set term. When the parents came with a younger brother, they took him on and extended the time for the older one another half year. The apprenticeship having fortunately ended, he could actually work anywhere he wanted, but generally, the apprentices remained with their old masters. They were used to one another; they forgave old offenses, came to terms for a year or a set time and then stayed in the workshop until they became head masters themselves.

Hand stitchers were generally from good Hasidic families or were tailors' daughters who worked in the home until the younger daughters grew up and took the older one's place.

Those workshops that developed in such a way that the apprentice could become a journeyman hummed along, and the working hours there were like other workshops, so that the normal (or abnormal) workday was, in the summer, from six in the morning until eight at night. Later, a program began of pressing twice a week and doing floor work. There was no midday lunch hour. One ate at the pressing table or at the [sewing] machine.

If one subtracts the four meal times of the day that took an hour and a half, the workday lasted thirteen hours. But this did not really apply to the master.

For the master, the workweek began Saturday night. Well-rested after Shabes—it was quiet in the house, restful, no one disturbed him—he could calmly work until after midnight. The master actually stood at the table with big scissors in hand, humming a tune to himself. On Sunday, at five in the morning, he arose, and he awakened the group. First of all, the apprentices, who slept on the sleep benches that served as ironing boards. At night, the plank was removed, and inside was a straw mattress, a pillow, and a cotton blanket. Then he woke up the journeymen, who slept on the iron cots that stood in the corner of the house. It took an hour until the people climbed out of the "nest" and the mess was cleaned away. If he was able to, the master got in a little *davening*, and they went to work.

A group of young men from the scout organization Gordonia.

On Sunday, the work did not proceed at the usual tempo. The journeymen were worn out, having done a lot of dancing the entire Shabes night and having downed a couple of beers; they felt tired on Sunday. Perhaps the apprentice fought with a gang from another town and came home with a lame foot. Well, the master had to complete the day with an additional two hours of work, but on Sunday, this did not bother him. He still had reserves from the Shabes day. In the second half of the week, generally Thursday, when they worked the entire night, it happened that the master, always at the table, took a little chair and laid his head on the table, and the assistants helped him out and work slowed down. But this lasted about a quarter of an hour. The master would jump up with a start, wipe his eyes, and notice that the group was dreaming. He would yell out, "Get moving!" and begin to tell a story:

"In the land of the pyramids, there was a king, angry and evil."

The journeymen helped him:

"You have suffered uselessly so that Manchuria should remain yours. Give a look at whose flag flies there and who is in there. Russian, you should bury yourself, your head bowed with shame; you will still have *tsurelekh* [little troubles], your heroic courage diminishes."

The hand stitchers helped a little:

"I loved a girl who was from Vienna, I loved a girl who was from Vienna."

And the assistant machine worker does not want to be left out (incidentally, the *birzhe* [office] of the Bund had already been established), and began to sing:

"Oh, you foolish Zionists with your clogged up minds, the Turks cheated you and will not give you the land!"

One hears again the soprano of the apprentice, "Come, come home, Isroelik! Come home to your own land! . . ."

Again the work went full steam ahead until four in the morning. Then they sent the apprentice to Majer the baker to buy two dozen warm bagels. It was warm in the house from the press irons and the bright lights that illuminate Court Street and Goat Lane. Thursday night must substitute for the short winter Friday. In practice, it seemed different. For the journeymen, the night stretched until nine to ten in the morning, but the master and the apprentices were also seen late into the dusk in the Brzeziner streets with little packets of pressed work when tall Bobes had already shouted, "Candle lighting!" [signifying the beginning of the Sabbath].

Three generations of the Kochberg family (picture is from 1912).

Top row from right to left: Syma Kochberg (Herszel Litvak's daughter)—perished in the annihilation, Szmul-Dawid Kochberg (Toronto, Canada), Chaja-Sura Ranis (Los Angeles), Jakub-Szlama Kochberg (Toronto), Sura Kochberg (Toronto), Elka Milner (Toronto), and Aszer-Zelig Kochberg (Toronto).

Second row: Aron-Lajb Kochberg (perished in the annihilation), Icek-Majer Kochberg (perished in Łódź ghetto), Hersz-Mendel Kochberg (died in 1924), Jerachmiel Kochberg (Toronto), Ita Kochberg (died in 1937 in Toronto).

Third row: Rutcia Kochberg (perished in the annihilation), Abraham Kochberg (Toronto), Ester Szafman (Toronto).

Brzeziner Rabbis and Hasidim (pp. 44–45)

S. Pinczewski (Tel Aviv)

I do not know if among those Brzeziners of my generation left alive there are any who know about the former old Brzezin, of the time of the Kotsker Khsides [Kock Hasidic movement]. Already then there was a Kotsker *shtibl* in Brzezin that was known among the Kotsker Hasidim for its eminent personalities—such as Reb Icek Brzeziner, Reb Mendel, and Reb Jokisz. Some, I remember from the time when I was a child, such as Reb Szlama Reb Icek's, Szlama Reb Mendel's, and Szaja Jokisz. Having been brought up in a Hasidic neighborhood, I myself had the opportunity to know personally a lot of such people from the Brzezin of the past.

I heard about the *makhloykes* [quarrel] in Brzezin over the *khazn*, Moszke Bialystoker [from Białystok]. At that time Brzezin was to take on a new cantor in the manner generally common in the Tfutses Yisroel [Jewish Diaspora]. When a town was to take on a new cantor, the candidate, before he was hired as cantor, first had to *daven* on a Shabes as a trial. So the new cantor, Moszke, came from Białystok to Brzezin. He was a marvelous cantor and *bal-tfile* [prayer leader]. He had an enormous voice. Right after the first prayers on that Shabes, the group of community leaders promptly hired him, and they actually would not let him leave town, wanting him to remain as cantor in Brzezin. But there was a problem with that Moszke in that he was an *alter bokher* [older bachelor], and according to the *Shulkhn Orekh* [book of rules governing the life of Orthodox Jews], it was objectionable that someone who did not have a wife should be a representative of the community. But the leaders did not want to consider that, since Cantor Moszke promised that he was going to get married.

The Kotsker Hasidim of that time were outright opposed to this. This brought about a feud in the town between the Hasidim and the community leaders. It went so far that they hit each other with sticks in *shul*.

My grandmother related that she locked my grandfather, Reb Naftali, an old Kotsker Hasid, in the house, so he could not go into the *shul* and fight with the leaders. She was afraid that he would come home battered.

The result was that Moszke, the cantor, had to leave Brzezin, because the *rov* [official town rabbi] was on the side of the Hasidim.

Reb Naftali Hersz, the *bal-musef* [leader of *musef*, extension of morning prayer] from the Gerer [Góra Kalwaria] *shtibl*, related seeing a young man *af kest* [boarding with in-laws], who by chance was going through the courtyard of the *shul* when Moszke Bialystoker was praying. He stood there, charmed by his praying. He could not tear himself away from the spot, but being a Hasid, he could not go into the *shul* [which was Orthodox, not Hasidic], so he climbed up in the attic of the *shul* and lay there hidden during the entire prayers.

In those years, Brzezin was a small, poor *shtetl*. A portion of its inhabitants supported the family by producing *talesim* [prayer shawls]. These were poor weavers who would produce prayer shawls in a primitive way on a make-shift loom that was in the home. The other portion of the inhabitants of the town consisted of small storekeepers and various artisans, among whom were several tailors who did mending and alterations. They would travel through the villages the entire week and sew for peasants for their home use; they repaired various old clothing and made over old furs. For Shabes they returned home to their wives and brought back from the villages a few potatoes, a few eggs, maybe a little produce or a chicken. There were a few prominent men in town who were better off, but in general Brzezin was then a poor town.

From the maker of prayer shawls evolved the great well-to-do man Reb Szlama Silski, later the *dozor* [overseer] of the Jewish community—one with a firm hand. The *rov*, together with the other religious personnel, had more dealings with him than with any of the other community leaders. He was lame. Earlier, while still a poor prayer shawl weaver, he married a mute woman with whom he had a daughter. Later, the mute wife died, and he married a second woman, Mirel. He made a *yikhes-shidekh* [match with someone of distinguished lineage] for his daughter from his first wife. Being very wealthy, he was able to become connected by marriage to a special family, with the Radomer *rov*, and took as a son-in-law the fine young man Reb Arje Dawid Perlmuter.

Reb Arje Dawid Perlmuter, *e"h* [may he rest in peace], the Radomer *rov*'s son, later grew to be a great philanthropist with a generous heart. He was one of the most eminent personalities that I remember in town.

I recall the fine Jew of stately appearance Reb Naftali Hersz, *e"h*, the *bal-musef* [leader of *musef*] during the Days of Awe in the Gerer *shtibl*. Although he had plenty of opponents—even among the Gerer Hasidim—he was nevertheless superior to all of them.

The Brzeziner *rov*, Reb Zalman Borensztajn, *zts"l* [may the memory of a righteous person be blessed], who had the reputation throughout Poland as a great scholar. The Nazi villains murdered him in a tragic manner.

Of the Hasidim from the Gerer *shtibl* whom I remember, I rarely found ordinary types. Icek Majer Berger was a very dedicated Hasid. His insights and Jewish charm were rare. He who has not seen his dancing and singing on Simkhes Toyre [festival marking the completion of the cycle of reading the Torah] at the Hakofes [procession with Torah scrolls], does not know what a Hasidic dance is.

From my childhood I also still remember the elderly distinguished scholar Szlama Reb Mendel's, son of an old Kotsker Hasid, the famous proofreader of *seyfer-toyres* [Torah scrolls], the great grammarian and scholar. He was then already a blind man from whose eye sockets looked out ancient generations of Jewish martyrology. While he was alive, he grew as a legendary personality in the town. He looked like an ancient *gaon* [eminent scholar].

Even the contemporary ultra-religious from the Gerer *shtibl* also had their peculiar charm. Here I mean the Hasidic impractical ones—Chanina Lipman and others. There also were other Hasidic personalities, such as Reb Mojsze Majer Gutkind, the dark Sura's, and Reb Perec Jakubowicz. Also, in the other Hasidic *shtiblekh*, such as the Aleksanderer [from Aleksandrów], the Grodzisker [from Grodzisk], and the Ostrovtser [from Ostrowiec], there were many fine Jews of whom Brzezin could be proud—such as Reb Josef Michał's, Reb Dawid Lajb Masza's, Reb Jerachmiel, the rabbi's [son], Reb

Szlama Pabianicer [from Pabianice], the red-haired Eliezer. There also were Hasidic *shtiblekh* with younger leaders, Hasidic scholars such as Reb Jekiel Nachum's, Reb Szymszon Erlich, Reb Jehuda Krongold, Reb Hersz Icek, Reb Fajwel Majer, Reb Chaim-Icek Ajnbinder, Reb Hersz Ledershniter, Reb Szmul Khazn, Reb Dawid Hersz Shoykhet, and Reb Hillel Shames.

There also were Hasidic *maskilim*, modern, enlightened, with a secular education. The elders of that time were Reb Nachman Gutkind, Reb Szmule Krongold, Reb Chaim-Icek Grynfeld, Reb Wowe Halberstam, and many others. All those listed were distinguished Hasidic scholars of whom Brzezin had nothing to be ashamed.

Finally, I want to recall the last two Brzeziner rabbis whose remembrance all Brzeziner Jews hold dear. The *rov* Reb Izrael Dwarter, z"l, was a great scholar and skilled in Shas [Talmud] and *poskim* [post-Talmudic commentaries]. His judgments were heeded even in Ger as the ultimate truth. He was considered one of the greatest scholars in Poland for whom even his opponents had respect. His teaching was in the manner of later *poskim*. He was not a *bal-pilpul* [hair splitter] nor shrewd. In teaching a lesson in Talmud he distinguished himself more with mastery than with cleverness. He was truly a great scholar. In contrast, in worldly matters, he was less proficient. He was not very friendly, and because of this, he had a lot of opponents in the town. But this did not diminish his authority as a great scholar. He had a son, Berl, with whom I studied. He was a contender for the Brzeziner rabbinate. He was quite impractical but at the same time a great scholar.

The Brzeziner *rov*, Reb Zalman Borensztajn, z"l, hi"d [may the Lord avenge his blood], was kneaded from an entirely different dough. He had a gentle heart. Aside from the fact that he was a great scholar, he also was open and friendly, a person worthy of love. He understood how to treat people, especially ordinary people. Everyone loved him. It was said about him, quoting from the *maymer khazal* [wise sayings from the Scriptures repeated in the Talmud], "A person who is received with pleasure by mankind will be also by God." His manner of living was that of a scholar. In teaching, he had the manner of his father, the well-known *moyre hoyroe* [rabbi who renders decisions on matters of rabbinic law], the author of the book *Sanhedrin Ktane* [Lesser Sanhedrin/ religious courts]. About such personalities as the two Brzeziner rabbis, one can only say, as the Gemore expresses it, "Woe, that the best of the best should ultimately decay in the dust, and woe, for the loss."

The Jews of My Generation (pp. 46–55)

Jacob David Berg

With great respect for the luminaries in the holy community of our devastated hometown Brzezin, I step forward to write about them and bring them to the forefront of people's memory.

No Jewish trace remains of our *shtetl* now. Even the *matseyves* in the cemetery were ripped out, and you can no longer find the essence of the precious Jews who beautified our Hasidic tailoring town—just as the famous writer Z. Segalowicz described Brzezin after the destruction in his dirge, the poem "There."

We must immortalize their illustrious names in this *Sefer Brzezin* [Book of Brzezin], and I hope that my own recollections will serve me well enough to be able to recall them all. The future generations should know who the Jews were of my generation in our destroyed hometown.

I call my town "Brezin" because that was what the town was called when it belonged to Czarist Russia. Brezin was famous then for its tailoring industry. The town provided the large Russian market with ready-made clothing, and this brought employment and earnings. Russian merchants from distant areas used to come twice a year and buy merchandise from us. Entrepreneurs, *magaziner*s, gave precut material to the tailors, and they sewed the clothing. The town was full of work and life. No one knew then of want. And so it continued until World War I.

After World War I, when Poland became independent, our town lost the name Brezin. The new rulers called it Brzeziny. Jews shortened the name to Brzezin. The main change, however, consisted of the fact that our town had lost the large Russian market and become quite impoverished.

Here I want to recall with great affection the *kehile* [community] of my generation in the town that I remember from before World War I. Our Brzezin justly earned the name Hasidic tailoring town. Although the majority of Brzeziner Jews were not Hasidim—but were simple, observant [Orthodox] Jews, who would fill up the *besmedresh* and the great *shul*—the influence that the Hasidic Jews had on the entire community life was quite substantial. They were the "Shabes-*Yontov-dike Yidn*" [Sabbath-Holiday Jews] of I. L. Peretz [famous Yiddish writer] among us, and they infected the entire town. Whoever came to Brzezin felt at once that the town carried the stamp of a generations-long Hasidic style of living.

One recalls the Fridays when in the afternoon, one could already feel in the air of the town and among everyone the inner excitement of preparing to greet the Holy Sabbath. The assistant *shamasim* [sextons], Psilke and Bobes, used to go through the town and call out, *"Likht tsindn, likht tsindn!"* [Candle lighting time!]. Right after that you heard their second call, *"Yidn, in shul arayn!"* [Jews, into the synagogue!], and at once the Hasidim of the town appeared in the streets in their *shabesdike* [fit for the Sabbath] outfit, in a satin *żupica* [caftan]. Some also wore *shtraymekh* [caps edged with fur]. The beards and *peos* [long side curls] were still wet from the *mikve* [ritual bath]. As if with a magic wand, all the shops were closed. And you saw clearly how the Sabbath Queen descended over our town. The Hasidic *shtiblekh* became very crowded, and the ardent prayers of Sabbath eve coming from there could be heard far and wide. In their Shabes clothing, ordinary Jews, non-Hasidim, filled the synagogue and the *besmedresh*. Emptiness spread throughout the market square. Two or three Christian taverns and the *goyish* apothecary's shop stood orphaned.

My memories extend further, and I remember the Yomim-Naroyim [Days of Awe, between Rosh Hashanah and Yom Kippur]. With what a shiver we caught the first blast, when at the beginning of the month of Elul, they began to blow the *shofar* [ceremonial ram's horn]. We, the school children, began to feel, together with all the grownups, that something was beginning—preparation for the great judgment. Then came the fervent night of *slikhes* [penitent prayers], the Holy Days after Rosheshone, the Days of Repentance from Rosheshone to Yonkiper, the eve of Yonkiper—the night of *Kol Nidre* [plaintive prayer on Yom Kippur eve], when I stood wrapped in my father's *talis* while he said the Tfile Zaka [prayer on Yom Kippur forgiving others]. My father's tears also made me wet. And although I was a nine-year-old boy, I already felt grown up, and I joined in and recited the prayers.

And on the morning after Yonkiper—today I still see the picture before my eyes—in every courtyard people were busy putting up *sukes*, and from all around, you could hear the sound of hammers. And when the holiday of Sukes came, the leaders walked proudly in the streets to the *shtiblekh* and to the *shul* and back home, carrying large bunches of *lulavim* [palm branches] and *esrogim* [citrons]. Simkhes Toyre was really our holiday, a holiday for children. How much pleasure we children had, ending with the flags, with the little candles stuck into red apples! And the Khevre Kedishe [Burial Society] divided honey cake—each piece of which was as big as a brick—among its members.

In addition, the preparation for the holiday Pesakh! Arising before daylight to bake *matse* [unleavened bread]! The Hasidim had their own bakeries, where they themselves kneaded, rolled, made punctures on the *matse*, and baked the *matse* under strict supervision.

Lag b'Omer [end of period of mourning for the destruction of the Temple] was finally entirely our own holiday, the holiday of school children. We used to march around beyond the town with bows, literally like soldiers from a Jewish army.

I still remember the happy days of Khanike [Hanukkah—Festival of Lights] in my town, how we children would not let go of the Khanike *dreydlekh* [spinning tops] and how we were proud of the heroism of Judah Maccabee. I still see before me the happy uproar when Purim [celebration of deliverance of Jews from Persian tyrant Hamen, with reading of Book of Esther] came. The *Purim-shpilers* [Purim reenactment players] went around from one corner of the town to the other, and there were open doors for them everywhere. We children had the *mitsve* of taking around *shalakhmones* [presents exchanged by friends and neighbors on Purim], and, incidentally, from this we were left with a few kopeks in our pockets.

We had a fine observant Jewish life in our town. And when our Brzezin earned the name Hasidic tailoring town, it was not without good reason. We had Hasidim from all the Hasidic *rebbes*' courts in Greater Poland. First place was taken by the Gerer [Góra Kawalria] *shtibl*, which had the greatest number of Hasidim. Next in line were the

Aleksanderer [Aleksandrów], Grodzisker [Grodzisk], and Ostrovtser [Ostrowiec] Hasidim. We also had several Radzyner [Radzyń] Hasidim, who were distinctive because they wore blue *tsitses* [ritual tassels on the four corners of undergarments].

Thanks to the Hasidic influence, our clergymen were also Hasidim. Our *rov*, Reb Izrael Dwarter, was a Gerer Hasid, a distinguished *tish-zitser* [follower] of the Gerer *rebbe*, the *shfas-emes* [source of truth]. Reb Izrael's learning was renowned over all Poland. Our old *moyre-hoyroe* [rabbi who renders decisions on matters of rabbinic law], Reb Abraham Szaja Heszl [Borensztajn], was a Grodzisker Hasid, the author of an important scholarly book *Sanhedrin Ktanim* [Lesser Religious Courts]. The Grodzisker *rebbe* came to his funeral.

After his passing, his son, Reb Zalman Borensztajn, took over the *kase rabones* [rabbinic seat] and became rabbi. After the death of Reb Izrael Dwarter, he became the Brzeziner town rabbi and remained town rabbi until the Nazis, *im"w* [may their names and memory be blotted out], murdered him.

When our superb synagogue was finished, instead of the town cantor, Reb Szulem Lerer, son of the Zgierz rabbi, we brought in a Grodzisker Hasid, Cantor Reb Mojszl Sterns, from Warsaw. He was a *mohel* [performed circumcisions], a *shoykhet*, and a good student of the Talmud. Reb Mojszl was a great musician. He brought with him from Warsaw a group of fine choirboys. Everyone enjoyed his prayers a great deal, and the tailors sang his *nigunim* [melodies] sitting at their work in the workshops.

Our *bal-shakhres* [leader of morning service], Reb Dawid Hersz Szulzinger, the chief *shoykhet*, a sincere leader of prayers, came from the town of Drobnin. He was a Gerer Hasid. I also want to take this opportunity to recall his two sons, Szlama and Chaim Baruch, who both played a big role in post World War I Brzezin, the first, with the Gerer Hasidim, and the second, with the Zionists. Reb Fiszel Shoykhet and Reb Hillel Shames were both Aleksanderer Hasidim. We also had Reb Aron Shames, an ordinary Jew who once served in the military and was, therefore, so we used to say, versed in city affairs.

Not all the people in our town were Hasidim. We also had non-Hasidim who belonged to a very fine middle-class station and played a large role in our community life.

When various *meshulokhim* [solicitors of money for yeshivas] and *magidim* [itinerant preachers] came to our town from Łomża, Telz [Telsiai, Lithuania], Maków, Wołożyn [now Valozhyn, Belarus], and other places, they would leave very pleased. They considered Brzezin among the few towns in Poland that gave to yeshivas with an open hand.

This is how I remember the town of my birth and the familiar Jews of my time.

Among the first of the fine Jews in the town I see before me is the bright figure of Arje Dawid Perlmuter, the son of the Radomer and later the Warszawer *rov* [Rabbi Abraham Cwi Perlmuter] and a senator in the Polish Senate. Horav [title for rabbi] Perlmuter was the son-in-law of the *dozor* (head community official) of our town, Szlama Silski. With his stately appearance, Arje Dawid Perlmuter looked like a noble, intellectual aristocrat. He was a great scholar and a generous *bal-tsdoke* [charitable person], one of the most distinguished Gerer Hasidim in our town. He was beloved literally by all the Jews in town.

Of the older Hasidim, Szlama Reb Mendel's, a great grammarian, was well known in town. He was a *bal-magiye* [examiner of Torah scrolls, *mezuze*s, etc.], and he would be summoned from neighboring towns to inspect newly-written *seyfer-toyre*s [torah scrolls].

Of the very oldest Jews, I remember Reb Jecheskiel Malech [angel], who presented a very interesting appearance—small in stature but with an unusual stately appearance and adorned with a long, beautiful, white beard. Reb Jecheskiel, who always wore a satin *żupica* [caftan], was a Grodzisker Hasid and a *bal-mekubl* [mystic]. The entire town came to see him with tears in their eyes when, in his deep old age, he departed for Eretz Yisroel and settled in the Cabalist city of Safed, where he died.

Reb Abraham-Pejsach was a fervent Hasid who had a haberdashery shop in the first building on the market square. However, Reb Abraham-Pejsach devoted himself more to communal matters than to his business, and for a time, he was also a *gabe* [trustee] of the Khevre Kedishe. His wife, Chana-Golda, a true woman of valor, took care of the business.

Distinguished Leaders of the Town

Picture taken in Jerusalem on opening day of University of Jerusalem (Hebrew University), Mt. Scopus.

First row (at the bottom) from right to left: M. Najman, Aron Fogel, W. Zagon.

Second row, from right to left: A. Frajnd, Mojsze Rubin, Funt, Chaim Gotlib, Sułkowicz, Jechiel Mojsze Gotlib, M. I. Frankensztajn, Z. Goldberg, Sułkowicz.

Third row: Raszewski, Fuks, Szulzinger, Buki, Herszel Lachman, S. Sułkowicz, A. Szafman, Rochwerg, A. Rozenberg.

Fourth row: H. B. Gotlib, Kejzman.

A little further in the market square was the flour shop of Josele Hercke, a Grodzisker Hasid. He had four sons and also a daughter—Icze [Icek] Ber Hercke, my *kheyder-khaver* [school friend], Mojsze Aron, and the youngest of them, Wolf, who died in America. His son-in-law, Herszel Lachman, who came from Skierniewice, had a shop in the very same building. He was a very interesting type, a Grodzisker Hasid, and, in addition, a *maskil* [supporter of Enlightenment], and an ardent Zionist. He was one of those who read *Hatsefirah* [The Dawn—a Hebrew-language newspaper], and he was very interested in world politics. At the beginning of the thirties, he left his shop and together with his two daughters went to Eretz Yisroel to settle in the Jewish homeland. Nowadays, his five sons—Ralph (Jerachmiel), Sam (Szulem), Mordechai, Mark, and Steve live in Miami Beach. He made a living as a *menaker* (one who removes forbidden fat and veins from meat). During my visit to Eretz Yisroel in 1938, I gave Herszel greetings from his sons. I told him what kind of successful businessmen they were in America, that they were owners of large hotels, that they were doing very well materially. Whereupon he looked at me with a bright smile and said to me, "Jankiele, if I were sure that my children had it as good in America as we have it in Eretz Yisroel, I would be happy." Reb Herszel Lachman died in Israel.

The family of Abraham, the kasha maker, was very well known in our town. He lived on Court Street and drew his wretched livelihood from grinding kasha, at which his wife, Dobryś, a very fine housewife, helped him greatly. They had four children—Chaiml, Chana, Aron, and Syna. The sons were already busy making their own living, especially with tailoring. But the name Kashamakher followed them. When people wanted to mention the name of Abraham's son, they said Chaiml, the Kashamakher's, and that is how they called the other sons.

Reb Abraham was the only Mogielnitzer [Mogielnica] Hasid in Brzezin, and on every *yortsayt* [anniversary of death] of the Mogielnitzer *rebbe*, in the month of Elul, he would pack his *talis* and *tfilen* [phylacteries] in a bag and a few small things for the journey, and he would set out, on foot, the ten miles to Mogielnica, in order to pray at the grave of the old *rebbe*.

Reb Dawid Lajb Masza's, well known by us, was an unusually fine figure, an exceedingly noble person from whose face always shone a kind, warm goodness. Day and night he spent on Torah and in divine service. Reb Dawid Lajb was one of the most respected Ostrovtser *rebbe*s, a *tish-zitser* and an intimate of the great Ostrovtser *rebbe*, Reb Jechiel Majer, *z"l*.

Lajbele Zychliński, son of Szulem, the *shoykhet*, was well known in our town. His grocery shop in the market square was a sort of club for Hasidic *maskilim* who used to gather there and discuss Jewish and general news. One could also get *Hatsefirah* and *Hamelitz* [The Advocate] to read, as well as the Petersburger *Der Freynd* [The Friend].

Lajbele Żychliński had five sons and one daughter, Ruchel. His oldest son, Chaim, was one of the first young men from our town who emigrated to America. His younger sons were named Syna, Szmul, Fiszel, Lazar, and Jume, who was my *kheyder-khaver*. No one remains from that family. Three of his sons died in America, and the Nazis assassinated Lazar.

My grandfather on my mother's side was named Icek Szotland. He had two brothers—Josef and Fiszel—and also two sisters—Sura-Bluma, the mother of Chaim-

Icek Grynfeld, and Fincia-Laja, the wife of Michał-Lajb Bercholc and the mother of Herszel Shakher. My grandfather Icek Szotland had three sons and five daughters. The sons were named Dawid-Lajb, Abraham-Machel, and Mojsze. The daughters were Marjem, Fajga, Gila, Frymet, and Chajela, my mother, *e"h*. My uncle Dawid-Lajb is the father of the well-known family Szotland that lives here in America.

An old Jewish couple in Brzezin, Lajbele Żychliński and his wife, Fajgele.

My uncle, Abraham-Machel, had a covered wagon from which he sold food in the market square. Of the entire family, which consisted of four daughters and two sons—the daughters Ester, Dwojra-Laja, Rywa, and the youngest, Fajgele, plus the two sons, Icek, and Efroim—no one remains. All with the exception of Efroim were slaughtered. Efroim died in California. Rywa's daughter is in Medines Yisroel [State of Israel]. Fajgele's son Matys, also one of the rescued, now lives in Winnipeg.

I remember Many Blat (Nafthendler [kerosene dealer]) with his sons; the oldest son, Berl, was the *shoykhet* in Koluszki, and his son, Mojsze, was killed in Haifa in 1938 in a battle with the Arabs. The second son was called Icze, and the third son, Szabtaj, was my *kheyder-khaver*. One of his daughters was the mother of Mojsze Światłowski, who lives in Israel. His fourth son was named Rywen, and the youngest, Chaiml—who had lived in Chicago and is now in Israel.

Many Nafthendler's neighbor was Lajbuś-Mendel Działoszyński, with his food shop. His wife was called Chana the Lodzerin [woman from Łódź]. They had four children— Icze, whose daughter is now in Israel, Mojsze, and Aron. The latter died some years ago in America, and the younger son, Josel, died in England.

I also remember well the family with the nickname Korekh—Herszel Korekh, Abraham Korekh. The Hamer family.

Herszel-Mendel Pinczewski, born in Ostrowiec, an ardent Gerer Hasid, was a Brzeziner son-in-law. He had a tailoring accessories shop in Jechiel Mojsze Gotlib's house. His wife was named Dwojra-Chana, daughter of Naftali Brzeziner. Hersz-Mendel had three sons—Henoch, my *kheyder-khaver*, Szlama, and the youngest, Naftali, who died in Israel. He also had a daughter, Fajga.

Until the outbreak of World War II, Szlama and Naftali Pinczewski had a large textile factory in Łódź that was well known as the Brothers Pinczewski Factories. Szlama Pinczewski settled in Medines Yisroel.

I recall Perec Jakubowicz with his sons Abraham, Szymon, and Pincia. They were all Gerer Hasidim. They were counted among the biggest *magaziner*s [owners of small clothing enterprises] in town. Pincia's daughters—Bruchecia, the wife of Mojsze Szydłowski, and Laja—are in Israel.

Naftali Hersz, one of the most distinguished of the Gerer Hasidim, was a *bal-tfile* [prayer leader] and often *davened* in Ger from the *rebbe*'s lectern. This was considered a great and rare honor.

The family of Srulke [Izrael] Shuster [shoemaker] Sułkowicz was well known in our town. As I recall, the family lived on Opteyk-Gas [Apothecary Street] in the courtyard of the *dozor* Szlama Silski. Srulke Shuster had his shoemaking workshop in one room, and in the second room was his sons' workshop, the tailors Aba-Hersz, Jukiel, Jojne, and Szmul. One of his sons, Dawid, was different from the rest of the family. He was a diligent student of Talmud and grew up to be a great scholar and an ardent Gerer Hasid. The Sułkowicz brothers later grew up to be *magaziner*s, and they and their wives were active in community affairs in the town.

In the 1930s Szmul Sułkowicz and his family emigrated to Palestine, to Eretz Yisroel. However, Szmul was very close to his brothers in town, and he would actually come to visit them often on vacation. In 1938, when Szmul was on holiday in Brzezin, he decided not to return anymore to Eretz Yisroel and to bring his family back to the town. His wife, Chanele, *e"h*, in no way wanted to return to Poland. Szmul had no other choice but to return to his wife and children in Eretz Yisroel. And so he and his family were saved by a miracle from the Nazi assassins. Szmul was one of the chief leaders of the Brzeziner committee in Israel who gave a great deal of help to the newly arrived *landslayt* [fellow townsmen]. Szmul died 27 Kislev [around December] 1951. His wife, Chanele, is also no longer among the living.

* * *

It was at the time when commerce was developing in Brzezin, and the town became the place to make a living, not only for the locals but also for the *mishpokhe*s [families] that came from surrounding towns and villages—and even from deep Russia—who began to settle in Brzezin. Brzezin conducted a lot of business in deep Russia, and the intermediaries were Jewish *komisyonerin* [agents on commission]. Several *komisyonerin* actually came with their families from distant Russian towns and became Brzeziner residents.

These new arrivals brought with them a way of life that carried with it a certain foreign flavor. I remember several of their names—Gracz, Aron Kiszenover [from Kishinev], Nikolajewski, Szechtman, Raczkowski, and Jamalut. They dressed differently, behaved differently. Also, their harsh Russian Yiddish sounded strange to us. And although they exercised no particular influence on our own way of life, they brought color to our everyday existence. Their Yiddish and Russian songs, which rang out so beautifully through the open windows of their apartments, made an impression on us. Through them, we heard for the first time Warshavsky's song "Oyfn Pripetchik" [At the Hearth], which our young people enjoyed very much.

Two families that settled in Brzezin in the early nineties of the last [nineteenth] century are sharply engraved in my memory. First of all, the *yikhesdike* [distinguished] family of Reb Szulem Maliniak Waynshenker [wine shopkeeper], who came to us from Warsaw. Reb Szulem was a Gerer Hasid. He opened a wine shop, modernly equipped for that time, in the house of Malya Fuks, who was a neighbor of my father's stationery shop in Golda Khazn's house.

This Maliniak family brought some kind of big city style to our Brzezin, both with their bearing and with their way of life. Even their shop itself was different from all the other shops in Brzezin. Reb Szulem sold not only raisin wine for benedictions. From the shelves of his shop shone down the more profane multicolored wines from foreign lands, adorned with all sorts of colored labels. His wife, Fajgele, wore a *sheytl* [wig] and was always beautifully and neatly dressed. She gave the impression of being an aristocratic Hasidic woman. They had four daughters and four sons. The daughters were named Chawecia, Chajele, Symele, and Bruche. Chajele died in Israel. Symele lives in the State of Israel. Their sons were named Wowcie, Szlama, Josel, and Icek.

Next door to Reb Szulem Maliniak's wine shop was the large grocery store of the Grodzisker Hasid Tojwen Luzer Krongrad. Reb Szulem Maliniak's son married Reb Luzer's daughter, Sura. Reb Josel is actually the father of our Fishel Maliniak in New York.

Luzer Krongrad had three brothers—Jehuda, Jakub-Hersz, and Szymele. Of them Jehuda and Szymele were excellent scholars. Szymele also was a Zionist activist. Jehuda Krongrad's son Fiszel lives in Israel.

To this day, I also remember very well a second family that aroused great interest in the town in those days. After expulsion from Moscow, a family of three appeared in Brzezin—a man, wife, and daughter. He, the husband, was a tall, sturdily built Jew, and his dark brown face was adorned with a beautiful beard, woven through with silver threads. We called him "the Moskver" [Muscovite]. His wife impressed us as a woman with a particularly Russian face. Their daughter, Chanele, was a lovely, refined child. This family created the impression in town as if they had come from another planet. With their bearing on the one hand, and on the other, with the figure they cut in their attire, they completely stood out from our Polish Jews. The man opened a large tailoring accessories store, and, although it somehow sounds strange, this particular Jew, who came from a very different area, from a remote place, quickly got used to living among us and became close to the Hasidic crowd. He later prayed in the Grodzisker *shtibl*.

I also want to recall the widow Malya Fuks; her husband was Majerichie. He was called this because he came from the Kalisz area. He died young. Six sons and a daughter were left. Her sons were Lajbuś, Lipman, Herszel, Icze, Syna, and Abraham. The very beautiful daughter married Szulem Winter. Two sons, Syna and Abraham, live in America.

The widow boasted about her sons. The eldest, Lajbuś, excelled with his self-taught education. He taught himself the Russian language and used to write petitions, which at that time was a very important matter. Of the entire family, only Syna and Abraham Fuks, who are deeply beloved by our *landslayt*, remain.

The family Szeps was well known—Luzer Szeps and his sons. One of them was called Wolf. Wolf's son-in-law is our *landsman*, Jechiel Erlich, who now lives in Israel. Jechiel's mother-in-law is also in Israel.

The family of Dan-Aszer Beker [baker] had two sons—Symche-Binem and Aron. The younger, Aron Kujawski, emigrated to America. He was much loved by the *landsmanshaft* [society of fellow townspeople] of which he was the president for many years.

His son-in-law, Benjamin Beker, had six sons who carried the names according to the order of the Patriarchs—Abraham, Izak, Jakub, Mojsze, Aron, and Melech. One from this large family, Jacob Fogel, is now in California. Mojsze died in Israel.

Let me also recall Icze Baron, the only teacher in our town who taught how to write in Yiddish. His son Josef Hersz was almost an attorney and wrote petitions; Charlie, his second son, was one of the first Brzeziner youngsters who emigrated to America. He was a founder of the Brzeziner Society.

The Tuszyński family. Abramele Tuszyński's coaches carried passengers to Koluszki and Rogów, our railroad stations. He came from a very fine family. His patriarchal appearance did not fit in at all with his trade as a wagon driver. He conducted his transportation business with a sense of importance—and with the growth of business in Brzezin, his enterprise grew into a large transportation firm.

A fine type among us was Zalman Furman. His only son, Abraham-Aron, was my schoolmate. Zalman Furman had a mark burned on his neck. The mark came from a difficult experience when, as a youth during the time of the Cantonists [forced conscription of Jews into the Czar's Army], he was seized to serve in the Russian Army for twenty-five years. They tried to force him to convert, but he resisted. The burn mark remained from that torment. That is what was said about him in the town. He was a fine person and an observant Jew.

Chaim-Icek Ajnbinder [bookbinder], father of Jacob David Berg

Josef Efroim Herszenberg, or as we called him in Brzezin, Josef Machel's, was a person of stately appearance, a truly patriarchal figure. His wife, Perla, in her *hob* or *kupke* [bonnet worn by pious women], with satin and silk ribbons, also looked like a queen, and she was such a beautiful woman that they called her "Beautiful Perla." They had eight children—four sons and four daughters. Josef Machel's was a Grodzisker Hasid, and since he was a sincere *bal-tfile* [prayer leader] the *rebbe* Reb Elimelech made him the *bal-musef* [leader of *musef, part of morning prayer*] for Rosheshone and Yonkiper. His oldest son, Szmul, lived his entire life in Pabianice.

His second son, Benjamin-Icek, the author of the *seyfer Pardes Dovid* [Paradise of David], married Sura, from the aristocratic Joskowicz family. After the death of Benjamin-Icek, she became the wife of *Harov* Perlmuter of Warsaw, the father of our *landsman* Arje Dawid. The third son, Eliezer, lived in Jeżów, where he was considered as one of the outstanding residents.

The fourth son was Jekiel, the *magaziner*. He married Rechel Gotlib, a sister of Jechiel Mojsze Gotlib. Ruchel was the eldest daughter—who gave out food to the poor at her stand in the middle of the market square—and everyone called her "Ciocia Ruchel" [Aunt Ruchel]. Even her very observant husband was known as Reb Mordchele Ciocia Ruchel's. The second daughter was called Kajla-Rywa. She was the wife of the Kotsker Hasid Herszel Ledershniter [leather cutter]. The third daughter was called Laja. She was the wife of the wealthy Mordechai Ikka. The youngest daughter was called Ester, and her husband was Berl Gurt, the cotton [padding] maker. A son of theirs lives in Australia and is a university professor. Another son of theirs, a pianist, lives in New York.

The family of Reb Lajbele Hendrykowski was known in our town. He was short in stature, his face ringed with a fine Herzl-like beard. He was an honorable, noble man, from the old-time *maskilim*. His store, a kind of modern *tchayne* [teahouse], was in the market square at the corner of Court Street. It was a gathering place for intellectual young men and women.

Reb Lajb was an ardent Zionist, and it was said that he had attended the First Zionist Congress in Basel. He had even corresponded with the founder of political Zionism, and we include here a photostat of a letter to him in 1898 from Dr. Herzl.

Our *landsman* Jechiel Erlich is from a fine family. The Erlich line extends back from his mother's side until the *rebbe* Reb Fiszele from Stryków, Reb Fiszele Szpiro. Jechiel Erlich's mother, Małka Chana, was a daughter of Reb Abraham Froman, who the Brzeziner Jews called Reb Abraham Warszawer. He also had a son, Reb Icek Froman.

Reb Abraham Froman was a son-in-law of Reb Mojsze Szpiro. Brzeziner Jews called him Mojsze Reb Jankiel's. Reb Jankiel Szpiro was the one-and-only son of Reb Fiszele Szpiro—the Strykower *rebbe*. Jechiel Erlich's father was named Szymszon Michał. He was a son of Reb Icek-Eliezer Erlich, who Zduńska Wola Jews called Ajzyk Brzeznicer (Brzeznica lies near Radomsko). Reb Ajzykl Brzeznicer was a son of the Zhatatsiner [Działoszyner?] *rov*—Reb Izrael Erlich, author of a *seyfer* with *droshim* [interpretations] on Psalms. He came from fourteen generations of rabbis.

A fine family of ours was the Rozenberg family. Elija Rozenberg, a harvest merchant, better known as Elija Cypora-Ruchel's, was an Aleksanderer Hasid his entire life. His aunt, Cypora-Ruchel, raised the early-orphaned Elija, a descendant from rabbinical lineage. That is certainly how he got the name. Together with his wife, Dwojra, better known as the Elijeta, he brought up a large family. Their two sons were well known among our *landslayt* in America. Feivel, the eldest son, lived and died in New York. The youngest son, Michał, died in California. Most of Elija Rozenberg's grandchildren are in Israel and America. One of them, Abraham Rozenberg, is very active in the Brzeziner Society in New York and played a large part in the preparation of our Yizkor Book.

Fajgele, the baker, was the only daughter of the well-to-do Ruta Laja, the baker. Chaskiel Najman was one of her brothers. Her husband, Herszel Fogel, an artisan, was a Jew, a Hasid, a fine person, and one of the few, at that time, into whose home a daily newspaper came. Their children received a good Jewish and secular education. Their grandchildren are in America and Israel. One of them is the well-known community leader Aron Fogel in Israel.

I see before me the fine figure of Eliezer Szeps, son of a rabbi. He ran a tavern on Apothecary Street. He was of tall stature, distinguished by his yellowish white beard. He was an Aleksanderer Hasid. He had two sons, Josef and Wolf. His son Wolf was the father-in-law of our well-known Brzeziner *landsman*, Jechiel Erlich, who participated in this Yizkor Book.

The two brothers Abraham Icek and Jakub Josef Garber were well known. Of Abraham Icek's six sons, three were rabbis in neighboring towns. His youngest son, Aaron Selin, is a respected member of our Brzeziner *landsmanshaft*.

I see before me the family of Mojsze Aron Szwab. I remember his sons; the older, Jecheskiel, was my schoolmate, whom I took with me to the yeshiva in Łomża. But he missed his warm home badly and returned home in mid-semester.

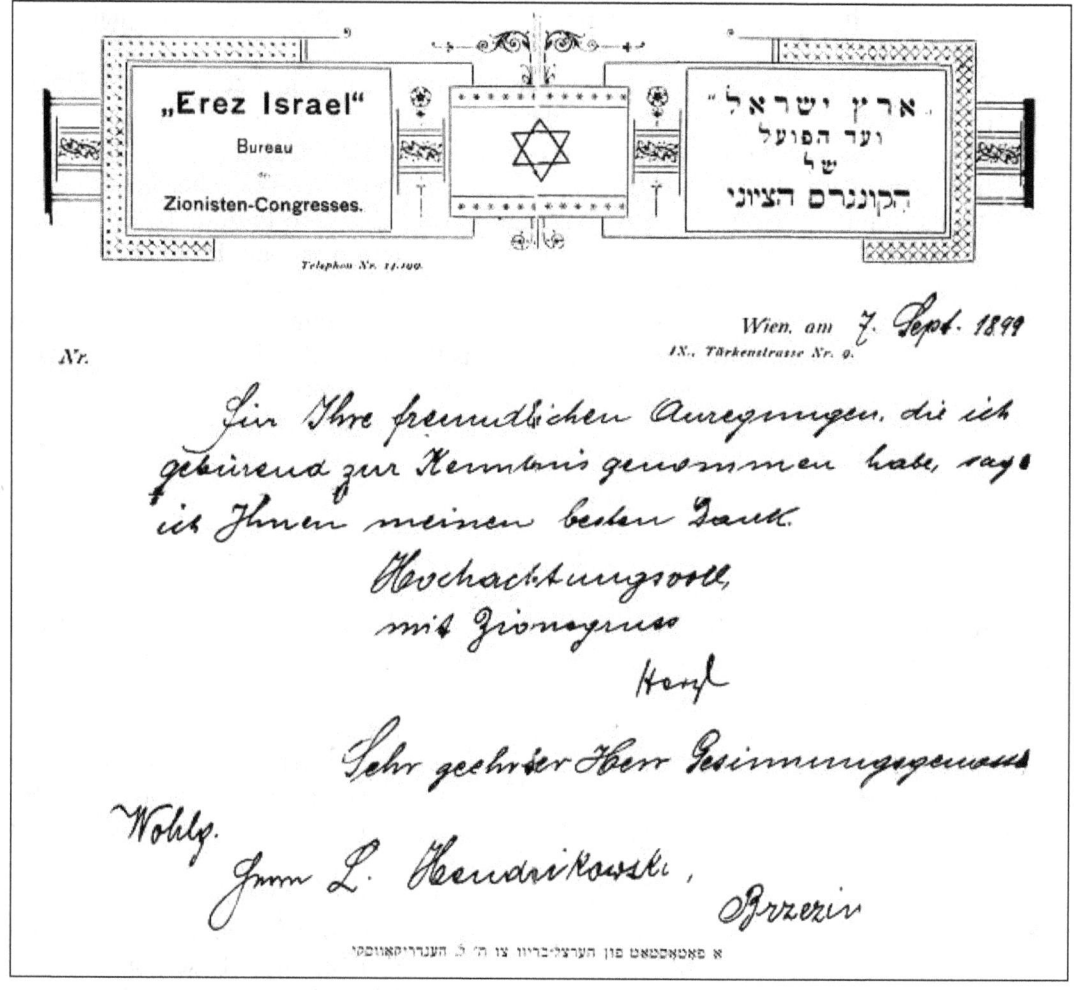

Photostat of Herzl's letter to Herr L. Hendrykowski.

I still remember the *gaboim* [trustees] of our Khevre Kedishe—Abraham Szaja Grosman, a tall, proud man, Judel Meler, who had a flour business, Abraham-Pejsach, Aba-Hersz Watemakher [cotton padding maker], and Zachariasz Tandejter.

Abraham Szaja Grosman was a Rozprzer [Rozprza] Hasid. His sons were well known—Hersz, Emanuel-Ajzyk, Icze, and Jeremia. Among them, Emanuel-Ajzyk was distinctive; he was one of the largest *magaziner*s in Brzezin. He later emigrated to America with his family. His son David is well known among our *landslayt*.

We had a fine Khevre Khayotim [Tailors Society], where the observant artisans, the tailors of our town, assembled. At the head of the Khevre Khayotim stood Zachariasz Tandejter. I remember that the Khevre Khayotim commissioned a *seyfer-toyre* to be written and celebrated on a great *yontov*. I remember from my youngest days the way they carried the *seyfer-toyre* with a great parade through the streets of the town and brought it into the synagogue. It was a march with torches and with music. The entire town took part in the *simkhe* [joyful celebration].

The distinguished families Dymant, Funt, and Gotlib had multiple branches. I also remember our *klezmorim*. Jankiel Kordelas, the *klezmer*, had a *gantse geshikhte* [whole story]. He had participated in the Polish Uprising of 1863, and because of that, the Poles took very good care of him. He used to tell an awe-inspiring story. The Russians were already taking him to the gallows after they had caught him as an insurgent. He begged them at the last minute to let him play his fiddle before he would have to take leave of his young life. They granted his wish. He began to play on his fiddle such sweet heartfelt *tfiles* [prayers] that even the brutal Cossack, the officer, was deeply moved and therefore spared his life. All his life, Jankiel Kordelas told this story to everyone. Among the Poles he was listed as an insurgent from 1863, and when he died after World War I, high-level military representatives came from Łódź to his funeral. They placed a wreath on his grave. At the open grave the Poles delivered patriotic speeches and showed respect for Jankiel the *klezmer*.

Mojszl Khazn [Sterns], who was renowned throughout Poland for his *negine* [vocal melodies]. (This picture was taken when Mojszl was a guest in America in 1925.)

In our town, Fiszele was another well-known *klezmer*. He left for the Russian army and became a *kapelmayster* [conductor] there. I remember how Fiszele Klezmer came to our town as a visitor and wore an officer's uniform with great pride.

A third *klezmer* was called Dawid Hersz. He played the bass. There was a fourth *klezmer* whose name I no longer remember. There were four in our town's *kapelye* [band].

I want to recall the Froman family. One of them—Icek Ajlszleger they called him—had a son, Ezriel. The family occupied a prominent place in our town.

In addition, I remember Mojsze-Majer Gutkind and his wife, the dark Sura, and their sons Abraham-Icek and Icze-Majer, well-known Gerer Hasidim.

Well known in our town was the family of Aszerl Garber. He had two sons, Aron and Dawid Melech. Two of Dawid Melech's children were rescued from Nazi concentration camps. His daughter Regina is now in Israel, and his son Aszer lives in Stockholm, Sweden.

I remember the family of Abraham-Nachum Piotrkowski and his son Tuwia. A son of Tuwia's, Harry Peters, was secretary of our Brzeziner Society and passed away not long ago.

I want to recall Josef Aszer Kornblum, the son-in-law of the widow Gela, whose brother left Brzezin for far away places and transformed himself into a Turkish pasha. (A separate chapter about him is published in our Yizkor Book.) Josef-Aszer Kornblum's children died in California. Two grandchildren remain alive; one lives in Israel, and one lives in Australia.

The family of Dawidl Garber and his sons Mendel and Noech were known in the town. Noech's son Herszel is now in America.

Among the prominent families were included Kalman Rozenberg and his sons Abraham, Aron, Mojsze, and my friend in *kheyder*, Josef. Josef's daughter was rescued from the Nazi *gehenem* [hell] and is now in America.

Josef Lukekhbeker [pastry baker], who immigrated to Palestine and died there.

Judel Soyfer [scribe], a Gerer Hasid, was an esteemed Jew in the town. We considered him to be one of the most distinguished Jews.

I recall the *magaziner*s of my generation. The most important and extremely exalted, who were in the most prominent position, were the two brothers-in-law Mojsze Aron Szotenberg and Emanuel Zygmuntowicz, both former tailor apprentices. When I was a *kheyder-yingl* [schoolboy] and studied with Jankiele Melamed, I used to go through the courtyard where Szotenberg's father—his name, I believe, was Icze-Ber—had his workshop. At that time, Emanuel Zygmuntowicz worked for him. Subsequently, these two tailor apprentices worked their way up to such an extent that their names as great *magaziner*s and fine people became well known in all of Poland and Russia. They helped a great deal in financing other smaller *magaziner*s. Although they were very rich men, they behaved democratically and were friendly with everyone. During World War I, they transferred a portion of their business to Russia. Both were murdered during the civil war in Russia after World War I. They played an important role in community life.

When the tailoring industry in our town grew, names began to appear such as Jechiel Mojsze Gotlib, Chaim-Ber Dymant, Perec Jakubowicz, Roman Winter and his brothers, and also smaller *magaziner*s—Majer Horn, Pejsach Grynszpan, Dawid Benkel, the brothers Sułkowicz, and Perec Mizes, (Izroelke Sułkowicz's son-in-law). Majer Horn's sons were Luzer and Lemel. Luzer Horn was the secretary of our relief committee for many years. He died in New York several years ago. Lemel Horn, who had settled in Eretz Yisroel, was the president of the assistance committee there for Brzeziner *landslayt* and expended considerable effort and money helping the *landslayt* in Eretz Yisroel. He died several years ago. His wife Blume and her three daughters and one son live in Israel.

Old Fuchs would make the entire town laugh with his jokes and tricks.

The custom tailors occupied a separate place. They made very fine clothing. Among them, Szmul Bendkower and his son Jecheskiel excelled; the two brothers Sosek and the Gritser [from Grójec] tailor. They maintained a distance from the other tailors. They considered themselves artists in their vocation.

A new phenomenon in Brzezin was the modern "big city-like" haberdashery store with fine men's shirts, hats, and ties that the recent arrivals from Russia began to wear.

* * *

Finally, I would like to say that I have written about all those I remember, and it is possible that I have left out several important families. I want to apologize here. My intention was to recall everyone and immortalize all the Jews of my generation whom I knew in the town of my birth and whose sacred memory I carry in my heart to this day.

Our Melamdim (pp. 56–58)

Jacob David Berg

Our town, just like other towns and villages in Poland, is now destroyed. Generations of Jewish life have been eradicated. The butchers have even destroyed the graves of our ancestors and disgraced their consecrated memory. They paved the sidewalks and streets with the *matseyves* so that they could step on them and trample them with their dirty feet. With sadistic pleasure they trod on the letters of the paved gravestones, so that they could in that way dishonor the Hebrew letters and, at the same time, the memory of past generations.

It is now my intention, in memory of the great Nazi destruction, to record the intellectual life of our town in my generation with regard to Jewish education. As much as my memory will serve me, I will try to describe the religious education system—the children's schools and their *melamdim* [teachers]. Although here and there my recollection may be a bit playful, I recall these teachers with deep respect.

The children's schools were divided into three categories: 1) *dardeke* [youngest children] from *alef-beys* [ABCs] to Khumesh [Torah], 2) some Tanakh [Holy Scriptures] and 3) some Gemore.

Jankiele Melamed

Jankiele Melamed held the first place among the *dardeke* teachers. Most of his *talmidim* [students] in *kheyder* [Jewish elementary school] were middle-class Hasidic children. He himself, that is, Jankiele, was small in stature, which is probably why they called him Jankiele [little Jankiel]. A sincere, good-natured person. He possessed an immense love for small children. He aroused an eagerness among youngsters to look into the *sidurl* [daily prayer book] by promising them that he would let them play with his [Torah] pointer made of bone. He was a fine, quiet man. Those from my generation who remember him speak of him with respect and love.

Abraham Mojsze

The second one in the first category of teachers was Abraham Mojsze. Tall in stature, with a white beard and a severe face. His method of impressing children was precisely the opposite of Jankiele's. He used to influence the youngsters by instilling fear and dread in them. In a moment of anger he used to grab a bread knife and threaten the youngsters that he would immediately cut off his beard if they would not learn and remember what they had learned. Or, he would run to the ceramic stove that stood in the middle of the room and scream that he was going to knock over the stove, or he would overwhelm the small pupils with a terrible fear by warning them that he would cut off his wife's head with the bread knife if they did not get rid of their foolishness and do a better job with *sheytl ivre* [a reading in Hebrew in traditional elementary education].

Although on the surface this teacher and his method of influencing the group of youngsters do not create the impression of a likable person, he still left his stamp on our generation. He was among the mentors who introduced the small child to the world of *yidishkeyt* [Jewish customs]—in his curious way and according to a certain pedagogical style of that time, which seems to be so foreign to us today.

Szlama Perec and Luzer

The other two schools—of Szlama Perec and Luzer Melamed—were already on a higher level. Most of the students in these schools were from rich Hasidic parents. Of the two, Luzer Melamed especially excelled. He became famous because he prepared the children thoroughly for the Khumesh [Torah] celebration. This celebration had a very important place in his instruction, exactly like the *bar mitsve* celebration has for us here in America. The celebration was carried out with a ceremony that was prepared weeks ahead. The Khumesh boy was dressed up in a special small silk coat and a small velvet hat and had prepared a well-rehearsed *droshe* [sermon] for the great occasion. This ceremony was performed in a theatrical manner. The boy had a fellow player, a second youth, who asked him: "What are you learning, little boy?" and the Khumesh boy answered, "Khumesh." "What does 'Khumesh' mean?" asked the fellow player, and the answer came, "Five." "What does 'five' mean?" and the answer, "The Torah has five books—Breyshes, Shmoys, Vayikro, Bamidbor, Dvorim [Genesis, Exodus, Leviticus, Numbers, Deuteronomy]. And then the boy let loose with his prepared *droshe* and a famous *posek* [verse of sacred text]—*ani* [and if not] . . .

The people around the tables thoroughly enjoyed themselves.

A class from the *kheyder* "Jesode Hatorah" [Foundations of Torah] with Jehuda Fuks, teacher.

Tate-mame [Papa and Mama] beamed with great *nakhes* [pleasure]. Luzer stood with a mixture of fear and happiness. He was afraid the little boy would suddenly get confused and mix things up or actually burst into tears and thereby spoil his reputation. But Luzer had tremendous pleasure when everything went smoothly and the weeks of work were not wasted.

After the four *dardeke-melamdim* comes the second category of religious schools. Just as with the first category, where everyone had his own style and method of teaching, so also with the second.

Herszel Litvak

Herszel Litvak, [from Lithuania] a tall man with a black beard already sprinkled with silver. A fine person. He related to children with love. When a student excelled in learning, he would point him out as an example and would hand him something sweet—something his wife used to sell, since the small tuition fee was far from enough for a teacher to make a living, even if his requirements were far from luxurious.

His subject consisted of Khumesh with Rashi [Torah with Rashi commentaries], a little Tanakh [Holy Scriptures], a little Gemore [second part of Talmud, commentaries on the Mishne]. His students still speak of him today with affection because he was a good and sincere person.

Icze-Majer Melamed

Icze-Majer Melamed was exactly the opposite of Herszel Litvak—still a young person but morbid and irascible. Most of his students were from the well-to-do class. The subject—a little of everything. He used to strike the students with sadistic delight until he would collapse in a faint. His sweet wife, the daughter of Mojsze Pabianicer [from Pabianice], lamenting, used to pull him away and calm him. Among the elements of his subject matter, the *pshetl* [hair-splitting argument] about Pesakh that he began at Khanike held the most important place. He was extravagant with blows over this *pshetl* that a boy had to be able to say at the Seder on Pesakh. It is now fifty years since that time, but many of his students still remember that famous *pshetl* that he knocked into their heads with many blows.

Henoch Melamed

His brother Henoch was an entirely different person. He possessed a fine character. He even had more of a system, more order in his teaching. He believed in the rule of fewer blows and more teaching.

Gimpele Melamed

Gimpele Melamed was short in stature, a quiet, unassuming, good-hearted person. Most of his students were well-to-do children. The subject was similar to that as described above.

* * *

The majority of students virtually ended their education with these two categories of schools. A completely different element attended the other schools, which were actually schools of an even higher level.

These *khadorim* [pl. of *kheyder*] from the third category had stronger Gemore teachers. The instruction was more systematic and introduced the student to a broader world of learning. Naturally, measured by today's methods of pedagogy, these *khadorim* were very limited, and what the students learned who succeeded in completing these *khadorim* was not much broader or more diverse than the learning of the students in the categories of schools mentioned before.

The Lutomiersker

The Lutomiersker [from Lutomiersk] Melamed—I believe hardly any of his students knew his real name, since among us he was known only as the Lutomiersker, from the name of the town from which he came. He was tall in stature. His great beard completely surrounded his earnest, severe face. His large front teeth increased the severity of his stately appearance, which strongly resembled Michelangelo's sculpture of Moses. A smile rarely appeared on his face. Always engrossed and absorbed in distant thoughts. His subject—Gemore—severe and serious. Also a little *Maharsho* [1555–1631 commentary on Talmud]. His type of students, who came from Hasidic parents, intended to continue their studies. His weapon was the well-known *korzhen* (a dried up tail of an animal), which he seldom used. The students used to brag about the small number of blows they received from that famous *korzhen*. It used to be said in town that a student who, during the course of three semesters, received no more than seven such *korzhanes* certainly should be considered a good student.

The Glovner

The Glovner [from Głowno] Melamed must also be counted among the few Gemore teachers. He, just like the others, had his own individual methods and manner. The fact that his students remember him and speak of him with reverence is a sign that his influence was widespread. Among the *khadorim* that exerted an influence over Brzeziner youth, his *kheyder* must occupy a prominent place.

The Glovner Melamed.

Luzer Tabak

Luzer Tabak's [*tabak* = snuff] *kheyder* was on a higher level. A hoarse voice. A strict Gerer Hasid who sought to exert influence over his students so that they would become the Gerer *rebbe*'s future Hasidim. Although most of his pupils had parents who happen to have been Hasidim from other Hasidic courts, such as the Aleksanderer or the Grodzisker, he would, with forceful ardor, always describe his impression of the Gerer *rebbe*'s *tish* [court]. He was a passionate user of snuff. With a certain air of confidence, he would stuff a pinch of snuff into his nostrils without losing any of it. We, the students, waited for a great, strong sneeze, but it ended with a deep, satisfied sigh, "A-ah!" As a result of too much snuff, he had a half-burned mustache.

He taught us well and we learned thoroughly.

Abraham Kaluszyner

Abraham Kaluszyner [from Kaluszyn] also belonged to the category of the better teachers in town. The same type of student went to him as went to Luzer Tabak—future *besmedresh bokhoyrim* [prayer house young men, i.e. religious students].

Mojsze Pabianicer

Last but not least, Reb Mojsze Pabianicer's small *kheyder* with a few students. Not everyone had the rare privilege to study with him. Every student had to be able to read a page of Gemore on his own. There one learned Yoyre-Deye [second part of the *Shulkhn Orekh*, code of Jewish laws] and Khoyshen Mishpet [third part of the *Shulkhn Orekh*]. Most of the students were already *khosn-bokhoyrim* [marriageable young men]. A student of Pabianicer was a candidate for a fine dowry and several years of *kest*.

The Two Mendels

The two Mendels should also be remembered among the teachers of my generation. In truth, Mendel Kop was not considered among the better teachers in our town, although he excelled as a *melumed* [learned man]. Everyone knows he was strict and even a bit of a prankster with his students, delivering a blow if someone got distracted. Later Reb Mendel wondered if he had not, God forbid, hurt the playful child with his own hand.

The second—Mendel Yezhover [from Jeżów]. In Brzezin he was certainly considered among the better teachers. He was a Gerer Hasid, a Jew, a *talmed-khokhem* [scholar]. Most of the students whom he prepared for the *besmedresh* came from Hasidic well-to-do parents. He certainly did not use a whip on their sharp *gemore-keplekh* [Gemore-learned heads], but he was very fastidious in his manner of teaching. I remember him as being not of tall stature, middle aged, and an asthma sufferer. He used to smoke all the time, thinking that smoking was a remedy for his rasping, tormenting cough. He was continuously busy rolling his own cigarettes.

* * *

These were the teachers of our town who had an immense influence over several generations. Naturally, over the years, other teachers with new methods of teaching came, but those of our generation will, with deep respect, remember these, our first teachers, who introduced us to the spiritual values of Judaism. True, they did it in a very primitive manner, which was the style of Jewish education in those years, but thanks to them, it awakened in us an eagerness toward general education—to familiarize ourselves with worldly, progressive, and revolutionary currents, which began to flow into our social lives. These very educational institutions, which we have only outlined with a few cursory strokes of a pen, are no longer there in our town, just as everything about our town is now eradicated by the devilish hands of the villains. But we will remember those intellectual institutions of ours as long as the pulse of the Jewish people beats.

Benjamin Melamed (pp. 59–60)
Melech Herszenberg

As long as I can remember, my father was always a very impractical man in worldly matters, and whenever my mother would complain to him and ask questions, he would always have a justification ready. "What should I sacrifice myself for? Since, all told, this world is just a passageway, an antechamber to the true palace that is the *oylem-habe* [world to come], which is the only worthwhile thing!"

Right after their wedding, he enlisted his brother-in-law in a "business undertaking"—they published a *seyfer* [religious book], *Pardes Dovid* [Paradise of David]—and he lost both his *nadn* [dowry from wife's family] and a thousand rubles of his Uncle Dawid's money.

My mother quickly understood that she had to bear the yoke and carry the burden of making a living on her own weak shoulders. She began to sell "lottery tickets." And since this was not enough, she agreed to take in to our room-with-a-kitchen an old senile woman, who was a relative of the rich Landsbergers from Tomaszów. They paid five rubles a week for her and also gave my mother the privilege of buying leftovers of wool from their factory. We called them *leystn* [remnants]. When I recall the misery my poor mother had to suffer over that old woman, my hair stands on end! More than once our neighbors came to bring us the message that the old woman wanted to undress herself in the middle of the street; and to bring her into the house was not very easy.

From time to time, my father would help make a living with his teaching. The wealthiest rich men of the town would bring him their sons, the *khosen-bokhoyrim* [marriageable young men], in order for him to teach them. It never lasted more than one term and often not even that long. My mother used to beg him with tears in her eyes, "Benjamin! Have God in your heart! Don't hit them! It's really a shame, such fine children! They're really rich children! Their parents certainly won't tolerate it!"

But my father had his justification. "I will not sell my soul for a few rubles! The parents gave the *shkutsim* [smart alecks] to me so I could teach them Torah! During the few hours a day that is set aside for the Torah, they will learn from me, not look out into the field at the *shikses* [non-Jewish women]!"

Since he quickly lost his students, he began to write a *seyfer* by the name of *Shoymer Emunim* [Guardian of the Faithful], but he could not find a partner with funding, and it was never published. When I once asked him, "What is holding up the little book?" he yelled at me, "*Sheygets* [smart aleck]! This is not just some sort of little book! This is a small *seyfer*! It states how important it is to observe and to repeat every '*omeyn*' [amen] while praying." He then added, "Every '*omeyn*' is worth more than a million rubles!" I knew I risked getting a smack in the face, but I could not hold myself back and asked, "Why don't you exchange a couple of '*omeyn*s' for small change and give it to Mama to make Shabes?" My cheek still burns today!

My oldest brother, who was a well-known child prodigy (by the age of nine he knew the entire *mesekhte* [Talmud tractate] backwards and forwards), was betrothed to a girl with one shoulder higher than the other, the daughter of a rich alcohol brewer in Gozlin. At that time my brother was ten years old, and the girl, thirteen. He was to get *eybike kest* [room and board from in-laws] for the rest of his life, so that he could sit and study. There was no limit to my father's happiness—one child provided with "*olyem-habe*" ...

My mother cried and begged him, "Benjamin, dear! He is truly still a child!" But the only thing he gave in to was that they would wait six years before the wedding.

Since my father had no dowry for my oldest sister, he got for her an observant young man named Josef Całek, the son of the hoarse Szyja. The young man took after my father completely, both with his piety and also with his impracticality. My mother used to call them the "father-in-law son-in-law team."

Right after the wedding, the young couple opened a food shop, and they had enough to eat, until they ate up the store. . . .

A meeting was called, and it was decided that my brother-in-law should become a *soyfer* [scribe]. He went to Łódź for a couple of months, and he returned home a trained scribe. Since the town knew very well how pious Josef was, it did not take long until he was bombarded with work.

Pious Jews were willing to pay for a *mezuze* or *Tfilen-parshes* [passages of the Torah placed inside phylacteries] five or six times more than they would pay another *soyfer* for the same work. But he did not become a rich man simply because he had to go to the *mikve* each time before he wrote down the *Shem* [the name of God].

Suddenly, he decided he would not write any more! My sister cried and begged him, "Josef! Don't do it just for me! But our four children, they will surely, God forbid, die of hunger!" He gave her an answer a bit reminiscent of my father's, "I will not sell my soul! I am not pious enough to do such holy work!"

In his mid-sixties, my father fell ill, and all the Lodzer and Warsaw doctors helped little.

I was already married then and ran a candy store that once belonged to Icek Landau. In the town I was considered a *shtikl gvir* [something of a rich man].

It was six o'clock in the evening at the beginning of the month of Shvat [January–February], the second day of the month. At just the time when I was very busy in my shop, my mother came in with tearful eyes and said, "Run quickly to your father; he wants to say something to you!"

I felt that something bad was about to happen, and running quickly, I thought: what will he say? He would surely say, "Melech! You must remember that your mother, unfortunately, will now be left alone!"

As soon as I came over to the sickbed and saw my father's face, I stood amazed—his eyes gleamed, his whole face shone, his entire bearing gave the impression that he was preparing himself for a great celebration. His sunken cheeks had a reddish color that I had not seen on him for a long time. He took my hand in his emaciated but hot hand, and pulling me nearer to him said, "Melech! You must never forget that you are a Jew!"

Suddenly he heard Mother crying in the next room; he shouted to her, "Surcia! Don't cry! The soul suffers from agony, and it will be hard for it to part from the body!"

My mother quickly wiped her eyes and came in. My father called her over and said, "Surcia! I guarantee to you that it will yet be so good for you that they'll be ringing your doorbell . . . ."

Then, I was sure that the fever made my father speak that way. I thought to myself: All her life she suffered and did not make a living, and now she would suddenly have good luck . . . but I must now say that my father's words completely came true, one hundred percent. My mother later was married a second time to her uncle, the Warsaw Rabbi Perlmuter, and she lived her last few years as a queen.

At that time, however, my father's words sounded very strange to me. Suddenly, my father noticed that a grandchild of his who was a *Koyen* [Cohen—a descendant of the priestly caste] was standing at the bedside, and he shouted at him, "Mojszele! What are you doing here? You know you are a *Koyen*! Go away and don't come back! Better run up to Aunt Ruchel and tell her to come here right away and bring all the children from the biggest to the smallest." Later, I found out why he needed them. His brother Jekiel, who had died in Russia, had left here in Brzezin a cemetery plot already paid for that my father wanted to use. He wanted all the children and the aunt to give him their hands, to pardon him for asking, and allow him the right to use this cemetery plot. As soon as they consented to his wish, he breathed easier and spoke out to Zachariasz Tandejter, the *gabe* of the Khevre Kedishe, "Zachariasz, don't be ashamed and do only what is necessary. You should forget that you were my student. You see exactly how things are! And I would like to be ready before *Reshkhoydesh* [first day of the new moon] is over!"

With lowered head and quivering fingers (not at all like his usual manner) Zachariasz laid a feather under his former rabbi's nose and began to recite with him *Videh* [confession of sins]. My father repeated every word, and when it came to the word "*Ekhod*" ["One," as in "God is One," the last words of the prayer "Shema Israel" (Hear, O Israel)], my father breathed out his sacred soul. . . .

A king, I think, could not have wished for a more beautiful death.

Two Mishpokhes [Families] (pp. 61–68)

Aron Mendlewicz (Tel Aviv)

The *tate-mame* [papa-mama] of the two great and many-branched Brzeziner families Halbersztadt and Mendlewicz were Reb Mojsze Zyndel Goldberg and his wife Perla.

Reb Mojsze Zyndel Goldberg himself was born in Amshinov [Mszczonów] near Warsaw. Perla Goldberg was a native of Brzezin. I do not remember what her maiden name was. I only know that she was part of the Brzeziner family that we called the "*Cofniks*" [backward ones].

Perla Goldberg was born in Brzezin roughly in the year 1815 or 1816. She died at the end of the nineteenth century, about 1898 or 1899, when she was some eighty plus years old.

Reb Mojsze Zyndel Goldberg was a well-to-do, prominent man in town, a distinguished person. Government officials relied on him a great deal and often sought his advice. It was said in the family that he was once invited to go to Piotrków to see the governor, to be consulted about whether a railroad station should be built in Brzezin— and the Warsaw-Vienna railroad line sent through it. There was a condition attached to it, that Brzezin would not be a *powiat* town [county seat]. In other words—either the railroad or the *powiat*. He concluded that Brzezin should be the *powiat* town and that the railroad stations should be located in Koluszki and Rogów. His thinking was that if it was a *powiat* town, one would be able to receive a contract from time to time to build a highway or the like. But what can you expect to get from a railroad station?

It seemed, people said, that Reb Mojsze Zyndel Goldberg was busy with various government contracts for paving highways. However, his principal business was liquor. He owned and maintained in Brzezin the *propinacja*, that is, a large wholesale business selling alcohol. In those days such a business was tied to a government franchise. He got the franchise because he was highly esteemed as a leader by the town and by the government officials of the time. This business existed until the Russian government instituted a government monopoly over alcohol, in approximately 1897 or 1898. After the death of Reb Mojsze Zyndel, the business remained in his family, and finally, in the last years, the business was owned by my father, Fajwel Majer Mendlewicz, *e"h* [may he rest in peace], one of Reb Mojsze Zyndel's, *e"h*, grandsons.

Reb Mojsze Zyndel Goldberg and his wife Perla had four children—four daughters. Two daughters died young, when they were still girls. One, named Blume, died in Warsaw, apparently in a hospital. The second, named Laja, died in Brzezin and was buried there. Her mother, Perla Goldberg, loved her very much, and right after her beloved daughter's death, she bought from the Khevre Kedishe a cemetery plot for herself next to her daughter's grave. And actually, forty-five or fifty years later, when Perla died, she was buried at the foot of her daughter. According to her will, one large tombstone was erected over both graves.

The remaining daughters—the older, Cyril, and the younger, Tyla—were my grandmothers. Cyril married Reb Aron Halbersztadt from Warsaw, and the younger, Tyla, Reb Herszel Mendlewicz from Pabianice, who was called in Brzezin—Reb Herszel Mojsze Zyndel's.

Reb Mojsze Zyndel Goldberg presided over sizeable businesses. Besides the wholesale sale of liquor and highway contracts, he also dealt in lumber. He was a very rich and successful man.

Reb Mojsze Zyndel died sometime between 1860 and 1870, reaching the age of fifty or more. I do not know exactly. After the death of her husband, Reb Mojsze Zyndel, my great-grandmother, Perla Goldberg, whom I remember, lived another ten or so years as a widow. She did not marry again. She dedicated her entire life to her grandchildren and great-grandchildren. She gave generously to *tsdoke* [charity]. She sent a lot of money to Eretz Yisroel to various institutions—old-age homes and others. She was a great patriot for Eretz Yisroel and for the *yishev* [Jewish settlement] of that time. Almost all the revenue from her big house [apartment building] in Brzezin near the corner of the Market Square and Apothecary Street (Market Square and Saint Anna Street) she used for these purposes. She needed almost nothing for herself.

As I remember, she spent all day at the home of her son-in-law, Herszel Mojsze Zyndel's, and his wife—her daughter, Tyla. She only went home at night to sleep. She planned, upon reaching the age of eighty, to travel to Eretz Yisroel, and she wanted to take me with her. But her illness and then her death destroyed her plans. And I came to Eretz Yisroel alone, not as a six- or seven-year-old boy but thirty-six to thirty-seven years later, in 1933. Every night before Perla Goldberg went to sleep, she would stop off at our house and also at her grandson Melech Halbersztadt's in order to be sure that her grandchildren were already asleep and that they were not, *kholile* [God forbid], uncovered.

In my great-grandmother's apartment stood, among the old style furniture, an iron strong box and a glass *serwantka* [glass cabinet]. It was a small cupboard with glass panes from top to bottom; only the wall was made of wood. The *serwantka* was full of expensive sets of dishes and various receptacles made of expensive porcelain and crystal. Over a period of many years, along with the porcelain cups and the crystal bowls and goblets, my great-grandmother had collected *esrogim* [citrus fruit used in celebrating Sukes]. The *esrogim*, which had lain there over a period of twenty years, were so dried out that they looked like walnuts. Therefore, when we opened the *serwantka*, the whole apartment smelled from *esrogim*.

During the period between 1880 and 1890, the great synagogue was built in Brzezin. The main initiator for this was my grandfather, Reb Aron Halbersztadt, *z"l*. He died before I was born; I was actually named after my grandfather. He put a lot of money and effort into the project to build the synagogue.

Reb Aron Halbersztadt was a child of a lovely *meyukhesdiker* [of aristocratic lineage] Warsaw family. The founder of this family was a *rov* from the Polish town Łęczyca.

This was approximately two hundred fifty years ago, around 1710–20, when the king of Poland was August [II] of Saxony. The Jewish community of that time in the Saxon town of Halberstadt had taken as their rabbi the previously mentioned Lentchitzer [from Łęczyca] rabbi, and he then took the family name Halbersztadt. This family spread throughout Poland, Galicia, Germany, and Hungary. One branch of the family, in Galicia, called itself Halberstam. To this family also belong the rabbis of the Tsanzer [Sącz] Dynasty, whose founder was the Hasidic *rebbe* Reb Chaim Halberstam, *z"l*, from the Galician town Tsanz [Nowy Sącz]. (The aforementioned Lentchitzer and later Halbersztadter *rov* is recalled and mentioned [as being] in Brzezin in the historical account written in Hebrew, *Yad Vashem o Sukhan Ha-Melech* [Everlasting Remembrance or The Agent of the King] by A. Cukerman.) I read this historical account forty-five or forty-six years ago.

Reb Aron Halbersztadt traded in grain (wheat, corn) and in lumber. He had a large granary near the railroad station in Rogów. Later that granary belonged to his oldest son, Reb Melech Halbersztadt, who was for a long time a Brzeziner *dozor* (at that time, that is how a member of the official Jewish community council was called). Reb Aron Halbersztadt was a *talmed-khokhem* [learned man]. He had a special Shas [Talmud] in a small format in addition to a large, rare printing of the Shas. As my mother, *e"h*, his daughter, told me, he would take on his journeys, beside his *talis* [prayer shawl] and *tfilen* [phylacteries], also a small Gemore. En route he was also occupied with studying Torah.

He was a Hasid and *davened* [prayed] in the Gerer *shtibl* [small prayer house]. Once during a *yontov* [holiday], when he came into the *shtibl* in a white shirt and an ironed, stiff collar, Reb Naftali Hersz, then the *gabe* [trustee] of the Khevre Kedishe, took soot from a lamp and rubbed it on his white shirt collar. From then on, he [Reb Aron] left the *shtibl* and prayed in the *besmedresh* [Orthodox, not Hasidic, house of prayer].

As I mentioned previously, Reb Aron Halbersztadt died prematurely and relatively young, at the time when they were building the great synagogue in Brzezin. My mother, *e"h*, told me that he caught a cold at that time, became sick in his throat, and died. He was considered a very rich man for that time. His children, as did also the children of my second grandfather, Reb Herszel Mendlewicz, each received a ten-thousand-ruble dowry. In those days, that was a considerable sum. When my grandfather Reb Aron Halbersztadt died, the Khevre Kedishe took six thousand rubles for the grave, and then, during many weeks after that, held dinners [honoring him].

My second grandfather, Reb Herszel Mendlewicz, or as he was known in Brzezin — Reb Herszel Mojsze Zyndel's [Reb Herszel, Mojsze Zyndel's son-in-law] — was born in Pabianice, near Łódź. He was, so far as I know, an only son. The Pabianicer Działoszyńskis were also among his relatives.

Reb Herszel Mojsze Zyndel's had a textile business all his life; in Brzezin this was called a dry goods business. From time to time he also dealt in lumber, that is, he would buy a tract of forest from neighboring landowners and cut it down. From the trees he cut logs and sold them to wood merchants or directly to those who built new houses. I remember when I was eight or nine years old, we, that is, our family, and also my uncle, Reb Melech Halbersztadt's family, lived during the summer in such a forest, a few kilometers beyond Koluszki, that my grandfather Reb Herszel had bought and cut down. Some ten *goyim* [non-Jews] or so worked there clearing the forest and sawing the trees into logs, and with them, in charge, was a *vald-shreyber* [forest scribe, overseer who kept track of the books], a Jew from Łódź, I believe.

My grandfather, Reb Herszel, was a very observant Jew. In his home in the parlor stood a large book cabinet overflowing with *seyfrim* [books], Shas [Talmud], and *poskim* [post-Talmudic commentaries] and all the *meforshim* [commentators]. As I remember, in addition to Khumesh with Rashi [Torah with Rashi commentaries] and other *meforshim*, he studied essentially *medroshim* [commentaries] and Eyn Yankev [certain stories from the Talmud]. The *seyfer* that he loved, that always lay on the windowsill so that when he had a free minute he would always be able to take a look at it, was the *Medresh Tanchem* [commentaries by Tanchem].

Reb Melech Halbersztadt and his wife Genendel.

He also had a habit that was a great novelty at that time—praying, not the way all the others did, "by heart," but from a *sidurl* [small daily prayer book]. I remember when I was still a small child I always wondered why all grown-up people prayed by heart; only my grandfather prayed from a prayer book as I and other children did who did not yet know the prayers by heart. When I asked him why he did it, he answered that he was afraid he would, God forbid, leave something out when praying or make an error. He was a Grodzisker Hasid and prayed at the Grodzisker *shtibl*. I often went there with him to pray.

My grandfather had some kind of a feud with a government inspector. I recall it as if in a dream. In our house an uneasy mood reigned. A Friday evening is engraved in my memory when my mother, *e"h*, took out of the cabinet under the mirror a large sum of money and, on Saturday, took it with her and left. As my parents told me later, this was the story.

As I already said above, at that time, my father conducted (during the last years before the establishment in Russian Poland of a government monopoly over strong alcoholic beverages) a large wholesale and retail business in alcoholic beverages and had a *rozlewnia* [bottling works]. He brought the alcohol in large iron barrels directly from the *gorzelnia* [distillery] and poured it, mixed with water, into small and large flasks. He sold 45–50 percent alcohol and other liquors. The business was inspected by government controllers and inspectors. There were different kinds of inspectors—mild and forceful, permissive and unresponsive, humane and inhumane. They changed all the time; each time different ones came. They would always come without notice and conduct an inspection. My father, *e"h*, conducted the business and above all the bottling precisely according to the government statutes.

Just as he was an observant Jew and in his entire life had never digressed a hair from the *Shulkhn Orekh* [code of law] and *dinim* [religious laws], he also, in conducting his bottling works, did not digress, God forbid, from government regulations. Once, a new inspector came, and, as it seemed to my mother, *e"h*, he began to harass her and without good reason tried to find fault with something. This took place in the presence of my grandfather, *e"h*, Reb Herszel Mojsze Zyndel's. My grandfather explained the way the work was done, but the inspector answered him crudely and insulted him. Then my grandfather punched him.

Don't ask what happened after that. There was litigation against my grandfather in the Piotrków County Court. The best lawyers defended my grandfather. The litigation took a long time and cost a lot of money, but my grandfather won the case, and the inspector lost his post. My mother, *e"h*, used to say that it was a very expensive punch; it cost fifteen thousand rubles.

My grandfather, Reb Herszel Mojsze Zyndel's, was a devout, observant Jew. He was known as a simple, affable, but at the same time proud man, who always insisted on his rights and enforced that in his life. For many years he carried out a complicated litigation with a Rogover landowner over a house in Rogów that was left as an inheritance from my great-grandfather, Mojsze Zyndel Goldberg. The house belonged to my great-grandfather and stood, it seemed, on land that belonged to the Rogów region. The Rogover owner of the land [where the house stood] did everything he could to make my grandfather's property rights to the house unpleasant. He surrounded the house on all sides with mounds of earth. Since there was practically no access to the house, no one wanted to live there, and if someone was finally found willing to rent the house, he did not pay any rent. But my grandfather was satisfied that—to spite the landowner and make him fit to burst—a Jew still lived in the house.

The landowner started litigation against my grandfather and all the other heirs of my great-grandfather, Reb Mojsze Zyndel, and requested that they take down the house and clean up the ground. The litigation dragged on for many years; it was conducted by important lawyers and went as far as the highest level of that time, the Senate in St. Petersburg. The Senate ruled in favor of my grandfather, Reb Herszel, that he did not have to take the house down and that the Rogover landowner had to pay for the entire house. The verdict was for a large sum to be paid for a house that was almost a ruin and was truly worth nothing. When the verdict arrived from St. Petersburg (I was then a small boy, but I remember it very well), it caused great joy in the family.

Perla Goldberg, wife of Reb Mojsze Zyndel Goldberg

My grandfather, Reb Herszel, immediately took the Piotrków *komornik* (court officer) and traveled together with him to Rogów to the property. There he took possession of the whole inventory—he confiscated all the horses, cows, the machinery, and everything that he found in the barnyard. He returned home a happy man and said that the Rogover landowner would have carried out the judgment of the Senate in the same manner. He wanted to teach the *Soyne Yisroel* [anti-Semite] a lesson, and he accomplished that with the confiscation.

As I mentioned earlier, he had a dry goods business. This was his business during his entire life, from after his wedding until he died. With him, prices were firm, that is, if he quoted a price, then he never lowered it. Also he had a custom that was an exception in that time. All stores were open until late at night, almost until midnight, but my grandfather closed his store—summer or winter—at dusk, and after locking up, he went to the Grodzisker *shtibl* to *daven minkhe-mayriv* [recite afternoon-evening prayers].

In the courtyard next to his house, the gate was always bolted. In this courtyard he raised several turkeys or geese and fifteen to twenty hens. He ate only twice a day. He died of a stroke in 1902 or 1903 at less than sixty years of age.

Now I shall again return to my great-grandmother, Perla Goldberg, *e"h*. As already mentioned, she gave a great deal to charity and also to the Jewish community. One of her good deeds was to donate the beautiful *ornkoydesh* [Holy Ark where Torah scrolls are kept] for the great synagogue in Brzezin. The Holy Ark was a masterpiece of carving. For months famous Warsaw Jewish cabinetmakers and wood carvers stayed in Brzezin until they erected the Holy Ark on the eastern wall of the synagogue. Almost two-thirds of the eastern wall was covered with carvings from ceiling to floor. My mother, *e"h*, said that with the money spent for the alcohol that was drunk during the construction and completion of the Holy Ark, one could have bought the nicest house in Brzezin. And who could have guessed that fifty years later no remnant of that superb Holy Ark would remain, not even a photograph. The Nazis burned down the synagogue along with the Holy Ark.

* * *

In the first years after my grandmother Cyril Halbersztadt became a widow, she ran various businesses alone. In the early 90s (approximately 1891–92), she even bought a forest in Pania (a village near Rogów) and had it cut down herself. She only paid the first installment for the forest—sixty thousand rubles. She had the forest cut down and the felled trees sawed into lumber. Later, around 1899–1900, she built a wall around a large house on Apothecary Street. The house was later bought from the heirs by Jekiel Froman. Later my grandmother became ill and nervous and began to go to doctors. She went to Warsaw to Dr. Platau and others and went to health spas in other countries. She died during World War I at the end of 1916 or the beginning of 1917 at the age of over seventy.

My second grandmother, Cyril Halbersztadt's younger sister, Tyla Mendlewicz, occupied herself, in addition to the management of the house, with important things connected with the dry goods store. My grandfather bought the goods, and she sold them. Besides all that she ran a *gmiles khesed* [interest-free loan fund] by herself and with her own capital. In many instances, she took as pawned items valuable objects such as rings, earrings, and watches. She had a lot of trouble with the pawned items. When the one who pawned an object was having a celebration, she would give back the object in order to beautify the celebration, and the objects were not always returned. On such an occasion, she would often actually repeat her mother's—my great-grandmother Perla's—words, "It is always better that they should owe me than I them, even when the debt is lost. Because whoever does not pay a debt, it is a sign that he has no money, and it is better when it is the other person who has no money. . . ." Grandmother Tyla Mendlewicz died at more than seventy years of age.

Aron and Cyril Halbersztadt had five children. The oldest son, Melech Halbersztadt, my oldest uncle, lived long years with his wife Genendel from Warsaw. She was a close relative of Reb Joel Wagmajster, Warsaw *dozor* (member of Jewish community council) for many years. Reb Melech Halbersztadt conducted various businesses. He had my grandfather Aron Halbersztadt's granary near the railroad station in Rogów, near Brzezin, and ran a large grain business. He also dealt in wool and other goods. He had a very good name.

In the years before World War I, when there was no bank in Brzezin yet, he was the contact person with the big banks in Warsaw and Łódź. The Warsaw and Łódź banks sent him to collect promissory notes that were made out and signed by Brzeziner merchants and *magaziners* [owners of small clothing enterprises]. In 1904–5 and later, he became a *magaziner* and managed a large business in ready-made suits and overcoats for men. He had eight children—three daughters and five sons. He was a highly esteemed man of stature in Brzezin and was a Brzeziner *dozor* for many years together with Reb Szlama Silski. He spent his last years living in Łódź. He died in either 1917 or 1918 in Otwock and was buried in Warsaw.

Reb Aron and Cyril Halbersztadt's only daughter—my mother—Szyfkele (Szyfra-Golda) married her cousin—my father—Fajwel-Majer Mendlewicz, the oldest son of Reb Herszel and Tyla Mendlewicz. Reb Aron and Cyril Halbersztadt's three sons were Chaim-Szlama, Dawid-Lajb, and Wolf. Chaim-Szlama's wife Małka was the daughter of the Zgierzer [from Zgierz] *rov*. They had a son, Aron. Chaim-Szlama died very young.

Reb Fajwel Mendlewicz and his wife, Szyfkele (Szyfra-Golda).

Dawid-Lajb Halbersztadt married the daughter of the rich merchant and respected Aleksanderer Hasid from Mlava, Reb Josel Goldsztajn. His daughter, Blume Goldsztajn, was a cousin of Wiktor Alter—later leader of the Bund in Poland—who, during World War II, was killed with his associate, attorney Henryk Erlich.

Dawid-Lajb Halbersztadt was a great merchant and engaged in trading wood. Later, in 1903–8, he had a large lumberyard in Warsaw next to a railroad siding, where all the Warsaw wood merchants brought and stored the wood they had purchased and brought in on the railroad. My uncle, Dawid-Lajb, financed these transports until the Warsaw merchants paid a deposit. There, at that site, near my uncle Dawid-Lajb's place, was the Warsaw wood exchange. About 1907 he became ill with a serious throat condition and was ailing for several years. For many months he lay in hospitals in Berlin and Vienna and was in many spas. He went through two throat operations and exhausted his large fortune.

During the last years before World War I, between 1910 and 1914, he lived in Brzezin and managed the Jewish Brzeziner Savings and Loan Bank, which was supported by the JCA [Jewish Colonization Association] of St. Petersburg. During World War I, 1914–18, he again moved to Warsaw. He had five children—three sons and two daughters. He died around 1927.

Wolf Halbersztadt married Gucia [Gustawa] Herszenberg, daughter of the well-known manufacturer from Łódź Reb Mojsze-Szyja Herszenberg. She was a cousin of the famous Jewish artist [Samuel] Hirszenberg. Wolf Halbersztadt was, as were his brothers, a Talmudic scholar and also versed in worldly knowledge and languages. He learned all this, not, God forbid, in [secular] schools, but by himself. In his young years, when still a lad, he, together with Nachman Gutkind, my uncle Icze (Icchak) Mendlewicz, Chaim-Icek Grynfeld, and some other friends, established a group Khovevei Sfat Ever [Lovers of the Hebrew Language] in Brzezin where they spoke traditional Hebrew to each other. Chaim-Icek Grynfeld, *e"h*, told me this during his last years in Tel Aviv.

Wolf Halbersztadt had five children—one son and four daughters. Together with his two brothers-in-law, Cudek and Nute Herszenberg, he owned a large woolen fabric factory in Łódź that employed some hundred workers and a large merchandise warehouse at 3 Kościuszko Street in Łódź. They also owned several large houses [apartment buildings]. Wolf Halbersztadt died in 1935 with a good name, having reached the age of sixty-three or sixty-four.

Reb Herszel and Tyla Mendlewicz had three sons—Fajwel-Majer, Aron-Lajb and Icze (Icchak). Fajwel-Majer Mendlewicz—my father—had, as was already mentioned, married his cousin Szyfkele, the daughter of Aron and Cyril Halbersztadt. He was a very devout and observant Jew, a great *talmed-khokhem* [talmudic scholar]. So also were his two younger brothers. He studied a lot, day and night, mainly Gemore with *toysfes* [supplementary commentaries] and other commentators. As I recall, he would rise after midnight, between one and two o'clock, and study until morning, between six and seven o'clock, when he left to go to the *besmedresh* to pray with the *minyen* [quorum of ten males]. Also, during the day and in the evening, he used to use every free minute to study. Even so, he was not overly bookish. He knew excellent bookkeeping, which he learned through correspondence in Hebrew with "Marek" in Libava, Latvia, who was then a teacher of bookkeeping well known in all of Russia.

As mentioned above, the first business my father ran after his marriage was the alcoholic beverages warehouse, *en gros et détail* [wholesale and retail]. Later, when a government monopoly for dealing with alcoholic beverages was introduced in all of Russia and Poland, he managed a leather business for two to three years in partnership with Herszele Ledershniter (Reb Josef Machel Herszenberg's son or son-in-law, I believe). After that, in partnership with Reb Abraham Gips (Nachman Gutkind's brother-in-law), he took on a contract to build a highway near Częstochowa. After that he managed a Brzeziner magazine of ready-to-wear clothing for Russia. In the beginning he was in partnership in the magazine with Szyja Ikka (son of Reb Szlama-Josel Ikka-Fuksel). After separating from his partner, he conducted the magazine on his own, and finally, he moved the magazine to Warsaw in partnership with his brother, my uncle Aron-Lajb Mendlewicz. They had the merchandise sewn in Brzezin and shipped the finished goods to the Warsaw warehouse.

After the death of my grandfather, Reb Herszel Mendlewicz, *z"l*, in approximately 1903, my parents took over the dry goods business. The dry goods business was principally conducted by my mother, *e"h*, with the capable assistance of my grandmother, Tyla, *e"h*. My father became more and more deeply involved in studying Torah. He was really a great *talmed-khokhem*, proficient in all Shas and *poskim*. He was an Ostrovtser [follower of Ostrowiec *rebbe*] Hasid and an observant, devout Jew. In approximately 1911–12, he retired from all business.

At the time of World War I and afterward, my father was a member of the town council of Brzezin and worked on various town commissions. These were the only years that he was active in public affairs, and at that time, he also bemoaned the contempt for Torah, which had an effect on him. He was a Hasid but not a fanatic. At the time of the elections to the Sejm (Polish Parliament), the Warsaw Rabbi Perlmuter from Agudas

Yisroel [non-Zionist Orthodox party] and the lawyer Icek Grynbaum of the Zionist Organization were campaigning for office. Representatives from Agudas Yisroel came to him—as to "one of us" religious Jews—to ask him to vote for and work for the victory of Rabbi Perlmuter, their candidate. However, my father, with quiet humor, asked them, "What is it today, elections for a *rov* or elections for a Jewish representative in the Polish parliament?" They answered him, "Of course, today is the election for parliament." Then he said to them, "If so, then one has to select a lawyer, because a lawyer knows what he should complain about and how to make a speech. But a *rov*? Why do we need a *rov* in the Sejm? Does one have to decide questions of ritual purity? I will now vote for the lawyer, and I promise you, when elections for a *rov* come up, I will on no account vote for a lawyer, only for a *rov*, because then one has to pick a Jew who is knowledgeable and can decide questions of ritual purity."

* * *

My mother, *e"h*, always worried about the poor and the sick. Every midday before serving us, while in the kitchen, she would put aside in a little pot a portion of the soup and meat for poor sick people. My father and mother had agreed that she would cook more for Shabes so that there would always be enough for an *oyrekh* [guest, usually one visiting from another community] for the Sabbath. And every Friday night, my father would come from *davening* with a guest for the entire Shabes. All the other worshipers had their turn to take a guest home for Shabes. Everyone knew when it came to his Shabes [his turn]. This was all done when there was more than one guest for Shabes. But if there was only one guest, then, of course, my father always brought him to his home. Everyone already knew that it was his right.

My father's brother, Aron-Lajb, was also an observant and very pious Jew, a great Talmudic student and *talmed-khokhem*. He married Perla, a daughter of Michał Temkin, a very rich man, a wine merchant from Siedlce. My uncle, Aron-Lajb, lived in Warsaw. He had one son and three daughters and also several grandchildren. They all perished in the Warsaw ghetto during World War II at the hands of the Nazi murderers.

Icze (Icchak) Mendlewicz, my father's youngest brother, was, like his two older brothers, a great *talmed-khokhem*. He obtained *heter hoyroe* [permission to function as a rabbi] from the Yezhover [Jeżów] *rov* when he was scarcely fourteen or fifteen years old. He also obtained *heter hoyroe* and *smikhes* [ordination] to the rabbinate, while he was still a young man, from the rabbis of Siedlce and Piaseczno and also from other rabbis. My uncle, Icze Mendlewicz, was also devout but still a so-called *hyantveltiker* [modern] Jew and person. He understood Russian and Polish. He was a member of the association of Lovers of the Hebrew Language in Brzezin.

He married Taubcia Wolman from Lublin. She was the daughter of a great Lubliner rich man and important grain and timber merchant, Szoel Wolman. He ran a large iron business on the main street in Lublin, Krakowskie Przedmieście, with his father-in-law, Szoel Wolman, and his brother-in-law, Mojszel Hajnsdorf.

My uncle Icze Mendlewicz had three sons. The oldest, Mojsze, was a lawyer, his second son, Pinkus, an electrical engineer, and his third son, Heniek, also completed university. My Uncle Icze, with his wife and both sons, the oldest and the youngest, perished either in the Lublin ghetto or in the concentration camp Majdanek near Lublin.

Only his middle son, the engineer, Pinkus, was left alive, since he was abroad at the outbreak of World War II.

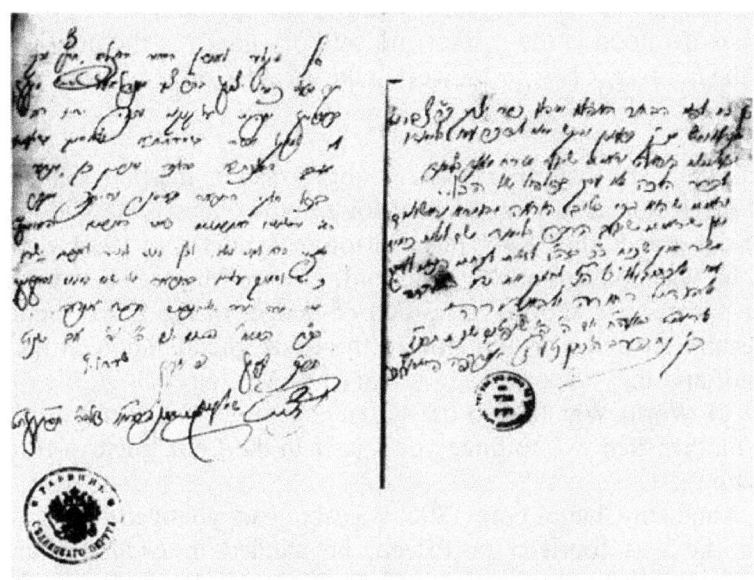

On the right hand side: *heter hoyroe* from the Piaseczner *rov,* HaGaon Reb Noech, *z"l,* and Reb Natan Nute, *z"l;* On the left hand side: *heter hoyroe* from HaGaon Reb Szymon *rov* Anielik, *z"l.*

My parents had three sons. I, Aron, was the oldest; the second son was Mojsze-Mordechai, and the youngest son was Abraham-Chaim. I married Hinda Majranc from Kutno. My wife's father, Jehunsen Majranc, *e"h,* ran a big business in coal, coke, tar, cement, tar-board, and other building materials. My wife comes from a rabbinical family. Approximately three hundred years ago her great-great grandfather, by the name of Reb Abraham Abele Gombiner [from Gąbin], was the *rov* in Kalisz. He was a great *poysek* [arbitrator] and an author of many religious books. His major book was the commentary *Mogen Abraham* [Star of Abraham] on *Shulkhn Orekh Oyrekh Chayim* [first section of *Shulkhn Orekh,* code of law]. In the rabbinic world he continues to be known today under the name *Mogen Abraham.* My father-in-law was a student of the famous Kutner *rov* and *gaon,* Reb Jehoszele Kutner [from Kutno], *z"l.* At that time he also wrote for *Hamelitz* [The Advocate]. He was a *dozor* for the Jewish *kehile* and, 1920, also a member of the town council.

I lived in Kutno—in Sholem Asch's town—from 1926 until 1933. There I was selected by the Zionist organization as chairman of the Jewish community council 1923–27 and also as a town council member (called *ławnik*) in 1920–28.

* * *

My teachers in Brzezin were—in turn—the *dardeke-melamed* [teacher of the youngest children] Reb Luzer Betcajg, then Gimpele Melamed, Reb Icek-Mendel from Radzyń, and the teacher Reb Jeremia (I remember that we called him the *vzvodny* [platoon commander], because he had been a soldier in Czarist Russia). Then I studied with Reb Szmul-Lajb, son of Mojsze Pabianicer (Beserglik) and with Mojsze (a son-in-law of the aforementioned Radzyner *melamed,* Reb Icek-Mendel, *e"h*). Finally, at the age of thirteen or fourteen, I studied with my last teacher, Reb Mojsze Pabianicer, *e"h.*

With Reb Mojsze Pabianicer, *e"h,* I studied alone. He did not want to take any tuition from my father for my instruction. At that time, he was already an old man. He had a few thousand rubles. He used to say that my father was one of his first students and so also were my uncles on both sides, the children of Reb Aron Halbersztadt and of Herszel Mendlewicz. Therefore, for me, his last student, he would not take any tuition. He was a refined, observant Jew. His wife stood in the market and sold dry goods to the peasants. Every Rosheshone he was the *bal-tekeye* [*shofar* blower] in the great Brzeziner synagogue.

* * *

My brother Mojsze-Mordechai, who was five years younger than I, married Taubcia Nowomiast (daughter of the Kutno textile merchant Mojsze Nowomiast). He had one son, named Herszele, after our grandfather, Reb Herszel Mojsze Zyndel's. In 1939, when World War II broke out, he was about fourteen years old. Mojsze-Mordechai lived in Brzezin together with our parents. He and his wife died of hunger in the Łódź ghetto. Also, his son, Herszel, became ill with consumption in the Łódź ghetto. The Germans caught him in a police raid, and they deported and killed him. My father, *e"h*, died in Brzezin in the first winter of World War II, two days after Purim (1940), at more than seventy years of age. My mother died two to three years later in the Łódź ghetto—from hunger, hardship, and loneliness.

My youngest brother, Abraham-Chaim, born 1896, was six years younger than I. He was a phenomenon. Until he was fourteen or fifteen, he studied in *khadorim* and yeshivas. Until then, he did not know even one word of any European language and did not have the slightest idea what science was. He only knew about one thing—studying Torah, studying Gemore with *toysfes*, studying *Shulkhn Orekh*, and other *poskim*. But at fifteen or sixteen, he suddenly began studying European languages, mathematics, and other sciences, also philosophy. He studied it by himself, not in any school or *gimnazjum* [secular secondary school]. And he achieved marvelous results. He knew Polish, Russian, German, French, and English well, spoken and written. He learned Hebrew, mathematics, and philosophy thoroughly. Most of all, he mastered the German language. He read and wrote German better than any student who studied in the German *gimnazjum*. About 1927 or 1928, he published a book in the German language entitled *The Tense State of Matter*, in which he discussed the physical and philosophical problems of the structure of matter and the universe. Several years later he wrote to me in Eretz Yisroel that he had written a second work, with charts and calculations, a complement and commentary to his first, already-published book. By then he no longer had the opportunity to see his second book published. During the war it was destroyed together with him. The Nazis killed him.

They told me that at the time of Purim in 1942, when the Germans demanded that the Jews in Brzezin deliver and surrender ten Jews, men or women, so they could hang them as punishment for the hanging of Haman and his children two thousand years before, my brother Abraham-Chaim, of his own free will, then presented himself to the *Judenrat* [Jewish Council]. He asked to be sent to the Germans as one of the Jewish victims to be hanged, but the *Judenrat* turned down his request.

You can just imagine how desperate my brother was then and how disappointed he had become in the last year of his life in "humane and European progress" and "German culture." Maybe he only wanted, by his sacrifice of death on the gallows, to be useful after all and rescue another Jew.

Abraham-Chaim was in the Brzezin ghetto in 1942. Two days before Shavuos, he, along with all the other Brzezin Jews, was deported. But at the time when most of the Brzezin Jews arrived in the Łódź ghetto, Abraham-Chaim was not with them, and from then on, all traces of him disappeared. He was, it seems, murdered by the Germans on the way from Brzezin to Łódź, or he was deported directly from Brzezin to some concentration camp and killed there.

When he was murdered, he was forty-six years old. He was not married.

* * *

When World War II broke out, two great-grandchildren of Reb Mojsze Zyndel and Perla Goldberg and one great-great-grandchild were outside Poland. They were 1) Aron, son of Fajwel-Majer and Szyfra-Golda Mendlewicz, the writer of these lines, 2) Pinkus, son of Icek (Icchak) and Taubcia Mendlewicz, who now lives in Spain, and 3) Pinkus-Elimelech, son of Mojsze and Sura Halbersztadt, grandson of Reb Melech Halbersztadt. He is a captain in the Israeli army.

Of the other members of the Halbersztadt and Mendlewicz families—the grandchildren, great-grandchildren and great-great-grandchildren of Mojsze Zyndel and Perla Goldberg, relatives that added up to a hundred *nefoshes* [souls], only seven souls were saved from Hitler's hands and survived the frightful destruction. Of those, four were the children—three daughters and a son—of Wolf and Gucia Halbersztadt from Łódź. Immediately, on the first day of the war, they escaped to Vilna and then through Lithuania to Sweden. From there three of them departed through London for Sao Paulo, Brazil. One daughter and her husband still live to this day in Stockholm, Sweden.

Only three of the family were saved out of the ninety to a hundred members of this great family who fell into the hands of the German assassins—who captured Poland and destroyed so many innocent Jews. Three members of the family survived the German oppression in the Łódź and Warsaw ghettos and the annihilation camp Oświęcim [Auschwitz]; they endured and lived to see liberation. They were 1) Blume Lachman, granddaughter of Dawid-Lajb and Blume Halbersztadt, 2) Ratkel, granddaughter of Melech and Genendel Halbersztadt, and 3) Tyla (Tola) Weksler, daughter of Abraham-Icze, son of Melech Halbersztadt. For the last ten years, she has been in Israel with her husband and little daughter.

This is the history of our great and lovely family, and such was the fate of our family—the same fate that befell the six million Jews in Europe who were annihilated in the worst destruction that befell our people in two thousand years.

A Bundle of Memories (pp. 69–71)

Mojsze Frank

I want to rekindle here my memories of Brzezin, the town that is so engraved in my heart, as if I had been born there. But first I want to write a bit about my childhood years and how it was that I came to Brzezin.

I was born in a small town called Biała, Piotrków province. Of course, we know that in a small town in Poland, when a youngster became twelve years of age, one had to start thinking about a practical occupation for him. What should he be? Make him a craftsman? My papa, *olev hasholem* [e"h—may he rest in peace], said—a tailor. I said, if a tailor, then a custom tailor, not an ordinary one. They looked for a good tailor, and they turned me over to him for three years to learn. After three years, I received a vest as supplementary payment.

Everyone knows well what an apprentice had to put up with. He had to carry wood and carry water; he had to do everything he was told to do. And if with the help of God you lasted the three years, you came out half a tailor. That meant you could work with a full craftsman, helping to sew pants or a jacket or an overcoat. Making a piece of work alone—this you could not do yet. You had to go and work at least three terms—three half years—until you became a full tailor.

So I went to a tailor who did work for local landowners, that is, for the well-to-do, and I worked for him three half years. I earned twenty rubles the first half year and thirty rubles the second half year, and the last half year, I already earned forty rubles. This was a lot of money at that time, and I became an expert tailor.

Now came the proper time to think about where one should go to work. In a big city? Someone called Abraham Polewinczyk happened to live in Brzezin. He was married to a woman from Biała. I decided to go to Brzezin. Brzezin had many tailors. They actually produced cheap magazine goods, but they themselves liked to wear good custom-made clothing.

I did not think about it a long time. I took a ride with the first wagon driver who was going to Skierniewice, to the railroad station. I arrived in Koluszki [station nearest Brzezin] and there indeed found the Brzezin coaches. One was Tuszyński's, and the other was Lemel Lefkowicz's. They called him Lemel Byk [bull], and you knew right away who he was. I went over to the wagon driver, Lemel, and told him to whom I was going, and he, of course, drove me to the right family.

I introduced myself and said why I had come. I explained to him that I was a custom tailor. He at once pointed out five tailors—the best ones, Chaskiel Szmul Bentkewe [Bendkower?] and Syna Szmul Bentkewe and a Gritser tailor [from Grójec]. And then he said to me that there were two brothers called the Soseks [pacifiers], named Majerowicz. One was named Berysz and the other was named Abraham, but in Brzezin, if you did not use their nickname, nobody would know who they were. That is how I came to work for Berysz. He lived on Apothecary Street. Opposite them lived a family by the name of

Fuks; they were called Malarz [painter]. A very fine family. They had four sons, very fine young men. I still remember, as if it were today, that they were already *daytchish geklayt* [dressed like Germans, i.e., modern]. One son was named Lajbuś, the others—Icze, Syna, and Abraham. Abraham was the youngest. They had a sister named Ester. She was very beautiful and very charming—a true Ester *hamalke* [the Queen]. If she ever looked out of the window, and if we, the workers, happened to notice it, we immediately set aside our work to take a look at her. She was that beautiful.

In this way I worked for Berysz a short time until I went to work for his brother, Abraham, because with him, you worked with a larger volume.

Abraham Sosek lived on Hoyf-Gas [Courtyard Street]. The house was called Mojsze Kopel's house. There were actually lots of tailors in that house. Mordechai Winter and Joel Lajfer and the tall Jankiel, as well as a family called Jaskółka [swallow], all lived there. As I said before, nobody in Brzezin knew them without their nicknames. Another family called Hayvens [yeast/midwives] also lived there. They had several daughters who sewed pants.

I Work for Abraham Sosek

Now I will describe my new place, where I began to work for Abraham Sosek. He managed an entirely different tailoring shop. There were *magaziner*s [owners of small clothing enterprises] in Brzezin—Mojsze Aron Szotenberg and Zygmuntowicz—who were among the largest *magaziner*s in Brzezin. They introduced a better type of magazine work, almost like custom-made, except that we did a little less work—but it had to be very good work.

We worked by the piece. The price was two rubles for a piece of work. I worked in partnership with another worker. We both needed to make twelve pieces of work during the week, and in addition, we made two extra pieces of work. As you can imagine, the work hours were very "short," from six in the morning until twelve at night, and Thursday, all night, since on Fridays, we worked only until four in the afternoon.

Once it happened that the kerosene in the lamp ran out at eleven o'clock. My master tailor and I went around looking for kerosene. In Brzezin, in the middle of the market, was an eating place where all the carts that came from the small towns and were traveling to Łódź would pause and give the horses something to eat, and they, the wagon drivers, also grabbed a bite. Therefore, you could get kerosene there. Since we had gone to bed earlier, we got up earlier, at four in the morning. That is how we evened out the hours.

The boss lived in three rooms. One large room was the workshop; in the second room slept the workers, and in the third slept the boss and his wife. We were five workers, and the boss was the sixth. The workshop contained only two machines, since we sewed a lot by hand. We worked it out so that each one sewed what he needed on the machine and after that sewed by hand.

The eagerness to work was so great that we used to sneak into the workshop before daybreak in order to get more work done. We used to leave the hand sewing to be done before daybreak, since making fourteen pieces of work a week by machine was a lot.

One had to pay the master craftsman for food but not for sleeping. A housewife who was not a very strong person would never have been able to cook the midday meal on time. When it reached two o'clock, we used to get hungry, like wolves. She used to put out a herring with bread; it was finished in a minute. We decided to look for a place to eat at midday.

In Brzezin a shoemaker lived in the middle of the marketplace. His wife was called Blume the *stolerkes* [carpenter's daughter?]. She used to cook for strangers. That is how we began to eat at Blume's. At two o'clock, on the dot, we used to go there to eat at midday. This was very good for us, since in the meantime we got a little rest, because to walk from Mojsze Kopel's house to the market and back was very pleasant.

The General Situation in Brzezin

Now I will write about the general situation in Brzezin. Some light began to shine little by little. They began to organize parties—Zionist, Poale Zionist, and the Bund. On Shabes, every party member would try to influence others to come to a talk. They would discuss every question. Everyone wanted to convince everyone else that their party was the most just, the best. I still remember the names of certain party leaders—"the blind Chune," Jakub, and Josel Lodzer [from Łódź]. And so it went for some time.

Then later, organizers began to arrive from Łódź, and they used to call meetings of all the parties, about what touched everyone's interests—to improve the situation and shorten working hours.

It did not take long until one time a man arrived from Łódź called Baruch Hoyker [hunchback]. He really was a hunchback. He was a very capable and intelligent person. He was sent by the Lodzer worker movement, and he actually stayed in Brzezin long enough to organize all the workers. A strike committee with a secretary was appointed. Everyone had to pay twenty-five kopeks [100 kopeks = 1 ruble] a week.

That is how the work went for a few weeks until they called a strike.

Now I will describe for you the strike in Brzezin. "The union group has rebelled." That's how the bosses spoke among themselves. "We have to see about doing something." Mordechai Winter called together a committee of the workers and bosses, and they began to confer. We had struck for shorter working hours. It took a few weeks, but we won the strike.

Since my boss, Abraham, loved me, and he saw how hard I had worked during the strike, he sent my parents a letter that they should take me home—to rest up a little—since I had worked very hard during the time of the strike.

When my parents heard this, my father, *e"h*, immediately came to Brzezin and took me home to the small village Biała to rest up a bit. When I was at home a week, a letter arrived at my parents saying that I should not dare to return to Brzezin, because they had arrested all the workers. Cossacks had gone through all the homes in which it was known just that someone was living there who had helped carry out the strike. One certainly could no longer talk about going back to Brzezin. That is how my loyal boss, Abraham, saved me from a lot of *tsores* [troubles].

I Travel to America

Now we started to think about what to do next. My family decided that I should go to America. It sounds simple—going to America. You needed to have one hundred and ten rubles for expenses. Where do you find such a sum of money? I had saved sixty rubles, I recall, from my entire earnings. I still needed fifty rubles. We went to borrow from family members. One pawned a silver watch, a second pawned the *makhzoyrim* [holiday prayer books] and *sidurim* [daily prayer books], until they put together the money, and I, *mit mazl* [with luck], left for America.

I traveled to America through Russia, since it cost less. I went to Libava, where I boarded a ship called *Smolensk*. It took three weeks, and we arrived safely in America. When we arrived at Castle Garden [prior to Ellis Island], they asked me how much money I had. I told them I had two rubles. The man made a gesture with his hand that I could go. I took my basket and began to leave. At once a man came over to me and said that he was from a Jewish organization and I should go with him; he would take me wherever I wanted to go.

I came through an organization that at that time was called Hakhnoses Orkhim [hospitality to guests]. Today the organization is called HIAS [Hebrew Immigrant Aid Society], which does wonders for newly arrived immigrants.

It was a practice that every Shabes the *landsmanshaftn* [societies of fellow townsmen] would look for people who had come from their towns. The Brzeziner *landslayt* [fellow townsmen] also used to come and look for their acquaintances. The Brzeziners, if they found anyone who had just worked in Brzezin, he was already counted as a Brzeziner.

The first *landsman* I found in New York, I recall, was the Glovner *melamed*'s [teacher's] son. He was named Luzer. He immediately took me home and treated me to a fine meal. Later, he took me to the *landslayt* and introduced me. There they provided me at once with a job to work and a place to live.

At that time, the *landslayt* lived in a certain neighborhood. This was Eleventh Street. There you could find out about everyone. It was a sort of *birzhe* [office]. A family that we called Braszes also lived there. They had a delicatessen where one could eat something, and it was also a meeting place where you could learn something about friends and acquaintances.

By this time, the Brzeziners already had a society, and they stuck together. I became a member of the society at once. We used to hold meetings twice a month. Every meeting was a *yontov* [holiday] for me. It was a great pleasure to get together, because you were with your own *landslayt*. You felt at home; we believed and felt as if we had found ourselves in Brzezin. That is why a lot of *landslayt* who only worked in Brzezin became members of the society.

Since I was already a member of the Brzeziner society, the *landslayt* made a match for me with a girl with Brzeziner parents. She was Menes Shveyger's [dairyman's] daughter. Her name was Fajgele. We got married and have, thank God, a lovely family. We brought up three sons—they should be healthy—all well married.

For me, born in Biała, Brzezin is as dear to me as my own hometown. I actually plead with the Brzeziner *landslayt* to instill in their children an affection for Brzezin and to keep the memory of the love of Brzezin alive, so that it will remain in memory for generations.

Three Bercholc families from Brzezin: The picture was taken on the way to Szymaniszki, to the soccer field. Herszel Młynarzewski is also there among the families.

A Brzeziner Jew — A Grand Vizier in Turkey (pp. 72–74)

Izrael Kahn

For many years in Brzezin a story circulated about a young man, Gedalia Fiszel Frajnd, son of Reb Szlama Frajnd, who left home, lived a tumultuous life, and achieved distinction in the court of the Turkish Sultan Abdul Hamid.

Izrael Kahn, the murdered Jewish journalist from Łódź, who before the war was editor of *Lodzer Togblat* [Łódź Daily Newspaper], wrote a marvelous story before World War II about Gedalia Fiszel Frajnd in a series of articles in the Warsaw *Moment* [Yiddish newspaper]. We print here a condensed version of Izrael Kahn's longer description.

It happened after the Polish Insurrection of 1830. In the small Jewish towns that had suffered so much, both from the uprising and later also from the Cossacks, the memory of the bloody events was still fresh. They had had many years to give accounts of various stories and experiences about that turbulent time. Fiszel Frajnd, the hero of our story (born 1828 in Brzezin), holding his breath, had always listened to these stories that his father, Reb Szlama Frajnd, a respected leader in town, told with such passion. His imagination was sparked. He lost his interest in learning. He used to go around like a person in a trance. In his young mind serious plans began spinning and weaving, and in his fantasy he began to imagine different scenes about wars, battles, awards, and heroics.

The young man from Brzezin who became a Grand Vizier to the Turkish Sultan. Hamid Pasha (Fiszel Frajnd), born in Brzezin in 1828, died in Beirut (Turkey) [Lebanon] in 1885.

His father, Reb Szlama, strove to make his youngest son Fiszel into an adult. He was hot-headed, with a lot of ability, but he did not want to learn in *kheyder*. His father did not have any other choice, and after his *bar mitsve*, the father turned him over to a watchmaker as an apprentice.

Since Fiszel was to be a secular person, Reb Szlama also hired a teacher to teach him a little Polish and German.

The thirteen-year-old Frajnd really loved to learn languages, for which he possessed many distinct abilities. It did not take long before the student outpaced the Brzeziner professor in knowledge of languages.

The young Fiszel, however, did not at all feel suited to the task of spending entire days at the tedious craft [watchmaking], and his head was always full of plans how to launch himself into the wide world to satisfy his thirst for passionate experiences and adventurous journeys.

An opportunity to realize his goals arose sooner than his imagination had pictured for him. His father, who was a deputy collector of lottery tickets, played a part in his luck. One of the tickets that happened to have been left unsold was the grand prize winner.

Fiszel became prosperous. Not thinking about it very long, he immediately—as soon as his father received the prize money—seized an opportune moment, got at his father's hoard, grabbed a considerable sum of money, and took to his heels.

He wandered around for some time through Germany, was left without a farthing in his pocket from all his fortune, and arrived in Hungary starving. In Budapest, Fiszel Ferdinand (that is what he was called then) obtained work in a wine business. There his luck began to turn.

His liveliness, nimbleness, and very careful attention to even the smallest detail of anything he undertook attracted the attention of one of the frequent visitors to the wine business. This was a Hungarian high-ranking officer, an old cavalry man. He became interested in the solitary young man, in whom he recognized uncommon abilities. He took the "little Polish Jew" home, made him an orderly, and at the same time set about to educate him in earnest.

The military man came to love his Ferdinand like his child. Seeing that he could not accomplish anything more for him, he decided to send him with warmest recommendations to his friend, the famous Hungarian folk hero, Kossuth [Lajos Kossuth, the "Father of Hungarian Democracy"].

At that time, Hungary was on the eve of the Magyar Revolution of 1848.

The Brzeziner youth threw himself into the fight for freedom at the side of Kossuth himself.

The young fighter quickly advanced to the level of officer and received a long list of distinctions.

But Kossuth's fight for the freedom of his people was not crowned with success. Austria defeated the Hungarian Revolution, and vicious persecutions of Hungarian Jews also began, because of their participation in the insurrection.

Fiszel Ferdinand left for Turkey at that point, and there he really had a marvelous career that sounds like a fantastic story from *A Thousand and One Nights*.

At that time, Turkey had to contend with partisan warfare. In the Sultan's empire, the insurrections multiplied among the dissatisfied portions of the population. Fiszel Ferdinand "put on the fez" (in later years that is how he expressed his conversion and his adoption of Mohammedism) and joined the Turkish army.

He distinguished himself greatly in the fight against the insurrectionists, and his military career advanced with fantastic speed.

When the year 1853 arrived, the Crimean War broke out between Turkey and Russia. Fiszel Ferdinand strove to get into the war and demonstrate his heroism. However, enemies denounced him as a former Russian citizen. They concocted the claim that he was a Russian spy and that he had received a "keg of gold" from the czar. The result was that he was exiled to the Isle of Rhodes for the entire war period.

During that difficult time, Fiszel Ferdinand found a completely unexpected defender—the great Polish poet Adam Mickiewicz.

When, in 1853, Mickiewicz came to Constantinople to create a Polish legion in Turkey and heard the story about Fiszel Ferdinand from Brzezin, he became deeply interested in the fate of his unlucky fellow countryman.

Mickiewicz, by persuading the Sultan, assured that a new investigation would be conducted concerning Fiszel Ferdinand. The investigation actually determined that the guilty verdict was false, and the Brzeziner hero was brought back from Rhodes to Constantinople, where the Sultan himself later protected him.

Turkey rapidly got into a second war—with Montenegro. Fiszel Frajnd, or, as he now called himself by his Muslim name, Makhmed Hamid, experienced a great deal of combat in the war. In one of the battles he had a difficult struggle with the commander of his division, a Turkish general. Fiszel Ferdinand had a suspicion that the general wanted to surrender to the enemy, so at a certain moment—so the story goes—he cut off the head of the general. The story reached the Sultan, who summoned Fiszel Ferdinand (Makhmed Hamid) to him.

The hero from Brzezin gave his account to the Sultan, and as a result, the Sultan was very pleased with Makhmed Hamid's action and immediately, on the spot, elevated him to the rank of general, also giving him the title Pasha.

That is how the youth from Brzezin, Reb Szlama Frajnd's youngest son, came to be a Turkish Pasha.

In the meantime, the war became complicated. The attempt at peace negotiations with Montenegro and Serbia—which was also in the battle—fell through. And it came about that Russia again declared war against Turkey in 1877. England was on the side of Turkey.

Fiszel Ferdinand Frajnd—now already Hamid Pasha—took part in the new war as a commanding general, and thanks to his heroism, achieved the title of Field Marshall. He received many high military awards, among them, also, one from the English Queen Victoria.

During this Turkish-Russian War, a serious situation arose in Syria, which was a Turkish province at that time. The Sultan needed an efficient, faithful governor-general for Syria and selected Hamid Pasha for the post.

While in Syria, the Jewish heart awoke in the Brzeziner hero who had so greatly achieved distinction, and he did many favors for Jews there. In general, he had great success in that post, and he also came to be beloved by the entire population.

After the end of the war, in 1878, the new Sultan, Abdul Hamid, appointed Fiszel Ferdinand Hamid Pasha as his closest counselor, with the title of Grand Vizier.

This was the first and only time that a Jew—even a former Jew—was elevated to such a high office in the Turkish Empire.

The story continues that upon rising to the highest level of power, influence, and honor, Hamid Pasha, the Grand Vizier, completely befriended his fellow Jews in Turkey. He succeeded in getting a government salary for the *Khokhem-Bashi* (Chief Rabbi) Mojsze Levi in Constantinople. Thanks to Hamid Pasha, the Sultan introduced the custom of sending to the *khokhem-bashi* before every Passover eight thousand francs so that he could distribute alms for Passover needs to the poor Jews in Constantinople.

When a great fire destroyed the Jewish quarter of Constantinople, Hamid Pasha succeeded in getting the Sultan to send aid for those who suffered the great loss. At that time, thanks to the Brzeziner Jew, a number of Turkish Jews also received high government posts.

* * *

Gedalia Fiszel Frajnd—that is how he was listed in the registration book of birth certificates in the Brzeziny town hall—achieved such grandeur but also did not forget his family in the old country.

The Pasha sent money to be divided among his relatives in Brzezin—separately, however, for his sister, the wife of Brzeziner resident Reb Izrael Kriger. She was later supported by him during her entire life.

Then Reb Izrael Kriger, who had until that time drawn his livelihood from a small haberdashery and dry-goods business, decided to make a trip to Constantinople to visit his brother-in-law and see what had truly happened to him. He took off his long garments, dressed himself in the German manner [modern dress], and went on his way.

This difficult journey took place under very trying conditions, but Kriger absolutely did not regret his efforts. Aside from the many gifts and curious greetings he brought with him from Constantinople, he returned with the title—Pan [Sir]! Sir Izrael Kriger!

The Grand Vizier did not forget to also send with Kriger a gift for the then Brzeziner *rov*, *Harov gaon* [rabbi and eminent scholar] Reb Syna Sapir (author of *Seyfer Olas Khodesh* [book of sermons about the new moon])—a beautiful, carved little tobacco box.

Upon parting, the Pasha asked his brother-in-law to come and visit him again very soon, this time together with his sister (Kriger's wife). That also came to pass.

Kriger's second visit to Turkey was very poignant and solemn—this time with his wife and also with their son-in-law, Sorkin.

They spoke of this trip among the family in Brzezin for many years and of the way Fiszel Ferdinand Hamid Pasha had received his own [family] in his palace.

Fiszel Ferdinand Hamid Pasha, toward the end of his extraordinarily tumultuous life, allegedly was even preparing to come for a visit to his people in Brzezin. However, he became seriously ill with malaria. His relatives in Brzezin stopped getting letters from him and became very anxious. Finally, Kriger sent off an inquiry to the Russian ambassador in Constantinople.

The ambassador answered with a sad letter. In the letter, written to "Herr Pan Kriger in Brzeziny, Piotrków Gubernia," the First Secretary of the Consul reported the news that Hamid Pasha had died on 15/27 [Julian/Gregorian calendar] August 1885, and on the order of the Sultan, a mausoleum was to be erected over his grave. Hamid Pasha died in Beirut, where shortly before his death, he had once again taken over the office of governor-general of Syria.

That is how the wonderful story is told about the Brzeziner Jewish young man who ran away from home and became a Grand Vizier under the Turkish Sultan.

The old Brzeziny Town Hall in Jukiel Brzeziński's house [building].

List of Brzeziner Jews Who Were Contributors to Keren Kayemeth in 1913 (pp. 75–77)

From Collection Plates in Synagogues on Yonkiper Eve 1913

This is a long list of the names of Jews in Brzezin who had, on Erev Yonkiper (1913), put donations for the settlement of the Land of Israel in collection plates placed at *minyen* [quorum of ten men needed for prayers] services in small Orthodox synagogues—[a practice] observed until today.

The list was a report of the donations made on Erev Yonkiper for the good of the community in support of Jews who worked on the land and for the purchase of land in Eretz Yisroel. [This paragraph is written in Hebrew.]

In fact, this was a campaign for Keren Kayemeth LeYisroel (Jewish National Fund) through the traditional collection on Erev Yonkiper during the afternoon prayer session in *bote-medroshim* [small Orthodox houses of prayer] and *shuls*. The Odessa Committee centralized the collection that was also conducted in the *gubernia*s [provinces] of the Russian Poland of that time.

The list of donors in Brzezin is one of the most interesting and important documents for the history of the Jewish community in our hometown (the designation "K" is for kopek, and "R" is for ruble). [100 kopeks = 1 ruble.] The report consists of a total of the donations in every *bes-tfile* [house of prayer] separately.

BRZEZINY
(Powiat Piotrków)

[This list was originally organized in groups by the name of the collector and within groups by how much the person gave. In order to aid those researching their family history, this list has been reorganized and alphabetized by surname. At the end is a key to who collected the contributions.]

	Rubles	Kopeks	Collector		Rubles	Kopeks	Collector
Ardenbaum, J.		20	e	Berchan, Awigdor		20	a
Aronow, Abraham		25	e	Berchan, Icze		20	e
Aronowicz, Abraham		20	c	Berchan, Mordechai		20	a
Aronowicz, Mojsze		50	b	Berchman, Mojsze		45	b
Auer, Herszel		20	a	Bercholc, Herszel		20	a
B(W)alensztajn, Eliezer		20	a	Bercholc, Mordechai		20	d

	Rubles	Kopeks	Collector		Rubles	Kopeks	Collector
Berkan, Jechiel	20		a	Fogel, Elimelech	30		a
Berkan, Mordechai	20		a	Fogel, Icek	25		i
Berliner, Baruch	20		a	Fogel, Jakub Szlama	20		a
Bialek, Pinkus	20		a	Fogel, Lejzer	20		a
Bialek, Wolf	20		a	Fogel, Mojsze	1	–	i
Bilinkin, Josef	50		b	Fotel, Ch. B.	20		c
Birenbaum, Icze	25		d	Frajdenrajch, Josef	20		j
Bimka, Izrael	20		f	Frajnd, Ch.	50		a
Blacherowicz, Ch.	50		b	Frank, Abraham	36		b
Blankert, Syna	20		a	Frankensztajn, Pinkus	20		f
Blatt, Chaim	20		a	Frenkelsztajn, Icek	20		a
Blatt, S. J.	20		g	Frydman, Josef	20		a
Bochkowicz, Abraham	20		a	Frydman, Mojsze	50		b
Bocian, Abraham	20		b	Fuks, Daniel	25		f
Bocian, Beryl	50		a	Fuks, Herszel	20		a
Bocian, S. M.	20		f	Fuks, Josef	20		f
Borensztajn, I. M.	50		b	Fuks, Juda	20		a
Borensztajn, Lajbel	20		b	Gelbard, J. M.	25		i
Born, Majer	20		a	Gerszoniak, Lajbuś Mendel	30		a
Breitbard, Mojsze	20		a	Gerszt, Jekel	20		a
Brenner, Jeb [Jakub?]	25		b	Giewerc, L.	20		c
Celcer, Eliezer	30		c	Ginsburg, M. W.	30		f
Chacko, Mojsze	25		b	Gitman, Ch.	25		b
Chajfec, B.	50		b	Gitman, Grisza	20		a
Cuker, Mordechai	30		a	Goldberg, A. A.	20		a
Cukerman, Cwi	20		a	Goldberg, Bencion	20		a
Cymerman, Lajb	50		b	Goldberg, Nute	25		b
Daszewski, Fajwel	25		a	Goldenberg, Mojsze	20		a
Dawidowicz, S.	25		d	Goldkranc, Jakub H.	20		a
Dorfman-Rabinowicz	30		e	Gotlib, Emanuel	25		a
Dymant, Herszel	40		d	Gotlib, Judel	25		h
Dymant, Naftali	30		a	Gotlib, Sura	35		a
Dymant, Oto	50		d	Gotlieb, J. M.	1	–	a
Dymant, Sura	25		a	Grodziński, M.	30		b
Dymant, Wolf	50		c	Grynberg, Mojsze	20		a
Dymant, Zelig	50		d	Grynfeld, H. J.	25		a
Eksztajn, Josef	30		e	Grynszpan, Pejsach	20		f
Elbaum, J.	20		e	Gutkind, Nachman	50		a
Elsztajn, Mojsze	20		a	Gutkind, Szulem	25		a
Enoch, Mojsze	20		a	Gutsztadt, Elchanon	20		a
Erlich, Jechiel	20		a	Halbersztadt, D. L.	20		a
Erlich, L.	20		a	Halbersztadt, Laja	40		a
Feldman, Josef	50		a	Halbersztadt. A. J.	25		a
Fidler, C. D.	20		a	Hauzer, Chemil	30		e
Fiszelewicz, Szmaje	25		c	Hauzer, Eli	20		a
Fiszhof, Lajbuś	20		b	Hauzer, Hercke	20		a
Flam, Abraham	20		a	Hauzer, Jechiel	20		a
Flamholc, Mojsze	20		a	Hauzer, Mojsze Jechiel	25		a

CONTRIBUTORS TO KEREN KAYEMETH IN 1913

	Rubles	Kopeks	Collector
Hauzer, Wowe		20	a
Hendrykowski, Chaim Zelig		30	a
Herszenberg, A.		30	h
Herszenberg, D. A.		25	a
Herszenberg, Jekel		20	a
Herszkowicz, Bracha		20	a
Hicirowicz		25	f
Horn, Gecel		20	a
Horn, Lemel		40	f
Igielski, Abraham Lajb		20	a
Iglicki, M. M.		25	b
Iglicki, Szlama		20	b
Ikka, Dawid, hb' [unmarried]		20	a
Ikka, Mordechai		20	a
Indyk, Szmul		20	a
Jakubowicz, Ch. D.		50	a
Jakubowicz, Mojsze		20	a
Jakubowicz, Pincie		25	a
Jankelewicz, S.		50	b
Jeruzalski, Abraham		20	a
Kahn, Awigdor		20	g
Kalisz, A. J.		20	c
Kalisz, Abraham		25	a
Kalisz, Mendel		50	b
Kalisz, S. M.		47	b
Kejzberg, J. S.		20	a
Kejzman, Elimelech		20	a
Kejzman, S. A.		25	a
Kiszke, Jakub		25	b
Klajnbard, Mordechai Lajbuś		25	a
Klajnblum, Mojsze		25	d
Klajnman, Efroim		75	a
Klajnman, Laja		20	a
Kleinert, Ch.		20	a
Kochberg, C. M		20	a
Kochenberg, H.		20	a
Kochenberg, S. D.		20	a
Kolf, Icek		20	d
Komoryński, Mojsze		30	c
Korman, Dr. S.		50	a
Kornblum, Abraham		25	a
Kozak, Majer		20	a
Krakowiak, Szmaje		30	b
Krawiecki, Henoch		20	a
Krawiecki, Majer		20	e
Krawiecki, Mendel		50	j
Krell, Mojsze		20	a
Krengel, Fiszel		50	a
Krongrad, Fiszke		20	a
Krongrad, Szymon		20	a
Lajchman, Cwi		20	j
Lakinicki, Mojsze		25	b
Landau, Jechiel		38	b
Landau, Icek		20	f
Lauster, Jakub		20	b
Lechtreger, Abraham, hb'		25	c
Lechtreger, Aron		20	a
Lechtreger, S.		50	b
Łęczycki, H.		30	a
Lehrer, Aron		20	e
Lenger, D. M.		20	a
Lenszczyński, Nosen		20	a
Lew, Chaim Dawid		50	b
Lew, Gerszon		25	f
Lewitin, Ajzyk		50	a
Lewkowicz. J. D.		25	a
Lindner, Szlama		30	a
Lipszyc, Abraham		50	b
Lipszyc, Aron		50	b
Lipszyc, Jechiel Majer		20	a
Lohs, Hersz Mendel		20	a
Lustig, Dawid		20	c
Malamut, Icek		30	e
Malamut, Josef		50	e
Maliniak, Icek		50	h
Malinowski, Lajbuś		20	f
Mandel, Josef		20	j
Mandel, Mojsze Aron		20	a
Mendelewicz, A. Ch.		30	a
Mendlewicz, Aron	1	–	a
Michrowski, Pinkus		20	a
Milgram, Dawid		20	k
Miller, S.		20	a
Minc, Fajtel		20	c
Miniawicz, M.		50	a
Mizes, Perec		25	f
Moskol, Chaim		30	b
Najfeld, Jakub		20	j
Najman, Szlama		30	c
Najman, Zysman		20	b
Nisenberg, Mojsze		20	a
Nowak, Achim		30	b
Ojzer, Jechiel		20	a
Ojzer, Pinkus		20	a
Opolion, Eliezer		20	j
Pakula, Judel		25	a

Name	Rubles	Kopeks	Collector
Perla, Judel	20		a
Perlmuter, A. D.	50		h
Perlmuter, Izrael	30		a
Perlmuter, Lipcze	25		h
Piasek, Lajb	25		c
Piekarek, Abraham	25		b
Piksztajn, Batya	50		b
Piotrkowski, Mojsze	20		a
Piotrkowski, Syna	20		a
Płocker, A. M.	30		b
Poleszak, S., Uman	40		e
Poliwoda, Majer	20		a
Poznański, Chaim	20		a
Praszker, Fajwus	20		a
Princ, Henoch	25		b
Przytykewicz, Dawid	30		b
Rabinowicz, R.	50		a
Rachelnik, S. J.	20		a
Rajchenberg, Izrael	30		h
Rajchenberg, J. J.	25		h
Rawicki, Jekel	50		b
Rojtblat, G.	20		d
Roszakowski, Szlama	50		b
Rozen, Efroim	50		d
Rozen, L. M.	25		b
Rozen, S. B.	25		a
Rozen, Syne	30		a
Rozenbaum, Szlama	20		a
Rozenberg, Fajwel	20		a
Rozenberg, Jekel	25		c
Rozenberg, Josef	20		a
Rozenberg, Mojsze	25		c
Rozenberg, Nachman	20		b
Rozenberg, Wolf	20		a
Rozenblat, Emanuel	20		c
Rozenblum, Ajdel	25		a
Rozenblum, Icek Hersz	20		a
Rozenblum, J.	20		a
Rozenfarb, Chaim	20		a
Rubin, Mojsze	20		c
Sapirsztejn, M.	50		b
Spirtus, Benjamin	25		b
Sułkowicz, Aba H.	50		a
Sułkowicz, Dawid	25		a
Sułkowicz, Jakel	50		a
Sułkowicz, Jona	20		a
Sułkowicz, S.	30		b
Szafman, Chaim	50		a
Szlamas, Abraham	20		a
Szmidt, Szmul	25		a
Szmukler, Szyja	20		a
Szotenberg, M. A.	50		b
Szotenberg, Pinkus	50		b
Szotenberg, Szlama	40		b
Szotland, Efroim	25		c
Szpiro, Szymon	25		c
Sztajnberg, Binum	20		a
Sztajnberg, Icek	20		a
Sztern, Lajbuś	30		d
Szufleder, Herszel	25		f
Szufleder, Mordechai, hb'	20		c
Szulzinger, Ch. B.	1	–	a
Szwalb	20		a
Szwarc, S. G.	25		b
Tajbat, Szmul	20		a
Takse, B.	20		a
Topolowicz, Abraham	20		e
Tuszyński, M.	50		b
Tuszyński, Majer	20		a
Tyl, Mojsze	30		d
Tyl, Mordechai	30		d
Wachler, Chaim	25		a
Wachler, Icze	50		c
Waldman, Gedalja	20		a
Waldman, M. B.	50		a
Wasilkowski	50		b
Widka, Icze	20		a
Widowska, Dora	20		f
Winter, Jerachmiel	50		b
Winter, L. M.	20		b
Winter, Picers/Ficers	30		b
Winter, Pincie	25		b
Winter, S. and Fuks	50		a
Wolf, Lajbuś	20		a
Zagan, J. M.	25		a
Zagan, Szyja	50		a
Zajd, Dawid	25		b
Zajdner, Abraham	25		c
Zelig, Mojsze Pinkus	30		a
Zeliwiański, Josef	50		e
Zelman, J.	20		c
Zinger, Wolf	20		a
Złocze, Abraham	20		a
Złotnicki, Josef	50		a
Żółtowski, Mojsze	30		f
Żychliński, Icek	25		a

CONTRIBUTORS TO KEREN KAYEMETH IN 1913

	Rubles	Kopeks	Collector
Żychliński, L.		50	a
Zygmantowicz, Bella		25	a
Zylberwaser, Judel		20	a
Zylberwaser, M.		20	a
Zylberwaser, Mojsze		50	c
Zylberwaser, Szlama		20	a
Zyman, Jakub Joel		20	a

	Rubles	Kopeks	Collector
Prominent synagogues	3	60	a
Miscellaneous	1	60	a
Pledges		55	d
Pledges		20	f
Pledges	3	–	g
Pledges		84	i
Pledges		51	j
Pledges		57	k
Bote-medroshim [small synagogues, houses of prayer] pledges	1	–	a
Bote Hasidim Ger [Ger Hasidim houses of prayer] pledges		82	a
Bekhakneset Hasides Dostrowtse [other Hasidic houses]		53	a

GRAND TOTAL: 102R 13K

Amount Collected	Name of person(s) who collected the contribution
51R 50K	a. Aron Mendlewicz, Ch. B. Szulzinger, Szyja Zagan, Izrael Perlmuter, Josef Złotnicki, M. B. Waldman, and B. Bocian
20R 56K	b. Josef Bilinkin
6R 40K	c. Mojsze Rozenberg
4R 70K	d. The *minyen* "Bney Lita" as above [through Mojsze Rozenberg]
6R 40K	e. Josef Zeliwiański
4R 05K	f. The "*magaziners minyen*" through M. W. Ginsburg and G. Lew
3R 40K	g. Jerachmiel Lajchman and Awigdor Kahn
2R 35K	h. Icek Maliniak
2R 34K	i. Mojsze Fogel and M. Gelbard
2R 01K	j. The Grodzisker Shul Through Cwi Lajchman
77K	k. The Aleksander Shul Through Dawid Milgram

Toward a History of the Brzeziner *Kehile* [Jewish Community]

(General Features of Past Community Life in Poland) (pp. 78–83)

Joseph Shaibowicz

In the Poland of the past, Jewish life was well organized. Everyone had to be connected to the Jewish *klal* [community] unless he had converted. The Jewish community of the town had full legal rights to impose taxes and control the life of every individual. It could also sentence one for crimes, even with the death sentence.

At the head of the community stood the *parnesim* [elected leaders], or *roshim* [heads]—*roshekool* [community leaders]. Every *parnes* presided over the community for a month, therefore, he was called *parnes hakhodesh* [monthly leader], and he was responsible for everything for that month. The *parnesim* had to swear a loyalty oath to the king and had to be certified by the *wojewoda* [governor of the province], who was the king's representative. In towns that were under the jurisdiction of noble landowners, the landowner had to certify each *parnes*.

The Brzeziner *parnesim* had to be certified by the noble landowner Lasocki. In addition to the *parnesim*, there also were *tuvim* [elders] or *tuvey-hoyir* [esteemed elders] (usually former *parnesim*). Their task was to help the *parnesim* carry out their work. In addition, there also were *memunim* [appointed officials], *gaboim* [trustees], and *meshgikhim* [supervisors], who had to take care of health, *kashrus* [rules of kosher], honest weight and measure, of good behavior, of the *malamdim* [teachers], etc. The community also had supervision over schools and *klekoydesh* [clergy] (rabbis, *dayonim* [communal judges], *khazonim* [cantors] and *shokhtim* [ritual slaughterers]), *mikvoes* [ritual baths], cemeteries, and social welfare. There also was an important commission of *shmayim*—appraisers. They had to figure out the tax that everyone had to pay. Apparently, if poor people could not pay even the head tax, the community paid it to the king for them. Aside from these, the community also had state functions in the realm of administration and court business. As early as the fourteenth century, we see laws where one could not sentence a Jew without the participation of Jews in the judgment.

The *rov* [official town rabbi] was the highest authority; his judgment was law. The strongest device was *kherem* [excommunication]. The *shames* [sexton] of the *kahal* [community council] occupied a different important position. He was the community's representative in the government offices and also a kind of *shtadlan* [intermediary] with the landowner. There also was a *nemen* (treasurer). The *kahal* also maintained a *royfe* [health practitioner], who treated poor sick people at the community's expense, a barber, a midwife, and a pharmacist.

Over the individual communities stood the Va'ad Haglil (District Council), which was selected at a convention of the leaders of the communities of the district and of special delegates. The chief of the Va'ad Haglil had the title Parnes Haglil. The Va'ad Haglil met once a year to take care of all the important items and measure out the taxes for each community in the district. The Va'ad Haglil had a district *rov* (*av-bes-din haglil* [chief judge] of the district), a government *shtadlan* [intermediary], a writer, *shamesim* [sextons], and a treasurer. Over the Va'adi-Haglilim in Poland stood the Va'ad Arba Aratzot [Council of Four Lands, which included Greater Poland, Lesser Poland, Red Ruthenia (Galicia and Podolia), and Volhynia]. This central administrative body consisted of delegates from the Va'adi-Haglilim. Large communities used to send up to four delegates, smaller, up to two, and the smallest, one. The Va'ad Arba Aratzot never had more that seventy-one members, and its executive body consisted of twenty-three members. Jews wanted to support the tradition of the Sanhedrin [Judicial Supreme Court in ancient Palestine], which consisted of seventy-one members, and the Sanhedrin Ktane [Lesser Sanhedrin], which had twenty-three members.[1]

This was the time of Jewish autonomy in Poland. The Va'ad Arba Aratzot was a kind of government within a government. It controlled all Jewish life in Poland. The finance minister of Poland often took part in the sessions of the Va'ad, and the Va'ad was the officially recognized representative of Polish Jewry before the king.

The growth of Jewish settlements in Poland led to the fact that many Jews settled on land owned by the nobility. As long as the settlements had been small, they had been mostly concentrated on land owned by the king, and the king had protected them as his own, since he did not want to lose them—because of the large income he received from them.

In 1539 the nobility won a big victory over the king, and the Sejm (parliament) that convened in Piotrków decided that all Jews who lived on noblemen's land would become the absolute property of the landowners.[2] This created two categories of Jews. In towns belonging to the king, Jews were on a higher level. In the towns and villages of noblemen, Jews were subject to the caprice of the landowner. If the nobleman was a fine person, he protected his Jews from hatred, the burghers, guilds, ecclesiastical organizations, and random anti-Semitism. If, however, he was a Jew-hater, he would often blackmail the Jews in order to extort even more money. The Jews were powerless, because they no longer had royal protection.

There were, however, also cases where the position of the Jews truly improved, and Jews actually stood up to the anti-Semitic plague.

The noble landowning family Lasocki in Brzezin—the owners of Brzezin in the sixteenth, seventeenth, and eighteenth centuries—continually improved the town, built churches, and always needed money. The Lasockis put the Jewish taxes and *loy yekhrets* [hush money] to good use. Therefore, they did not permit any persecution of Jews and often supported Jews against raids from the burghers (townspeople) and the guilds.

* * *

The dawn of Jewish life in Brzezin is not known. There are legends about Jews in Brzezin as early as the twelfth century.[3] Today it is difficult to determine when the communities in Brzezin and its environs came into existence. Our historians and chroniclers, alas, did not understand the importance of registering a newly-established

---

[1] Dr. M. Shifer, *The Creation of the Arba Aratzot* [Four Lands]. (Author's Note)
[2] Majer Edelbaum, *The Jewish City Mezritch* [Międzyrzecz]. (Author's Note)
[3] See "Central Historical Commission of the Central Committee of the Freed Jews in Poland." Historical Questionnaire 596, YIVO, New York. (Author's Note)

settlement. The majority of communities suddenly appeared in the historical chronicles shortly before or just at the time of the Chmielnicki Uprisings [uprisings in Ukraine in mid-17th century, in which countless Jews were killed]. It is certain, however, that they already existed a long time before then. The oldest date of the certain existence of a Jewish settlement in Brzezin is 1564.[1] Kutno, which at that time also belonged to the Lentchitser Województwo [Łęczyca Province], is mentioned as having Jews in 1513. The supposition that when King Casimir the Great gave Brzezin the privilege of becoming a town in 1366, a significant Jewish community was already there—has not been confirmed.

The Polish writer Sarniecki wrote in 1558 that there were skilled artisans in Brzezin whose products were sent to other towns in Greater Poland. A large number of the skilled artisans were Jews.

During the seventeenth century, the general conditions in Poland seriously worsened. The Jewish situation became catastrophic. Chmielnicki descended on hundreds of Polish towns and killed off entire communities. Swedish troops came to help him in the battle, which was a rebellion against the king of Poland, and overwhelmed entire Jewish communities. The Swedes caused great destruction in Brzezin, but the greater tragedy came later. Although the Jews were among the most loyal supporters of Polish power, this did not prevent the church from taking advantage of the alleged "miracle of the Madonna of Częstochowa [a portrait in Częstochowa Cathedral]," thought to have caused the defeat of the Swedes. The priests instigated doing away with unbelieving Jews (the Swedes, as Protestants, had also counted them as unbelievers) and called for pogroms against the Jews. In 1656 a terrible pogrom occurred in Brzezin. Forty Jewish families were murdered by Hetman [military chief] Stefan Czarniecki's troops.[2] The Brzeziner Poles helped, and it is thought that at that time the majority of the Jews of Brzezin met a violent death.[3] Pogroms carried out by similar gangs also took place in Kalisz and Piotrków. In Piotrków they slaughtered fifty families, the entire Jewish population.[4]

A short time later, however, the Jewish population in Brzezin, as in many other Polish towns, increased greatly, not only from natural growth, but also principally from a large immigration into Poland. Jews who had been banished from Austria, Bohemia, Silesia, and the German provinces came to Poland in droves. A portion of the banished settled in Brzezin.[5]

---

[1] See Mgr. A. Feldman, "Pages Before History," *Younger Historians*, no. 3, Warsaw, 1934. Distributed through the historical circle of the society YIVO in Warsaw. (Author's Note)

[2] See *Encyclopedia Judaica*. (Author's Note)

[3] I. Lewin, *Die Judenferfolungen in 2 Schwedisch-polniczche Kriege*, 1901. (Author's Note)

[4] According to Dr. I. Schipper, on the eve of the evil decrees, T"Khes [8 Tevet/Tamuz] 1615, there were half a million Jews in Poland. On the basis of this statement it appears that 330,000 Jews were slaughtered as a result of these evil decrees. Others believe that even more were killed. (Author's Note)

[5] See Mendlewicz's chapter in this book about his family Halberstadt. (Author's Note)

JEWS IN BRZEZIN IN 1764

Subsequent to the time in Poland when the Va'ad Arba Aratzot was dissolved in 1764, a census of Jews was conducted in Brzezin, as in all Polish towns.[1] The count for the head tax was applicable to all Jews without any distinction as to gender and social standing — except for children who were not yet nine years old.

In order to establish the statistical validity of this census, it is necessary to point out that the census was carried out by a special "inspector" who had to be a nobleman, together with the *parnes hakhodesh* [monthly leader of Jewish community council] and the *rov* [official town rabbi] and *shames* [synagogue official] of the town. They had to go into all the Jewish homes and record the family names and given names of all the souls in town. The Jews from the surrounding villages had to come to the town and, under oath, register all the souls in their families.[2]

The Jewish population in Brzezin and its environs in 1764 was given as 243. Two hundred and three Jews lived in Brzezin, and forty Jews lived in the surrounding seven villages that belonged to the Brzeziner Jewish community. Koluszki was at that time a village with eight Jews that belonged to the Brzeziner Jewish community.

After carrying out the census, the inspector had to travel to Łęczyca, the capital city of the province, and deliver the registers into the hands of the official counters who were appointed by the Sejm. Then the Jewish inspectors had to swear an oath in the synagogue that they had omitted no one. But, in spite of all the precautions of the law, the registers did not show the true number of Jews in Brzezin. Paying two gulden a year per head led many Jews to find means to conceal themselves from the count. In 1775 the head tax was raised to three gulden and, in 1779, by another half gulden.

Still, the count of 1764 is considered to be of extraordinary importance. First, it took place 215 years after the first Jewish census in Poland, and it showed the great change that had come about in Jewish life. Second, the first census had been at the beginning of the Va'ad Arba Aratzot (Jewish autonomy), and the new census was carried out when the Va'ad Arba Aratzot was dissolved—and with it, Jewish self-government also declined.

From this census we get a little idea about Jewish life in Brzezin during that time. Thirty houses belonged to Jewish leaders. Among the Jews were 1 tavern keeper, 1 distiller (whiskey distiller), stallkeeper, 3 tailors, butchers, baker, lace maker, glazier, 1 *balbider* (kind of *felczer*) [health practitioner], and *shamosim*. Two *parnesim* had two *meshorshim* [servants] each and one *parnes* had three *meshorshim* (a servant girl, a servant in the shop, and a wagon driver). There were Jews who lived as lodgers in strangers' houses. One leaseholder in Brzezin held the lease on the collection of the market fees (*arendarz targowy* [market leaseholder]).

Of all the towns in the Łęczyca province, only Brzezin is remembered as having a Jewish bagel-baker[3] and a *parnes* who had three *meshorshim*. In Brzezin there were also municipal lessees. This means leaseholders who leased from a landowner most of his

---

[1] Dr. Rafał Mahler, "Town of Brzezin in 1764" (*Lodz Scientific Writings*). (Author's Note)
[2] See also the statistical supplement about Jews in Brzezin and the surrounding villages. (Author's Note)
[3] Rafał Mahler, *Jews in Former Poland in Light of Numbers*, 129. (Author's Note)

income-producing businesses, for example, distillery, brewery, inn, toll collection (*przewozowe*) [transport fees], market fees, and sometimes mills.

Jews in Brzezin According to Their Civil Status in 1764[a]

Total # of Jews older than 1 yr	Men / Women	Married	Independent	Widowers / Widow	Married sons & sons-in-law *af kest* / Married daughters & daughters-in-law *af kest*	Widows *af kest*	Unmarried sons / Unmarried daughters	Unmarried servants and orphans	Journey men / Servants	Owners of houses	Tenants	Heads of families
	102 Men	50	43	2	7		40		10	30	19	49
	Women			Widow	Married daughters & daughters-in-law *af kest*	Widows *af kest*	Unmarried daughters	Unmarried servants and orphans	Servants			
203	101	50	4	4	7	4	38	5	5			

Total of 60 families, averages 3.4 *nefoshes* [souls] per family.

In the Eight Villages That Belonged to the Brzeziner Jewish Community[b]

Total # of Jews in 8 villages	Men / Women					
	18 Men	9	11	1	2	5
40	22 Women	11	2	2	-	8

Total of 14 families, averages 3 individuals per family.

Altogether from the town and the villages, 243 individuals belonged to the Brzezin Jewish community. The general Brzeziner population in 1764 amounted to about 642 individuals; this means that approximately one-third of the population was Jewish.

Table Footnotes:
a. Dr. Rafal Mahler, *Jews in Former Poland in Light of Numbers*. (See also tables 8, 24, 41 and 63 [in Mahler's book]). (Author's Note)
b. Koluszki, with eight Jews, was a village at that time, and belonged to Brzezin. (Author's Note)

In the seventeenth and eighteenth centuries, a fine Jewish life bloomed in Brzezin that was well known all over Poland. There were *rebbes* [Hasidic rabbis] in Brzezin who were considered famous people in the Jewish world of the time in Poland. From Brzezin they spread Hasidism far and wide all over Poland. A notable example from that generation of "good Jews" was Reb Fiszele (Efroim) Szpiro,[1] who was a *rov* [official town rabbi] in the neighboring town Stryków and was known as Reb Fiszele Strykower. Always absent-minded and pensive, a homebody who knew nothing about the shape of a coin, he always ate in his private room in the service of Torah, always practicing mortification of the flesh and fasting while the Spirit was in the Disapora. The "Holy Light" [from title of book he wrote], as the Hasidic literature called him, came from Podolia, the cradle of Hasidism. His father, Reb Josef Lajb, who was dubbed "Hasid" because of his strict piety, was a student of Reb Jakub Josef from Polonnoye, one of the major students of the Baal-Shem-Tov and author of the well-known Hasidic *seyfer Toldes Yakov Yosef* [The Story of Jakub Josef]. Reb Fiszele Szpiro was born in Belotserkovka, where his father was the *rov* (1743).

Because of the Haidamak [paramilitary bands, mostly Cossacks] slaughters and massacres of Jews under the leadership of Gonta and Zheleznyak (Tamuz [June-July] 1768), Reb Josef Lajb, with members of his household, fled to Balta and became a *maged meshorim* [itinerant preacher] However, soon afterward, the Turks dominated this town on one side and the Poles on the other. Not having time to run away to the Turkish side, which many Jews had done, Reb Josef Lajb remained on the Polish side.

However, he could not remain there long either. Because of the frequent wars, he had to take his wandering stick and get under way with his family. On the way, in various towns, he gave sermons and lived on alms, and upon coming to Brzezin, he settled there. He became a preacher and taught grown young men, and from this, frugally maintained himself. There his family branched out into tens of families.

His son, Reb Fiszele, left Brzezin and stayed a long time with Rebbe Reb Ber, the Mezritcher [Międzyrzecz] *maged*, and also with Reb Elimelech from Lizhensk [Leżajsk]. While at the latter's, he studied and devoted himself to *kabole* [Jewish mystical philosophy], together with the Kozhenitser [Kozienice] *maged*, Reb Isroel'cze. Then he returned to Brzezin, married his second wife there, spent many years *af kest* and later was accepted by the neighboring town of Stryków as *rov*. He had children in Brzezin—Reb Jekiel Brzeziner and Reb Icek, later *rov* in Żarnów. His son-in-law, Reb Ruwen Kosher, was *rov* in Ujazd.

In Brzezin, as in the entire region at that time, the Hasidim did not have any home base. Becoming a *rov*, Reb Fiszele established a nest there for Hasidism, from which he became the spiritual leader of the movement. Being very famous as a *kodesh* [holy man] and a *bal-moyfes* [miracle worker], he had a large following around him, and the great *rebbes* of Poland sent Jews with heavy hearts to him, and they were helped by him.

They showered him with "red *matbeyes* [coins]," that is, what he called the "little golden rubles," but he himself did not want to use the *pidyones* [payments for advice]. He lived on the few gulden the town paid him every week as *rov*. He used to give away the gold coins to poor people so they would have some prosperity, gaining great pleasure from the fact that the poor could have such delight from them.

---

[1] Mojżesz Fajnkind, *The Good Jews in Poland*. The same author also wrote the history of Piotrków. As a young man he studied in Brzezin under the supervision of his father, the old Brzeziner *rov*, Reb Izrael Fajnkind. (Author's Note)

The *rebbe* Reb Fiszele had strange, one would say, non-Hasidic methods in his leadership. He gave no one *sholem* [greeting] with his bare hand. His hand was always covered with a kerchief or a towel. A story arose that once the *rebbe* Reb Bunem from Pshiskhe [Przysucha] came to watch him perform the benediction. In addition, he brought with him the *rebbe* Reb Henoch from Aleksandrów. Reb Fiszele gave the *sholem* with his bare hand. On the spot the *rebbe* Reb Henoch edged forward and also received the greeting with the bare hand. It immediately dawned on Reb Fiszele that he had given *sholem* without a covered hand to some stranger, causing him great consternation. He calmed himself only after the Pshiskher told him who and what Reb Henoch was.

Rebbe Reb Henoch and the Tshekhanover [Ciechanów] *rebbe*, Reb Abramele, then became his closest Hasidim, serving at Rebbe Reb Fiszele's side for many years.

Then the following story was told:

> A complete upheaval suddenly occurred in the *rebbe*'s court. The *rebbe* Reb Fiszele closed himself in his secluded chamber and would no longer permit anyone near him. One could rant as long as one wanted—it was useless. There was a commotion in the Hasidic world. There was no one to defend the Jews during bad times occuring then in Poland because of the wars with Russia. Rebbe Reb Bunem learned about it and came running at full speed to see what was happening there. Rebbe Reb Fiszele could not refuse him and opened his closed door. When asked why he closed himself in, Rebbe Reb Fiszele naively responded as follows:
>
> Some time ago, a man came, very bitter, who was burdened with a large family but had no way to support them. Rebbe Reb Fiszele advised him to play the lottery, and he promised him that he would be successful. The man actually obeyed him, but when the man did not have enough money to redeem the ticket at the final stage, the collector sold it to another man, and the other man actually won the grand prize. And so, Rebbe Reb Fiszele then justified himself before Rebbe Reb Bunem—that the Almighty did not implement what he as a *tsadik* [saintly person] had decreed, and there was nothing more he could do— *basta* [enough]."
>
> The Pshiskher explained to him that a *tsadik* must not dictate to the Almighty how he is to help a person. "Because what right do you have to say what is to be done?" A *tsadik* must express the wish, and Providence will then find the means to implement the *tsadik*'s wish.

Rebbe Reb Fiszele immediately opened his door to all those with heavy hearts, and the people again came to cry their eyes out and find comfort.

What happened then is that Napoleon the Great, in his war with Russia, marched with his great army through the Łódź-Brzezin region, but on account of the great dense forests, the army got lost and could not find its way to Brzezin and Warsaw. He demanded that the Łódź population give him a guide, but the town of Łódź was afraid, so they ran to Rebbe Reb Fiszele for advice. He told a Jew from Brzezin who, at that time, lived in Łódź—Reb Szmul Berman[1] or Reb Szmul Pachter (well-known as Reb Szmul Brzeziner)—that he should be the guide. Reb Szmul Brzeziner knew the local forest roads well. Since "*sar vgodl npl veyisroel*" [a prince suddenly came to the people of

---

[1] According to Abraham Arzi-Tenenbaum in *The History of the Jews in Łódź*, Reb Szmul Brzeziner was one of the first Jews in Łódź. He was a very important community leader and one of the first *dozor*s in Łódź. (Author's Note)

Israel] and Napoleon was a great *sar* (interpreting the initials from the word "npl" to mean that Napoleon had dropped in amidst the Jews), Reb Szmul Brzeziner led the army to Brzezin, from which there was a wider road to Warsaw.

The story continues that finding out from Reb Szmul Brzeziner where the great miracle worker [Reb Fiszele] lived who had instructed him [Brzeziner] to show the way, Napoleon sent his adjutant with the Jew to thank the *rebbe* for the favor and reward him. But how astounded the Frenchman was to see before his eyes a hunchbacked old man with a snow-white long beard, sitting in *talis* and *tfilen* in a poor, utterly dark room in a half-sunken little house. The officer was overcome by a great reverence for the great *tsadik* [saintly person], and he asked him to express his good wishes for the French army to win the war. With that he poured out onto the table a considerable amount of gold pieces as *pidyen* [payment]. Then for the first time Rebbe Reb Fiszele understood that the "red pieces" were valuable coins with which one could buy something.

It was told in another story that a frequent visitor at Rebbe Reb Fiszele's was a poor little tailor for whom the *rebbe* had high regard. Once, at the time of Sukes, the little tailor had a lot of work. Now it was already the eve of Sukes, and the *rebbe* did not have the *suke* ready, so the little tailor abandoned his work—"What do I care about scissors? What do I care about ironing?"—and he began to build the *suke* for the *rebbe*. Rebbe Reb Fiszele, thoroughly delighted with the little tailor, asked him what he wanted for the work—riches or long life. The little tailor asked that the *rebbe* sit with him in *Gan-Eden* [Paradise]. The *tsadik* promised him. It did not take long before the little tailor became sick, and on the same day—17 Tevet [December–January] 1822—that Rebbe Reb Fiszele, the saintly Jew, died at the age of eighty, the little tailor also died, and he was buried next to Rebbe Reb Fiszele, just as he wished.

* * *

Rebbe Reb Fiszele left two sons, Reb Jekiele Szpiro in Brzezin and Reb Icek in Żarnów, and a son-in-law, Reb Ruwen Kosher, who was *rov* in Ujazd.

Reb Jekiele Brzeziner married off his son, Reb Jeszajele, to the daughter of a doctor to *rebbe*s, Reb Dawid-Chaim Bernard from Piotrków, who had become a *bal-tshuve* [newly observant] at an advanced age. The Hasidim grumbled a great deal to Rebbe Reb Fiszele over this *shidekh* [match]. He consoled his Hasidim that because of that *shidekh*, "a cure will come into the family." And when Reb Jekiel Szpiro became ill, he actually traveled from Brzezin to his *mekhutn* [daughter-in-law's father], the doctor, to undergo treatment. Reb Jekiel died 19 Sivan [May–June] 1840 in Piotrków.

In Brzezin Reb Jekiel Szpiro was a prominent merchant, a military contractor, and a successful man; on account of animosity, his competitors created serious disturbances and rebelled against permitting him to be the successor to his great father, so the dynasty ended with Rebbe Reb Fiszele Strykower. After the death of Reb Fiszele, his student, Reb Szmul Aba, became *rebbe* in Żychlin and founded the Zhychliner dynasty.[1]

The subsequent famous *rebbe*, Reb Wolf Strykower, was a son of the Tshekhanower *tsadik*, Rebbe Reb Abramele. Reb Wolf married someone from Stryków, and being a

---

[1] Menasze Unger, "The Historical Dynasties" in *Tog-Morgn Zhurnal* from November 1959. (Author's Note)

Strykower son-in-law, he settled there in the residence of the great Hasidic *rebbe*, Reb Fiszele. The Kotsker *rebbe*, Reb Mendele, used to say, "The illustrious first *rebbe*, Rabbenu Icchak Majer [from Ger/Góra Kalwaria], is my '*gaon*' [eminent scholar], Reb Hersz Tomashover [from Tomaszów] is my 'Hasid,' and Reb Wolf Strykower is my '*khokhem*' [sage]."[1]

At that time, when *rebbe*s in Poland lived on *pidyones* from their Hasidim, Rebbe Reb Wolf ran a large timber business in partnership with his wealthy Hasidim, and he himself became a very rich man. He was renowned far and wide for his great wisdom. He was an affable, popular person. He loved workers, and in his businesses he employed only Jews. He helped the poor *mit rat un tat* [with advice and deed].

Later, Reb Wolf relocated to Łódź and died in 1891; he was more than eighty-three years old.

* * *

In the second half of the nineteenth century, Jews in Brzezin began to develop the clothing industry. During a period of some ten years, Brzezin grew to become the greatest tailoring center in Poland. This was the glorious epoch of Brzezin, when its production and its workers were known throughout the entire world (see the chapter "Tailors in Brzezin").

Hundreds and hundreds of Jewish young people came to Brzezin from near and far to work and learn tailoring. Later, they spread the trade and the name of Brzezin over many lands. The boisterous growth of the new industry was a completely Jewish accomplishment, and that is how it remained, with insignificant exceptions, until the Nazi destruction.

With their effort and virtuous hard-working lives, Jews elevated the status of the town Brzezin and the surrounding towns. From approximately three hundred souls at the end of the eighteenth century, the number of inhabitants in Brzezin reached nine thousand at the beginning of the twentieth century. The Jewish population multiplied from 27.1 percent, in 1827, to more than double in 1913. At that time, Jews were 54.4 percent of the inhabitants and formed the absolute majority of the population of the town.

Even during the time of the vicious extermination, there were still a thousand Jews employed in the garment trade in Brzezin. On 24 April 1942 the Jewish firm "Vorsteher and Bunger" asked the ghetto management in Łódź not to allow the thousand Jews that worked in their establishment in Brzezin to be deported until they finished their military order.[2]

The response was that one could not oppose Hitler's command to put a curse on all Jews.

---

[1] See Mojżesz Fajnkind, *The Good Jews in Poland*. (Author's Note)
[2] Żydowski Instytut Historyczny [Jewish Historical Institute in Warsaw], *Eksterminacja Żydów na Ziemiach Polskich* [Extermination of Jews on Polish Soil], 238. (Author's Note)

The Great Synagogue in Brzezin (p. 84)

The great synagogue in Brzezin, because of its architecture, was famous throughout all of Poland. In several articles in this Yizkor book, the history of the destroyed synagogue was reported in detail, including information about those who were involved with building this beautiful synagogue, which brought such honor to our town.

The Jews in Brzezin took great care of the Great Synagogue and sought to beautify it and treat it with honor. After World War I, it was necessary to perform a thorough renovation of the building, and the synagogue committee undertook it as a holy task. This can be seen from the documents from the summer of 1925 that we present below.

Synagogue Committee in Brzezin

Brzezin, Tamuz [June–July] 1925

To the Jewish Population in Brzezin!

Exodus 25:2: "and the Lord spoke to Moses, saying, 'Speak to the children of Israel that they bring me an offering.'"
Exodus 25:3 : "of every man whose heart prompts him to give, you shall take my offering."
Rashi: "A separate amount you will offer me as an offering."

For years, the structure of our local town synagogue (*beysakneses*) had been in a ruinous condition. No longer talking about the fact that during a period of approximately forty years, ever since the synagogue was built, we did not take the time to paint it or to create an enclosure that would be appropriate for such a *beysamigdesh* [temple in Jerusalem]. In recent years, thanks to our carelessness, to our great shame, it has been transformed into a ruin. The entire foundation is ruined, bricks were torn out, the roof full of holes, so that the rain, unhindered, thoroughly soaked the ceiling, and every time we came to the synagogue, the doors were broken, the floor rotted, etc. etc.

Leaving the synagogue that was built with such dedication and effort in such a state would be a great crime on our part, for which we could not forgive ourselves, neither from a moral nor from a material standpoint.

Now is the best time to carry out both inside and outside a thorough renovation of the synagogue structure, in general, to restore the structure to the state that it deserves for such a holy house.

The newly organized synagogue committee has taken on this task and used its own money to start the work.

It appears, however, that restoring the synagogue to the proper condition demands a much greater sum of money than we had originally thought, and, therefore, we must turn to every one of you with the passionate appeal:

Help us to carry out the holy task!

What Jew would not want a share in this holy building!
Who wants to be left out of this great *mitsve* [good deed]!

All Jews from our town, men, women and children, too, must bring significant amounts of donations. Each and every one must voluntarily tax himself with proper sums of money and with all that is possible to help, so that our synagogue can be restored to its proper stature.

With respect,

The Synagogue Committee of Brzezin

Part Two

Between Prosperity and Destruction

Brzezin Between Two World Wars (pp. 87–96)

Fishel Maliniak

When the shooting of the cannons had stopped and the air was cleared of the suffocating gun powder, people came out of the trenches and saw that all the bridges to the outside world had been cut off.

Everything that had been built over the period of generations with effort and toil was no longer there. The chaos was almost total. Business and industry that had been built and developed were altogether destroyed. The large Russian market that was developed by the pioneers from the Brzeziner clothing industry had disappeared entirely. The institutions that were created along with them had also disappeared.

The worst happened to the pioneers themselves. Most of them sought to save themselves in great and deep Russia. But with few exceptions, they all perished, some from the revolution in Russia and others from various afflictions and misfortunes that multiply in times of war and unrest.

The result was that our town looked like the world after the deluge, and the entire population stood as if before the time of Creation.

Anyone with a little imagination can envision the picture of that time. Each person by himself and everyone together had to begin anew. Consequently, it is no wonder that the years after World War I brought with them a great exodus of the younger set. Emigration was either to the United States or to France and Belgium. A small number of idealists emigrated to Palestine, to Eretz Yisroel [Land of Israel]. One way or another, they had to start from the beginning, so they started at least where there were opportunities, both financial and spiritual!

However, the majority remained and made great efforts to organize a new life in every way—economic, social, and cultural.

It is remarkable that in all areas, new elements and new strengths arose. In almost all cases, the leaders of the different institutions were people who had played no role at all before World War I. The war had brought an immense psychological revolution, and the crisis in every strata of the population was so great that that of itself is worth a study by sociologists—especially since all this happened in a natural, democratic, and evolutionary manner, without bloodshed, in a manner that today one could barely imagine possible.

The world has reverted considerably from that liberal, democratic springtime that dominated the period after World War I, but my task is not to bemoan that lost era. My task is to record briefly what happened from that time until the destruction, the total destruction of our town.

IN THE ECONOMIC AREA

As the Torah has already stated, *Im eyn kemakh eyn toyre* [If no flour, no Torah]. It is therefore necessary to begin with how our town earned its first bit of bread during that time.

From the accounts in this book, it is already known that our town consisted only of tailors. Not, God forbid, that one did not find other trades, only that for us, without scissors and an iron, nothing could get started. My grandfather, who came from Warsaw and was called "the tavern keeper" in town, used to say that when he went to Warsaw to visit his parents' graves, they asked him, "Reb [title of respect] Szulem, is it true that your rabbi also sews pants?" You understand that these were exaggerations, and as for exaggerations, I think, no one had a better pedigree than our Brzeziners. Not, God forbid, because they were bad people, but only that they had imagination. And often this was all they had. But in this case, it actually helped.

Therefore, when the Polish war began—and a war surely requires an army, and an army must certainly be clothed—as you can probably guess, the first order to outfit the new Polish army was actually filled by Brzeziners. Tailors cleaned off the heads of their machines, and they took to the work with gusto. One could feel such a fervor in the town, as if everything had renewed itself; the machines, nature, and especially the feeling of again becoming a productive element grabbed kith and kin, and the tempo increased from day to day.

I myself was still a child, but I remember how the town blessed two men for this accomplishment—Pincia Jakubowicz and Szlama Szwarcpelc. The first was a son of Perec Jakubowicz, who was already renowned as an important *magaziner* [owner of a small clothing enterprise] before the war. And the second, who did not play any kind of significant role in the industry before World War I, made the projects possible because of the fact that he could finance them.

After them others came. It did not take long before the Brzeziners had outfitted the Polish army.

What else? There were no longer any sales markets. Russia was shut tight with seven locks, especially from Poland. The economic situation began to worsen again. But this time it was after a period of relative prosperity, and as we know, it seems harder if it follows a time when one has had the taste of better times.

People were very embittered. At that time help came from America. Not only from our countrymen, but also general help came by way of JOINT [American Jewish Joint Distribution Committee], an organization that was very well-known in those days, and also from miscellaneous other American Jewish charitable institutions.

Then various economic institutions were created—first of all, a bank that would help develop commerce, a master-tailors' union that would organize the masters from the small workshops, and together with these a workers' union, a union that would speak in the name of all workers. Also as a result of the organization of the working class, the *magaziners* and also the other merchants of the town organized themselves.

Almost the entire town was organized, the worker sector as well as the *balebotishe* [boss/owner] sector. And everyone, each in his own way, worked intensively to improve the economic situation of its members.

It is also interesting to add that most of the organizations had their own *minyens* [quorum of ten males] where one also went on Shabes [Sabbath] to *daven* [pray] together.

THE ORGANIZATION OF CLOTHING PRODUCTION

In the interim, the situation in the country had begun to improve. The Polish government received large loans from America, and the peasants in the country (71 percent of the population) began to clothe themselves for the first time in their history. The Brzeziners developed the production of clothing to such a high level that one could get a pair of trousers practically for *groszy* [small change], so that at least once a week, Sunday, one could go to church in a pair of new pants. The pants did not last long, but in the meantime, they sewed new pants, and many of the new entrepreneurs (*magaziners*) became well-to-do.

One of those new *magaziners* was Mojsze-Icek Frankensztajn. He had already worked his way up and had begun to travel around the world looking for new markets where inexpensive goods made by Brzeziner tailors could be sold. He discovered what we all already know today, that most of the world goes around unclothed—some because they have nothing with which to buy clothing and others who did not believe in dressing themselves. In any case, there were still enough places to market pants, men's jackets, vests, greatcoats, overcoats—in one word, "We had plenty to do."

In this way, a new stampede for foreign markets began in the town. And prosperity came again for a time—until they saturated one foreign market, and then they had to find a new market. So we see the cycle of "boom and bust," always an attendant phenomenon of the entire economic life of our town.

It is interesting to describe a few features of the work process itself, how it was all organized:

The *magazine*r was the one who worked to fill orders or to generate stock. He bought material for winter clothing such as bolts of fabric and material for linings in Łódź, Zgierz, or Białystok. The wagon driver brought home the material late at night. The town already knew that they would be "cutting" [the material] at such and such a *magaziner*, and so all the master tailors set out to go there to get work. Some sewed pants, some made jackets, and some made vests. Each tailoring workshop made one part of the suit, and later the garment was assembled. It was usually on Friday that the various craftsmen brought back the completed work to the magazine.

It was an interesting scene when all the gates opened to send forth the apprentices, no bigger than Lilliputians—so that they could barely be seen under the stack of jackets that they carried on their small bellies. They ran to turn in the work to the *magaziner* before candle lighting time.

Only on Saturday night did they return to settle accounts. The *magaziner* would find all sorts of defects in the work—there a sleeve hangs a little twisted, there the fold was not properly pressed. All, you understand, aimed at one thing—to take off a *tsenerl* (10 *groszy*) from the piece of work. But in the end they came to an understanding and asked when Reb Chajkel would again be "cutting," meaning when would they have a new batch of work.

Most of the time, among the different craftsmen, the vest tailor came off the best. They criticized him the least. And it is interesting that they were the most respected. It is still a mystery to me today why this was so. After all, it was the least important part of the suit, and yet these craftsmen were more respected than the other tailors. It seems the secret was in the people themselves. The vest tailors were a more intellectual group. They were also small in number, and consequently, they kept themselves a little apart from the larger mass of tailors.

With time, a large number of entrepreneurs developed. I want to list here just a few of them—the firm Frankensztajn-Wołek and Tuszyński, two firms of the brothers Sułkowicz, the brothers Dymant, Mojsze Raszewski, and the Celcer brothers.

Among the tailors, there were a number of very respected Jews who played a role in the community's social life. Later, a number of them became *magaziners* themselves and worked themselves up, not only financially but also to occupy important positions in various institutions. Among them, it is worthwhile to mention Zachariasz Tandejter, Chajkel Grynszpan, Mojsze Fryde, Mote Bercholc, and others.

OTHER CRAFTS AND INDUSTRIES

Often when you speak or think about our town, it seems that the impression that my grandfather's friends in Warsaw had about Brzezin was justified. But the truth is, there were other elements in town. As in the saying we had: "As the wheel turns (meaning the wheel of the machine), so also turns the town."

So, for example, there were a number of spats makers who made the boot legs for the shoemakers, both in town and also in the surrounding areas. Jews were also the owners of three brick factories that were put up beyond the town—Mojsze (Kalmus) Rozenberg, my older uncle Jehuda Krongrad, and Chaiml Dymant. An attempt was also made to bring a new industry into town—stocking makers, but the attempt did not succeed. In this area, a great deal was accomplished in other towns around Łódź, such as in Aleksandrów, Zduńska Wola, and others. Brzezin was, until the last moment, a center of tailoring in the best sense of the word. Its goods were varied both in quality and in quantity.

A printing shop, which was always in Jewish hands, also existed in town. The first owner was a certain Herr Gutsztadt, who later emigrated to America. Then for a short time, the printing shop was taken over by the yellow-haired Natan Łęczycki. The only Jewish typesetter in town was Eli Mote, a Gerer Hasid who was called by his wife's name—Eli Mote Genendl's. This went on until the beginning of the war for Polish independence.

Then a Leipzig printer named Landau arrived in Brzezin and took over the print shop, and in that very place, the writer of these lines received his vocational education. Later Wolf Szeps opened another printing shop, which was later managed by his son-in-law, Jakub Potasiewicz, a Tshenstokhover [from Częstochowa] young man who took Wolf Szeps' daughter, Ita-Małka, as his wife.

FINANCIAL INSTITUTIONS

In order to develop industry and really help individual merchants get through difficult times, a number of financial institutions were established. The most popular and best managed of them was the cooperative bank that was supported by the *Fundacja* (Foundation), which was a division of JOINT. At the head of the bank for many years was Aron Buki, Szaja-Ber Bialer, and Mojsze Froman. In addition to his [Szeps'] son-in-law, Jakub Potasiewicz, the Tshenstokhover, the salaried clerks were Dawid Ikka, Brucha Jakubowicz, Rajza Maliniak, and others. The bank had a very good reputation and was managed well until the thirties, when quarrels began that caused the downfall of this fine and useful institution.

Magaziner Bank. The *magaziners* created their own financial apparatus to help them carry out big projects that from time to time required larger investments.

Gemiles-Khsodim-Kase [fund for interest-free loans]. A *gmiles-khosodim-kase* also existed that gave interest-free loans to owners and other needy people. However, the loans had to be guaranteed and paid back. Mordechai Winter was at the head for many years.

Most of the payments for work and other debts were made by promissory notes and *kvitlekh* [informal IOU notes]. The promissory notes were obligatory contracts and were furnished with stamp marks, where their price was a specified percentage of the sum for which the promissory note was drawn. By contrast, a *kvitl* was a private obligation, as with an IOU for us in America, and it was good only when and if the one who drew it up was willing to pay. Legally, the *kvitl* had no value.

In addition, two government banks also existed—PKO [Polish Guardian Bank] and Kasa Oszczędnościowa [Savings Bank]. There was also a private German bank. All worked with businesses and were able to exist thanks to the enterprise of the Jewish population.

HASIDIC SHTIBLEKH [small houses of prayer]

It is impossible to write about Brzezin and not include the everyday way of life of all segments of the population. It would be no exaggeration if I were to say that our town was a miniature of the entire Jewish population in Poland. So, for example, one found there Hasidim, the middle class, the enlightened, the simple people, and the intellectuals of all kinds. There were a few of each type. Let me now tell you bit by bit a little about each of them—just a little.

I will begin with the Hasidim. In the town there were all sorts of followers of Polish *rebbes* [Hasidic rabbis] such as the Gerer [from Ger/Góra Kalwaria], the Aleksander [Aleksandrów Łódzki], the Grodzisker [Grodzisk], the Skernievitser [Skierniewice], the Radzyner [Radzyń], the Ostrowtser [Ostrowiec], and the Amshinover [Mszczonów], as well as two local *rebbes*—one actually born in Brzezin. True, he did not have a great name, but he conducted a *tish* [*rebbe's* table where followers gathered], and women would run to him with *kvitlekh* [notes of supplication]—in a word, a *rebbe*. He lived amid great poverty on Court Street at Mojsze Kopel's [building], and his fortune was also not grand. I do not know his name or his origins; perhaps others do. The second *rebbe* was an out-of-towner from somewhere. He lived at Mojsze Kalman's on Apothecary Street (its correct name was St. Anna Street), and there he conducted a *tish* for some time with the craftsman group, but in the end he had to leave Brzezin because the Hasids did not think highly of him, and he was unable to gain any respect in town.

Gerer *Shtibl*

The primary Hasidim were the Gerer. The most distinguished inhabitants of the town belonged to this group. Several of them, such as Reb Lajbuś-Mendel Pinczewski and Perec Jakubowicz, were even *tish-zitsers* [followers] at the Gerer *rebbe*. Also well known were Arje Dawid Perlmuter and Chanina Janower and his father-in-law—husband of the dark-haired Sura—who was named Mojsze-Majer (incidentally their son Abraham-Icek later became the *moyre hoyroe* [rabbi who renders decisions on rabbinic law] in town). Then there was an important resident like my great uncle, Abraham-Pejsach, who was the treasurer in the Gerer *shtibl* and for some time treasurer of the Khevre Kedishe [Burial Society]; Szmul-Zeinwel Broder; Josef Soyfer; Benjamin Herszenberg; Benjamin Światłowski; my grandfather; and the Gerer *khazn* [cantor] (Łęczycki). Later younger Hasidim joined who were no less prominent and, in most cases, were more aggressive in the domain of piety and *Yidishkeyt* [Jewishness]—as they understood it.

Among the younger Hasidim were Pincia Jakubowicz, Pincia-Noech Parzęczewski (Fiszel Shoykhet's son-in-law), Fiszel and Lajb Gostyński (Jancze's two sons), and others. They were the *pirkhei kehune* [young disciples] who also took upon themselves to fight against the growing *apikorses* [heresy] in town.

Quarrels and fights in public places broke out when the young and "free" desecrated the Sabbath in public. Some of those who desecrated the Sabbath were worshipers from the Gerer *shtibl*—who were thrown out of there for wearing a necktie or some another offense. In later years, this behavior was not seen, since most of the children of the Hasidim remained within the confines of tradition and grew to such strength in the town that all groups drew their leaders from among them.

The Gerer *shtibl* was located in Szotenberg's building and took up two large rooms, which were always crowded, both during the week as well as on Shabes. The din was very great. Someone was always arguing with someone else, sometimes about study, sometimes about politics, and often about business. In a word, the *shitbl* was the center of all kinds of activities—religious, educational, and political, as well as economic.

Although there were other places than the *shtibl* for carrying on business, nevertheless, all arbitration and controversies were settled there by the Hasidim, strictly among themselves. About *tsdoke* [charity]—it was arranged. The Hasidim knew what was going on among themselves, and they saw to it that whoever needed it got help. One must understand that everything was discreet. Retaining a confidence was not always successful, but nevertheless things were done with tact and good intentions.

The *shtibl* subsisted on small fees paid by those who were better off. The poor Hasidim were not charged any fee. The chief income of the *shtibl* was from the *aliyes* [calls to read from the Torah] that were purchased every Shabes before the Torah reading. Anyone who wanted to buy a prestigious *aliye*, like *Shishi* [sixth *aliye*, a very desirable portion] or *Mafter* [special *aliye* before the reading of the Haftorah], had to pay well.

Those interested in "good" *aliyes* were not lacking, and dramatic scenes were played out during the purchase of *aliyes*. And they had readings in both rooms. They did *daven* together, but the reading of the Torah was arranged so that one could buy the *aliye* twice for the same *minyen*.

In the first room, where the less ardent Hasidim—or the youngsters who also loved to *schmooze* [chat]—were getting ready to read from the Torah, the *aliye*s were a little cheaper, and the competition was not as great. There the *bal-koyre* [Torah reader] was Eliezer-Mendel Rozen (Majer Melamed's son); in the second room, where it often came to quarrels and rivalry, Jakub-Aron Badower was the reader, a nice quiet man who would not hurt a fly. Often, however, he was pulled into various political games about which he himself had not the slightest notion.

For example, this is what happened once during an election campaign when my father got a desire to have *Shishi*, but no matter how much he raised the price, Henoch Pinczewski always outbid him. And when Henoch grew tired, the yellow-haired Natan (Łęczycki) raised the price until my father gave up his desire to have *Shishi*.

I myself was by that time a less ardent Hasid and prayed in the first room. While chatting, I overheard Fiszel Szulc (Lipman's son), and he related with great excitement that Josel Szulem's (Maliniak) [the author's father], a member of the Mizrachi party [Orthodox Zionist], had been properly taught a lesson—he had a yen for *Shishi*, that *Tsinist*! [Zionist]. And since I was involved in the story, and my father's honor was also important to me, I, in the Gerer Hasidic manner, did not think about it a long time and threw a punch at him, so that he saw his great-grandmother [saw stars].

There was a racket and a shouting until my father came in and first properly slapped my face for raising my fist—and especially on Shabes. In short, my father decided to leave the Gerer *shtibl*. If it actually comes to punches and indignities, this is no place for us, he said, and we actually left for home immediately.

But before I leave the theme of the Gerer *shtibl*, I want to relate one more episode about an odd custom among the Gerer Hasidim.

As I previously mentioned, everyone had to pay a membership fee. But very rarely did everyone pay on time, and the *shtibl* found itself in financial difficulties. Therefore, once a year on Shabes, they would take away the *talesim* [prayer shawls], and since no one could possibly be without a *talis*, then for sure everyone would have to redeem the *talis* immediately at *moytse-shabes* [close of Shabes].

What tricks went on during such a Shabes in the *shtibl* is not hard to imagine. People fought like lions, sprang through the windows. No one wanted to give up his *talis* of his own free will. They were taken from everyone—from those who had paid and also from those who did not have to pay because of poverty—so that no one would be shamed. At *moytse-shabes,* the *gaboim* [synagogue trustees] went around to everyone and returned the *talesim* to those who were not guilty and squared accounts with those who were in arrears, and after that, everything went along normally until the next seizure of *talesim*.

Aleksander *Shtibl*

The Aleksander *shtibl* was located in my uncle Jehuda's (Krongrad) building. They *davened* there for many years. They did not conduct any widespread activity like the Gerers did. Also, they were not the same sort of Hasidim as the Gerers—no great scholars were to be found among them. But the people were middle class and distinguished. Among them were Hersz-Icze Edelson (Abraham-Pejsach's son-in-law), Szymsi Erlich, Abraham Szafman (secretary of the Jewish community), Fiszel Shoykhet (Lasker), Chaskiel Najman, Szaja-Ber Bialer, the tall Szlama, and others. Actually, the tall Szlama had a building in the market square and a large vacant square behind the building that he donated to the Hasidim so that they could build a building for themselves there. They did accomplish this, and the Aleksander *shtibl* was the only one that had its own building.

The Aleksander Hasidim did not behave like the Gerer, but piety was not lacking there either.

Ostrowtser *Shtibl*

Among the Ostrowtser *rebbe's* Hasidim was the *rov* [official town rabbi], Reb Jekutiel Zalman Borensztajn. Although he had to pray in the town synagogue among the ordinary middle-class people, he nevertheless found occasion several times a year to pray in the *shtibl*.

The *shtibl* boasted about the rare visits of the *rov,* and a greater number of people always attended on such a happy occasion. My uncle Jehuda was also an Ostrowtser Hasid.

My *rebbe*, Reb Szmul-Mojsze (Litvak) Gajer (although not a Hasid), also prayed in the Ostrowtser *shtibl* (we also studied there and in those years it was almost the largest *kheyder* [Jewish elementary school] in town). His father-in-law, Reb Judel Soyfer [scribe], who was a tombstone engraver—incidentally, the only Jewish tombstone engraver in town—prayed there also.

In the Ostrowtser, as in almost all the other *shtiblekh*, with the exception of the Gerer and Aleksander, they only came together on Saturdays and holidays. During the week there were no *minyens* [quorems] there.

Grodzisker *Shtibl*

The Grodzisker *shtibl* was a kind of modern center. Even active Zionists were found there, such as Herszel Lachman and Uncle Szymele (Krongrad), who not only aspired to have their own land but made *aliye* [emigrated to Palestine] themselves and lived out their lives in Eretz Yisroel. On the other hand, one found people like Szmul-Lajb, the *bal-musef* [leader of *musef*, extension of morning prayer], who happened to believe that only the Messiah could deliver the Jewish people and carry them into the holy land. The only Jewish farmer in town, Joel Bialek, was also one of the Grodzisker Hasidim. He was truly a real farmer. In addition, he was an observant Jew and a saintly man. He spoke in a shrill voice but was very easygoing. They called him the "kosher brother," because that is how he addressed everyone he called upon. He never got anyone angry, and he himself never got excited. In the town they said that his wife, Ester, was an educated woman and even read French. Nobody had heard her, but everyone had respect for Reb Joelsie, the "kosher brother."

Among the more highly esteemed Grodzisker Hasidim were Reb Mojszl (Khazn) [the cantor] Sterns, who always prayed in the Grodzisker *shtibl,* as, according to his contract, he did not have to pray in the [great] synagogue; Jekiel (Szydlowcer) Amzel; Jakub Herszenberg (who was the *bal-shakhres* [leader of morning service] in Grodzisk with the *rebbe* during Yomim-Naroyim (Days of Awe between Rosh Hashanah [New Year] and Yom Kippur [Day of Atonement]); Eliezer Krongrad (my grandfather), the ample Eliezer, and his son-in-law, Mojsze-Josel Opolion, and also Berl Lachman. Berl Lachman contributed to the industry of the town. He had taught his children to be mechanics. They were the only ones who knew the trade of servicing sewing machines and, because of this, assisted in the development of the tailoring industry in Brzezin.

JEWS IN THE BRZEZINER TOWN COUNCIL

When Poland became independent and Brzezin was declared a *powiat* town (a county seat), the impression was often created that the town was under the rule of an external power. The reason for this was that the town proper was completely Jewish, but the surrounding areas were Christian; in addition, the leadership of the county lay in Christian hands.

While elections to the town council (municipal authorities) were in reality Jewish elections, nevertheless, a number of liberal Christians were also elected. One of them was the long-time mayor of the town, Herr Niedźwiedź. He himself was a former freedom fighter and a leader of the Polish Socialist Party, the PPS.

The small number of Christians who lived at the edge of the town did not take any great part in the social life.

However, this situation changed along with the "sobering up" of the Polish masses from their strivings for freedom and their retreat to national chauvinistic slogans.

At that time, several neighboring villages were assigned to Brzezin with the clear intention of reducing the Jewish majority in town. The number of municipal representatives of the Jewish population then became smaller, and their influence continued to decline.

But in the first years of independent Poland [after World War I], the leaders of the town council were, with the exception of the previously mentioned mayor, exclusively Jews. Among them were the vice-mayor, a well-known Zionist, Mordechai Wolf Ginsberg, and all *ławnik*s (members of the town council): Mojsze-Pinkus, Pincia Jakubowicz of the Gerer Hasidim, Jekiel Rochwerg from the business owners, and Natan Wolf from the tailors—all councilmen.

It is also no wonder that the majority of the councilmen were Jews, since, in fact, Brzezin was almost a Jewish town. When you think about it today, that there is not one single Jew in the town, it is impossible to comprehend, since once there were entire streets where, with the exception of the caretaker, there was not one single Christian to be found.

It remained that way for many years. It is also understandable why Brzeziner Jews never felt that they were in a ghetto, which was the case in the majority of towns in Poland.

Over the course of time, the socio-political face of the population changed. On the one hand, the proletariat element grew among the Jews, and on the other hand, the Christian portion of the population increased. In 1929 the left wing of the Poale Zion [Zionist Labor Party], together with the professional unions, succeeded in electing a number of Jewish councilmen to the town council. At the same time, the local Endeks [National Democratic Party] (reactionary right-wing Polish party) elected a large number of councilmen, thanks to the artificial districting of the town. A demonstration started while Mordechai Biedak, the leader of the Jewish workers' faction, was reading a declaration in the town council in Yiddish. The session exploded, and this was the beginning of subsequent conflicts between Jews and Christian Poles in the town council.

That is how the situation continually deteriorated until the Jewish population realized that future cooperation in the town council was not possible.

ZIONIST GROUPS AND AGUDAS YISROEL

The attention of the leaders of the different Jewish groups and parties was at this time dedicated to greater internal consolidation.

A group of Zionists in Brzezin.

The leftist Poale Zion party, which had been able to attract a young and energetic membership, created evening courses for adults. Many of the working youth got their only education there. The Poale Zion party also had a well-run library. Among those who energetically carried on this work was Perla Majerowicz, daughter of the "custom tailor" Sosek (that is how we called him). Later she was also elected to the town council. Among the younger ones were Chaim Rafał Rozenblum, son of the coal dealer; the Szajbowiczes, Monisz and Josef (now in America); the glazier's son, Jankiel-Mojsze Zygmunt; Mojsze Kalmus, a son of the *dardeke-melamed* [teacher of the youngest children]; and others. Most of them were children from poor families.

The Aguda [Agudas Yisroel]—as we called the political party of religious Jews [non-Zionist Orthodox party], of which most were Gerer Hasidim—organized the Shiri Erev [Evening Prayer Group], where we studied Tanakh [Holy Scriptures] and other subjects every evening, and where questions about everyday life were discussed.

This very group deserves to be specially described, since from it came the leaders of almost all the other political and social organizations in town.

At the same time, the Zionist element remained almost without a following—but not for long. Soon a group emerged, actually from the Shiri Erev group, which had, together with a number of intellectual workers and with the help of the leaders of the older Zionists in town—Chaim Baruch Szulzinger, Gerszon Krauze, Wolf Zagon, Aron Fogel, M. W. Ginsberg, and Szymon Mandel—created the Hitachdut Party [Socialist-Zionist labor party]. This party was based on the foundations of Labor Zionism. Its sister party in Eretz Yisroel was the Hapoel Hatzair [non-Marxist labor party]—the present day Mapai.

The teacher or mentor of the group was Reb Mordechai Kochman, an interesting type of observant Jew, who was thoroughly knowledgeable in worldly matters. A poor man himself and burdened with a sick wife and sick children, he would basically come to life when he would meet with his grown-up students every evening and educate them with love and attention, inculcating in them a respect for education and an attitude toward work that revolutionized the entire way of life of the town. The young people with whom

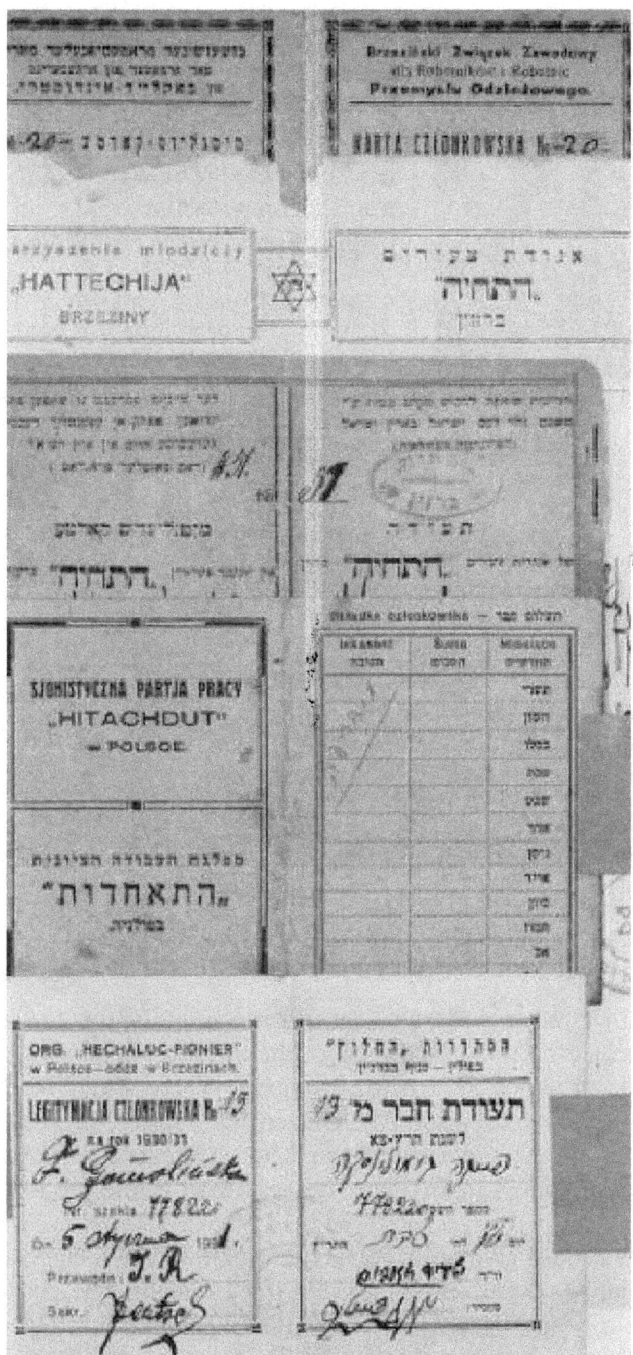

he spent time were not students but friends. And it would not be an exaggeration to characterize Reb Mordechai Kochman as the educator and mentor of youth, about whom much would have been heard had it not been for the war and its terrible tragedies.

Among the more promising of the group were the brothers Szulc, the brothers Gerszt, the brothers Światłowski, Jakubowicz, and others. At the head of that group were Fiszel Mitelsztajn, Izrael Bundowski, Szaja (Zeygermacher) [watchmaker] Rozenblum, and the writer of these lines. Later other leaders of the group developed who expanded the work and created the Hechalutz [Hechaluc in Polish] [pioneers] that devoted itself to preparing the youth to make *aliye* [emigration to Eretz Yisroel] as *chalutzim* [pioneers] of the present day Medines Yisroel [State of Israel].

Another organization that played a big role among Brzeziner youth was Gordonia, the youth movement of the previously mentioned Hitachdut Party.

Membership cards and identification papers for various organizations that functioned in Brzezin.

Intensive courses were conducted for the young through local means and by invited guests from Łódź, the nearby large city.

Aside from this, Hebrew teachers were brought from afar to teach Hebrew to the young, all a part of Zionist pioneer education.

A group of young girls from the chalutzim organization Gordonia [pioneer youth group].

Several earnest attempts were made to organize a Hebrew day school, but it was very difficult to implement because of the heavy costs associated with it.

There was a time when these organizations—Hitachdut, Hechalutz, and Gordonia—were the only active ones in the socio-cultural domain among Jews of Brzezin.

A group of Zionists in Brzezin.

JEWISH EDUCATION

Of the three state public schools in Brzezin, one was set aside especially for Jewish children. The head of the school was Herr Kopler, and most of the teachers were brought from Galicia [southeastern Poland, province of Austria-Hungary before First World War]. Among them were Hanka Erich, Zosia Auster, Mr. Glazer, Mr. Gąsior, Professor Rozenblum, Spiegel (today a leader of the Communists in Łódź), Kujawski, Regina Wajsberg, and others. Most of them remained in Brzezin; they got used to the job there and married young Brzeziner Jews.

The school was located in Majer (Olek) Dymant's house on Mickiewicz Street. Later the school moved to a building that was built especially for it by Chaiml (Blacharz) [tinsmith] Fiszer. The building was in Nowe Miasto [New Town] near the glazier's place.

Besides this, there was a *gimnazjum* [secular high school] in town, on Koluszki Street, in which many Jewish children studied after they completed the public school. The *gimnazjum* was on a very high level and had good teaching personnel who were brought in from other cities.

In addition to the lessening of Jewish rights and the strain on making a living, the number of students in the *gimnazjum* also dropped. For example, it had been accepted that children of observant parents were not required to attend school on Shabes. This right was later withdrawn under pressure of the rising anti-Semitism.

During all the years of the existence of the *gimnazjum*, it was the Jewish sector that actually financed the school. The Christian students—with few exceptions—were exempt from tuition. Consequently, it was natural, with the lessening of the number of Jewish students, that the school closed in 1930. Brzeziner Jewish children who wanted to continue studying were able to do so in Koluszki, where a Polish *gimnazjum* existed, financed by the government, for children of railroad workers.[1]

Jewish Private Schools

Efforts for their own Jewish education began with great ardor. Right after World War I, a number of educational institutions of which Jewish Brzezin could rightly be proud were created.

The first large institution was the *kheyder* Jesode Hatora [Foundations of Torah]. All the teachers in town were admitted to the general educational institution, and they gave up their own unsanitary, and in many cases, shocking *khadorim*.

The united *kheyder* was organized in a modern fashion and divided into classes. Also, the students from the *kheyder* were excused from attending the state public school. This was a concession on the part of the government in return for their having given up their separate *khadorim*, which were, in most cases, conducted in the homes of poor teachers in the kitchen or bedroom, often the teacher's only room. However, the students had to study general, worldly subjects, and our *landsman* [fellow townsperson] Judel Fuks (now in America) was employed as the teacher for subjects like Polish and arithmetic.

The director of the Jesode Hatora *kheyder* was a son-in-law from a distant place, Mr. Joel Dymant. He led the institution with an iron hand. And immediately quarrels arose among the teachers. One must understand that a political battle almost arose from this. The teachers who participated in the united *kheyder* were Icze-Dawid, Majer Rozen, Szmul Mojsze (Litvak) Gajer, Szmul-Jekiele, Mordechai Kochman, Nechemia Melamed, Luzer Watemakher [cotton padding maker], and Szyja Teitelbaum. After lengthy quarrels, the director, Joel Dymant, was removed, and Pinkus Parzęczewski, a son-in-law of Fiszel Shoykhet from Łódź, was appointed in his place—an ardent Agudnik [member of Agudas Yisroel] and Gerer Hasid.

The quarrels, however, were not quelled; just the opposite, they flared up even more. The new director led the educational institution in a much more sectarian manner. And consequently, a private *kheyder* was created by the very same former director, Joel Dymant. A large number of the children transferred to him. He took the teacher Szmul Mojsze Gajer with him, and it did not take long before Jesode Hatora closed completely.

The new *kheyder*, under the leadership of Mr. Joel Dymant, lasted for several years, and the teacher of general studies was Mr. Spiegel, son-in-law of the well-known Doctor Korman. The teachers who had been dropped because of the liquidation of Jesode Hatora

---

[1] Koluszki was a great railroad center in Poland and was located seven kilometers from Brzezin. The railroad in Poland was operated by the state. (Author's note)

returned to private teaching in their homes. The competition between them was intense, and the poverty, even greater. There were fewer students all the time because of the pressure to begin working at an early age and because many parents were not able to pay tuition.

Under such conditions, it is easy to imagine the increase in ignorance among the Jewish youth of the town and the immense burden that was placed on the youth organizations to offer a minimal Jewish education.

Beit Seyfer Javneh.[1] The teacher, Jehuda Fuks, and the director, Lachman.
In the second row from the bottom, one can also see Abraham Rozenberg.

If this did not succeed in systematizing and developing Jewish education for the [male] youth in our town, it is worthwhile to note that in the field of education for daughters, it actually did succeed.

In the town, during all the years between the two world wars, an observant girls' school existed under the name Beis Yakov [House of Jacob]. The school had a large number of supporters and was conducted like a supplement to the government public schools. The school elicited great fondness and operated under the intellectual influence of Dawid and Ester Sułkowicz. Later the administration was officially taken over by Judel Grynbaum, Jekiele Kishkemacher's [*kishke* maker's] son, a gentle young man who also later became the leader of a religious *kheyder* for youth—Khorev.

Only a few years before World War II did they succeed in establishing a kindergarten, where Jewish children of school age received a Jewish education and also a

---

[1] School named after the great rabbinic academy established in Jamnia/Javneh in southwest Palestine after the destruction of the temple in Jerusalem.

food supplement. The writer of these lines, who was then working in the Tarbut [Zionist educational organization] Center in Warsaw, dispatched for the cause one of the best Froebelian [followers of German educater Froebel] school teachers to direct and teach in that kindergarten, which functioned until the outbreak of the war.

SPORT CLUBS

Several sports clubs existed in the town; two of them were the HaPoel of the Hitachdut Poale Zion and Stern [star] of the leftist Poale Zion. However, they were not active in proportion to what they should have been because of the lack of interest in sports on the part of the leaders of the political parties.

There was, however, a Jewish club in town that included all groups. The managers of the club were Icze Lechtreger (now in Argentina), Dawid Szotenberg, Tuwia Krawiecki, Jecheskiel Bercholc, Izrael Tryber, and others.

The club had a good soccer team that played every Saturday afternoon. The competitions took place with clubs from the surrounding towns and caused great interest among the public. On Saturday afternoons, hundreds of Jews used to go to the play area on Koluszki Street, which was designated for that purpose by the town authorities. Previously, the play area was in Szymaniszki, and they used to have to walk three miles to attend a soccer game.

Counted among the best players were the brothers Kornblum, Stach Krengel, Moniek and Janek Zygmuntowicz, and Benisz Piotrkowski.

Finally, it is worthwhile to mention that the people of Brzezin were very keen about theater. In another article in this book, this striving is described and the manner in which it came to be expressed by the local intellectuals. Here, I only want to mention that the finest Jewish and also Polish troupes used to come to Brzezin to perform, including the Wilner Troupe, the Ararat [Yiddish Theater in Łódź], and also American actors such as Jack Rechtzeit, Julius Adler, and others.

Aside from these, in almost every organization, a drama circle existed that used to offer several presentations a year with their own home-grown talent. An orchestra was also organized by Hitachdut headed by Fiszel Kleinert, the *felczer*'s [medical practitioner's] son. This very group not only appeared in Brzezin itself but also traveled throughout the province, to places such as Stryków, Jeżów, Szydłowiec, Głowno, and elsewhere. Everywhere they went they brought joy and life to the lethargic Jewish youth from small Polish towns. Its every appearance, whether in Brzezin itself or in the surrounding neighborhoods, was a holiday-like event.

Election of Rabbis in Brzezin (p. 97)

Fishel Maliniak

As a rule, in the monotonous life of most Polish towns, the election of *rabonim* [rabbis] was one of the high points that brought a little excitement and often left behind it squabbles for the entire year.

Such an election of *rabonim* occurred in Brzezin in the 1920s. Usually, two candidates would have run—the *moyre hoyroe* [rabbi who renders decisions on matters of rabbinic law] at the time, Reb Jekutiel Zalman Borensztajn, and Reb Berl Fajnkind, the *rov*'s [official town rabbi's] son, the natural candidate and the unofficial *rov* of the Gerer Hasidim.

But Reb Berl had declined to run because of the large business he managed in Łódź (together with his sister); consequently, the Gerer Hasidim were left without a candidate.

The Gerer Hasidim, together with the Agudas Yisroel, set out over the land to find a suitable *rov* candidate. After lengthy searches, they agreed upon Harov [Rabbi] Gutentag (Yontov), a man from Warsaw and a pious man.

When Harov Gutentag came to Brzezin for the first time to deliver a sermon, the entire town came to hear him. He made a good impression on everyone who came in contact with him.

However, inasmuch as the Zionists, the Mizrachis, and the ordinary middle class had earlier made up their minds that the *moyre hoyroe* should become the Brzeziner *rov*, absolutely nothing could be done.

The Agudas and the observant Gerer Hasidim employed all their ammunition. All the important leaders from the big cities of Łódź and Warsaw—such as Zysio Frydman, Icze Majer Lewin, and other notable personalities of that time from Agudas Yisroel and other entities—came to town to the Gerer court.

Mojsze-Pinkus, son of Zelig, a well-known community leader in Brzezin town government.

Meanwhile a debate unexpectedly took place in town. There were those who did want the outside candidate—but only because he was the representative of the Agudas. Regardless of the fact that he was personally an affable person and from his entire person there shone out the saintliness a town rabbi had to present, people could not bring themselves to vote for Harov Gutentag.

The commotion went on until the election. The candidate, Harov Gutentag, stayed with Reb Szmul Broder, himself a relative of the Gerer *rebbe*. People by the thousands came to say goodbye and apologize to the candidate. However, they voted for the local candidate, Reb Jekutiel Zalman Borensztajn. In addition, another issue arose, that Reb Abraham-Icek Gutkind, who was also a *moyre hoyroe* and a grandson of the old Brzeziner *rov,* was also running. So good Gerer Hasidim were forced to vote for the local candidate.

The most interesting part, however, came after the election, when it turned out that Harov Gutentag was quite a Zionist and a leader of the Mizrachis in Warsaw, and Brzezin had lost the opportunity to have as their rabbi one of the nicest personalities that modern Jewish Poland had at that time.

It was already too late. The voting ballots were already counted, and until the last day, Reb Jekutiel Zalman Borensztajn and Reb Abraham-Icek Gutkind, of blessed memory, remained *rov* and *moyre hoyroe*.

Brzezin's Way of Life (pp. 98–103)

Abraham Rozenberg

Until the rise of the tailoring industry, the way of life of the Brzeziner Jews was almost the same as that in hundreds of settlements in contemporary Crown Poland [Kingdom of Poland].

As for making a living, they lived a lot better. A large number of the villages that surrounded Brzezin were settled by German peasants, who, thanks to their well-known industriousness, became fat and rich from the fertile Mazovian soil.

Brzezin was beautiful. Superbly beautiful she was, with fruit-laden orchards and cool forests within which the town was set like a diamond in a green frame. Brzezin lay in a valley. From the market square, which was in the center of town, the streets and paths that went to and fro from the surrounding towns spread out like veins.

In the blue summer predawn—long before the sun rose from behind the meadows—in wintertime's extreme cold, dozens and dozens of Jews, either by foot or by cart, set out from the surrounding towns and villages.

From the villages, the cobblers, glaziers, butchers, grain merchants, and horse dealers made their way. From the neighboring towns traveled old clothes dealers, hat makers, the not so well-off dry-goods merchants, bakers—carrying bread, *stritsl* [type of strudel], baked *ferfel* [pellet-shaped noodles], and pastries with them—and petty merchants with various beads and inexpensive jewelry. These were wholesome Jews, not some kind of weaklings. Trudging over the Polish side roads in heat, cold, snow, and rain, enduring the highly pitiful competition at the market fairs—where you often had to fight until you drew blood for a better space—the people earned a living with such hard work that seldom did anyone dare to pick a quarrel.

Brzezin presented an entirely different picture on Thursdays, when the weekly market fair, which was the major source of earning a living, took place. The stars still shone in the heavens when Jews *daven*ed *hashkoma* [first prayer upon awakening] and barely had time for a meal in expectation of the big day. On all the roads that led to town stretched great numbers of wagons, with entire peasant families loaded down with all kinds of food—poultry, grains, and fruit, fresh butter made from sweet cream wrapped in green leaves, soft and hard cheeses, sour cream, green onions, radishes, parsley, carrots, berries, fresh-picked cherries, apples, pears, strawberries, currants, and green gooseberries. Behind the wagons, which could barely move because of the lack of space, were cows, calves, often a goat and a horse. In cages that were attached to the wagon were hens and roosters, turkeys, ducks, and geese.

The four-sided market square and a part of Łódź Street were so overcrowded with stands that you could not toss a pin on the ground. The stalls were stuffed with everything good. There they sold cotton *burkas* [hooded cloaks], jackets, trousers, colorful vests, caps with leather visors, fur hats, boots, gaiters, women's shoes, slippers, *trepes* (shoes with wooden soles), men's underwear, women's bloomers, colorful slips, blouses, aprons, colored ribbons for braids, combs, beads, tin or brass finger rings, bracelets, and cheap watches.

There were stalls with all kinds of *nosheray* [snacks]—caramels, candies, sweet and sour candies, and halvah. The ginger cake baker sold sweet baked goods—honey-ginger cakes, cheesecakes, pastries filled with berries or cherries, long strudels, and sweet *griskelekh* [buckwheat cakes]. At the fair there also were jugglers, organ grinders with parrots, blind beggars, the cripples—who sat on the ground near the old church in the market square and begged and sang heartrending "moralizing" songs—and pickpockets.

Horse and animal trading was done at the pig market. That was "man's realm." The robustly built butchers and horse-handlers, whose blood just about spurted from their necks from strength, with much experience in critiquing, looked at the horse's teeth, felt the beasts, haggled in fluent peasant Polish, and at the end, clasped the hands of the peasants with such force that they just about caught their breath. The peasant women sold fowl in the market square, dairy foods, and fruit. The *goyishe* [non-Jewish] youths wandered about the market square, gaping, examining, and touching everything. After selling their products, the *goyim* [non-Jews] took off among the stands to the deep dark hardware shops where you could get anything from shovels to glittering scythes.

The peasant women and their daughters descended upon the dry-goods stores. Just before dusk, the *goyim*, faint from a day of haggling, clappings on the shoulders, and vigorous handshakes, set out for the taverns. There they allowed themselves to have a fling with roasted goose, chicken livers, gizzards, boiled peas, marinated or shmaltz herring, sour pickles, foaming light or dark beer, and various kinds of liquor—from aquavit to 90 percent alcohol, followed by hard, salty cheese and a hard roll.

There was no lack of fighting at a fair. It could be a peasant who got drunk and had to be thrown out of the tavern, or a pickpocket who was caught red-handed, or even a braggart who annoyed a good-looking *shikse* [non-Jewish girl]. The tavern keepers were somehow all strong and able to handle things by themselves. In exceptional cases, when a tavern keeper could not manage, the butchers with hatchets and the wagon drivers with crossbars joined in.

At Icek Bialek's [the tall Icek's] pond.

Late in the evening, when the peasant wagons gravitated toward their homes, the market square and the side streets looked as if after a battle. The Jewish merchants were weary, barely standing on their feet near closed shutters, counting out the *pidyon* [payment, here, presumably for a place in the market] from the day's earnings.

Brzezin was also the capital of the *powiat* and served as the administrative center of the entire county, which included such cities as Tomaszów and towns like Ujazd, Stryków, Głowno, and Koluszki. The *kaznodziejstwo* [church rectory] and all bureaus of the civil authorities were in the town. Although no Jews worked for the government—in town hall there was one administrative office employee, Chaskiel Najman—this [presence of government offices] added to their income.

Also the annual *los* [drawing of lots] (conscription) was a source of income. Annually hundreds of conscripts would descend on the town to report to the military commission. The Jews of the town had several anxious days. The recruits—especially the Christians—were usually lawless and went wild. The reputation of the Jews of Brzezin was such that no real disturbances took place. Only a very few occasions are known when the fights were out of control. There are maybe a few stories about the strength that Jewish youth displayed on these occasions.

Although there was no lack of flour in Brzezin, there was no Torah center [reference to the saying "If no flour, no Torah"]. Observant and God-fearing, the Brzeziner Jews packed the Hasidim *shtiblekh*. Almost all Hasidic *rebbes* had followers in town, with the Gerer and Aleksanderer in first place. The old *besmedresh* [house of prayer] was packed at all the *minyen*s. Men and women wore traditional clothes. They even frowned on women who wore wigs instead of *kupkes* [bonnets]. They sent the youngsters to *kheyder*. It may be that there was not a single Jewish boy who did not know some Hebrew, but there was no yeshiva [school of advanced religious instruction] in the town. True learned men were very rare; few people had a secular education. Also the Haskalah [Enlightenment] movement that was wide spread in those years in Galicia, Lithuania, and in the larger cities in Crown Poland, had practically not reached Brzezin.

In this manner, Brzezin lived a quiet life, traditional, almost an idyllic life, until long after the second uprising in 1863 [against the Czar], until the waves of industrialization, beginning slowly but surely, undermined the firmly established generations-long way of life that had dominated this Polish Jewish town.

Many causes contributed to the rapid and tumultous growth of the tailoring industry in Brzezin. The proximity to Koluszki, which was one of the most important railroad junctions; the nearness to Tomaszów and, principally, to Łódź, which, in a short time, had become one of the greatest textile centers in Europe; and the fact that in Brzezin, tailoring in general was a widespread trade. Also, the majority of Brzeziner tailors produced finished clothing, contrary to the custom tailors who sewed garments made to measure.

Stream near Probaken where Brzeziner youth played during the summers and carried on love affairs during moonlit nights.

Third, was the lack of a Torah tradition that in other towns gave rise to a sharp resistance to the new way of life accompanying industrialization. All these factors transformed Brzezin in a very short time into one of the largest centers of the ready-made clothing industry in the Russian Empire of that time.

Brzeziner Jews displayed amazing ability to be enterprising. It is worthwhile to take the opportunity to point out the fact that those who were most energetic, daring, and with the most creative ideas, came from the deepest Brzezin poverty.

Without secular education, with rare contact with the world outside the four corners of their isolated town, they reached as far as the most neglected corners of European and Asiatic Russia. The growth of production was so immense that the annual export reached the sum of eight million rubles.

The golden deluge radically changed the face of the town. From Bessarabia and Wołyń [Volhynia], from Lithuania and Ukraine descended traveling salesmen, brokers, agents on commission, and bookkeepers. These were very different Jews, another tribe. Although very Jewish, they sounded *goyish* to the residents. And not only very Jewish, their Jewishness was also foreign, not the same as that of the Brzeziners. One could sense strangeness, bizarre behavior, and scandal from them. Among themselves they spoke Russian and called themselves by their Russian names. None of them forgot that he had left a wife and children somewhere.

The town did not have a lot of time to occupy itself with the "Litvaks" [literally Lithuanians, but used to refer to the Russians]. All of Brzezin became one immense workplace. From Shabes after Havdole [end of Sabbath] until Friday close to *likhtbenshn* [lighting of candles], the town worked. The working conditions of that time were dreadful. From three in the morning until late in the evening. Thursday, Jews sewed, cut, and pressed all night long. The need for working hands was great, the wages, good. Even Jews who boasted that they did not have any craftsmen in their family were not able to resist the temptation. Nine to ten-year-old youths were taken out of the *khadorim* and sent for apprenticeships. But such Jews did not make their children cutters or buttonhole makers, which was considered a bit superior. The entire commerce revolved around tailoring. Shops of accessories, linings, and yarn sprouted up. Mechanics came to town to repair the out-of-order sewing machines. The town grew.

Because of the growth in the population and the need for a place for workshops, a shortage of apartments prevailed. The entire family was involved with the work. In two little rooms—one was the kitchen—stood several sewing machines, pressing irons, and small tables for the women hand stitchers. In the midst of the noise of the machines and the charcoal fumes from the irons, in the midst of youngsters who had the measles, cut teeth, and were sick with all the children's illnesses, entire families ate, worked, and slept, together with apprentices and journeymen from distant places who had hired themselves out for room and board.

The role of the apprentices was difficult, especially for those who came from distant places. They came from towns where poverty reigned and a hopeless future awaited them. They got the opportunity to begin again amid the plenty that prevailed in Brzezin. The prospect of success forced them to leave their poor but warm homes at an early and tender age. In most cases, such a youngster, without a relative, was hired for room and board to learn tailoring. During the first term, the youth was a servant; he carried out the garbage, prepared the pressing irons, carried the basket of the master tailor's wife in the market, carried the work to the *magaziner* or to the buttonhole maker, tended to and rocked the children, and suffered from the practical jokes of the older workers.

Because of the crowding, such a youth did not have a place to lay his head. They prepared a bed for him on the floor together with their own children. He would make the pillows wet with his tears of loneliness. It became easier and better for him when he finally became a finished craftsman. Although these pleasant, nice youngsters used to be badgered and asked for "*pretensje*" [money claimed to be owed], most of the time most of them would adjust, adopt Brzezin, fall in love, and marry girls from the town. They grabbed the prettiest ones. Until today, scattered over the entire world, they identify themselves with Brzezin and speak of the town, especially about the wives of their masters and the Brzeziner kinds of food, with warmth and nostalgia.

The sanitation and the working and living conditions were only one side of the coin. There was plenty of opportunity to earn a good living. One can say without exaggeration that in no city or town did Jews eat as well as in Brzezin. My father, may he rest in peace, used to tell me what they used to eat at his home on Shabes. After the Shabes *davening*, there was sweet liquor with ginger cake, sweet and peppered *gefilte* fish [ground fish patties] with *challah* [braided holiday bread], chopped liver with onions—a short intermission for *zmires* [Sabbath songs]—*cholent* [dish of meat and vegetables kept warm from previous day so as not to cook on the Sabbath], grated potatoes and roasted mutton, sweet *kugl* [noodle pudding], cooked plums with apples, all washed down with a couple of glasses of tea. After a nap, "*gute brider*" [good brothers, comrades] went to the tavern where they ate a quarter of a goose and peppered peas with a keg of beer. Four or five glasses was the average. There were those who drank down twenty glasses! For *shlush sudes* [evening meal at end of the Sabbath] there was herring and jellied little calves' feet (*ptscha*). In wintertime for *shlush sudes*, they served *borscht* [beet soup] with marrow bones, potatoes, and fried cutlets. If, after that they played "oke" [a card game] or "telephone," which used to last until late at night, they would again drink beer and eat fried liver.

True, here we are talking about a group of well-off tailors and buttonhole makers, but, in general, one can say that with respect to eating, the craftsmen lived very well.

In those days, we did not know about vacations. The difficult working conditions almost literally forced the tailors to invent tricks to ease the burden of work. A system was put into place to stop work right after Purim [festival celebrating saving of Jews by Queen Esther] until a few days after Pesakh [festival celebrating exodus from Egypt]. This long awaited holiday, yearned for and awaited during the long winter nights, when the town was covered with snow and frost, was celebrated not only as the freeing of the Jews from Egypt, but also as the freeing from one's own heavy yoke.

They took out the double windows, and homemakers washed, brushed, and cleaned. The well-off craftsmen used to travel to Łódź to buy wines, mead, expensive silk clothes, and expensive shoes for the womenfolk for the holidays. They themselves and the young boys were also not neglected. The custom tailors, artists in their trade, the *kamashnmakher* [spats/gaiter maker] did not have time to breathe before the holiday. At prayer time on *erev* [eve of] Pesakh, Jews and their children, with haircuts, bathed, dressed up in their best clothes, gravitated toward their friends and to the *shul*. In the light of the brightly lit *bote-medroshim* [small Orthodox houses of prayer], Jews with a critical eye fingered the new clothing, sometimes even finding a defect, and wished each other to wear it in good health. In the morning at prayers, and especially after noon, the tailoring people seized the opportunity to go to Rogów and Koluszki Streets, where the wealthy lived and sat on their balconies to watch the parade of silk and satin. During Pesakh, Brzezin smelled of spring, of the odor of very familiar food, and of full stomachs and peace of mind.

Khalemoyed [days between first two and last two days of a holiday] was even more relaxed than the holiday days. They did not work, they ate just as well, but one was freer to go about. What didn't they do in those days? It was the *shidukhim* [matchmaking] season, when one came to look over brides and grooms. They traveled to Łódź to enjoy themselves and see a Yiddish theater presentation. They went for visits and came back. How odd that although the town was small, parents seldom went to visit their children. *Khalemoyed* was the exception.

When the season was a good one, they bought new furniture, a second-hand sideboard, a mirrored closet, a dresser, and an oak table with upholstered chairs. The home was freshly painted, the table covered with a green, plush tablecloth, and freshly pressed curtains were swaying lightly from the mild spring breeze. On the table—red wine in polished little glasses, brown nuts and golden yellow mead, dark brown honey cakes, and sliced sugar cakes. The odor of fried *bubele* [matzo meal pancakes] came from the kitchen, and boiled, strong tea with lemon.

My grandfather used to sit at the head of the table and keep silent. The *kheyder* student, in his holiday clothes, could hardly wait until the guests left. His friends were waiting for him outside to play a game with nuts.

During *khalemoyed*, journeymen changed masters, masters changed *magaziner*s. They used to hire new teachers for the term for the youngsters. After the hard winter, the several weeks of rest, milder weather, the knowledge that during the summer they did not have to work such long hours blew a new soul into the Brzeziner tailors, who were very weary from their heavy toil.

During the summer, they mostly worked until sundown. The crowding in the house was lessened, because the small children played in the street. The days were sunny but not too hot. Doors and windows remained open, wide open. The outdoors—which smelled of fields, forest, and blooming orchards—drew, called, and lured them. Apprentices and journeymen and even masters were often unable to resist the temptation to stretch out on their backs under a tree or to submerge themselves in the cool waters near Probaken, Stawianen, or in the *rzeka* [stream]. After the harsh winter's groats and bread and garlic borscht, it was a delight to eat sorrel borscht with new potatoes, crumbled farmer's cheese with green onions, and the early summer vegetables and fruit.

Sfire [counting of the Omer, the 49 days after Passover] was counted until Shavuos [holiday commemorating the giving of the ten commandments], which was the crowning holiday of the summer. The town was flooded with bright sunshine, steeped in green plants, lilacs, and blossoms. The houses and houses of prayer were decorated with leafy branches and long grass that produced a screaming sound when blown upon. With great efficiency Brzeziner homemakers used to cook and bake dairy dishes and pastries that would give their men great pleasure.

A market day in Brzezin. Stalls and booths with all kinds of merchandise and foods.

It was difficult to part with the summer. It was not so much the fear of the Days of Awe [Rosh Hashanah and Yom Kippur]. The early autumn days were shorter and cooler. The Polish autumn blazed with all the colors of the rainbow. The red flaming sunsets, the bare fields, the falling leaves, the blowing of the shofar, and the chilly dawns reminded one of the passing of summer, of the long, harsh Polish winter.

Although the town was then a little more "enlightened," a little less God-fearing, the Yomim-Naroyim [Days of Awe] were observed according to all the Jewish religious laws and customs. During Sukes [Feast of Tabernacles], they used to eat in common *sukes* [booths]. Brzeziner homemakers on this occasion did not bring shame to their men.

Although *khalemoyed* Sukes was casual, just as the Pesakh one had been, the upcoming winter covered it with gloom. At that time they used to think about double windows, a few cartloads of coal, a small wagonload of wood, and warm clothing. The expected rains, the snowy blizzards, the fear for the older generation, whose sons would have to take part in the lottery for military service, lay heavily on their mood. Simkhes Toyre [festival marking the completion of the cycle of reading the Torah], when Jews danced, sang, ate, and drank until oblivion, was like the last spree of a recruit before he went off to serve his four years.

* * *

With the tumultuous growth of the clothing industry, the population also grew. The shortage of apartments for personal use, as well as for the expanding *magaziner*s, became even more intense. The newly rich merchants and the better paid craftsmen wanted to live better, more comfortably.

In the early years of the twentieth century, a building boom began in town. On the sites of the old small wooden houses, solid brick buildings were erected. Just before World War I, the two most modern houses [buildings] were completed for the Ikka brothers in the market square on Rogów Street, which, by then, even had running water.

Only building for personal use was limited. The new *shul* was one of the most gorgeous and expensive synagogues in Poland. The impressive building—the highest in town—stood near the meadows, opposite the old *besmedresh*, whose walls had absorbed the prayers and tears of generations of Jews. The prayer house and the new majestic, richly decorated synagogue symbolized the old and the new Brzezin more than anything else.

For the new *shul* they brought a new *khazn*. Although Reb Mojszl Sterns was devout and observant—he was also the *shoykhet* [ritual slaughterer]—he was far from an outmoded preacher. As a former synagogue choirboy with *khazn* Gerszon Sirota—a fine musician, violin player, and music expert, he adhered to the modern style of cantorial art. One could feel the influence of worldly music in his compositions. A capable conductor, he established a first-rate choir. Shabes Reshkhoydesh [first Sabbath of the month] during the Yomim-Naroyim, the synagogue was packed with youngsters from the *shtiblekh*, friends, and even Christians, who came to hear his *kdushes* [prayers of sanctification], which he and the choir performed. His musical pieces were heard and sung for months by the journeymen in the workshops.

Parallel to the industrial growth of Brzezin, a series of far-reaching and radical occurrences took place in the life of Jews in Eastern and Central Europe—the rise of Polish Zionism, the rise of the Bund [Jewish Socialist Party], and the blossoming of modern Yiddish literature. Their echo, like distant thunder, was also heard in Brzezin. People began to subscribe to and read the Jewish press in all languages—Yiddish, Hebrew, and Russian. A private library was established that had the works of the classics and younger writers. Half-organized groups of Zionists arose that sold *shekels* [coins/certificates of membership in the World Zionist Organization] and collected money for Zionist causes. The bold slogans and the agitation of the Bund, the revolutionary winds that blew over Russia, the economic crisis that was a result of the Russo-Japanese War also had their repercussions in Brzezin—among the working youth and the youth with precarious professions, such as bookkeepers and so forth. It did not come to any serious disturbances, but there were a number of arrests, and one of the Bundist leaders, Iser Rozenblum, was exiled to Siberia.[1]

The Czarist reaction to suppress the freedom movement was successful. The Zionist movement became semi-legal, the Bund went underground; however, the seeds of unrest and revolt that they sowed did not go to waste.

Although the economic situation in town became normal—and the outlook very good—a discontent that took several forms was, nonetheless, apparent in town, especially among the working youth. The mass emigration to America was one factor. In truth, a large number that left came back, because the conditions in America then were no better than in Brzezin. These "Americans"—with their modern attire, the few English words that they had grasped and used at every opportunity (whether or not they were

---

[1] His son, Majer, a talented painter, was liquidated by the Bolsheviks in the 1930s. (Author's note)

appropriate), the couplets from American operettas and melodramas they sang, the poems they recited and sang (from popular revolutionary poets such as Edelstadt, Bashever, and Morris Rosenfeld), which had become widespread—also contributed a lot to the dissatisfaction and vague longing.

The old way of life no longer fit in with the new Brzeziner atmosphere. The Hasidim, the older middle class, held on, tooth and nail, but they were a minority. Most of the Jews had been transplants from other areas, a number of them half-assimilated sons-in-law with a little worldly learning, who had already dabbled in the Enlightenment; workers who simply had no time to observe the laws and customs; and those who returned from foreign lands and had lost their traditional baggage during the trip. These elements could no longer be content with the generations-old style and had, without confidence, shakily begun to build a new one.

Iczele Mydlak, one of the town fools.

Characteristic of that state of mind was the group Lines-Hatsedek [society to care for the sick]. Outwardly it was a group like all other groups—a place where one prayed and helped the needy. Actually, however, it was something else.

The composition of the group was mixed. There were more better-off tailors, cutters, buttonhole makers—trades that were considered among the more "elite"—small *magaziner*s, and a number of former Americans. Although most of them outwardly behaved traditionally, their side curls were cut a little shorter and their beards trimmed. The majority were secular and pro-Zionist. In their homes they were already less strict about *kashrus* [keeping kosher]. At the conclusion of the Sabbath or get-togethers on Shabes nights during winter, instead of singing *zmires* [Sabbath hymns], they sang, with a glass of beer, "There near the cedar tree," "Hatikvah" [Jewish national anthem], and songs from the Jewish theater repertoire.

This was a generation born and brought up when Brzezin was already an industrial town, which had been pulled into trade or business at an early age, whose knowledge of *Yidishkeyt* was slight, and the old way of life no longer satisfied.

It is not hard to see in advance what kind of spiritual and physical appearance Brzezin would have had, had it not been for the war in 1914, which engulfed Europe like a forest fire and singed the flourishing *yishev* [Jewish settlement]—Brzezin.

The Workers Movement in Brzezin (pp. 104–7)

Abraham Abramowicz

In the beginning of the twentieth century, a violent political storm was already raging over the entire length and breadth of the Russian Empire. Its aim was to put an end to the absolute monarchy of Czar Nicholas II (Nicholas Aleksandrowicz reigned despotically from 1894 to 1917).

Poland, which had many times before raised its flag for national freedom, was particularly sensitive to the development. When the uprising of 1905 spread, it naturally did not bypass any industrial area where socialist activity was already taking place.

The industrial town Brzezin at that time already had a socialist movement that was a part of the socialist movement of the country.

And in those days, just after Russia had lost the war with Japan (1904–5), after the bloodbath of 22 January 1905—known in history as "Red Sunday," when thousands of workers marched to the Winter Palace in St. Petersburg with demands for reforms and were, as a result, killed and wounded—at that time, a socialist leader from Łódź came to Brzezin.

Baruch, the socialist leader, was a good speaker and a capable organizer. The flames of the revolution that blazed over the Russian Empire also reached our town, which was not isolated.

On that day, the tailors' wheels did not turn. The tailors were out on strike!

On the second day, about forty tailors were arrested. There were rumors that certain *magaziner*s let the police authorities know who the revolutionaries were, so that those arrested would be exiled to Piotrków—where they indeed were banished.

This provoked an absolute fury among the workers—the wives of those arrested broke almost all the windowpanes at the *magaziner*s' in retaliation for their denunciation.

Disturbed by the extraordinary happenings mentioned, a number of the important *balebotim* [leaders] of the town intervened and disputed the charges leading to the arrests—and were thus instrumental in freeing the tailors.

The main leader of the Akhdesnikes [United Youth] in town was known as the Finnish doctor. Among the leaders were the pale Abraham Mojsze, Icze Poznański, N. Bundkin, and others.

The Bojowy Komando [fighting squadron] was the executive organ, which had the assignment to carry out all the plans that the central committee authorized.

The participation of the Brzeziner Akhdesnikes and their contribution to the uprising can only be correctly understood when one takes into consideration that the uprising of 1905 rocked and undermined the throne of the Czar and forced him, for the first time, to agree to a concession—the establishment of the Duma (parliament) and a number of other reforms. True, not broad enough, no great satisfaction for the workers, but nevertheless a step forward.

A number of the Akhdesnikes had to run away from town. It became too "hot" for them there. Others were very disappointed because socialism had not been victorious. For many of them, pessimism and passivity were the "natural" results of the "unsuccessful operation."

During the time of World War I, in 1914, Brzezin had been a major strategic point between Łódź and Warsaw, and the inhabitants experienced all kinds of trouble. Hunger, death, and destruction were normal phenomena.

A considerable number of the *magaziner*s left town. They sought safety in the East, in Russia, far away from the war front.

Who can forget the terrible tragedy of the day when the Russians took Jewish fathers and sons from a great number of homes and carted them off to the eastern market square—where the sound of shooting rifles announced that gunfire had killed innocent lives!

The revolution in Russia in 1917 sped the process of freedom.

In November 1918 the news came from Lublin that a socialist peoples' government was established there under the leadership of A. Muraczewski. On 13 November the Red flag was hung on the Royal Castle in Warsaw, which acted as a call to action to all socialist units.

Could such a new event that took place in the land pass Brzezin unnoticed? Certainly not! The occurrences of 7 November 1918 in Lublin and of 13 November in Warsaw reverberated like a flash in the tailoring town.

The Hilfs-Komitet [Relief Committee] of the Brzeziner town council decided in 1932 to relieve the great unemployment that had at that time prevailed in the town. The picture shows how Jewish and non-Jewish workers were widening the river at Łódź Street as one of the service projects.

THROUGH THE TAILORING TOWN

On the day when workers took over the management of the town, the workers' council had before it a very serious question about providing food for the long-suffering, hungry inhabitants.

The workers' committee issued orders to a number of *magaziner*s the first day, to others the next day, and so on, continuously, to prepare meals for groups of fifteen, twenty, or more workers. So it continued for the short life of the workers' council.

News arrived from Warsaw that Andrzej Muraczewski had begun to talk about a coalition with the capitalist parties, which, one must understand, would undermine the workers' councils and also the very existence of the Muraczewski government. And that is what happened; the life of the Brzeziner workers' council was thus cut short.

Brzezin became an important place, where the struggle of the new parties was carried out with an unexpectedly amazing momentum in an effort to win the following of the masses.

Party debates were not lacking there. Major leaders of the directorate used to come from Łódź and from centers in Warsaw. They were such frequent visitors that they were soon rightly called Brzeziners.

Their lectures were multi-sided. Beside political ones, a great number of their lectures were on historical, scientific, and literary themes.

Their contribution struck deep roots that surely influenced later events in town; progressive activity blossomed there as never before. Drama groups sprang up, sports clubs, libraries, and also other activities.

The struggle between the old and the new, between the new philosophical ideas, between parents and children—who had in large numbers begun to go in new directions—naturally changed the intellectual character of the town.

In many homes where life had been conducted according to the traditions of great-grandparents, crises occurred. Under the new circumstances of the town, the appearance of worldly ideas in the homes was simply unavoidable.

The thing that really was unusual in the town was the rapidity of the tempo spurring on the radical process, the very extreme attitude to issues, the general, boundless fanaticism that helped no one.

I will never forget what happened in the town on Shabes Shuvah [Sabbath between Rosh Hashanah and Yom Yippur] 1927.

The Yevsektsiia [special section for Jews in the Communist Party] had invited the editor of the Polish *Fraydenker* [Free Thinker], Długoszewski, who came from Warsaw, to give a lecture on the day of Shabes Shuvah on an anti-religious theme. The news spread quickly through the town. From minute to minute, the atmosphere became more strained.

In the *shul*, in the *besmedresh*, and in the *shtiblekh*, all over, they talked and called on the worshipers to go to Fireman's Hall on Łódź Street—with the rabbi in the lead—and not to tolerate such blasphemy.

On the other side, again, the radical interests joined together to prevent the lecture from being disrupted. The day arrived. On that day, when holy dread spreads through the heart and soul of the religious Jew, on that day, they got ready for battle.

An hour before the room was to open, Łódź Street was already chock full of synagogue-going Jews. They poked and pushed each other in the direction of the doors. There was no question of tolerance. From the angry and loud shouting and violence that drifted from the entrance, they soon came to blows. Many raised their hands, others, their feet. The police chased and pursued them and even shot over their heads; the police chased not only those who came to disrupt the lecture but also the defenders.

So the lecture was not held. The rabbi and the Jews from the synagogue were euphoric, delighted with their victory.

Certainly the lecture did not have to take place precisely on that day, but at that time, those in charge did not see it that way.

After the Shabes Shuvah incident, friction began again among the leftist parties. The left-wing Poale Zion contended that they and they alone were the one and only representatives of the Jewish workers and had the right to represent the Jewish working class. They brought out their heavy artillery, the Borochovism [Marxist-Zionist views of Ber Borochov], and they contended that this was the Marxism of the Jewish street and that proletarian Zionism was the most important and most consistent way to solve the Jewish question.

But the Yevsektsiia denied them the right to be the representatives and contended that their own program possessed the *refue shleyme* [complete recovery] for all people, which also included, of necessity, you understand, the Jewish question. And in the meantime, it was lively in town.

In 1927 Left Poale Zion took part for the first time in the town council election. Among the speakers who came from Łódź for the election campaign was the Brzeziner teacher Judel Fuks. He, like the others, and perhaps more so, was extremely influential and contributed with his heartfelt lectures to the great victory in the election of the first Jewish councilman, Mordechai Biedak.

This Jewish worker-councilman (from Left Poale Zion), in his behavior and actions in town hall, was nothing like the other Jewish councilmen—who did not represent Jewish workers.

For the first time, the town council heard such an "astonishing" proposal—that assistance, such as potatoes, coal, and flour, should be distributed to the unemployed and the needy. The usual "silence" in town hall came to an end.

The violent struggle of that time and the wide support for this proposal among the population, after a number of violent sessions of the town council, compelled the majority not only to accept M. Biedak's proposal, but also to carry it out. It is, therefore, no wonder that the same party, in later elections, sent two additional representatives to the town council, Mesdames Ester Winter and Hamer.

THE STRIKE

Brzezin was known throughout Poland as a tailoring center.

Workers from many towns used to come there. The earnings of Brzeziner tailors were a good deal less than, for example, those in Łódź or Warsaw. Here the workers worked almost twice as many hours a day as in other known towns. Brzeziner products were specifically for export. And the export, ever since the end of the war, had decreased. At that time, the population was larger and the tailoring season shorter. And this had a bad effect on the situation of the craftsman.

The worker's life was made even harder by the fact that in order to get immediate necessary cash, one had to give up from ten to thirty percent of the value of promissory notes [legal contracts] and *kvitlekh* [informal IOU notes] written for dates three or six months into the future.

At that time, a group of tailors joined the Clothing Exchange, which was in Warsaw and controlled by the Bund. After the exchange of a number of letters, the agent from the Warsaw Clothing Exchange, Herszel Himelfarb, came to Brzezin. The meeting was held in the home of Melech Akerman, who belonged to the Bund. The writer of these lines participated in the meeting. We, the initiators, were unhappy with the decision of Herszel Himelfarb not to give the charter (status) to the founders of the professional union—only to his Bundist friend Melech Akerman. But, under the circumstances, we did not have any other alternative. And we got down to the work of forming a union.

The tremendous difficulty that we encountered was due to the fact that there were many hundreds of small workshops in which only relatives were employed. But all these difficulties were overcome. Their own children, sisters and brothers, struck against their parents. The strike did not last long. The tailors now had their union and also won a ten-hour workday. Before this, the tailors used to work about eighteen to twenty hours a day.

Then the professional union drafted conditions that made the life of the tailor easier and more comfortable. A little later, after the time when I left town (in July 1928), the tailors won the eight-hour workday.

People standing in line for bread in front of Sara's bakery on Apothecary Street during the German occupation in 1915 or 1916.

THE FIRST OF MAY

The First of May (Socialist Labor Day) used to be celebrated in Brzezin by not going to work. This was already considered a great accomplishment. But who among the progressive worker-leaders dared to dream of a May Day demonstration in Brzezin?

In 1928 this was no longer a daring dream. Negotiations were conducted among the socialist parties to find common ground for a united May Day demonstration, and such a unanimous resolution was accepted. On the first of May, the various factions marched with their slogans and flags up to the market square. There the great demonstration was formed.

It was still early, and the market square was already full of people. With red flags and banners, the march moved noisily in the direction of Rogów Street. Chants and slogans in Polish and Yiddish deafened the streets through which the demonstration moved. From Cloister Street [Reformacka] the march turned into Apothecary Street [Święty Anna/ Saint Anna Street] and stopped in front of the town hall. The *burmistrz* [mayor], Wacław Niedźwiedź, who was a member of PPS [Polish Socialist Party], came out and placed himself at the head of the demonstration, which extended from there into the market square. The speeches and slogans were warmly received by the assembled crowd.

We gave the Left Poale Zion Party (I was then the party secretary) the honor of bearing the flag. The flag was so heavy—and the wind made it even heavier—that to this day, I feel its weight.

The flow of life carried me to Canada. The thousands of miles between the two points did not separate me from my town.

During World War I we had partial losses in the town, but in World War II, the Nazis destroyed all that was dear and valuable to us.

A Stroll Through Our Shtetl (p.108)

by Jechiel Erlich

I try, in my imagination, to stroll though our *shtetl* Brzezin when our town was still full of Jewish life. I begin in the *rynek* [market square] at Nachman Gutkind's, *e"h* [may he rest in peace], tailoring accessories shop. Right after his place is Chaim-Dawid Klinger's *galanteria* [haberdashery], and then Reb Abraham-Pejsach's haberdashery shop, where his wife, Chana-Golda was in charge of everything. Later the shop was taken over by Reb Mojsze Tajerman, Reb Hersz Icze's older son-in-law. When Reb Mojszele Tajerman became rabbi in another city, Hersz Icze's second son-in-law, Berysz Rozenblum, *e"h*, took over the shop. Then I see before me Reb Josele Hercke's; Icze-Ber Mandel's father's *kashemakheray* [kasha-making shop] and food store; Reb Herszel (Shakher) Bercholc's tailoring accessories store; Reb Herszel Lachman's haberdashery; Reb Chanina Janower's haberdashery; Reb Szmul Jecheskiel's, Shenker's son-in-law's, haberdashery shop; Lajbuśl's, Jecheskiel Shenker's son's, food store; Godel and Henoch Fidler's hardware shop; Reb Szlama Hasid's, the big Szlama's, dry-goods shop.

And further on—Reb Wolf Szeps' lamp and blue enamelware store; Reb Hersz Icze's haberdashery; Lajbele Żychliński's tobacco, cigarettes, and sugar shop; Icze-Ber Mandel's grocery store; Reb Elija Rozenberg's dry-goods shop—Elija Cypa-Ruchel's, as he was called. He was the father of my friend, Fajwel Rozenberg.

I go further—Chana's beer tavern; Reb Mojsze-Kalman, Hajker's son, Rozenberg's paint and kerosene store; Wolman-Jankielewicz's *apteczny skład* [drugstore]; Reb Mojsze Froman's cigarette store; Reb Szymele Krongrad's haberdashery; Reb Hersz Mendel Pinczewski's tailoring accessories shop; Reb Szoel Fogel—a baker, Aron Fogel's father; Reb Welwel Żydek's son-in-law—haberdashery; Reb Dawid Kaufman—paper and writing instruments store; Herszel Srocker—tailoring accessories; Reb Lajbele Hendrykowski—teahouse; Herszel Mojsze Zyndel's dry goods store—his wife Tyla was the shopkeeper; and Aron-Mojsze Jukiel's flour shop.

And from the market square, we go over to Apothecary Street [Saint Anna Street]—Reb Chaim Icek Ajnbinder, Jakub-Dawid Berg's father—paper, books, and writing materials; Bendet, Fajga-Machel's husband—a butcher who had the Varshever *yatke* [Warsaw butcher shop]; Reb Jankiel Froman—grocery store; Zysman Beker—cotton wool factory; Reb Hersz Liberman—grocery store; Reb Kalman Rozenberg—paints; Aron Kalman's, Reb Mendel Liberman, and Henoch Princ—textiles; Reb Abraham Szaja Grosman, the "fat Szaja"—grocery store. Later Ezriel Froman took over the grocery store; Reb Jecheskiel Kolwizner—grocery store; Reb Dawid Hanower—dry goods; a store belonging to the dark-haired Chana-Beila; Herszel Lederman's son-in-law—grocery store; Jankiel Froman, in Małka Chana Erlich's building—a grocery store; Małka Chana Erlich—a soda-water factory; Mendel Liberman—a grocery store.

We go on from Apothecary Street.

Reb Mendel Hanower—a dry-goods store; Etja the herring vendor, Pesa Nar's mother, the tall Abraham's wife. A little further on Surele, the borscht vendor, had her shop. There you could get pickled bran borscht and beet borscht, as well as sour pickled cucumbers. Luzer Melamed also lived in the same house.

And further on is Reb Emanuel Cemak—a small grocery store; Reb Dawid Jakubowicz—made *chlebny kwas* [drink made from fermented bread]. He used to make it in Goat Lane and carry his wares to the peasants who enjoyed themselves greatly with the *kvas*. A little further—Reb Eliezer Opolian's grocery store; we called him the "fat Luzer."

That's how our town stands before my eyes, with its Jews from the past and their ways of earning a living.

Łódź Street. The needleworkers' union and the workers' council were in the house on the right.

My Gate to the Great World (pp. 109–11)

Icchak Janasowicz[1]

Born in the small town of Jeżów, I took my first step into God's great and broad world by way of Brzezin. I do not remember exactly when I was in that town for the first time, but I am sure that the trip was the first *khalemoyed* [period between first two and last two days of Pesakh or Sukes] trip of my life. I must have been about eight or nine at that time, and I remember very well that this trip was an award for the zeal I had displayed studying the *mesekhte* [tractate] "Nedarim" [vows] with Rashi [comments by Rashi]—during the entire winter with the old Yezhover [Jeżów] rabbi, Reb Menachem Mendel HaCohen Segal, *zts"l* [*zeykher tsadek livrokhe*—may the memory of a righteous person be blessed]. At that time, he, our old *rov*, took me with him to Brzezin for a day, together with his grandson Issachar—who was my companion in studying with him during the long winter evenings in his not very warm house and not very homey *besdin shtub* [room where rabbi's court was held].

Between Jeżów and Brzezin stretched a road that one could traverse, with a decent wagon driver, in two and a half hours. Jeżów did not have its own river or its own hospital. If a Jew, heaven preserve us, got sick in Jeżów, and reciting prayers and the *felczer* [medical practitioner] did not help, they used to take him to the Brzeziner doctor. If the *sholem bayes* [domestic harmony] in a Jewish family was disrupted, and now the *tsvelf shures* [divorce] had to be written, they used to go to the Brzeziner rabbi. If God helped, and a man married off a son or a daughter, he used to bring both the klezmer band and the entertainer from Brzezin. If one sold or bought property, he used to go to Brzezin to the notary to sign it over. For a lawsuit in court, you had to go to the Brzeziner court. To take out a passport or get a permit for an amateur theatrical performance, make a large purchase, repair a sewing machine—the way always went through Brzezin, the *powiat* town [county seat] to which our town belonged administratively and in police matters.

Brzezin and Jeżów were, as we say in plain language, a kind of house with an alcove. A Jewish child grew on the Yezhover soil with imaginary fantasies about the big city Brzezin where there was such a thing as electricity. Brzeziner Jews, on the other hand, came to the Yezhover fairs, bought oak-tanned oxen pelts from Yezhover tanners, and sold all kinds of merchandise that twinkled with glistening sheen and quaintness. During *khalemoyed*, Yezhover grooms went to their Brzeziner brides, and the Brzeziner brides were invited by their Yezhover *mekhutnestes* [in-laws]. The strolling about of these brides on Brzeziner streets was a review of the latest styles before the town, and from them, one found out the trends in public attire. Generally, all the news used to come to us

---

[1] Icchak Janasowicz [also known as Yitzhak/Isaac Janasowicz] is a well-known Yiddish writer and poet who is currently a resident of Argentina. His *A House in Town* celebrates and mourns the town Jeżów, near Brzezin. His book *With Soviet Jewish Writers* acquired a reputation throughout the entire Jewish world. (Author's note)

from Brzezin, and we were closely linked to that town and bound through thousands of familial, economic, social, and cultural threads from which were woven our common life on Polish soil.

Jeżów was located approximately fifteen kilometers from Brzezin and approximately twenty-five kilometers from Rawa Mazowiecka. So we were farther from Rawa, and we seldom had any contact with it at all. There were two streets in town—Rawa and Brzezin. People used to go along Rawa Street to the *besoylem* [cemetery], and it would have looked strange if one of the young people had gone out walking on that street. The way to go for a walk from the town was on the street that led to Brzezin. Middle-aged Jews used to go up to the first bridge and turn back. Young people would go walking up to the second bridge, near the windmill. The dreamers like me were really not particular about *tekhum-shabes* [distance an observant Jew did not exceed on Shabes] and used to stray all the way to the state garden. Thereby they came closer to Brzezin, which really was a piece of the wide world, and even more, the gate to that world to which we were bound through our constant dreams of the future.

Brzezin was located on the fat, black soil of Mazowia, surrounded by thatched villages with forests and fields, hills and rivers. The peasants in the villages around Brzezin still lived the life of old feudal Poland. There they still split a match into two. They still wore homespun woolen clothing that was distinguished by its Łowicz [town known for colorful folk costumes] colorfulness; they traded with Jews and consulted them on all sorts of things. The main worry was not to be left in the winter without salt or in the early spring without seeds.

The Jews in towns around Brzezin still maintained the old ways, baking their own bread, and in the poorest homes, right after Sukes, they piled up a cellar full of potatoes and prepared a shed full of wood. Both the village and the town kept far away from the big cities, and in business matters, they strove to avoid them. However, in that respect, Brzezin was an exception. By that time, Brzezin was itself a sort of big city and through its local industry was exposed to remote places. With its sewing, Brzezin reached out to Siberia and, even further, to China.

I do not know what kind of town Brzezin was before the rise of Łódź to become the "Little America" of Poland. In my time, it was a town that had both big city momentum and also small town coziness. The momentum came from the rhythm of work that characterized Brzezin life. Naturally, in Brzezin there were shops, merchants, and *kleykodesh* [clergy]. But Brzeziner Jews, for the most part, were the needle trade's proletariat, who filled all the streets and lanes. The sound of the sewing machines came from every window and filled all the courtyards. The rhythm of work was modern and smelled of the "sweat shop," except without all the industrial mechanization. The fact that the Brzezin Jewish craftsmen did not work for their own local use but for export, and also because they had to use the *magaziner*s as intermediaries, made them big city workers of the industrial era. In this respect, Brzezin was the child of the second half of the nineteenth century, which brought into Poland the sound of rising capitalism with all its ramifications for social life.

On the other hand, the Brzeziner Jew, nonetheless, had his distinctly old-fashioned life style and psychologically did not allow himself to be turned into a proletarian. Even in the years between the two world wars, when the town already had a considerable awareness of social issues and militant youth and well-organized professional unions, a definite patriarchal quality was still preserved in the way of life and left a certain stamp on the battle between wage earners and the master and between the master and the *magaziner*.

True, in Brzezin they carried out the same social battles as in Łódź, and strikes there were not infrequent, but all the battles lacked the sharp bitterness of the large cities, and they almost never led to the outbreak of serious hatred as in some other places. In Brzezin the capitalist and also the master and the worker were from good families, and even though I would not want to exaggerate the idyllic quality in their attitudes in comparison to other towns, there certainly was an idyllic quality. At least, the kind of separation in Brzezin was not as great or deep as the separation of the classes in other places.

Masza Żychlińska was one of the first to open a library in Brzezin.

Measured by the present American scale, Brzezin was a small town bordering on technological primitiveness. According to our views of life at that time, however, it was a town with all the frills. True, the local electric plant furnished light only for a few hours in a twenty-four-hour day, and the shine from the ancient Edison bulbs was pale yellow and stung the eyes with its radiant quivering rays. Also true, the sewing machines were powered by foot. I am doubtful that you could find in all of Brzezin even one sewing machine that was run by an electric motor. But nevertheless, the town for us, the inhabitants of the smaller towns, was truly a big city. When my small town Gemore [second part of Talmud, commentaries on the Mishne] teacher wanted me to translate from the *maymer* [learned treatise] called *Yeshivot Krakhim Kashe* [Yeshivas of the Big Cities], he would use Brzezin as an example, its three-story houses and its cobblestone streets on which, according to him, you "twisted your ankle" as you walked along.

Now, after my wandering over the towns of the world on three continents, I would really have to smile at my Gemore teacher's notion of urbanization, as well as at our own concept. My smile is, however, frozen on my lips in a grimace of sorrow when I remember that all the large cities on the terrestrial globe have never brought forth the emotion that Brzezin brought forth in me, in my youth, the town that was the first *trep* [flight of stairs] of my climb, or descent, on the ladder of life.

I cannot write about Brzezin the way a resident could; I cannot, however, utter the word Brzezin as a stranger, because I was not a stranger in that town. I had relatives and friends there, and I left there a piece of my youthful fluttering heart. In those streets and lanes, life wrote chapters about my youthful happiness and sorrows with the handwriting of naive illusions and rosy expectations. Although my first steps on God's earth were not taken in Brzezin, Brzezin was, nevertheless, the town where I took my first step into that near and far world in which my adult life was formed and matured.

It is remarkable that when I remember Brzezin, I always think of it as that town of good Jewish workers, which, until the last moment of its downfall, was not damaged by the assault of assimilation in Poland. Naturally, in the last years before World War II, there were already a lot of young boys and girls who studied in Polish *gimnazjum*s and spoke fluent Polish. In general, however, Brzezin was still a natural Jewish fortress, and both the language and the life were and remained fundamentally Jewish. How that tailoring industrial town defended itself from the winds of assimilation that raged so strongly in the thirties is a surprise to me to this day. Apparently, the value of the folk style of life and the traditional patriarchal way of life gave them the strength to withstand and maintain their own generations-long Jewish countenance.

Brzezin was only one of the hundreds of cities and towns that the enemy wiped out from under God's heaven. But even so, it was a town with its own color and its own scent. Writing these lines leaves me only with the mournful satisfaction that a part if its uniqueness will be sealed in the pages of the Yizkor book that its devoted sons and daughters publish with such great effort and love. I pray that in the sea of love and longing my tears shall not be left out and that in the chorus of the painful *kadesh* [mourners' prayer] will be my own sincere *kadesh* for that world that was so beautiful and everlastingly radiant and is no more.

A class of children in a state school in Brzezin. The *lererin* [teacher] is in the middle.

Two Victims: Memories of the First World War (pp. 112–13)

Welwel Rozenblum

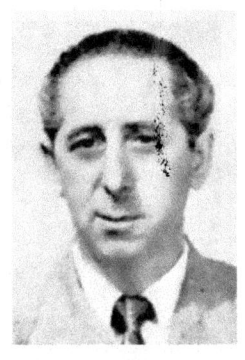

In our *Sefer Brzezin*, I wish to recall the memory of two casualties from our town. They were from two diverse worlds, two completely distinct types. They lived differently and died differently, but both deserve to be remembered and paid tribute.

My memories of these two casualties are, incidentally, bound up with World War I. The worst tragedy that our town lived through in those hard times was the slaughter of ten Jews, carried out by the Cossacks. They took out ten innocent Jews from their homes, took them away somewhere in a field, and shot them—without rhyme or reason. Among the casualties were Abraham Paja with his father, both from Głowno, and another father and son, and other holy martyrs whose names I cannot remember to my greatest regret.

For a long time the town mourned the innocent victims. Every year, they used to go to the cemetery to commemorate the *yortsayt* [anniversary of death] and to say *kadesh* at the common grave for the martyrs.

The Cossacks killed another victim, but not at once. They attacked him and beat him mercilessly, and he died a short time later from the blows. The victim was Herszel Litvak, the Gemore teacher, Tema's husband. Herszel Litvak was one of the most virtuous, observant, honest Jews in town. A pure, holy soul, who all his life, with the highest devotion, served the Creator of the Word and studied the holy Torah.

Since they were our neighbors, I knew them well. Tema had a little grocery store in Josef Grosman's building in Nowe Miasto and never, or seldom, found time to devote to herself, because she, Tema, was, in her great poverty, the finest saintly woman in town. She was always busy helping people in need—the sick, the feeble, orphans, widows. A poor bride was to be married—they came to Tema; attention needed for a poor, sick pregnant women—also to Tema. Somewhere there was not enough for Shabes or for *yontov*—Tema took my mother as her helper, and they took care of the needy. My mother was always Tema's first assistant. One call from Tema was enough; my mother would leave her kit and caboodle and set out with her, door-to-door—to collect alms to provide for someone for Shabes or *yontov*. The wedding of someone who was alone in the world had to be made beautiful. Tema came adorned with her decorated cap from which sparkled pearls, corals, and different beads, and she was as happy as if at the wedding of her own daughter. Also the opposite. If, God forbid, a poor woman died, Tema came with her *khevre-kedishe-yidenes* [women from the burial society] and gave the deceased her due. Wherever, God forbid, a tragedy occurred in a Jewish family, they ran to Tema for help, and Tema never refused. Even if it was necessary to pawn her gold chain and earrings, it did not stop her from helping with an open heart.

Tema also helped free young men from conscription. How this Jewish woman, who was not dressed according to the latest fashion, was able to call on the authorities, on Dr. Stodółkiewicz, and be received and ask for the freedom of many young men was a mystery—but if you will, it was no riddle at all. All laments, all secrets were brought to Tema; she received everyone as a guest, she sought to help everyone, because she was everyone's mama.

But her own house, her own family, her own grocery store, she neglected in order to help others. And if a customer finally showed up in the store, Reb Herszel had to interrupt his studies with the *bokhoyrim* [students] and go into the store. But he stood there as if lost; he did not know what to do in the little shop. He would stand inept, and like a child who looks for its mother, he would give a groan, "Ay, Tema, Tema, where are you?"

While Reb Herszel was absorbed in another world, in a world in which one had to serve the Creator of the Word with complete devotion, with heart and soul, he had to awaken me continuously to tell me to be pious. "Welwel, Welwel," he would encourage and practically beseech me, in his Litvak Yiddish, to *daven* every day and recite a chapter of the Book of Psalms. "If you can't recite all day, at least one chapter," he used to beg me. The great goodness, the great love shone out from his deep, clever eyes.

The Family of Reb Herszel Litvak
Sitting in the first row from right to left: Jakub-Icek, Reb Herszel's wife, Tema (known as the mama of the city), Sima with her child Isroelik on her lap, Cywia, and Sura-Chana. Standing from right to left: Cyna-Ruchel, Josef-Henoch and Hersz-Chaim.

"One has to prepare, Welwel," he would always remind me. All his life he continuously prepared and fulfilled *mitsves* [commandments] with *maysim-toyvim* [good deeds], until on a cloudy, dreary day before noon, when the entire town was in hiding from the Cossacks who were killing and carrying out a pogrom, they grabbed him, Herszele, and murderously beat him. He could not survive long after the death blow, and his saintly, pure soul departed.

They had to bring the body to burial. A double fear dominated everyone. The town was bombarded from all sides by the Germans. They were afraid to lift their heads from their hiding places, and they trembled and shook even more over the Cossacks. While the town was not in anyone's hands, empty both of Germans and of Russians, my father and the tall Mene, *e"h* [may he rest in peace]—they both were on the board of the tailors' association and members of the Khevre Kedishe [Burial Society]—they, and also other neighbors, began to prepare for the burial. But they could not get any hearse in which to lay the body and take it to burial. They finally succeeded in getting a small peasant wagon and a horse. They lay the body inside and covered it with straw, and in great haste and with great fear, they reached the cemetery. They dug the grave quickly, and Reb Herszel Litvak was buried in a quiet, safe place, without any fear of the Cossacks or other killers of Jews.

Josef Henoch, his son, crying all the while, said *kadesh*. But before returning after the burial, shooting flared up again, and bullets flew over their heads. My father, the tall Mene, Tema and her children, and the few neighbors miraculously—but barely—made it home alive, and they again had to hide themselves from danger.

All his life Reb Herszel prepared himself. He was very pious, very observant, righteous, and faultless. Cutthroats came and murdered this saintly Jew, and together with the other ten martyrs, an eleventh was also murdered, martyred as a Jew—Reb Herszel Litvak, *e"h*.

* * *

The war in our town quieted down and was carried over to other fronts, each time further away and deeper into Russia. During that time, the Germans took power and governed with a strict hand. They requisitioned everything, took it over and sent it to Germany, and for the population in Poland, there was little left to make a living. They struggled and did everything possible in order to be able to exist. However, the Germans of that time gave the population a certain freedom. They were permitted to organize various associations.

The youth used it and organized a Zionist association—Hattechija [The Revival]—a people's association, a Bundist one, and many others. Libraries were created around the associations. Lecturers were brought from Łódź or Warsaw. They arranged evenings of entertainment and lectures, established drama groups. I myself joined the Zionist association Hattechija and later became a member of the Zionist youth organization Hashomer Hatzair [Young Guard]. We had a wonderful, sincere youth group of fine boys and girls.

Majer Rozenblum is the one most strongly engraved in my memory. We had the same last name, but we were not related. Majer was very gifted and artistically inclined. He painted with an artistic talent and also possessed other abilities. His grandfather, Mojsze-Jojne Rozenblum, raised him. His father, Hersz-Iser, was in prison and was also deported to Siberia because of his revolutionary activities. If his mother was alive and shared the same fate as his father, I do not know. I only know that Majer was a delicate, dreamy young man, with dark-brown, sparkling eyes. His youthful mischievousness very often banished the sadness that would spread across his refined face.

On the various excursions we made together with our friends from surrounding towns and villages, our Brzeziner Hashomer Hatzairnikes [members of Hashomer Hatzair] always excelled in various ways. One of those occasions was in Głowno, at a well-to-do landowner's. We played various sports games and sang Yiddish and Hebrew folksongs. Majer drew caricatures and good-naturedly made fun of everyone. Together we authored humorous songs and helped create a joyous, sincere, friendly atmosphere.

We ate near the estuary, cooking in the camp kitchen. We slept in barns and carried out our joyous singing until night disappeared and morning stars showed that a new day was born. We returned to the town singing and marching in rows and dedicated ourselves once again to our organizational tasks.

We had success in the field of theater plays. I dramatized the recently published Yizkor Book, which depicted the heroic fight and death of our guardians of Eretz Yisroel. I wrote a play in three acts. The entire winter we prepared, rehearsed, and learned our roles. During Khalemoyed Pesakh, we raised the curtain before a large crowd in Firemen's Hall. My heart trembled; I was scared. Would we succeed in portraying the dramatic battle, the sacrifice of our guardians in Eretz Yisroel? Would we pass the test? When the curtain came down after the last act, the people applauded loudly and showed great pleasure and recognition for the Hashomer Hatzairnikes and for the memorial play.

Not long afterward, shocking events occurred. The Germans began to lose the war on all fronts, and the revolution broke out in Russia. Poland became an independent country. In 1920 I was forced to flee and save my young life. Luck was in my favor, as I came to America. My friend Majer Rozenblum and many other friends of mine, unfortunately, remained stuck in anti-Semitic Poland. Repression, pogroms, and political and economic oppression induced my friend Majer to join the Communist Party.

It did not take long before he was arrested. Then began his horrible suffering in Polish prisons. When he was finally freed, his health was already undermined. But Majer had one desire—to get out of Poland and run to the "Socialist Garden of Eden" [Russia]. After great difficulty, he finally succeeded. He thought that he was finally rescued, but there, new troubles began for him. They looked at Polish-Jewish Communists with a particular suspicion, and at the time of the great purges, Majer Rozenblum was also purged, with a bullet to his head.

Majer Rozenblum came from a family of idealistic revolutionaries. His father, Hersz-Iser Rozenblum, was a well-known Bundist activist. When Majer was very young, his father and mother were exiled to Siberia for revolutionary activities, and the child was brought up by his grandfather, Reb Mojsze-Jojne Rozenblum. Because of this, he called his grandfather "Papa" and his grandmother "Mama." Only later, after many years, returning from exile, did he get to know his real parents well.

His aunt, Basia Rozen, Syna Naczelnik's [director] wife, the mother of several grown children at that time, was put forward by the United Workers in Brzezin as the first member to the town council. The list, however, was declared void. She would certainly have been elected.

Majer read a great deal, was a sensitive young man with a fine sense of humor and satire, physically weak, with an artistic sense for painting. His portrait of Ber Borochov [Marxist-Zionist leader] adorned the Poale Zion library in Brzezin and was praised strongly by art connoisseurs from Warsaw and Łódź. He had the possibility of a far-reaching future, and they predicted a great career for him as an artist. But his path was destined to be different.

After the decline of Hashomer Hatzair, he, together with several friends from bourgeois homes, organized the Communist Party in 1924. He, more than the others, involved himself with boundless, unlimited devotion and idealistic fervor with the active workers from other workers' unions and especially with the professional unions, participating in cultural evenings and discussions, teaching the workers the importance of class struggle.

Majer became secretary of the Communist Party in the Brzezin region and also party operations manager. Under his authority were the local operational people who carried out rigorous covert conspiratorial work, such as spreading illegal literature, hanging out flags and banners at important places—even under the nose of the police—with antigovernment slogans, calling on the workers and the people to rise up and revolt.

Because he was a photographer with his own studio and conducted business with different strata of the municipal population, his address was less suspicious. As a matter of fact, illegal meetings were held at his home, but that did not last long. In March 1927 his apartment, on the third floor of Arje Dawid Perlmuter's house, was surrounded by the police. As secret agents were coming into his room, he still had time to throw a considerable amount of illegal literature out of the window, which the police, standing outside, found and later brought to court as evidence against him. After the search, he and other active leaders—such as Lajb Sieradzki, Jankiel Dawidowicz, and others—were arrested and sent to the political prison in Łódź at 13 Długa Street, where he stayed several months before being sentenced to four years in prison.

After the Warsaw appeals court confirmed the sentence, despite a good defense by two first-class lawyers, he was sent to the famous Łęczyca prison for political criminals. The prison regimen there was not severe. Majer had special privileges because of his artistic ability, painting large portraits of the prison head's family. At that time, in addition to Communists in the Łęczyca prison, there were also Ukrainian and White Russian nationalists who were striving to secede their territories from Poland. A great percentage of intellectuals, writers, and important political leaders, as well as former Sejm [Polish Parliament] deputies were there. Majer also took a course in the Russian language and studied with great zeal.

However, in a year and a half, even the milder prison regimen undermined Majer's weak health. Efforts were made to exchange him for a Polish political prisoner in Russia, but this would have taken a long time. After great effort, he got a six-month health furlough. After the six months, he was supposed to return to prison; also every day that he was free, he was to report to the police. Majer used the health furlough to flee to the free city of Danzig, with the idea of going to Russia. After waiting several months, he and his wife, Lyuba (youngest daughter of the late Mojsze Aron Szotenberg, a wealthy man) traveled on a Soviet ship to the land of "freedom and equality" for which he had so longed. Later his friends from prison also went there—Lajb Sieradzki, Aron Rozenberg, and later Judke Lechtreger.

In 1933 Majer and all his friends, because of their Russian comrades, were shot there as spies.

A tragedy, Majer, that your young life was so dreadfully, horribly cut short. If you had not been seduced by false Messiahs, perhaps you would now be in Israel, in America, or somewhere else in the free world. You would have had influence and perhaps been famous as a Jewish artist. I often think of you, and it grieves my heart. Even now I shed a tear for you. Blessed is your saintly memory!

Left Poale Zion [Zionist Labor Party] in Brzezin in 1931

In the Poale Zion Almanac of 1931 a list was published of all the members of Left Poale Zion in Brzezin who were active that year. The names that are listed here were signed on a greeting for the 25th-year jubilee of the Poale Zion movement. Only a few of the listed individuals remained alive after the destruction.

1. Benkel
2. Liberman, Melech
3. Pakula, Zelig
4. Rozenblum, Chaim Rafał
5. Szajbowicz, Monisz
6. Biedak
7. Winter, A.
8. Brejtsztajn, F.
9. Krauzchorn, H.
10. Minc, Z.
11. Pajczer, R.
12. Pajczer, S.
13. Rozman, H.
14. Kon, P.
15. Lisman, M.
16. Cynamar, B.
17. Kalmus, L.
18. Lerer, I.
19. Szajnzylber
20. Zygmunt, R. L.
21. Rotsztajn, I. L.
22. Hamel, W.
23. Rotsztajn, F. L.
24. Dajcz, R. L.
25. Szwarc, M.
26. Sztajnberg, Sz.
27. Gerszonowicz, I.
28. Mandel, H.
29. Kolski, M.
30. Kalmus, A.
31. Frydman, A.
32. Grynszpan, I.
33. Majerowicz, D.
34. Herszkowicz, L.
35. Fogel, Melech
36. Pajczer, A.

Herzl Society in Brzezin (p. 116–17)

In 1904 a Zionist organization was created in Brzezin and took the name Agudas Herzl [Herzl Society]. This occurred several months after the death of the creator of political Zionism and founder of the World Zionist Organization, Dr. Benjamin Zav (Theodor) Herzl. In order to especially honor the memory of the immortal leader, the founders decided to call the organization by his name.

The founders of Agudas Herzl in Brzezin were immediately in contact with the Zionist representative in Łódź, the well-known rabbi, Dr. Jelski, preacher from the "German" [Progressive] synagogue in Łódź, who was one of the first Zionists in Poland and had under his jurisdiction the Zionist organizations in Łódź and the Łódź area.

We bring here three documents concerning the founding of Agudas Herzl in Brzezin. The documents were written in Hebrew, which demonstrates the attachment of the first Zionist leaders in Brzezin to the old-new language of the Jewish people. We print here a Yiddish [now English] translation of the three documents.

Document 1

Herzl Society in Brzezin

Founded on *moytse-shabes* [the end of the Sabbath] occuring at the beginning of the Torah portion *Lekhlikhol*, Genesis 12.1, version 1, eighth month of the Hebrew calendar—October 1904.

The Committee:

Chairman: Chaim-Icek Grynfeld
Vice-Chairman: Mojsze Ber Hamer
Secretary: Mojsze Fiszman
Treasurer: Szymon Krongrad
Controller: Arje Nubiński
Organizational Representatives:
    Lajbuś Fuks
    Jakub Sułkowicz
    Nachman Gutkind
    Herszel Cwerner

Statute of the Organization:

1. Every Jew may become a member only with the approval of the chairman.
2. The list of members is maintained by the vice-chairman, and new members have to apply to him.
3. Every member must pay monthly dues, in accordance with his ability, for the organization and for the general Zionist organization.

4. The money collected from the monthly dues goes to our local organization, and the rest of the money, according to the vote of the committee, which meets at the end of every year, that is, at the end of the month of Elul.

5. Every member who sells five *shekels*[1] to people who do not belong to our organization and also buys a share (in the Jewish Colonial Trust) will be included as an honorary member and will have the right to participate in committee meetings.

6. Every new member must pay, upon joining the organization, the sum that the committee decides.

7. Two members of the committee will collect the dues on a monthly basis.

8. A member who does not pay his monthly dues over the course of three months will be removed from the organization.

Document 2

b"h [*borkhashem*—Blessed be God's Name], Tuesday, *parshat Vay-khi,* Tevet, (December 1904), Brzezin.

To harav hakhokhm [the sage] Dr. Jelski
Warsaw
Zionist Circle—Łódź

In response to your letter of the third of Kislev [11 November 1904], page 10, Number 61, we have the honor of enclosing the minutes of our last meeting with the names of the committee and the bylaws according to which our organization operates. In the next few days in Łódź, one of our group, Warszajnlich, the chairman, will visit you concerning our organization, and he will purchase the amount of *shekels* we need, also forty pamphlets of "The Shekel." We received the ten pamphlets of "Doctor Herzl," and we distributed them among our members. We thank you very much for the pamphlets. We can assure you that this will help spread our great concept in our town.

Finally, we ask you again to certify our organization and to send us letters and circulars. We also ask you to send us twenty-five receipt booklets to record the payments of installments for the shares (in the Jewish Colonial Trust) that we are promoting among the friends of our movement.

With respect and with *Tsion* greetings [Zion is in our hearts]

Chaim Icek-Grynfeld

---

[1] The Zionist *shekel,* named after an ancient Jewish coin, was a certificate in the World Zionist Organization and was proof of payment of membership fees. Buying the *shekel* was a condition for the right to vote and eligibility for election to the Zionist Congress.

Document 3

Minutes of the meeting of the Herzl Society

Moytse-shabes parshat Mikets [parsha read during Khanike], the third of Tevet (January 1905)[1]

A. The chairman opened the meeting and read aloud the answer from Dr. Jelski of Łódź to the letter regarding the establishment of the Herzl Society in Brzezin.

B. The treasurer gave a report that to date the sum of nineteen rubles from monthly dues and other income has been collected by our members.

C. The bylaws were unanimously accepted by all members, and it is determined that they should be written into the organizational book by the chairman.

D. The motion of the vice-chairman, Mr. Dawid Hamer, not to obligate the members to buy shares in the Jewish Colonial Trust, even in installments, was tabled until the next meeting.

E. The motion of member Szulem Litwin concerning reading Tanakh [Holy Scriptures] and chapters of Jewish history every Shabes before the members, was rejected by a majority vote, because the local conditions are against it and could damage the development of our movement in our town.

F. The meeting came to a close with the singing of Zionist songs.

---

[1] According to calculations, 3 Tevet was actually 11 December 1904.

Chaim-Icek Grynfeld, *z"l*

Reb Chaim-Icek Grynfeld was a Hasidic *maskil* [adherent of Haskalah—Enlightenment] and occupied an honorable position among the distinguished people of the town. He was among the *rashoynim*, the first prophets, of the Zionist movement in Brzezin. At the time when political Zionism was still in its early days, Reb Chaim-Icek Grynfeld came and created the first Zionist organization in our town, the Agudas Herzl. This was in the year 1901. Important documents about the previously mentioned organization have been cited above.

We also want to relate here a very tragic episode in the life of Reb Chaim-Icek Grynfeld, which had at that time provoked a storm of protests from the inhabitants of our town, both Jews and non-Jews. We have in mind here the historic situation when Brzezin was occupied by the Germans during World War I and the occupiers had condemned to death, among others, the leader of the community, Reb Icek Grynfeld, who, at that time, occupied an important post in the *kehile* [Jewish community council] of Brzezin.

Reb Chaim-Icek Grynfeld, founder of the Zionist organization in Brzezin.

"In the year 1914, Friday, *Parshat* Noah" [day on which that Torah portion is read], his son, who is now in Israel, told us, "Jews and Christians went to plead that the person condemned to death be freed. The protest activity on the part of the general population had such an effect that the very next day, a commission from the general staff in Warsaw was brought in, and after they had listened carefully to all the details, he was freed." On the day he was freed, he took upon himself a voluntary oath to observe a fast every year on that day, and he indeed did observe it as a pious Jew.

Between the world wars Reb Chaim-Icek Grynfeld emigrated to Palestine and died there. *Koved zayn ondenk!* [Honor to his memory!]

Jewish Sports in Brzezin (pp. 118–21)
Abraham Rozenberg

Brzezin, between the world wars, was like a two-sided coin. On one side, the blooming of a community, secular life, elementary education for children, libraries, lectures, cinema, and theater-performances—on the other side, economic decline and hopelessness.

After World War I, Brzezin did not recover. The hermetically sealed Russian marketplace and the anti-Semitic governmental policy had a strong and catastrophic effect on the tailoring industry, which was Brzezin's only source of income.

With difficulty and bitterness the town struggled for a piece of bread. The more difficult conditions, the hopeless outlook for the young, the mass emigration that took away the best and most active young people, and perhaps a premonition of the future catastrophe—weighed heavily on the mood. And when one falls into such a mood, one looks for escape in secular pleasure, living in the present moment. One of these pleasures, which captured the hearts and minds of the small town youth, and older people too, was sports—physical culture in all its forms.

Before the end of World War I, physical culture and organized sports were unknown in Brzezin. Of course, Jewish children played, ran, leapt, swam, skated, and wrestled. But this was rather instinctive, before taking care of the body became so popular.

Before Brzezin became a tailoring town—in the early 1890s—most of its Jewish inhabitants were famous for their strength. It was not an accident that even the elderly could not remember a pogrom, not because their Polish neighbors loved the Jews so much, but just simply because they were afraid to pick a quarrel.

The closeness to nature, the fresh, delectable air from the surrounding fields and forests, and the resulting satisfaction, made the children of the town physically sturdy.

Shabes, *yontov*, after *cholent* [baked dish of meat and vegetables kept warm from the day before Shabbat], when the parents took a nap, young people went out in the street, onto the meadows, and let loose their accumulated energy. We sprang over the *rzeka* [stream], carried on *walka*s [fights], and played various games. One of the most popular games was *palant*. This was a team game with a *piłka* [ball] and a *klipeh* [a sort of stick], very similar to the American game of baseball.

The rise of tailoring had a negative physical effect on the state of health in the town. The crowding, the unsanitary conditions, the long hours of work, and sending children at an early age into stuffy workshops contributed to a physical decline.

World War I changed the situation radically. The clothing industry became paralyzed overnight. Need, simple hunger, as well as the Germans, took over the town.

How strange! Although Jews suffered from hunger, it did not show outwardly on their faces. They were forced to resort to their former occupations. Traveling through the villages, smuggling—which involved immense, physical risk—and the difficult treks over the highways and through the forests, these straightened out the bent backs and returned color to the pale emaciated Brzeziner tailors. The generation that was brought up in those four years was taller and more robust than their parents.

The period 1917–20 was the springtime period of secular community life in Brzezin. All the secular parties and organizations came into being at that time. One of the first was the Zionist youth scouting movement—Hashomer Hatzair [Young Guards].

Hashomer Hatzair, modeled after the English scouting movement, in addition to spreading the Zionist ideal among youth, popularized and promoted the slogan "in a healthy body, a healthy spirit." Its members engaged in elementary gymnastics, gymnastic formations (such as pyramids), and quasi-military exercises. On their overnight trips, they slept in tents on the bare ground in fields or forests. In khaki shirts and knickers, they marched through the streets of the town in military formation, keeping time to music with Hebrew songs.

Hashomer Hatzair lasted but a few years, but it left an enduring stamp on the youth of the town, who had become almost entirely disconnected from the old way of life. The changes manifested themselves both in style of clothing and also in the satisfaction derived from being in the open air.

On sunny Shabes afternoons, in the summer moonlight, the young people played on the lakes near Probaken and sang sweet haunting Russian romantic, Zionist, and worker songs. In addition, in winter, when the frost crackled, we skated there on steel ice skates or rode in sleighs.

The predominant political and spiritual set of circumstances caused an increased emphasis on the value of the balance between muscle and mind, body and soul. This led to the rise of the sports movement at the beginning of the 1920s.

The first to take part in athletic games were the children of the Brzeziners who had been evacuated with the Russian armies at the beginning of World War I and had come back to Brzezin after the revolution.

About 1921, in Szymaniszki, about two *verst* [1 verst = .66 of a mile] from the town, opposite the Tadzin Forest, on a flat field that was ideally suited for soccer, the children of the former Brzezin aristocracy began to play—the brothers Zygmuntowicz, Dawid Szotenberg, the distinguished goal keeper Stach Krengel, the Bercholc brothers, and others.

Brzeziner Jewish children in a sports competition.

Because they were few in number, they encouraged, gathered, and taught the young ones, who were captivated and threw themselves with might and main into sports.

In a short time, hitting the ball took on epidemic proportions. At dawn on Shabes summer days, instead of going with one's father to pray, the young people, through roundabout detours, in order to avoid the "evil eye," were drawn to the playing field. There, they threw off their Shabes clothing, put on short pants, shirts, and special shoes and with great zeal took to training. During the week, they hit balls at all the vacant lots, in the courtyards, and in the streets. Little by little, a group emerged that dominated the sport, and they were ready to participate in the game in an organized way.

In 1924 the BKS (Brzeziński Klub Sportowy) [Brzezin Sports Club] was formed. The founders and lead players were Stach Krengel, the brothers Janek and Moniek Zygmuntowicz, Dawid Szotenberg, Abraham Abramowicz, the brothers Izrael and Szyja Kornblum, the brothers Chaskiel and Dawidke Bercholc, Anczel Lustig, Aszer Bocian, Syna Zylberman, and others. The club consisted of several *drużyny* (teams), part of the Polish soccer league, Class C. Later the club moved up to Class B. The club had a number of first class players and competed with such masters as LKS (Łódzki Klub Sportowy) [Łódź Sports Club] and Lodzer HaKoakh [power]. In addition to soccer, there were also sections for ping-pong (table tennis), cricket, tennis, and recreational activities. The club had its own premises on Rogów Street.

In 1926 the sports club Stern (Gwiazda) [Star], which was under the influence of the Left Poale Zion [Zionist Labor Party], was formed. Among the founders and players were A. Abramowicz, Majer Ber Szwarc, Mojsze Goldman, and others. In additon to soccer, they had a section for recreational activities. Mostly, they devoted themselves to excursions (*wycieczki*) in the surrounding areas, which were distinguished by their natural beauty. Their premises were on Court Street at Mojsze Kopel's.

In the year 1927–28 the TMS (Towarzystwo Miłośników Sportowych) [Society of Sports Lovers] began. Among the founders and players were Dan-Aszer Fogel, Nachum Nowak, Icze Mandel, Lajbel Jerozolimski, Szmul Rozenkranc, Lajbel Szyftman, Benjamin Bonian, Zelig Frydman, and others. This club, which was not associated with any political party, had the following sections—ping pong, bicycling, and recreational sports. Their premises were on Apothecary Street.

Besides those mentioned above, at a lower level, existed the club HaKoakh, the Sports Association of Hitachdut, and the Prąd (Stream), under the influence of the leftists. These clubs did not last long.

Besides organized sports clubs, the youth were strongly devoted to swimming, ice skating, bicycling, tennis, and gymnastics.

* * *

As described in this chronicle, the reader can get some notion of the role that sports competitions, matches that usually took place on weekends, played in the life of the young. The excitement, the nervous tension, the glee or sorrow when the town club won or, *kholile* [God forbid], lost a match. If I may be so bold, both as an onlooker and often as a participant, I will try to describe the precious picture that is left engraved in my memory of those wonderful days, of my own unforgettable childhood years, of the superb youth of my generation, of our passionately beloved town Brzezin that was so terribly annihilated with fire and sword.[1] May the cold fire that still smolders in ashes that cover that desert Brzezin warm us in the autumn cold.

A Shabes afternoon in summer, right after eating *cholent*, the young people begin to shuffle out of their houses. From all the streets and lanes, groups are drawn to Nowe Miasto [New Town] on the way to the playing field. Near the German church, where the

---

[1] *Fire and Sword* is the title of a well-known Polish novel by Henryk Sienkiewicz.

highway begins, the mass of people becomes denser—most of the girls in white dresses, young boys in short pants in bright summer suits, and Hasidic young men in their Shabes long black coats, which makes them stand out on the silver-pebbled highway.

The road goes uphill. At the very top, on the left, the Tadzin Forest shines green. The sky is a deep blue, here and there interwoven with small silver-white clouds. A midsummer sun burns with pale fire over the yellow-green corn-covered fields, which sway slightly in the barely felt breeze. In the plush green meadows, black and white cows graze contentedly.

A Jewish Football Team in Brzeziny

On the field, dressed in multicolored uniforms, the players practice, surrounded on all sides by living walls of onlookers. The nervousness, the tension, makes the midday heat seem even stronger. We wait impatiently for the *sędzia*'s (referee's) whistle. With something like spite, the opposing players from the other town practice with such cold-bloodedness and skill that our feelings of uncertainty increase. Decent, nice boys look over the opposing players with a critical eye and promise themselves quietly whom they would teach a lesson if he were to become a *pętak* [jerk]. Now begins the usual ceremony. The captains greet each other. A whistle cuts through the overheated air. Play begins.

The Brzeziner Sports Club "BKS."

The first minutes go according to the previously adopted plan. Each player is at his position. The ball goes from player to player, as agreed, as was planned during endless practices. But something happens here. The opponents go on the offensive; they bring the ball to our goal. They have already torn through the defense. The only hope lies with the stretched-out goalie. He runs out of the net, grabs the ball, and falls to the ground. The opponents try, with their feet, to take back the ball. He is injured. The wall of onlookers, with an angry roar, rush to help their beloved player.

A fight that does not last long breaks out. Cooler heads, older saner onlookers, and the referees step in. The play continues.

The opponents get the upper hand. Twice already they have kicked the ball into our net. The splendid goalie, who is constantly bombarded, plays miraculously and heroically and is rewarded with grateful shouts and applause. The game is coming to a close. The players, covered with perspiration, are almost dead on their feet. The opponents bombard, the goalie skillfully grabs the ball and throws it deep into enemy territory. It is overtaken by the center forward who gives it, *blitz-shnel* [lightning fast], over to the right wing. He carries it all the way to the corner, centers it, and, with the power of a bomb, it is driven into the opponent's net. A wild, triumphant shout rips out of hundreds of breasts. The match is really lost, but our honor is rescued.

The sun has finally gone down behind the meadows when the dense masses reach Nowe Miasto. A cool evening breeze caresses and cools the agitated crowd. The church bells have rung. Through the windows that blaze in shining purple from the setting sun is heard the sweetly sung *nign* [melody] of "God of Abraham" [a woman's prayer marking the end of the Sabbath].

By the time the crowd reaches the market square, the first stars are already twinkling. Some go home, a number go to *daven* the weekly *mayrev* [evening prayer]; others go to the bar at Szotenberg's, where, with a glass of beer or tea, they soberly analyze the lost match.

The players on the opposing team, although conquerors, behave modestly, swapping compliments and mutual appreciation. Etiquette demands that we accompany them to the bus that takes them home.

On thickly tree-lined Koluszki Street, where the players depart, a dark-blue sky can be seen. When we reach Wolfschmidt's orchard, the full moon shines forth.

Clouds of dust, the smell of gasoline, outstretched hands, of *hidd* [bravo], *do widzenia* [good-bye], and the bus disappears in the blue distance. We cut through the orchard, the deep, grassy fields, and the trails among the rye and come out on the Rogów highway.

From the valley, where the town lay half asleep, here and there a small fire sparkled. On the edge of the horizon, the outline of the nocturnal secretive forests shone darkly. The forests shone in the pale-golden light of the full moon swimming in the dark blue sky. The night lay still, heavy and fragrant. We had finally sung all the songs. We did not want to go home. The pleasure of the past day slowly evaporated. The morning ahead lay gray and cheerless. Only one song was left to be sung, a song that fit the spirit, which was overburdened with sadness, longing, and gloom.

On Rogów Street, in the gloom, in the shine of stardust immersed in moonlight, the doomed generation sang Icchak Kacenelson's song:

> World, world, you don't worry,
> Soon the day arises.
> But eternal is my sadness,
> Eternal is my lament.

Somewhere a dog howled heartrendingly in the silence of the night. Like shadows we dispersed for home. Like shadows in the night, like eternal shadows in the eternal night.

Icchak Kacenelson in Brzezin (pp. 122–24)

Welwel Rozenblum

In our town Brzezin, during the time of World War I, various organizations existed that spread not only enlightenment but also presided over great cultural activity. In this area, the Zionist youth organization Hattechija excelled the most. Various important speakers from Łódź and even from Warsaw gave lectures on Yiddish literature. All the lectures were well attended and received with great interest, but only one speaker succeeded in transforming his every appearance into a great event. The members, not only of Hattechija but also of all the other organizations, were overwhelmed with joy when they found out that the beloved and revered Yiddish-Hebrew writer Icchak Kacenelson[1] was coming to their town to deliver a lecture and read his own poems.

Icchak Kacenelson

Weeks before, they began to prepare for the festive evening. Hattechija's own hall, which was large enough for various other get-togethers, was too small on this ocassion. Therefore, they had to take the largest hall in town. For an evening of Icchak Kacenelson, everyone dressed up in his or her most beautiful and best clothing and hurried to Firemen's Hall. It did not take long before all the seats were taken. Many more wanted to come in, but there was no room left. A tension was felt in the hall. When the members of the committee, with great respect, led the writer out onto the stage, a storm of applause spontaneously broke out; everyone stood up and began singing the writer's beloved and famous song "The Sun Goes Down in Flames."

The love that we had for Icchak Kacenelson was boundless. He charmed us all. His lectures on Yiddish literature were instructive and interesting. When he began to read his poetry, it was as if he had bewitched everyone. Rarely did anyone, so splendidly and with so much talent, present poems the way he did. He had a touching voice that charmed and caressed and carried us away on the wings of the writer's poetry to a world of spiritual exaltation.

Frequently, after such an impressive evening, the members of the organization met with a number of invited guests at the home of Lea'le Bialek, a beautiful and charming Brzeziner woman. Her house was the meeting place for the intelligentsia in our town. Beforehand Lea'le had already prepared a *simkhele* [small celebration]. At covered tables

---

[1] Known in Israel and the United States as Yitzhak Katzenelson, he is the author of a well-known poem, written in the Warsaw ghetto, "The Song of the Murdered Jewish People."

with a smaller group, an intimate atmosphere was created at which the amiable personality of Icchak Kacenelson was unveiled. He was relaxed, friendly. His humor overflowed with spice and charm. He was incomparable in his singing and interpretation of Yiddish folksongs. He had the magnetic charm to infect everyone with his joy and optimism. It was a great pleasure to spend time in his company.

He visited Brzezin quite often, and we always received him with great enthusiasm.

* * *

I also had the great pleasure of meeting with Icchak Kacenelson in New York when he came here on a trip after World War I in 1921. It was great exciting news for me when I learned that he was in New York. At that time, he was warmly received by the Yiddish press. He published his fine poems in *Morgn Zhurnal* [Morning Journal].

A group of Lovers of Yiddish Literature with the famous Yiddish-Hebrew poet, Icchak Kacenelson, who is seated in the middle of the second row.

My first meeting with Icchak Kacenelson in New York was in the home of the now deceased poet I. H. Radoszycki, who had earlier been a resident of Łódź and belonged to the group Yung Yidish [Young Yiddish]. He greeted me warmly and inquired in detail about the Brzeziner *landslayt* living in America. At that time, I met with him very often. I would accompany him on various occasions during his visits and appearances in New York. Everywhere he visited he was received with affection and hospitality. The students in the Hebrew schools showed a very great interest in him; they would meet him with delight, song, and great honor. In New York Icchak Kacenelson also had intimate friends from Poland and from his home town in Lithuania. He used to invite me to go along with him to visit them. I remember a Davis family in Brownsville, marvelously sincere people, and also other friends of his in various parts of New York. Everywhere, at every get-together, the hosts invited their friends, and a little celebration was held in honor of Kacenelson, and they always sang his beloved song "The Sun Goes Down in Flames."

When Icchak Kacenelson began to prepare to return home to Łódź, we, the Brzeziner *landslayt*, the first arrivals in America after World War I, together with several of the *landslayt* from earlier immigrations, arranged a farewell evening for our beloved writer, held in the home of our *landsman* Sam Fox, in Jamaica, Long Island.

We, the Brzeziner *landslayt* in America, responded to Icchak Kacenelson with the same love and honor as we had earlier in our hometown Brzezin. An intimate, friendly atmosphere was created at once, with the tables covered with plenty of good things arranged and prepared by Mrs. Fox. We ate, drank, and were happy. But a silent gloom came over us, like a cloud—our beloved writer was going away from us and when would we see him again?

Finally, the writer took his leave of us and thanked us for the friendship we had shown him in a foreign land.

When he finished his speech, a sort of strange silence came over us. At once, without any kind of prompting, we all rose and sang his elegy "The Sun Goes Down in Flames." It seemed to us that this time we sang the song completely differently than on previous occasions—with more longing and with a hope that we would once again greet and enjoy ourselves with our beloved writer. Therefore, our voices flowed together as if in a group *tfile* [prayer].

Even today, I see the image before me, and it still rings in my ears, the way we sang Icchak Kacenelson's song:

> The sun goes down in flames, the sun, we barely see
> So my hope goes down, so my dream is extinguished.
> The night is dark, the night is mute and black,
> So seems my mourning, so seems my heart.
> World, world, you don't care, soon your day will rise,
> Eternal is my mourning, eternal is my lament.

Who could have foreseen the *khurbn* [destruction], the annihilation, the laying waste? Who could have believed that our dear, beloved writer would be devoured in a black, dark night, that all his hopes, all his dreams would be extinguished and "eternal would be his mourning, eternal his lament"—as he had sung in his elegy some forty years earlier, before his martyr's death.

The writer-martyr Icchak Kacenelson perished together with our six million brothers and sisters in Nazi Europe. We stand enveloped in deep mourning at the frightening tragedy, at the terrible misfortune, and we cry for the writer Icchak Kacenelson, together with his assassinated Jewish people, as the song of lament that he left for us has risen from his writer's soul.

"Eternal will be our mourning, eternal will be our lament."

Yiddish Theater in Our Shtetl (p. 124-25)

Malka Rose (Rozenblum)

In 1910 Jewish life in Brzezin was flowing along like a quiet stream. Every *mishpokhe* [family] had its own way of life. Young and old were struggling hard to make a living.

Besides the *kheyder* [Jewish elementary school] and higher studies for children, there were no other educational institutions. Cultural organizations, where young people could derive satisfaction and develop spiritually, absolutely did not exist in our town in those times.

However, there was a class of Jews in the town who lived very well, and their children, even better. These children, therefore, got a better education. Since Brzezin did not have the necessary schools, their parents brought teachers for them from larger towns; others sent their children to larger communities where there were high schools. The very wealthy sent their children to study in foreign lands.

These youths, or some of them, who had acquired a good education, felt a need for and sought to bring in a little spirituality and cultural education. Mrs. Isz, a newcomer from Russia, who was well educated and had an intelligent and perceptive personality, helped in this undertaking. Thanks to her initiative, an amateur theater group was formed that served two purposes—first, to perform plays of the better Yiddish playwrights so as to develop more of a taste for Yiddish theater among the Jewish people for their own enjoyment, and second, the income was to be used for charitable purposes.

Fortunately, at that time another person was found, also a newcomer in town, Syngalowski, an employee at one of the magazines. He was a highly gifted person with higher education and leadership ability. He took charge of the drama group, and a glorious chapter of Yiddish amateur theater began in Brzezin.

The group was made up of the following persons—women: Bela Zygmuntowicz, Surele Gotlib, Ruchele Dymant, Małka Rozenblum, Aneta Stajn, and Chajka Malamut; men: Motel Lechtreger (the tall one), Motel Lechtreger (the short one), Zelwiański, Dorfsman, and Epsztajn.

The majority of the women were Brzeziner natives; the remaining women and also the men were newcomers from Russia.

We had rehearsals two or three times a week. The work began with several lectures on theater and performance. The director also explained to the players the essence of each of the characters in the play. The director's first commandment was that the performer must not allow himself to be dragged down by the audience; on the contrary, he must lift up the people with him to a higher artistic level.

Rehearsals were held in the homes of various members of the company. Every rehearsal was a holiday and a joyful gathering. And in this joyful mood, we would go out into the town and fill the streets with our singing. The windows of the workshops would still be lit up, the clanking of the presses would mix with the sound of the machines and with the workers' songs, and our singing in the street would penetrate into the midst of it.

After an entire winter of rehearsing, we began to prepare for the performance, which was to take place during Khalemoyed Pesakh [between first two and last two days of Passover]. But in order to perform Yiddish theater, one had to have a special permit from the government. Friend Isz had to travel to Piotrków, exert influence, and give a bribe, and only then could we rent *Strażacki* [Firemen's] Hall to accommodate the performance.

On the day of the performance it was not *khalemoyed* in the town but a real *yontov* [holiday]. Everyone got ready to go to the theater. They also did not forget to bring with them various foods and *nosheray*, which was the custom at that time.

Even before the theater doors were opened, the windows were already besieged by students who wanted to peer into the theater.

When the actors arrived, they were greeted with various outbursts, with a clamor and whistling. The caretaker had to come and chase the people away.

Behind the scenes, they were already causing a commotion, setting up props on the stage. Funt, the *felczer* [medical practitioner], began to put makeup on the actors. The hall was fully packed all the way up to the gallery. When the third sounding of the bell was heard, all became still, and Lewandowski, the caretaker, raised the curtain with a cord. The play began, and the people sat on the edge of their seats and enjoyed themselves.

Drama circle of the Society for Evening Courses (Poale Zion), picture taken in 1930. Epsztajn, the director, is in the center.

The first two pieces that the amateur group performed were Perec Hirschbein's *Di Nevole* [The Infamy] and Sholem Aleichem's *Mazl Tov* [Good Luck]. Mojszele Szotland played the two children's roles in *Mazl Tov*.

We also performed *Shema Yisroel* [Hear, O Israel] by Osip Dymov; *With the Stream* by Sholem Asch; *The Unknown, Khasye the Orphan,* and *The Jewish King Lear* by Jacob Gordin; *People, A Doctor,* and *The Divorce* by Sholem Aleichem; and *The Eternal Song* by Mark Arnstein.

After every performance, we would take out the benches from the hall into the courtyard, and the Brzeziner *klezmorim* [musicians] played one dance after another. In this way, the people and the actors danced and enjoyed themselves until daybreak. This was the beginning of Yiddish theater, as performed by the first amateur group.

With the out-break of World War I, everything came to an end. The noise of the machines and the singing in the workshops stopped—and so also did amateur groups performing Yiddish theater.

In 1916, after Poland had already been occupied by Germany for two years, cultural life was reestablished. The young people organized themselves into a cultural association. Immediately, a fight broke out between two political factions—the Zionists and the Bundists [Jewish Socialist Party].

The Zionists won after a violent fight, and the organization Hattechija was born. At once, the organization formed a drama section with the following people—Ginsberg as director, Melech Herszenberg, Maks Tuszyński, Hamer, Epsztajn, and others. Among the women were Abraham Gips' daughter, the hatmaker's daughter, Ajdele, and Małka Rozenblum.

At that time, a young man showed up in town, a teacher by trade and very gifted in the dramatic arts. He was drawn to the amateur group and became not only its director but also a fellow actor. The young man was Josef Grynberg, later the well-known actor of the Vilna Troupe and of Maurice Schwartz's Art Theater [in New York]. He was also popular later as the producer of Yiddish films under the name Joseph Green.[1]

Under his direction, the drama group in our town blossomed and had success in several fine performances.

The chapter of Yiddish theater in Brzezin extended even further. A youth organization, Hashomer Hatzair, founded by the Zionist organization Hattechija, also began to play Yiddish theater. The very young Welwel Rozenblum succeeded in producing a play in three acts that he composed from the then recently published Yizkor Book, dedicated to the heroic fight of the fallen *shomrim* [guardians] in Eretz Yisroel. This Yizkor commemoration was performed under his direction and assistance. Participating were Mojsze Badower, Abraham Dymant, Hamer, Kempner, Majer Rozenblum, and others.

In later times, the Brzeziner Jewish youth again performed Yiddish theater, similar to that which we, the first amateur group, had begun.

The chapter of Yiddish theater in Brzezin ended along with the destruction of Jewish youth and the entire Jewish *kehile* [community] in our town, annihilated by Hitler (may his name be erased).

---

[1] Joseph Green 1900–1996, produced such classic films as *Yidl Mitn Fidl* (Yidl with a Fiddle), *Der Purimshpiler* (The Purim Jester), *Mamele* (Little Mother), and *A Brivele der Mamen* (A Letter to Mother).

Poems (pp. 126–29)

Nachum Summer

MY SHTETL BRZEZIN

Nachum Summer

My splendid *shtetl* Brzezin
That the butchers annihilated,
Wounded forever
My heart my soul . . .
I remain a mourner since the
great disaster,
Since then, I search for words
of comfort;
Words to expel the grief, the gloom —
And helpless is my search . . .

My tongue stammers out unintelligible speech —
And suddenly — as from a spring
A stream of tears rushed out,
That I could not quell . . .
Goyisher villains
Poisoned my heart with gall —

And from my lips stream out
Curses, words of blight,
Against assassins' hands
That annihilated, ravaged
My splendid *shtetl*, Brzezin . . .
It is well-known that the enemy,
In his malice, sought
Its total destruction.
The enemy did not completely succeed
In his devilish plan, —
Woe unto us, —
Impoverished men are left, heirs
Spread throughout the world's parts,
Who will the great epic
Of my *shtetl* and its holy martyrs
Relate for generations, for eternity . . .
We will tell —
Of the beautiful, tender, chaste mothers;

Of persons of stately appearance, virtuous, observant fathers;
Of the toiling, ordinary, simple,
Scissors-and-iron journeymen,
The shoemakers who shod the young and old;
The butchers' boys, the jolly wagon drivers,
The bakers, the hatmakers, the porters,
Who carried their weekly burden
With a Yiddish song ringing out . . .
We will tell of your Shabosim and *yomim-tovim* [holidays].
We will tell
Of your streets and your domains
About your happiness and your pain;
About your sages and your buffoons,
Who sweetened your burden, your poverty,
With *roshinkes un mandlen* [raisins and almonds] . . .[1]
We will remember
Your *melamdim* [teachers] and your *bal-tfile*s [leaders of prayer],
Who nurtured us for generations.
We will tell
About your streams and orchard gardens,
That spread graciously
Over Rogów and Koluszki Streets,
Where Brzeziner youth
Spent many sweet days and nights . . .
We will roll up the *Megile-Brzezin* [scroll of story of Brzezin],
Which is preserved in our memory.
We will tell of a beautiful past
And the surviving witnesses will also tell
Of the last flickering, sunset days,
Of extinguished lives . . .

The Brzeziner earth became parched! . . .
The rhythm of the week and holidays
Was by murderous hands stifled, choked . . .
Who could have foreseen such a gloomy dream,
That Brzezin would be a town — without Jews? . . .
No longer the dear, beaming
Shabes-Yontovdike [Sabbath-holiday] Jews of our *shtetl*,
Who sang out their *nign* [melody] —
Of weekday poverty and Shabes rest . . .
Only memories of long ago remain —
For generations to spin . . .

---

[1] "Roshinkes un Mandlen" was the title of a popular Yiddish lullaby.

You will become holy, my splendid *shtetl*
In your greatness and your simplicity . . .
We light memorial candles
For young, cut-off lives
From near and far —
That the brutal hand of Cain
Has savagely killed . . .
The *kadesh* that I recite collectively —
Is a holy vow,
That I will not forget the legacy
Of the tormented, suffocated, gassed
Hero martyrs of my once home . . .
Of my — Brzezin! . . .

OUR BESMEDRESH (a Ballad)

Going toward Nowe Miasto [New Town],
In the direction of the market square —
Stood our *besmedresh* [Orthodox house of prayer].
The building — far from a marble palace;
The exterior walls
Painted white —
More gray than white
From spring rains
And wintry snowy blizzards,
Which, year in, year out —
Whipped and thrashed them . . .

Once it was lively here,
The ten *minyonim* of Jews —
Who prayed three times a day
And their prayerful supplications
Directed to the Reboyne Sheloylem [God Almighty] . . .
Late in the night
The generation-old
Gemore-nign [chant with which Gemore is studied] broke through to the outside . . .
The simple, the overworked scissors-and-iron Jews,
Found, in reciting Psalms, their redemption
From troubled spirit —
And often actually let a tear fall,
Onto the yellowed pages —
As a hint of the burden of exile . . .

Oh, how clear it is in memory
The *yomim-tovim* [holidays] in our town! . . .
The Pesakh — of cleaning and koshering
And the bell-like sound
Of the small rascals
While they played *nislekh in griblekh* [game played with nuts] . . .
Shavuos—of leaves and blossoms in all the homes, —
Also the *besmedresh*, smells of forest and field . . .
The Yomim-Naroyim [Days of Awe] —
For which the entire town
Prepares itself with dread and reverence . . .
Sukes — the holiday of joy and Torah
And the showing-off
Of the young housewives
With their serving portions of fish
In the *Suke* booths —
Who can forget it! . . .

Or — there goes
A woman very heavy with child,
Or, somewhere in a home
Lies a dangerously sick person —
Close family, relatives
Rend themselves with lament before the Holy Ark . . .
Jews, recite Psalms! . . .
At once someone stands before the *omed* [synagogue lectern]
And begins in a low fearful tone —
Blessed is he who walks not in the counsel of the ungodly [Psalms 1:1] . . .

The *maged* [preacher], who from time to time
Would come to town,
Chastise people, whip them with reproaching words,
Threaten with hell-fires, call to *tshuve* [repentance]
And weed out sin from among them . . .
All the community quarrels, debates,
That sparkled between the walls
Of our *besmedresh* . . .
All that is no more
Than a flash in my memory. . . .

There once was a town — Brzezin
And is no longer . . .
Like a joke from bloody madness
Our *besmedresh* remains
But stands vacant without Jews . . .

The walls covered with dirt and cobwebs,
On the roof green moss grows.
The broken windows,
On all sides stale dampness permeates . . .
On the floor lie the scrolls of the Torah
Plucked, dishonored . . .
In the corners where destruction began —
And rats walk among piles
With Exodus from overturned Torah Arks . . .
The stream has been dried up
That had fertilized our community —
The Brzeziner earth no longer sprouts
With the prayer of Jewish psalms . . .
The sound of Torah
And weekly speech has become silent.
No longer are there *daveners* in our congregation . . .
Only memories of the past remain
For generations to relate —
Yisgadal v'yiskadash shmei rabo! [opening words of *kadesh*, the mourners' prayer]

A TRIBUTE TO JUDEL THE WATER CARRIER

Yesterday you
Carried water
For the town.
Hard was
Your life.
For old and young;
For small and large —
You were the butt of ridicule . . .
But, you, —
Silently
Smiled at everyone you met.
Kheyder-yinglekh [school boys]
Did not let you walk through the streets.
Funny jokes,
Biting words,
Youngsters would
Whip across your face.
And you, —
Instead of anger, wrath —
Only love and goodness
Did you show the pranksters . . .
Your fate,
Is — you said — fixed on high . . .

Therefore you
Met your hard fate
With a *gamzu letoyve* [it's all for the best].
You also did not
Avoid Hitler's destruction.
They, the devils,
Tormented you
With horrible pain . . .
They flayed your flesh
With inhuman torture.
Your faith —
The swine could not break . . .
For the God of Israel
You had no complaints.
All the affliction
You bore in silence,
Perhaps predestined from on high . . .
The executioner tightened
A noose around your neck.
In your last step to the gallows
You murmured words
To yourself;
Words made holy
In the great folk disaster,
That will, in their simplicity
Make your name eternal
For coming generations;
. . . "Yesterday, to you, I was
Judel the water carrier
Tomorrow, I will be
Judel *kodesh* [holy martyr]! . . ."
Like an incendiary
Your last testament words fell
On the face of the murderer.
Those very simple words
Will Brzeziners
Remember forever.
Your life and your death,
Place you
On the list of our
Great folk *kdoyshim* [holy martyrs].
Our writers and artists,
Will, from your simple life
Find inspiration,
And will raise word-monuments to you . . .

THE OYEL OF REB SZYMON BAL-RAKHMONES[1]

Not satisfied,
The murderous hands,
When they drove into the gas chambers
The old men and old women;
Our women and men;
Our children and suckling infants . . .
They, who
Brought down
The Creator and His creation —
Man!
To the lowest low,
With the
Bloody hand of Cain,
They sought out, on the cemetery
The remains of the long dead;
Of our furthest,
Of our nearest, —
Their skeletal remains,
In earthly concealment,
Nazi villains —
Dishonored, trampled
With beastly feet.
Left as a symbol,
For future generations —
There in Brzezin
The very much loved *oyel* [structure over grave]
Of the great scholar Reb Szymon,
Who passed through our town,
And not wanting to desecrate the Sabbath,
Stayed in our town for Shabes.
And when the Jews lit the *Havdole* [ceremony at close of Sabbath] candle —
The soul of Reb Szymon Bal-Rakhmones
Was gathered into Eternity . . .
The Brzeziner community
Awarded the great scholar,
The most beautiful spot
In their *beysakvores* [cemetery].
Later the Brzeziner religious community
In memory —
Of the great *bal-mide* [person of high moral character]
Raised an *oyel* . . .
Since then, Jews —

---

[1] Bal-Rakhmones means "man of compassion."

When paying their respects at the graveside of their parents
Have also included the grave of this holy man
Leaving there their worries and troubles.
We begged the great Bal-Rakhmones,
He should intercede for us in heaven . . .
With little stones and *kvitlekh* [notes of supplication],
That observant women
Left there,
Was raised
A little hill towered toward heaven . . .

The murderer —
Plowed up, trampled,
Our cemetery . . .
Like a God-given miracle,
The grave of the great scholar
Remained as a witness
To the great disaster of our people . . .
No longer are there Jews
Who used to come
To his grave to let a tear flow.
The villain annihilated
Our sacred community —
Even our dead
He did not spare . . .
But, the grave remains,
From which Jews,
In time of trouble had drawn solace,
As a memorial to the great Jewish destruction —
And as a message to coming generations:
Jews, don't give up hope! . . .
To the gas-ovens was sent . . .
Jewish flesh,
Wrapped in tongues of fire;
But the *Kol Yaakov* [voice of Jacob]
Of the great soul,
The murderous hand
Did not burn up, did not annihilate . . .

New Jewish lives will rise
Upon the background of burned bodies,
And in remembrance of the past —
Will raise up the great qualities
Of a Szymon Bal-Rakhmones. . .

Shnayder-Yinglekh [Tailor Apprentices] (p. 130)
by Nachum Jud

(A Fable)

Three tailor apprentices, very new at their work,
Argued among themselves at the master's table;
Each one was striving to show —
What was actually the most important for the garment:
The scissors,
Or the needle, or the iron?
Over this they
Fought so heatedly,
That oh-oh — and fists would have flown! . . .
But an experienced journeyman, who to one side
Sat bent over his work,
And all the time
Was listening and kept silent,
Remarked to them, calmly, from a distance,
"Why, little young men, should you fight,
And make a racket, argue over and over?
You are all correct, each of your views is correct!
Since every cut and prick,
And every stroke is important for the garment . . .
But in the end —
The essential part is the material!"

PART THREE

ON THE RUINS OF OUR SHTETL

The First Victim (p. 133)

A letter from a rescued Brzeziner landsman

In 1939 Nazi agents grabbed the nineteen-year-old young man Aron Efroimowicz, threw him into an automobile, and took him away to the nearby Rogów Forest. There, those despicable beasts took off all his clothes, bound him to a tree, and beat him with murderous blows—without rhyme or reason. His screams from the terrible pain were carried to the heavens, but no one came to help him. The villains answered his imploring pleas with more blows, with sticks over his naked, tortured flesh, until he fell unconscious from the barrage of blows. Seeing that their victim was barely moving and his wailing cries had become a dying groan, they shot him with revolvers and ran away, leaving their victim to die.

Aron Efroimowicz, the first victim in Brzezin.

Not far from the Rogów Forest lived a Brzeziner Jew, a *shveyger* (milk dealer), by the name of Pachczer [Pachciarz?], who came running into the forest to help, hearing the reverberating echoes from the horrible screaming. As he came into the forest, he could hear the quiet death rattle of someone dying. When he looked around, he saw the tragic, gruesome scene of the dying nineteen-year-old young man who was bound to a tree. His body and his face were black and blue and bloodied so as to make him unrecognizable. These were the last moments of his final breath. Then he looked around the forest for some evidence of who the victim was. He found his clothes, and from the pieces of paper in his pockets, the man found out that this was the observant Hasidic young man Aron Efroimowicz of Brzezin, who studied in the Gerer *shtibl* [Hassidic house of study/prayer].

Reb Pachczer immediately ran to Brzezin to inform the community and the young man's close relatives about the horrible assassination by the rotten Germans and that they needed to bury the victim. When the milk dealer gave the young man's mother the terrible news, she immediately fainted. Later she went through the streets with a candle in her hands and asked everyone to come to her son's graveside.

Aron Efroimowicz, the pious young man who sat in the Gerer *shtibl* day and night, was the first victim, the first martyr of the Nazi bestiality of our holy community. May his soul rest in the Garden of Eden. . . .

The First Shocking Encounter (p. 134)
Aron Fogel

Aron Fogel (Ester-Laja's, the baker's son) was one of the first survivors from our town who returned to Brzezin after the war. He had just been freed from a Nazi concentration camp, where, by a miracle, he had managed to stay alive.

In a letter to our *landsmanshaft* [society of fellow townspeople] in New York, Aron Fogel gave the first shocking report from destroyed Brzezin. He wrote:

Arriving in Brzezin at the beginning of February 1945 at four o'clock in the afternoon, coming alone from the camp, I did not imagine I would find the town as it was before, but how could I not find a few dozen Jews? There were, after all eight thousand souls who were living there before! One easily says and writes "eight thousand," but let me, as much as possible, try to give here the details of what it had been like. The creativity, the activity, the work, the bustle, the coziness, the informality, the quarreling between givers and takers of work, the travelers, wagon drivers, tailors, shoemakers, elegant Jews, Hasidim, friends, intellectuals, semi-intellectuals, the *shuln* [synagogues], *bote-medroshim* [Orthodox houses of prayer], Hasidic *shtiblekh* [Hasidic houses of prayer], *mikvoes* [ritual baths], organizations, Jewish banks, charitable institutions—I believe almost all of Brzezin passes before your eyes. And imagine—nothing. As in Genesis—*toye-voye* [a void]! Not one single Jew, literally, none.

I, myself, who had seen the great Hell, where, in a few days, thousands of our brothers were taken away and never came back, was not able to understand how it was possible. What happened to all the people? Where are our children—the infants, the schoolchildren? Where are the *talmetoyres* [Jewish elementary schools]? And it moved me emotionally so much that I decided to go to the *besoylem* [cemetery] first thing in the morning. I will rip open the graves and demand answers from the dead. Those of ours lying and resting in their graves for generations, do they know that their *yishev* [Jewish settlement] was exterminated, their martyrs burned up and annihilated, that never again will anyone say Yizkor [memorial prayer] at their graves nor El Mole Rakhamim [memorial prayer for the dead], to commemorate the ceremony?

I did not sleep at all that night. I waited for daylight as if for redemption. And the way everything passes, so did the night. Early in the morning, I immediately ran to the cemetery, but unfortunately, I had no one to whom I could unburden my bitter heart. They, the assassins, also had not preserved our dead. The cemetery was torn up, the gravestones gone, the fence ripped out—the *mekhitse* [separation] between the living and the dead torn apart. And with a broken spirit I left that holy place; before my eyes it had revealed to me our entire tragedy.

It was, it seems, not enough. Only in the light of day did I find massive barricades in the streets of the town made from the gravestones of our dead, and I thought to myself—souls of the dead, both generations-old and recently perished, float around in the air of our town; and heaven is filled with holy souls that are even greater than the souls of the *asore-haruge-malkes* ["the ten martyrs"—sages put to death by the Roman Emperor Hadrian]; because after their deaths, there still was a holy remembrance, but our tormented ones have no redress at all. And a force, a tremendous one, began to push me—run away, run away from the *klole* [curse] inflicted on our town! And I made a vow that wherever I might be, and at every opportunity, I would recite the *Megile Eykhe* [Book of Lamentations].

On the fifth *yortsayt* [anniversary of death] of the annihilation of the Brzeziner community, Mendel Frydman (Aron Shames's grandson) spoke in the presence of Brzeziny town officials.

I Saw the Destruction of Our Shtetl (pp. 135–39)

Dr. Stanisław Warhaft

RECOLLECTIONS OF THE GHETTO DOCTOR

The outbreak of World War II found Brzezin, along with all the rest of Poland, unprepared. The town was already bombed from the air in the first days of September 1939. There were many victims among the Jewish population. We lived in fear and worry—what will happen when the Germans occupy the town? Many men left town, mostly the young. A number of them returned after a time; a number of them succeeded in escaping to Russia.

At that time I was at the front as a Polish reserve officer. On 14 October I returned to Brzezin. The town was occupied by the Germans. The local Germans, who now felt like the "chosen people," were helping them. Already the situation for the Jews was difficult—Jewish stores were closed; on them was written *Jude* [Jew], and no one would sell any food to Jews. Jews could only appear in the streets from six in the morning until five in the evening.

On the streets, Jews were beaten and insulted. They were grabbed on the streets and in their homes for forced labor. The local Germans helped the German soldiers ransack Jewish homes, where they stole everything possible.

The merchandise of *magaziners* [owners of clothing enterprises] was confiscated by the gendarmes and shipped off to special camps. Jewish working families, who never had to worry before about making a satisfactory living, had not earned a *grosz* [coin worth 100th of a *zloty*] during the last two months. Hunger began to appear in the homes. All Jewish social institutions were shut down. From the Jewish *kehile* [community council], only the chairman, Icek Dymant, and the secretary, Abraham Szafman, remained. Their task then was to supply Jewish workers daily to the Germans; often they were beaten and insulted for not providing the required number of workers. Immediately the command went out that Jews must wear the *Yudn-late* (yellow Star of David).

On 5 October I was arrested as a Polish reserve officer. Thanks to my former German patients, I was freed. At that time we came together secretly at Icek Dymant's—Jakub Zagon (Jasza), the dentist Irlicht, and I. We took stock of the situation and came to the conclusion that we must create a people's kitchen at that time, as quickly as possible, and that the workers supplied by the *kehile* every day must be paid.

But where could we get the means to make it happen, since the community chest was empty? We then decided to carry out a voluntary collection of monetary resources among the population, and anyone who wanted to free himself from work duty would have to pay for a substitute worker—the sick and elderly were completely exempt.

Jaszka Zagon had, however, another way to generate money. The magaziners goods lay confiscated in a special camp—and the Germans demanded workers to sort them out. Jasza got a special group of workers who had the assignment of smuggling out new suits of clothing, coats, etc. every day or twice a day, by wearing them on their bodies. The clothes were stored and then sold. Lajzer Zagon, Szyja Zagon, Mordcha Szufleder, and others belonged to this group. This brought us a very nice sum of money—morally we felt this sort of dealing was appropriate.

In the first days of November, rumors spread that the Germans would carry out arrests among the Polish people, since their [the Poles'] holiday fell on 11 November [World War I Armistice Day, which finalized the defeat of Germany]. On 9 November German soldiers actually appeared in the street with local Germans in attendance. They arrested many Poles, but they didn't forget the Jews.

Assembly in memory of the Brzeziner martyrs. Dr. Warhaft, the doctor in the Brzeziner ghetto, is the speaker.

The Brzeziner rabbi, *Harov* [town rabbi] Borensztajn, Dr. Klajnhaus, Dr. Irlicht, Attorney Drucker, Attorney Jakubowicz, and others were arrested. I also expected them to come after me at any moment. One of my former patients appeared and told me that I could rest easy. They would not arrest me. Those arrested were held on the premises of the Bajka movie theater, where they were tortured and beaten.

On the evening of 9 November, the Germans set fire to the synagogue. A notice in the German Łódź newspaper stated that the Jews and their rabbi had set fire to their synagogue. "The provocateurs were arrested." In a few days, those arrested were taken to Łódź; they were held several months in special camps. Later they were sent to other towns. They were not allowed to return home (some did come back later).

At that time, the Germans divided occupied Poland into two parts: 1) Warthegau and 2) General Government. Warthegau was annexed directly to Germany [including Łódź and Brzeziny]. Many towns got German names: Łódź—Litzmannstadt, Brzeziny—Löwenstadt near Rogów. At that time, the border between the two lands was located in Kolacin, with a customs office and a border guard.

On 20 November a section of the Gestapo came to Brzezin, and in a matter of a few minutes, I had to vacate my residence for them. I got a room at my wife's grandmother's. The Gestapo chief announced that only the Gestapo had the right to handle all Jewish questions. They asked the *kehile* to supply workers to serve them and demanded various other things. Among the workers that the *kehile* sent was Fiszke Ikka. Over time, through various tricks, he managed to become the only important Jew to the Gestapo.

Later, the Germans decided that in Warthegau the towns must become *Judenrein* [cleansed of Jews]. The Brzeziner Germans also adopted the same decision. On a cold winter day at the end of December 1939, they chased the residents of Court Street [ul. Staszica] out of their homes; the Gestapo permitted the Jews to take with them only a little clothing, and the residences were sealed. The keys were given to the gendarmes.

I turned to the mayor (a German Brzeziner manufacturer) with a request that he stop the deportation. He said he would hold off the deportation for two days until I came back from Łódź with an answer from the authorities. A delegation traveled to Łódź—Icek Dymant, Chajkel Grynszpan, and I. There was a terrible frost.

A group of surviving Brzeziner remnants in Stuttgart. Some are now in America.

We traveled to Łódź by wagon—Jews were not allowed on the bus. With heavy hearts we went to beg mercy from the Nazi beasts in Łódź. A few steps from the entrance to the German *Kreischef* [district head], my companions, Dymant and Grynszpan, were grabbed to be laborers; I got out of it, thanks to my insignia that I was a doctor on an assignment.

I went to see the head of the district. After a long wait in the corridor, I was received by a young German in military uniform. He sat, and I, with my yellow patch front and back, stood. I told him that the local authorities had decided to make Brzezin *Judenrein*. The times were not favorable; it was a severe winter, already there were cases of people being frozen. In the name of the Jewish community, I asked him to permit the order to be carried out in stages, so that we would be able to provide those who left Brzezin with food and some money.

He heard me out without giving me any answer but told me to wait in the corridor again. After ten to fifteen minutes, he called me in and told me that the German authorities had received my request. Jews would have to leave Brzezin by the first of April 1940—every two weeks, five hundred people. The Jewish community would carry out the deportation. The Jewish Doctor Warhaft would be responsible. The local gendarmes would supervise.

The outcome of my intervention was completely unexpected. Later I met Icek Dymant and Grynszpan, and we traveled home with lighter spirits but with one question: What do we do now?

While we were in Łódź, Ikka carried out his first assignment. He pointed out to the Gestapo ten *magaziners* and other well-to-do people from whom money could be extorted after they were arrested. All were freed after paying up to one thousand marks [German currency].

We returned home with our order that no one had to leave town at once by force. Again we created a small committee that consisted of Dymant, Jasza Zagon, Grynszpan, Szafman, and me. We consulted together on what to do next. Since the gendarmes allowed us to buy back workers with money and gifts, we decided to deliver a list of five hundred people who had "abandoned" Brzezin. In reality, it was a list of the residents of Court Street who were living with their relatives on another street. The list was backed up with money, and the experiment succeeded. Again, we won a little time.

A group of friends—*landslayt* [fellow townspeople], the majority of whom had been tortured in various camps in France and Germany.

At the same time, Jasza Zagon got wind of the fact that in Łódź there was a German firm, Schwarz, that distributed work to Jewish tailors and also organized shops for Jewish workers. After long negotiations, work was finally procured for Brzeziner tailors, who worked in their homes and also in "shops" [German workshops]. The assigned materials were picked up from the firm by the Jewish community. The *kehile* got paid for the work, and it paid the workers. From the amount that the community got from the Schwarz firm, it took ten percent as its share.

The *kehile* also provided resources for living. It had its own shops, bakeries, and butcheries. Almost all of the inhabitants worked. From time to time, the Germans would make trouble for the Jews. Still, it was already a little easier.

In May 1940 the Germans designated a part of Brzezin as the ghetto. Jews were not to be found outside the ghetto. The Gestapo designated Fiszke Ikka as head of the ghetto. He took over the *kehile* proceeds under the title *Judenaltester* [Jewish elder]. He created the ghetto police. He designated Seweryn Perlmuter as its commander. A health center was created in the ghetto. Since Jews did not have access to the general health fund, it was decided that every Jew in the ghetto was entitled to free medical care.

I was the only doctor in the ghetto. I took the *felczer* [medical practitioner] Kleinert and the nurses Tuszyńska and Rozenberg to help me, also the midwife Buki. Abramowicz and Fraulein Mizes ran the pharmacy in the ghetto. Since sick Jews were not taken to the hospital outside the ghetto, we had the task of creating a small hospital with twenty-five beds. We got a house at 6 Court Street (Majer Dymant's). The women went from house to house collecting beds, linens, dishes, and other necessities. The former schoolteacher Auster (all schools were forbidden in the ghetto) was designated to be in charge.

We all worked competently and until then had no casualties. In the beginning, I also got permission from the Germans, in cases of serious surgery, to take the sick person from the ghetto to Łódź. Later, this was forbidden. I lost a sick patient who needed to undergo serious abdominal surgery only because I could not take him to Łódź.

Ikka ruled as a dictator in the *kehile*. He gave out community money without any kind of community control. In times like these, he knew how to provide himself with gold and diamonds—he bought them with community money or extorted them from various people. Any attempt at opposition was suppressed by him and his German helpers. An attempt to forward a message to the German powers that they should select someone else as head of the *kehile* ended with the arrest of Zagon, Grynszpan, Stark, and Sender. They were tortured in Brzezin and then taken to Łódź. From there they were dragged to the prison in Sieradz. After a long time, Grynszpan, Jasza Zagon, and Stark came back to the Brzeziner ghetto. Sender was killed.

A Jewish children's school in Brzezin

That is how ghetto life looked until June 1941. At that time, unofficially, *Harov* Borensztajn, Jakub Sułkowicz and his family, Mordechai Winter, and others returned to the ghetto. According to official reports, no one came back.

In June 1941 the Germans took one hundred fifty healthy young people to dig peat in the neighborhood of Stryków. Because of the hard labor and hunger, after two months, skeletons returned to the ghetto. One of the group was very viciously beaten until he died from the blows and torture. During his burial, the *gabai* [trustee] of the Khevre Kedishe [Burial Society], Fajbisiak, died of a heart attack at the cemetery, while begging forgiveness of the dead.

During that same period of time, the former *kehile* chairman, Icek Dymant, also died of a heart attack.

News began to reach the ghetto from people who smuggled themselves in that all the small ghettos in Warthegau were being liquidated by the Germans. They sent away a portion of the men and women who were able to work, but they took away the sick, the old, and the children, and no one knew what happened to them. There were reports about mass shootings, about burnings, but precise information was not known. We had no contact with the outside world; we were surrounded on all sides by Germans—civilian and military. We had no newspapers and no radios.

In the ghetto, the dictator ruled with his police. Maybe he knew something, but he said nothing.

That is how it stood until 1942. There was less work. In individual homes people were already starving. There were already cases of sickness from hunger. Typhus appeared. The epidemic spread fiercely, yet we did not receive medical supplies from the authorities to give inoculations against the illness.

The Gestapo and other Germans began to appear more often in the ghetto. We felt something in the air, that a change in our situation was coming. We were told to take an exact census of the inhabitants of the ghetto immediately. We were ordered to appear before a medical commission, where we got a stamp on the chest with the mark "A" or "B"—but what that signified, we did not yet know.

A group of young Jewish Brzeziner children with their teacher in 1939

At the time of Purim, 1942, ten men and women were hung, and all inhabitants of the ghetto were required to attend. The Germans took photographs. Ikka made a speech that the ten (innocent victims) were hung for sabotaging the demands of the authorities. The *kehile* supplied the victims—a couple of mentally handicapped, sick people, and two arrested for smuggling. Ikka also exploited his hatred of Stark and arrested him. He was among the candidates to be hung, but at the last moment, he was forced to be a participant, together with the police, as the hangman in the execution.

In April 1942 I was suddenly called to the *kehile*. A German from the Gestapo was waiting for me. He said that they knew that there were cases of typhus [spotted fever] in the ghetto, the kind of illness the German hygiene doctors have had little experience handling ("Jews have lice," they said). I was told to prepare a transport of my patients with typhus, and they would be taken to a special sanatorium. I could also send along my personnel—but if they were not up to the task, the German doctors would take over.

The offer seemed very suspicious to us. We decided to send home all the sick. Only a few on their death beds remained. In the morning, a large closed truck arrived. The sick were put inside. They also took a few people who had been arrested. The doors were hermetically sealed, and on the way to Łódź, they were all suffocated by gas fumes from the truck.

The Jewish hospital was in fact liquidated. We had many ill with typhus in private homes.

May 1942—we already knew that the ghetto in Brzezin would be liquidated; some would be taken to the Łódź ghetto, and a small number would remain in Brzezin.

Ikka created a circle of his helpers—police and others—who believed that they would save themselves if they remained in the ghetto. He proposed that I remain in the ghetto (the king of the ghetto still needed a *Leib-arzt* [physician]). I said, however, that I would go together with those who were leaving the ghetto.

We knew that the *kehile* treasury still had enough money. The camps also had resources to keep people alive. I requested of Ikka that everyone deported from the ghetto receive a few marks and some food. At the beginning, Ikka stated that the dead don't need anything. But after a serious argument, I actually extracted ten marks and bread for everyone deported.

According to a list that was created by the *kehile*, the old, the weak, the sick, and mothers with children up to ten years of age were assembled in the town square. During the night, the mothers were torn away from their children, who were thrown into automobiles and carried out of the ghetto. Actually, later we learned that all the children were gassed in Chełmno, near Koło.

On 14 May 1942 we were again assembled. The Germans made a selection based on age and appearance. Many healthy men were immediately sent off to work in camps. I believe none of them ever came back. The rest were split into various groups. They took us to Gałkówek. There we were loaded into railroad cars. At that point, Mojsze Raszewski's son was severely beaten and fell dead. We traveled to Łódź in sealed railroad cars. There, a large part of our group was again deported—from the Łódź ghetto—and every trace of them vanished.

Those left began a new hard life in the Łódź ghetto. Many died of hunger and need, others from illnesses. Rabbi Borensztajn, whom we smuggled into the Łódź ghetto, died in Łódź. Abraham Topolewicz died there, as did the teacher Auster, and many, many others.

And then came the liquidation of the Łódź ghetto in September 1944. Again, the small group of Brzeziner Jews still found in the Łódź ghetto were carried away with the tide. A great number were murdered in the gas chambers of Auschwitz (among them my in-laws, Fiszel Dymant and his wife, and our uncle, Zelig Dymant); others were sent away to various work camps. Only a very small group of them survived all these camps and are now scattered all over the world. Most of them are in our old-new land Medines Yisroel [State of Israel].

This is my history. That is how I myself lived through the destruction of our Brzeziner *kehile*.

Joseph Szaibowicz addressing a *Yizkor* [memorial] meeting in Paris, France.

Destruction of Brzezin (pp. 140–43)

Abraham Blankiet-Sułkowicz[1]

We want to report here to the *landslayt* the "dry facts" about the destruction of Brzezin under the Hitler regime. We could have used florid language with the facts, but what is the point in using such language when each word was forged in chains and description is hopeless? Great masters of the word and the pen have not yet found appropriate artistic forms nor the proper perspective to describe the terrible tragedy of the destruction of six million Jewish martyrs in the Fascist-Nazi epoch in Europe. So let me here relate to you the prosaic, plain facts—facts that pertain mainly to our town—the town that bound us with thousands of familial, intimate threads. Today this very town is for us only a geographic concept that exists in our memory—that in reality, is no more.

Once we had a cemetery there—where rested the physical remains of our nearest and dearest—that the German murderers also destroyed, so that there is no remembrance left even of our graves.

The superbly beautiful synagogue that Brzeziners were so proud of—the pride of our town—was set on fire by the assassins and disappeared in smoke and flames. The beautiful Brzeziner synagogue is no more.

For us, it was a Jewish Brzezin, which bound together today and yesterday with beautiful, bright, orderly traditions. That Brzezin does not exist any more for us. Only a few Brzeziner mourners are left; they are orphans—bloodied, like limbs torn from a tree, thrown into all corners of the world. These very Brzeziners remain the living witnesses to recite the *Megiles Eykhe* [Books of Lamentations] of Brzezin, all the horrors and atrocities that they lived through during the time when the German assassins were slaughtering, burning, and persecuting. They can relate moments when plain, simple, toiling Brzeziner Jews lifted themselves up to the level of sacred martyrs; moments of *kdushe* [saintliness] and—about those past restful, sunny, light-filled days, when the plague of Nazism had not yet reached this world.

* * *

September of 1939 will remain a tragic date in world history and certainly for the Jews of Poland. In that year the German assassins assaulted Poland with their totally sadistic malice. Soon every town and city was in a hail storm of flying destroyers with fire-spitting dynamite bombs. There was a stampede, an attempt to escape. Buildings began to fall like houses of cards; immediately there were the dead and the wounded—and among

---

[1] The author of these bloody documents is Syna Blankiet's son, who was left an orphan when he was young. He was brought up by the Sułkowicz family. As a result, with deep gratitude, he adopted the name Sułkowicz. Everything he relates, he himself lived through and experienced. By a miracle, he survived death and remained a living witness to relate the horrors and terrors of the Brzeziner community. [Yiddish edition editor's note]

them, small innocent infants—yes, the villains, with distinct sadistic pleasure, snuffed out the little souls of nursing infants; it is unbelievable, but it is the absolute truth!

The German murderers brought devastation and destruction to Poland. In our town, as in the surrounding towns, there was gloom. People left all their belongings, possessions accumulated during difficult years of drudgery and toil, and wandered about aimlessly to save themselves from the flying devils. But the planes were all over; nowhere could they be avoided. With systematic brutal calculation, they attacked the unprotected, unarmed civilian population, which tried to escape to shelter and safety.

It soon became clear that Poland had lost the war. The Germans became total masters over everything. Many people fled to the east in order to find protection with the Russians. Others made peace with their fate and remained where they were. Many of the Jews who ran away from our town met the Angel of Death along the way; others succeeded in finding provisional shelter with the Russians. But the majority returned to town when the enemy fire began to abate.

But now, in fact, began the real trouble for Jews. The Germans from our town, such as Wolfschmidt, Bach, Lutomski, and others, with whom we had lived as neighbors quietly and in peace for years, suddenly began getting *khutspe* [nerve] and displaying their German superiority in relations with the Jews, with whom only yesterday they had been friendly and polite. They began systematically to persecute and steal goods from Jewish shops. Yes, Jewish property became ownerless, and every outcast and degenerate began to order Jews around, harassing them with jokes and ridicule.

They began to enlist the cooperation of the Jewish underworld and ordinary degenerate elements. They were elevated to high position and given rank. With the help of these degenerate elements they sought to break the solidarity of Jewish bonds and deliberately incite quarreling and denunciations by one Jew against another. By this method they sought to bring confusion and bewilderment to the Jewish existence and, in general, to undermine and reduce Jewish morale.

This odious "game of sport" partially succeeded. Soon their vile intentions became clear, however, and people began to adjust themselves to the cat-and-mouse game.

Then the villains began to install the infamous bloody ghettos in various cities and towns throughout Poland. The Jewish community was imprisoned behind walls armed and reinforced with barbed wire. They began "systematizing" their devilish and murderous deeds with their sadly well-known precision. They began documenting and registering. They wanted to have an accurate accounting of their victims. Woe to the individual or to the entire camp if anyone dared to run away or generally shirk the harsh procedure of registration and selection. This registration had to be precise. There one had to furnish the entire family record, what possessions were owned, and those who were not merchants had to state their occupation.

The Brzeziner ghetto was established in April 1940 under the harsh supervision of the Nazi murderer Kopmann. The ghetto housing was located on several streets—Apothecary Street, Court Street (Staszica Street, where Szotenberg's house was), Synagogue Street, and Butcher Street. Incidentally, it should be mentioned here that the streets themselves were strictly forbidden to Jews. If one Jew wanted to see another Jew who was located on another street, they had to devise their own paths and trails through the courtyards in the back of the houses. Often they risked their very lives in order to see a relative who was imprisoned in the ghetto prison on another street. But we did it. We were not afraid.

The Germans selected Fiszke Ikka as the "elder" of the Brzeziner Jewish ghetto, who, with all due respect, did not play a very sympathetic role. True, he was bound by the German murderers, but many others also found themselves in similar positions and still found a way to get themselves out of an uncomfortable situation. But we will not judge here. Because who can presume to judge a person who is forced to carry out the orders of an executioner? There were other "petty people," whose names we will not mention here so as not to shame the memory of their families, who played a very ignominious role by helping the Jew haters. These disgraceful, worm-like elements performed their vile work with a determined fervor in order to be rewarded by the villains. These very "small souls" were themselves later annihilated by the ax of the villains.

In Brzezin there were also established large tailoring factories under the supervision of the German company Gunther and Schwarz. The entire community was harnessed to hard labor to produce military equipment. If truth be told, at the beginning of the terrible years, we felt "happy" that we were working, because at least there was enough to eat for a meal—it was certainly a very meager meal, but a meal nevertheless. Later, in the course of months and weeks, the situation seriously deteriorated. The meals began to shrink and shrink. Under these conditions, the production in the factory naturally began to fall—but the villains became more savage and harsher. The SS [Schutzstaffel—elite military unit of Nazi Party] began to use rubber sticks and loaded revolvers. Those physically weakened were naturally the first to fall under the harsher regimen in the workshops. But as bad as it was on the war front, the situation was more horrible in the ghettos. The Nazis became more arrogant and murderous. Their devilish management became more brutal and unbearable. Repressions and severe punishments became an everyday phenomenon. They began a systematic annihilation in the camps.

Haskore [memorial service for the dead] in Paris, France, in honor of Brzeziners who perished.

In the early months, here and there, they tortured someone to death—and it was done unofficially. It had the character of an "unfortunate accident." This is what happened in our town. They dragged the Hasidic young man Efroimowicz (a nephew of Ester-Lajele, the baker) and a Yezhover [from Jeżów] *shoykhet* [ritual slaughterer] who was in Brzezin at that time by chance, into the nearby woods. They dishonored them and then hung them. When they were found hanged several days later, the assassins tried to justify themselves—yes, that was the beginning. We wore the yellow patches. We were abused and crudely insulted. Here and there we were punished with whipping.

But later, the situation began to be horrible and barbarous. Later, the treatment took on the character of wildness and brutality toward a wounded animal.

Because of some sort of a smuggling incident in town, they ordered the "elders" of the Jewish ghetto to deliver ten Jews to the gallows as punishment. The elders tried to bring to bear all means to have the punishment revoked but without success. With broken spirit they "chose" ten Jews for the German executioner. Among them were several who were already at the disposal of the German assassins because of previous "crimes" and others who were abnormal or mentally ill.

This "hanging spectacle" took place in the first months of 1942. The villains undertook to arrange this tragic spectacle with holiday pomp, so that it would make the "proper impression." The gallows were raised behind the synagogue, by the river. The entire Jewish community had to be gathered there. The German schoolchildren were also nearby and contributed their share by yelling out loud, "Heil Hitler! Heil Hitler!" The entire German killing crew of our town were there all dressed up in their finest military uniforms. The "elder" of the Jewish ghetto, Fiszke Ikka, gave the "festive speech" in which he had to say that this spectacle is just an example of the "superior" morality of the German people. There will be worse examples if Jews do not behave "more appropriately." Hitler's ethics are the accepted ones, and his orders are sacred.

Now came the tragic moment when they took the ten doomed people to the gallows. As if it were not enough that we selected the victims for the assassins for their bloodthirsty aims, the villains ordered that the Jews should be the hangmen. The majority of the ten Jews were mentally ill, but they went to the gallows normally, quietly, conscious of their status as Jews—sons and daughters of a long-martyred people.

Here are the names of the martyrs: Judel Sochaczewski, a Kutner (Kutner's grandchild), who'd studied so long and hard that it affected his mind—a water carrier from our town; Jankiel, the Kuke's [looker's] son; Mojsze-Icek Frankensztajn (the tailor's son); the old water carrier (name not known); Mizia the *meshugene* [crazy one] (Idel Beder's daughter); Fajgele with the pigtail (Icze Mydlak's sister). The others, who were from Łódź, found themselves in the Brzeziner ghetto; their names are unknown.

While they were throwing the noose over his head, Judel Sochaczewski said the following words, words that are etched in memory and cannot be forgotten by those who had the mournful luck to have heard them: "Yesterday, I was Judel Sochaczewski; tomorrow I will be Judel *hakodesh* [the martyr]" Yes, simple words, but from their content breathes the history of an ancient persecuted people.

But the "Black Day" of the Brzeziner Jews was still to come. This was 15 May 1942. The villains issued an order that Jewish parents must deliver their children. And on the designated day, Jewish mothers had to part from their children. That was the evil decree. Neither crying, nor begging, nor asking for mercy helped. Jewish mothers had to bring their children before the sacrificial altar of the German rulers. The day when the parents took leave of their small children and infants for the last time was the most awful day, the culmination of the German bestiality against the Brzeziner Jewish community. The lament and the wails of the unfortunate parents, while their children were torn from them and taken in trucks to the death camps to be annihilated, was something that words are too inadequate to describe.

Another black evil decree was the deportation of the elderly of our town. The enemy had previously tormented and bullied them. Earlier, before they sent them to the crematoria, they had been ordered to come before an alleged medical commission. The commission ordered the men and women to undress until completely naked, and they packed them all into a small room. Then the German doctors made jokes about our elderly. They pricked and tugged at the breasts of the women and the sexual organs of the men. The behavior of the doctors was the behavior of loathsome, odious sex maniacs.

These two evil decrees were terrible symbols for the Jews of Brzezin. With these two, they were robbed of the past and the future. Brzezin was left *Kinderrein* [cleansed of children]. What could have been more terrible than these two evil decrees?

Brzeziner martyrs in German death camps.

The miserable remnants went around like lost sheep, their spirits completely broken. The devil had completely achieved his aim. After these two evil decrees that are described, the butchers began to liquidate the Brzeziner ghetto. On 18–19 May 1942 the ghetto for Jews in Brzezin was formally closed. Those who remained were transported to the Łódź ghetto. While they were dispatching them, the Jews were ruthlessly and murderously beaten by German SS men. It should be noted here that many Brzeziner Jews met their death while on the way between Brzezin and Łódź.

The chapter of martyrdom for the Brzeziner Jews had not yet ended when they entered the Łódź ghetto. As soon as they arrived, a new "selection" began, and the number of Brzeziner Jews remaining from that day on was severely reduced. Of the six thousand Jewish men, women, and children who had been located in the Brzezin ghetto, twelve hundred children and elderly were sent to Auschwitz to the gas chamber, forty-three hundred were sent to the Łódź ghetto, and ten were killed in the Brzezin ghetto. The majority were annihilated little by little in the Łódź ghetto. A very small number escaped to the Soviet Union. Before and after the war, a number of Brzeziners succeeded in getting to Eretz Yisroel, where they were materially and spiritually assisted. Right after the war, about a hundred and fifty returned from Soviet territories and went to Łódź. All of them fled at once from the place that embodied within it such a mournful, terrible past.

This is the sorrowful summation of the Brzeziner Jewish community, and we believe, that this summation does not need any commentary.

There Once Was a Jewish Shtetl Brzezin (pp. 144–46)

Dawid Tuszyński

There once was a town of Jewish tailors—Brzezin. From early dawn until late at night one could hear the music of the Singer sewing machines. It was the music of hard work, of intense anxiety, of a hard life, but also of noisy youth, semi-intellectuals, observant Jews, and Hasidim who lived and had aspirations in the small Jewish town Brzezin.

The Nazi savages extinguished this life forever, transformed it into ashes. Only a few Jews from the tailoring town Brzezin by some miracle remain, scattered over the entire world, individuals who were witnesses to the German cannibalism.

May these words, frail in print, but inscribed not with ink but with blood, be a modest contribution to the *matseyve* [gravestone] for my native town, Brzezin.

* * *

Brzezin was one of the oldest and most popular Jewish communities in Poland. When this community was established, it carried the name Krakówek [Little Kraków]. At that time, the community extended from the Strykower highway to beyond the Jewish *besoylem* [cemetery] to the surrounding hills. The Polish noblewoman, Anna Lasocka, had brought the first weavers from afar into this community. Then the community developed even further and began to broaden its borders. At that time, the town already carried the name Brzezin.

Jewish tailors came to Brzezin from many places, and after several generations, the town developed its own type of tailoring industry by which it was known all over the world. A cottage industry was the main occupation here. As early as 1772 Brzezin was famous for its mass production in tailoring. Until 1914 the great Czarist Russia was flooded with the inexpensive products of Brzeziner tailors. In the years between the two world wars, the export of Brzezin industry was spread over many lands in Europe and into other parts of the world. In this, the great Jewish *magaziners*—exporters such as Frankensztajn, Tuszyński, Sułkowicz, and others played a great role.

The Jews in Brzezin did not only work, they also participated actively in the sociopolitical and cultural life of the town, had their representatives on the town council in town hall, and they had their religious and secular, educational, cultural, and social organizations. Materially, it was a life of Jewish poverty, but spiritually, socially, and culturally, it was rich.

* * *

September 1939

The Germans are on the move. Mobilization and turmoil. From western Poland, thousands of Jews are fleeing in panic. Masses pass through Brzezin heading toward Warsaw. Brzeziner Jews leave their sewing machines and go out into the streets in order to give assistance to the transient Jews passing through. They share food, give medical help, and provide beds for those who are delayed for a day or two in town.

Wednesday, the sixth day of the war. Brzezin gets bombed. Fire and smoke cover the town. The streets—Saint Anna Street, a part of Pilsudski Street, and Rogowski Street—disappear in smoke. At that time, many inhabitants and refugees from Łódź, Kalisz, and other communities are killed.

Several days later the Germans enter our town, and a series of persecutions begin—house searches and looting, round-ups for work, insults, humiliation, beatings, and torture. A large number of Jewish intellectuals and various leaders are arrested and deported. They never came back, and since then nobody knows what became of them.

Yonkiper, after the Germans had set fire to the synagogue, they led old Rabbi Borensztajn into the street and set fire to his beard. Goaded, beaten, exhausted, and ridiculed, he was dragged away to the train and shipped off to Kraków. Broken and sick, he came back to Brzezin several days later, only to be deported later to the gas chamber with all the elderly.

Round-ups for work take place daily. A portion of those seized are sent away outside of town, on the way to Gałkówek, where people are tortured and then buried alive. Spread out along the roads that go from Brzezin to Gałkówek, Witkowice, and Koluszki—and also into the surrounding forests—are mass graves of Brzeziner Jews who were buried alive.

In the second half of December 1939, the SS man Kopmann arrived, and several days later, the first curses began. From an entire group of streets, Jews were rounded up in order to be deported. After great effort on the part of the Jews Zagon and Klajnbaum—who made it clear that these Jews, tailors by trade, could be used to work for the army—and, most importantly, with the help of a gigantic sum of ransom money in cash and in gold, the abuse was stopped. Workshops to serve the military were created in Brzezin.

Where the Jewish cemetery was before the Nazis dishonored it.

In the first months of 1940, a ghetto was established in Brzezin. The *Judenrat* (Jewish Council) was formed with Fiszke Ikka at the head and [Seweryn] Perlmuter, known by the name *Shmayde Fiak* (complete drunkard), as the police commander. As if there were not enough Germans, we also had to put up with bitter torment even from Jewish "leaders."

In the ghetto, despite hunger, cold and repression, the work went on in the tailoring workshops. They made clothing for the Germans. From time to time German "visitors" used to come to Brzezin. Especially known were the names of the Gestapo men—Fuchs,

Richter, and Swinto. Those names evoked terror and horror among the Jewish population in the Brzezin ghetto. Using various methods and means, they took from the Jewish population the last remnants of their possessions—gold, jewelry, and furs. They used to get drunk, and the *Judenrat* would have to supply alcohol—wine, liquor, and cognac. They wanted women, and the *Judenrat* had to provide women. "Chairman" Fiszke docilely obeyed, carrying out all that was demanded of him.

Nevertheless, life in the ghetto during the year 1940 passed, one could say, "normally"; we somehow survived. Later, the situation worsened beyond comparison. Already in the first days of January 1941, a command suddenly came to furnish ten Jews who must be publicly hung. On the site of the burned-down synagogue, a gallows was erected. The *Judenrat*, according to the command, had to furnish ten Jews—and the *Judenrat* carried out the command.

The entire Jewish population of the ghetto was brought to the execution and had to view this event. At twelve noon, with hands bound behind their backs, the ten Jews were led to the gallows. Among the victims was a mentally ill Jewish woman, Mundzia; there was another woman among them, Fajga the water carrier. The rest were men; among them were Judel the water carrier, Urbach, Hauzer, and others. Hauzer went to the gallows with the outcry, "We go to a martyr's death; take revenge!" Judel the water carrier called out, "Until now I was a simple water carrier; tomorrow I will be among the holy martyrs!"

After that it was quiet for several weeks, and then it began again.

A command was issued that all the elderly and sick must be brought in to be "branded." All the elderly and sick were collected in Badower's building—men and women. All had to undress completely naked. First the SS men arranged entertainment. The naked men and women had to dance and demonstrate various things that are simply impossible to describe. They forced the Jews to perform various distinct scenes, beat them on their naked flesh, and kicked them. After that, when the SS men had finally had enough of this "exhibition," they began to stamp all those that were there. They put the stamps on their sexual organs. The healthy ones returned home, those that got branded with the letter "B." The rest were sent away to die.

On 14–15 May 1942 a gang of SS men came into the Brzeziner ghetto with the chief, [Hans] Biebow. Biebow's name already had a reputation at that time. That name of his aroused horrible fear in everyone. Biebow issued a command that mothers had to bring their children to him, up to the age of ten. It rained on that day in Brzezin; it rained torrentially, and through the streets of the ghetto came neatly dressed Jewish children with their hair freshly washed and combed, led by their mothers. The mothers were crying, and the children calming them, trying to quiet them, "Mama, don't cry. Why are you crying?"

The children were all assembled around the town square near the town hall; they remained there the entire day with their mothers. Night fell, the tired children fell asleep on the ground near their mothers. Some children cried, begging, "Mama, let's go home. Why don't we go home? Why is it so dark? Why don't we turn on some lights?"

Suddenly, at three o'clock in the morning, there was a great commotion. A drunken clamor awoke the children. A command was heard—turn over all the children—and right after that, they began to tear the children away from their mothers. A lament from the mothers and children, a cry, an entreaty, and the SS men tear the children away from their mothers' clenched hands. Children scream and cry, "Mama, I want to go with you, *Mamusia* [Mommy]!" The mothers fall at the feet of the SS men in entreaty, kissing their filthy boots. The SS men kick them with their boots, strike heads, prod them, and a contemptuous laughter echoes through the hall, mixed with the sound of pointed tips of rods on the flesh of the crying mothers. The mothers plead, "Take us along also; we want to go together with our children." It does not help.

From the Brzeziner children's colony in 1938

They take the children away, and in the hall remain the battered, aching, and sobbing mothers. One of the Gestapo, Zeifert, shouts out, "The mothers must so perish," and goes out. A reverberation of child-like screaming and crying is heard from outside. After several minutes, it becomes entirely still. At daybreak, the SS men come in to the mothers, and with shouts and beatings, they chase them outside into the street.

The next morning, the Brzeziner ghetto was empty of children. No longer were there children in the ghetto. Only one mother remained in the ghetto with a child; this was Mira Rozen. The *Judenrat* took a chance for her, and the Germans were so magnanimous that, for the time being, they pardoned the life of a Jewish child.

When the mothers turned to the chairman of the *Judenrat* with the question "What happened to our children? Where did they take our children?" the chairman answered, "The children are in Łódź, with Rumkowski [head of *Judenrat* in Łódź ghetto] in Marisin; they are there in a children's home. You will see them soon."

Several days later, they did the same thing to the grown-ups that they did to the children. The liquidation of the Brzezin ghetto had begun. People were rounded up from their homes and shops and carried away to their deaths.

Within a short time later, the Brzezin ghetto was liquidated—Brzezin was cleansed of Jews.

BRZEZINER JEWS IN THE ŁÓDŹ GHETTO

From *In the Years of the Jewish Catastrophe*, an anthology by the Bund [Jewish Socialist Party]:

In the month of July 1942, the Jews of Brzezin began to be brought into the Łódź ghetto. Those who came told of terrible things, the way the liquidation had taken place in Brzezin. Through special gangs—we called them *Rol-komandes*—who were called into the town, the Jews were driven together into one place, shot, murdered, robbed, and a selection carried out. The healthy ones were packed one hundred to one hundred and fifty people at a time into one train wagon. Many women with children and sick people were taken away to Chełmno [death camp].

A Jew from Brzezin brought a postcard from the Grabów *rov*, in which he reported that he had spoken to three Jews who had fled Chełmno and told him what was happening there.

The card was brought to a meeting of the ghetto committee in Łódź.

What we lived through then is hard to communicate. By then we knew everything. It was decided to inform all parties about it, as well as Rumkowski, the *alteste* [elder] of the *Judenrat* in Łódź, so that Rumkowski would no longer be able to say that he did not know what was happening to people. We told him that he should no longer be an accomplice of the Germans and that he should no longer attempt to buy off the evil decree—a tactic that Rumkowski categorically rejected.

* * *

Comrade Abraham Apowski [Opatowski], former member of the town council in Brzezin, was brought in as a member of the Łódź group (of the Bund) to direct the self-help activities in the ghetto. The Bundist party group from Brzezin amounted to fifteen men.

I Saw the *Khurbn* [Destruction] (pp. 147–48)

Dora Zagon-Winer

I will never forget the dark Shabes day, a week after the outbreak of the war, when the Nazis marched into Brzezin and the destruction of our hometown began.

Very early on Shabes the Germans took Brzezin. We Jewish citizens waited in our homes, terrified because of the forthcoming events. Night came, a death-like stillness spread over the town. Suddenly, a flame lit up the heavens, caused by the burning down of our beautiful synagogue.[1]

The German murderers brought to the site of the fire our Rabbi Borensztajn, an elderly man upon whom we all looked as the spiritual father of our *kehile* [Jewish community]. He was forced to sign a document that he himself had set fire to the synagogue. Hitler's fire setters thought this would wash away the sin that they had committed against the Jewish population of Brzezin.

Then began the terrible persecutions inflicted upon us by German soldiers, together with the Brzeziner *Volksdeutsche* [ethnic Germans].

The first victims were the wealthy families. Killings and robbings, as well as beatings with murderous blows without any reason, were daily occurrences. The "hero" of the first barbarous action was a local German, a former friend of ours by the name of Bach, a member of the sports club BKS, the *bramkarz* (goalkeeper) of the local soccer team.

Brzezin, the regional capital, became the focal point for the assembly of regular German army battalions. A regiment of the German *Wehrmacht* [regular army] was stationed in Brzezin. The local police were quartered in Korolenki's building on Sienkiewicza Street. The Gestapo [secret police] and the SS [Schutzstaffel—elite military unit of Nazi party] occupied Dr. Warhaft's private home.

Day and night without end the Stormtroopers [Nazi paramilitary group] would rampage through the streets of our town. The *Obersturmführer* [head of Stormtroopers], Manen Kopmann, a terrible sadist, would invade Jewish homes and issue orders for men, regardless of age, to gather in the courtyard in rows of five. Then he would begin to torment them with military drills. "Get down! Get up!" And during this orgy he would beat the poor wretches with revolvers and kick them in the head with his boots. At the end, he used to pick out several elderly men and cold-bloodedly beat them with blackjacks.

---

[1] According to other information, the synagogue was burned down 9 November 1939 during a German military holiday. (Author's note)

According to the Warhaft story, p. 135 of the Yizkor book, the burning of the synagogue occurred on 11 November, the anniversary of the day Germany had surrendered and signed an armistice ending World War I (11 November 1918).

The SS men set up a real butcher shop in their quarters. They summoned rich Jewish citizens, beat them, and forced them to give away all they possessed. Afterward, they sent the unfortunate Jews home, half bloodied and battered.

The systematic campaign to rob Jews lasted until the month of May. The murderous work was carried out with German "precision."

In addition to the evil decrees, they humiliated us morally at every step. Often a German sadist would stop a Jew and cut off his beard, while a group of onlookers would stand around and amuse themselves by laughing and applauding the merriment. We Jews had no right to walk on the sidewalks—only among the pigs and on lanes in the middle of the street. This would be the filthiest part and the most dangerous. We wore yellow patches on our chests and backs. Under penalty of death, we were not allowed to appear on the streets after four o'clock in the afternoon.

Later we found out that the Nazis had decided to liquidate us, drive us out of town, and drag us away to the crematoria. With great self-sacrifice, Jasza Zagon, together with Dr. Warhaft, carried out a plan to help during this terrible time. They persuaded a German officer who had shown mercy for Jews to travel with them to Łódź to the *Handelskammer* [chamber of commerce] to present a plan to the Germans and convince them that the Jewish tailors from Brzezin could be of use to the German Reich. This helped a bit, and they put us to work.

On 15 May 1940 they stuffed us like animals into the ghetto, fenced in with barbed wire. We worked twelve hours a day for the firm Gunther and Schwarz. The living conditions were horrible. Two families occupied one small room, without any facilities. Hunger, deprivation, and cold reigned in the ghetto. Several diseases spread rapidly.

In the ghetto and at work, the Nazi sadists tortured us terribly. They were "artists" in discovering all sorts of methods to shorten our lives. Depressed and hungry, we surrendered. But they did not break our spirit. In every tortured Jew a spark of hope lived that the horrible hellish suffering would end and the moment of revenge would come.

The black day when the Hitler assassins herded the Jewish population onto the streets to be present at the "hanging spectacle" of ten Brzeziner Jews.

In March 1942 posters appeared on the walls of the ghetto that the execution of ten so-called criminals would take place on Purim. They would be hung, and the entire population of the ghetto must witness the execution.

On the designated day, the gallows were raised not far from the Mrozica River (that the Jews called the *rzeka* [river]), amid the remains of the half-burned outside walls of our beautiful synagogue.

Militiamen, specially recruited for the purpose, forcibly dragged out every Jew who refused to be a witness. It was thus that all the Jews of the ghetto were assembled at the site of the gallows. Many of us were torn apart; the nerves couldn't stand it. Indescribable screaming and crying were heard from the crowd. The desperate cries were borne up to the heavens.

But then an SS man suddenly appeared and with his high, strong voice gave the order: "Be silent! If not, everyone here will be shot!" In an instant there was a deathlike stillness.

Those condemned to be hung were brought out. Upright, with heads held high, they approached the gallows without displaying the slightest fear of death. One, a homeless beggar, Judel Sochaczewski, who in his entire sad life never hurt a fly, cried out several times as he was climbing the steps to the gallows: "I go to a martyr's death for the whole town!"

After the execution, all the Jews had to march past the gallows with their faces toward those who'd been hanged.

In the month of May another dreadful piece of news swept through the ghetto—the announcement of the liquidation of the ghetto and the deportation of all Jews from the town.

One day Jewish mothers with children up to ten years of age had to gather in the market square. The unfortunate mothers experienced a short-lived happiness. They thought, in their naiveté, that they were being taken to a rest home with their frail children. How terrible was their disappointment!

The market square was immediately surrounded by SS men. Large trucks came to the square where the mothers and their children were gathered. The "action" [deportation] had begun.

These were the last Jews in Brzezin. Josef Bialek Jobrusz, the waggoner's grandchild.

In a bestial manner, the SS men tore the tiny children from their mothers' arms. Heartrending scenes were played out there; the shrieking and screaming reached the heavens. The mothers fought for their children like lionesses, but they had to surrender.

That is how they loaded thousands of children onto trucks and carried them away to the crematoria.

On 15 May the Nazis drove the entire Jewish population of the ghetto out onto the streets. On 19 May six thousand Jewish souls were deported from Brzezin. Of these, only a small group remain alive.

That is how our Jewish town was destroyed.

Our Two Writer Martyrs (pp. 149–53)

Chaim-Lajb Fuks

JAKUB-BER GIPS

J. B. Gips, the poet and Yiddish teacher from Brzezin, was an unusual person.

Always eager for action, for teaching, and for beauty, he devoted himself wholeheartedly to the new Yiddish culture and literature. They occupied his entire being and replaced the *Gemore* [second part of Talmud] and *Haskole* [Enlightenment] literature, imbibed during his earlier youth between the walls of the *besmedresh* [house of prayer].

Born in Brzezin in 1892 into a middle-class family, Jakub-Ber displayed, at a very young age, in his *kheyder* [Jewish elementary school] years, an extraordinary passion for learning. At the age of five, he already knew *Khumash* [Torah] and chapters of *Tanakh* [Holy Scriptures]; by twelve he had outgrown the traditional religious school with the *Gemore* teachers and had to travel to Łódź and Skierniewice to study. In Łódź, his *rebbe* [Hasidic rabbi] was Reb Chaiml Kotsker [from Kock]. From him he heard many, many Hasidic stories, and through him, he began to become absorbed in the world of Jewish mysticism. All through the night he read books about *kabole* [Jewish mysticism], about the search for the infinite, about the essence of life.

Through this his ideas matured; through this he acquired his own view of the world. From there he was drawn to worldly knowledge. In those years his second home was the Yiddish section of the TKO[1] library, which satisfied his thirst for knowledge. There he came to understand Yiddish literature, which opened wide horizons to him and engraved in his blood the longing for a national way of life. In the Łódź Poale Zion [Zionist Labor Party] circle he matured into someone who also responded to world problems, political issues, questions concerning the awakening Jewish workers' movement, and the revolutionary happenings in Russia and in the world. He became one of the early members of the first circles of writers and poets just beginning to be formed in Łódź.

Gips sought out the evening courses that Lazar Fuks and the attorney Anders arranged for young people free of tuition. From that time on, Jakub-Ber Gips became an enthusiastic admirer of Labor Zionism, of the left-wing Poale Zion party, and of Jewish culture.

He dreamt of becoming a teacher—and particularly a teacher in the folk language, in Yiddish. His dream was interrupted when World War I broke out.

Like all those who had lived in the *shtetlekh* [small towns], he was drawn back home during that time. He came back to Brzezin during the terrible days when, because of the war, all activity was completely brought to a standstill. The tailoring machines that

---

[1] TKO—Possibly Towarzystwo Kultury i Oświaty [Society for Culture and Education].

previously had clothed half the world were silent. Songs were no longer heard—those melodies of a new time that the Jewish worker had sung about, when he'd been able to bring bread into the house.

The town, which drew a great deal of its livelihood from Łódź, was confused and discouraged. The manufacturers and merchants had saved a little, but not the Brzeziner tailors, who had barely made a living from their day-and-night toil.

Jakub-Ber did not rest. Already in the first week, when operations had been suspended and the Germans had occupied Łódź and Brzezin, a meeting was called at Jakub-Ber's initiative, and the first savings and loan bank, the first cooperative, was founded as a department of the *arbet-heym* [workers home]; the main institution was in Łódź.

In those days he created his first poems, which he brought to Icchak Kacenelson. The first poem that gave him recognition was published in the first number of Lazar Kahan's *Folksblat* [People's Newspaper]. He even wanted to return to Łódź, but duty to his Brzeziners dispelled any such thought. He had to be in the place where he was most needed. He was cofounder of a number of institutions. He made use of his time to complete the preparation of his life's aim—to become a teacher of Yiddish. Since a position became available in the town of Łowicz, he went there and also took over, in addition to the Yiddish courses, the entire Poale Zion party and its cultural work.

In 1922 he settled in Łódź. There, new journals were born every month—*Yung Yiddish* [Young Yiddish], which presented the new tone of stirring poetry, and three Yiddish daily newspapers. And Jakub-Ber Gips came to Łódź with only his poems and his dreams. The young writers group received him as one of their own, which signaled his future destiny. He became, with all his heart and soul, a friend and co-builder of Yiddish culture.

In those days Jewish secular schools were expanding. Thousands of Jewish children drank in the growing fruits of the Yiddish Folk School.

Jakub-Ber Gips became one of the teachers in the large Borochov school in Łódź [named for Marxist-Zionist leader Ber Borochov]. He taught the children Jewish history, the subject that he loved most in the world and that he felt would help build a Jewish people's homeland. He instilled in his students the spirit of *chalutzim* [pioneers] through the ancient sources of *Medresh* [creative interpretations of the Scriptures] and *Tanakh* [Holy Scriptures]. He did not teach the children only from books but also recreated, through his visions and images, the times of the past, when Jews were a people on a par with other peoples. The children loved him like a good friend, like a father. He was very happy. His dream had sprouted wings.

In those days he was unusually creative. He published his works in newspapers, in the periodicals of the young Łódź writers group—*Vegn* [Paths], *Shveln* [Doorsteps], *S'feld* [Domain], in the Poale Zion press, and several in the publication *Das Kind* [The Child], where he considered himself a founder. He wrote poetry, public affairs commentary, and literary criticism.

In 1925 he became an editorial staff member of the new daily newspaper *Lodzer Morgenblat* [Łódź Morning Paper], which was later merged with the *Ekstrablat* [Extra Paper]. There he also wrote about Jewish politics and set the tone for the daily issues of Jewish life in Łódź and in Poland in general. With Izrael Rubin and Chaim-Lajb Fuks, he became coeditor of the *Literarishe Vokhnshrift* [Literary Weekly], which later opened for him the doors of the editorial room of the oldest Łódź newspaper, the *Lodzer Togblat* [Daily Paper], where he became a very important member of the staff. There he also published, in addition to current events, political articles, fiction, book reviews, plays, and a number of original and translated novels. A very important work of his was the publication, in every pre-holiday number, of one of his translations of our old *tfiles* [prayers], like *Akdomes* [hymn recited on the first day of Shavuos] and *Tfile Zaka* [prayer on Yom Kippur forgiving others]. He also translated *Khad Gadye* [An Only Kid—in the Passover Hagaddah] and *Shir Hashirm* [Song of Songs] into very fine poetry.

He also wrote the majority of the lesson books for the *Beis Yakov* schools [for girls] in Poland. Of great significance were his revisions of the *zikhroynes* [memoirs] of the Łódź *rov*, Reb Eliahu Chaim Meisels. Both parts of the memoirs were published by Grubsztajn's publishing house. He edited them with his friend Izrael Rozenberg.

J. B. Gips also translated several books from European literature, which were published by the publishing house of the Goldfarb Brothers, such as Blasco Ibanez' *The Victim of Fanaticism*, as well as books of Russian writers—Gorky, Fadayev, and others. He wrote under many pseudonyms: B. Zajdów, Jack Beer, Brzeziński, and others.

For a time, while the Nazis occupied Łódź, he went into hiding. The German Nazis, who had a list of all the Jewish writers, and especially of those who had carried out a fight against them (among them Jakub-Ber Gips, who, in *Togblat*, had very boldly urged the boycott of German goods and had written critical articles about the expulsion of Polish Jews from Germany), searched for him. He dressed like a peasant with long hair and a Polish coat and barely reached Siemiatycze alive. From there, a few days later, he traveled to Białystok.[1]

A group of Zionists gathered together to say goodbye to friends Emanuel Gotlib and Adela Rozenblum upon their departure abroad. The third from the left, standing, is Jakub-Ber Gips.

He could not get work from the Bolsheviks or the right to live closer than one hundred miles from the border. He also had to give up the idea of being a Yiddish teacher. The Yiddish schools were closed, and in their place, Belarussian ones were opened. The new areas that the Soviets had taken over, in general, did not have many schools. The politics was to Russify even

---

[1] Białystok, in the northeastern corner of Poland, was occupied by Russia from 1939–41 and invaded by Germany only in 1941.

more, and Jakub, the faithful Yiddishist, was in great despair. There was less and less news from the other side of the border all the time, and the hope that those closest to him would be able to reach him, grew fainter. He was a desperate man until he accepted an offer to be a Belarussian teacher in a faraway, secluded village.

During the first days of July 1941, when the Germans occupied Belarus, he was captured by the Nazis and martyred.

POEMS OF JAKUB-BER GIPS

Bones Speak[1]

The old world trembles, temples crash,
Blue heavens, golden princesses.
Quiet princesses, recite final prayers
During the Shabes afternoon hour,
Tranquil rest.
Bones speak!
Winds blow in the hearts, mortal man
Who now stands naked, strives.
Iron voices of trumpets wheeze,
Strings of the old-woman-fiddle scrape, relaxed.
Bones speak!
One immense skeleton sings out, bone-like
The last song of the last generation . . .

Woe to the Days

Woe to the days with the dead hours,
That lie shrouded in mist —
Consumed streets and yellowed people
Who drag,
On stairs
Of precipitous ways, the burden of years
Wrapped in rags, in shirts.
Among them, I go around, a stranger
With a breast open wide
And play, a last liturgical poem
About small coins and *groszy*,
About everything living
Everything dead . . .
Oh, woe to the days with hardened heavens,
And leaden stars
And clouds suspended

---

[1] Many years earlier, in his poem "Bones Speak," J. B. Gips had a premonition of the coming destruction. (Author's note)

Before your eyes —
And catch up with winds
That wheeze with death
Snagged in their teeth . . .

The Last One

With mouth singing out loud and drunken head
The last generation of Europe sings
On banks and lanes the last song . . .
The voices wander into the graves of the dead,
The voices wander into the channels of
The not-yet born,
The voices wander around,
Like roaming souls, searching for redress
And merge together
In one great outcry of woe!
A voice thunders: Go, go.
Search for everything, since of generations
You are the last!
— He goes
And wherever he goes, stones sing out
And wherever he goes, flames blaze out
And everything sings, everything burns —
And walls fall
Before the last song-sound,
And generation to generation, stretches out a hand.
But, hey, what's the matter? A wall —
And bones, bones, bones —
Shards! — — —

MELECH FOGEL

Melech Fogel had a completely different character. Under the influence of Gips, he began to write poetry and aspired to be regarded as a writer in the minds of Jews.

He was a very interesting type, both in his attitude toward people and also especially in his ambition to become well-known, to extricate himself from small town life and go out into the wider world.

Born in 1898 into a working family of bakers, he barely finished *kheyder* but taught himself to write not only Yiddish but also Polish and a little Russian and German. And the little that he learned, he had to acquire after his working hours in a tailoring workshop.

After he had finally become a "perfect" pants sewer and was making a good living, he did not think about getting all dressed up and going out to the dance halls as most of his kind did; in his free evening hours, he devoted himself to community work in the *arbet-heym* [workers home], which brought him closer to the Left Poale Zion. However, he did not become a party member, and, as a sympathizer, he helped with the work—more on account of his love of people than of the party. In those days, when Gips began to play a role in the new Yiddish poetry, Melech Fogel was also fascinated by the desire to write poetry.

He made many plans to establish his own platform, his own publication in Brzezin. However, nothing came of it. The poems that reflected his populous nature—his virtuous being, his in-love-with-someone soul—were too old-fashioned in style and form to be printed in the publications of the young writers' group in Łódź. He was only published in humorous sections of newspapers, such as "Lamtern" [Lantern] in the *Lodzer Togblat* [Łódź Daily Paper] and "Shrapnel" in the *Folksblat* [People's Paper], but this did not satisfy him. An idea occured to him. He would pay for the publication *S'Feld* [Domain] that we published in those days, on the condition that his poems would be printed in it.

That is how Melech Fogel's poems got published in two numbers of *S'Feld*. But again, he was not satisfied, and he decided to publish his own small books of poems. In the years between 1926 and 1939, he published eight books of poems, almost all of which were devoted to local Brzeziner matters—for example, *The Terrible Murder in Brzezin*, which was published in 1926, and others. This separated him even further from the literary group, which saw Melech Fogel as deviating completely from the usual taste of people and as looking only for his own popularity instead of, as in the beginning, being concerned with Yiddish literature. This, however, did not deter Melech Fogel. And his books more and more had even less to do with poetry.

However, until World War II, he always maintained contact with the Łódź writers. He attended every literary event and continued to pay for each issue (knowing that his works would not be printed). In the last weeks before September 1939, he had prepared a large book with old Brzeziner stories and poems for publication and had made an arrangement with a printer (Liebeskind) to distribute it. This was supposed to be his swan song, his contribution to literature and to the hometown that he loved so much, to which he paid tribute in the manner of plain people and dreamt about with tears (he would sing his poems with appropriate melodies and shed tears while singing). But it was not to be that he or his *landslayt* would enjoy his work of many years.

In the first days of September 1939, after the Germans had already bombed Poland, he came to me with inquiring glances and silent looks, and that is how we ran from one cellar to the other, hiding from German bullets.

During the night of 6 September 1939, I decided to leave Łódź and go to Warsaw on foot. On the morning of 7 September, I told him that he should come with me to Warsaw. I went to another house to rest myself from the journey and the unmercifully tormenting heat. A half hour later, German planes flew over and bombed almost every house. By some miracle, I narrowly escaped. But when I later went over to Fogel's house, the house was in flames, and Melech Fogel had perished in the flames.

May my words be a memorial candle to their dear souls, for the young lives that so beautifully shone upon the familiar and beloved, poor but sincere, Jewish Brzeziner way of life. They put their holy lives at the service of Jewish people, and Jews will remember them with love.

A Tailoring Song by Melech Fogel (from before the destruction)[1]

1
Oh, this is a good time,
The tailors come to life,
They beat the cotton jackets
They cry: an end, an end.

2
Sew, sew little tailors,
As long as you have strength.
If you'll have enough for Shabes,
Only the one God knows.

3
They do not look at what they earn,
Just to sew as much as they can,
From early to very late at night,
Let the wheel turn.

4
A good tailor is only one
Who makes the jackets trim;
One who does not save
On a piece of soap.

5
The tailor lives very well.
During the week he has bread to eat,
Except the child who does not work—
That child must suffer need.

6
The machines make a lot of noise,
Nearby stands the little wife
And wraps the merchandise,
Like the motorcycles.

7
A boy who is eight years old
Is already a grown-up —
A jacket up to his elbow
That he himself made.

8
A boy who is four years old
And cannot yet sew,
They find for him a little work
  anyway
Winding spools.

9
Young children here
Mature very early—
In one little hand—a doll,
With the other he smears soap.

10
Small children are
Not spared from work—
One child irons the seams,
The second sews buttons.

11
No matter how small children are,
Sometimes they can be put to work,
One threads a needle,
Another turns a spool.

12
A child who barely stands on his feet,
He still shuffles along near the wall,
They put him on a little bench,
With a pressing iron in his hand.

13
A child who still lies in the cradle
They don't even let him rest—
They give the child a job,
To pull threads.

14
He who has no children,
Him they mock—
That tailor must then starve,
He can't make any jackets.

15
Sew, sew, little tailor,
As long as you have strength;
How long you can hold out,
Surely only the one God knows.

---

[1] This poem was written in the style of simple plain folk, as if the author actually had no artistic pretensions. (Author's note)

The Wretched Cry (p. 154, col. 1)

Genia Brandszaft

I will never forget that dark day of 15 May 1942 in our town Brzezin. On that day, when it was spring everywhere else in the entire world, a heavy cloud descended over our heads. Hitler's murderers had issued the evil decree that mothers who had children younger than ten years old must report to the market square. The well-known "curse" that meant "go to the slaughter" had begun. . . .

But at the gathering place itself, it was the most horrible. The Nazi beasts began to tear away the mothers from their children and the children from their mothers. Even now, the wretched crying of the children resounds in my ears, the heartrending cries of fathers and mothers. And above all, I hear the cry of lament of my own child, my little daughter. . . . Those voices will continue to ring in my ears as long as I live.

I gathered up my courage, I ran up to a Nazi and tried to beg him to take me with my child. But instead of an answer, he began to beat me with his horse whip, all over my entire body, until I fell unconscious in a pool of blood. Until today, I have the wounds all over my body as a "reminder" of that day in our town Brzezin.

And after that we shared the tragic fate of our brothers and sisters in the destruction. The Łódź ghetto, hunger, humiliation, suffering . . . And after that came the road to Auschwitz—undress yourself naked . . . shaved heads . . . the gas-chamber and the crematorium. Who can even describe those horror scenes? Who is able even to recount them? How can you write about the separation from your husband, from those near and dear?

But in my old days and nights, as for many of our people, one feeling and one desire was dominant—REVENGE! To take revenge for the murder of our fathers and mothers, brothers and sisters, and REVENGE for the spilled blood of our children!!!

I do not know by what miracle or through what kind of merit I remained among those who lived. Perhaps only for the reason that I should actually live to see the longed-for revenge. I should see the end of Hitler and his band, and I should have the rare honor to live to see the birth of the Jewish state . . . and great was my feeling of revenge when I lived to see the punishment in the Jewish state of the bestial murderer Adolf Eichmann, may his name be erased.

In the Tragic Years (p. 154, col. 2)

Rywka Tajczer

In the worst times, when I struggled between life and death, the thought was always dominant—the hour of revenge must come; we should be able to take revenge on the murderers for our pain and suffering, for our brothers and sisters who were so tragically and brutally murdered. . . .

Yes, twenty years have sped by since that tragic era, but the wound has remained painful and fresh; the entire horror stands clearly before my eyes. A deep wound will remain engraved and seared in my memory, in my heart, that will follow me until the end of my days. I will never forget it, nor forgive it!

When I was in Oświęcim [Auschwitz], in those terrible times, I thought that if it were to be my fate to survive the horrors of the war, I would take a vow never again to walk on the accursed Polish earth. And so it was. In 1946 we left Poland. We set out illegally with the aim of going to Israel.

In 1947 we were on the ship *Exodus*. Once again we lived through terrible, painful days and nights. My husband and I and my only child, who, unknowingly, was already a fighter, a soldier for Medines Yisroel. Alas, to my great sorrow, my child could not survive the difficult journey and died prematurely en route during the perilous trip to Israel. My child was born 4 September 1947 and died 20 September of the same year . . . an innocent victim of that tragic epoch . . . another wound in a mother's heart that will remain engraved in memory until the end of her days. . . .

A memorial gathering of *landslayt* in Israel, held in the meeting hall of Shikkun Brzezin [Brzezin housing project].

Matseyve [Gravestone] in Bergen-Belsen (p. 155)
To the memory of the victims of our town

On 27 July 1947 (Tisha b'Av) the unveiling of a memorial as a remembrance of the Brzeziner martyrs took place in Bergen-Belsen, Camp One, at the site where the crematorium stood, where Jewish lives were brutally extinguished—among them our own dear ones from Brzezin.

Landslayt from all over came to the memorial gathering. The *landslayt* in America, on this occasion of the fifth *yortsayt* of the liquidation of the Brzeziner ghetto, sent the following telegram:

Dear Sisters and Brothers,

> On this anniversary day of our great annihilation, we are together with you, immersed in deep sorrow. Let us with combined strength help to rebuild the life of the survivors and give honor to our fallen heroes. Undertake this with courage, and may your hearts be strengthened to meet the tomorrow that will shine over our people and also our own land.
>
> We are with you!
>
>   For the *landslayt* in America,
>
>   Jacob David Berg, Joseph Diamond, and Fishel Maliniak

The Brzeziner Jewish Community During the Time of the Ghetto (p. 156)

Rywka Hendler-Gociał

The activity of the Jewish *gmina* [community] in the time of the ghetto years 1940–42 was, in general, different from the normal activity of the Jewish community before the war.

Because of the unusually difficult situation that Polish Jewry found itself in, also in the spiritual realm, all religious activities unfortunately ceased.

The *gmina* served only to carry out administrative functions. Under its supervision the following offices operated: 1) the finance department, 2) the housing office, 3) the provisions office, 4) the post office, 5) the clothing manufacturing committee, 6) the court, 7) social welfare—the hospital, the police, and other offices.

The chairman (*Judenaltester*) [Jewish elder], Fiszke Ikka, was not selected by the *kehile* [Jewish community council] but picked by the Germans.

The work of the secretary, Abraham Szafman, *z"l* [of blessed memory], was very difficult. Very often he was forced to provide various statistical lists for the German authorities. Once it was a work list—to send people away to a camp, another time, a list of smugglers, and later, lists of small children and the elderly, and so forth. It was quite evident that the lists were not accurate, but they could not conceal everything.

The housing office, under the leadership of Icek Dymant, *z"l*, began its activity with the establishment of the Jewish ghetto. After that, as a greater number of Jews were forced to leave their homes and locate within the ghetto area, the housing office saw to it that no one remained homeless.

The provisions office, in which Tobiasz Krawiecki, *z"l*, worked, was concerned with giving out the limited supply of products and clothing, distributed in the cooperative under the leadership of Ezriel Eksztajn. Only bread rations were distributed by the bakers. No other businesses existed.

As a former member, I can accurately describe all that pertains to the manufacturing committee. Its operational work was carried out by Fiszel Dymant and Izrael Tryber, *z"l*. The committee was concerned with all kinds of production that was connected with manufacturing work. It created tailor shops in which thirty to thirty-five workers were employed. They also calculated the prices for the masters, apprentices, and hand-stitchers, according to their work qualifications, and also set the rates for machine buttonholes and hand-made buttonholes.

Later, the manufacturing committee also created a shop to make netting, in which children aged nine to ten were employed, to protect them from being sent away.

In addition to that, the committee also resolved different conflicts that occurred between the workers and the masters and dealt with the appropriate distribution of work to buttonhole makers and women hand-buttonhole makers.

As is known, the town was saved by a miracle from liquidation, until May 1942, because of the manufacturing work for the German armies in which approximately ninety percent of the Jewish population was employed.

Among the statistics listing the wages earned through that very committee were included names of children, in order, in this way, to avoid paying the head tax, which was calculated in accordance with earnings, and at the same time to show a larger number of those employed.

In comparison to other ghettos, life in the Brzezin ghetto was not the worst.

However, the situation became very bad several months before its liquidation in 1942. Little by little, production began to stop. Then the committee began to distribute funds to the unemployed. When little work came in, they distributed fewer funds. During the last weeks, however, the work stopped altogether. Every week the committee distributed funds to the needy tailors, which were virtually their only income. However, this improved the situation very little, since, at the same time, the ghetto was more closely guarded, and it was not possible to smuggle in food; so hunger began to reign in the ghetto.

In the social welfare group, the wife of Doctor Warhaft worked as honorary chairperson, along with Ezriel Gotlib, *z"l,* and carried out her activity as best she could. She helped the sick, widows with small children, and so forth. She also established a people's kitchen, where the needy got soup daily without having to pay.

Because of the difficult housing situation, various conflicts also arose in the ghetto, and so once a week, trials were held. The judge was Icek Dymant, *z"l.*

In order to make it easier for workers to receive their weekly wages, ten people were employed by the community to go around distributing the payments. Working in this capacity were Nechemia Szajnberg, Jakub Maroko, Raszewski, Josef Pas, *z"l*, and others whose names I cannot recall.

No cultural activities existed in the ghetto, since they were not permitted.

The Germans only needed the great production, and when the work stopped, their curses and murderous evil decrees began.

Visiting Ancestors' Graves in Brzezin in 1960 (pp. 157–59)

Rhoda Hendrik-Karpatkin

Brzezin! My father's birthplace has always evoked in me a feeling of romance and enthusiasm. My father, *e"h* [may he rest in peace], never tired of talking about Brzezin. Very early in my life I developed a longing to see this Polish town Brzezin and its people. I fantasized about Brzezin as if it were in an enchanted fairy tale. Is it a *shtot*, a *shtetl*, or a *dorf* [a city, a town, or a village]? When my husband and I made our first trip to Europe in 1960, it was natural that we should also add Poland to our travel plans—first, in order to visit the part of Europe that had spawned and nourished Yiddish culture in all its forms and that was so savagely destroyed by the Nazis, and second, and primarily, to see the town of my longing, the very town where my ancestors had lived. But I was heartsick seeing what had become of such an important Jewish cultural and population center. Just as with all the other Jewish cities and towns, Brzezin lay in ruins, in ashes.

Brzezin! Just a two-hour trip from modern Warsaw—but today, it is an entire century behind.

We traveled from Warsaw to Łódź on an electric express train. On the train we met a Polish officer, about forty years old, a polite and fine person. He told us horrible things that had happened in the recent past; his father and brother, professors, had been murdered in Auschwitz, and his mother and her sister had been stabbed to death by the Nazis for listening to the forbidden English radio. We heard many such similar stories from Poles and Jews.

In Łódź the officer took us to the address of the Jewish community, which is an official branch of the Social and Cultural Association of Jews in Poland.[1] There, the secretary, S. Web, befriended us and accompanied us all over. It was he who arranged our trip to Brzezin. We got a luxury automobile (a Russian limousine) with a chauffeur. After a side detour from the main route, we came to a modest summer colony for Jewish children outside Łódź, and, accompanied by the director of the colony, we arrived in Brzezin. All at once we fell back into the nineteenth century.

Of course, we had heard that many hundreds of cities and towns were now free of Jews. Here, Hitler had won the war, a full one hundred percent. But a choking painful feeling came over us when we saw that Brzezin, my father's birthplace, was no more. We lost Brzezin doubly—first, the pulsating Jewish life was cut down, and second, because of that, our life-long dream also vanished.

Not having found any living Jews, we decided to look for the Jews who had had the good fortune to die a natural death—in the Brzeziner cemetery.

Sholem Aleichem said that the pride of Kasrilevke was its *beysakvores* [cemetery], whose half-wrecked *matseyves* dramatized the history of an entire people. Here, in the

---

[1] Towarzystwo Społeczno-Kulturalne Żydow—TSKŻ.

Brzeziner cemetery, the murderers had not allowed even the dead to rest in their eternal sleep. Certainly the bare field, where the cemetery had been, is even more tragic because of the fallen gravestones, which could have told the history of a people who had lived on that very soil. The Nazis and Poles tore out the gravestones and paved the sidewalks with them; the earth was plowed, everything that was sacred to us was dishonored and made unclean. Yet the history-rich Warsaw cemetery, on the border of the Warsaw ghetto, remained almost untouched.

Also the Łódź cemetery was not desecrated, although it is not properly looked after because of the small number of surviving Jews. There the only thing that stands out are the spires of the monument of the great Poznański.[1] But the Brzeziner cemetery no longer exists. Our Polish guides remembered something about a small mound with a stick inserted in it to symbolize the slaughtered Jewish population. Even now old bones can be found lying around the plowed field. Today only the memories that are so deeply engraved in the hearts of the surviving Brzeziner Jews have survived—the only remembrance of the former Jewish Brzezin.

In our pain and sorrow we tried to find out something about my family, the Hendrykowski family. Taking into account the young age at which my father, *e"h*, left Brzezin, we turned to older people, who would be the most likely to know something about them.

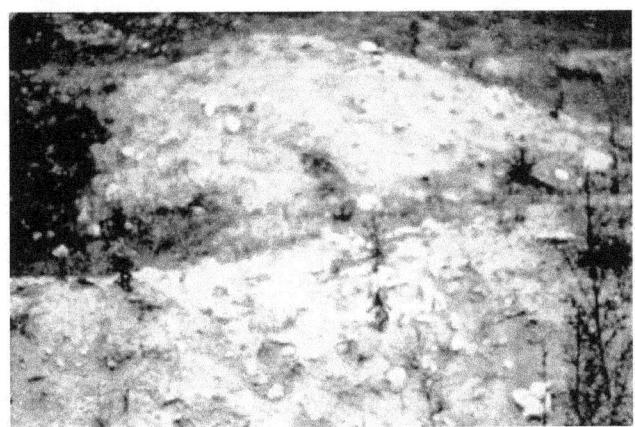

Once the cemetery of Brzezin stood here. The mound that is visible in the picture is a mass grave for the collected skulls that were found after the great destruction. The picture was taken in 1960 by the author of this article, grandchild of Lajbel Hendrykowski and daughter of Jechiel Hendrik.

They pointed out to us a small house. Our Łódź guide and translator explained our mission and then took us into a peeling, poor peasant hut. There lived an old man—probably more than eighty years old—with a long yellowish beard. He lay curled up in bed. He was certainly talkative, yes, he remembered my family well and even saw some of them in the Łódź ghetto. He recounted how he was forced by the Nazis to carry sick and old Jews to Łódź with his horse and wagon. This very old man pointed out where our house stood on Kościuszko Street (Łódź Street), over the bridge.

And indeed it was actually a substantial, two-story brick house—20 Kościuszko Street—which stood on the street corner. The year 1906 was engraved on a brick, and on the brick wall a tablet was mounted with the name "Hendrykowski, Eli" (my father's

---

[1] Wealthy Jewish industrialist in Łódź.

older brother). This was just a relic and a reminder of another era in Brzezin. In the neighboring home were four women—one barefoot—and they remembered the extinct Hendrykowski family. They looked at us curiously and without warmth. Across the street a thin, barefoot youngster of about ten looked at us with baffled wonder.

This very spot was actually my family's Brzezin—an old house with deep holes like pock marks from bombs and shrapnel. The town suffered badly during the murderous fighting, when the Russian army chased the Nazis and surrounded them near Łódź. The entire surrounding area was darkened like the swollen legs of the women who stood about.

Over the outmoded, crooked, cobblestone streets, weary people were dragging themselves with horse and wagon. The wheels were wrapped in heavy iron hoops (our automobile was the only one of its kind to be seen). Bent-over women were carrying heavy bundles of hay on their backs. Present-day Brzezin was one hundred years back in time; they were thrown back to a time before the Industrial Revolution of the nineteenth century. In truth, we did see one newly-built house of red brick; this was the medical clinic. One of our group was among the first to need help and actually got immediate and friendly medical attention there.

The Hendrykowski house on Łódź Street, which remained intact.

A Jewish historian, whom we met in Warsaw, informed us that before 1939, Brzezin was an industrial city, one of the great tailoring centers in Poland; intellectual and communal life existed there. There was a cultured youth of various Zionist and socialist ideologies, a middle class, workers, and sports organizations. Today Brzezin is dead; there is no industry there, no culture, no development. It is a primitive agricultural village. Present-day Brzezin, with its six thousand souls, poor and backward, is not even a reflection of its former close-to-twenty-thousand, a dynamic and prosperous town.

The Jewish population gave Brzezin life, vigor, and culture. With their diligence, entrepreneurship, and hard work, Jews made the town great and famous. Those who murdered the Jews wiped out, at the same time, the life and existence of the town of Brzezin.

My father's Brzezin is gone forever, but a rich legacy remains. The intellectual and cultural movement, the respect for learning and for human improvement, the zeal for justice—the eternal Jewish words—were imparted to Jewish children wherever they settled. The children and grandchildren of Brzeziner Jews brought with them this very spiritual baggage to America and Israel and everywhere they went. The publication of this monumental book, where our most loved and dearest ones are made eternal, is another ring in the golden chain that gives *koved* [honor] to all the generations of Brzeziner Jews. I strongly hope that the younger generations emanating from Brzezin will also continue to put to use all that was worthwhile and exalted in Brzeziner Jewish life.

An election meeting near the *besmedresh*, most likely in the year 1921, during the vote for the Sejm [Polish parliament].

Brzeziner Jews in the Wide World (pp. 160–61)

Jehuda Fuks

According to all the reliable sources, the number of Jews in Brzezin in 1939—that is, on the eve of World War II—reached about ten thousand.

At present, there is information that in Brzezin, all told, there is only one Jewish family left—which, according to the old tradition of our town, is engaged in making inexpensive clothing.

This is, unfortunately, the horrible truth, which says that this town of ours, about which we write this very Yizkor book, remains *Judenrein*, orphaned. There is not even anyone to take care of the destroyed cemetery. After Hitler's bombardments, which left the town in ruins, the Poles paved the streets with the gravestones that had been torn out of our holy cemetery. The Jewish institutions have been destroyed; only the name Brzezin is left.

According to the map of our town that was in use, Jews occupied residential streets according to their occupation and financial status. The *magaziners* lived on these streets: Koluszki, Rogów [Sienkiewicza], and a part of the market square [Rynek] up to the corner of Rogów Street. Merchants took up the entire main market square up to Synagogue Lane [Joselewicza]; smaller shops were on Apothecary Street [St. Anna].

The tailors, the majority of the town, were concentrated on the poorer streets, where rent for an apartment was not exorbitant—for example, Pig Street, Zieliński's [Moniuszki?], Cloister Street [Reformacka], Court Street [Staszica], Small Street [Krótka?], Łódź Street [Kościuszki], and New Town [Nowe Miasto].

How do we look today? Where are those who, by a miracle, survived the ghettos, concentration camps, and Siberian *taiga*s [forests]? To be precise, how many Brzeziners are left spread far and wide over the entire world?

The number of remaining Jews is, unfortunately, terribly small in comparison to the Jewish population of our town before the war.

Of the ten thousand souls, approximately four thousand remain in total who can be found today in the following lands:

1. United States of America	450	families	2000	individuals
2. Canada	40	"	160	"
3. South America (Brazil, Argentina)	30	"	120	"
4. Australia	15	"	50	"
5. France	50	"	160	"
6. Belgium	15	"	48	"
7. Sweden	10	"	30	"
8. Germany	20	"	45	"
9. Poland	15	"	48	"
10. Africa	10	"	25	"
11. Israel	350	"	850	"
12. Russia	probably? -		50	"
Total	1005	families	3536	individuals

During the past ten years, the writer of this article visited a series of countries and personally met with the majority of Brzeziners.

A group of Brzeziner Jews in Australia with guests from America, Dr. Ester and Jehuda Fuks.

When, why and how were our Brzeziner people dispersed so far and wide, even to Australia? The emigration of the Brzeziner tailor-workers had begun some sixty years earlier. At that time, the most popular land was, of course, America. In 1896, sixty-five years ago, the number of Brzeziners in America was already large enough that the Brzeziner Sick and Benevolent Society was founded in New York and served all those years as a gathering place for newly-arriving immigrants.

Brzeziner families who could not readily obtain American visas settled in Canada. A number of families went to South America—Brazil and Argentina—at the urging of friends or relatives. France attracted young people as they aspired to the greater world; so also did Belgium and Germany, where the number did not increase. The approximately twenty families that are now found in Germany consist of those who were rescued from Hitler's concentration camps and remained on German soil.

The gathering of surviving *landslayt* on the fifth *yortsayt* of the liquidation of the Brzeziner ghetto, Łódź, 1947.

There are a number of Brzeziner Jews in Poland who settled in Upper Silesia [territory ceded to Poland by Germany], those tired of wandering and also a number of people repatriated from Soviet Russia. A total of fifteen families went to Australia, several through Shanghai, China, and others who left France as soon as they could, when there were rumors of a third world war in Europe.

The Brzeziner Jews in Australia are concentrated in one city—Melbourne. Among them there are already several independent contractors and *magaziners*. All are employed and make a good living.

In another part of this book there are details written about the Brzeziner Jews in Israel. Eretz Yisroel attracted a number of young Brzeziner Jews in 1918, right after the Balfour Declaration. Individual Brzeziner Jews who have already raised two generations born in Israel can be found there. World War II caused the number of Brzeziner families to increase by various means to three hundred fifty.

It should be emphasized here that we have in Eretz Yisroel a "little Brzezin" that the American Relief Committee built. That is the Shikkun Brzezin (Brzezin housing project) on Keren Kayemet L'Yisrael soil in a suburb of Tel Aviv, where we built dwellings for Brzeziner families, with a common room in which there is a rich Jewish library (for details see "Shikkun Brzezin" in the reports of the Relief Committee reprinted in this book).

From the widely-known tailoring center in Brzezin, Poland, a series of small clusters in twelve countries from all parts of the world remain, with barely one-quarter of the souls compared to the number in 1939.

A group of Brzeziner *landslayt* in Israel at the reception for a guest, Jehuda Fuks. First row, below, from right to left: Perec Zagon, Krongrad, A. Najman, I. Sułkowicz. Second row: D. Rozenberg, Lemel Horn, Aron Fogel, Jehuda Fuks, S. Sułkowicz, Dawid Zycher, Z. Szajnbach. Third row: Fiszel Benkel, Fiszel Krongrad, Mrs. Krongrad, Mrs. Guta Mer-Goldkranc, Mrs. Sułkowicz, Jakub Rozenberg, Gerszon Frankensztajn. Fourth row: Mrs. Zycher, Mrs. Szajnberg, Mojsze Szajnberg, Gedalja Waldman, Bronia Sułkowicz, and Frajda Sułkowicz.

Jews in Brzezin Before and After the Destruction (p. 162)

The document that we publish here is in answer to a questionnaire that the historical section of YIVO Institute for Jewish Research distributed to the survivors of the various cities and towns just after the war.

The name of the provider of the information from Brzezin is not known. It appears that several known details are not entirely accurate, but in general, the document is an important one.

Those rescued from Brzezin gave the following answers to the questions presented:

1) In 1939 there were up to six thousand Jews in Brzezin. The major sources of income were tailoring, various handcrafts, and small businesses, mainly in the clothing industry.

2) There existed there a *kehile* (organized community), the Society for Workers Evening Courses, a great synagogue, eighteen *bote-medroshim* [prayer/study houses], a *beysakvores* [cemetery], an old-age home, a children's home, Lines Hatsedek [Society to Care for the Sick], a seven-grade secular school, six libraries, four drama groups, two cooperatives, two banks, *gmiles khsodim* [interest-free loan] funds, a professional workers' union, and two artisans' unions. Among the political parties were the Left Poale Zion, Right Poale Zion [Zionist Labor Party], Bund [Jewish Socialist Party], Hitachdut [Socialist-Zionist Labor Party], Agudas Yisroel [Orthodox non-Zionist Party], Mizrachi [Religious Zionist Party], various other Zionists, WIZO [Women's International Zionist Organization], revolutionists, and Communists.

3) The most important event in the town from the beginning of the war (September 1) until the Nazi occupation was the annihilation of dozens of people during the bombing.

UNDER NAZI OCCUPATION

On 9 September they took as hostages the former *moyre hoyroe* [town rabbi who renders decisions on matters of rabbinic law] Jekutiel-Zalman Borensztajn, Dr. Klajnhaus, Dr. Irlicht, and attorney Jakubowicz. The Nazis confiscated all Jewish possessions, created a ghetto, and cut off beards. On 18 November 1939 a decree was announced that one must wear the *gele late* [yellow patch]. Jews were taken for forced labor from the first day of the occupation.

The Jews from the town of Stryków were brought to Brzezin.

At the very beginning of the occupation, eighteen-year old Efroimowicz was murdered. Ten Jews were hung at a forced assembly of all the Jews of the town.

On 14 May 1942 all Jewish children from the age of one day to ten years of age were taken away. Together with the elderly people, they were sent to Majdanek and Treblinka.[1]

On 15 May 1942 the Jews of Brzezin were sent to Łódź, except for three hundred people who remained in the town. Not one of those three hundred Jews is now alive. How

---

[1] Both Warhaft and Tuszyński state in their accounts that the children were taken to Chełmno.

they were killed, we do not know. Those who were sent to Łódź had the same fate as the Łódź Jews. In August 1944 the remaining Jews were deported from Łódź to Auschwitz.

The number of Jews from Brzezin who were left alive is two hundred sixty. They survived all the concentration camps: One hundred seventy were rescued from the camps, and ninety were in Russia; a total of two hundred sixty.

Important Jewish leaders in Brzezin before the war:

Agudas Yisroel—Izrael Dawid Sułkowicz, Chanina Janower, and Lipman Szulc

Mizrachi—Josel Zylbersztajn, Josef Zyskind, and Działoszyński.

Zionist—Chaim Baruch Szulzinger, Ginsberg, and Jukiel Sułkowicz.

Right Poale Zion—Budkowski, Mitelsztajn, and Dan-Aszer Kujawski

Left Poale Zion—Chaim Rafał Rozenblum, Mojsze Zygmunt, and Dawid Szymkowicz.

WIZO—Rywcia Sułkowicz, Mrs. Irlicht, and Mrs. Dymant.

Bund—Abraham Opatowski, Herszel Rozenblum, and Majer Holc.

Part Four

Brzeziners in America

Our *Landsmanshaft* (pp. 165–81)

Nachum Summer

In November 1956 the sixtieth-year jubilee of the Brzeziner *landsmanshaft* [society of fellow townspeople] in the United States was celebrated in a festive manner. Now, during the preparation of this monumental work, in which we want to show generations to come the history of our town in all its phases and aspects, it is especially important to have them learn about the rich history of our *landsmanshaft* here in America.

More than sixty-five years ago, the first Brzeziner families began to arrive here. As is usual for people in a foreign land with an unfamiliar way of life, they felt depressed, deserted, and lonely. Longing for home gnawed away at them, and spiritual desolation prodded them. Individual Brzeziner families began to cling closely to each other. At that time, an idea was born to organize themselves into their own society in order to recreate a familiar environment and also to maintain the ties linking them to their town, to their own roots. They tried to transplant the traditions, the customs, and the spiritual institutions of their town to American soil.

New York was the point of disembarkation for the majority of the immigrants. You must understand that our first Brzeziner pioneers also fell into that great "melting pot." Certainly, the immigrant here in the early years did not have it so easy. Those were difficult years, physically and spiritually, for those far from home. Thus they clung so ardently to their own, to their *landsman*—people from their own town.

In 1896 Brzeziners organized officially and received a charter under the name Di Breziner Untershtitsung Farayn [The Brzeziner Benevolent Society]. This is the way the first minutes read, found years later among our archives, written by Gerszon Dymant [George Diamond], who was the recording secretary from that time until the time of the first official election. The authenticity of the minutes was actually later confirmed by the first secretary and also by other original founders. Here are the minutes of that historical, first founding meeting:

> On 30 March 1896 the first meeting of the Brzeziner *landslayt* [fellow townspeople] was held at the home of Hyman Rechseit on East Second Street. At this gathering it was decided to organize the Brzeziner Benevolent Society. The following *landslayt* attended this meeting and registered as members: George Diamond, Hyman Rechseit, Sam Cohen, Sam Newman, Jack Wolborsky, Morris Drengel, Morris Krengel, Hershka Weinberg, Jacob Hillel, Izrael Rozenkrantz, Kive Rubinstein, and Daniel Glicklich. Jacob Hillel was elected temporary secretary-treasurer until the election of officers.
>
> G. Diamond reported that he mailed out twenty postcards to *landslayt*. The purpose of the current meeting was described in the postcards. Only twelve people attended the meeting. It was resolved that everyone who registered as a member in the organization should pay $.25, and this should be in effect until the election, which would take place at the first meeting in July. Then the initial fee would be raised according to the decision

of the members. It was also decided that those members who wished to register today should pay their $.25 dues from now until the first meeting in July, which amounts to the sum of $1.25. It was also decided to meet in private homes until election time, since our financial situation does not allow us to rent a meeting hall. Brother Diamond was requested to send out postcards so that all Brzeziners who live in New York, and also outside New York, would be informed of the founding of the society. It was also resolved that those who join as members at this meeting or at the next meeting would be considered the founders of the Brzeziner Benevolent Society.

G. Diamond, Temporary Recording Secretary

About the language—which we have not changed—notice the signs of German influence that were strong at that time. And not only is the language strongly affected by English expressions and ideas, but also the names were changed very quickly. The majority of them who only a short time ago called themselves Abraham, Mojsze, Szlama, and Dawid—already are called Abram, Morris, Sam, and David.[1] They Americanized quickly, and a great deal of the homey familiar traditions and customs underwent a transformation, although, when they came together with familiar *landslayt*, they were nostalgic about their youthful years in Brzezin.

From that small cluster of people mentioned by the founders in the first minutes, an organization sprang up, which at the time of the fiftieth-year jubilee, celebrated in 1946, consisted of about four hundred members. Achieving this number is certainly the greatest accomplishment in the history of our *landsmanshaft*. In 1956, when the sixtieth-year jubilee was celebrated, many of the first of that pioneering generation were no longer with us. Nevertheless, our *landsmanshaft* now consists of approximately a thousand members, *keyn-yirbu* [may they increase].

Hyman Rechseit's home was the assembly point for the assimilated residents who had already been in America several years and were already accustomed to the new land. This house was also a well-known gathering place for newly-arrived immigrants, who, in the beginning months, really needed substantial, immediate help.

Also, in those early years, A. Barasz's delicatessen on the East Side served as a club for Brzeziners. After a hard day's work in a factory, they gathered there in the evenings over a glass of tea and talked about all sorts of things, especially, you understand, about the *landslayt*. They enjoyed themselves just as they did in the *besmedresh* in Brzezin— but in a secular atmosphere. They talked over the events of the day, about what was going

---

[1] The spelling of surnames in this chapter, in so far as possible, is that which was used in the United States, especially if the people were listed in the 80th Anniversary journal. The spelling of the same surnames in Poland was more likely to have been as follows: Cwern (Zwerin), Dymant (Diamond), Fuks (Fox), Goldkranc (Goldkrantz), Grynszpan (Green), Hajman (Hyman), Hauzer (Hauser), Hilel (Hillel), Kalisz (Kalish), Kon (Cohen), Kujawski (Kuyawsky), Lomanec (Loomanitz), Najman (Newman), Pajczer (Peizer), Pakula (Pakull), Rechtszajt (Rechseit), Rubinsztajn (Rubinstein), Silski (Schilsky), Szajbowicz (Shaibowicz), Sobowinski (Sobovinsky), Szwarc (Schwartz), Tuszyński (Tushinsky), Wajnberg (Weinberg), and Wolborski (Wolborsky). Names beginning with "Roz," such as Rozen and Rozman have been kept with the original spelling to be consistent, even though in America some of them may have been written as Rosen or Rosman.

on in the country, especially details about the *landsmanshaft*. Here they created the future plans of the society. Here they also did not escape various frictions and quarrels over insignificant things, but in the end, they would reconcile again, as was usual in those days.

Extremely interesting is that this Mr. Barasz was not even from Brzezin. He was a native of Białystok, and yet, he became very interested and involved in Brzeziner "politics" and had heard about and was familiar with every little street in Brzezin, even though he himself had never been there. This Barasz was a curious and interesting person, who willingly adopted Brzezin as his hometown and became a member of the organization. His wife was also closely linked and bound to everything that had a connection to Brzeziners. She had the warmth and tenderness of a loyal mama. In her shop on the former East Side, she was involved with the bright beginning of our *landsmanshaft*.

A group photograph of Brzeziner *landslayt* in New York. Here can be seen former leaders who unfortunately lie in the dust, among them Aaron Kuyawsky, Toviah Peizer, Alter Rozenfeld, Izrael Cohen, and others.

So the years passed swiftly by. The situation of our hometown went from bad to worse. As soon as it was possible, people fled; they emigrated. And the majority of the emigrants were drawn to the United States. There were also many who went to Eretz Yisroel; others traveled to South America and settled there.

The great majority of those others were drawn to South America. In the first place, because they already had relatives and friends there who could give support in time of need, and secondly, because they received encouraging reports from *landslayt* already living there under reasonable circumstances.

In general, the economic situation was much better here. The conditions in the tailoring trades began to improve with the rise of the trade union movement. This certainly encouraged the younger tailors in Brzezin to emigrate to a distant and free land.

Emigration brought here ever greater groups of our *landslayt,* and with the new emigrants, the local *landsmanshaft* grew and prospered. Soon, as usual, people began to show their dissatisfaction with the old, established leadership. The younger, the newer element, and even among them some of the older ones, came with a bunch of complaints and raised questions that provoked dissent. And the dissent brought about a rift.

This rift occurred in the years between 1908 and 1910. Twenty-six members broke away from the mother organization and created their own independent group. They even took out a charter under the name "The Brzeziner Progressive Society," so that the newly-created organization would have a legal standing. The leaders of this newly-created organization were Abraham Icek Rozman, president; Alter Rozenfeld, vice-president; Charlie Baron, secretary; and M. Rozman, treasurer. They held their meetings in Springers Hall on Avenue B.

A. Barasz, whose delicatessen on the East Side was the first destination for immigrants from Brzezin.

It should be noted that among the stated number of those who officially split off, there were also those *landslayt* who kept their membership in both organizations simultaneously. Those members who remained loyal to the old Brzeziner Society tried, in this way, to act as go-betweens in order to make peace again between the two separate factions. In the last analysis, the rift was not caused by, God knows, some kind of terrible ideological clash over who should have authority, in which the possibility for both sides to make up would have been altogether lost.

This voluntary mission on the part of those who remained in the old organization was successful. In the scant two years that the new group had functioned, after the entire dispute was brought to court because of stolen books and in order to maintain the legal right to speak in the name of the Brzeziner *landslayt*, peace was finally reestablished between the feuding factions. The newly-created organization agreed to support the decisions and regulations of the mother organization.

The organization again operated with its usual routine. The membership continued to grow with newly-arriving immigrants. That is how things proceeded until the outbreak of World War I.

During the war years, there was little opportunity to keep in touch with those nearest and dearest whom we had left behind in our town. By indirect means we received news of the terrible impoverishment of our hometown, Brzezin, but there was little likelihood of easing the pressing need. Our help could not reach our loved ones.

Finally, after those difficult war years, when armistice was declared, the old ties were reestablished, and the *landslayt* began to think about sending a messenger directly to Brzezin.

It must be understood that during the time of war, the *landslayt* here did not rest. They prepared a plan for the time when the first opportunity would arise to help our starving sisters and brothers on the other side of the ocean.

The first one who reconnected and linked us again with our town was our *landsman* Hyman Funt, *e"h* [may he rest in peace], who traveled to Brzezin immediately after the war. He actually went on a visit to the town and willingly carried our messages. The society had entrusted him with a great mission.

He, Hyman Funt, belonged to the pioneer generation of our local *landsmanshaft*. His clothing factory was a haven for Brzeziners. A great number of undertakings were planned and dreamt of in his shop. The sweatshop system that predominated in those days in various trades was well known, and in that respect, his shop was an exception. Our *landslayt* tailors boasted to other *landslayt* about his fair and humane treatment. This was not the way other bosses behaved, who seriously exploited and used their *landslayt* brothers to promote their own interests.

He had a very difficult mission on his visit to Brzezin. In order to distribute the first relief funds that the American *landslayt* had entrusted to him, he used a lot of common sense, and, in general, his handling of those who had suffered was very judicious.

There were also other *landslayt* who visited Brzezin later and were, at the same time, our ambassadors, who represented the local *landsmanshaft* on behalf of the relief work.

At various times the following *landslayt* visited Brzezin: J. D. Berg (who was, incidentally, the leading spirit in the great relief and rehabilitation work after the more recent great catastrophe of our people—a bright chapter of its own that will be told in later accounts), Icek Rozman, and Jacob Fogel.

As already mentioned above, the work of the society in those postwar years was concentrated mostly on sending help to the victims of war. A Relief Committee was formed, consisting of Aaron Kuyawsky, Toviah Peizer, William Green, Benny Loomanitz, Louis Horn, Alter Rozenfeld, Jacob Leib Wald, Izrael Cohen, and Jacob Fogel. The majority of the *landslayt* mentioned are unfortunately no longer with us. Every one of them contributed in his own way to the *landsmanshaft*. There were even *landslayt* who took an active role in the relief work who had not yet officially joined as members of our society. They felt, however, the responsibility of the moment and wanted to have a share in the very important assistance to our town.

Certainly, the form of help in those days did not take on the character or establish such concretely defined objectives as after the recent great disaster, of which we will give an account later.

After World War I, the town began to recover. The Jewish population remained, although its status was certainly not the same as in the thriving prewar years. A portion of the working class began to turn to the outside, toward the world, for the simple reason that the sources for earning a living had seriously dried up. Many left for America—in the first place, because, in those days America was prospering economically, and second, after a Polish government was reestablished, the entire socio-political climate was not favorable for Jews. However, the great majority of Brzeziner Jews remained in the town, and many were living in miserable circumstances.

Between 1918 and 1936 the Brzeziner Relief Committee sent the sum of approximately seventeen thousand dollars to Brzezin. It can be seen that the amount of aid during this time period was not very significant. However, one must not minimize this limited form of relief and rehabilitation work of our local *landsmanshaft*.

It was a different time, and from the beginning, the committee set about its work on a minimal basis. In those years, when the Jewish population of our town became seriously impoverished, any form of assistance made things easier and reduced need.

In the meantime, week-in, week-out, Brzeziner *landslayt* began arriving in America, immigrants both young and middle-aged. Of course, the new type of immigrant was cut from a different cloth. He was of the more modern, enlightened type. He had already been exposed to and infected with the agitation of various kinds of Jewish factions during the war years in Eastern Europe. Quite a large percent had belonged to or were active in the various Socialist and Zionist organizations. In one word—a progressive, cosmopolitan element.

Coming here, encountering the local *landslayt*, attending meetings of the society, the entire style and leadership of the *landsmanshaft* seemed strange and very conservative. The established ritual for coming into a meeting, standing at attention like a soldier, the hand over the heart—this all felt old-fashioned, out-of-date, and did not at all appeal to the newly-arrived immigrants.

They began immediately to rebel against this archaic form and strove to introduce new ways, a new style in the life of our society. Of course, this did not go entirely easily. As always, they did not permit the new generation of immigrants to approach the Eastern Wall [take a place of honor]. They (the old-timers) took a dim view of them, regarding them with suspicion and mistrust. They criticized them, saying that they came disturbing the peace and that their new ways and methods would bring about the downfall of our entire structure. Disputes and flare-ups between the older residents and the new generation of immigrants did indeed take place. They could not live together in peace.

This state of affairs led to a new rupture in the solidarity of the society. Most of the new immigrants, with the help of several older leaders, founded an organization called The Brzeziner Culture Club, which later was transformed into Workmen's Circle, Branch 472. There, the influence of the new immigrants was evident.

Among those especially active in the Culture Club were Jacob David Berg, B. Loomanitz, Joseph Diamond, Velvel Rozenblum, and B. Brakash (the last was not even a Brzeziner *landsman*). They conducted their meetings according to modern ideas and standards. They, the *landsmen* who had already partaken of the ideas and ideals of the various movements in Jewish society, really did not feel comfortable at the meetings of the old Brzeziner Society. The spirit that the society had adopted from the Hungarian and German way of operating was, as already stated, not to their taste. It also had very little relationship to the town of Brzezin. That is why the Culture Club, which wanted to bring in a new style and modern concepts into communal work, came into being.

At the meetings conducted by the Culture Club, the order of business was not so important; they were mainly concerned that the gathered group should hear an interesting lecture about an important topic. They thus brought to almost every meeting well-known writers and lecturers, and the people were satisfied and enjoyed themselves. Brother Diamond tells us that in that interesting time they not only tried to educate and teach people but also to entertain and amuse them in an appropriate way. From time to time, they arranged concert evenings with well-known and gifted artist groups from the Jewish stage.

But Fate willed it that the new culture club, just like the earlier progressive society, would not last long. The overwhelming majority of the Brzeziner *landsmanshaft*, united in their sentiments, again prevented a victory. The newly-founded organization dissolved, and the old and the new elements flowed back together and established a lasting peace. Both sides agreed to the compromise. The old leadership relaxed their domination a little, and new, fresh blood began to make its appearance in the leadership. The meetings began to have a different character. Little by little, a lot of the out-of-date methods, which had the smell of the former mysterious ways of operating, were eliminated or repealed.

A great number of the pioneering generation, because of their advanced age, no longer participated actively in the society's work. Many of the founders and leaders from the old generation had passed away. New faces appeared, and new leaders, along with new ideas about communal work.

Of the leaders from the old generation, we still had the rare privilege of having among us nice, sincere, unpretentious, ordinary people. I will mention several. Toviah Peizer, a real veteran, who tried to adapt to the later conditions in the society. Nevertheless, physically and psychologically, he remained fixated in the past. It would cause him to muse: "Once it used to be . . . ," and his face would practically light up. He evoked beautiful, shining recollections from the familiar past. He got carried away by his own speech while he painted a picture for us of the first ten years of the life of our local *landsmanshaft*.

Aaron Kuyawsky—or the way he was called among the *landslayt*, Aaron Dan-Aszer's [son of Dan-Aszer]—also belonged spiritually to the earlier generation. He was not of the "leadership type," but he always filled important posts and was deeply loved among the *landslayt*. We really rarely complained about his actions—although they were not, God knows, of any great stature. We knew, however, that our Aaron had honest and fair intentions. He did not put on airs; he did not have any great pretensions. He did not even get angry when someone stepped on his toes. Often it seemed that Aaron, the "Pop" (father)—the title that many of the younger generation respectfully gave him—felt unjustly treated because of this or that action. However, he always found a justification for everyone, rationalizing that they could not have acted differently.

And, of course, Alter Rozenfeld was very active. When you leaf through old record books, you find that already at that time he was an ardent participant in the discussions that used to stretch late into the night. Alter Rozenfeld was active in our society for many years, almost until the last day of his life. He held office as our president many times. Already all kinds of legends about Alter's constant "presiding" have spread among our *landslayt*. He was a person with a fiery temper, and he suffered from a "father complex." It always seemed to him that the leaders of the younger generation continuously sought to harm the reputation of the society. He, as the founder, would not permit "his" society, perish the thought, to be destroyed because of the strange behavior of the new leaders. But with all his faults, he was good for the society.

In their naiveté, in their plain-folk simplicity, the old leaders accomplished wonderful things. We, the present-day leaders, remember them with admiration and respect. Thanks to their persistence and devotion, this all came about.

Activities

During our many years of existence, our activities were not limited exclusively to organizational routine. We displayed an interest in all the important events in Jewish life.

In addition to our usual meetings, at which specific Brzeziner matters were taken up and handled, we always expanded our activities to all things associated with the Jewish people. From time to time general Jewish problems were raised and discussed at our meetings.

We arranged dozens of lectures and papers on various topics connected with Eretz Yisroel. We discussed, when it was timely, the matter of Jewish settlements in lands other than Eretz Yisroel. We also saw to it that the members were more or less informed about the details. We invited distinguished and prominent personalities to lecture about all these problems, so that our members would have an objective picture of what was happening in the Jewish community.

Jewish literature in its many forms was also not an unusual topic for us. We listened to lectures on various cultural issues that held a broad interest for Jewish people. Among the distinguished representatives of Jewish organized society, and from Yiddish literature, who made presentations to us were: S. Niger, H. Leivick, Perec Hirschbein, N. B. Minkoff, Mordechai Dantsis, Dr. E. Naks [Izrael Knox], Lajbuś Lehrer, N. Meisel, Aba Gordin, Dr. Seikin, B. Shefner, Sasha Zimmerman, Dr. Emanuel Pat, B. Kaplan, and many others.

When the Yiddish theater blossomed in the Jewish community, and the people were younger, the Brzeziner Society organized theater performances almost annually, as was the custom in those early years.

The Brzeziner Society also responded to appeals from important fund-raising campaigns for the Jewish people of that time. The Brzeziner Society took a very active role in almost all important collections of money administered by responsible Jewish community organizations. In our record books, financial contributions were noted to such distinguished organizations as the United Jewish Appeal, the Joint Distribution Committee, ORT [Organization for Rehabilitation and Training], Keren Hayesod [United Israel Appeal], Histadrut [Israeli Workers Union], Keren Kayemeth [Jewish National Fund], HIAS [Hebrew Immigrant Aid Society], World Jewish Congress, American Jewish Congress, Red Magen David [Israeli Red Cross], the Red Cross, and various health organizations and institutions that served the interests of the Jewish community.

It also must be recalled here that during the time when weekend picnics were in vogue during the hot summer months, the Brzeziners were not behind the times in that aspect relative to other organizations. We spent the entire day in good spirits under the open skies, sang Yiddish folk songs, played pinochle, and the women prepared delicious snacks and drinks. Often we had a keg of beer, just like in the good old days in our former hometown.

The banquets and concerts that the *landslayt* arranged for various occasions, especially to celebrate some important event, really deserved a prize for their grand style.

The fortieth-year and the fiftieth-year and even the recent sixtieth-year commemoration will live long in the memory of those who had the rare honor to participate in those celebrations.

The special journals that were published for the jubilee celebrations under the editorship of Nachum Summer have been renowned for a long time. These very beautiful journals hold a place of honor in most Brzeziner homes throughout the world. Distinguished literary critics also wrote warmly about them. These journals are of great historical significance. They certainly served as an important source for our present *Sefer Brzezin* [Book of Brzezin—Brzeziny Yizkor Book].

For the sixtieth-year commemoration, a new booklet was also published with illustrations and pictures about the ten years of our relief work.

Since we are speaking about important journals, it must also be noted that for the sixtieth-year birthday celebration of our distinguished *landsman*, Jacob David Berg, a beautiful journal was published with important comments about the *yubilar*'s [honoree's] many activities, both as a culture builder and also as an important leader in the work of our *landsmanshaft*, especially in our relief work.

The memorial monument that the *landslayt* erected at the cemetery on Long Island must be mentioned as an important accomplishment in the effort to immortalize the martyrs of our destroyed *shtetl*. There, in the Beth David Cemetery, we have come together on various occasions in order to pay tribute to the martyrs of our hometown and also to recall those *landslayt* who died here.

Since this monument was erected, it has became a tradition in the month of May to arrange an evening of commemoration for the Jews from our Brzezin who were gassed and murdered and also for the members of our *landsmanshaft* who died prematurely.

I have not exhausted the history of our *landsmanshaft* with this account. We have only reviewed here the most important moments in the sixty-year existence of our Brzeziner Society.

BRZEZINER LADIES AUXILIARY

Since the relief work after World War I had not reached any significant goals, it was abandoned almost at once. The small amount of work that was still being done was taken over exclusively by the Ladies Auxiliary, which actually came into existence during that period.

In 1925 several activists from the Brzeziner *landsmanshaft* agreed to give serious thought to including our women in active community work. We had a young, good element, whose specific activities would surely be a constructive addition to the general work of our *landsmanshaft*.

The participants in that conversation, as it was reported, were Aaron Kuyawsky, Toviah Peizer, Izrael Cohen, Alter Rozenfeld, Feivel Rozenberg, Abe Miller, and maybe some other brothers also.

This initial committee already had in its possession a small sum of money that had been raised by the women in order to begin the work. After a series of meetings held by the committee, it was agreed to call an organizational assembly.

At this first assembly, they talked over the necessity for such a branch—in as much as the women represented an important element and could, most importantly, engage in constructive work of a broad and far-reaching scope for the benefit of our *landsmanshaft* here and, at the same time, also serve as an important connecting link with our *landslayt* overseas.

One did not have to do much campaigning to convince the majority of the women at that founders' assembly of the importance of such an organization. They were a mature, good group, capable of carrying out such work. They actually moved very quickly from talk to action.

That same evening, a provisional working committee was formed, consisting of the following sisters: Katie Sobovinsky, president; Helen Kalish, vice-president; and Sara Hauser, treasurer. In order to encourage the work, Brother Izrael Cohen was appointed financial secretary, and Brother Sam Hyman, recording secretary.

The first official installation of the newly-elected officers took place in March 1927. Brother J. D. Berg, in an impressive manner, conducted the meeting, and he had the honor of swearing in the newly-elected officers of the newly-founded branch of our *landsmanshaft*.

The first public endeavor as an organized effort consisted in taking over a part of the relief work of the men's organization. The very first act consisted of providing for poor and sick pregnant women in Brzezin. In that area they did a lot of work of which they can certainly be proud. It was a good and successful beginning.

Their second action was really a greater challenge. This time they took under their maternal wings a project to provide clothing and shoes for impoverished children in Brzezin. Brzezin had a lot of small children whose parents, because of the seriously deteriorating economic condition of the postwar years, could not provide them with basic needs. This work was under the auspices of our Ladies Auxiliary.

Later, with the cooperation of the entire *landsmanshaft*, they took over more concrete, constructive work.

They helped finance a children's camp in Brzezin. This children's camp was located in a village near Brzezin and provided the opportunity for seriously pale and emaciated small children to enjoy several weeks of summer vacation and breathe fresh country air. At the same time, they could strengthen their weak little bodies,

Summer colony for Jewish children in Brzezin.

under the special supervision of the children's director, especially through eating healthy, nourishing food.

The Ladies Auxiliary carried out a regular correspondence with Mrs. Rywka Sułkowicz from Brzezin, who was the head of this children's camp, and also with the teachers and the children's camp counselors. In their correspondence, they reported and talked about every single detail of their activities.

Thanks to this intensive work on the part of our Ladies Auxiliary, it encouraged and made possible the rehabilitation and relief activities in Brzezin itself to expand and include the outskirts of the town.

They regularly distributed food packages to impoverished families in the town. They took care of the sick, the pregnant, and the unemployed craftsmen. The responsible committee members who devoted themselves to this extremely important work made sure that middle-class homes hit by the recession, which dominated almost all of Poland, would not have their Shabosim [Sabbaths] and holidays spoiled. In a tactful way, they selected clean clothing and especially dressed and shod our little Moyshelekh and Shloymelekh, in order that they could go to *kheyder* [Jewish elementary school] neat and clean.

In order to create the necessary financial resources that would enable Mrs. Sułkowicz—and the committee she established in Brzezin—to function and plan appropriately, here in America, the sister organization, with the assistance of the entire *landsmanshaft*, organized various campaigns to raise money. They arranged all kinds of ventures of a diverse and interesting character. They organized trips, theater benefits, banquets, and also small gatherings on various occasions. Smaller committees were assigned to find cost-free rooms that would make it possible to minimize expenses and increase profits.

Year in and year out, the Auxiliary also arranged New Year celebrations. These holidays really became a tradition. For these evenings, the women themselves baked, cooked, served, and even brought food and drinks from their own homes, so that the organizing committee would have fewer expenses. Their happiness was truly great when an undertaking of theirs was a social and, most important, a financial success, because it really meant that a greater sum of money could be sent to Brzezin.

It must also be said, to the credit of the sister

The children's home in Brzezin directed by Mrs. Rywka Sułkowicz, who can be seen in the picture.

organization, that their work was not limited only to fund raising, food packages, and clothing for the impoverished in Brzezin. They also had a considerable list of activities concerning Brzeziner families who were, from time to time, in need of concrete, substantial help even here in our local Brzeziner colony. They did this work in an appropriately circumspect manner, with aid given discreetly, so that no one would feel embarrassed.

The organization also handled all kinds of holidays and private celebrations for various occasions. These celebrations in honor of this or that deserving family were carried out in a stately, impressive manner. Those who had the great honor of attending any of the celebrations and intimate small gatherings will surely not forget them.

Ruth Hauser became president of the Ladies Auxiliary in 1941. Ruth Hauser is one of our most capable and gifted sisters. She acquired this reputation thanks to her energetic, intensive work. She has a long list of accomplishments.

The year 1941 was difficult both for Jews and also for Americans. The world was involved in a bitter armed conflict. Hitler had invaded Poland, and at once we had started to get news from there.

Another group of Jewish children from Brzezin. Director Dr. Warhaft

The work among the Brzeziners for our *landslayt* overseas came to a halt. The mood was strained and downcast. We knew what was now awaiting the Polish Jews under the domination of Nazism, including our own near and dear ones from Brzezin. . . .

In December 1941 America declared war against the Japanese and Nazi enemies. Our children were mobilized into the American armed forces and were sent to all the battle fronts. At that time, the local women's organization carried out an active campaign to send letters and food packages to our children in the armed forces. Ruth Hauser, as president, with her thoroughness and energy, especially excelled in this important work.

When the war ended, the women's organization was again involved in its interrupted relief activities. They directed a broad range of projects on behalf of Hitler's victims from our destroyed town. They capably participated in all sorts of activities to send food, clothing, and medical supplies to the survivors in various countries.

When the Brzeziner *landsmanshaft* became engaged in the great project of building homes in Israel for the remaining refugees, the women's organization very energetically took part in this work. For this purpose, they raised nearly ten thousand dollars. When taking into consideration that the majority of the husbands of these women had already, separately, contributed to the same project, it is of very great significance. Without their devoted work, the great project in Israel—of which we are all proud—surely would not have been realized with such enormous success.

Rachel Rozenblum, close to one hundred years of age. She is the oldest woman in America and maybe the entire world.

It was truly a pleasure to attend the meetings of the Auxiliary. They were conducted in an interesting, simple, and easy manner and ended in an intimate way, with a pot of coffee and pastries.

Among the sisters who especially excelled in the many activities must be recalled the following: Sister Ray Bergman, many-times president, who, with her simplicity and popularity and with a constant smile on her face, is very beloved; Sister Gussie Pakula, one of the older sisters, has worked for the Auxiliary since the beginning and expended a great deal of effort and endured sleepless nights so that the various activities would be crowned with success; Anna Hayman, *e"h*, almost always filled the post of recording secretary and used to read aloud the driest details of a meeting as if recounting a children's story. With her fine Litvak Yiddish, she also excelled in reading stories from Sholom Aleichem and other Yiddish writers, so that the meeting would be interesting and inviting.

Ruth Hauser, who has already been mentioned, in addition to being president, also filled the office of financial secretary (since our brother Louie Horn died, she also took over his post in the Relief Committee which she fills in a worthy manner) and is generally active in every important working committee. Although she is American born, she displays a lot of feeling and warmth for the work of our *landsmanshaft*. Fannie Tanenbaum, who also excels in the field of the Auxiliary's finances and is always the secretary for all undertakings of our sister organization, is a capable and devoted leader who is truly a great prize for the entire *landsmanshaft*. Mary Lehrer is the one who reports to us all the personal celebrations, such as births, marriages, and various celebrations among our *landslayt*. She offers a lot of congratulations to everyone. Rose Lefkowitz occupies the

Children in the fresh air taking pleasure in a summer meal.

office of vice-president and is represented on various committees. Renee Lasky, *e"h*, was an unassuming, capable leader for the welfare of our large *landsmanshaft*. Masha Green, who is also very dedicated to various activities, particularly loves to give reports on weddings and celebrations. Our late sister, Helen Kalish, also excelled in various offices and functions. An important leader, she also had been president. Also Minnie Frank, Esther Shapiro, Anna Zwerin, Anna Pakull, Molly Schilsky, Fannie Gamzon, Sarah Levy, and many others.

All of them worked and continue to work like a well-organized "team" in the interest of all of us and for the good of every Brzeziner no matter where he might be. The Brzeziner Ladies Auxiliary holds a very important place in our history.

THE WORKERS UNION

The bitter, critical years after 1929 seriously damaged the economic stability of the country. The great unemployment directly and indirectly affected the majority of workers in America. Certainly, that oppressive state of affairs did not bypass the clothing industry in which such a great number of Brzeziner *landslayt* were employed.

In those difficult years, all kinds of groups and clubs began to develop in the Cloak and Dressmakers Union, each trying to exert its influence on the broad masses, who were victims of the bad economic situation in the country. Among some of the groups, you must understand, elements of swindle and deception were also not lacking. There were people who had ill intentions and used the bad situation entirely for political ends that had absolutely nothing to do with the interests of those who suffered directly from the crisis. It was also the period of the Right-Left conflict that flared up so strongly within Jewish society during those sad years.

This fight flared up sporadically within our circles, but it can be said with pride that in our community, among us *landslayt*, the fight between the Right and the Left did not take on such an ugly face as in other *landsmanshaftn*. This was thanks to the farsighted and healthy attitude on the part of our leadership, who, right from the beginning, sought to avoid bringing the outside battle into our society.

However, at that time, the problem of more substantially helping our *landslayt* who were employed as cloakmakers and dressmakers arose. This could only be accomplished through the creation of an independent organized body that could, by appropriate methods, exert influence on the leadership of the union on behalf of our members.

As a result, on 4 December 1930 a meeting took place of Brzeziner *landslayt* and *landslayt* from nearby towns employed in the dress and cloak industry. The purpose was to organize as an independent body with the aim of gaining more influence within the union, and, in that way, directly and indirectly, to use that strength to secure more favorable conditions for our *landslayt* in the shops.

To give an accurate historical account, it should be stated here that the Brzeziner Workers Union was founded two years later, but it was this important meeting that was the driving force inspiring the formation of an independent organization.

In the minutes of this first meeting, we find the following statement that expresses the aims of this Brzeziner Workers Club: "The arguments within the workers movement over the last four or five years have moved us to reflect on the sad state of affairs in which our own *landslayt* are also involved, and we must organize as an independent body in order to gain influence and respect in the union movement."

Soon the Workers Union acquired a reputation with its activities. The members rented their own meeting rooms on Eighth Avenue in the garment district. At one time they reached two hundred members. Meetings were held every other week in which important problems relating to conditions in the shops were discussed, as well as ways to broaden our activities to reach beyond the confines of our own circle. They also arranged lectures on different subjects and about specific problems that concerned the interests of the trade union movement.

The events that the organization arranged from time to time, where people enjoyed themselves with a keg of beer and herring with bread, were so warm and intimate that they provided a homey atmosphere and brought back the flavor of the distant, distant past.

Certainly, a major goal was for each of us to help the other cooperatively, such as trying to get work for an unemployed *landsman* or generally helping him get settled in a shop where badly needed communal aid was available. The union also tried to educate and culturally elevate the Brzeziner worker, so that he could fight for his social and community rights on a more conscious level and also so that he would not be crushed in the great quarrel between the Right and the Left within Jewish society.

During the short period of its existence, the Brzeziner Workers Union clearly demonstrated its accomplishments, both on behalf of its own craftsmen and also with respect to influence and prestige within the trade union movement.

The chairman of the union was brother Joseph Diamond; L. Hauser was financial secretary, and Nachum Summer, recording secretary. The following brothers also took an active part in the work: Jacob Leib Wald, Izrael Cohen, Louis Horn, A. Kuyawsky, B. Loomanitz, Sam Hyman, and others.

Joseph Diamond really had an extremely great influence on the union because of his long years of accomplishments in the local Jewish trade union movement. Over the course of many years, he was the chairman of the union and was really the driving force in the activities of the Brzeziner Workers Union.

OUR LEADERS

No organization can exist if it does not have numerous individuals who dedicate their time, energy, and devotion to the support of the organization or institution. In that regard, we are no exception.

Not only should we remember the founders, the pioneers, the builders, who, unfortunately, already sleep in the dust, but we must surely acknowledge with gratitude those who remain at the helm to this day.

We will try to outline here some current observations about our leaders, thanks to whom it was possible to celebrate the sixtieth year anniversary of our local *landsmanshaft*, certainly an important milestone in our history. Several of our leaders who devoted years of their lives have already been mentioned in other chapters.

Jacob David Berg

Jacob David Berg is truly a great wonder among Brzeziner *landslayt*. It seems that he was not one to just remain in Brzezin. While still young, he went away to learn in yeshivas [schools of advanced religious instruction]. He traveled to Kalisz, Brisk de-Lita [Brest-Litovsk], Szczuczyn, Warsaw, and Vilna [Vilnius]. The town was small and could not satisfy him intellectually. In addition, he was orphaned at the age of four, and a stepmother appeared in the house. Since he was of a mischievous nature, the young stepmother apparently took a dislike to him. It began to be too crowded for him in a house full of little children.

Berg actually writes about it himself:

> My sensitive father noticed it with distress. Surreptitiously, he would sometimes press me to him and, with tears in his eyes, recall the name of my mother. "When you get older," he would whisper, "you'll go away to study. . . ." Feeling my father's helplessness, because he did not want to spoil the *sholem bayes* [domestic harmony], I quietly looked forward to the day when I would finally be grown up enough to go away to study in a yeshiva.

Though not residing in Brzezin, Berg was deeply anchored and rooted in Brzeziner soil. He had been restless in the small Jewish *yishev* [settlement], where the environment was confining and too monotonous for his dynamic, restless spirit. With a tremendous passion, he was magnetically drawn to life in the big city, and yet, the love for his hometown grew within him with a tremendous passion. He was entwined by a thousand threads to the place where he had first seen light, despite the spiritual restlessness that propelled him out into the world.

During his interesting life, he came into contact with colorful personalities who exerted a strong influence on Jewish spiritual life, in general, and on him, in particular. Still, it was Brzezin, the small village, which remained the source from which J. D. Berg drew his spiritual nourishment.

Every time Berg comes together with *landslayt*, he turns the conversation to Brzezin and Brzeziners. He is a wonderful conversationalist, and with nostalgia and fervent longing, he talks about his younger years in his beloved *shtetl* and about those years when, as an already grown-up and successful businessman in the community, he returned to Brzezin for a visit. He expresses a warmth for Hasidic middle-class Brzezin. As he concludes his reminiscences about those years, about that generation, you actually sense that a tear appears in the corners of his eyes: "Brzezin of the past was beautiful! The Jews of my generation were beautiful! You *shnekes* [squirts] really didn't know my generation," he warms up. "That really was a generation of *tsadikim* [saintly people]."

When the younger Brzeziners, those from the second generation, want to disagree with Berg, he protests very strongly, and it is not easy to convince him that in his generation, during his time, there were also quite a few shadowy aspects. But no, and no, he would not allow any blemishes to be ascribed to the "beautiful people" of his generation.

This mighty love for his town, which is now more dream than reality, strongly influenced Berg to undertake this work with great zeal and determination, in order that Brzeziners might immortalize their town through a verbal monument. He plunged in under formidable, objectively difficult circumstances, in which a person of weaker character and less conviction might have been badly discouraged and, perhaps, in general, not have dared to proceed with such a risky undertaking.

Berg, the eternal man of faith, made light of the unfavorable conditions and obstacles. He was inspired by the idea that the world should become acquainted with his town, with his generation, and with all the past and future generations of Jews from Brzezin that the Nazi murderers had annihilated forever. And, as a result, we have this great book-monument about the destroyed Brzezin community!

Berg is a colorful personality within the turmoil and turbulence of Jewish organized society. Everywhere he is the same, an unpretentious man. There is not an activity, an institution of communal significance, where Berg does not occupy a place of respect.

But the focal place for his spiritual interests—is the Sholem Aleichem school movement. He was once granted the honor of being the president of the Sholem Aleichem Folk Institute.[1] He has put his heart and soul into this work during most of the time he has been in America. His house was a gathering place for people from the Yiddish world, of the Yiddish spirit. Important meetings of cultural leaders and people for whom Yiddish and Yiddish literature were near and dear always took place there. His home was a *bes-vaad lekhokhmim* [wise men's house of council]. Berg boasts that important institutions dedicated to the preservation of Yiddish culture in America were planned and created there, and he has the right to be proud.

Along with his work for educational and cultural endeavors, he certainly does not forget his *landslayt*. He is very active in the area of relief and rehabilitation work. Under his leadership, the Brzeziners in America built a housing project in Israel with a cultural center and library, the crowning glory of the sixty-year old Brzeziner *landsmanshaft* in America.

Certainly, at the beginning, when this great project came up for discussion, a considerable number of *landslayt* had doubts about the possibility of an undertaking of such magnitude. They were afraid that it was beyond our capability, since the majority of the members were craftsmen. Berg, the great man of faith, encouraged and cheered us on, and the Brzezin housing project is today a reality. In Kfar-Ono, not far from Tel Aviv, a Jewish village is located as a remembrance of the destroyed and martyred Brzeziner Jewish community. Hundreds of Brzeziners from all parts of Israel converge there for various occasions.

Jacob David Berg's work, in connection with the great Israeli project and with his general effort throughout the entire world on behalf of the American Brzeziner *landsmanshaft,* is a great historical accomplishment.

Willie (Vevche) Green

There was a separate group in our *landsmanshaft* that primarily showed their talents in practical everyday acts. Among these leaders, the outstanding *hadres-ponem* [person of stately appearance] was Willie Green, or, as the *landslayt* called him with love, "Vevche."

---

[1] The Sholem Aleichem Folk Institute provided supplemental schools and camps where Yiddish was taught.

He had a serious attitude toward his work, even if it was the smallest task. He was neat and tidy in his attire, and that is how he habitually conducted himself in his work. If he took on an assignment, he sought to carry it out to the minutest detail. During the time he worked among our *landslayt*, he occupied various posts, and his personality lent a special importance to the lowliest office.

Before his premature death, he held the respectable office of financial secretary of the local Relief Committee. He put an endless amount of hard work into this task, and we must understand that the hours he devoted to it he wrested from the pressure of work in a cloak shop. He belonged to those leaders who loved more effort and less noise. He did his work like a good, proficient businessman. He was very precise, and he hated those leaders who continually got away with shouting "much ado about nothing." May he be remembered with honor.

Joseph Diamond

Our Joseph Diamond has recently reached the "golden age" when one begins to withdraw from active work, but knowing Diamond, a person of community responsibilities, we know that he is still far, far from bringing his work to a close. He will undoubtedly free himself from the difficult physical shop work, but as for community work, he will surely not rest on his past laurels. He will not be able to just sit on his hands and warm himself by the fires of history.

Diamond has a very great interest in the trade union movement, but most of all, it seems to us, he was—and is—bound up, body and soul, with everything that has a close connection to Brzeziners.

When we leaf through the pages of forty years of Brzeziner *landsmanshaft* in America, Diamond occupies a very respected place there, an extremely prominent spot. Leafing through the books of the minutes of our society, there is truly not one important project in which he does not figure very significantly.

Diamond is a community leader in whom word and deed are harmoniously combined. He belongs to those leaders who don't just don the frock coat and top hat but also are always among the "doers." He not only tells others what to do but actually "puts on the overalls," as our fine *landsman*, Aaron Selin, once splendidly characterized our active leaders.

Diamond, the leader, the man, often had complaints, grievances that are a part of community work. They were, in most cases, fair complaints, of justifiable merit. He knew things should have been different. It would certainly have been healthier for us, but these resentments and grievances were, it seems, unavoidable in community work.

In his broad community responsibilities, Diamond had decidedly aimed to achieve the maximum, and often because of his strong zeal and temperament, someone seemed to step on his toes. However, he never lost sight of the forest for the trees, that unique individual. Especially in his attitude toward neighborly relations, Diamond particularly had great merit. Almost every one of the hundred *landslayt* families can find a commendable instance somewhere in which Diamond found time and lent an attentive ear to their private communications, their individual concerns. It is a great plus in an account of his life that must be greatly valued. It is of great importance in a *landsmanshaft* like ours to find leaders of Diamond's caliber. They are true diamonds in the crown of our accomplishments.

Diamond recently moved to sunny California. We here, the New York *landslayt*, are encompassed by a kind of feeling of sadness, because so many *landslayt*, friends, are recently missing from our get-togethers and meetings—and certainly, we will sorely miss this dynamic, energetic person who spent forty years with us in New York. It is certainly not a small thing! We know that although he has become a resident of California, he will, nevertheless, remain closely bound to us. Diamond, the leader, will surely not sit on his hands and isolate himself within the confines of his own four walls. Most important, he should only be healthy and enjoy many, many more years.

Luzer (Louie) Horn

L. Horn, occupied a prominent place in the list of our active society leaders.

Horn belonged to those leaders who could not remain indifferent when they noticed a wrong. He was very sensitive and argued with opponents with fire and feeling. That sensitive trait of his was not a pretense. That is how he was even in his private life.

But regardless of his overly sensitive nature and the indelicate adjectives and expressions he used in arguing with his opponents, he was, nevertheless, a great asset to our organization. Those individuals in L. Horn's category are winners in every organization. They are the constant guardians who make sure that, God forbid, some strange element does not find its way into the work. They often disturb the tranquility of many of our leaders, but their moralizing and stern speech often spur others on to more work and greater effort. In that light, they are constructive and a factor that brings life and zest to the work. They break up the monotony and the apathy that often intrude into routine, everyday activities.

Let me mention here a characteristic feature of Louie Horn's biography. As all of us know, Horn came from a middle-class, well-to-do family, but not everyone knows that Horn was not very happy with his father's overly harsh manner in dealing with craftsmen and that he promised himself not to follow the same, well-worn, traditional path as his father. In protest, Louie decided to become a worker himself and set out on the path of radical and socialist elements that were striving to free the world and the individual from exploitation and injustice. And here in America he became very active and involved in various radical groups, most particularly, in the Cloakmakers Union, in which he himself was a member. Later, because of his service, he became the business agent of Local 117.

Horn did a great deal of important work, both as president and also as recording secretary and, most especially, in his tireless work on behalf of our children who were on all the battle fronts.

His activities on behalf of our Relief Committee were also tireless. He held the important post of financial officer in the Relief Committee for many years, until his sudden death in his sixty-fourth year. At the Kfar Ono housing project, for which Louie worked so energetically, trees have been planted in his memory.

Syna (Sam) Hyman

When we leaf through the minutes of our society for the last ten years, we notice that Sam Hyman occupies a very prominent place in them. In those archival documents are registered and recorded Hyman's ideas and views about various phases and aspects of our work. He always had something to say, something to improve, something to add, that others did not think of. His views were based on logic. He sought the practical, the constructive, in every action.

Hyman is not a person who is satisfied only with putting forth a view or a thought and then his mission is fulfilled. No, he belongs to the category of active leader. In our community life, there are certain known types who take great pleasure in being active in communal affairs by causing a commotion, by talking, by pursuing grievances, and scolding others for not doing enough. But they themselves stand on the sidelines and don't participate. They exclude themselves from the rules. We must really work, we must, we must—but not themselves, only others.

Hyman does not belong to the type that tells others to do the work and sees himself only as the leader. In the Relief Committee, in the sorting of the clothing, he himself truly did an enormous amount of work. All the clothes had to be sorted, mended, packed, and delivered to the necessary agencies. He practically did this work by himself, and you must understand that he could only do it in the evenings, after a hard day's work in the shop.

Hyman served in nearly every office in our society. He was also instrumental in the founding of the Brzeziner Workers Union and was truly very active in it for many years. No task was too small or too big. He did not measure the work by the amount of honor he would get from it—only by the importance of the work itself. His motto was always "if the work is important, action is important; it must get done."

Now Hyman belongs to that great multitude of craftsmen who enjoy their "golden years" in retirement. He now summers and winters in sunny Florida. In his retreat he still holds close to his heart warm feelings and nostalgic longings for our Brzeziner colony in New York. And if he should once drop in on us in New York, he would actually see all those *landslayt* with whom he spent so many pleasant evenings.

Luzer (Louie) Hauser

L. Hauser, just like Hyman, also belonged to the group of active leaders in our organization. He also tallied up a lot of accomplishments, without which our society would have been a lot poorer. Hauser is a good listener to others' opinions, to others' views—this is a great attribute. If we could have had good listeners, people who were tolerant of the ideas of others, a lot of misunderstandings and confusion could have been avoided in our communal life.

Usually, most of the leaders are in love with themselves and their petty notions—therefore, their ideas, in most cases, are without substance or vitality.

We do not want to create here the impression that Hauser is only a good listener. No, he also has his opinions and his judgments about matters connected with our work. What he says is of significance, although he often breaks in, in his usual manner of expression, with a note of doubt, of "what if the opposite . . ." It is because Hauser wants to be clear and see in everything logical connections, a logical basis. He dislikes vagueness and distortions. He wants to see a serious consideration of everything, a purposefulness. Therefore, he would often call for more information from the chairman, more particulars, more clarity in the matter that was being so hotly debated by people.

Hauser is also considered among us as an expert in the field of finance. In almost all financial discussions and in all matters that had a connection to financial affairs, he occupied a very prominent place. Incidentally, Hauser was the first financial secretary of the Brzeziner Workers Union and put a lot of effort and energy into it. For many years, he occupied the responsible post of financial secretary in the society and truly brought clarity and system to the books. A good public accountant would testify to that.

Our Louie, although already a grandfather, is still young. Let us wish for him that he should hold on to his youth for many, many years and continue to grace our *landsmanshaft* with his right-to-the-point, practical suggestions.

Aaron Selin

Aaron Selin belongs to the older generation of our leaders. Now he is surely not as active as in his younger years. Recently, his eyes do not serve him so well, and he does not have the energy to come to our meetings so often—and yet, he is still closely bound to our activities.

Our Reb Aaron—the title we are accustomed to use for him—reminds us, with his entire manner, of the old community leaders we respected so much. He belongs to that type of leader that is becoming a rarity among us; every expression and idea has to be supported with a parable or lengthy passage from our sages. When Reb Aaron says something, we are eager to listen. His thoughts are always intertwined with pearls of wisdom and Torah witticisms of past generations.

We do not have many of them, these Aaron Selins. He should really be aware that we are proud of him—and may he for many, many years favor us with the treasures and pearls of wisdom that he gathers from our ancient sages. As the *peyrek* [chapter from a holy text] says, speaking in Reb Aaron's language, good is the one who gathers pearls and words of the Torah, and good is he who pays attention to the wise speech of the sages.

Fishel Maliniak

Fishel Maliniak, who had served as Hitachdut [Socialist-Zionist labor party] leader in Brzezin, occupied a prominent place in the Hebrew-language school system in Poland, and was also involved with Tarbut [secular Zionist educational organization] publications in Warsaw, very quickly gained a respected place among the local *landslayt*. He especially excelled in the work of the Relief Committee. He managed its extensive correspondence, and thanks to his great efforts and intensive work, he succeeded in making contact with hundreds of refugee *landslayt* who found themselves cast away in various displaced persons camps. He found them in remote parts of the world, where they had wandered far from home. Thanks to the contact, they found a word of consolation, an answer to their call for help. These impoverished individuals, who had lost so much during their wanderings, felt immediately that they had not been left orphaned and alone.

Thanks to the fact that Fishel Maliniak is employed in a printing shop, he is completely responsible for the fact that our publications and printing work these last years are so lovingly and accurately published. Also, in the planning of this book to memorialize our *shtetl*, we had to rely greatly for practical instructions and recommendations on the person who is an expert in the printing trade. In summary, Fishel belongs among our important leaders from the younger generation.

Jehuda Fuks

Jehuda Fuks [Julius Fox], personally, by a miracle, survived the executioner's ax, although he did not come out of the great destruction of our people unscathed. He was left with a wound that will surely go with him to his grave. When sometimes they try to talk to him about the mass destruction of six million souls, you see his countenance change, and tears appear in the corners of his eyes.

Here, on American soil, he adjusted. It was not easy for him. For a teacher from the Polish-Yiddish schools, the local style and local cultural situation were difficult for him to grasp. Thanks to his community activities, he was able to overcome many difficulties.

In his varied community work, he does not neglect his *landslayt*; those small town Jews from whom he drew his *shoyresh-neshume* [roots of his soul].

He became active here with the local *landslayt*, mainly in connection with the relief and rehabilitation work, helping to rescue the uprooted, the impoverished. His pleading and warmly emotional speeches, intertwined with silent sorrow and poetic lyricism, make an impression on our *landslayt* and prod them into action.

In the assembling of this *Sefer Brzezin* [Brzeziny Yizkor Book], he also contributed by word and deed.

Sam Fox

Sam Fox has been active in our *landsmanshaft* already for a good number of years. He is by nature a quiet man, silent, almost shy. He was not one of those clamoring for a place of honor.

He was always involved in all kinds of activities. He was one of our several regular committee members. Without the practical, matter-of-fact leaders, a great many of our accomplishments over the years could not have been realized. Thanks to the quiet, modest leaders, our *landsmanshaft* did not remain stagnant or fall into disarray due to the infirmities of old age.

They, the quiet, modest leaders, were always ready to do their assigned work without cymbals clanging, without whims or biases.

Sam Fox held various offices with us and even served several terms in the office of president, and his modesty and simplicity added dignity to the office.

Harry Peters, *e"h*

Harry Peters—formerly Piotrkowski—belonged to the group of quiet, modest leaders. God had not blessed him with great talent as a speaker; he was not one of the initiators among us with great, gigantic plans. However, he occupied a respected place in our work.

For many years he was engaged in bookkeeping, with managing our finances. It is responsible work, requiring a lot of diligence and knowledge. He was our financial secretary for many years. That very office is in fact the key office in our administration, and we must not forget that Peters worked with his own hands and earned his bread in a cloak factory, where he had to wrest free time from his hours of rest and family duties for his work.

Finally, in his later years, when working became difficult, he practically fought "tooth-and nail" to remain in that post and, indeed, did remain there until the last days of his life. He was devoted and loyal all the years that he carried the heavy burden of financial secretary. *Koved zayn ondenk* [Honor to his memory].

Morris Krengel

Krengel was surely an interesting type, and he justly earned the right to be included in the ranks of our leaders.

Krengel was a person of strong character—which means that he would impose his opinions on everyone with whom he came in contact.

We don't know whether this "bossy" element would be so charming and desirable in our community life today. Years ago, because of entirely understandable and extenuating circumstances, this type of Jewish community leader was an important component of our community life. The accomplishments of these people with iron-clad principles and opinions were numerous and important. They were not to be found among the soft-hearted and wishy-washy people who could not decide important issues.

Jewish society was ruled by these kinds of people, and our small movement also had that kind of element, of which M. Krengel was a typical example.

We say that Krengel never officially held any office in the society, but, in fact, he was the boss of our organization. If he wanted a certain project to go through or not to go through—the final decision was always the way he wanted it. The sentiment of the people could have been for carrying out a certain proposition, but if Krengel said no, it could not go through. Indeed, he prevailed in most cases.

We do not say these words about him to criticize him, because we know that, in essence, he was a constructive, reliable member with the best and purest intentions for the welfare of our society.

That powerful element may appear odd today and naive, child-like, but in those beginning years, it was not at all childish and certainly not at all naive.

Abraham Kuyawsky

When we leaf through all the journals that the Brzeziner *landsmanshaft* published for various occasions, many faces that were once prominent rise up before your eyes; they were fervently involved with the work. Great is our sorrow when we also notice there the young face of Abraham Kuyawsky, who was cut down so early. He left this world for eternity when he had barely reached forty years of age.

Our Abraham was full of life, bursting with energy. Often, it seemed to us that his sparkling vigor was a bit excessive. He had to react to every detail. Nothing was regarded as someone else's concern. Where there were two, he became a third in the debate. You could have a conversation about literature, about great personages in Jewish life, about politics, trade union questions, our own society matters—he always had something to say, an idea, a saying in his own direct style. He had something of a peculiar manner of presiding over and engaging in conversation. He was often extremely pointed, and his words could pierce like a sword. We took it in a friendly manner, good-naturedly, because we knew from whom it came. He was quick to get very upset and angry, but his anger just as quickly dissolved, cooled off.

He occupied many administrative posts in the Brzeziner *landsmanshaft*. In an entirely different position, he also excelled as financial secretary.

For the fortieth-year jubilee of the local society, Abraham Kuyawsky was very active in putting together and distributing the very fine journal that was published at that time. He contributed valuable historical and cultural material and, most especially, he was involved with the technical work in connection with the journal.

While we are now preparing the great *yizkor* book, we are aware that we would not have been able to write the history of our local *landsmanshaft* without Abraham Kuyawsky's having laid the groundwork, and though he was taken from us so early, we want to thank him for having been such an energetic, active leader among us.

Izrael Cohen

In spite of the fact that Izrael Cohen's cradle was not in Brzezin, he grew to be so much at home among the Brzeziners, that he actually adopted the "Brzeziner tempo" (cynics should not make a joke of it; there really is a specific Brzeziner character).

Izrael Cohen became one of the most active, energetic leaders of our organization. For many years he was in charge of our finances, and it is extremely responsible and difficult work. And we must take into consideration that almost all of our officials were hard-working, toiling workers in the cloak and dress shops. And under these conditions, Cohen carried out his duties to complete satisfaction.

At the founding of the Brzeziner Workers Union, Cohen was one of the most capable leaders of the union and occupied important positions there. It is worth mentioning here that, in fact, in the later years of the union's existence, he was the facilities manager. Every time we came into the clubrooms of the union, the large premises were clean and neat. On a cold, frosty, wintry late afternoon, you could also find a delightful hot glass of tea, thanks to his effort.

Landslayt appreciated it and really thought of him as a unique person in our midst; as an important leader on our board. It is unfortunate that he left us so early.

Feivel Rozenberg

We, the closest coworkers and friends, knew that Feivel's heart had been seriously affected. In his last years, he was practically forced to withdraw from active shop work, not because of advanced age, but only because his weak heart could not bear the heavy work in the factory. Every strenuous movement, every effort was deadly for him. Nevertheless, he wanted to be in the thick of things, to be active in community affairs, involved with community matters, carrying on the responsibilities himself. He did not want to isolate himself in the confines of his own house, although he had a warm home and a fine wife who watched over him as over a helpless child.

Yes, he lived and breathed for Brzezin. Our dear friend, J. D. Berg, long may he live, once said: "Brzeziners, that is somehow like a different tribe." When you saw the ardor, the kind of fervor when the late Feivel Rozenberg spoke about Brzezin and its residents, you would understand that Berg's statement was not a meaningless saying but is actually characteristic of Brzeziners. Yes, they are somehow kneaded from a different dough— with all their faults and shortcomings. For us, our Feivel was, in fact, one of those who knew Brzezin like his ten fingers. Among us, he was actually the living memory with regard to the history of our *shtetl*. We remember a particular instance about some sort of historical episode concerning our *shtetl*, when Feivel immediately helped us to disentangle and clarify the seeming problem in the incident. And of late, with the monument to memorialize our beloved *shtetl*, we actually intended to take advantage of Feivel's knowledge of Brzezin. He left us too soon, and we really miss his knowledge.

It is somehow not easy to get used to the thought that this quiet, modest Feivel is really no longer among the living. There he sits in the president's chair and carries out the functions of the president's office with quiet modesty. He was a man of the people, an ineffectual speaker and not skilled enough to respond to certain "subtle questions" regarding our members. He regretted afterward that he had lacked significant arguments with respect to this or that matter. Sometimes he felt somewhat helpless in his role as the president of the local *landsmanshaft*—and, nevertheless, his straightforwardness crowned the office with respect. Those with the "subtle questions" surely did not have any evil intentions, and he with his ineffective answers meant them for the benefit of all.

He left a great legacy that remains in the possession of the people of our community. We should not minimize this legacy for our people. His remembrances will live on with us. Somewhere, Hasidism has maintained that mourning must be accompanied with a melody of ascent, of future existence, and continuation. And in the last years, Feivel drew near to the universal concept of Torah Judaism. Let us cherish his legacy regarding our *shtetl*, which, as everyone knows was in the Hasidic spirit.

Joseph Shaibowicz

Joseph Shaibowicz is one of the few refugee immigrants who occupies a respected place among the leaders of our *landsmanshaft*.

He belongs to the quiet, unassuming, dignified leaders. His words are significant, and one is always ready to listen to him, because we know that he has a serious attitude. He substantiates his spoken thoughts with logical arguments, and, most important, he is also a person of deeds.

He likes to carry things out precisely and thoroughly. When we talked about getting authentic, historical documents of the history of our *shtetl*, he did not let us get away only with talk. He immediately made contact with the appropriate authorities and ran daily to the libraries in order to get the necessary sources and information. The significant work that you find in this book is the result of his zeal, industriousness, and thoroughness.

As the recording secretary of the society these last few years, he has added dignity to the office and brought thoroughness and clarity to the beautifully written minutes.

Joseph-Hersz Goldkrantz

Joseph-Hersz Goldkrantz was among the first young people who emigrated from Brzezin to America. In those years he found a harsh, thorny terrain here. Separated from friendly surroundings, it was hard for him to sink his teeth into the gray American reality. One lovely day, early in the morning, he boarded a ship and returned to Brzezin.

Because of worsening economic conditions and the mood of revolution and war that filled Russia and Poland, he decided to leave Brzezin again and return once more to America. He came with a background of long community service gained in Zionist circles in Brzezin, but here he did not take an active part in Zionist community life. Here, he is extremely busy and weary with toil to support his family.

But he takes part in various *landsmanshaft* activities. Once he held the office of recording secretary and was a member of various committees. As a traditional Jew, well-versed, he observes Shabosim and holidays. Over the years he was drawn into orthodox life. He became a *bal-tfile* [prayer leader] and a *bal-koyre* [Torah reader]. He is drawn back to his roots.

Although in his later years Joseph-Hersz Goldkrantz was not active in Zionist affairs, he had, however, great *nakhes* [pleasure] from his two daughters who settled in Eretz Yisroel. One of his grandchildren, Michrowski, about whom we have written in detail elsewhere in this book, died as a hero in the War of Independence. These meager facts about Joseph-Hirsh Goldkrantz are certainly not a full description. Here we have only sketched the outlines of his profile. May his memory be honored.

Relief Work and Shikkun Brzezin [Brzezin Housing Project] in Israel (pp. 182–92)

Nachum Summer and Fishel Maliniak

When we now record the history of our relief work and want to analyze how it was possible for us to successfully carry out such a project, we can only characterize it as an episode in the history of Brzeziners in America that in its scope had no equal, not only among our *landslayt*, but also among other similar organizations in the country.

The Brzeziner Relief Committee. Sitting from right to left: Abraham Rozenberg, Rachel Bergman, Joseph Diamond, J. D. Berg, Morris Hendricks, Louie Horn, *e"h*, Fannie Tanenbaum, and Fishel Maliniak. Standing from right to left: Sam Hyman, Masha Green, N. Summer, Izzy Schilsky, Joseph Shaibowicz, Max Tushinsky (Tyson), Sam Fox, Harry Peters, *e"h*, Willie Rozenfeld, Feivel Rozenberg, *e"h*, Alter Rozenfeld, *e"h*, Gussie Pakula, and S. Fuks. (Missing in the picture were, among others, Aaron Selin, J. Rozenblum, Meyer Lasky, Renee Lasky, Louie Hauser, Szlama Schwartz, Sam Maliniak, Jehuda Fuks, and Manny Snyder.)[1]

We should not forget that the period 1945–56 was a very intense time in the lives of the American Jewish community. It was the time of the United Jewish Appeal — preparation for the rise of the *yidishe medines* [Jewish state] in Eretz Yisroel, and from all sides came urgent appeals for help and monetary support. Nevertheless, a small group of Brzeziners succeeded in collecting over $50,000, which was in addition to other donations Brzeziners had made to national institutions, as well as their contributions to the general Jewish community life in America, both as individuals and as an organization.

---

[1] See footnote on p. 250 regarding name changes.

In order to understand this, one must place oneself in that time period, into that terrible emotional frame of mind in which American Jews were living. On the one hand, there had been the destruction of all the cities and *shtetlekh* [small towns], which most of the still-living community in America had once called home; and on the other hand, was the arrival of salvation—one could see with one's own eyes the rise of Medines Yisroel [State of Israel].

A meeting, on behalf of refugee *landslayt,* of the well-known union leader Sasha Zimmerman with representatives of the Brzeziner Relief Committee. From right to left: Max Tushinsky, Rachel Bergman, Joseph Diamond, J. D. Berg addressing the people, Sasha Zimmerman, A. Rozenberg, and Fishel Maliniak.

And when you add to this the personal element of finding a relative or a friend—and, in most cases, the only rescued relative from thousands of family members who had been annihilated—one can understand the willingness for self-sacrifice displayed by various individuals among us in America.

Therefore, we can ascribe the success of our work not just to the leaders of the Relief Committee, without whom nothing would have been accomplished, but, most of all, to the aroused compassion of our *landslayt*.

A second factor was the organization of the project. Although the entire project was carried out on a voluntary basis, the plans for the work were prepared in great detail, and the meetings and general conferences were well planned. The people who were at the head of the committee had enormous experience in organizing Jewish life, not only in America, but also in Europe. For instance, the chairman was Brother Jacob David Berg, president of the Sholem Aleichem Folk Institute for many years, while the vice-president, Brother Joe Diamond, was an active trade union leader. The situation was the same with Brother Louie Horn—after the death of Brother Willie Green—who was an intelligent person and had been a businessman. The secretary, Brother Fishel Maliniak, came to America in 1941 with long years of experience in administrative leadership at the headquarters of the Hebrew language school system in Poland—the Tarbut Center in Warsaw. In addition, the following were also members of the committee—Jehuda Fuks and Louie Hauser. And we were

Willie Green, *e"h,* former secretary of the Relief Committee

fortunate to have among us the capable, energetic Ruth Hauser, who took over the work from Louie Horn when he left us so suddenly. As can be seen, the best people that the *landsmanshaft* in New York possessed were placed at the head of the committee.

And now, a history of our project. Immediately at the outbreak of World War II, in 1939, the leaders of the Brzeziner Society created a committee dedicated to the collection of special funds for the needy among Brzeziner Jews. At that time we hoped, first of all, that the war would not last long and, second, that Jews here would be willing to help as long as the war continued. Members of the Society, members of the Ladies Auxiliary, and respected *landslayt* whose participation lent dignity to the committee were represented on that committee.

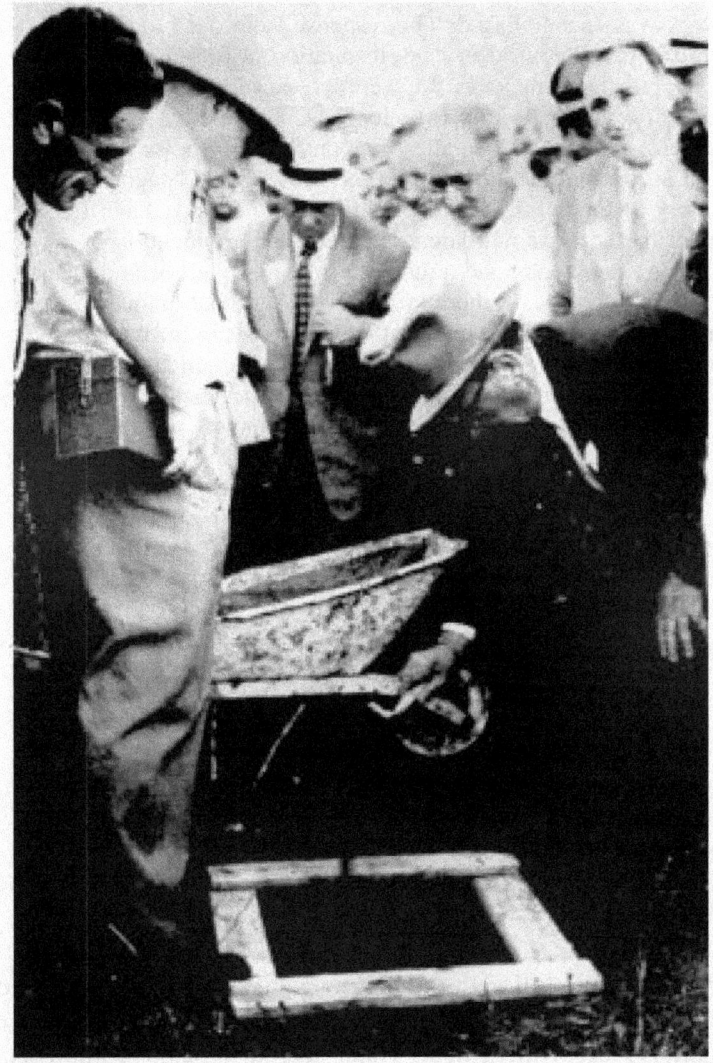

However, it soon became clear that the committee could accomplish very little and that this war was different from World War I. Therefore, the committee discontinued its activities after a short time.

Then, at the beginning of 1945, when it appeared as if the war would end soon, an urgent meeting of the Society was convened to revive the committee.

The laying of the cornerstone for Shikkun Brzezin in Kfar-Ono in Israel. In the picture can be seen Jacob David Berg, chairman of the Brzeziner Relief Committee in America, Lemel Horn, Har-Jaffe (Szajnberg), Abe Berg, and other *landslayt*.

We reproduce here the appeal as a characteristic expression of the mood that predominated in those times among all our leaders:

Distinguished Brothers and Sisters,

Six dark, terrible years have passed since the Nazi enemy assaulted Poland, and since then, for us, every source of information about Polish Jews, in general, and about our Brzeziner Jews, in particular, has been cut off.

In order to maintain the tradition of continually staying in touch with our *landslayt*, we created at the very beginning of the war a Relief Committee, with the purpose of gathering the minimal sum of $10,000. This was to be ready when the appropriate time came, so that we would have the apparatus in place and not be delayed in our relief work.

The first part of the work was accomplished. The response from our brothers and sisters was very heartening. Their enthusiasm and inspiration was, unfortunately, hindered by the bloody developments of the war. We were left powerless and helpless. We waited with fear and hope for the smallest opportunity to be able to offer assistance. But the German hangmen did not permit the smallest amount of help to reach Polish Jews. In helpless desperation, we were forced to interrupt the work we had begun.

Now, thanks to the victory of the heroic Allied armies, Poland is once again free, free from the wild barbarism of the Nazi murderers! In truth, the culmination of six years of Hitlerism in Poland has been bloody and tragic. The barbarians left behind them desolate victims in every city and town. But there is still hope here that among those Jews who were left alive may also be our sisters and brothers, *landslayt* from Brzezin.

It is now our sacred duty—we, the lucky ones, who are in free America—to again establish our connection with our unfortunate *landslayt,* whom the terrible war has uprooted and scattered to far-off lands wherever there was the remotest possibility of saving oneself.

All those whose hearts ache and bleed—because of the dark devastation of the tragedy—for our people, in general, and for our *landslayt,* in particular, have, through an urgent summons from the president of our society, challenged themselves to actively participate in a large

Mass Meeting

called by the Brzeziner Society to take place

Sunday, March 11, 1945

with brotherly greetings,

For the committee:

Abraham Fox, vice-president   Jacob Berg, chairman

Willie Green, secretary

At the meeting, held 11 March 1945, the following *landslayt* were selected for the Relief Committee: Alter Rozenfeld, Joseph Diamond, Sam Fox (Syna Tauba's), Feivel Rozenberg, Sam Hyman, Louie Hauser, Ruth Hauser (later secretary of the committee), Sam Fox, Fishel Maliniak, J. D. Berg (chairman), Ray Bergman (from Ladies Auxiliary), S. Schwartz, Abraham Fox (vice-chairman), Moishe Hendricks, Louie Horn, Abraham

Rozenberg, Fannie Tanenbaum, Masha Green, Willie Rozenfeld, Gussie Pakula, Jehuda Fuks, Max Tushinsky, N. Summer, E. Snyder, J. Rozenblum, Harry Peters, Aaron Selin, Meyer Lasky, Renee Lasky, *e"h*, Sam Milstein, and Izzy Schilsky.

A resolution to collect money was passed on the spot—and carried out with but short interruptions. Over the course of ten years, with only brief interludes, money was raised for various causes.

The committee also undertook the task of finding out, first of all, if there were any *landslayt* still left alive. Soon, information began to come from various places that here and there a few souls had survived.

Examining a sign affixed to the wall of the houses in Israel built with the help of the American *landsmanshaft*. In the picture from left to right: Lemel Horn, J. D. Berg, a boy (a child of one of the residents of Shikkun Brzezin) and Szlama Pinczewski.

The dedication of the building project Shikkun Brzezin. At the microphone is Dr. Pinchas Hurgin, *e"h*, president of Bar-Ilan University.

The beautiful hall of the Culture House in "Shikkun Brzezin," Israel.

The first news came from the camps in Germany—Bergen-Belsen, Stuttgart, Bad Worishofen, Munich, Bad Reichenhall, Camp Fernwald, Feldafing, and many others.

As soon as we received news from a *landsman,* or about him, a letter was sent, as well as food, and, where possible, money, also, in order to let him know that he was not alone. We put together lists, and in many cases helped to unite families.

After the first contacts with individuals were established, we organized district committees where help was consolidated, and the relief work was carried out through these committees.

At the same time, an intensive campaign was conducted to raise money needed to satisfy the requests that came daily from various camps and countries, once our *landslayt* learned that there was a committee in New York helping Brzeziners.

There were many cases in which strangers who never belonged to the *shtetl* but heard of the Brzeziner aid turned to us for support. Although in several instances we knew that these were "imposters," nevertheless, we helped them. The slogan of our chairman, Brother Berg, was: "*In boydkin mizoynes*" [when someone asks for food, give it to him without questions]. If someone turns to us for support, it doesn't matter if he is trying to fool us; we have to help him in order to succeed in making him believe once again in humanity.

In a few months the work had so expanded that we had to engage a secretary to answer the large amount of correspondence—which was carried on by our secretary, Brother Maliniak, all over the world and with more than half a dozen organized committees. (Such committees existed in Stuttgart, Bergen-Belsen, Sweden, Łódź, Paris, and Tel Aviv.)

Meanwhile, we also advertised in the Jewish world press, and in that way we reached almost one hundred percent of the surviving Jews from our *shtetl.*

A special chapter is needed to cover the group of *landslayt* saved by the Red Cross in Sweden. There, at the head of the committee stood Mrs. Rywka Grosman, who was well known to the secretary, Brother Maliniak, because he had worked with her before in a Brzeziner youth organization.

Our *landsman* friend, Jehuda Fuks, whose assignment was to personally look for *landslayt* and also to distribute help according to their need, traveled there later.

Soon the possibility arose to send money, food, clothing, and medical supplies to Łódź, where Jewish survivors who had returned to Poland were concentrated.

In those days significant sums of money were raised that were sent directly to the surviving *landslayt* in Poland. Understand, that for such work great effort was needed among the *landslayt* to campaign for funds. Large mass meetings of *landslayt* were called in order to rouse the *landslayt* and tell them about the concrete needs of the survivors.

Through an agreement with the organization CARE, hundreds of packages of food were sent. The same was done with medical supplies. As soon as someone needed a particular item, not easily available in those days, like medicine, it was quickly arranged.

Somewhat later, a clothing campaign was organized, in which Brother Sam Hyman clearly excelled. It should also be noted here that Chicago was very successful in this campaign. Thousands of pounds of good and clean clothing were collected and sent.

At the Sixty Year Jubilee for Jacob David Berg. In the name of the Brzeziner *landsmanshaft*, Brother Moishe Hendricks presents to J. D. Berg, as a gift on his becoming sixty years of age, a check for the benefit of the Relief and Rehabilitation Committee of which Berg is chairman. In the picture, seated, is J. D. Berg. Standing from right to left: Luzer Horn, *e"h*, Fishel Maliniak, Rachel Bergman, Abraham Rozenberg, Isaac Hemlin (a guest at the gathering), Joseph Diamond, Moishe Hendricks, and Fannie Tanenbaum.

As a rule, the work was carried out according to the requirements of the time.

For example, the first step was establishing the connection and satisfying the major needs—this stage we can call "immediate help."

The second stage was linking the survivor with his family and with setting up a local district committee where help could be organized though the local cooperative—which understood the situation better than we did here in New York. This period can be labeled "team help."

The third stage was involved with the exodus of the survivors from their camps. An enormous task was accomplished in this area.

The fourth stage was the constructive assistance that was given to our *landslayt* in Paris. The first opportunity opened up for us when our brothers in Paris began to return to their homes. Most of their houses had been plundered and destroyed. In the great conflagration they had all lost everything and had to start all over again from the beginning. Then came the Relief Committee, which brought sewing machines. Since the majority were tailors—a trade inherited from our *shtetl*—they took our practical means of help with immense gratitude. In this undertaking we had the cooperation of ORT, which immediately supplied over seventy machines of all kinds. These machines were not at all easy to get, even for money. In organizing the project to get the machines, we also helped interested relatives by providing them with machines, so they could also take part in the work. The *landslayt* were literally brought back to life. This gave them the ability to support a family through their own work. We still remember very well their letters of thanks with *brokhes* [blessings].

Finally, comes the crown of our work—the Shikkun Brzezin that was built in Israel.

We also carried on activities to help our uprooted *landslayt* come to America. Later we helped them settle here by getting them jobs and visas. In this respect, the following

J. D. Berg and Har-Jaffe (Szajnberg) at the opening of the library named for the Berg Family

shall be recognized here. When the International Ladies Garment Workers Union obtained the prospect of employing a greater number of tailoring factory workers in Canada, we also did not let the moment pass.

Through our influence in the local trade union movement, particularly thanks to the capable and energetic effort on the part of our distinguished *landslayt* Joseph Diamond, Louie Hauser, Abraham Rozenberg, and Louie Horn, *e"h*, we succeeded in getting a greater number of visas. This permitted several dozen Brzeziner refugee families to settle in Canada as qualified tailoring craftsmen. Here the Jewish Workers Committee also cooperated with the company's community organizer and the manager of the International [International Ladies Garment Workers Union] in Canada, Friend M. Shein.

The same thing took place again when the International gained the opportunity to bring a greater number of tailors to America. Nearly thirty families were brought to the United States at the expense of the government, and with the help of our *landslayt*, they were all accommodated. Also, Friend Sasha Zimmerman, then head of Dressmakers Local 22, assisted us in this, and also B. Kaplan, manager of Cloakmakers Local 117.

Calls for help from refugee *landslayt* who had succeeded in saving themselves and had immigrated to Eretz Yisroel began to reach us. We knew their difficult situation very well. This call for assistance on the part of our *landslayt* did not let us rest. However, we decided that our help should have a more constructive character than it had possessed up to that time. We should not be satisfied with just sending food packages, clothing, medical supplies, and a little cash. The assistance should have a more solid, a more lasting foundation.

Then all sorts of plans and proposals were brought up regarding the appropriate way to help the surviving *landslayt* in Eretz Yisroel.

At that time we had even developed the idea of building a tailoring cooperative in conjunction with the Histadrut. Certainly, it was plausible, since Brzezin was then well-known for its clothing industry. And with Brzeziner Jews, who for generations had worked in that trade, such a project as a tailoring cooperative, particularly with the collaboration of the Histadrut, would be sure to succeed.

But when we proceeded to think about the project concretely, various difficulties and complications arose, especially after the well-known Jewish workers' leader, Benjamin Kaplan, who had visited Eretz Yisroel at that time, actually talked with our *landslayt*. He spoke to them about this matter and about other plans and about what they could use immediately that would also have lasting value.

At that time we also had more detailed accounts from our own *landslayt* from America—Julius Fox and Fishel Maliniak, who had also been in Israel during those years and were deeply interested in the problems of the *landslayt* there.

Friend Berg decided to go to Israel. You must understand that the *landslayt* gave him a mandate on the spot to investigate the entire matter and actually see what was the most appropriate way to perpetuate the memory of our destroyed *shtetl* and, at the same time, to help in a tangible way the surviving *landslayt* who had managed to save themselves in Israel.

The well-known journalist M. Tsanin wrote about this in an article in the New York *Forverts* (published 9 August 1953):

> A few years ago, a Jew by the name of J. D. Berg, a Jew from America, but for whom America had never erased his attachment to Brzezin . . . that which he, as a young man had absorbed in that small *shtetl* was never eradicated. And in Israel, that Jacob David Berg got wind that "his" Brzeziner Jews, who had come to Israel as immigrants, were still sitting in transit camps, hoping to see a home where they might once and for all unpack their bags and become just like Israeli Jews. Jacob David Berg opened his Brzeziner heart: "What is this, my *landslayt* sitting in transit camps? Who ever heard that Brzeziners should allow such a thing?"

The signing of the contract with the "Rasko" building contractor. Seated from right to left: Abraham Fox, Joseph Diamond, Ray Bergman (chairman of the Ladies Auxiliary), L. Horn, e"h (who had held the office of financial secretary of the Brzeziner Relief Committee), and Alter Rozenfeld. Standing from right to left: Fishel Maliniak, Fannie Tanenbaum, J. D. Berg (chairman of the Relief Committee), Mr. Louis Berg (attorney for the Brzeziners at the closing of the transaction), P. Imber (representative of Rasko) Ruth Hauser (later financial secretary of the Relief Committee), and Sam Fox (then president of the Breziner Society).

Berg called together the long-time residents in Israel and said to them: "We want to build Brzezin in Israel. Those unfortunate individuals who arrived in Israel, rescued after enduring all the anguish and horrors that they lived through before coming here—that our minds can never grasp—we cannot allow them to wander about in holes, in dens, and live again under inhuman conditions."

And so it was. When Berg returned from his trip to Israel, he reported on all that he had seen and heard among the *landslayt* in Israel. Berg contended:

> It is our duty. History has decreed it for us. Since we certainly cannot restore the entire world, we should at least take care of our own *landslayt*, whose plight is so dreadful. We must no longer leave them in such terrible conditions. Specifically, we must build a housing project. We must provide those who remain in these wretched shelters with decent housing, so that they may become normal people once again.

J. D. Berg addressing the meeting of the Relief Committee. On the platform are, from the right: Fishel Maliniak, Jehuda Fuks, Joseph Diamond, Louis Horn, *e"h*, and Abraham Rozenberg.

An appeal to our *landslayt* all over the world was issued at once, and we read in it:

To all Brzeziner *landslayt* dispersed throughout the world:

To our *landslayt* whose cradle was in Brzezin near Łódź, to all who learned the alphabet in that Hasidic tailoring town of toiling, honest, noble folk, it is to you we turn with this appeal. We hope that the call for help will reach all Brzeziners that Fate has scattered all over the world.

The matter about which we turn to you is of such great importance that we want all Brzeziners to acquaint themselves with it, to agree at once that they wish to have the honor of being among those who have assisted in the realization of the project.

It is the matter of the Shikkun Brzezin that is to be built in Israel to put a roof over the heads of all our *landslayt* who were rescued from Nazi hands and now find themselves and their children in canvas tents in Israel, imperiled by all kinds of weather, bringing them to the brink of desperation. For those Brzeziners who came through hell and arrived in our homeland to find their permanent home—we must care for all of them so that they may settle down as human beings and be able to live a normal life. We, the Brzeziners in America, as brothers who were concerned about all the survivors and helped them when they were found in the camps, we must now provide them with a roof over their heads.

In order to carry this out, a *shikkun* [housing project] will be built in Kfar-Ono near Tel Aviv, a *shikkun* of forty three-room apartments, ten four-family houses, and also a gathering place. We must contribute $44,000. The New York organization has raised half that sum. Now we have to complete the project. If we do not get the help from our *landslayt* around the world, we will not be able to see the plan finalized. The construction work has finally begun!

For the Brzeziner Society: Alter Rozenfeld, president
For the Brzeziner Relief Committee: Jacob D. Berg, chairman
Abe Fox, honorary chairman
F. Maliniak, vice-chairman
Louie Horn, finance secretary

Of course, it was not as easy as it sounds. It required a lot of determination and effort on the part of our *landsmanshaft* in New York and the *landslayt* in California, Chicago, and Paris.

Many raised their eyebrows. They could not believe that we were capable of accomplishing such a big project. We were not many in number; most of the *landslayt* consisted of craftsmen working in the tailoring trades, small wage-earners. "It will get stuck in the middle. It is far beyond our strength," well-meaning *landslayt* advised.

Nevertheless, the plan succeeded in being implemented. Not only were nine buildings built in Kfar-Ono, where one hundred and thirty souls live, but there is also a beautiful culture center, where the walls are adorned with pictures of the once remarkably beautiful *shul* [synagogue] of Brzezin, of the great *rabonim* [rabbis], and especially with the picture of Harov [Rabbi] Jekutiel Zalman Borensztajn, *zts"l* [may the memory of a righteous person be blessed], whom the Nazis beat murderously while they were burning the *shul*.

At the Beit Ha-am [House of the People], the gathering place for all our *landslayt* in Israel, trees were planted in memory of our dead brothers, the secretaries of our Relief Committee—Willie Green and Louie Horn—who put in so much strength and effort that everything might be completed.

We must also recall that there is also a very fine library there, which was donated as a gift by the J. D. Berg family. The equipment and furniture in the hall was a gift of our member Morris Frank and his wife. He himself was actually born in Biała but voluntarily adopted Brzezin as his second hometown.

We also had the great *mazl* [luck] to have a most wonderful ladies auxiliary such as ours, which raised the sum of $7,000 and helped make it all possible. They encouraged us so that our great undertaking might succeed.

As was already stated, the greatest part of the needed sum came as direct donations from our *landslayt* in New York, California, and Chicago. We must certainly remember here with thanks several of our well-to-do *landslayt* who donated larger amounts. Among them were Abraham Fox, the honorary chairman of the committee, who donated a building in the name of his deceased

Child actors from Shikkun Brzezin in their roles.

mother, Mollie Fox, *z"l*; the Brothers Max and Charlie Kalish; Szlama Schwartz; and several others.

The *landslayt* from Paris, who had been helped only recently, also had a hand in that work. They contributed several thousand dollars to the historic project that is our great crowning work—of which we can truly be proud.

Fishel Maliniak, on behalf of the Relief Committee, addressing a gathering of *landslayt*. On the dais can be seen Joseph Diamond, J. D. Berg, and Ruth Hauser.

In connection with activities to raise larger sums among the *landslayt* in Chicago and California, it should be noted here that our Brother Joe Diamond, who had the opportunity to make several trips to various places, used his private travels for all sorts of projects related to the Brzeziner Relief Committee. The Brzeziner Relief Club of California, with J. Fogel at its head, carried out independent relief work on behalf of our surviving *landslayt* and should be mentioned here.

When Friend Berg traveled to Israel for the second time, for the dedication of a building of the Shikkun Brzezin, the Israeli correspondent Tsanin of the *Forverts* wrote about it:

> It was not an ordinary commemoration but a real wedding, where the most essential person was the representative of the Brzeziners in America, J. D. Berg, for without the Brzeziner *landslayt*, the entire celebration would not have taken place.
>
> The Jews in the transit center did not even dream of having such palaces, so the celebration was enormous. They laughed, and they cried . . . but it did not end with that. Places to live are certainly a good thing. Only now will they be able to have a real sense of their own home in Israel—but that is not enough. Brzezin was not an ordinary *shtetl* of "scissors-and-iron folk," but Brzeziner tailors knew Talmud, carried on a cultural life with libraries, with books, with lectures and talks. And that is what they also wanted in Israel. One has to take care of the soul. And at the ceremony at the opening of the apartments, the cornerstone was laid for a culture center.

The culture center and the library about which M. Tsanin wrote in the above-mentioned article in *Forverts* is already a completed fact. A wonderful library functions there now with Yiddish and Hebrew books, newspapers, and journals from all over the Jewish world.

When our distinguished *landsman*, Har-Jaffe (Szajnberg), came to America, he expressed thanks that this great project brought the *landslayt* in Israel closer to the *landslayt* in America. A bridge was created between them and us. Actually, there are now two great communities of Brzeziner *landslayt*—in America and in Israel. They represent Brzezin from long ago and from the present.

Brzeziners and Lodzers in California (pp. 193–94)

The Jewish *yishev* [settlement] in California has grown greatly in recent years; Jews have come from various states and cities. Of course, the good climate for which California is known has been an extremely strong influence.

Of course, there already had been Jews in California for many years, but they did not come with the stream of "gold hunters." Most of the Jewish residents came looking for the "gold" of the sun.

Brzeziners came to sunny California with *yikhes* [distinguished lineage], with tradition. Jews from Łódź also came. They kept close together; they felt as if they were related, because, geographically, Łódź and Brzezin were almost like a room with an alcove. They began to come together, and as a result, the Brzeziner-Lodzer Society was established.

On 21 November 1929 we convened at the home of Morris Badower, and there the cornerstone was laid that united the highly developed industrial Łódź with the small tailoring town of Brzezin. Since then, they have lived in harmony as in a good marriage.

At the founding meeting the following *landslayt* were present: Morris Badower, Charlie Baron, S. Berkowitz, Jack Diamond, A. Diamond, Morris Gribs, B. Miller, C. Newman, M. Piotrkowski, J. Rozenblat, S. Rubinstein, W. Walter, and Sam Zigman.

The following were appointed temporarily as the first officers of the united Brzeziner-Lodzer *landsmanshaft*: Morris Badower, president; B. Miller, vice-president; and Charlie Newman, treasurer.

Over the years, they carried out various community activites. Here is a list of important organizations they supported: the American Red Cross, City of Hope, the Cancer Fund, the Community Chest, and the California Home in Recido—as well as Jewish organizations and institutions, such as Keren Kayemeth, Histadrut, United Jewish Welfare Fund, and many others.

With respect to our account about California, permit me to cite from "Impressions from a Trip," which Joseph Diamond printed in his booklet, released by the Brzeziner *landsmanshaft* on their Fiftieth Anniversary Jubilee:

> My personal pleasure in meeting with those near and dear to us also had an additional place in our plans. A meeting of the Brzeziner Relief Club was arranged at once, and I was warmly and cordially greeted that evening as the guest of honor. Although that club consists of just a small number of members, they nonetheless created a warm and friendly atmosphere.
>
> The warmth with which our *landslayt* were welcomed that night, was—we thought to ourselves—not personal, not an expression of pleasure toward an individual, but only because that evening I was the embodiment of the *landslayt* in New York. Perhaps in that feeling of pleasure was the expression of a buried longing, which lies in the depth of our souls, toward that former place, for the town where our cradles had stood. . . . I was so overwhelmed by that poignant pleasure that I could not stop talking about it. . . .
>
> This particular society [Brzeziner-Lodzer Society] has a majority of non-Brzeziner members. Therefore, it is natural in their collections of money for their rescue work that they would express the wish to participate in general Jewish relief work. They did not

want to localize their relief work—all of those in need are victims and must therefore be helped. This organization made a good impression on us, particularly their method of conducting their meetings. Their leaders are very likable people, and they demonstrated interest and a sincere attitude toward our recommendations and suggestions.

The Brzeziner Relief Club there is an organization that was created at the outbreak of the war. It should be noted here, incidentally, that Brother Fogel dedicated a great deal of effort and work in support of the club. The purpose of that Brzeziner club became clear to me. It was motivated principally by the idea of having their own corner in which to be able to live in their own Brzeziner manner. Fate had also willed that because of the horrible world situation, they should feel obligated, as to one of their own, to come to the aid of Hitler's victims from Brzezin. They began to carry out independent fund raising, sending clothing and food packages directly to the unfortunate who had survived Hitler's hell.

After several meetings with them, we succeeded in persuading them that substantial work for the victims can only be done in a united way and that the New York relief organization should be the central body to carry out the rescue work.

As a result of these negotiations, they actually began at once to send contributions to the Brzeziner Relief Committee in New York. . . . At my farewell evening there were representatives already from both of the local organizations sitting at one table and discussing common problems.

The present board of the Brzeziner-Lodzer Society consists of the following members:

J. Haber, president; Harry Newman, vice-president; Celia Zigman, recording secretary; Jack Lax, financial secretary; and Sam Zigman, treasurer.

Chairmen of committees are: Nathan Chernick, executive board; Rudy Chernick, loan and relief; Sam Stein, cemetery; Esther Haber, membership; Edward Jaloff, culture and publicity; Henry Bernheim, entertainment; Ida Apelbaum, hospital visits; Herbert Segal, management; Berta Kaufman, management; and Hetty Miller, executive.

IN MEMORIAM

Sam Apelbaum	B. Miller
Morris Badower	Jacob Miller
J. Baron	Morris Piotrkowski
Malia Becker	Herman Ratner
Fanny Berkowitz	Isidor Rozenblat
Morris Berger	Ana Rozman
Sol Berkowitz	J. Rozman
William Brown	Carl Rubinstein
Sam Simon Cohen	Emanuel Samuels
Tesia Cooper	Bessie Sheinholtz
Jack Diamond	Henry Sheinholtz
Noel Irwin Fox	Sara Weinberg
George Horn	William Walter
Celia Kalish	Celia Zigman
Harry Kaufman	Abe Zigman
S. Kronin	Alex Zimmerman
Max Lang	Alex Zwilling
S. Lasman	Mary Zwilling

During various times, the following list of *landslayt* held the post of president of the Brzeziner Society in America: A. Blas, S. Baron, M. Drengel, G. Diamond, Joseph Diamond, William Green, J. Hillel, M. Horowitz, A. Toping, H. Kesler, L. Fogel, Sam Fox, A. Kuyawsky, S. Newman, Toviah Peizer, A. Rozman, M. Rozenberg, Feivel Rozenberg, Alter Rozenfeld, J. H. Rozenkrantz, Aaron Selin, M. Sher, J. Silverstein, and Manny Snyder.

Jankiel Chaim-Icek's (p. 195)

Lajbuś Lehrer

In cheerless, difficult days and in view of our many sins—and they certainly are not lacking—how easy it is to become locked inside oneself and throw away the key. But, still, sometimes one becomes tired of *tfile belakhesh* [prayer under one's breath], and one becomes overly saturated with dark shadows surrounding one's thoughts. Then one thinks that soon today's guest will come and force a bit of a vague hope on us. And a telephone is also an instrument that can carry within it a lot of unexpected surprises.

And so it is; the telephone rings. "It's Jankiel Chaim-Icek's speaking."[1] The self-confident voice, with the smile of mischievous familiarity, announces that Jacob David Berg is paying a visit by telephone. The words flow in a gushing stream. He weaves a constant conversation with all the nuances and innuendos of his typical humor. Berg has complaints; he is not happy. He has undertaken a sizeable project, but there is no one to carry it out with him. One is a "lazybones," the second a "do-nothing," and a third is nothing but a "foot-dragger." Jankiel Chaim-Icek's has his own spirit and his own way of expressing himself. It begins with a smile and advances to a force that bites into the problem facing him and ends with: "But we have the strength and the will to carry it out."

The words flow in a rhythmic manner. Little by little, something catches on. It becomes brighter all around. We are reminded how much money was lost in dark moments. But now, it suddenly becomes clear. The lost money is seemingly lying on the lighted floor. We only have to bend down, pick it up, and right away, we feel we've become richer. That is how Berg goes among us with the light, from: "Don't give up hope!" to the never ceasing command: "Have Faith!" His friends bend down, find what is needed, and rise up.

Exactly as in private life, also in community life, in secular circles, Jacob David Berg, with his own hands, built for himself his respected position. Those who could not go along with him were pushed out by the considerable current that he stirred up around him. It carried him forward on the waves of his fantasy, and those who wanted to stop him with cold calculations fell apart like broken ships in a violent sea.

In every undertaking, he voices the message of unexpected hope, of great assurance, maybe never to be realized, but the strong drink of pleasure in the present is intoxicating and lulls to sleep any sober consideration of the future. He is quite often the central focus that attracts, stimulates, and puts wings on the slowest ones plodding ahead on foot. That is how Jacob David Berg became a person of renown—and probably not just among the followers of Sholem Aleichem, for whom he played such a leading role.

But when Jacob David Berg undergoes a small transformation and becomes Jankiel Chaim-Icek's, then the Divine presence of his *shtetl* Brzezin shines through in him. He then displays the most common traits of his people, both the discontentment and the

---

[1] It was customary in Brzezin to call a person informally by his given name plus the name of his father or mother. Jankiel Chaim-Icek's meant Jankiel (Jakub), son of Chaim-Icek.

charms with which God blessed the Ukrainian, Tevye the Milkman, in his modern Polish edition, Jankiel Chaim-Icek's.

He possesses the *ahavat yisroel* [love of Israel in the broad sense], a satirical humor that attacks with silken threads, and a friendship that caresses with a warm *lekhaim!* [to health!]. What would infuriate Jacob David Berg, Jankiel Chaim-Icek's, can lightly pardon with confidence. He is permeated with a traditional Jewish spirit, but he never worships the god of vengeance and jealousy. His closest theological reality draws spiritual nourishment from *av-horakhamim* [God of mercy].

Nachum Summer, the Brzeziner[1] (p. 196)

Mordechai Dantsis

Neither I nor my forefathers nor their forefathers have ever been in the *shtetl* Brzezin. I only know that this town is located not far from Łódź. I say that it is not far from Łódź. More accurately, it was once there, before Hitler's curses destroyed it. Today, as with hundreds of other towns and cities, there is nothing more than mounds and graves left.

When they used to ask a Brzeziner Jew where he came from, the answer was, "From Brzezin, not far from Łódź." Why they attached Brzezin to Łódź, I do not know. From what I have heard about Brzezin, I am sure that the *shtetl* could have stood on its own feet and that it had its own *yikhes*.

But that is how it was with the small *shtetlekh* in the old country. They always liked to warm themselves in the sunlight of the larger places. I know that from my own *shtetl*, where I was registered [had legal residence]. If you asked one of our residents what place he came from, he did not reveal the truth that he was a Zhvanetser, but his answer was, "I am from Odessa." You should know that from Zhvanets [Zwianiec] to Odessa took several days by train.

Other Zhvanetsers used to refer to themselves as being from Kamenetz [Kamieniec]. Why Kamenetz? Because that was the biggest city neighboring my *shtetl*. For this reason, it is not so puzzling that Brzeziner Jews add that their *shtetl* is "not far from Łódź."

* * *

As I said, neither I nor my forefathers nor their forefathers have ever been in Brzezin. And when I recall that *shtetl* here and do it in a manner as if I were a Brzeziner *landsman*, two people are responsible for this—one is the well-known Jewish cultural leader Jacob Berg, the other, the young writer Nachum Summer. Jacob Berg and Nachum Summer are both Brzeziners. In a brief conversation that Berg had with me, he told me several curious facts about his *shtetl*. From the hodge-podge of details, a complete picture came into being for me.

"Our *shtetl*, you should know, was a very interesting *shtetl*," Berg told me, "and Nachum Summer is our *landsman*, who is very important to us. . . . Brzezin clothed half of Russia with ready-made garments. When you went into its small streets, the sound of irons and scissors could be heard, the sound of the Singer sewing machines mixed with the singing of the tailoring apprentices." Jacob Berg ended his story about his and Nachum Summer's *shtetl* with, "We have here several hundred Brzeziner *landslayt*."

* * *

How does Nachum Summer enter into this? And why have I suddenly written so much about Brzezin? That's a story in itself.

---

[1] The writer Mordechai Dantsis, *e"h*, published this as "*Lekoved Shabos*" [To honor the Sabbath], about N. Summer, in the New York *Der Tog* [The Day] on 15 April 1950. (Author's note)

Nachum Summer is, as we said, a young writer. He wrote a very fine biography of the unforgettable Ze'ev Jabotinsky, the only biography of Jabotinsky in Yiddish. He also published biographies of the founders of the Zionist movement—Max Nordau and Ahad Ha'am [pen name of Asher Ginsberg]. Recently Nachum Summer published a collection of his essays, *Man and Word*.

All this was no small intellectual accomplishment for a young writer like Nachum Summer. Nachum Summer, incidentally, is not one of those writers who pushes himself forward. He does not beat a path to the doorways of editorial offices. He does not hound any editors. He writes for himself. He publishes his books using his own money—and his reward for writing is the satisfaction that those who read his works enjoy them. Those who are *meyvinim* [connoisseurs] can judge his fine style, his solid approach to the questions that he addresses in his essays, and his intimate acquaintance with the life and the fate of the people about whom he writes.

Nachum Summer upholds the Brzeziner tradition. He is a craftsman. He works at the Singer sewing machine. In his free time, he withdraws into his own secluded, spiritual world.

I and the young Nachum Summer were especially close. I remember him from the time when I was active in the Zionist-Revisionist movement. I see before me the red-headed Summer as he sits in a corner, patiently paying attention to the often tedious speeches and negotiations, seldom saying a word—sitting, listening, quiet and modest, then silently slipping out. . . .

It was Berg who acquainted me with his *shtetl* and, at the same time, also told me about Summer's work among the local Brzeziner *landslayt*.

A Letter From a Landsman (p. 197)
Aszer Grosman

Dear Brzeziner *Landslayt*:

When you read the Yizkor Book, you will be reminded of many moments from your past life.

It will raise the question among many *landslayt* how our *shtetl* is different from other *shtetlekh* in prewar Poland. And in what area— economic, social, or cultural-communal?

When Jewish life in Poland became more and more difficult everywhere, we emigrated and settled in various *yishuvim* [settlements] throughout the world, maintaining constant contact with the former Jewish leaders of Poland. Each of them informed us of the great accomplishments that were being made by them and what still remained to be done in the future.

I personally have made an effort at every opportunity to indicate that I am a descendent of Brzezin, the town of tailors and craftsmen. I point out how Brzezin stood out even from other great towns. First, our town was entirely a worker's town. Jews from distant provinces, from all sorts of backgrounds, who had a desire to work, found it easy to settle in Brzezin. Each of us, even those who lived only a short time in our town, thought of himself as a Brzeziner.

Everyone had great confidence in Brzezin, and this was because our town created a different type of person, a working person. By way of illustration, in the years 1900, 1902, and 1908 in Brzezin, there was a strong revolutionary movement. Many participants in this movement were persecuted by the Polish regime and were forced to leave town and emigrate. This was actually the beginning of the emigration before World War I.

Our *landslayt* were simple people, but they possessed a communal sense, and in foreign lands, they organized right away into *landsmanshaftn*, so that immediately after World War I, representatives from our *landslayt* were already coming to see us in the *shtetl* and helping a great deal with the needy.

Through the years our *landsmanshaftn* in various lands throughout the entire world developed and increased considerably, thanks to the fact that many from our *shtetl* emigrated. Especially our young people strove to go forth into the broader world, and indeed they brought new life to our *landsmanshaftn*. I must, however, add and stress that in every case and at every opportunity, we displayed our bond to our hometown and were proud of Brzezin and of its past.

On every ocasion, whenever we meet, we talk about our *shtetl*. We recall the very familiar friends from our past and maintain the spirit of Brzezin.

After the destruction in Poland, in which our Jewish Brzezin was erased, we, the *landslayt* throughout the entire world, immediately contacted the survivors, the small number of brothers and sisters from our *shtetl* who remained alive, and we assisted them with everything possible.

On this occasion, I express my best wishes and thanks to all those who helped and still help at every opportunity to enhance the name of our town and our people. May their work be blessed! And may they again forge a link to our destroyed town Brzezin.

A class of children and the teacher, Mrs. Wasserman, who was practically an institution in Brzezin. (The picture was taken after World War I.)

A group of children at a Brzeziner children's camp.

Part Five

Brzeziners in Israel

The First Brzeziner *Chalutzim*[1] [Pioneers] (pp. 201–2)

Mojsze Har-Jaffe (Szajnberg)

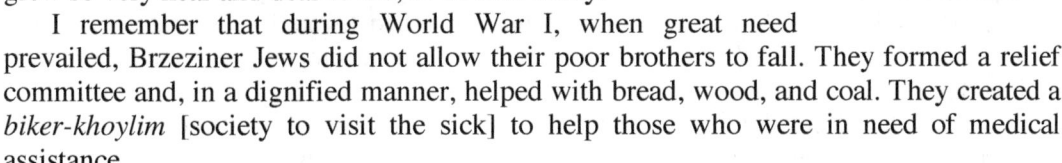

I came from Piotrków to Brzezin with my parents at the age of five, several days before the outbreak of the war in 1914. In Brzezin I studied in a *kheyder* [Jewish elementary school] with various *melamdim* [teachers], later in the *kheyder* Jesode Hatora [Foundations of Torah], and finally, with Reb Mordechai Kochman and others. I learned secular subjects with the teachers Jehuda Fuks, Spiegel, and others.

Together with the studies, I absorbed a lot of what was good about Brzeziner Jewish life. I became a real Brzeziner, as the town grew so very near and dear to me, even until today.

I remember that during World War I, when great need prevailed, Brzeziner Jews did not allow their poor brothers to fall. They formed a relief committee and, in a dignified manner, helped with bread, wood, and coal. They created a *biker-khoylim* [society to visit the sick] to help those who were in need of medical assistance.

When the war ended, the *shtetl* began to get help through support from the Brzeziner *landslayt* [fellow townspeople] in America.

Life in Brzezin began to return to normal. The *magaziner*s [owners of clothing enterprises] and tailors resumed their work, and everything sparkled again with life and creativity. They threw themselves into their work; the sewing machines hummed in every house from before dawn until late into the night—and all night on Thursdays.

Some time later the workers became organized, and a workday of twelve hours was established. Then the youth had more time, and there was an opportunity to get involved in culture and sports. A great Yiddish library was created with a reading room, and everyone enjoyed it. It was a very rich library and included a variety of cultural publications.

In approximately 1923 the organization Poale Zion [Zionist Labor Party] was founded under the leadership of Mr. Biedak, Mr. Jakub Benkel, and others. In a short time they succeeded in enlisting the young people, since at that time, this was the only place in Brzezin where Jewish youth could enjoy themselves socially. A sports club was also created under the name Stern [Star].

So time passed, and parties were formed in Brzezin, such as the Bund [Jewish Socialists], the Folkists [for autonomy within Poland], general Zionists, Mizrachi [Orthodox Zionists], and Agudas Yisroel [Orthodox non-Zionists]. Brzezin took part in all the movements. They collected money for Keren Kayemeth [Jewish National Fund] and for all the other funds. At the same time, Brzeziner Jews continued to study in the *bote-medroshim* [prayer and study houses], *talmetoyres* [free Jewish elementary schools],

---

[1] The Polish spelling used in Brzeziny was *chalucim*, but the more common spelling in Israel and the United States is *chalutzim* [Yiddish: *khalutsim*].

supported orphans, and fulfilled the *mitsves* [commandments] of giving *gmiles-khsodim* [interest-free loans] and offering hospitality to guests.

In 1924, when the call was heard for a great *aliye* [immigration] to Eretz Yisroel, Brzeziner Jews joined in. A substantial group left Brzezin and traveled to Palestine, but a number of them returned to Brzezin. It probably was not their fault. They simply were not properly prepared to live in Eretz Yisroel at that time.

In 1927 a sizeable group of Brzeziner youth—such as Mojsze Szajnberg, Fiszel Maliniak, Abraham Herszenberg, Chaim Igielski, Pruszyński, *z"l*, [of blessed memory], Abraham Zylbercan, *z"l*, Fiszel Mitelsztajn, *z"l*, Szaja Rozenblum, *z"l*, Jakub Butkowski, *z"l*, and others—formed the Hitachdut [Socialist-Zionist labor party] in Brzezin and the youth organization Gordonia [pioneer youth group]. Their task was to help the Brzeziner youth understand better the problems of Eretz Yisroel and to prepare them to be good pioneers for the building of their new home there. In the course of a short time, a substantial group of youth became members of Hitachdut, thanks to those who played a very active role in this movement. A very fine library was created, as well as a sports club and a Jewish orchestra, which marched through the Brzeziner streets during celebrations. The *shtetl* hired Yiddish actors and arranged theater performances and readings.

In 1928 the Hechalutz[1] [pioneer movement] was formed in Brzezin. We were preparing ourselves and began the appropriate training for immigration to Eretz Yisroel.

In 1929 Brzezin sent its first pioneers to undergo training. These were Mojsze Szajnberg, Jehuda Bialer, and later, Menachem Rajchman, Icek Herszenberg, and others. When we came to the training grounds at the firm Szlit near the Nemen River, we Brzeziners were not ashamed. We showed our devotion to work and the bond with our people and our readiness for everything. Thanks to our competence, we immediately took part in all the work at the training place and were approved to make *aliye* to Eretz Yisroel.

In 1930 Brzezin sent its first pioneers to Eretz Yisroel. The entire *shtetl* said goodby to us and arranged a *sude* [celebratory meal] by the river near Icek Bialek's. They accompanied us to the train at Koluszki, from which we traveled to Warsaw, to the Hechalutz central office, before completing the last part of the journey to Eretz Yisroel. Our friends, relatives, and hundreds of Brzeziner Jews awaited us in Koluszki. Brzezin bid good-bye to their pioneers whom they were sending off to Eretz Yisroel. The pioneers who were about to leave danced, sang happily, and cried with joy, together with the Brzeziner Jews. The train left Koluszki, and from far, far away was heard the shout of hundreds of Brzeziners: "*L'hitraot b'Eretz Yisroel* [See you in Eretz Yisroel]." Until today, the last "*Shalom, shalom, l'hitraot!*" [Goodbye, goodbye, we'll be seeing you!] resounds in my ears.

Arriving in Eretz Yisroel we found a small group of Brzeziners such as Szymon Krongrad, *z"l*, Chaim-Icek Grynfeld, *z"l*, Lemel Horn, *z"l*, Mojsze Ginsberg, Isachar Fiszer, David Poliwoda, Fiszel Froman, Gedalja Waldman, Michał and Chana Benkel,

---

[1] The Polish spelling in Brzeziny was Hechaluc, but the more common spelling used in Israel and the United States is Hechalutz.

and perhaps several more Brzeziners. We contacted them and began to organize a separate Brzeziner group.

We did not forget that we were the first Brzeziner pioneers and many more were yet to come. We were three in one room and lived a communal life. Almost all the Brzeziners who came during that time stayed with us. Although we ourselves did not have an easy life, nevertheless, we shared what little we had, and we invigorated the new pioneers with our strong spirit. That made it easier and helped them overcome any difficulties. So it went until everyone had adapted, and the Brzeziner families in Eretz Yisroel grew and lived happily.

During this time Jews came to Eretz Yisroel by various methods, such as through Maccabi [Jewish sports league] sports events, exhibitions, excursions, and by other so-called illegal *aliye*s. In all this, Brzezin had a part; in every endeavor, Brzeziners came. Our *landslayt* did not embarrass Brzezin; they took part in building the land, actively participated in the Haganah (self-defense organization), and were always ready to sacrifice themselves for their people and their land.

During the War of Independence, all Brzeziners in Eretz Yisroel, together with the entire *yishuv* [Jewish community], took part and fought heroically—and sacrificed seven of their dear ones, who, with their Brzeziner blood, together with all the others, consecrated the victory of Medines Yisroel [State of Israel].

Our *Landslayt* in the *Yidisher Medine* [Jewish State] (pp. 203–6)

David Poliwoda

According to our history, Jews have never lost their connection to Eretz Yisroel. Brzeziner Jews, also, have never forgotten the land of our forefathers.

As early as 1910 Reb Nachman Gutkind, a Jew from Brzezin, traveled to Eretz Yisroel on a visit—one of the first *maskilim* [supporters of the Enlightenment] from our town. When he returned home, almost the entire town came to welcome him back and to learn what was happening in the Holy Land.

Several years later, but still before World War I, a few Brzeziner Jews were already candidates for settling in Eretz Yisroel. Among them was the Szotland family, which lives in Israel to this day, and Isachar Fidler, who went there in 1913 in order to buy a cemetery plot on the Mount of Olives. He died in Jerusalem during World War I.

After World War I, when Eretz Yisroel was already under the British Mandate—right after the Balfour Declaration, while the Jewish community was small and work was very hard to get—as early as that time, Brzeziner Jews were coming into the land in spite of the difficult conditions. In 1920 there were already in the country two Brzeziner tailors—Josef Złotnicki (Zahavi) and Isachar Fiszer (Abraham Blecher's son). They worked in an orange grove or at other manual labor.

Brzeziner Executive Committee in Eretz Yisroel. First row, standing, from right to left: Gutkind, Szajnberg, Poliwoda. Second row, from right to left: Mendlewicz, Benkel, Lencicki, *e"h* [may he rest in peace].

In 1921 these Brzeziner Jews came: Gedalja Waldman, Monisz Gutkind, and Michał Benkel. They worked on the highways and at various public service jobs, with the view that they would fill these work slots for the good of the national Jewish cause. At that time that was the motto of the Zionist organization. The salary the central committee paid at that time was very low in comparison with other private jobs.

In 1921, during the time of the anti-Jewish pogrom in Jaffa, Jakub Cymerman and his family came to the country. They settled in Tel Aviv, and they are Israeli citizens to this day.

Presidium of the first assembly of *landslayt* in Eretz Yisroel. Seated from right to left: David Rozenberg, Izrael Fiszer, Szmul Sułkowicz, Lemel Horn, Mojsze-Icek Frankensztajn, Chaim-Icek Grynfeld, Jechiel Erlich, Josef Szajnberg, Jechiel-Michał Herszenberg, Dawid Zycher, and Har-Jaffe (Szajnberg)

In 1922 Michał Benkel brought in his cousin Sarah Blachowicz and his sister Chana. In that same year, the Khovevei Zion [Lovers of Zion] Brzeziners—Chaim Grynfeld and Mojsze Fogel—also came. Their families, which are still in the country to this day, came later.

In 1923 a tailoring cooperative of Brzeziners was founded. Those who joined the cooperative were Złotnicki (Zahavi), Fiszer, and later, also David Poliwoda, who had come at that time from Germany. The tailoring cooperative exists to this day. In general, the Brzeziners were already active in the Haganah [underground paramilitary organization], Histadrut [Workers Union], and in all other organizations in the country.

Gathering of the Israel *landslayt* at the laying of the cornerstone for Shikkun Brzezin [Brzezin housing project].

At the main table are seated the *landslayt* Abraham Fuks (from America), Lemel Horn, and Har-Jaffe (Szajnberg).

In 1925, when there was a great crisis in the land and severe unemployment reigned, several Brzeziner families left the country. At the same time as the difficult economic situation occurred, the following Brzeziner Jews came to Eretz Yisroel: Szymon Krongold with his family, Lemel Horn and his family, who had survived harsh and bitter times, and Mojsze-Icek Grynberg, who had also sampled the taste of unemployment and harsh conditions. Reb Szymon Krongold had a printing shop in those days. He was a very good and kind person to all and, in particular, to his workers.

In 1929 pogroms broke out in the land. The British Mandate government closed the gates of Eretz Yisroel. At that time in Poland, the Hechalutz was blossoming. During the time *aliye* was difficult, when the way to enter the land was restricted, the Brzeziners sent four pioneers: Mojsze Szajnberg, Icek Herszberg, Judel Bialer, and Mendel Rajchman. One should not forget that at that time finding work was unlikely; nevertheless, this did not stop our Brzeziners from leaving home. In 1932, at the time of the Maccabi sports events, the following came to the country: Wolf Zagon, Fiszel Benkel, the family Markowicz, Sara Działoszyńska, and Izrael Kornblum and his family. They were all in danger of being expelled from the country, but they managed to remain. In 1933 the following came into the country: Aron Mendlewicz, Jechiel Erlich, and Melech Michrowski. In 1934 Zebul Poliwoda arrived with his family. Later Reb Szmul Sułkowicz and Mojsze-Icek Frankensztajn came. In 1935 Reb Josef Erlich, a man in his sixties, came. He lives in Jerusalem today and studies with a congregation of Orthodox Jews in the Akhava synagogue. Chuna Waldman, the *shoykhet* [ritual slaughterer], and Reb Dawid Zycher (Reb Nachman Gutkind's son-in-law) came—all with their families.

In 1938 Jacob David Berg made his first visit to Eretz Yisroel. He unexpectedly met Aron Mendlewicz, who introduced me to Friend Berg for the first time. It was not peaceful in the land at that time. Friend Berg was not able to visit the country properly because of the unrest.

Planting a tree in front of the *Bet-Am* [House of the People—cultural center] in Israel, in the name of Louie Horn, secretary of the Brzeziner Relief Committee for many years. From right to left: Morris Frank, Benkel, Lemel Horn, e"h, and Har-Jaffe (Szajnberg)

At the opening of the Shikkun Brzezin in Israel.

In the picture can be seen the well-known journalist Tsanin, who wrote about Shikkun Brzezin in the New York *Forverts* [Forward].

CONTACT WITH THE *LANDSLAYT* IN AMERICA

At that time, we had, in fact, already broken our ties with the American Brzeziner brothers. The Brzeziners in America had already had a society for many years. We, in Eretz Yisroel, at that time, maintained that in Eretz Yisroel all Jews who arrived should join together without exception and that there was no need for any *landsmanshaftn* [organizations of fellow townspeople].

A group portrait of Brzeziner *landslayt* in Medines Yisroel.

World War II broke out, and Tel Aviv was bombed. Eretz Yisroel stood on the brink of war. At that time, we certainly did not think about creating an organization. When the country was a little calmer and the enemy had withdrawn from the borders of the land, we met in 1942 at Friend Szmul

Sułkowicz's home and founded the Brzeziner Society. The outcome of the war was not known at that time, but we understood that we had to collect relief money for the people who had remained in Brzezin. We did not know that the end would be so tragic.

The following friends were members of the committee: Frankensztajn, Mojsze Icek Szajnberg, Lemel Horn, Fiszel Benkel, Jechiel Erlich, and Szmul Sułkowicz. During that time, a considerable sum of money was collected in order to be able to assist the Jews remaining in Brzezin.

Unfortunately, Fate determined otherwise. Instead of helping those remaining in Brzezin, we had to help the survivors all over the world.

Our first deed was to send packages to Łódź and oranges to Sweden.

Shortly thereafter Jews from Brzezin began to arrive in the country. The committee began to provide financial assistance. At that time none of the committee members expected that the money they had distributed would be returned to the treasury. Fifteen hundred pounds [Israeli currency] was distributed, and in those times, that was a great sum of money. Dissatisfaction then arose among the new arrivals. As with all community work, here as well, many of the newly-arrived had complaints about the committee.

The first connection between the Brzeziners in America and the Brzeziners in Eretz Yisroel was through Jehuda Fuks, who was on his "Joint Appeal" visit in Eretz Yisroel at that time. He left one thousand dollars, which at that time was over three hundred pounds. When Fuks returned to America, the Brzeziners took upon themselves the obligation to commemorate the destroyed life of the Jewish community in Brzezin, the Brzeziner *kedoyshim* [martyrs]. The cooperation of the American and the Israeli Brzeziners grew into a close relationship. In 1950 our friend Jacob David Berg came to Israel in order to create a tailoring cooperative or a *shikkun* [housing project] in memory of the Brzeziner martyrs.

A secular school with its teacher. In the second row, in the center, is the teacher Penina Horn-Kaufman.

After basically exploring the situation, it was decided to build a *shikkun* and a community center and to publish a Yizkor [memorial] book. After the *shikkun* was erected, Friend Berg came especially for the dedication of the buildings.

Thirty-six Brzeziner families live in the *shikkun*. A number of them had previously lived in tents or barracks and, in general, under very difficult conditions. At the same time, a cultural center was created in the name of the Brzeziner martyrs as well as those who fell in the War of Independence in Israel.

How the Shikkun Brzezin Was Built (pp. 207–12)

(Activities Report from the Brzeziner *Landsmanshaft* in Israel for the years 1940–60)

A.

The *landsmanshaft*, under the name Irgun Yotzei Brzezin b'Yisrael [Organization of Former Residents of Brzezin in Israel], was founded and began activities in 1940 with the following persons: 1) Jechiel Erlich, 2) Fiszel Benkel, 3) Lemel Horn, *z"l*, 4) Mojsze Har-Jaffe (Szajnberg), 5) Gedalja Waldman, 6) Wolf Zagon, 7) Aron Mendlewicz, 8) Szmul Sułkowicz, *z"l*, 9) David Poliwoda, 10) Aron Fogel, and 11) Mojsze-Icek Frankensztajn, *z"l*.

The only role and activity of the *landmanshaft* in the first years after its founding was to collect money from our *landslayt* in Eretz Yisroel, in order to be ready and able to send help to Brzezin when World War II ended.

The fundraisers at that time were, in addition to the already mentioned founders, also the following *landslayt*: 1) Jehuda Bialer, 2) Rywka Benkel, 3) Sara Goldberg-Działoszyńska, 4) Cypora Har-Jaffe, 5) Chana Waldman-Łęczycka, 6) Gitel Janowska-Ardenbaum, 7) Bluma Markowicz-Erlich, 8) Chana Sułkowicz, *z"l*, and many others.

Considering the difficult economic situation during the war years, the Irgun Yotzei Brzezin b'Yisrael succeeded in collecting what was in those days a significant sum of money. That money was held by the treasurer at that time, Szmul Sułkowicz, *z"l*.

When the world war ended, sadly, the great tragedy that befell the Jewish world in Europe and, among them the Brzeziner Jews, was revealed and brought to light. It was evident that there was no longer any Brzeziner Jewish community and that the Brzeziner Jews, men and women, the elderly and the children, had been assassinated and murdered in a horrible and brutal manner by the merciless beasts, the Nazi assasins. Only a very small number of Brzeziner Jews remained alive. Through great miracles, they had managed to survive and escape from the inhuman, murderous hands. These Brzeziner Jews who remained alive were spread out over many displaced person camps in all the countries of Europe.

The previously mentioned money that was collected was then used to send packages of food and clothing to the surviving *landslayt* in the various displaced person camps and, later, to the *landslayt* in Sweden and Łódź, where, after the war, a few surviving Brzeziner Jews had assembled.

B.

At the end of 1948 *landsman* Jehuda Fuks visited us from New York, following which contact was established between the two largest and most important Brzeziner *landsmanshaftn*, in New York and in Israel.

At that time, Friend Jehuda Fuks brought with him $1,000 from the Brzeziner Society in New York and presented it to our *landsmanshaft* in Israel. This was then exchanged into our currency and was worth 329 Israeli pounds, an extraordinary sum.

Later the New York *landsman* Fiszel Maliniak visited us and gave us ninety pounds.

With these above mentioned sums, together with the money that had been collected by the *landslayt* in Israel, the *landsmanshaft* in Israel conducted a new relief activity for those Brzeziners, newly arrived in the country, who had been saved from the cataclysmic war. Every newly-arrived Brzeziner who turned to us received a sum between ten pounds and seventy-five pounds, all according to the situation of the new arrival and according to our financial capability at the time.

In order not to shame the needy person, help was distributed in the form of loans, and although all of those new arrivals, thank God, became settled, only a very small number paid back the aid they had received. The sums that were repaid were again used for the same purpose.

In 1950 and 1951 the *landsmanshaftn* in New York and Israel proposed two projects to help the needy Brzeziners in Israel: 1) the founding of a tailors' cooperative or 2) the building of a *shikkun* (housing project) for Brzeziners in Israel.

During the time of New Yorker *landsman* J. D. Berg's visit to Israel in 1951, these two projects were thoroughly considered and fully defined, and with his cooperation and influence, it was decided by both *landsmanshaftn* to select and undertake the project of building the *shikkun* in Kfar-Ono.

On 30 November 1951 the contract to build the apartment project for the Brzeziner *shikkun* in Kfar-Ono in Israel was finalized between the New York Brzeziner Relief Committee and the Israeli construction firm, the Rasko Corporation.

The New York Brzeziner Relief Committee selected and approved the following people as the Israeli Building Committee to act on behalf of the New York Brzeziner Relief Committee: 1) Lemel Horn, *z"l*, 2) Fiszel Benkel, 3) Aron Mendlewicz, 4) Mojsze Har-Jaffe (Szajnberg), 5) David Poliwoda, 6) Aron Fogel, and 7) Majer Sułkowicz.

Nine buildings were constructed—four apartments in each building—altogether thirty-six apartments. The Brzeziner Relief Committee in New York sent word to assign one of the apartments to a Jewish family from Romania. Of course, the Relief Committee in New York received $1100 for that apartment from the New York relatives of that family. As it turned out, the Brzeziner Relief Committee in New York paid the Rasko Corporation for thirty-five apartments, $1100 per apartment—altogether $38,500 (according to the rate of exchange at the time of one Israeli pound for one dollar, that came to 38,500 Israeli pounds.)[1]

The thirty-five apartments were allocated and sold to:

1) Brzeziners who were living in *mabarot* (temporary camps) and
2) Brzeziners who were living in very bad conditions but not in *mabarot*.

Because of the fact that the Brzeziners who lived in the *mabarot* did not have sufficient funds to buy an apartment, we were compelled to allocate the loans from the relief money differently. Not $1100 per apartment but more for the camp dwellers and less for the others, as listed below. Otherwise, the camp dwellers, in general, would not have been able to afford an apartment.

---

[1] It seems from what follows that this amount did not pay for the apartments entirely but served as a subsidy for each apartment, at the rate of $1100 per apartment. The Relief Committee in Israel decided to allocate the subsidy loan based on need, rather than being uniform for each apartment.

The final price for which the apartments were sold was:
1) For the camp dwellers:
    Cash Payment   I£[1]   460
    Loan (with interest)   <u>I£   800</u>
Total   I£ 1260
    Interest-free loan from the relief-money $1450

2) For those who were not camp dwellers:
    Cash Payment   I£ 1475
    Loan from Rasko Corp. (with interest)   <u>I£   600</u>
Total   I£ 2075
    Interest-free loan from the relief-money $ 900

This was the decision of the Building Committee in Israel in order to make it possible for the Brzeziner *oylim* [immigrants] who were in the camps for the homeless in the worst conditions to also be able to get a good place to live.

This was the decision—and in fact, the relief money was distributed in the following manner:

27 loans of	$ 900 =	$24,300
1 loan of	$1,010 =	$ 1,010
5 loans of	$1,450 =	$ 7,250
1 loan of	$1,480 =	$ 1,480
1 loan of	$1,100 =	$ 1,100

Altogether: 35 loans for the sum of $35,140

The Brzeziner Relief Committee in New York had given the Rasko Corporation in New York $38,500. We allocated from this 35 loans for the sum of $35,140. The amount of $3,360 remained. This amount, which at that time equaled I£ 3,360 was credited to the building of the cultural center, Beit Ha-am al Shem Kdoshei Brzezin [House of the People in Memory of the Martyrs of Brzezin].

C.

The building of the Beit Ha-am al Shem Kdoshei Brzezin cost by the end of 1956— I£ 19,700 and in 1957, 1958, 1959, an additional I£ 1,400 was spent. Altogether, the Beit Ha-am cost I£ 21,100 by the end of September 1959.

This sum grouped together in the following way:
1) Building costs according calculation of the Rasko Corporation   I£ 14,857.00
2) Fence around the site of the Beit Ha-am   I£   1,275.00
3) Lighting supplied by the electric company   I£   320.00
4) Painting the fence   I£   46.50
5) Installation of electricity and lamps   I£   247.00

---

[1] I£ is the symbol for the Israeli pound/lira

6) Pictures and signs	I£	253.00
7) Planting and maintaining the garden around the Beit Ha-am	I£	241.00
8) Furniture	I£	2,283.00
9) Changes and improvements	I£	102.00
10) Books purchased	I£	72.00
11) Miscellaneous expenses	I£	<u>69.50</u>
Total through the end of 1957	I£	19,676.00

In the years 1957–58 and through the end of September 1959:

1) 3 electric fans and 6 fluorescent lamps	I£	327.00
2) 6 oven vents	I£	110.00
3) 20 small tables	I£	320.00
4) Table linen and curtains	I£	54.52
5) Glasses, saucers, and platters	I£	55.60
6) The garden at Beit Ha-am	I£	283.00
7) New books for the library	I£	149.50
8) Payment for handing out books to readers (for being on duty three times a week up to two hours in the course of three and a half months)	I£	<u>105.00</u>
Total for 1957–58	I£	1,394.62
Total costs for Beit Ha-am	**I£**	**21,394.62**

The above expenses—for building, fixing up, furnishing, and also maintaining the Beit Ha-am, the library, and the garden—amounting to the sum of I£ 21,070, were put together in the following manner:

1) The remainder from the $38,500 for the houses built $3,360.00 = I£ 3,360.00
2) The participation of the Relief Committee in New York to build Beit Ha-am, sent directly to Rasko Corporation—$4,500.00 (at rate of 1.80 I£ to the $) = I£ 8,100.00
3) Contribution from Mojsze Frank in New York for chairs I£ 1,500.00
4) From the Brzeziner *landsmanshaft* in Los Angeles $450.00 = <u>I£ 807.55</u>
Total **I£ 13,767.55**

The rest of the building costs for Beit Ha-am, in the amount of approximately I£ 7,300, were covered by:

1) Three repaid loans by residents of the Shikkun who left Kiryat Ono and sold their apartment (during 1954–56)—together I£ 2,700.00
2) From the donations collected by the Brzeziner *landslayt* in Israel <u>I£ 4,600.00</u>
Total **I£ 7,300.00**

D.

Now our greatest attention turned to developing the *gmiles-khsodim-kase* [interest-free loan fund] in the name of the Brzeziner heroes who fell while freeing and defending our country.

The *gmiles-khsodim-kase* began its activities in January 1957 and joined the Israeli central organization of *gmiles-khsodim-kase*s and was under the supervision of that central organization.

From the Brzeziner Relief Committee in New York, we received as a contribution to the *gmiles-khsodim-kase* two bank transfers: 1) $1,500 and 2) $500, altogether $2,000 — which was changed into I£ 3,600.

Every *landsman* who was in need and turned to the *gmiles-khsodim-kase* with appropriately good references received an interest-free loan up to the amount of I£ 400 — insofar as our financial condition allowed.

You must understand that if the Brzeziners who lived in the houses in Kiryat Ono had held to their obligation and repaid in monthly installments the monetary loans that they got in 1952 — when they entered the apartments in the Shikkun — then today we would have much greater financial reserves, and we would be able to distribute to Brzeziners in need more loans and in greater amounts.

Until now — in the course of the three-year activity of the *gmiles-khsodim-kase* — the *kase* has not had any losses, and all the borrowers have paid their installments precisely and promptly.

E.

Now we present here a summary of everything we said before in numbers:

According to the joint account balance 1) Irgun Yotzei Brzezin b'Yisrael (our *landsmanshaft*) and 2) Yad Hashisha kupat gmiles-khesed shel Irgun Yotzei Brzezin b'Yisrael [The Helping Hand Fund of the Organization of Former Residents of Brzezin in Memory of Our Six Fallen Martyrs] (our *gmiles-khsodim-kase*) show, up to September 1959, the following activities:

1) Cash in the bank	I£ 4,357.71
2) 27 building loans to the residents of the Shikkun	I£ 27,940.00
3) Regular loans	I£ 4,756.00
4a) The Beit Ha-am, according to real estate evaluation amounted to	I£ 18,000.00
4b) According to the calculation of expenses	I£ 3,070.00
	I£ 21,070.00
Together, our assets	**I£ 58,123.71**

We have no outstanding loans whatsoever to anyone.

Besides these assets that we have according to the account balance up until 30 September 1959, we have to take into consideration that during the time between 1940 and 30 September 1959, that is, during the last twenty years, we have had expenses: 1) sending help to the surviving Brzeziners in camps, 2) distributing relief to needy Brzeziners who came to the country after the end of the world war, 3) arranging projects, collections, *haskore* [memorial services], etc., 4) entertaining guests from abroad, 5) administrative expenses, such as writing materials, printed matter, postage stamps, etc., and 6) various other expenses.

These expenses during the entire period of our activities — during the last twenty years — come to a sum of about I£ 12,000. And this outstanding sum of I£ 12,000 was recorded as expenses, without omitting even the smallest, most insignificant amount in the balancing of the account. But before we spent the money and distributed it, we had to collect and accumulate it.

To restate all the previously enumerated expenses, from the total of about I£ 70,000, we received from the Brzeziner Relief Committee and from the Brzeziner Society in New York, during twenty years, the already previously mentioned sums:

1) From *landsman* Jehuda Fuks, $1,000.00	I£ 329.00
2) From *landsman* Fiszel Maliniak	I£ 90.00
3) Via the Rasko Corporation for the houses built—$38,500.00	I£ 38,500.00
4) Via the Rasko Corporation for building of Beit Ha-am—$4,500.00	I£ 8,100.00
5) For the *gmiles-khsodim-kase*: 2 transfers $2000.00	I£ 3,600.00
Received from the Relief Committee and the Society in total	**I£ 50,619.00**
6) From *landsman* Mojsze Frank	I£ 1,500.00
7) From Brzeziner *landmanshaft* in Los Angeles	I£ 807.00
8) From 8 repaid building loans—I£ 900 each	I£ 7,200.00
Together	**I£ 60,126.00**

The rest—a sum of I£ 10,000—we gathered and received from our *landslayt* here in Israel through voluntary contributions and donations, income from meetings and memorial services for the dead, and other revenues.

F.

In brief, we must remember that during these years we also dedicated ourselves and spent much time and effort in order to help particular individual *landslayt* in the country with employment and making a living.

Also, from time to time, we had to settle and straighten out conflicts between the residents of the Shikkun.

The entire account above describes the activities of our committee in Israel; the difficult work, which took a great deal of time and effort and often resulted in grievances and even worse, aggravation.

But nevertheless, after the tasks that we had undertaken were completed and the Shikkun and the Beit Ha-am were built and the *gmiles-khsodim-kase* began its activities and all had the opportunity to develop and to grow, it brought all of us great pleasure and satisfaction, and we were proud of the results of your and our effort during the last twenty years.

In the name of:
Brzeziner Landsmanshaft in Israel and
Brzeziner Building Committee in Israel

S. Mendlewicz   David Poliwoda
Menachem Gutkind

Tel-Aviv, 8 August 1960

Fallen in the Defense of Israel (pp. 213–15)

Mojsze Blat, *z"l*

Born in 1900 to Hasidic parents. His father was a *shoykhet* in Koluszki, eight kilometers from Brzezin. The Blats were a family of honest and courageous people. He inherited courage from his father; from his mother, who was also full of goodness, Mojsze inherited his devotion to friends.

Being a Zionist, he sought to travel to Eretz Yisroel when he was still a youngster, and in 1921 he came to Israel against the will of his parents. When he came, he worked in construction. Not happy with this, he voluntarily joined the border police. He served for five years as a corporal. Having learned Arabic and English, he traveled through the entire land and became familiar with every segment of the population.

After five years in police service, he returned to civilian life. In 1925 and 1926, when unemployment spread throughout the country, he experienced many difficulties as an unemployed person. His friends extol the virtues of his attitude toward other friends during that difficult time. In 1927 Mojsze Blat left Eretz Yisroel and went to America, with the intention of returning to Eretz Yisroel.

He returned in 1933 and settled in Jerusalem, later in Tel Aviv. With the outbreak of troubles [between Arabs and Jews] in 1936, Mojsze Blat received an important assignment in the defense of the Tel Aviv suburban housing project Hatikvah.

In 1937 Mojsze Blat came to the forests of Carmel, near Haifa, and was responsible for guarding this strategic position. The conditions were very difficult there. He lived in cramped quarters. Winter brought rain. He was cut off from the city of Haifa and often did not have any means to bring in enough food. Mojsze accepted this all with dedication, and he made an effort to lighten the difficult life of his companions and encourage them.

In those days he showed who he was with his admirable behavior. While in the forests of Carmel, he did not sit still; he energetically researched the area and developed good relations with the Arab neighbors. His involvement was also great in the purchase of land in Carmel and the development of Yaarot HaCarmel [Carmel Forest].

Many times Mojsze complained that they did not make good use of the fertile land and that there were not more Jewish settlements in this part of Carmel. His aspiration was to build a series of kibbutzim in Carmel. Unfortunately, he did not live to see the realization of his hopes, because his life was cut short before his time.

On Carmel his companions mourned a long time for him. He fell in Yaarot HaCarmel on 29 September 1938.

Koved zayn andenk [Honor to his memory!]

Chaim Flam, *z"l*

Born in 1927 in Brzezin. Chaim'l was a grandson of Krok; his father was Abraham Krok. In 1942, during the deportation from Brzezin, he was dragged away by the Germans to a concentration camp. He succeeded in escaping to the partisans, where he remained until 1945. After liberation, he joined a kibbutz in order to go to Israel. In the meantime, he was sent on a trip to Poland in order to transport survivors to Germany and from there to Israel.

In 1946, when he was on his way to Israel, the English captured his ship and sent the survivors to Cyprus. At last, in 1947, he came to Eretz Yisroel and lived in Nesher. In 1948 he participated in the War of Independence, in fighting around Haifa in the Hativat HaCarmel [Carmel Brigade]. He fell in the fight near Kibbutz Yagur in a clash with the Arab League and was buried in the cemetery of Kfar Hasidim.

Koved zayn andenk!

Abraham Michrowski, *z"l*

Son of Elimelech and Chaja, a grandson of the esteemed Brzeziner businessman, Jakub-Hersz Goldkranc. Born 13 October 1926 in Łódź. He emigrated to Eretz Yisroel in 1933 with his parents and worked there as a locksmith. When he was seventeen and a half, he was mobilized as a *gafir* [constable]. Later he joined the Jewish Brigade[1] as a corporal. He experienced all the ups and downs that took place in the Brigade, and finding himself in Holland, he was sent to organize the *bricha* [escape] of the Jews of Eastern Europe to Israel. He was arrested but managed to escape.

After liberation, he returned to the Haganah and was made head of a company. In the War of Independence, he and his unit fought in the "meshulash" area [near Natanya] and captured Migdal Tsedek, Rosh Ha-Ayin, Qalanswa, and many other Arab villages and positions. When he returned from the attack on Latrun, he said to his mother, "It

---

[1] Unit of the British army formed in Palestine; it was later involved in helping survivors flee Europe and immigrate illegally to Palestine.

would not have bothered me if I had fallen in battle, if only I knew that we had recaptured Latrun.

After the capture of the village Kolah in a ten-day battle, he was assigned to hold the position, but during the night of 17 July 1948 the position was suddenly surrounded by fifteen armored cars with machine guns from the Arab Legion. He was one of the first to fall, without saying goodbye to his loyal friends, who fell to the last man.

On 19 July 1948 he was laid to eternal rest in the cemetery of Natanya.

He was awarded the rank of lieutenant posthumously.

Szlama Lipszyc, *z"l*

Son of Cwi Dov and Mina, born in 1913 in Brzezin. He received a good Jewish education, and he prepared himself to come to Eretz Yisroel and to work in a kibbutz. In 1934 he came to Israel as an illegal immigrant. He worked at various enterprises. He got married in Israel, and his son was born. He was a quiet person. In his later years, he lived in Jerusalem.

He fell in the War of Independence on 31 May 1948 at Sheikh Jarrah. On 10 September 1950 his grave was moved to Mount Herzl.

Koved zayn andenk!

Dan-Aszer Fogel, *z"l*

Son of Icek and Brucha. Born in 1913 in Brzezin. After completing elementary school and high school, he began to work as a tailor. He was much loved by the youth of Brzezin, and he was also active in communal life. In 1939, when World War II broke out, he joined the Polish army.

In 1944 he came to Eretz Yisroel with the Anders Army by way of Russia.[1] Being very desperate and heartbroken, he regained his good humor and courage after

---

[1] When the Polish army collapsed in 1939, Fogel must have escaped to Russia and ended up in Siberia as a Soviet political prisoner. In 1942, as part of the lend-lease agreement with the Allies, former Polish political prisoners in the USSR were allowed to form an army under Polish General Anders. They left the USSR and came through Iraq and Iran to Palestine. There were 4,000 Jewish soldiers among them, of whom about 3,000 left the Anders Army, like Fogel, and remained in Palestine. Some then joined the British army, others, the Haganah or the Jewish Brigade. Those who remained in the Anders Army fought in Italy as part of the British Eighth Army.

meeting *landslayt* in Eretz Yisroel. He returned to work in tailoring and was active in the establishment of the organization of the Brzeziner *landslayt* in Eretz Yisroel.

In the War of Independence he distinguished himself with his heroism on almost every front, and not far from Kfar Ono, he fell in battle on 11 June 1948.

He left a wife and a son who was born after he fell in the War of Independence. His son also carries his name—Dan.

Koved zayn andenk!

Arje Wald, *z"l*

Arje Wald was from France, the son of Jakub Wald, who had previously lived in Brzezin. After the liberation of France, as a seventeen-year-old young man with a sparkling soul and heart, he did not remain idle but gathered the orphans among the *sheyres-hapleyte* [few remaining survivors] and organized them.

Arje Wald came to Eretz Yisroel and participated in the difficult struggle to free the country.

He fell near the Arab village of Dir Alban and was buried in the cemetery in Kibbutz Kiryat [Anavim], amid the mountains along the way to Jerusalem. Since he was in Israel only a short time and had stayed in Petach-Tikvah, he is recorded in Yad Vashem as a citizen of that colony.

Koved zayn andenk!

Jakub Lasker, *z'l*

Jakub Lasker, son of Fiszel the *shoykhet*. He worked in the refineries in Haifa. He died when a wild group of Arabs attacked his workplace.

Koved zayn andenk!

David Lencicki,[1] z"l (p. 216)
G. Waldman

Dawid was born in 1894 to his parents Reb Natan and Marjem Łęczycki, *z"l*, in the *shtetl* of Ujazd near Tomaszów Mazowiecki. Being a son of Hasidic parents, from God-fearing and sincere people, he received a strong religious education. At the age of eight, he began to study Gemore [commentary on the Mishne]. He possessed an excellent memory. Even in the latter years of his life, he remembered what he had studied with *melamdim* [teachers] in *khadorim* [Jewish elementary schools] in the little *shtetl* Ujazd.

Since his parents' earnings were meager, they moved to Brzezin. Reb Natan Łęczycki, *z"l*, bought a buttonhole machine and became a buttonhole maker. In those years, fine Hasidic young people took up that trade. Dawid continued to study with *melamdim* in *kheyder* until he was thirteen or fourteen years old. Then he had to contribute toward making a living, and he, also, became a buttonhole maker. In 1914 the Great World War broke out. The Brzeziner accessories industry came to a standstill. You must understand that this also happened to the Łęczycki family; they looked for a new way to eke out a living—with new worries.

The Prussian Junkers [German aristocrats], who ruled Poland at that time, ruined the Jewish means of making a living in a vicious, cruel manner. However, they permitted the youth to engage in cultural activites, such as, for example, opening libraries. In that way, Brzeziners got permission to open a library. The writer of these recollections and Dawid Łęczycki took on the task of collecting books for the library. We gathered up several hundred books. Dawid was a great enthusiast of Yiddish literature. He had read all the classic Yiddish writers and remembered them well. This also contributed to his ethnic consciousness in his later years.

In 1929 Dawid left Brzezin and went to Brussels, Belgium, where he worked as a buttonhole maker. After five months, he brought his family there as well. Dawid Łęczycki's house, during the time he lived there, served as a typical Jewish hospitable home for all Brzeziners who came to Belgium by chance or were passing through as their exile spurred them to wander. Dawid and his wife, Chajce, *z"l*, possessed the special, traditonal Jewish characteristic of welcoming and offering hospitality to all Brezeziners who crossed their threshold.

Photo of David Lencicki, *z"l*

Dawid, through his honest work, gave his children a higher education; he also knew how to influence his children to remain resolutely faithful Jews and not be swept along by the stream of assimilation in strange surroundings. He prepared them to become Eretz Yisroel-like *chalutzim* [pioneers] and liberators in the difficult struggle of the battle for independence.

---

[1] In Israel, Dawid Łęczycki became David Lencicki.

They certainly felt and still continue to feel it. During the time Dawid lived in Belgium, he was active in the Zionist movement and also in his line of business; all the members of his family supported and honored him for his activities. Unfortunately, Hitler's era ruined his health and that of his wife. Dawid was left with a bad heart. His wife died in 1948.

Dawid came to Israel in 1949 and settled into his trade. He married again and lived a beautiful, honorable life. His children treated his gracious, respectable home with honor.

David Lencicki, *z"l*, was an advocate of the idea of a *yizkor sefer* [memorial book] of Brzezin and contributed important documents to the book that now lies before you, like his chapter about "Tailoring Families." Unfortunately, however, he did not live to see the realization of his idea.

Shabes [Sabbath] 29 March 1958 he began to feel ill, and he died within two days on 1 April 1958, 11 Nisan 5718.

Let us honor his memory!

The *Matseyve* on Mount Zion (pp. 217–18)

Jakub David Berg

When the *matseyve* [tombstone] was erected, our *landsman* Mojsze-Icek Ginsberg delivered a eulogy for the martyrs from our *shtetl*. In his eulogy, he said:

> Brothers and sisters, fathers and mothers, our dear and devoted friends. We, the *sheyres-hapleyte* [few remaining survivors] from our town, Brzezin, have today convened on the mountain of Jerusalem, Har Hatsofim,[1] in Martef HaShoah [Chamber of the Holocaust] to pay final tribute to our annihilated community and to consecrate their memory by the placement of a memorial tombstone.
>
> We fulfill our holy duty to the future ages, in this holy moment, as their purified souls are now here with us and soar above our heads. They proclaim to us and to the coming generations, the people of Israel, the great exhortation: "Jews, be strong. Be as steadfast as an armored outer wall; stretch out your brotherly hand one to the other so that such a terrible tragedy shall not, *kholile* [God forbid], happen again in our history."
>
> They, the virtuous souls, say to us as we stand here now: "Be brave."
>
> We, the survivors, are full of pain and sorrow. In this difficult time, we shed tears over their terrible fate. Here we stand next to the dishonored *seyfer-toyres* [Torah scrolls], near the soap that was made from the exhausted bodies of our virtuous parents and of our small children who could not distinguish good from evil, near the venom with which they poisoned them, near the coats sewn from *seyfer-toyres* in which was written "Thou Shall Not Kill," near the bloody *talesim* [prayer shawls] in which Jews had wrapped themselves and prayed early every morning for the world and humanity, to reform the world through the ruler God Almighty. Together with the six million Jews, they were murdered by the villains.
>
> At this moment, as we stand on Har Tsion [Mount Zion] in Jerusalem, the symbol of peace, we want to cry out so that those who are the conscience of the world might shudder, beat their chests, and repent, crying out, "*Ashamnu*"[2] [We have sinned] . . .
>
> There are scarcely any Jewish souls left from our Brzeziner Jews. We, the survivors, the living orphans, eternally pledge to you: "As long as we breathe and our eyes see the light of the sunrise, our hearts and thoughts will be turned to the tombstone on Har Tsion in Martef HaShoah in Jerusalem, this holy place."
>
> And to all these memorial stones for the destroyed communities, which the survivors have placed to honor their memory; to all those who were annihilated as tragically as our own dear ones, eternal in a common fate, we pledge, in this sad moment, that we will come and pay homage, with pain in our hearts, before the caskets of earth and ashes and before the tombstone that we unveiled today in memory of the destroyed community of Brzezin.

---

[1] This must be an error. Har Hatsofim is Mt. Scopus, located to the north of Jerusalem. The Chamber of the Holocaust is located to the south, on Har Zion [Mount Zion], as mentioned later.

[2] Prayer recited on Yom Kippur.

* * *

May I be permitted to convey here, in a few words, what I myself experienced when I participated in the laying of this symbolic tombstone on Har Tsion in Jerusalem for the martyrs of our *shtetl*.

This tombstone was placed on Har Tsion in memory of the communities that were destroyed.

When you come into Martef HaShoah, into the "Cave of Horror," and you see the *yortsayt* [memorial] candles that are lit there for the destroyed communities—grieving in your heart from mourning and pain, and tears flowing from your eyes over the terrible destruction—the holy images of the victims of the Nazi beasts appear before your eyes. You are reminded of your relatives and friends who were suffocated in the gas chambers and thrown into ovens with lime. You feel your souls fluttering here, in the Martef HaShoah, on the holy mountain in Jerusalem.

In a corner lie bloodied *talesim* that were brought from the death camps, torn sheets of parchment from Torah scrolls rescued from the dreadful destruction. Small *matseyves* of marble were erected here, grouped together. Each tombstone recalls a *shtetl* of Jews who were massacred and died a violent martyr's death.

We, too, have erected a tombstone for the destroyed community martyrs from our *shtetl* Brzezin. A large number of our *landslayt* in Eretz Yisroel came to Jerusalem, to Har Tsion, to dedicate this tombstone. The arrangements were made by our esteemed *landsman* Ginsberg. Among those gathered were those who themselves had experienced dreadful suffering in the Nazi camps and were, by some miracle, saved. They still carry with them the scars of their torment.

With broken hearts, in tribute to the memory of the martyrs from our *shtetl*, we stand on Har Tsion at the unveiling of the tombstone. Our *landsman* in Israel, Ginsberg, gave a moving funeral oration in Hebrew. He turned over to me the unveiling of the tombstone. And I eulogized, in Yiddish, the massacred brothers and sisters from our *shtetl*—as the representative of our *landslayt* in America and over the entire world.

Full of sorrow, we parted, promising each other to honor for eternity the memory of the martyrs from our home *shtetl*.

May the few words concerning what I experienced on Har Tsion in Jerusalem find their place in this memorial *sefer* that we publish about our *shtetl*, establishing a permanent memorial for future generations.

Jacob David Berg

At a *yizkor* gathering in Shikkun Brzezin for the martyrs of our holy community.

Our Leaders in Israel (pp. 219–21)

Aron Mendlewicz

Aron Mendlewicz belongs to that generation of idealists, the pioneer generation, that was in love with the idea of Zionism and always intended to make *aliye* to Eretz Yisroel. He became a bookkeeper in the Kupat Kholim [Workers Care and Insurance Cooperative], where he has been employed for many years. He is also active in all sorts of community projects.

Being the descendant of a great and extended Brzeziner *mishpokhe* [family], he also has not forgotten his origins, although he lived from 1916 to 1933 in Kutno, a well-known *shtetl* in Poland, where, incidentally, he was a town councilman. (This *shtetl* became famous due to the classic writings of Sholem Asch.) He became particularly active in the Brzeziner colony after the great destruction, and of late, he is the financial officer of the local *lay-kase* [credit union] that is regulated by and under the control of the Israeli government. He is represented in our *sefer* with an important chapter in which two Brzeziner families are described. In the depiction of these extended families, we see a portrayal of an old, deeply rooted Jewish life in Brzezin.

S. Pinczewski

Szlama Pinczewski is the descendant of a Hasidic middle-class family. He received a traditional education and later studied a great deal on his own. He also became knowledgeable about world literature. The Pinczewski brothers became prominent industrialists in Łódź, with a reputation throughout all of Poland. Certain historians regard them as co-creators of the great Łódź textile industry. Szlama Pinczewski was not only well known in the business world; he was also a dynamic personality in our Jewish communal society, with all its problems and concerns.

His entire family was murdered in the great destruction, among them, his daughter, who was a gifted artist. It is only by chance that he came to Yisroel. He came as an impoverished man. He lost everything in the great destruction, all his possessions. It so happens that years ago, he had invested a little money in a certain Eretz Yisroel business undertaking, which now provides him with the means to manage his affairs. At the beginning, the business did not do very well. Over time, things got better, and he was able to succeed in a very middle class, comfortable way.

In those years, he was not active in *landslayt* circles. When Shikkun Brzezin came into existence, he became active and would often show up in Brzeziner circles. With J. D. Berg's arrival in Israel, an old friendship was renewed that went as far back as their *kheyder* years. They both had studied with the same teachers. Now they carry on a regular correspondence, and Pinczewski is strongly interested in all *landsmanshaft* matters. He is also represented in our book by a significant chapter, "Brzeziner Rabbis and Hasidim," which describes an important part of the Brzeziner Jewish community.

Fiszel Benkel

Fiszel Benkel belongs to the old settled residents among our *landslayt* in Israel. He is a son-in-law of Herszel Lachman. He is a refined and proper person. With self-sacrifice he devoted himself to the work of the Brzeziner *landslayt* in Israel. When he speaks of our great accomplishments, he speaks with such warmth and sentiment that he is practically moved to tears. He is one of the extremely important people of that small group of leaders in the Irgun Yotzei Brzezin b'Yisroel [Organization of Former Residents of Brzezin in Israel].

David Poliwoda

David Poliwoda belongs to the practical leaders of our circle in Israel. He is a person with common sense and a lot of community experience as a former leader in the circles of Mapam [United Workers Party]. He belongs among the first organizers of the Brzeziner cooperative and is among the very first who helped, with body and soul, to build the Shikkun Brzezin in Ono. After the annihilation of our people, when our *shtetl* was wiped out in Poland, where it had reigned for so many generations, he was strongly interested in transplanting into our own land the way of life of our past generations that had been so violently cut short. He therefore displayed an intense interest in all the needs and affairs of the survivors. He is a member of the Irgun Yotzei Brzezin.

Mojsze Har-Jaffe (Szajnberg)

Mojsze Har-Jaffe belongs to the younger generation. Although he is not originally from Brzezin—his cradle was actually in Piotrków—nevertheless, he was closely linked with everything that had a connection to Brzezin and Brzeziners. In Brzezin, he was one of the founders of the pioneer youth movement. He went with a group for preparatory training and later emigrated to Palestine. The first years in Eretz Yisroel were certainly not easy. Others were broken under the stress of the harsh realities and returned to their *shtetlekh* [pl. of *shtetl*]. He remained in Israel and became an active builder of his own independent life in the land.

In Israel he is close to our *landslayt*. They organize themselves into their own circle and look for mutual assistance from each other. Mojsze Szajnberg once traveled to America, and he wanted to build a bridge between the American and Israeli *landslayt*. He believes that there has to be closer contact between these two communities, because the majority of our remaining *landslayt* are concentrated within them.

In Israel he is one of the most active of our circle, and he was involved, with heart and soul, in the work when the housing project of Kfar Ono was being built. Szajnberg is also represented in this *sefer* with an important chapter about the youth and pioneer movement in Brzezin.

Monisz Gutkind

Monisz Gutkind is a scholar, a great lover of Yiddish literature, a great admirer of our classical writers, Mendele and Peretz. He is the descendant of an enlightened Hasidic family. Since his father, Nachman Gutkind, was one of the first Khovevei Zion [Lovers of Zion], he was surely influenced by that path, and he always aspired to live in Eretz Yisroel.

He has also been in Israel for a long time and has become acclimated to the way of life here, although he is not estranged from the past. He feels that the endeavor to immortalize our *shtetl*, both through the buildings in Israel and through this *Sefer Brzezin*, is truly a holy work. He is an honorable and devoted leader among our *landslayt* in Israel.

Aron Fogel

Aron Fogel (son of Ester-Laja, the baker) went through the sorrowful and painful wandering path of the survivors. He was among the first who sent us the shocking report from our annihilated community about the horrors and nightmares of the Nazi camps. When he was liberated from the Nazi camp, he was among the first to go to Brzezin and see with his own eyes the enormous devastation, the annihilation of our idyllic, prewar *shtetl* Brzezin. . . . He ran away from the curse that had been inflicted on our *shtetl* . . . and he made a vow that everywhere and at every opportunity, he would recount the *Megiles-Eykhe* [Book of Lamentations] of Brzezin.

At one time, before the deluge, he was a central figure in Brzezin's communal organizations. Now he lives quietly and modestly in Israel and is active in the community—though certainly not as before in Brzezin—and he is also in close contact with the local *landslayt*. He is represented in our book by an excellent chapter encompassing generations of Brzeziner life. He relates how Brzezin first became a tailoring center, and he describes the various segments of Brzezin's organized society in his interesting account.

Jechiel Erlich

Jechiel Erlich is a descendant of a learned Hasidic family. His *yikhes* [distinguished lineage] on his mother's side extends all the way back to Rabbi Reb Fiszele from Stryków. He himself received a thorough traditional education. Since Brzezin did not have a yeshiva, Jechiel became a *besmedresh* [house of prayer] scholar, just like a lot of other young people of his kind.

He has lived in Eretz Yisroel for many decades. He was among the first to settle in Eretz Yisroel, with pure unconditional love. He lived through the difficult, thorny ways of *chalutzism* [pioneering]. He lived in Kfar Saba, where he was engaged for many years in raising chickens and also had a small soda water factory. All the years he has been in Eretz Yisroel, under all sorts of conditions, he has remained true to the roots of his soul. He is strongly committed to religious Judaism. He lives as his ancestors did. Ideologically, he is close to Poale Mizrachi [religious Socialist Zionist party].

His daily discourse and the occasional *droshes* [sermons] that he gives before an audience are always intertwined with *maymer khazal* [wise sayings] and with simple examples and sayings of our old *khokhmim* [wise men].

Although his home is far from the main center, he is bound with all his being to the activities of the *landslayt* of our *shtetl*. When the Shikkun Brzezin was built in Kfar Ono, he thought of it as a symbolic accomplishment, since the way of life of our Brzeziner generations that had been destroyed could now continue in our own land. Many years ago, he was in America on a short visit, and he left a good impression, with his observant piety and simplicity.

This observant and Hasidic, scholarly world, of which he alone is heir, permeates his beautiful composition in our book.

Lemel Horn, *e"h*

Lemel Horn, *e"h,* came from a middle class, well-to-do home. He received a very fine Jewish upbringing. He was thoroughly at home with the wisdom of PaRDeS [acronym for the four levels of understanding of the Scriptures]. He was also an expert on sayings and their meanings.

He was closely tied to political Zionism, with the idea of building his own independent, nationalistic life on his own Jewish soil. When he was already in Eretz Yisroel, he turned Revisionist and became allied with the extreme right wing of the Zionist movement.

He came to Eretz Yisroel through Russia, where he was active in Zionist circles, and in order to support his family, he engaged in trade. He built a leather factory. Although not a very wealthy man, he became respectably middle class.

He is extremely busy with his business and also with community matters, but he never forgets for one minute his Brzeziner *landslayt*. He is always involved with activities for his Brzeziners.

When the relief work began for the survivors, for those who were rescued from the Nazi death camps by a miracle, he threw himself, with heart and soul, into this holy work. He became chairman of the Israeli Relief Committee, a position he held until his untimely departure to the eternal world. He virtually gave his life for this work. He did not spare his own health, because he felt the extraordinary importance of organizing assistance for the victims of Hitler.

When the building of the Shikkun Brzezin was completed in Kfar Ono, he viewed the great historical accomplishment of our *landslayt* as a purely personal triumph, as a great *yontov* [holiday] in his life. He was practically breathless and feverish over this work. We know of many letters he sent to *landslayt* in America; he spoke to them with terrific enthusiasm and warmth about this accomplishment of ours. He could foresee that the disrupted generations would again spin our Brzeziner way of life on Israeli soil.

When he saw the progress of this *Sefer Brzezin*, he was overcome with tremendous joy. First, we had raised a monument of concrete and brick, meaning the Shikkun Brzezin, and now, with this third endeavor, we would end with a written memorial for future generations in which we would describe the destruction of our Brzeziner community and the generations that existed before the deluge.

Unfortunately, to our great sorrow, he did not live to see the great moment of the conclusion of this project. It would certainly have given him great pleasure. He also intended to contribute an important, significant chapter about certain aspects of the Brzeziner way of life. He did not even have time to prepare it, which is truly a great pity, but even greater is the loss of his own illustrious personality.

He had his home in Jerusalem. He considered it a special rare honor to live in the holy city.

He leaves his wife, Blume, three gifted, intelligent daughters and one son, all devoted heirs to his life's dreams.

Koved zayn ondenk! [Honor to his memory!]

A group of Brzeziner intellectuals.

Photographs of Brzeziner Jews in Paris (pp. 222–24)

Presidium of the memorial evening in Paris with representatives from both societies [Israeli and French]. From left to right: Mrs. Flam, Kujawski, Flam (blocked), Freed, Frajm (chairman of the Society), "Mutualité de Monmort," Morris Horn (honorary president), Khazn [Cantor] Pinkas (president of the Brzeziner Society), Zajdenberg, Horn, Kaziv, Bernard Fryde, Homel (all were among those who had been deported).

Brzeziner *landslayt* at the Ner Tamid [Eternal Light] of the Memorial of the Unknown Jewish Martyr [Mémorial du Martyr Juif Inconnu].

Brzeziner *landslayt* in Paris at a memorial gathering in 1961. From right to left: Zajdenberg, Simon, Khazn Pinkas, Horn, Frajm, Fryde, Flam, Kujawski.

The former deportee to Auschwitz, Zajdenberg, says *kadesh* for the victims at the Ner Tamid of the Memorial of the Unknown Jewish Martyr.

People in the hall at the memorial evening 8 June 1961.

Our *Landsman* Abraham Rozenberg (p. 225)

Abraham Rozenberg was born in Brzezin. He studied in *khadorim* [Jewish elementary schools] and the Hebrew day school Javneh, as well as completing the *powszechna* [Polish elementary] school. He was one of the founders of the leftist Poale Zion youth movement in Brzezin. He was also active in cultural and sports groups. He came to America through Argentina. Here he attended high school and went to work in a women's clothing factory. He became active in the circles of the local trade union movement and became an officer in Local 22 of the "International" [International Ladies Garment Workers Union], of which David Dubinsky is the president, and participated actively in the cultural work of the organization.

Although he is not among the most active leaders in the local Brzeziner colony, he stepped in, however, when the Relief and Rehabilitation Committee undertook various projects to help the survivors. He became very involved when the Shikkun Brzezin was being built in Israel and gave his enthusiastic support for the work of publishing this book.

Abraham Rozenberg inherited the love of our *shtetl* from his father. He displayed this affection in his lyrical, nostalgic portrayal of the Brzeziner way of life and his account about sports that are included in our magnificent yizkor book.

From right to left: Lajbuś Lehrer, Mrs. Lehrer, Mrs. Millie Berg, Jacob-David Berg; Isaac Hemlin, leader of the Histadrut Campaign, who is speaking, Joseph Diamond, and Fishel Maliniak.

* * *

Harov Reb Chaim Szotland, z"l (p. 225)

In the Hague, Holland, at the age of seventy, the Brzeziner *landsman* Harov [Rabbi] Reb Chaim Szotland, *z"l*, passed away.

The deceased, one of the remaining members of the older generation, was known, while living in Moscow, in religious circles all over Russia. His home was a meeting place for wise men, and ignoring all the exhortations, he provided help to every *talmed-khokhem* [scholar] in need.

After World War II, Harov Szotland, *z"l*, settled in the Hague. There, in Holland, he also opened his home to everyone traveling by, to every emissary from a yeshiva, and to every Jew who wanted to eat kosher food. It was quite evident that all these people found his home to be welcoming.

The Sephardic chief rabbi, Harov Pereira, made a special effort to come to his funeral, and a great crowd of Jews from the Hague and other places participated in it. The deceased [Szotland] had previously given the eulogy at a funeral of the Hague chief rabbi, Harov Dr. Benjamin Ze'ev Benedict Sklita, who, only a short time before, during the end of the reading of a tractate of Talmud, had given Harov Reb Chaim, *z"l*, the title *moyreynu* [our scholar]. The chairman of the Hague Jewish community, as well as Herr Zadoks, Herr Strykowski, and the *khazn* of the Hague, Herr Mosel, also gave funeral orations.

All of them stressed the great loss that the Jews of the Hague had suffered because of the passing of Harov Reb Chaim Szotland, *z"l*.

Oh, for those who are gone and cannot be replaced!

Icek Fajgenbaum

Heartfelt Thanks! (p. 226)

We thank the following contributors who have made the publication of this *Sefer Brzezin* possible:

Jacob David Berg, Abe Fox (New York); M. Winter (Melbourne, Australia); David Grosman, Jan Dymant, the Lachman brothers (Florida), Szymon Lachman (Florida); Abraham-Jacob Gotlieb (California); the Brzeziner-Lodzer Society of California; Fishel Maliniak, Morris Frank, Jehuda Fuks, the brothers Max and Charlie Kalish; Bernard Kujawski (Paris), Szlama Schwartz, and Anna Rozenblum in memory of Isidor Rozenblum.

We also thank all those who made smaller contributions.

The Brzeziner Book Committee

My Father, Chaim-Icek Ajnbinder (Nisenberg) (pp. 227–28)

Jacob David Berg

Chaim-Icek Nisenberg

I remember my father as an already old man with a stately beard and a large family to care for, in a house with many children. For a very long time, I had not been in my father's house. When, at the age of four, I became an orphan because of the death of my mother, who was my father's second wife (the first wife was my mother's sister), my father married for the third time a younger widow, a *bas talmed khokhem* [daughter of a scholar], and I, at my young age, had a taste of what it is like to have a stepmother. At a very early age, I began to think about leaving my father's house, and when I was barely eleven years old, I left to study in a yeshiva.

One can say then that I saw my father for approximately eight years while growing up. However, he has remained dear to my heart and in my memory forever after.

I will describe here in a few strokes, albeit in a lackluster manner, an attempted portrait of my dear father as I knew and understood him with my entire being.

My father, *e"h*, was the only son of his parents. He was born in the small *shtetl* Ujazd, near Tomaszów.

His father—my grandfather—was an intelligent Vorker [from Warka] Hasid. He had moved to Brzezin when my father was still a young boy. In Brzezin, my grandfather became a *melamed* [teacher] and, as with every *melamed* in a small Polish *shtetl*, he had a nickname. They called my grandfather, my father's father, "the yellow [yellow-haired] Izrael." My father, probably because he did not want to be a *melamed*, decided to learn a trade, and he chose the bookbinding trade. So together with his trade, my father was also stuck with the nickname Ajnbinder [bookbinder]. It followed him until his last days; although he had not been a bookbinder for a long time, he was called Reb Chaim-Icek Ajnbinder. The actual family name was Nisenberg (it was here in America that our name was first shortened to Berg).

My father became the son-in-law of the Brzeziner Icek Szotland. It turned out that my father was selected to go off for twenty-five years to serve the Russians, as was then the Russian law for military service. But the distinguished businessmen of the town forcefully intervened for the young Hasidic man, and he escaped from the Russians' clutches.

His [first] wife bore him three daughters and a son, but she died. My father got married again, to the sister of his deceased first wife. The name of the second wife was Chajela. She bore him five children. I was among the first three. After the other two boys, twins, were born, my mother died, at the age of twenty-eight. And I was then barely four years old.

My father, *e"h*, could not cope with the small children and with his business of selling writing materials and Christian religious books. He got married for the third time to a young widow, the daughter of a learned man. I got a stepmother, and even though I was young, I sensed it right away. It had become crowded in my father's house.

I felt that my father loved me very much. More than once I noticed a tear glistening in his eyes on my account. He showed me his quiet paternal love when he frequently pressed me to his chest, and then he would whisper into my ear the name of my mother who had died young, may she rest in peace. With this, it seemed to me, he wanted to appease me. That has remained in my memory all my life.

My father, who was known to everyone as Chaim-Icek Ajnbinder, was a distinguished resident of Brzezin, and he was treated with honor; they showed him respect. He was the *gabe* [trustee] of the Biker-Khoylim Society [society to visit the sick]; he was an intelligent Vorker Hasid just like his father, my grandfather. After the death of the Vorker *rebbe*, my father began to travel to the Aleksander [Aleksandrów] *rebbe*, Reb Jechiel.

As a fair-minded person in town, my father, *e"h*, was very often asked to resolve disagreements between people; he was often chosen as the arbitrator. He made peace between married couples. They paid a great deal of attention to my father's opinions.

I loved my father, *e"h*, with heartfelt love; on his part, I felt a quiet pity and compassion for me.

My father was respected not only by Jews but also by Christians and was also highly regarded by the authorities in town. In as much as my father was the owner of a writing materials business, he provided the town hall with various writing materials and thus had the opportunity to make the acquaintance of those with influence. He was friendly with the district doctor, and if one is able to sway the district doctor, one can also do a favor in regard to military conscription and intercede to free someone from having to serve in the Russian army. Because of this, my father's prestige in the town grew a great deal.

My father ran a gracious home. Every Saturday evening after *havdole* [ceremony at close of the Sabbath], the leaders of the town used to come to drink a glass of tea with cookies. His wife had the greatest respect for him, and she took good care of him in his old age.

It happened that a Jew from somewhere else came to Brzezin and opened exactly the same type of shop with writing materials as my father had, so his earnings began to diminish. In his old age, when his earnings were extremely small, my father was not at all ashamed. He bought a horse and a little wagon and traveled around among the German villages (many Germans lived in our area) and sold them books. Once, my father took me along with him to the villages, probably wanting to show his love for me in this way. He took along bread, cheese, and butter as food for the trip and bought milk from the German peasants. I was assigned to stay and watch the milking to make sure that the milk was not, *kholile* [God forbid], made *trayf* [non-kosher].

And although the burden of making a living became ever harder for my father, *e"h*, our home was still run in a nice, Hasidic, genteel manner. The Shabosim and the holidays brought happiness and pleasure to the entire family. And I, who was always in yeshivas away from home, could barely wait for the holidays, Pesakh [Passover] or Sukes [Feast of Tabernacles], when I would come home and join my father at the comfortable holiday table.

With pride I would give my father, *e"h*, the report from the head of the yeshiva, who used to write about my being a good student. This was the greatest pleasure for my father. And although I was away from home, my father's spiritual influence over me was great. I learned a lot from him, from his genteel habits and his good deeds. And foremost, I learned from him the virtue of love for the Jewish people.

* * *

After I finally became a young man away from home, having had free board in many homes in various towns in Poland while studying in yeshivas, I ventured out into the great world and, by chance, ended up in London.

And unfortunately, I did not see my father, *e"h*, any more.

Shortly before World War I, my father wrote to me that he would like to come to London to see me. You can imagine my great joy. I prepared for the reunion with my father, but I was not destined to realize this great joy. On 1 August 1914 World War I broke out, and our contact was interrupted.

I heard nothing from my father until 1916. Poland was then occupied by the Germans, and I was in England. I actually once wrote a letter to my father through a neutral country, but my letter came back with a notation from the German post office—deceased.

That was a great loss for me. I was by then already the father of two children, but as long as you still have a father, you feel you are still a child. I went around a long time in deep sorrow. I could not get used to the thought that I would never see my father again. I could not become reconciled to the fact that nothing had materialized of the plan for my father to be my guest in London.

I could only take comfort in the fact that my father had died at the dignified age of eighty-two. The news that reached me later, after arriving in America, that the entire town had been at my father's funeral was also a comfort to me. The shops were closed; everyone came to pay him their last respects—which he had earned from the Jewish community in our town by his virtuous and beautiful life and his good deeds.

In the deepest depths of my heart, all my life I have carried the holy memory of my dear, beloved father. He is of blessed memory, specially honored that his *yortsayt* falls on Erev Rosheshone [the eve of the Jewish New Year].

Part Six

Yizkor [Memorial] Section

Don't Forget My Soul (p. 229)

Z. Segalowicz

What I ask of you and have come to beg of you,
You should not pass by or avoid.
We cannot really rescue the dead—
Then let's rescue the suffering.

I pledge to you my oath
For other times . . . in peace,
You must remember the influence
And the significance of every Jew.

With song and divine fury
With blood, lament the loss,
Because God himself has now lost
The best *daveners* [reciters of prayers] of his Jewish community.

Our shuls—in ruins,
In the cemeteries that terrify,
You will find enough, enough
That can inspire and awake.

For generations may it be remembered,
For eternity to tell the tale . . .
The doom of Jewish Poland
On written and engraved parchment.

    from Song of Lament "Gone"

Page Design: Emanuel Szary

Introduction to Yizkor Section

It must be noted that the list of Brzezin martyrs that follows does not include all people from Brzezin who were killed in the Shoah. Not all victims' names were known. Thus only those people whose names were submitted by friends or family appear in this book.

All names listed in the original Yizkor Book were included here, even when there seemed to be duplication. In some cases a victim's name may have been submitted by more than one person, but it was difficult to tell whether the second name was a duplication or a second person with the same name. In some cases, the same person may be listed under more than one spelling, because different submitters spelled the surname differently. Thus duplication could not be avoided.

As mentioned in the "Foreword to the English Edition," transliterating names and surnames from one language to another is a very difficult task, and, in the case of Jews from Poland, the names have gone through several language changes over time. It is thus difficult to ascertain which is the "right" spelling—if one exists.

The policy we adopted in this Yizkor section was to spell names, in so far as possible, as they most probably were in prewar Poland. This was done in order to make it easier for researchers to trace their ancestors back to Poland and find official records there. As is the custom in Poland, the feminine surname endings "cka" and "ska" have been used for women (Sawicka, Kowalska) rather than the masculine surname endings "cki" and "ski" (Sawicki, Kowalski). Thus, in these cases, the women's names appear before the men's.

In the original edition, the list of martyrs was in alphabetic order according to the Hebrew alphabet. The list here is in alphabetic order according to the English alphabet.

Certain Hebrew letters can be transliterated differently depending on the vowel signs and the letters around them. For instance, Aleph may be transliterated "A," "E," or "O," Therefore, in searching through the list of martyrs, one should examine the different sections of the list in order to avoid missing any relevant names.

When searching for given names, it must be kept in mind that the same name may have different forms. Diminutives in Yiddish are often expressed by adding "el" or "le/la" [Hersz/Herszel, Fajga/Fajgela], while diminutives in Polish may be expressed by adding "ek/ka," [Josef/Josek, Rywa/Rywka] or "cia/sia" [Szajndel/Szańcia, Zofia/Zosia]. Lajb/Lajbuś/Lewek are different versions of the same name as are Jakub/Jankiel/Jankief and Wolf/Wowe/Welwel/Wołek. In addition, Hebrew equivalents of Yiddish names may be used interchangeably, such as Dov–Ber, Cwi [Tsvi]–Hersz, and Arje–Lajb.

For a guide to the pronunciation of names, please see page xiv in the "Foreword to the English Edition."

We apologize in advance for any errors in transliteration.

Fay Vogel Bussgang
Coordinator-Editor of English Translation

N.B. The Hebrew word *ben* in a name means "son of," while *bas* means "daughter of."

A PARTIAL LIST OF BRZEZINER MARTYRS (pp. 231–40)

The Book Committee made a search in order to find a complete list of those from our *shtetl* who were killed. We turned to the Brzeziny Town Hall and to the Jewish Historical Committee in Warsaw; to our great regret we were not successful in getting such a list. The files for the registered Brzezin community were destroyed by the Nazis during the liquidation of the Brzezin ghetto.

[Unknown], Chawa-Liba
Abba (the tall Abba)
Abramowicz, Cwi [Tsvi] ben Icek
Abramowicz, Dora
Abramowicz, Icek
Ast (Bercholc), Chana bas Mojsze
Ast, Izrael
Ast, Izrael-Icek ben Mojsze
Ast, Izrael-Icek ben Mojsze
Ast, Izrael-Icek ben Mojsze
Ast, Mojsze
Ast, Mojsze
Ast, Mojsze
Ast, Sura
Ast (Rozen), Sura
Awner, Szmuel ben Josef and child
Badower, Balcia bas Aron
Badower, Bencion [Bentsion] ben
    Lajzer-Dawid
Badower, Frajda bas Aron
Badower, Herszel ben Bencion
Badower, Hudes bas Aron
Badower, Ita bas Abraham
Badower, Rywa bas Berysz
Badower, Szlama ben Lajzer-Dawid
Baran, the entire family
Barber (Berberg), Abba ben
    Dawid-Hersz
Barber, Abraham ben Dawid-Hersz
Barber, Balcia
Barber, Dawid-Hersz ben Szlama-Lajb
    and wife
Barber, Jakub ben Dawid Hersz
Barber, Jochwet
Barber, Rajzla bas Szmuel-Jakub

Bas, Abraham
Bas, Chawa bas Abraham
Bas, Małka bas Abraham
Bas, Rywka bas Abraham
Bas, Szajndla
Bechler, Aszer
Bechler, Bajla
Bechler, Ester-Ruchel
Bechler, Mojsze-Hersz
Bekermus, Cypa [Tsipa] bas Wolf
Bekermus, Dobryś
Bekermus, Hania bas Wolf
Bekermus, Tauba-Rywka bas Wolf
Bekermus, Wolf
Benkel, Aszer ben Rywen
Benkel, Berl
Benkel, Chaim-Lajbuś ben Rywen
Benkel, Chaja-Golda bas Rywen
Benkel, Chajele
Benkel, Dwojra bas Rywen
Benkel, Elka
Benkel, Ester bas Szlama-Eljasz [Elijah]
Benkel, Ester-Laja bas Szoel
Benkel (Niekrycz), Fajga bas Dawid
Benkel, Fajga bas Dawid
Benkel, Fajga bas Rywen
Benkel, Fajwel ben Nachum
Benkel, Fiszel ben Szoel
Benkel, Henoch-Wolf ben Fajwel
Benkel, Icek ben Szoel
Benkel, Jankiel
Benkel, Jankiel ben Nachum
Benkel, Pawel ben Nachum
Benkel, Rajza bas Fajwel
Benkel (Bocian), Rywka bas Mordka

Benkel, Rywka-Laja bas Rywen
Benkel, Sender ben Fajwel
Benkel, Sura
Benkel, Sura bas Dawid-Hersz
    and husband
Benkel, Szajna bas Dawid-Hersz
Benkel, Szmuel-Dawid ben Fajwel
Benkel, Szoel
Benkel, Tauba bas Fajwel
Berholc, Abraham-Chaim ben Szlama
Berholc, Abraham-Fiszel ben Szlama
Berholc, Alter
Berholc, Chaim-Aron ben Szlama
Berholc, Chaim-Aron ben Szlama
Berholc, Chana bas Mojsze
Berholc, Fiszel ben Szlama
Berholc, Hercke ben Szlama
Berholc, Izrael ben Szlama
Berholc, Izrael ben Szlama
Berholc, Szlama ben Hercke
Berholc, Szlama with four sons
Bercholc, Andrzej
Bercholc, Chaja
Bercholc, Chana bas Jancza
Bercholc, Elja ben Juma
Bercholc, Fiszel ben Szlama
Bercholc, Hercke ben Judel
Bercholc, Hercke ben Szlama
Bercholc, Jancza ben Judel
Bercholc, Josef ben Judel
Bercholc, Judel ben Jancza
Bercholc, Mania bas Jancza
Bercholc, Masza bas Josef
Bercholc, Mojsze ben Hercke
Bercholc, Perla bas Chaim
Bercholc, Szmuel
Betcajg [Betseig], Chaja-Sura bas Lajb
Betcajg, Izraelek ben Lajzer
Betcajg, Lajbel ben Lajzer
Betcajg, Lajzer (melamed)
Betcajg (Monat), Szajna-Rywka
Bialek, Benjamin ben Abraham
Bialek, Benjamin ben Majlech
Bialek, Bluma bas Majlech
Bialek, Elja

Bialek, Elka bas Jankiel
Bialek, Ester bas Benjamin
Bialek, Fiszel-Ber ben Majlech
Bialek, Frymet bas Majlech
Bialek, Icek
Bialek, Icek ben Joel
Bialek, Jankiel ben Joel
Bialek, Joel ben Lajbuś
Bialek, Laja bas Mendel-Jojne
Bialek, Lajbuś
Bialek, Liba bas Rabham
Bialek, Luzer
Bialek, Masza bas Majlech
Bialek, Majlech ben Joel
Bialek, Mendel ben Jankiel
Bialek, Perla
Bialek, Pesel bas Abraham
Bialek, Pessa bas Majlech
Bialek, Rózia [Ruzha] bas Abraham
Bialek, Rózia bas Majlech
Bialek, Ruchel bas Mendel
Bialek, Szmuel-Majer
Bialek, Tema bas Jankiel
Bialer, Ester-Chana
Bialer, Izrael ben Szaja [Yeshaye]-Dov
Bialer, Menachem ben Szaja-Dov
Bialer, Rywka bas Szaja-Dov
Bialer, Sura bas Szaja-Dov
Bialer, Szaja-Dov
Biedak, Mordka Dawid
Bitkowska, Nechama
Bitkowski, Jakub
Blacharowicz, Herszel
Bocian, Aron ben Szmuel-Majer
Bocian, Abraham-Gerszon ben Dawid
Bocian, Baruch ben Hersz
Bocian, Berl ben Jankiel
    with wife and three children
Bocian, Cywia [Tsivia]
Bocian, Frajdl
Bocian, Hersz ben Baruch with wife
    and three children
Bocian, Izrael ben Jankiel
Bocian, Jankiel ben Hersz
Bocian, Lajele bas Izrael

Bocian, Masza bas Izrael
Bocian, Mojsze ben Baruch
    with wife and three children
Bocian, Mojsze ben Jankiel
Bocian, Pinkus ben Mordka
Bocian, Rafał ben Mordka
Bocian, Rajza
Bocian, Rywka bas Majer
Bocian, Szmuel-Majer ben Hersz
Borower, Nechemia and Pessa
Brajtbart, Gedalia ben Rywen
Brajtbart, Majer ben Gedalia
Brajtbart, Perla bas Mordka
Brajtbart, Rajzla bas Gedalia
Braun, Fajga bas Josef-Hersz
Braun, Majer ben Josef-Hersz
Braun, Towa bas Josef-Hersz
Brener, Mojsze
Brumer, Abba ben Jukel
Brumer, G. bas Abba
Brumer, Jukel ben Abba
Brumer, Ruchel bas Szlama
Brzezińska, Chana-Chaja bas Izrael
Brzezińska, Laja bas Chaskiel
Brzezińska, Małka bas Izrael
Brzeziński, Izrael
Brzeziński, Izrael ben Aron-Berl
Buchner, Berl
Buchner, Jojne
Buchner, Mojsze
Budkowska, Bina bas Izrael-Hersz
Budkowska, Ester-Małka
    bas Izrael-Hersz
Budkowska, Perla bas Izrael-Hersz
Budkowska, Rywka bas Izrael-Hersz
Budkowski, Aszer ben Izrael-Hersz
Budkowski, Icek ben Izrael-Hersz
Budkowski, Izrael-Hersz
Buki, Aron
Buki, Balbina
Buki, Lolek
Buki, Moniek
Bursztajn, Cyrla [Tsirla] (Rozenkranc)
Bursztajn, Dawid ben Szoel
Bursztajn, Fajga bas Szoel

Bursztajn, Mojsze ben Szoel
Bursztajn, Szoel
Butkowska, Laja bas Jakub
Butkowska, Nechama
Butkowski, Abraham ben Jakub
Butkowski, Jakub
Całek [Tsawek], Mojsze
Chajmowicz, Chaim
Chajmowicz, Elka
Chajmowicz, Ester
Chajmowicz, Ester bas Chaim
Chajmowicz, Mojsze
Chajmowicz, Ruchel
Cuker [Tsuker], Sura
Cuker, Cywia [Tsivia]
Cuker, Gitel
Cuker, Mojsze
Cukerman [Tsukerman], Aron-Majer
Cukerman, Chana
Cukerman, Chawa
Cukerman, Ruchel-Laja
Cwern [Tsvern], Chanina
Cwern, Jakub
Dajcz [Deitch], Basia
Dajcz, Chana bas Nechemia
Dajcz, Marjem bas Nechemia
Dajcz, Nechemia
Dajcz, Nechemia
Dajcz, Ruchel-Laja
Dobryszycka [Dobryshytska], Chaja
Dobryszycki, Hersz
Dymant, Abraham ben Zelig
Dymant, Aron
Dymant, Awramek
Dymant, Donia
Dymant, Fiszel
Dymant, Fiszel ben Majer
Dymant, Herszel
Dymant, Ita
Dymant, Leokadia bas Herman
Dymant, Maja
Dymant, Majer (Majerlik)
Dymant, Olek [Alexander]
Dymant, Romek ben Icek
Dymant, Róża bas Icek

Dymant, Tauba
Dymant, Zelig
Dymant, Zelig ben Majer
Dymant-Melamedson, Pola
Dymant-Melamedson, Sura
Dymant-Winer, Regina and child
Dymowicz [see Tymowicz]
Działoszyńska [Dzhalwoshyńska], Bajla-Ester
Działoszyńska, Chawa
Działoszyńska, Dwojra
Działoszyńska, Fajga
Działoszyńska, Gitel (Zemler)
Działoszyńska, Gucia
Działoszyńska, Ita
Działoszyńska, Matel bas Lajzer-Icek
Działoszyński, Aron ben Lajzer-Icek
Działoszyński, Chaim-Szulem ben Lajzer-Icek and wife
Działoszyński, Dawid
Działoszyński, Fiszel
Działoszyński, Fiszel ben Lajzer-Icek
Działoszyński, Juda
Działoszyński, Lajbuś-Mendel ben Lajzer-Icek
Działoszyński, Lajzer-Icek
Działoszyński, Mojsze
Działoszyński, Mojsze and his family
Działoszyński, Naftali
Działoszyński, Wolf
Eidelson, Lajzer
Elbaum, Jechiel-Majer and Marjem
Epsztajn, Alter ben Szmuel
Epsztajn, Ester bas Icek
Epsztajn, Icek
Epsztajn, Icek
Epsztajn, Jojne ben Szmuel
Epsztajn, Lajb ben Icek
Epsztajn, Motel ben Szmuel
Epsztajn, Sura
Epsztajn, Sura bas Lajbel
Erlich, Abraham ben Icek-Ajzyk
Erlich, Baszewa
Erlich, Bajla bas Icek-Ajzyk
Erlich, Chawa

Erlich, Cywia [Tsivia] bas Chaim
Erlich, Dina bas Icek-Ajzyk
Erlich, Efroim Fiszel ben Icek-Ajzyk
Erlich, Elka bas Icek-Ajzyk
Erlich, Fajga bas Wolf
Erlich, Icek-Ajzyk ben Szymon-Michał
Erlich, Icek-Lajzer ben Josef
Erlich, Izrael-Jakub ben Szymon-Michał
Erlich, Marjem bas Szymon
Erlich, Ruchel bas Mojsze
Erlich, Sura bas Lajzer
Erlich, Sura bas Wolf
Erlich, Wolf ben Josef
Erlichman, Chaja-Jehudes bas Mojsze
Erlichman, Ita
Erlichman, Mojsze
Erlichman, Szmuel-Dawid ben Mojsze
Erlichman, Tauba-Rywka bas Mojsze
Fajfer, Golda bas Icek
Fajfer, Hudes bas Josef
Fajfer, Icze ben Mojsze
Fajfer, Mojsze-Josel ben Icek
Fajfer, Pinkus ben Icek
Fajgenblat, Chaim
Fajgenblat (Fuks), Hania bas Abraham-Judel
Fajgenblat, Jenta
Fajgenblat, Josef
Fajgenblat, Mindel
Fajgenblat, Ruchel
Fajgenblat, Sura
Fajnkind, Abraham
Fajnkind, Berl
Fajnkind, Berl ben Izrael
Fajnkind, Ester
Fajnkind (Lipska), Ester and two sons
Fajnkind, Hessa
Feferman, Abraham-Josef ben Berysz
Feferman, Alta-Nechama bas Herszel
Feferman, Berysz
Fidler, Abraham ben Godel
Fidler, Ester bas Godel
Fidler, Godel
Fidler, Herszel
Fidler, Pola bas Godel

Fidler, Ruchel
Fidler, Rywka
Filater [see Pilater]
Filip (Szulzinger), Dina
    bas Pinkus-Szlama
Filip, Josef-Nahum
Filip, Laja bas Josef-Nahum
Fiszer, Chaim-Izrael ben Abraham-Ber
Fiszer, Chaja
Fiszer, Chana-Sura
Fiszer, Hercke ben Chaim-Izrael
Fiszer, Hersz-Josef ben Chaim-Izrael
Flambaum, Baruch ben Berl
Flambaum, Berl ben Bendet
Flambaum, Bluma-Gitel bas Berl
Flambaum, Chaim-Hersz ben Berl
Flambaum, Necha
Flamholc, Dwojra
Flamholc, Szmuel-Szaja [Yeshaye]
    ben Herszel
Fogel, Abraham-Josef
Fogel, Benjamin ben Icek
Fogel, Bernard ben Hersz-Cwi [Tsvi]
Fogel, Brucha bas Dan-Aszer
Fogel, Brucha bas Rafal
Fogel, Dan-Aszer ben Icek
Fogel (Karp), Dwojra
Fogel (Lewkowicz), Fajga bas Szlama
Fogel (Bercholc), Frajdal
Fogel, Heniek ben Abraham
Fogel, Heniek ben Rafal
Fogel, Hersz-Cwi ben Icek
Fogel, Icek ben Abraham
Fogel, Icek ben Dan-Aszer
Fogel, Izrael ben Icek
Fogel, Izrael ben Szoel
Fogel, Josef ben Abraham
Fogel (Rubin), Krajndel
Fogel, Lajb ben Icek
Fogel, Lajbuś ben Icek
Fogel, Rafal ben Icek
Fogel, Ruchel bas Icek
Fogel, Rywa bas Abraham-Mechel
Fogel, Rywka bas Hersz
Fogel, Rywka bas Icek

Fogel, Szajele ben Abraham
Frajnd, Abraham
Frajnd, Chaim
Frajndt, Abraham
Frajndt, Becalel ben Abraham
Frajndt, Gitel bas Abraham
Frajndt, Kajla bas Abraham
Frajndt, Laja
Frajndt, Ruchel bas Abraham
Frajndt, Syna ben Abraham
Frajndt, Szymon ben Abraham
Frankensztajn, Abraham-Mojsze
    and wife
Frankensztajn, Benjamin
Frankensztajn, Chawa
    bas Abraham-Mojsze
Frankensztajn, Dan-Josef
Frankensztajn, Dan-Josef
    ben Abraham-Mojsze
Frankensztajn, Dan-Josele
    ben Jakub-Icek
Frankensztajn, Ita
Frankensztajn, Jakub-Icek ben Dan-Josef
Frankensztajn, Laja
Frankensztajn, Lolek
    ben Abraham-Mojsze
Frankensztajn, Rywka bas Jakub-Icek
Frankensztajn, Sura-Hinda
Frankensztajn, Szlama ben Jakub-Icek
Frankensztajn, Tolba bas Jakub-Icek
Frankensztajn, Tolba-Buzi (Basia?]
Froman, Chaim
Froman, Jakub
Froman, Szulem
Frydman, Binem
Frydman, Dawid ben Hersz
Frydman, Dwojra bas Gerszon
Frydman, Icek
Frydman, Mordka
Frydman, Sura
Frydman, Szlama
Fuks, Abraham
Fuks, Abraham-Judel ben Majer
Fuks, Benjamin ben Abraham
Fuks, Cale [Tsale)] ben Mojsze

Fuks, Chaja
Fuks, Daniel ben Abraham
Fuks, Eljasz [Elijah] ben Abraham
Fuks, Erna bas Mojsze
Fuks, Ester bas Szymon
Fuks, Icek ben Abraham
Fuks, Jacha
Fuks, Jankiel ben Abraham-Judel
Fuks, Mindel
Fuks, Mojsze ben Mendel
Fuks, Pawa bas Abraham
Fuks, Rafal ben Abraham-Judel
Fuks, Ruchel bas Abraham
Fuks, Rywka bas Herszel
Fuks, Syna ben Abraham-Judel
Fuks, Szmuel ben Abraham-Judel
Fuks, Szulem and his two children
Fuks, Wolf ben Abraham-Judel
Gdalewicz, Fajga bas Mojsze
Gdalewicz, Mojsze
Gdalewicz, Pawa bas Icek
Gdalewicz, Perla-Laja bas Mojsze
Gdalewicz, Szajndla bas Mojsze
Gdalewicz, Welwel [Velvel] ben Mojsze
Geber, Pincia [Pinkus?] with children
Gerber, Abraham
Gerber, Alta with children
Gerber (Epsztajn), Chana with child
Gerber, Mojsze
Gerber, Motel
Gerszt, Rajzla-Laja
Gewirc, Fajga
Gewirc, Icek-Majer
    with wife and children
Gewirc, Mojsze
Ginsberg, Abraham-Chaim
Ginsberg, Chaja
Ginsberg, Ita
Ginsberg, Jakub-Szlama
Ginsberg, Marjem
Ginsberg, Ruchel
Ginsberg, Sura-Laja
Glazer, Icek
Gliksman, Josef with children

Gliksman (Szajbowicz), Rajzla
    bas Gecel [Getsel]
Glowińska, Marjem
Glowińska, Sura-Fajga bas Icek-Majer
Glowiński, Abraham-Chaskiel
    ben Icek-Majer
Glowiński, Icek-Majer
Gociał, Aszer-Anszel ben Josef-Dawid
Gociał, Bajla-Marjem bas Chaskiel
    Hillel-Jakub-Cwi [Tsvi]-Nechemia
Gociał, Hillel-Jakub-Cwi-Nechemia
    Harav [Rabbi] ben Josef-Baruch
Gociał (Elberg), Jehudes
    bas Josef-Baruch
Gociał, Lajzer-Dawid ben
Gociał, Małka-Laja
    bas Hillel-Jakub-Cwi-Nechemia
Gociał, Menachem-Szulem
    ben Hillel-Jakub-Cwi-Nechemia
Gociał, Naftali ben Josef-Baruch
Gociał, Ruchel bas
    Hillel-Jakub-Cwi-Nechemia
Gociał, Rywka-Perla bas Josef-Baruch
Gociał, Sura bas
    Hillel-Jakub-Cwi-Nechemia
Goldberg, Abraham
Goldberg, Anszel ben Wolf
Goldberg, Elka-Chaja bas Abraham-Ber
Goldberg, Ester-Małka bas Judel
Goldberg, Icek ben Hersz
Goldberg, Jakub ben Wolf
Goldberg, Mojsze
Goldberg, Perla bas Wolf
Goldberg, Rajza bas Mendel
Goldberg, Rywka bas Wolf
Goldberg, Sura bas Mojsze-Ber
Goldberg, Szajndla bas Icek
Goldberg, Telca
Goldberg, Wolf
Goldkranc, Abraham ben Chaim
Goldkranc, Dawid ben Icek
Goldkranc, Ester bas Pinkus
Goldkranc, Frajdl bas Jakub
Goldkranc, Icek ben Jakub-Hersz

Goldkranc, Icek ben Jakub-Hersz
Goldkranc, Jakub-Cwi [Tsvi]
    ben Abraham
Goldkranc, Ruchel bas Fiszel
Goldkranc, Rywka
Gomulińska, Cywia [Tsivia] bas Icek
Gomulińska, Sura
Gomuliński, Lajbel ben Szlama
Gomuliński, Mojsze
Gotlib, Berko
Gotlib, Mojsze-Bajnisz
Gotlib, Wolf
Granat, Alis [Alicia?] bas Mojsze
Granat, Mojsze ben Dawid
Granat, Pessa bas Josef
Grundsztajn, Chaja
Grundsztajn, Chana
Grundsztajn, Hersz-Icek ben Lajbuś
Grundsztajn, Jerachmiel ben Lajbuś
Grundsztajn, Jochwet
Grundsztajn, Laja
Grundsztajn, Lajbuś
Grynbaum, Chawa
Grynbaum, Frymet bas Jakub
Grynbaum, Golda bas Jakub
Grynbaum, Jakub
Grynbaum, Mendel ben Jakub
Grynbaum, Ruchel bas Jakub
Grynbaum, Rywka bas Jakub
Grynholc, Abraham Mechel ben Josef
Grynholc, Fajgele bas Abraham Mechel
Grynholc, Judel
Gutkind, Brucha bas Abraham-Pejsach
Gutkind, Dwojra bas Nachman
Gutkind, Jeremia ben Nachman
Gutkind, Lajbel ben Nachman
Gutkind, Nachman ben Mojsze-Majer
Gutkind, Szmuel-Aron ben Nachman
Gutkind, Szulem ben Nachman
Gutkind, Szyja [Jehoszua] ben Nachman
Gutkind, Tauba bas Nachman
Halbersztam, Mojsze
    ben Pinkus-Elimelech
Halbersztam, (Gotlib) Ruchel
    bas Jechiel-Mojsze
Halbersztam (Gotlib), Sura bas
    Jechiel-Mojsze
Halbersztam, Szymon ben Mojsze
Hamer, Chaim
Hamer, Dawid ben Lajbuś
Hamer, Golda
Hamer, Lajbuś
Hamer, Mojsze ben Lajbuś
Hamer, Pejsach ben Lajbuś
Hamer, Sura
Hamer, Symcha-Majer
Hamer, Szmuel
Hamer, Temar
Hamer, Zelda-Perla bas Lajbuś
Hauzer, Abraham ben Jakub
Hauzer, Brajndla
Hauzer, Chaim ben Icek-Lajb
Hauzer, Chawa bas Wowe [Vove]
Hauzer, Fajwisz ben Kalman
Hauzer, Frajdal bas Chaim
Hauzer, Golda bas Abraham-Ber
Hauzer, Icek-Lajb ben Kalman
Hauzer, Jakub ben Icek-Lajb
Hauzer, Kalman ben Icek-Lajb
Hauzer, Lajbel ben Wowe
Hauzer, Marjem
Hauzer, Mendel ben Wowe
Hauzer, Mojsze
Hauzer, Mojsze ben Jakub
Hauzer, Mordka
Hauzer, Rajza bas Chaim
Hauzer, Rajzla bas Kalman
Hauzer, Róża
Hauzer, Rywen ben Chaim
Hauzer, Szmuel ben Jakub
Hauzer, Szmuel-Mojsze ben Kalman
Hauzer, Wowe ben Icek-Lajb
Hendel, ??
Hendel, Abraham-Eljasz [Elijah]
Hercberg, Alter
Herszenberg, Chawa
Herszenberg, Szmuel
Hilcberg, Laja bas Abraham
Hirsz, Alte-Izrael-Aron
Hirsz, Bajla-Masza

Hirsz, Bencion [Benzion]
Hirsz, Hillel
Hirsz, Jakub-Lajbuś
Hirsz, Sura-Rywka
Hirsz, Szajndla-Hudes
Hirsz, Szlama
Hoferman [Huberman?],
    Chana bas Josef
Hoferman, Falki
Hofman, Josef
Hofman, Symcha
Holcberg, Fiszel ben Aron
Holcberg, Jankiel ben Aron
Holcberg, Szymon ben Fiszel
Ikka, Chana
Ikka, Mania
Ikka, Mojsze-Zundel and wife, Sura
Ikka, Pinkus
Ikka, Sura
Ikka, Sura-Hinda
Irlicht, the entire family
Izraelowicz, Onysz [Janusz?]
    with wife and son
Jakubowicz, Chaja bas Icek
Jakubowicz, Dwojra bas Icek
Jakubowicz, Icek ben Josef
Jakubowicz, Marjem bas Icek
Jakubowicz, Rywka bas Icek
Jakubowicz (Erlich), Sura bas Josef
Jakubowicz, Szmuel ben Icek
Jakubowicz-Łęczycki [Lenchitski],
    Chaim Dawid
Judkowicz, Bluma bas Icze
Judkowicz, Bluma bas Szlama
Judkowicz, Bluma bas Zawel
Judkowicz, Chawa bas Szulem-Lajzer
Judkowicz, Ester bas Zawel
Judkowicz (Pajczer), Golda
Judkowicz, Icze ben Szulem-Lajzer
Judkowicz, Liba
Judkowicz, Mania (Blajrarowicz)
Judkowicz, Mojszl ben Szulem-Lajzer
Judkowicz, Pinkus ben Szulem-Lajzer
Judkowicz, Rywka
Judkowicz, Szlama ben Szulem-Lajzer
Judkowicz, Zawel, ben Szulem-Lajzer
Kaczka, Dawid-Mendel ben Icze
Kaczka, Fiszel ben Dawid-Mendel
Kaczka, Marjem-Hinda
Kaczka, Surele bas Dawid-Mendel
Kalisz, Laja bas Zalman
Kalisz, Mojsze
Kalisz, Mojsze-Lajb ben Aron
Kalisz (Ast), Rajzla
Kalisz, Rajzla-Laja bas Mojsze
Kalisz (Pakula), Sura-Marjem
Kalmus, Aron
Kalmus, Luzer
Kalmus, Mindel
Kasztan, Chana bas Abraham-Icek
Kasztan, Ester-Laja bas Dawid
Kasztan, Ester-Marjem bas Josef
Kasztan, Izrael ben Dawid
Kasztan, Juda ben Josef with four sons
    and three daughters
Kasztan, Mirel
Kasztan, Sura Hinda bas Ezriel
Kejzman, Hersz ben Mordka
    with wife and child
Kejzman, Masza bas Hersz
Kejzman, Mordka ben Dawid
Kejzman, Sura bas Mordka
Kejzman, Szaja ben Mordka
Kempner, Szlama
Kiejlis, Dawid-Szlama
Kiejlis, Jedydia
Kiejlis, Josef
Klajnbaum, Mojsze
Klajnert, Chaim ben Majer
Klajnert, Chawa (Alter Kozeles)
Klajnert, Majer ben Chaim
Klajnert, Mania bas Chaim
Klingbajl, Lajzer
Klingbajl, Moryc [Morris] ben Lajzer
Knobel, Akiwa
Knobel, Chawa bas Akiwa
Knobel, Rajza bas Rywen
Kochberg, Juda-Lajb
Kochman, Mordka and family
Kohen, Abraham-Mendel

Kohen, Cyrla [Tsirla]-Rajzla bas Lajb
Kolska, Hindla
Kolton, Abraham and Chana-Perla
Kolton, Bajla
Kolton, Ezriel
Kolton, Jakub and wife Ita
Kornblum, Golda
Kornblum, Herszel
Kornblum, Josef
Kornblum, Sura
Kornblum, Szyja
Kozłowski [Kozwovski], Eljasz [Elijah]
Kozak, Majer
Kraushorn, Dawid-Hersz
    ben Mojsze-Juda
Kraushorn, Laja bas Chaim-Izrael
Kraushorn, Mojsze-Juda ben Pejsach
Kraushorn, Raszka bas Mojsze-Juda
Kraushorn, Szlama-Aron
    ben Mojsze-Juda
Kraushorn, Szymon-Mendel
    ben Mojsze-Juda
Krongrad, Chaja-Sura
Krongrad, Jakub-Hersz ben Fiszel
Krongrad, Juda
Krzywanowska [Kshivanovska], Hinda
    bas Dawid
Krzywanowska, Tauba bas Szmuel
Krzywanowski, Dawid ben Mendel
Kujawska, Ester bas Szyja
Kune, Jakub and wife Elka
    with four children
Kuperminc, Jakub ben Izrael-Dov
Kuperminc, Sura-Pessa
    bas Gerszon-Henoch
Lachowska/i [see also Lichowska/i
Lachowska, Cypa [Tsipa]
Lachowska, Hania with husband
    and children
Lachowska, Jochet with husband
    and two children
Lachowska, Jochwet
Lachowska, Jochwet bas Josef
Lachowska, Marjem-Brucha bas Josef
Lachowska, Róża
Lachowska, Szyfra bas Jakub
Lachowska-Fogel, Rózia bas Szoel
Lachowski, Abraham with wife
    and two children
Lachowski, Abraham-Icze ben Josef
Lachowski, Jakub
Lachowski, Jakub
Lachowski, Josef
Lachman, Dawid ben Szyja [Jehoszua]
Lachman, Laja bas Szyja
Lachman, Szyja and wife
Łęczycka [Wenchitska/Lenchitska],
    Chaja-Sura bas Mordka
Łęczycka, Chana-Laja bas Icek-Jakub
Łęczycka, Machla bas Mordka
Łęczycka, Tauba bas Mordka
Łęczycki, Fiszel ben Mordka
Łęczycki, Mordka ben Szmuel
Łęczycki, Nachman ben Mordka
Łęczycki, Szmuel ben Mordka
Lenge, Genia bas Szulem
Lenge, Hania
Lenge, Icze ben Szulem
Lenge, Pola bas Szulem
Lenge, Sura-Liba bas Kiwa
Lenge, Szulem
Lerer, Izrael
Lerer, Izrael
Lerer, Izrael ben Szaja [Yeshaye]
Lerer, Laja
Lerer, Mania
Lerer, Szaja
Lerer, Szaja
Lew, Jojne
Lew, Lila bas Chaim
Lewkowicz, Abraham
Lewkowicz, Bajla bas Mordka
Lewkowicz, Chaim-Mojsze
Lewkowicz, Chaja bas Chaim-Mojsze
Lewkowicz, Chana Ruchel
Lewkowicz, Daniel ben Izrael-Dawid
Lewkowicz, Dawid ben Josef
Lewkowicz, Gitel bas Chaim-Mojsze

Lewkowicz, Izrael-Dawid ben Szlama
Lewkowicz, Izrael-Szyja ben Chaim-
    Mojsze with wife and children
Lewkowicz, Jakub ben Izrael-Dawid
Lewkowicz, Jechiel ben Izrael-Dawid
Lewkowicz, Josef
Lewkowicz, Josef ben Icze
Lewkowicz, Lajbel ben Chaim-Mojsze
Lewkowicz (Najman), Marjem
    bas Szmuel
Lewkowicz, Menachem
    ben Izrael-Dawid
Lewkowicz, Mojsze
Lewkowicz, Mordka
Lewkowicz, Perla
Lewkowicz, Sura
Lewkowicz, Sura Rywka
Lichowska/i [see also Lachowska/i]
Lichowska, Cypa [Tsipa] bas Josef
Lichowska, Chana with husband
    and children
Lichowska, Jochwet bas Josef
Lichowska, Jochwet bas Naftali
Lichowska, Rajza bas Szoel
Lichowska, Szyfra bas Jakub
Lichowski, Abraham and wife,
    Chajka (Milsztajn)
Lichowski, Abraham-Icze ben Josef
Lichowski, Jakub
Lichowski, Josef
Liderman, Akiwa ben Josef
Liderman, Dwojra bas Mendel
    with husband and children
Liderman, Genendl bas Syna
Liderman, Hersz ben Szmuel
Liderman, Icek ben Josef
Liderman, Jakub ben Mendel
Liderman, Josef ben Mendel
Liderman, Laja bas Mordka
Liderman, Lajzer ben Mendel
Liderman, Majer ben Josef
Liderman, Mendel
Liderman, Perla bas Jakub
Liderman, Perla bas Szmuel
Liderman (Szajbowicz), Perla
    bas Josef-Baruch
Liderman, Rafal-Josef ben Mendel
    with wife and children
Liderman, Rajza-Gitel bas Mendel
    with husband and children
Liderman, Syna ben Jakub
Liderman, Szmuel ben Mendel
Lipkowicz, Abraham ben Fiszke
Lipkowicz, Ester Małka bas Hersz
Lipkowicz, Fiszke ben Szaja [Yeshaye]
Lipkowicz, Szmuel ben Fiszke
Lipkowicz-Winter, Rywcia bas Fiszke
Lipkowitz, Abraham ben Fiszel
Lipkowitz, Ester Małka bas Herszel
Lipkowitz, Fiszel ben Szaja
Lipkowitz, Szmuel ben Fiszel
Majerowicz, Dwojra
Mandel, Chana-Hinda
Mandel, Josef ben Mojsze-Aron
Mandel, Mojsze-Aron ben Josef
Mandel, Rywka bas Abraham-Ber
Mandel, Sura-Laja bas Mojsze-Aron
Mel, Ber
Mel, Chaim
Mel, Szmuel-Dawid
Melamedzon, Sura bas Majer
    and two daughters
Mendelewicz, Abraham-Chaim
    ben Fajwel-Majer
Mendelewicz, Fajwel-Majer ben Hersz
Mendelewicz, Herszel ben Mojsze-
    Mordka
Mendelewicz, Mojsze-Mordka
    ben Fajwel-Majer
Mendelewicz, Szyfka bas Aron
Mendelewicz, Towcia bas Mojsze
Mietkiewicz, Andrzej
Mietkiewicz, Bluma
Mietkiewicz, Golda
Mietkiewicz, Szlamek
Mietkiewicz, Zajnwel
Milberg, Cyrla [Tsirla]
    bas Gerszon-Henoch

Miler, Dawid with entire family
Milsztajn, Naftali ben Abraham
   and wife
Miodownik, Ita bas Jukel
Miodownik, Małkele bas Josef
Miodownik, Rajzla bas Josef
Mitelsztajn, Fiszel
Mizes, Josef ben Perec [Peretz]
Mizes, Perec
Mizes, Szymon ben Perec
Mordkowicz (Rozenberg), Bina
   bas Wolf
Mordkowicz (Eksztajn), Ester bas Wolf
Mordkowicz, Izrael ben Wolf
Mordkowicz, Ruchel
Mordkowicz, Wolf
Najdenberg, Chana bas Abraham
Najdenberg, Dina bas Izrael-Icek
Najdenberg, Hancia bas Dawid
Najdenberg, Izrael-Icek ben Rywen
Najdenberg, Jakub-Dawid ben Rywen
Najdenberg, Marjem bas Rywen
Najdenberg, Nechama bas Rywen
Najdenberg, Rywen ben Juma Lajb
Najman, Abba ben Lajbuś
Najman, Abraham ben Syna
Najman, Cypa [Tsipa] bas Lajbuś
Najman, Fajga bas Mordka
Najman, Hersz ben Syna
Najman, Izrael ben Rywen
Najman, Izrael ben Syna
Najman, Josef ben Lajbuś
Najman, Laja bas Lajbuś
Najman, Majlech ben Syna
Najman, Mordkele
   ben Szaja [Yeshaye]
Najman, Rajzla bas Szaja
Najman, Regina bas Rywen
Najman, Rywen ben Chaskiel
Najman, Rywka bas Baruch
Najman (Rozenkranc), Rywka
   bas Mendel
Najman, Rywka bas Mojsze
Najman, Rywka bas Szaja
Najman, Szaja ben Berl

Najman, Szmuel ben Chaskiel
Najman, Szmuel ben Lajbuś
Nekrycz, Chawa bas Hanan
Nekrycz, Hanan
Niewiadowicz, Aron ben Josef
Niewiadowicz, Chanela bas Josef
Niewiadowicz, Ester-Laja bas Josef
Niewiadowicz, Fajga
Niewiadowicz, Fajwisz
Niewiadowicz, Fajwisz ben Josef
Niewiadowicz, Fiszel ben Josef
Niewiadowicz, Herszel ben Josef
Niewiadowicz, Josel
Niewiadowicz, Róża bas Josef
Niewiadowicz, Szmuel
Niewiadowicz, Zilpa
Nisenbaum, Berysz
Nisenbaum, Chawa
Nisenbaum, Jakub
Nisenbaum, Mendel
Nowak, Abramele ben Mordka
Nowak, Bramcia-Laja bas Mordka
Nowak, Chawa
Nowak, Chawa
Nowak, Herszel ben Mordka
Nowak, Ita-Małka
Nowak, Majlech ben Mordka
Nowak, Mordka ben Szymon
Nowak, Pola bas Szymon
Nowak, Sender ben Mordka
Nowak, Szmuel-Dawid ben Szymon
Nowak, Szymon ben Bendet
Oberman, Aron-Majer
Oberman, Chana bas Aron-Majer
Oberman, Chawa bas Aron-Majer
Oberman, Ruchel-Laja bas Aron-Majer
Oberman, Rywka
Offenbach, Golda
Offenbach, Josef ben Mojsze-Icek
Offenbach, Laja bas Mojsze-Icek
Offenbach, Mojsze-Icek
Opatowska, Fajga bas Abraham
Opatowska, Frajda
Opatowski, Abraham
Opatowski, Dan ben Abraham

Opatowski, Fajwel ben Abraham
Opoczyński, Gerszon ben Josef
Opoczyński, Josef ben Icek
Opoczyński, Judel ben Josef
Oratowska, Basia
Oratowska, Rajzla
Oratowski, Pinkus
Orensztajn, Pinkus
Orensztajn, Zelda
Ost [see Ast]
Pajczer [see also Pitzer]
Pajczer, Abraham
Pajczer, Abraham ben Herszel
Pajczer, Bina
Pajczer, Chawa
Pajczer, Daniel ben Syna
Pajczer, Dwojra
Pajczer, Ester-Jetta bas Josef
Pajczer, Ester-Laja bas Herszel
Pajczer, Ester-Laja bas Syna
Pajczer, Fajgele bas Symcha
Pajczer, Herszel
Pajczer, Izraelek ben Syna
Pajczer, Jechiel
Pajczer, Josef ben Symcha
Pajczer, Lajbel ben Syna
Pajczer, Lajzer
Pajczer, Mojsze ben Syna
Pajczer, Perla
Pajczer, Rywka
Pajczer, Symcha ben Syna
Pajczer, Syna
Pajczer, Szymon ben Herszel
Pajczer, Zelda bas Syna
Pakula, Chaja bas Szoel
Pakula, Laja bas Szaja [Yeshaye]
Pakula, Rywka bas Szoel
Pakula, Szoel ben Aron
Pakula, Zelig
Perec [Peretz] (Tandeter), ??
Perelmuter, Aron ben Joel
Perelmuter (Wołkowicz), Dina
    bas Jakub-Mojsze
Perelmuter, Joel ben Mojsze
Pfefferman [see Feferman]

Philip [see Filip]
Pilater, Benjamin ben Chaim
Pilater, Chaim (Chaiml)
Pilater, Rywka
Pinczewska, Jochwet
Pinczewska, Luta bas Henoch
Pinczewski, Henoch
Pinczewski, Izrael ben Henoch
Pitzer [Pajczer?], Chawa bas Daniel
Pitzer [Pajczer?], Daniel
Pitzer [Pajczer?], Ester bas Daniel
Pitzer [Pajczer?], Herszel ben Daniel
Pitzer [Pajczer?], Rywka bas Daniel
Pitzer [Pajczer?], Syna ben Daniel
Pitzer [Pajczer?], Szmuel ben Daniel
Pomeranc, Ester
Potaszewicz, Ester bas Izrael-Jakub
Potaszewicz, Ita-Małka bas Wolf
Potaszewicz, Izrael-Jakub ben Berl
Pruszyńska, Chawa
Pruszyński, Dawid
Raszewska, Ester bas Szmuel
Raszewska, Fajga bas Mojsze
Raszewska, Gitel
Raszewska, Małka bas Mojsze
Raszewski, Icek ben Mojsze
Raszewski, Izrael ben Mojsze
Raszewski, Szlama ben Mojsze
Raszewski, Szmuel ben Jakub-Icek
Rozenberg, Abraham ben Menachem
Rozenberg, Andrzej
Rozenberg, Aron
Rozenberg, Beniek
Rozenberg, Chana-Jochwet
Rozenberg, Ester
Rozenberg, Gabriel
Rozenberg, Gecel [Getsel] ben Towia
Rozenberg, Gucia bas Towia
Rozenberg, Hadasa bas Abraham
Rozenberg, Hania bas Josef
Rozenberg, Hania bas Towia
Rozenberg, Hinda
Rozenberg, Juma
Rozenberg, Josef
Rozenberg, Josef

Rozenberg (Szajbowicz), Kajla
    bas Gecel [Getsel]
Rozenberg, Lajb
Rozenberg, Lajbel ben Towia
Rozenberg, Marjem bas Josef
Rozenberg, Mojsze
Rozenberg, Pawa bas Josef
Rozenberg, Pessa
Rozenberg, Rywa
Rozenberg, Rywka
Rozenberg, Sasza
Rozenberg, Sura bas Eljasz [Elijah]
Rozenberg, Surcia
Rozenberg, Szmuel ben Towia
Rozenberg, Szmuel-Chaim
Rozenberg, Towia
Rozenberg, Towia ben Lajb
Rozenblat, Benjamin
Rozenblat (Fogel), Chawa bas Icek
Rozenblat, Icek ben Emanuel
Rozenblat, Szyja [Jehoszua]
Rozenblum, Abraham
    ben Szaja [Yeshaye]
Rozenblum, Chaim-Rafal
Rozenblum, Chawa bas Hersz
Rozenblum, Cwi [Tsvi] ben Szaja
Rozenblum, Dawid-Mendel ben Szaja
Rozenblum, Hersz ben Jerachmiel
Rozenblum, Jerachmiel ben Hersz
Rozenblum, Mirel bas Szaja
Rozenblum, Motel ben Hersz
Rozenblum, Ruchel bas Motel
Rozenblum, Sura-Chana
    bas Dawid-Mendel
Rozenblum, Surka bas Jerachmiel
Rozenblum, Szaja
Rozenblum, Szaja ben Hersz
Rozenblum, Telca bas Hersz
Rozenblum, Zelda bas Hersz
Rozenfarb, Chaiml
Rozenfeld, Brucha bas Welwel [Velvel]
Rozenfeld, Josef ben Welwel
Rozenfeld, Mojsze ben Welwel
Rozenfeld (Fogel), Ruchel bas Icek
Rozenfeld, Szlama-Hersz ben Welwel
Rozenfeld, Welwel
Rozenkranc (Szajbowicz), Bajla
    bas Josef-Baruch
Rozenkranc, Chajcia
Rozenkranc, Dan-Josef
Rozenkranc, Fajga-Mirel bas Mendel
Rozenkranc, Mendel
Rozenkranc, Rywka-Ruchel
Rozenkranc, Szlama
Rozensztrauch, Chaim-Baruch
Rozensztrauch, Chaim-Baruch
    ben Majer
Rozensztrauch, Chana-Laja
Rozensztrauch, Ester-Laja
Rozensztrauch, Frymet
Rozensztrauch, Gitel
Rozensztrauch, Glika
Rozensztrauch, Henoch ben Mordka
Rozensztrauch, Kalman and wife
Rozensztrauch, Majer
Rozensztrauch, Menachem
Rozensztrauch, Mojsze
    ben Chaim-Baruch
Rozensztrauch, Mojsze ben Kalman
Rozensztrauch, Mordka
Rozensztrauch, Naftali
Rozensztrauch, Naftali ben Majer
Rozensztrauch, Perla bas Abraham
Rozensztrauch, Różele bas Mordka
Rozman, ??
Rubin, Dawid
Rubin, Mendel-Lajzer
Sabatowska, Chaja bas Jojne
Sabatowska, Pessa bas Jojne
Sabatowska, Ruchel bas Izrael
Sabatowski, Jojne
Sadorkiewicz, Abraham
Sadorkiewicz, Brajndla bas Abraham
Sadorkiewicz, Dawid ben Abraham
Sadorkiewicz, Frajda
Sandowska, Frymet
    bas Chaim-Mordka
Sender, Bernard ben Szlama
Sender, Leon
Sender, Leon ben Szlama

Sender, Szoel ben Szlama
Siedlowcer [Shedlovtser], Abraham
Siedlowcer, Tauba
Sieradzka, Laja bas Eljasz [Elijah]
Sieradzki [Sheradski], Judel
Skurnik, Bajla Liba
Skurnik, Berl
Skurnik, Chaim
Skurnik, Czarna
Skurnik, Dwojra
Skurnik, Izrael
Skurnik, Jakub
Skurnik, Pessel
Skurnik, Rajzla
Sochaczewski [Sohachevski], Icek
Strzyzewski [Shchyzevski], Izrael-Juda
   and wife
Światlowski [Shviatlovski], Berysz
Szafman, Abraham
Szafman, Abraham ben Mojsze
Szafman, Chaim ben Szmuel
Szafman, Chana
Szafman, Chana
Szafman, Chaskiel
Szafman, Eljasz [Elijah] ben Szmuel
Szafman, Ester
Szafman, Fajgele bas Abraham
Szafman, Golda
Szafman, Golda bas Szmuel
Szafman, Herszel ben Szmuel
Szafman, Majer ben Szachna
   with wife and three children
Szafman, Regina bas Abraham
Szafman, Ruchel bas Abraham
Szafman, Ruchele bas Abraham
Szafman, Rywcia bas Abraham
Szafman, Rywcia bas Chaskiel
Szafman, Rywcia bas Herszel
Szafman, Sura-Laja bas Abraham
Szafman, Szmuel
Szajbowicz, Abraham-Chaim
Szajbowicz, Abraham-Chaim
   ben Josef-Baruch
Szajbowicz, Bajla
Szajbowicz, Bajla bas Gecel [Getsel]

Szajbowicz, Bluma
Szajbowicz, Blumele bas Josef-Baruch
Szajbowicz, Chaim ben Mojsze-Majer
Szajbowicz, Chaim ben Rywen
Szajbowicz, Chana
Szajbowicz, Chana bas Abraham-Chaim
   with husband and children
Szajbowicz, Fajgele bas Rywen
Szajbowicz, Fajwel ben Gecel
Szajbowicz (Gotlib), Frajdla
Szajbowicz, Gecel ben Icek
Szajbowicz, Gecel ben Josef-Baruch
Szajbowicz, Gecel ben Lajb
Szajbowicz, Hersz ben Mojsze-Majer
Szajbowicz, Hudes bas Mojsze-Majer
   with husband and children
Szajbowicz, Icek ben Abraham-Chaim
   and children
Szajbowicz, Icek ben Gecel
Szajbowicz, Josef ben Icek
Szajbowicz, Josef-Baruch
   ben Abraham-Chaim and children
Szajbowicz, Josef-Baruch ben Lajb
Szajbowicz, Josef-Baruch
   ben Rywen and wife
Szajbowicz, Laja
   bas Chaim and children
Szajbowicz, Lajbel
Szajbowicz, Masza
Szajbowicz, Mendel ben Rywen
Szajbowicz, Mindel
Szajbowicz, Mojsze ben Gecel
Szajbowicz, Mojszele ben Gecel
Szajbowicz, Mojsze-Majer
   ben Josef-Baruch
Szajbowicz (Kaczka), Pessa bas Hercke
Szajbowicz, Rajca [Raitsa]
   with two children
Szajbowicz, Rajza-Gitel
Szajbowicz (Wencel), Rajza-Gitel
   bas Abraham-Chaim
Szajbowicz, Rajzla bas Icek
Szajbowicz (Gliksman), Rajzela
   with husband and children
Szajbowicz, Rechel bas Judel-Sojfer

Szajbowicz (Kuke), Ruchel
Szajbowicz, Ruchele bas Majlech-Majer
Szajbowicz, Ruchele bas Uri
Szajbowicz, Rywa
Szajbowicz, Rywen ben Josef-Baruch
Szajbowicz, Rywka bas Mojsze-Majer
Szajbowicz, Rywka bas Rywen
Szajbowicz, Rywka-Laja
    bas Abraham-Chaim
Szajbowicz, Szajndla bas Szulem-Lajzer
Szajbowicz, Szmuel ben Mojsze-Majer
Szajbowicz, Szulem ben Uri
Szajbowicz (Hauzer), Tema
Szajbowicz, Uri ben Josef-Baruch
Szajbowicz, Zalman ben Icek
Szajnberg, Efroim ben Nechemia
Szajnberg, Mojsze-Kalman
    ben Nechemia
Szajnberg, Nechemia ben Josef
Szajnberg, Rywka bas Josef
Szmirgold, Cema [Tsema]
    with two children
Szmirgold (Bocian), Chaja-Rywka
Szmukler, Golda bas Daniel
Szotenberg, Boris and family
Szotland, Abraham-Mechel ben Icek
Szotland, Icek ben Abraham-Mechel
Szotland, Izrael ben Icek
Szotland, Mojsze ben Icek
Sztajnberg, Laja
Sztajnberg, Marjem
Sztajnberg, Mojsze
Sztajnberg, Rywcia
Sztajnberg, Szlama
Sztajnberg-Frydman, Sura
Sztajnman, Abramele
    ben Mojsze-Lajb
Sztajnman, Berl
Sztajnman, Chaim
Sztajnman, Dwojra
Sztajnman, Ester
    with husband and children
Sztajnman, Ita
    with husband and children
Sztajnman, Laja

Sztajnman, Marjem
Sztajnman, Mojsze-Lajb
Sztajnman, Rajzla
    with husband and children
Sztajnman, Rywka-Bajla
Sztark, Jakub
Sztark, Sura-Liba
Szufleder, Mordka
Szulman, Fajga bas Mojsze
Szulman, Majer ben Mojsze
Szulman, Mojsze and wife
Szulzinger, Abraham-Icek
    ben Pinkus-Szlama
Szulzinger, Dawid-Cwi [Tsvi]
    ben Nusen-Majer
Szulzinger, Ester-Laja bas Dawid-Cwi
Szulzinger, Małka
Szulzinger, Pinkus-Szlama
    ben Dawid-Cwi
Szulzinger, Symcha ben Pinkus-Szlama
Szulzinger, Szajndla-Chasia
    bas Elja-Majer
Szulzinger, Taubele bas Dawid-Cwi
Szwarc, Aron
Szwarc, Aron
Szwarc, Motel ben Dawid
Szymkowicz, Dawid
Tabacznik (Fogel), Frajda bas Icek
Tabacznik, Heniek
    ben Mojsze-Mordka
Tabacznik, Mojsze-Mordka
Talkowska, Jomka-Fajgusia
Talkowska, Rajcia
Talkowski, Josi
Talkowski, Nusen
Tendler, Benjamin ben Szmuel
Tendler, Jerachmiel ben Benjamin
Tendler, Szajndla bas Jakub
Tendler, Szyfra bas Benjamin
Topolewicz, Abraham
Topolewicz, Abraham ben Izrael
Topolewicz, Icel [Itsel] ben Abraham
Topolewicz, Izrael ben Abraham
Topolewicz, Nachman
Topolewicz, Rywka

LIST OF BRZEZINY MARTYRS

Topolewicz, Szlama-Lajb
Tryber, Baruch ben Hersz
Tryber, Hersz ben Efraisz
Tryber (Sandowska), Hudes bas Efroim
Tryber, Rywka bas Hersz
Tryber, Sura bas Efroim
Tuszyńska (Zagon), Róża
Tuszyński, Abraham
Tuszyński, Arcze (Arje?)
Tuszyński, Elja ben Abraham
Tyll, Chaja bas Mojsze
Tyll, Icek ben Mojsze
Tyll, Icek ben Mordka
Tyll, Jechiel ben Mojsze
Tyll, Josef ben Mojsze
Tyll, Majer ben Mordka
Tyll, Małka
Tyll, Małka bas Mordka
Tyll, Mojsze
Tyll, Mordka and wife
Tyll, Rywka bas Mojsze
Tyll, Temar bas Mojsze
Tymowicz, Chaim ben Mojsze
   and family
Tymowicz, Elka
Tymowicz, Mojsze
Wachler, Aszer ben Szulem
Wachler, Ester-Ruchel bas Jakub-Icek
Wajnberg, Abraham
Wajnberg, Mania bas Majer
Wajnberg, Zysia
Wencel, Ester-Chana bas Jechiel-Majer
Wencel, Fiszel ben Jechiel-Majer
Wencel, Icek-Mendel ben Jechiel-Majer
Wencel, Jechiel-Majer
Wencel, Rajza-Gitel
Werdyger, Mojsze
Winer, Sala bas Wolf
Winer, Regina bas Majer
Winter, Cwi [Tsvi] ben Jakub
Winter, Ester
Winter, Fiszel
   ben Szlama-Eljasz [Elijah]
Winter, Genendl
Winter, Herszel ben Szlama-Eljasz
Winter, Jakub ben Mordka
Winter, Jakub ben Mordka
Winter, Majer ben Szlama-Eljasz
Winter, Pawel ben Szlama-Eljasz
Winter, Pinia [Pinkus?] ben Mordka
Winter (Lipkowicz), Regina bas Fiszel
Wiślicka, Golda bas Izrael
Wiślicka, Marjem
Wiślicki, Abraham ben Izrael
Wiślicki, Dawid ben Izrael
Wiślicki, Jojne ben Izrael
Wizel, Baruch-Mordka
Wizel, Gitel bas Baruch-Mordka
Wizel, Sura
Wołkowicz, Abraham
Wołkowicz, Abraham
   ben Chaim-Mordka
Wołkowicz, Abraham
   ben Jakub-Mojsze
Wołkowicz, Chaim-Mordka
Wołkowicz, Chaim-Mordka
   ben Jakub-Mojsze
Wołkowicz, Chana bas Pinkus
Wołkowicz, Dwojra bas Jakub-Mojsze
Wołkowicz, Fajga bas Aron
Wołkowicz, Izrael ben Jakub-Mojsze
Wołkowicz, Jakub-Mojsze ben Bendet
Wołkowicz, Laja bas Jakub-Mojsze
Wołkowicz, Lajbel ben Jakub-Mojsze
Wołkowicz, Małka bas Jakub-Mojsze
Wołkowicz, (Krengel) Marisia
   bas Fiszel
Wołkowicz, Mordka ben Lajbel
Wołkowicz, Perla bas Berl
Wołkowicz, Wolf ben Jakub-Mojsze
Wołkowska, Chaja
Wołkowska, Dina
Wołkowska, Matel
Wołkowski, Abraham
Wołkowski, Bernard ben Icze
Wołkowski, Icze ben Abraham
Wołkowski, Kalman ben Abraham
Wołkowski, Mojsze ben Abraham
   and son
Wołkowski, Moryc ben Icze

Wolman, Izaak
Wolman, Sura-Ita bas Lajb
Wrocławska, Rywka bas Szmuel
Wrocławski, Fiszel ben Herszel
Zagon, Elka
Zagon, Etka
Zagon, Gelusia bas Lajzer
Zagon, Icek ben Szyja
Zagon, Jochwet bas Hinda-Rywka
Zagon, Lajzer
Zagon, Lajzer ben Alter
Zagon, Różka (Jakub)
Zagon, Szyja ben Icek-Majer-Alter
Zagon, Witek-Gedajla ben Szyja
Zajdman, Icze
Zalcszajn, Szymon
Zalcsztajn, Binem Icek
Zalcsztajn, Bluma
Zalcsztajn, Brajndla
Zalcsztajn, Josef
Zalcsztajn, Szlama
Zelig, Abraham
Zelig, Efroim
Zelig, Genendl
Zelig, Icek and Perla
Zelig, Laja
Zelig, Majer
Zelig, Mendel
Zelig, Ruchele
Zelig, Szoel
Zelig, Szymon
Zelman, Alta
Zelman, Mendel
Zinger, Alter-Jechiel and Hania
Zinger, Icek ben Welwel [Velvel]
Zinger, Mojsze ben Welwel
Zinger, Welwel and Chaja
Zucker [see Cuker]
Zuckerman [see Cukerman]
Żychlińska [Zhychlińska], Regina
  bas Lajzer
Żychliński, Lajzer ben Lajbele
Żychliński, Szulem ben Icek and wife
Zygmunt, Hersz ben Mojsze
Zygmunt, Jechiel ben Mojsze
Zygmunt, Mojsze
Zygmunt, Mojsze
Zygmunt, Mojsze ben Elja
Zygmunt, Motek
Zygmunt, Rajzla
Zylberberg, Abraham-Jakub ben Ayjzyk
Zylberberg, Chaim ben Lajb
Zylberberg, Herszel ben Bencion
Zylbertson, Abraham
Żytnicka, Szprynca
Żytnicki, Zacharjasz

Alef (A)

IN SACRED MEMORY
of

Bursztajn, Szajndla (Abramowicz) bas Dawid, 50 years old, and her sons (from right): **Mordechai, Machel**, and **Abraham**—murdered

Abramowicz Machla
born 1875
died 1917

Abramowicz Dawid
born 1863
died 1916

Bursztajn, Jankiel—murdered

Bursztajn, Mojsze-Szmul ben Dawid—died in Brzeziny at age 64

Bursztajn, Perla-Laja bas Mojsze-Zev [Neifeld]—died in Łódź

Bursztajn, Rywen-Hersz ben Mojsze-Szmul, age 50
— murdered in the ghetto

Bursztajn, Fiszel ben Mojsze-Szmul
—murdered in World War I

Bursztajn, Josef—murdered at age 48

Estusz, Chaja-Gitla (Bursztajn) bas Mojsze-Szmul, age 48
— murdered in Auschwitz

Tobiasz, Jankiel, his wife, **Perla (Abramowicz)**, and their children: **Mechele (Marcel)**, 10 years old, and **Dawidl**, 7 years old—murdered

Walter [Wołek] Burstein (Philadelphia)

IN ETERNAL MEMORY

OF MY FAMILY

Murdered by the Hitler assassins

My father **Jakub Amzel (Szydlowcer)**
—murdered at age 78

My mother **Lipcia Amzel**
—deported from Brzeziny at age 72

My sister, **Jenta,** with her husband, **Mojsze Fensterman,** together with their daughter, age 20

My sister, **Chaja,** with her husband, **Lajbel Gerszon,** together with their two children: **Abrahaml**, age 19, and **Herszele**, age 14

Frymet and **Szmul Kohn**, age 25, with their children: **Mendel**, age 11, and **Herszele**, age 4

Icek Hersz Frydman, age 31

Icek Aufrychter, age 31

Chana Zylberwaser
(Paris, France)

IN SACRED MEMORY

Ikka, Trajna

born in 1845—died in 1927

TO THE ETERNAL MEMORY

Ikka, Jojne (father)
—murdered at age 62

Ikka, Pesa (mother, from **Zylberberg** family)—murdered

Ikka, Róża (sister)
—murdered at age 25

Ikka, Fela (sister)
—murdered at age 18

Ikka, Sonia (sister)
—murdered at age 14

Ikka, Ajzykl (brother)
—murdered at age 7

Helen Orensztajn (Ikka)
(Detroit, Michigan)

IN ETERNAL MEMORY

Badower, Ruchla, age 39,
and her sister,
Fox [Fuks], Libcia, age 43
murdered in the Łódź ghetto

IN ETERNAL MEMORY of
MY NEVER-FORGOTTEN SON

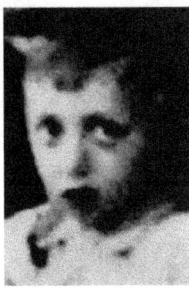

Bocian, Abraham-Gerszon, born in
Brzeziny 1930, murdered in Auschwitz 1944

Bocian, Dawid
(State of Israel)

Sura-Jachet
his wife
born in 1903
murdered in 1942

Bercholc, Luzer
born in 1903
murdered in 1942

[B] **Beyz**

IN ETERNAL MEMORY

Baron
Josef-Hersz

Baron
Abraham Majer

Fela Baron with her husband
Chaim Richter

IN ETERNAL MEMORY

Bekermus, Anszel ben Abraham
born in 1900, murdered in Brzeziny in 1941
Bekermus (Goldwaser), Chaja-Gitel
his wife, born in 1902
murdered in the Łódź ghetto in 1943

IN ETERNAL MEMORY
of

Blajman, Reb Abraham
died 11 Adar 1935 in New York
at age 72

Blajman, Laja
died 19 Adar 1943 in New York
at age 80

IN SACRED MEMORY
of all the victims

our sister, brother-in-law, and children:

Goldberg-Blajman, Basia
Goldberg Naftali

their children:

Towa-Ruchel, age 21
Dobryś, age 17
Icze-Mendel, age 16

Sylvia Keselman-Blajman
Jehuda Blajman

Blajman, Elisha, died in
1948 in New York at age 21

YIZKOR MEMORIAL SECTION

IN ETERNAL MEMORY

Fajgele bas Kasriel
third wife of
**Reb Chaim-Icek
Nisenberg**

His first wife
Marjem
died in Brzeziny

My mother,
Chaja-Dwojra
second wife of my father,
Reb Chaim-Icek,
died in Brzeziny
at age 28

**Chaim-Icek ben Izrael
Nisenberg**
died in Brzeziny
Erev Rosh Hashanah 1916
at age 82

Their Children and Grandchildren:

**Izrael
ben Chaim-Icek**
died in Tomaszów

Gitel
and her husband
Arje Rozenblum
(lived in Tomaszów)
and their children:
Manuele, Zlata-Laja,
and **Jechiel**, deceased

Rywka
with her husband
**Herszel Tajtelbaum
(Ajnbinder)**
deceased

Chajele
and her husband
**Lajzer Rozenblum
(Malarz)**
and their children:
**Marjem, Gołda,
Abraham-Dawid,
Różka, Mojsze, Arje,**
and **Bencion**
all were murdered

my brother
Kasriel
died in New York
in 1917

my brother
Jonah Berg
died in New York

my sister
Ruchel Grynfeld
died in Cardiff, Wales
(England)

my brother
Abraham Berg
died in New York in 1956

Reb Herszel Tajtelbaum
(Herszel Ajnbinder)

Szwarc (Tajtelbaum), Sura bas Herszel, her husband, **Chaim-Icek,** their daughter, **Marjem,** and their son, **Josef**—murdered

Rotman (Rozenblum), Marjem bas Lajzer, her husband, **Icek,** their daughter, **Gitel,** and their son—all murdered

Rozenblum, Sura-Gitel, **Zlata-Laja,** and **Fela**—murdered

Giml [G]

IN ETERNAL MEMORY

Grosman, Emanuel-Ajzyk
ben Abraham-Szaja
died 2 Iyar 1944
his wife
Ester-Chana bas Jechiel-Chaim
died 24 Iyar 1937

David Grosman

IN ETERNAL MEMORY
of

Grundsztajn Rywka (Manis)	Grundsztajn Abraham
deceased *yortsayt*: March 27	murdered by the Nazi villains

S. Stein (Los Angeles)

IN ETERNAL MEMORY
of
My Children:
Badower, Hudes, Frajdele, and **Balciele**
murdered by the Nazi villains
My Parents:
Badower, Luzer-Dawid and **Szajndel**
1858–1939

Aron Badower (Winnipeg, Canada)

Bursztajn, Mojsze-Szmul and family
See **Abramowicz**
Burakowski, Icek and family
See **Stal, Mojsze-Josef**

IN ETERNAL MEMORY
of my Parents
Bialek, Naftali ben Jakub, died 1905 at age 64
Bialek, Chana (from **Horn** family)
died in 1934 at age 93

Masza Bialek

Bercholc, Herszel (Herszel Shakher)

IN SACRED MEMORY
of
my mother **Bercholc, Ester**, deported from Brzeziny at age 60
my sister, **Bercholc, Chana**, murdered at age 28 with her husband and child

Szmul Bercholc (Paris, France)

IN ETERNAL MEMORY
of Our Parents
Bercholc, Jankiel and **Perla**
Wajnberg, Zyse and **Mania**
all murdered in the Łódź ghetto in 1943

*Zalman and Perla Berholz
(Toronto, Canada)*

Krakowiak, Lajzer, age 62, and his wife, **Pesa bas Izrael-Gerszon**, age 50
—murdered

Ginsberg, Mordechai-Wolf, age 43, his wife **Chana-Rywka bas Mojsze**, age 40, their children: **Nemi**, age 17, and **Benjamin**, age 12—murdered

In Sacred Memory of My Beloved Husband, **Maks Gukman**
—murdered in a camp at age 57
Tema Gukman (Paris, France)

Krauze, Gerszon
—murdered in Auschwitz at age 47

Michrowski, Dawid-Mendel, age 62, his wife, **Masza**, age 60, their children: **Laja**, 30, and **Chana**, 28—murdered
Grosman, Aszer (Stockholm, Sweden)

Oratowski, Lemel—died in 1914 at age 56
Oratowska, Fajga—died in 1924 at age 56
Benkel, Rywen—murdered in 1942 at age 42
Mrs. Ch. Farber (Toronto, Canada)

Ikka, Aron—murdered in 1942 at age 54
Ikka, Laja—murdered in 1943 at age 52
Ikka, Abraham (Toronto, Canada)

Goldkranc, Icek-Lajb ben Jakub-Hersz and his wife, **Regina**, their little son 3 years old—murdered
Szlama Goldkranc (Melbourne, Australia)

Gips, Reb Abraham—murdered
Gips, Szajndel—murdered
Gips, Jakub-Ber—murdered
Gips, Moris—murdered
Wajnberg, Abraham—murdered
Wajnberg, Róża—murdered
Rachela Gips-Blumsztajn (Melbourne, Australia)

IN ETERNAL MEMORY
of the Family
Dawid and Małka Gutkind

Icze Gutkind   Małka Gutkind   Maks Gutkind

Dawid (brother of **Mojsze-Majer**)
—died in 1897
Małka—died on the second day of Passover (April 1932)
Icze—died May 1956
Róża—died in 1934
Emanuel (Maks)—died in 1944

Goldkranc (Wiślicka), Rywka bas Dawid
—murdered at age 20

Grosman, Dawid-Melech, age 67, his wife, **Cywia**, age 52, their children: **Balcia**, age 25, **Laja**, age 23, **Ruchel**, age 22, **Wolf**, age 19
—all murdered by the Nazi assassins
Frajdenrajch, Ruchel (Grosman)
—murdered in Bergen-Belsen at age 22
Rozenberg, Sura-Frajdel bas Aszer
—murdered in the Łódź ghetto at age 64
Rozenberg, Ester bas Mojsze
—murdered in the Łódź ghetto at age 26
Rozenberg, Mania-Róża bas Mojsze
—murdered at age 24
Rozenberg, Aszer ben Mojsze
—murdered at age 20
Aszer Grosman (Sweden)

Wiślicka, Marjem bas Aszer
—murdered in the Łódź ghetto at age 65

Ikka, Icek ben Izrael Gerszon
—murdered at age 45

IN ETERNAL MEMORY
of my beloved parents

Dymant, Icze-Ber
— died 11 Heshvan 1915 at age 88
Dymant, Małka
— died 8 Tevet 1914 at age 78
Dymant, Jakub-Dawid
— murdered by the Nazi assassins

Gerszon Diamond

IN ETERNAL MEMORY

Tauba-Ruchel
his wife
born in 1856
died in 1928

**Dymant
Majer**
born in 1856
died in 1928

In Eternal Memory
Jechiel-Mojsze and Rywka Gotlib

among the outstanding upright people in town
and prominent community leaders

*Abraham-Jakub Gotlib
(Los Angeles, California)*

In Eternal Memory
Benjamin and Frymet Gotlib

Leon Gotlib (Los Angeles, California)

Grosman, Abraham-Izrael — deceased
Grosman, Ester-Chana
— died 24 Iyar 1937
Grundsztajn, Lajbuś
— born 1853, died in Brzeziny in 1935
Grundsztajn, Chaja
— born 1862, died in 1942
Grundsztajn, Jerachmiel — born 1896,
died in the Łódź ghetto in 1943
Grundsztajn, Chana
— died in the Łódź ghetto in 1943
Grundsztajn, Jochwet
— died in Russia in 1944
Grundsztajn, Hersz-Icze — murdered in
Gałkówek with 300 Brzeziner Jews

In Eternal Memory of My Family

Grynbaum (Zhirardover), Josef-Zanwel
— murdered at age 67
Grynbaum, Laja — murdered at age 66
Karger, Icek-Mendel, age 47, his wife,
Szajndel, and their son, **Hersz-Lajb**, age 17
Wajnkranc, Hercke, his wife, **Fania,** and
their daughter, **Mindel-Fajgel**

*Charles and Gertrude Grynbaum
(Los Angeles, California)*

Josef and **Fajga Grynholc-Szotland**
1886–1929

M. Grynholc (Winnipeg)

Gewirc, Naftali — murdered in 1941 at age 41,
his wife, **Sura** — murdered in 1941 at age 41
along with their children: **Arje**, age 19,
Heniek, age 17, **Szaja**, age 14, **Rajzel**, age 12

A. Gewirtz (Toronto, Canada)

In Eternal Memory of My Parents

Grynszpan, Szymon-Josef, age 43, his wife,
Chaja-Szajndel (Gerszt), age 42 — murdered

Herszel Grynszpan (Australia)

IN ETERNAL MEMORY
of

my mother

Chana (Sperling)

murdered in 1943
at age 63

my father

**Dymant
Aron-Hersz
(Urka)**

died in 1919
at age 46

my grandmother

Dymant, Rajzel

died in Brzeziny
in 1926
at age 93

my grandfather

Dymant, Eliezer

died in Brzeziny
during
the First World War
at age 86

from left to right:
Jakub-Dawid Dymant, **Fela Działoszyńska**, and **Jakub-Aron Badower**

Dymant, Blume, Sonia-Szajndel, and **Abraham**—murdered
Dymant, George—died in New York in 1946
Dymant, Jakub-Dawid—murdered in 1942 at age 63

Emilia, his wife—died in 1921; their daughter, **Stefa**
—died at age 9 in Moscow; **Bela**—died in 1924

Jan Dymant *(New York)*

IN ETERNAL MEMORY

Frymet
his wife
born in 1865
murdered in 1942

**Dymant
Josef**
born in 1861
murdered in 1942

Dymant, Ester
born in 1903 — murdered in 1942

IN ETERNAL MEMORY

Dymant, Mordechai-Icek — born in 1892
Szajndel-Bela, his wife, born in 1895
— murdered in the ghetto

Dymant, Abraham, born in 1889
Bajla, his wife, born in 1896, and their
sons: **Mordechai**, born in 1914, **Lajbel**,
born in 1920, **Majer** born in 1927
— all murdered in the ghetto

In Eternal Memory
Pauline Diamont, died at age 26

Leon and Paul Diamont

IN ETERNAL MEMORY
of my beloved parents, sister, and brother

Diamond, Chaim-Ber
died in 1936, age 74

Diamond, Alta-Laja
died in 1929, age 63

Diamond, Bajla
died in 1924, age 26

Diamond, Abraham
died in 1936 in New York
age 37

Dymant, Mojsze-Icek
died after World War II
in France

*Joan Diamond
(Los Angeles, California)*

In Eternal Memory

Dembiński, Mordechai
born in 1910 — murdered in 1942

IN ETERNAL MEMORY

Gołda, his wife
born in 1885

Hauzer, Chaim
born in 1883

their children:

Rywen

born in 1930—murdered in the ghetto

Róża
born in 1921

Frajdl
born in 1919

Hey [H]

IN ETERNAL MEMORY

Jochwet
his wife
died in Brzeziny
on 24 Nissan 1940

Szaja Hauzer
died in Brzeziny
on 24 Nissan 1940

Louis and Aba Hauzer

IN ETERNAL MEMORY

Hauzer, Majer ben Szaja
died in New York in 1949 at age 59

Hauzer, Pejsach ben Szaja,
and his wife, **Sala**—died
Hauzer, Majer—died
Hauzer, Wolf ben Szaja
—died in 1920 at age 14
Hauzer, Eliasz, with his wife and
children—murdered
Hauzer, Jechiel, with his wife, **Laja**
—murdered
Hauzer, Aron, and his wife, **Ruchel**
—murdered

IN ETERNAL MEMORY OF OUR FAMILY

Hamer, Abraham
murdered in Auschwitz
at age 36

Hamer, Gołda
died in 1930
at age 50

Hamer, Mojsze
died in 1935
at age 70

Brandszaft, Icek
murdered in Auschwitz
at age 31

Berger, Sura
murdered in Auschwitz
at age 38

Herszfinger, Chaja
murdered in Auschwitz
at age 45

Hamer, Gołda
born in 1930
murdered in the
Brzeziny ghetto
in 1942

The child is a grandchild
of **Reb Mojsze Hamer**
born on the ship Exodus
4 September 1947 and
died 20 September 1947

**Hamer, Tema
(Działoszyńska)**
born in 1900
murdered in the Łódź
ghetto in 1943

IN ETERNAL MEMORY

Hamer, Lajbuś
— murdered in 1944 at age 64

Hamer, Dwojra— died in 1917 at age 37

Hamer, Icek and **Dwojra (Golas)**
— murdered in 1942
with their five sons and one daughter

Hamer, Zelda-Perla, with her husband and son— murdered

Hamer, Mojsze and **Jenta**— murdered in 1942 with two sons

Hamer, Dawid and **Rywka**— murdered at age 25 with their child

Hamer, Małka— murdered at age 22

Hamer, Pinkus— murdered at age 20

Kujawski, Dan-Aszer— murdered at age 30 with his three children: **Dwojre-Laja**, 12, **Chaim-Hersz**, 11, **Abraham-Josef**, 9

Mr. And Mrs. S. Zysholc
(Toronto, Canada)

In Sacred Memory of My Husband

Hauzer, Josef, deported to Auschwitz on 11 July 1942 at age 48

Juliet Hauzer
(Paris)

In Eternal Memory

Hercberg, Gerszon and **Gitel**
both born in 1889
— murdered in Brzeziny in 1943 at age 54

Leon Hercberg
(Toronto, Canada)

IN ETERNAL MEMORY

Ruchel, his wife murdered by the Nazi villains

Jakub ben Josef-Efroim Herszenberg, died in Russia 27 Shevat 1920

their children:
Fajgele, Dawid, and **Sara**
all murdered by the Nazi villains

Herszenberg, Jechiel-Mechel— died in Israel 14 October 1959

Helen Hendrykowska
daughter of Lajbele Hendrykowski

Jechiel Hendrik

Reb Lajbele Hendrykowski
and his wife

Rhoda Hendrik-Karpatkin

IN ETERNAL MEMORY

Wald, Natan, long-time member of the Brzeziny Town Council
—murdered in 1942 at age 45

Cyrel, his wife, died at age 45

his children: **Abraham-Eliasz, Sonia,** and **Hencia**

—all murdered in 1942

Szymszon Wald
Israel

IN SACRED MEMORY

Wajnkranc, Naftali and **Chana**

Wajnberg-Zygmuntowicz, Gencia

Wajnberg-Szaldajewska, Gucia

Wajnberg-Śrubka, Mindel

all murdered in the Brzeziny and Łódź ghettos

Majer Wajnkranc (Bakel)
(Melbourne, Australia)

Vov [V]   (VovVov = W)

IN ETERNAL MEMORY

of

| my unforgettable mother | my unforgettable husband |

Waldman Perele
(from the **Windheim** family)
died in Brzeziny
in 1924

Waldman Menachem
murdered in
the Łódź ghetto
in 1944

my unforgettable father
Reb Szmul Waldman
beaten to death by the Nazi assassins
on the way to the Łódź ghetto

my dear sister, **Pesa,** murdered in 1944

Chana Waldman
(Israel)

Mojsze-Dawid Szperling, 4 years old, torn from his mother's arms 15 May 1942

Benkel, Szoel (uncle)

Benkel, Sara (aunt)

Benkel, Icek (cousin)

Benkel, Ester-Laja (cousin)

Benkel, Fiszel (cousin)

Benkel, Chajele (cousin)

Niewiadowicz, Josel, with his wife, **Fajga**

Niewiadowicz, Herszel, **Róża**, and **Aron**

Niewiadowicz, Ester-Laja, **Fajwisz**, **Fiszel**, and **Chanele**

IN ETERNAL MEMORY
of our dear parents, brother, and sister

Winter, Lajbuś-Mendel—died in Brzeziny in 1918 at age 68

Winter (Bursztajn), Gitel
—murdered in Brzeziny at age 48

Winter, Jechiel Estusz
—killed for carrying out an act of sabotage against the Nazis

Mr. and Mrs. M. Winter
(Australia)

IN ETERNAL MEMORY
of the Benkel family

Benkel, Abraham-Lajb
—died in Łódź ghetto at age 57

Benkel (Rozenstrauch), Dwojra
—murdered in Auschwitz at age 55

Benkel, Fiszel
—murdered in Auschwitz at age 30

Benkel, Elija
—murdered in Brzeziny at age 24

Benkel, Hil
—murdered in a camp near Poznań at age 18

Benkel, Dobryś
—died in Łódź at age 19

Aba Szperling
—sent away in a black wagon 13 May 1942 and gassed

YIZKOR MEMORIAL SECTION

IN ETERNAL MEMORY

Zajdman, Dawid ben Chaim
(Luzer Melamed's stepson)
died in New York at age 39

His wife, Dina Zajdman, and children

In Eternal Memory

Reb Luzer Betcajg
(**Luzer Melamed**)
died in 1941 in Brzeziny at age 72
and
my mother, **Szajna-Rywka** (**Monat**)
killed in 1942 in Łódź
at age 58

Helen Atlas
Boston, Massachusetts

In Eternal Memory
of my Unforgettable Parents

Zelig, Binem—murdered in the Łódź ghetto at age 53
Zelig, Sara—murdered in Brzeziny in 1941 at age 53

My Grandparents

Zelig, Reb Mojsze-Pinkus, long-time member of town council and community leader

Zelig, Ester—murdered

M. Klajn-Zelig
Toronto, Canada

Zayen [Z]

IN ETERNAL MEMORY

Żychliński, Syna   **Żychliński, Chaim**
(**Frankel**)

Żychliński, Icze

Żychliński, Frankel   **Żychliński, Luzer**

IN ETERNAL MEMORY
of our parents

Fajgele Tuszyńska

Icek Tuszyński

In sacred remembrance of our sister and brother and their families who were killed by the German villains

Tuszyńska-Szwajcer, Rywkele, murdered at age 50

Szwajcer, Berysz—died in the Łódź ghetto; his child died in 1928 at age 9

Tuszyński, Zajnwel—shot by the Nazis at age 46; his wife, **Dora,** and two children: **Fredzia** and **Izy**—murdered in Majdanek

Tuszyński, Szymon—died in 1932 at age 33

Tuszyński, Tewel—murdered in Auschwitz at age 43

Tuszyński, Hersz—murdered at age 37

Helen, Pola, and Welwel Tuszyński

In sacred memory of our parents

Tuszyński, Melech, age 50, and **Frajda**, age 42

Chaim Fiszel, age 23, and **Regina**, age 12

Uncles:
Tuszyński, Jechiel Majer, and his wife and children

Tuszyński, Abraham, and his wife and children

Mr. and Mrs. S. Rotholc
(Toronto, Canada)

Tes [T]

IN ETERNAL MEMORY
of our parents

Sura-Ita Tuszyńska Szymszon Tuszyński
and
Berg, Fajga, wife of **Chaim-Icek Berg**

MR. AND MRS. MAX TYSON
(Brooklyn, New York)

Chaja Sułkowicz

Herszel Tuszyński

In Sacred Memory

Loomanitz, Ester-Fajga

Buki, Aron-Ber—murdered
Buki, Bajla-Bina (Loomanitz)
 —murdered
Moniek and **Josef Buki**
 —both disappeared in Russia

In Sacred Memory

Hinda bas Abraham-Nachum, his wife, born in 1868 died in Brzezin in 1935

Lichtreger, Icek born in 1863 in Kishinev, murdered in Brzeziny ghetto

In Sacred Memory

my father, **Eli-Nisen Tuszyński**
 —died in Brzeziny in 1931
my mother, **Rywka-Laja**
 —died in Brzeziny in 1926

Syna Tuszyński
(Rio de Janiero, Brazil)

Lamed [L]

In Sacred Memory

Lachowski, Abraham
(adopted name
Milsztajn), age 41,
and his wife,
Chajka, age 41
murdered in France

In Sacred Memory

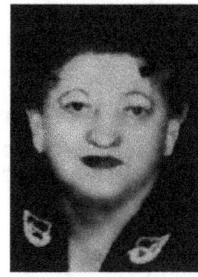

Małka Ruchel Laska, age 65
died 31 May 1961

In Sacred Memory

his wife, **Chana-Laja**

Łęczycki, Mordechai

murdered by the Nazis in the ghetto

IN ETERNAL MEMORY

Lefkowicz, Fiszel, born in 1875, his wife, **Ester-Małka**, born in 1879, their son, **Abraham**, born in 1914
—all murdered in the ghetto

Lefkowicz, Lemel—murdered at age 62
his wife, **Perla**—murdered at age 60
their children:
Lajzer, age 29, **Ruchel**, age 19
—all murdered

David Lefkowicz

In Sacred Memory

Lenga, Szulem—died in 1917 at age 32
Lenga, Henie
—murdered in 1942 at age 51
Fogel, Abraham
—murdered in 1942 at age 62
Fogel, Hudes—murdered in 1942 at age 53

K. Lenga
(Toronto, Canada)

In Memory of My Beloved Parents

Lustig, Alter and **Ruchel-Liba**
  my sisters and brothers-in-law:
Horn, Gecel and **Rywka**
Flamholc, Fiszel and **Ester**
Lustig, Anszel, Szaja, and **Wolf**

Bela Szyf-Lustig
(Melbourne, Australia)

Lamed [L]

IN ETERNAL MEMORY

Lachman, Reb Herszel
died 12 Nisan 1949 in Tel-Aviv

Lachman, Chaja-Sura
died 13 Heshvan 1915 in Brzeziny

Lachman Brothers
(Miami, Florida)

In Sacred Memory

Jakubowicz, Chaim-Dawid
—deported from Paris with his children:
Chana, Szmul, Josef, and **Abraham**

Łęczycki, Mojsze and **Chana**
—deported from France

Pinczewska, Perla-Laja—deported from Brzeziny with her children

Amzel, Mojsze; with four children
—deported from Brzeziny

Kirszbaum, Dawid; with his wife and son
—deported from Brzeziny

Kirszbaum, Sara, her husband (husband's name unknown), and children
—deported from Brzeziny

You will be engraved in my heart forever.

Mme. Jakubowicz
(Paris, France)

IN ETERNAL MEMORY

Lerer, Szulem ben Izrael-Icek and his wife, **Frajdel**—died in Brzeziny

Lerer, Symcha ben Szulem

murdered in the Łódź ghetto

Lerer, Szprynca (Gan)

his wife, murdered in the Łódź ghetto

Lerer, Jakub-Hersz
murdered in the Łódź ghetto at age 26, with his wife, **Hinda,** and their child, **Szulem**

Lerer, Szaja-Awigdor
murdered in the Łódź ghetto at age 20

Lerer, Mania
died in 1929 at age 21

Lerer, Izrael-Icek ben Symcha,
and his wife, **Laja** murdered in the Łódź ghetto with their little son, **Mojsze**

Richter (Lerer), Cypa, and her children: **Chaim, Izraelik, Aszer, Mania,** and **Nachman**—murdered in the Łódź ghetto

Kon, Szlama ben Szaja-Awigdor, age 56, and his children: **Jechiel, Jochwet, Nacha,** and **Małka**—murdered in Koluszki

Kon, Pinchasl, and his wife, **Frajdel** —murdered in the Łódź ghetto their son, **Hersz-Lajb**—murdered in Bergen-Belsen at age 32

Małka Lerer-Singer
(Montreal, Canada)

Lerer, Chaim-Wolf ben Mojsze
—murdered in Poznań at age 17

Lerer, Abraham ben Symcha
—murdered in Auschwitz at age 15

Lerer, Aron ben Szlama, and his wife, **Krajndl (Fuks)**, age 52, and their four children: **Chaiml, Mania, Izraelik,** and **Wolf**—murdered in the Łódź ghetto

Sara Lerer-Szajbowicz
(New York)

In Eternal Memory

of my children

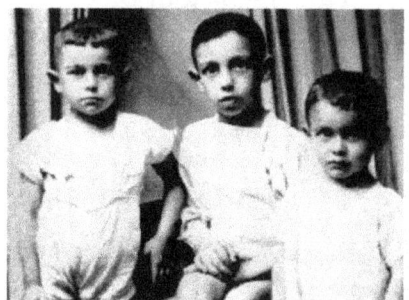

Herszel	Sender	Melech
born 1935	born 1932	born 1928

killed by the Nazi assassins

Morton Nowak
Los Angeles, California

In Eternal Memory

Miler, Majer—shot with 300 other Brzeziner Jews in the forest near Gałkówek

Miler, Chanka, his little daughter—murdered 15 May 1942 at age 2 years and 4 months

Tuszyński, Urcie, Mojsze-Izrael, and **Szlama-Szymon**—died in the Łódź ghetto

Tuszyńska, Chaja—died as a child

Tuszyńska-Topolewicz, Hendel—died

Tuszyński, Josef—died in 1939

Adopted parents:
Topolewicz, Chana—murdered in 1944
Topolewicz, Abraham—died in 1942

Fela Tuszyńska
(Melbourne, Australia)

In Sacred Memory

Moszkowicz, Sara, and family
(see: Aronów, A.)
Majerholc, Fajga
(see: Aronów, A.)

Mem [M]

IN ETERNAL MEMORY

Mojsze-Mordechai Mendlewicz
born in Brzeziny in 1895, died in the Łódź ghetto in 1942 or 1943

Abraham-Chaim Mendlewicz
born in Brzeziny in 1896, deported from Brzeziny when the ghetto was liquidated in 1942; from that time on, any sign of him was lost

In Eternal Memory

Mandel, Icze-Ber
born 1889

Fajga	Ita
his wife	their daughter
born in 1892	born in 1912

all murdered by the Nazi villains

IN ETERNAL MEMORY

Milsztajn, Cywia
his wife
died in Paris in 1934
at age 69

**Milsztajn
Chaim ben Abraham**
died in Brzeziny
in 1917 at age 54

**Fuks, Aron-Icek
(Tauba's)**
died in Paris in 1935
at age 62,
his wife, **Jachet
(Milsztajn)**
murdered at age 65

Milsztajn, Izrael, age 36
his wife, **Małka,** age 36

and their children:
Henri, age 11,
Jacques, age 8
all murdered in France

**Milsztajn, Josef ben
Chaim**
died in Paris in 1954
at age 62

Aufrychter, Szymon, 33, his wife, **Rywcia,** 33,
and their three children: **Cyna, Chajele,**
and **Herszel**—all murdered in France

Zylberberg, Szulem, age 55, his wife, **Cywka (Milsztajn),** age 53
their children:
Abraham-Michal, age 28, **Mordechai,** age 25, **Gitele,** age 19
—all murdered

Nun [N]

IN ETERNAL MEMORY

Nowak, Matel bas Jakub (Pakula)
murdered at age 49

Nowak, Zalman (Prusak)
murdered in the Łódź ghetto in 1942 at age 54

Nowak, Naftali ben Zalman—murdered at age 32

Nowak, Chaim-Nuchem ben Zalman
— murdered at age 25 with his wife,
Rajzel (Szydłowska)

Nowak, Chana bas Zalman
— murdered at age 28 with her two children:
Lajele, age 9, and **Josele,** age 6

Nowak Arcie ben Zalman
murdered at age 30

Igielski Henry ben Abraham-Lajb
died in Arizona at age 51

Igielska Chaja bas Icek-Luzer (Bimka)
murdered in Auschwitz at age 40

Igielski Abraham-Lajb ben Berl
murdered in the Łódź ghetto at age 53

**Pluśnik, Hudes
(bas Abraham-Lajb Igielski)**
murdered in Bergen-Belsen at age 29
with her husband, **Zalman,** and their
infant son, **Szajele,** only a few months old

**Najman, Surecia
(bas Abraham-Lajb Igielski)**
murdered at age 33 with
her husband, **Abraham,**
and their little daughter, **Chawcia**

Igielski, Dan-Aszer ben Abraham-Lajb, age 31, his wife, **Topcia (Klajnman)**,
and their 3-year-old **Chawciele**—all murdered by the Nazi assassins

In Eternal Memory of

Najman, Jecheskiel
deceased

Najman, Brucha
born 1870, died 1940

Harry, Machel, Wolf, and Charlie Newman
(Los Angeles, California)

In Eternal Memory
Nowak, Bajla-Chana bas Reb Motel
—died 31 March 1953 in New York

Ab. Nowak and children

In Eternal Memory of My Dear Parents:
Szymon and **Ita-Małka Nowak**

my brothers: **Szmul-Dawid** and **Mordechai**; my sister and brother-in-law: **Perla-Ruchel** and **Icek Goldberg,** and their son, **Wowe**; my nephew and niece: **Hersz** and **Fajgele Nowak**

Laja and Szlama Tajfel
(Lakewood, New Jersey)

In Memory of
my father, **Najman, Jojne,** and my mother, **Rajzel**; my brother-in-law, **M. Pilichowski,** my sister, **Bela,** and their two children; **Najman, Polia,** and her husband and two children; **Najman, Izraelik,** and his wife and two children; **Rozen, Abraham** and **Fela,** and their child

Najman, Fiszel (England)

In Eternal Memory of Our Parents
Aron and **Rywka (Bursztajn) Najman**
our brothers: **Mordechai, Pinkus, Izrael, Aszer,** and **Chaim**

Chana Lange, Mollie Frolich, Sally Weinrib, and Masza Kowalska
Isaac Kowalski and family

IN SACRED MEMORY
of

Najman Gołda-Kajla
bas Bajla-Perla
murdered

Najman Chaim-Jehuda
murdered in the
Łódź ghetto at age 62

Najman, Hendel,
and her daughter, **Perla (Percia)**

A. Dytman
(Brazil)

Ayen [E]

IN SACRED MEMORY
of my dearest ones

Efroimowicz (Szotland), Rywka
murdered in Auschwitz at age 52

Efroimowicz, Chaim-Majer—died in Brzeziny in 1922, age 36; had *heter-hoyroe* [rabbi credentials] and was a Gerer Hasid

Four daughters and a grandchild
Hasidic family of **Chaim-Majer** and **Rywka Efroimowicz**

Efroimowicz-Braun, Ruchel, and her little daughters: **Szyfrele, Esterl,** and **Marieml**
—murdered in Auschwitz at age 26

Efroimowicz, Ester
—murdered in Brzeziny at age 21

Efroimowicz, Blimele—murdered at age 20

Efroimowicz-Horn, Mindel
—murdered in Auschwitz with her husband, **Mojsze** (Fiszel Horn's son), and their little daughter, **Ester**

Dora Markus-Efroimowicz

To the Eternal Memory of **Maks Nusbaum**

Shirley Segal

To the Sacred Memory of
Newman, Ester bas Majer
—died in New York 17 March 1957, age 66
Newman, Isidor—died in New York

In Sacred Memory of our parents
Najman, Syna and **Rywa** (Kashe-makhers)

Mr. and Mrs. L. Rotter
(Toronto, Canada)

Samekh [S]

In Eternal Memory

Fajga Skurnik
born in 1878
died in New York
in 1957

Izrael Dawid Skurnik
born in 1878
died in 1924

In Sacred Memory

Sobowinsky, David-Lajb
—died in New York 23 Kislev 1939

Sobowinsky, Fajga-Brucha
—died in New York 9 Kislev 1939

Frankensztajn, Wolf
—died in Brzeziny 5 Shevat at age 49

Frankensztajn, Rywka
—died in Brzeziny 5 Elul at age 36

Sol Sobowinsky

In Eternal Memory
of my unforgettable
beloved husband
Frank, Abraham ben Szmul
died in New York
6 October 1959

Mrs. Minnie Frank

In Eternal Memory

Fiszer, Abraham-Ber, born in 1850
—murdered in the ghetto; his wife,
Frajdl, born in 1852—died in 1911

In Eternal Memory

Fiszel, Chaim-Israel
(Chaiml Blacharz)
born in 1874
murdered in Brzeziny

In Eternal Memory

Kraushorn, Mojsze-Jehuda and his wife,
Laja—murdered

Fiszel Kraushorn
(Rio de Janiero, Brazil)

IN ETERNAL MEMORY

Eksztajn, Fiszel (yortsayt: 19 Heshvan), his wife, **Zlata** (yortsayt: 21 Tevet), and their daughter, **Rajzel Lefkowicz**, who was murdered with her husband, **Dawid,** and their children

Rhoda Eksztajn-Czernik

Fey [F]

In Eternal Memory

Eliezer-Ze'ev ben Icek Fogel
died 22 April (13 Nisan) 1948 at age 51

In Sacred Memory

Fogel, Dwojra —murdered together with her four children: **Josele**, age 12, **Hersz-Wolf**, age 9, **Szaja**, age 6, **Icek**, age 3

Fogel, Icek, born in 1845—died in 1933

Fogel, Brucha, born in 1864—died in 1927

Abramcze Fogel (Toronto, Canada)

IN ETERNAL MEMORY

The Fuks family, from right to left:

Lipman Fuks, murdered by the Germans; **Icze Fuks**, murdered in Russia by the Denikin bandits; mother, **Molly Fuks**, died in Brzeziny at almost 90 years of age; **Ester Winter**, died; **Lajbuś Fuks**, died in Chemnitz, Germany, in 1926

Pola Fuks

Herszel Fuks

IN ETERNAL MEMORY
of

my murdered wife, **Tola**, and my two daughters: **Marja** and **Irena**

Fuks, Hersz ben Mojsze-Chaim
(a teacher in Brzeziny and Łódź) murdered in Auschwitz at age 42 with his wife, **Helen**, age 38, and their little daughter, **Laja**, age 5

The gravestone of **Mojsze-Chaim ben Szymon Fuks** (**Jehuda Fuks**' father) in the Brzeziny cemetery
Standing from left to right: **Jehuda**; his murdered wife, **Tauba**; mother, **Krajndel**; sister, **Masza-Chaja**; and brother, **Hersz**

Fuks Krajndel bas Jecheskiel
died in New York at age 76

Fuks Mojsze-Chaim ben Szymon
died in Brzeziny at age 33

Josef-Mendel ben Mojsze-Chaim
killed at age 21 during the Russian-Polish War

Fuks, Tauba bas Mordechai, a teacher (**Julius Fox**'s murdered wife) murdered in Auschwitz at the age of 45 with her two children: **Maryla**, age 17, and **Irena**, age 16

Pilichowski, Natalia—murdered in Auschwitz with her children: **Sławek**, age 20, **Ryś** [Ryszard], age 18

Tenenbaum, Mietek, age 44
Tenenbaum, Ruth, age 48
Tenenbaum, Henry, age 15
—murdered in Auschwitz

Krasowski, Dr. Władysław, age 50, his wife, **Nata**, age 48, their little daughter, **Alina**, age 6
—murdered in Auschwitz

Fuks, Josef-Mendel ben Mojsze-Chaim
—murdered while a soldier at the front at age 21

Nisenhaus, Rywen ben Michał
—died in Paris at age 65

Nisenhaus, Kuna
—murdered in Auschwitz at age 60

Nisenhaus, Michał ben Rywen
—murdered in Auschwitz at age 45

Pilichowski, Stach [Stanisław]
—murdered in the Łódź ghetto at age 50

Ester and Jehuda Fox
(New York)

In Eternal Memory

my mother **Marjem bas Josef**
—murdered in 1939
my father **Abraham Fuks**
—murdered in 1945

Max Fox (Miami)

In Eternal Memory

Szmul-Szaja and **Dwojra Flamholc**
Szlama-Hersz Rudnicki

Flamholc, Jakub,
Rudnicki, Henie

In Eternal Memory

Fuks, Abraham-Judel, and his wife, **Mindel** (Watemakher, also known as **Kolewizner** with the short finger)
—died in Brzeziny at age 57

Fuks, Mendel—died in Brzeziny, age 56

Fuks, Syna—deported and killed in France at age 58

Fuks, Szmul—died in Paris at age 50, long-time president of the Brzeziner Society in France

Fuks, Rafał—murdered in Dachau at age 56

Fuks, Wolf—deported and killed in France at age 37

Mojsze and Aron Fuks

In Eternal Memory of My Husband

Flajszer, Phillip
Active for many years in the Brzeziner Society and held various positions. Died in New York.

Mrs. Flajszer

In Sacred Memory

Frohman, Dwojre-Małka
murdered at age 66

Frohman, Jakub
murdered at age 63

Frohman, Szymon
murdered in the ghetto at age 33

Frohman, Fiszel
murdered in a camp at age 39

In Sacred Memory of My Parents and Family

who were murdered
during the great tragedy

Pilater, Emanuel ben Chaim
—died in the Łódź ghetto at age 55
Pilater, Perla bas Cwi-Mendel
—murdered in a camp at age 25[1]

their children:
    Matel-Fajga
      —murdered at age 35
    Towa—29
    Becalel—25
    Ajdel—26
    Ester—22
    Abraham—21
    Henoch—20
    Mariem—17
    Chaim—31

Nowak, Cwi-Jehuda ben Szmul-Dawid—murdered at age 8
Nowak, Gela-Fajga bas Szmul-Dawid—murdered at age 6
Szwarc, Jecheskiel ben Mojsze
—murdered at age 35
Gerszeniak, Mojsze
—murdered at age 27
Pilater, Rywka bas Abraham
—murdered at age 30
Pilater, Hinda bas Hersz
—murdered at age 28
Pilater, Gołda bas Jakub-Szlama
—murdered at age 21

Rywka (Rymer) Pilater
(Dayton, Ohio)

In Sacred Memory

Fuks, Icek-Icze—died in 1919 at age 34
my mother, **Rywka**
  —murdered in 1941 at age 54
my brother, **Maks**
  —murdered in 1942 at age 31
my sister, **Chana**
  —died in 1938 at age 22

Fox, G. (Toronto, Canada)

In Eternal Memory of Our Dearest
Whom We Will Carry in Our Hearts Forever

Fryde, Abraham (father)
—died in Brzeziny at age 58
Fryde, Małka (mother)
—died in Paris at age 71
Fryde, Natan (brother)
—deported from Paris in 1942 at age 49
with his wife, **Pauline**, age 42, their son,
Jonah-Jean, 14, and their daughter, **Dora**, 10

Hamel, Perla-Laja (sister)
—deported in 1942 at age 47 with her
husband, **Mordechai Hamel**, age 49,
their daughters: **Fani**, 19, **Rosette**, 15,
Marguerite, 13, and their little son, **Henri**, 11

Fryde, Herszel (brother)
—deported in 1942 from Paris at age 45
together with his wife, **Chana-Anna**, age
42, their daughter, **Klara**, 17, and their
little son, **Abraham-Albert**, 12

Fryde, Szmul (brother)
—deported to Pithiviers near Paris at age 35

Mojsze, Icek, Daniel, and Bajrech Fryde
(Paris, France)

---

1. Age probably meant to be 55.
For more information about the Pilater Family, as well as about many other families formerly in the Łódź ghetto, see "Lodz Ghetto Database" on the JewishGen Web site.

Pey [P]

In Eternal Memory

Pawe, Szlama-Jakub ben Abraham, age 59, and his wife, **Ester-Gitel** (from the **Joab** family), age 56—murdered

Josef Pawe

In Eternal Memory

Fryde, Kajla-Ita
born in 1877
murdered in 1942

Fryde, Aszer
born in 1877
murdered in 1942

Ester
their daughter
born in 1917, murdered in 1942

In Eternal Memory

Fajngold, Reb Berl (uncle), once a rabbi in Brzeziny, and his wife, **Ester** (from the **Lipski** family)

my cousins: **Herszel** and **Abraham Fajnkind**—murdered in the Łódź ghetto

N. Lipski (Antwerp, Belgium)

In Sacred Memory

Frankensztajn, Szlama-Judel, died in November 1948 at age 56

Mrs. Bess Goodman

In Eternal Memory

Frankensztajn, Dan-Josef (father)
—died
Frankensztajn, Sura-Hinda (mother)
—murdered

Balcia Frankensztajn-Grodzińska

In Eternal Memory

Fox, Sam (Syna Tauba's)
died 8 December 1949
in New York at age 67

Gussie Fox and children

In Sacred Memory

Piotrkowski, Perec and **Rechel**, 1852–1915
Jecheskiel-Dawid and **Jachet Wolman**
— murdered with their five children by the Nazi assassins

S. Zigman (Los Angeles, California)

In Eternal Memory

Piotrkowski, Pinchas-Hersz (father), age 52
my mother, **Ruchel**—both murdered in 1942
my sister, **Cywia**—murdered in 1944, age 32

B. Piotrkowski (Toronto, Canada)

Tsadek [Ts]

In Eternal Memory

Cuker, Gitel
born in 1918
— murdered in
Warsaw in 1939

**Cuker, Cywia-Necha
(Działoszyńska)**
born 1898 — murdered
in the Warsaw ghetto

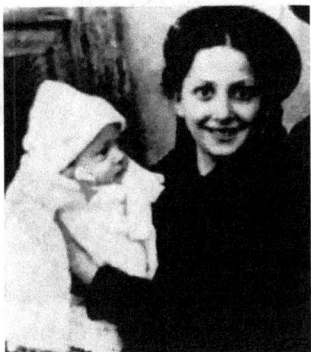
Cuker, Sura, born in 1928
— died in the Warsaw ghetto
(the child, **Mendele,** was a grandchild of
Welwel Żydek, born 1939 — murdered)

In Eternal Memory

Laja
his wife
born in 1876
murdered in 1942

Poliwoda, Majer
born in 1871
murdered in 1942

Poliwoda, Abraham-Elije
born in 1897 — murdered in 1942
his wife, **Zelda-Ruchel**
— murdered in 1942

Chana-Kajla
their daughter
born in 1917
murdered in 1942

*Dawid Poliwoda
(Israel)*

In Sacred Memory

Poznański, Majer
— died in Głowno 5 Nisan 1916 at age 67
Poznańska, Gela
— died in Głowno 17 Kislev 1929 at age 87

Phillip Pozner (New York)

IN SACRED MEMORY
of our murdered brothers

Urka and **Abraham-Josef Kalisz**

In Memory

of Our Beloved Parents

Mojsze and **Chaja Kalisz**
died 5 June 1933

In Memory

of our dear brother

Leon Kalisz

who died in America

Kuf [K]

In Sacred Memory
of

Kraushorn Raszka
died in the
Brzeziny ghetto
in 1940 at age 69

Kraushorn Eliasz-Pejsach
(Ajnbinder)
died April 1935
at age 71

In Sacred Memory
Kaczka, Marjem-Hinda

with her three children:
Fiszele, age 11, **Surele**, age 13,
Dawid-Mendel, age 15
all murdered by the Nazi assassins

ISAAC FREIFIR
(Brazil)

In Sacred Memory of the Kujawski Family

Mojsze (brother) — murdered in 1941 in the Brzeziny ghetto at age 21

Edzia Frohman (sister) and her husband, **Szulem**

Rywka (sister) — murdered in the Łódź ghetto in 1941 at age 37

Perla-Pola (sister) — murdered in the Brzeziny ghetto at age 23

Bronia (sister) — murdered

Brucha (sister) — murdered in the Brzeziny ghetto at age 26

Kujawski, Eliasz-Eli (father) — died in the Brzeziny ghetto at age 60

Kujawska, Jochwet (mother) — died in the Brzeziny ghetto at age 49

Piotrkowska (Peters), Sura-Ita (grandmother)

Kujawski, Anszel (brother) — murdered in Camp Drancy near Paris in 1942 at age 35

Kujawski, Szlama (brother) 1941

Bernard Kujawski (Paris)

In Eternal Memory

Kornblum, Sura, Gołda, Herszel, Josef, and **Szyja**

Ikka, Mojsze-Zyndel, Sura, Mania, and **Chana**

Morris Kornblum (Australia)

In Eternal Memory

Kejzman, Eliasz—murdered in 1943
Kejzman, Dina—murdered in 1943

Children of **Eliasz Kejzman** and his wife, **Szyfra Kejzman: Szmul-Aron** and **Rajza**
—murdered in 1943 with their two sons

Jurkiewicz, Dawid and **Ester-Małka (Mania)**
—murdered with their three children

Bajzer, Abraham and **Hendel-Ruchel (Cela)**—murdered with their son

Kejzman, Szymon-Josef and **Regina**
—murdered with their daughter

Młynarzewski, Abraham and **Perla-Rywka (Polja)**—murdered with their child

Mr. and Mrs. A. Young (Toronto, Canada)

In Eternal Memory

Kejzman, Abraham-Mordechai, age 58, **Masza**, his wife, age 55
—murdered in Auschwitz

Kejzman, Herszel and **Perla**, both age 36
—murdered with their two children

Kowalski, Sura and **Mojsze**, both age 25
—murdered with their two children

Kejzman, Szaja
—murdered in Brzeziny in 1942 at age 19

Kejzman, Sura
—murdered in Auschwitz in 1942 at age 27 with her three children: **Becalel**, age 6, **Chana**, age 4, and **Rywka**, age 8 months

Mojsze Kazman (Toronto, Canada)

In Eternal Memory of My Sister

Cywia (Celia) Cooper
died 22 July 1961 in New York
at age 62

In Sacred Memory of My Parents:

Kornblum, Josef-Aszer and **Pesa**

Chemia Kornblum
Los Angeles, California

In Eternal Memory

Kalisz, Mojsze-Lajb (Mojsze Moc)
—murdered in 1945 at age 48

Kalisz, Rajzel-Laja
—murdered in 1944 at age 42

Chajele Kalisz-Fogel
(Toronto, Canada)

In Eternal Memory

Kalmus, Chaim-Lajb, age 63, his wife, **Sura-Ester**, age 62
—murdered in Auschwitz with a grandchild

Abraham Kalmus (Israel)

In Eternal Memory

Rozenblum, Reb Lajb
(**Lajb Lekhernajer**)
died 2 Iyar 1943 in New York at age 78

In Eternal Memory

Rozenberg, Michał, son of **Elija** and
Dwojra (the **Elijeta**) — died in Los Angeles

In Sacred Memory

Buchner, Mojsze   **Rubin, Dawid**
born in 1911   born in 1911
murdered in   murdered in
Auschwitz in 1944   Poznań in 1942

Reysh [R]

In Eternal Memory

Raszewski
Mojsze ben Nisen

murdered in the Łódź ghetto
at age 65

Raszewski   **Raszewski**
Małka-Rojza   **Jakub-Icek**
died in 1929   ben Szymon-Josef
at age 69   died in 1921
                        at age 60

IN ETERNAL MEMORY of

Rozenblum, Jonah
died in New York
28 Shevat 1961 at age 75

Izzy (Icek) Rozenblum
died 1 Elul (13 August 1961)

An active leader in the Brzeziner Book Committee and, for many years, in business matters in the Workmen's Circle.

With his passionate interest in Jewish cultural organizations, with his dedication, he pursued a productive and intellectual Jewish life in America.

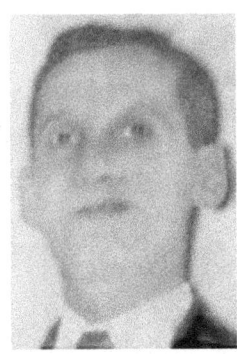

Rozenblum, Irving
died in New York at age 47

Rozenblum, Lajzer ben Chaim-Jona
— died in Brzeziny at about age 20
Rozenblum, Chaja
— died in Brzeziny in 1898
Rozenblum, Herszel ben Chaim-Jona
— murdered in a camp
Rozenblum, Dwojra
— murdered with her three children:
Chaja, **Symcha**, and **Chaim-Rafał**

Anna Rozenblum, children and grandchildren

**Rozenblum, Trajna
bas Lajzer Chaim-Jona**
with her husband and children
— murdered in the Warsaw ghetto

Rozenblum, Szymon
— murdered with his wife and children
Rozenblum, Małka
— murdered with her sons

IN ETERNAL MEMORY

Rozenberg, Feivel—born in 1884
—died October 1954 in New York

Rozenberg, Zelda—born in 1883
—died August 1930 in New York

Rozenberg, Eliasz-Chaim
—died in Brzeziny in 1934

Rozenberg, Dwojra
—died in Brzeziny in 1936

Fogel, Cwi-Hersz
—died in Brzeziny in 1920

Fogel, Bajla (Ajgele)
—died in Brzeziny in 1924

Abraham Rozenberg (New York)

In Eternal Memory

Rozen (Szwarc), Rywka
murdered in Łódź at age 52

Rozen, Luzer-Mendel ben Majer
—died in Łódź at age 52

Rozen, Ester
—murdered in Brzeziny at age 30

Rozen, Itka
—murdered in Lemberg at age 27

Rozen, Małka
—murdered in Bergen-Belsen at age 24

Rozen, Majer—died in Brzeziny

Rozen, Cypa (the Gerer *rebbe*'s daughter)
—died

Rozen, Szaja
—murdered with his entire family

Rozen, Fajga—murdered

Rozen, Sura-Laja—murdered

Szwarc (Bernholc), Necha—murdered

Szwarc, Mojsze—murdered

Ringrot-Rozen, Chana—murdered with her husband and three children

Gołda Kersztajn
Dwojra Lipko

In Eternal Memory

Rozenblat, Szaja (father), age 39
  Chawa (mother), age 39
  —both murdered in 1942
Rozenblat, Benjamin (brother), age 10
  —murdered in 1944

M. Rozenblat (Toronto, Canada)

IN ETERNAL MEMORY

Rozner, Josef ben Aba-Hersz
—died in Brzeziny at age 86

Rozner, Tyle bas Rafał
(teacher's daughter)
—died in 1918 in Brzeziny at age 65

B. Rozner

In Sacred Memory of Our Annihilated Family

all murdered by the Nazi killers

Rubin, Mojsze, and **Szprynca**
(parents)

Fogel, Krajndel, and her husband, **Fulka,** with their children

Łęczyńcka, Mindel, and her husband, **Chaim-Symcha,** with their son

Aronowicz, Welwel, and family

Aronowicz, Abraham, and family

Aronowicz, Mojsze, and family

We will remember you forever.

Aronowicz Family
(Paris, France)

IN ETERNAL MEMORY

Rozenberg, Mojsze-Icek
(father)
died 18 November 1960 at age 74

and grandparents:
Menachem Mendel and **Mindel Rozenberg**

In Eternal Memory of My Parents

Rozenberg, Chanina ben Kalman
and **Ruchel**

my sisters: **Ester**, **Sura**,
and **Chana** with her husband

M. Rozenberg (Melbourne, Australia)

In Sacred Memory

Rozenblat, Izzy—for many years a dedicated leader among the Brzeziner *landslayt*—died in 1951

Wife and Child

IN ETERNAL MEMORY

For my dearest

**Rozenberg, Josef
ben Reb Kalman**
murdered at age 54

**Wolrajch-Rozenberg
Chana-Jochwet**
(**Anszel Bronowicer**'s
granddaughter)

Rozenberg, Mariem—murdered in the Łódź ghetto at age 21

Rozenberg, Henie—murdered in Auschwitz at age 19

Rozenberg, Laja—died in Brzeziny in 1939 at age 10

Rozenberg, Josef—died 24 July 1942 in the the Łódź ghetto at age 54

Rozenberg, Chana—murdered in the Łódź ghetto at age 47

Rozenberg, Pawa—murdered in the Łódź ghetto at age 24

Regina Rozenberg-Jablonka
(Detroit, Michigan)

IN ETERNAL MEMORY
of my annihilated family

Szulzinger, Chaim-Baruch
born 1888, murdered 7 Iyar 1943

Szulzinger, Dawid-Hersz (the tall *shoykhet*)
Szulzinger, Bajla, Aszer, and **Ala**
Szulzinger, Szlama (*shoykhet*) and **Małka**
**Szulzinger, Symcha, Abraham-Icek,
  Resza,** and **Dina**
Kejzman, Aron, Rajza, Aszer, and **Natan**

*Nathan Schulsinger
(Brooklyn, New York)*

In Eternal Memory

Szyldwach, Ruchel   **Szyldwach, Tanchem**
daughter of Dawid   born in 1898
and Jehudit Miler   murdered
born in 1898   in Auschwitz
murdered in Auschwitz

In Eternal Memory
of our never-forgotten parents,
sister, and brothers

Szajbowicz, Lajbel ben Gecel and **Rywele
bas Jankiel**, their children: **Basia**, age 12,
Gecel, age 9, **Josele**, age 6—all murdered

*Roza Hoffman, Hessa Kapelusz,
Gucia Bekermus*

Shin [Sh]

IN ETERNAL MEMORY

of our most beloved and dearest, who were murdered by the Nazi assassins (may their names be erased). May these words be a tombstone for their saintly souls.

May Their Souls Be Bound Up in Eternal Life

**Szajbowicz   Szajbowicz, Uri
Pesa   ben Josef-Baruch**
our mother, age 59   our father, age 54
—murdered   died 21 March 1936
                             yortsayt 27 Adar I

Ruchel   **Szulem**
our sister, age 20   our brother, age 22
—murdered   —murdered

Josef, Monisz, Mendel, and *Gabriel
Szajbowicz*

YIZKOR MEMORIAL SECTION

IN ETERNAL MEMORY

Szotland, Dawid-Lajb
died September 1932

Szotland, Laja
died 26 February 1943

Gela Manhajm
Sister of **Dawid-Lajb Szotland**

In Eternal Memory

A. Z. Szotland

IN ETERNAL MEMORY

Szajnberg, Nechemia
born in 1910
murdered in Auschwitz

Szajnberg, Josef
born in Brzeziny in 1884
died in Israel in 1955

Szajnberg, Rywka
born in 1912—murdered with her two children in Brzeziny in the first selection

IN ETERNAL MEMORY

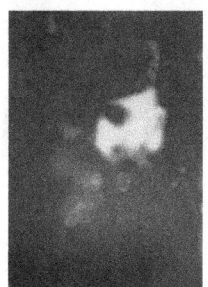

Gomuliński, Mojsze
born 1886—murdered

Gomuliński, Lajbel—born 1886
Gomulińska, Cywia—born 1886
both murdered in the ghetto

Cypora and Mojsze Har-Jaffe (Szajnberg)
(Israel)

IN ETERNAL MEMORY
of my parents

Szwarc, Dawid
died in Brzeziny in 1905
at age 86

Szwarc, Bina-Laja
died in New York in 1955
at age 97

my murdered brothers:
Mojsze and **Aron**,
and my sister, **Frajda**

Szwarc, Szlama
(New York)

IN ETERNAL MEMORY

Szwarc, Bluma   **Szwarc, Majer**
born 1902   born 1902

their children:

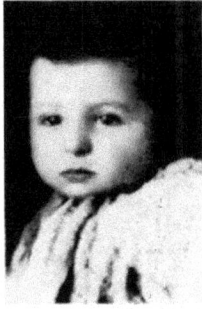 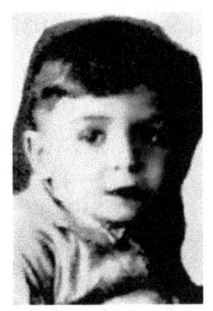

Icek   **Mojsze**
born 1936   born 1934

all murdered by Hitler's assassins

In Eternal Memory

Stal, Mojsze-Josef—died 1918 at age 37
his wife, **Brajna**, age 62,
their son, **Abraham**, age 35
—murdered in Auschwitz in 1942

Burakowski, Icek and **Chajka**, both age 40
—murdered in Auschwitz with their sons:
Mojsze, age 14, and **Szlama**, age 8

Stal Family (Toronto)

In Eternal Memory

Stal, Jechiel, age 45, his wife, **Brajna**, age 42, and their son, **Mojsze-Dawid**, age 19

—all murdered in Auschwitz

H. Stal (Toronto, Canada)

IN ETERNAL MEMORY

Działoszyńska (Fuks), Małka
—murdered in Koluszki at age 32

Fuks, Izak
—murdered in Koluszki at age 11

Fuks, Max
—murdered in Koluszki at age 32

Moskowicz, Izak
—murdered in Koluszki at age 30

We will never forget you!

Ludwig Dzialoszynski (Toronto, Canada)
Hanka Aronow (Melbourne, Australia)

In Eternal Memory

Ikka, Jechiel-Majer
—died Tel-Aviv 14 Sivan 1954 at age 64

Ikka, Hudesa
—died in Tel-Aviv 4 Shevat 1950 at age 50

Ikka, Leon-Lajbuś ben Mojsze Zyndel
—died 25 December 1953 at age 42 in Nancy, France

Ikka, Mojsze Zyndel
—murdered in Poland with his wife, **Sura**, and daughters: **Chana** and **Mania**

Ikka, Wolf, with his wife, **Matel**, and their son, **Szaja**

Zev Ikka (New York)

Aronów, Abraham
—died in the Łódź ghetto at age 44

Aronów, Ester Blima
—died August 1944 at age 47

Zimnawoda, Róża
—murdered in 1942 with her 7-year-old little daughter, **Karolina**, during the deportation from Brzeziny to Łódź

Aronów, Sala
—murdered in Majdanek

Badower, Gołda
—murdered in the Tomaszów ghetto at age 70

Benet, Motel, age 46, his wife, **Chaja**, and their child, **Abraham**, age 9
—all murdered in the Łódź ghetto

Majerholc, Szaja, age 43, his wife, **Bluma**, age 39
—murdered in the Łódź ghetto

Działoszyńska, Fajga
—murdered in Koluszki at age 58

Działoszyński, Kopel
—murdered in Koluszki at age 35

Moszkowicz, Sara
—murdered in Koluszki at age 30

IN ETERNAL MEMORY

IN ETERNAL MEMORY OF OUR PARENTS

Herszenberg, Benjamin
— died in February 1922

Herszenberg, Sara
— died in November 1937

Krawiecki, Szymon
— died in 1899

Krawiecka, Chana-Chaja
— died in 1927

Leah and Melech Hirsch
(New York)

IN ETERNAL MEMORY

Wołkowski, Abraham and **Matel**

Maks Wolkoff

IN ETERNAL MEMORY of OUR BROTHER-IN-LAW

Lichtensztajn, Chaim
— interned in Paris and deported 26 June 1942 to Auschwitz

His mother became paralyzed because of her grief.

Marie and Icek Hersz Benkel
(Paris, France)

IN ETERNAL MEMORY

Benkel, Fiszel (father)
1880 to 1935 — died

Benkel, Marjem (mother)
1883 to 1936 — died

Benkel, Małka Frymeta (sister)
1914 to 1942 — murdered

Benkel, Ester-Laja (sister)
1925 to 1942 — murdered

Benkel, Mojsze-Eliasz (brother)
1928 to 1942 — murdered

Benkel, Frajdel (sister)
1932 to 1942 — murdered

We will remember you forever!

Jakub Hersz Benkel and family
(Toronto, Canada)

IN ETERNAL MEMORY

Gross, Abraham
— died in New York at age 69

Gross, Rywka
— died in New York at age 67

Emanuel Gross (New York)

IN ETERNAL MEMORY

In Sacred Memory of Our Parents, Sister, and Brothers

Fajn, Jakub-Szlama
(**Herszel Litvak**'s grandson)

Fajn, Tauba-Laja

Fajn, Szymon-Josef and his family

Fajn, Majer-Wolf and his family

Fajn, Cyna-Ruchel

We will always carry you in our hearts!

In Eternal Memory

Zylberberg, Szulem
—murdered at age 55

Zylberberg, Cywka (Milsztajn)
—murdered at age 53

their children:

Abraham-Michal, age 28,
Mordechai, age 25,
Gitele, age 19
—all murdered

In Eternal Memory of

Chaskiel and **Brucha Najman**
—lived from 1870 to 1940

Machel, Wolf, and Charlie Newman
(Los Angeles, California)

In Eternal Memory

Sieradzki, Berysz—died in 1937

Sieradzka, Frajdel—deported from Brzeziny in May 1942

Wolf Sieradzki (New York)

CHICAGO

In Sacred Memory of the Landslayt and Members of the Brzeziner Society in Chicago Who Have Died

Brothers:

Abramowicz, B.
Adler, J.
Apelbaum, J.
Belkin, Harry
Braun, H.
Breitberg, M.
Brockstein, Ab.
Bruski, M.
Cohen, Joe
Cytron, Sam
Ehrlich, Bro.
Eizner, Louis
Fajnberg, M.
Feder, M.
Finkelstein, M.
Flam, Harry
Freund, Nathan
Friedman, H.
Friedman, J.
Friedman, Max
Greenbaum, Louis
Heft, Solomon
Holtz, Sam
Jacobson, J.
Jacobson, Max
Kabak M.
Kesler, A.
Korenstein, F.
Kron, Izydor
Lazarus, Jacob
Levitz, Nathan
Lewin, J
Lewin, J.
Luchen, N.
Melnick, Harry
Metz, Joe
Newman, Charles
Novak, Hyman
Rakowski, Sam
Selzer, Sam
Simon, Harry
Simon, Julius
Solomon, Ab.
Solway, H.
Stein, Jacob
Stein, S.
Szypman, N.
Tobias, F.
Wajnberg, D.
Walter, Willie
Weisdorf, H.
Wishni, Jack
Zandberg, David

Sisters:

Blat, Helen
Feder, Emma
Flam, Ida
Freund, Minnie
Galper, Gussi
Goralnik
Jacobson
Kesler, S.
Kron, Gussie
Luster, Esther
Metz, Anna
Sokolow, Esther
Solomon, Tillie
Stein, Esther
Weinberg
Weiner, Sara

Index

Certain conventions have been used in compiling this index to facilitate the identification of persons who may have been known by more than one name. Married women are listed under both their maiden name, e.g., Zagon, Dora m. [married name] Winer, and their married name, e.g., Winer, Dora b. [born] Zagon. The names of people who have changed their names are listed under both names, e.g., Berg, Jacob David b. [born] Nisenberg, and Nisenberg (Berg), Jakub Dawid.

What appears as a surname in the book may have been in reality a nickname, often indicating the person's profession. When this is known or suspected, the surname in the index has a [?] added after it. If the real (legal) name is known because of something mentioned elsewhere in the book, a reference is made to the real name. Thus, if a man is mentioned as Dan-Aszer Beker (Dan-Aszer the baker), but it can be determined that his real name is Dan-Aszer Kujawski, he will be indexed twice, as follows: 1) "Beker[?], Dan-Aszer, see Kujawski, Dan-Aszer"; and 2) "Kujawski, Dan-Aszer (aka Dan-Aszer Beker)" [aka=also known as]. The referenced page numbers are listed under his real name.

As is the custom in Poland, the feminine surname endings "cka" and "ska" have been used for women (Sawicka, Kowalska) rather than the masculine surname endings "cki" and "ski" (Sawicki, Kowalski). Thus the women with such surnames are alphabetized before the men.

For examples of alternate spellings of surnames used in America, please see the footnote on page 250 in the chapter "Our Landsmanshaft" by Nachum Summer.

When searching for given names, it must be kept in mind that the same given name may have different forms. For example, diminutives in Yiddish are often expressed by adding "el" or "le/la," while diminutives in Polish may be expressed by adding "ek/ka," or "cia/sia." The names Chaskiel/Jecheskiel may be used interchangeably, as may Eliahu/Eljia/Eliasz; Icchak/Icek/Icze/Izak; Jakub/Jankiel/Jankief; Jehoszua/Szyja [Joshua]; Jeszaja/Szaja [Isaiah]; Lajb/Lajbele/Lajbuś/Lewek; or Wolf/Wołek/Wowe/Wowcia/Welwel. The same person may have been called a different name under different circumstances or by different people. In addition, Hebrew names and their Yiddish equivalents may have been used interchangeably, such as Dov–Ber, Cwi [Tsvi]–Hersz, and Arje–Lajb.

In Polish, letters with diacritical marks are usually alphabetized after those written without diacritics. However, since most readers will not know whether the name is written with or without diacritics, diacritics have been disregarded in alphabetizing this Index.

Please note that the following lists of names were not included in the Index: "List of Brzeziner Jews Who Were Contributors to Keren Kayemeth in 1913" (p. 113–17), the memorial section of "Brzeziners and Lodzers in California" (p. 291), and the extensive "Alphabetical List of Martyrs" (p. 344–60).

Additional information helping to identify the person is shown in square brackets; nicknames and alternate names are in parentheses.

For help in pronouncing names, see page xiv in "Foreword to English Edition."

_____, = without surname
_____, [the Gritser tailor], 82, 104
_____, Ajdele [the hatmaker's daughter], 189
_____, Aron (the *shames*), 57, 72, 203
_____, Aron-Mojsze Jukiel's, 163
_____, Bendet [Fajga-Machel's husband], 163
_____, Benjamin Josef [son-in-law of Machel], 54
_____, Blume the *stolerkes* [carpenter's daughter?], 106
_____, Chana [had beer tavern], 163
_____, Chune (the blind Chune), 43, 45, 56, 106
_____, Cypora-Ruchel [aunt of Elija Rozenberg], 79
_____, Dark Chana, 52, 59
_____, Dark-haired Chana-Beila, 163
_____, Dawid [uncle of Benjamin Herszenberg], 89
_____, Dawid Lajb Masza's [Ostrowtser *rebbe*], 68, 74
_____, Dwojra-Laja, 54
_____, Eli Mote (aka Eli Mote Genendl's), 134
_____, Eliezer (aka the red Eliezer), 69
_____, Elija Cypora-Ruchel's, see Rozenberg, Elija
_____, Elija Mojsze (aka Mojsze Koyke, gravedigger), 55
_____, Elijeta, see Rozenberg, Dwojra
_____, Ester-Lajele the baker, see Fogel, Ester-Laja
_____, Etja [herring vendor], 59, 163
_____, Fajga the water carrier, see Mydlak, Fajgele
_____, Fajga-Machel, 163
_____, Fiszel [trumpet player], 57
_____, Frajde [daughter of Szlama the Hasid], 57
_____, Gecel [matzo dealer], 54
_____, Hersz Icek, 69
_____, Hersz Icze [father-in-law of Mojsze Tajerman], 163
_____, Hersz Icze, 57, 163
_____, Herszel Mojsze Zyndel's, see Mendlewicz, Herszel
_____, Icchak of Warka, 48
_____, Icek [son of Nuta], 59
_____, Icek [son of] Masza, 59
_____, Icze Ber (the Nosher), 52
_____, Icze-Dawid, 143
_____, Issachar, 165
_____, Jakub, 106
_____, Jakub Josef, 36
_____, Jankiel, the Kuke's [looker's] son, 215
_____, Jankiele (Jankiele the blind Kokis), 52
_____, Jekiel Nachum, 69
_____, Jerachmiel [son of rabbi], 68
_____, Josef Aszer, 36
_____, Josef Michał, 68
_____, Judel the water carrier, see Sochaczewski, Judel
_____, Luzer [the Glowner *melamed*'s son], 107
_____, Machel, 54
_____, Majer (the baker), 66
_____, Make [son of Nuta?], 59
_____, Matys [son of Fajgele Szotland ?], 75
_____, Mendel, 67
_____, Mendel, Chana's son, 36
_____, Mojsze (aka Mojsze Hon Dark Chana's), 52
_____, Mojsze (deaf Mojsze), 61
_____, Mojsze [played fiddle], 57
_____, Mojsze Kopel, see Kopel, Mojsze
_____, Mojszele [grandson of Benjamin Herszenberg], 91
_____, Mojsze-Pinkus, son of Zelig, 146
_____, Mordchele [husband of Ruchel b. Herszenberg], 78
_____, Mordkele (Mordkele the *gabe*), 36
_____, Naftali Hersz [Gerer Hasid], 67–68, 75, 94
_____, Natan Nute, 101
_____, Nechemia, 57
_____, Old Pinele, 61
_____, Pesa Nar [tall Abraham's wife], 163
_____, Pinkas [*chazan*], 330
_____, Pinkus Job, 61
_____, Rabbi Abramele of Ciechanów, 124, 125
_____, Rabbi Ber of Międzyrzecz, 123
_____, Rabbi Bunem of Przysucha, 124
_____, Rabbi Elimelech, 78
_____, Rabbi Elimelech of Leżajsk, 123
_____, Rabbi Henoch of Aleksandrów, 124
_____, Rabbi Hersz of Tomaszów, 126
_____, Rabbi Icchak Majer of Góra Kalwaria, 126
_____, Rabbi Isroel of Kozienice, 123
_____, Rabbi Jakub Josef from Polonnoye, 123
_____, Rabbi Jechiel of Aleksandrów, 337
_____, Rabbi Mendel of Kock, 126

INDEX 411

_____, Rabbi Noech of Piaseczno, 101
_____, Rabbi Szmul Aba of Żychlin, 125
_____, Roman [mail carrier], 55
_____, Sara [had bakery], 161
_____, Surele [borscht vendor], 163
_____, Szlama [son of Mendel, torah proofreader], 67–68, 73
_____, Szlama Perec, xxiv
_____, Szlama the Hasid, 57
_____, Szmul Jecheskiel, 163
_____, Szmul-Jekiele, 143
_____, Szmul-Lajb [*bal-musef*], 138
_____, Tamar, 57
_____, the pale Abraham Mojsze, 157
_____, the tall Abraham, 163
_____, the tall Jankiel, 105
_____, the tall Mene, 170
_____, the tall Szlama [Hasid, owned building in square], 137
_____, Zalmele, 59
_____, Zelig [son of] Reb Icek Masza's, 59
Abramowicz, 207, 367
Abramowicz, Abraham, v, 157, 181
Abramowicz, Dawid, 361
Abramowicz, Machla, 361
Abramowicz, Perla m. Tobiasz, 361
Abramowicz, Szajndla m. Bursztajn, 361
Adler, Julius, 145
Ajlszleger[?], Icek, see Froman, Icek
Ajnbinder, Chaim-Icek, see Nisenberg, Chaim-Icek
Akerman, Melech, 161
Akerman, Szmul, 30
Aksler [Polish fire chief], 55
Aksler, 61–63
Aleichem, Sholem, xxv, 188, 238, 261
Alperin, Aron, vi, xv–xvi
Alter, Wiktor, 98
Amzel, Chaja m. Gerszon, 362
Amzel, Chana m. Zylberwaser, 362
Amzel, Jakub (aka Jakub Szydlowcer), 362
Amzel, Jekiel (aka Jekiel Szydlowcer), 138
Amzel, Jenta m. Fensterman, 362
Amzel, Lipcia, 362
Amzel, Mojsze, 380
Anders [attorney], 226
Anders, General, 318
Anielik, Szymon [rabbi], 101
Apelbaum, Ida, 290

Apelson, Eliezer, 56
Apowski, Abraham, see Opatowski, Abraham
Arnstein, Mark, 188
Aronów, Abraham, 405
Aronów, Ester Blima, 405
Aronow, Hanka, 405
Aronów, Sala, 405
Aronowicz Family, 400
Aronowicz, Abraham (aka Abraham Aron Shuster's), 61, 63
Aronowicz, Abraham, 400
Aronowicz, Mojsze (aka Mojsze Aron Shuster's), 63
Aronowicz, Mojsze, 400
Aronowicz, Welwel, 400
Asch, Sholem, xxv, 188, 325
Aszer, Josef, 50
Atlas, Helen, 377
Aufrychter, Cyna, 383
Aufrychter, Chajale, 383
Aufrychter, Herszel, 383
Aufrychter, Icek, 362
Aufrychter, Rywcia, 383
Aufrychter, Szymon, 383
Auster, Zosia, 142, 207, 210
Baal-Shem-Tov, 123
Badower, 220
Badower, Aron, 367
Badower, Balciele, 367
Badower, Frajdele, 367
Badower, Gołda, 405
Badower, Hudes, 367
Badower, Jakub-Aron, 137, 370
Badower, Libcia m. Fox/Fuks, 363
Badower, Luzer-Dawid, 367
Badower, Mojsze, 189
Badower, Morris, 289
Badower, Ruchla, 363
Badower, Szajndel, 367
Bach [German], 213, 223
Bajbke, Dawid, 36
Bajzer, Abraham, 396
Bajzer, Hendel-Ruchel (Cela), 396
Barasz, A., 250, 252
Baron, Fela m. Richter, 363
Baron, Charlie, 77, 252, 289
Baron, Icze [Icek], 77
Baron, Josef Hersz, 77, 363

Baron, S., 291
Baruch [Łódź socialist leader], 157
Baruk [bookkeeper], 34, 45
Bashever [revolutionary poet], 156
Bazilewski [district chief], 58
Bazuk, [Baruk?], 45
Beder, Idel, 215
Beder, Mizia/Mundzia, 215, 220
Beker, Zysman, 163
Beker[?], Benjamin, see Fogel, Benjamin
Beker[?], Dan-Aszer, see Kujawski, Dan-Aszer
Beker[?], Joel [son of Majer], 59
Beker[?], Smoluch, 57
Beker[?], Zysman, 57
Bekermus, Anszel ben Abraham, 363
Bekermus, Chaja-Gitel b. Goldwaser, 363
Bekermus, Gucia, 402
Bel-Rakhmones, Szymon, 196
Bendkower[?], see also Bentkewe and Blianket
Bendkower[?], Jecheskiel, 82
Bendkower[?], Jecheskiel Szmul, 58
Bendkower[?], Szmul, 82
Benet, Abraham, 405
Benet, Chaja, 405
Benet, Motel, 405
Benkel, 306
Benkel, Abraham-Lajb, 376
Benkel, Chajele, 376
Benkel, Chana, 302, 305
Benkel, Dawid, 82
Benkel, Dobryś, 376
Benkel, Dwojra b. Rozenstrauch, 376
Benkel, Elija, 376
Benkel, Ester-Laja, 376, 406
Benkel, Fiszel, v, 244, 306, 308, 310–11, 326, 376, 406
Benkel, Frajdel, 406
Benkel, Hil, 376
Benkel, Icek, 376
Benkel, Icek Hersz, 406
Benkel, Jakub, 301
Benkel, Jakub Hersz, 406
Benkel, Małka Frymeta, 406
Benkel, Marie, 406
Benkel, Marjem, 406
Benkel, Michał, 302, 304
Benkel, Mojsze-Eliasz, 406

Benkel, Rywen, 368
Benkel, Rywka, 310
Benkel, Sara, 376
Benkel, Szoel, 376
Bentkewe [Bendkower?], Chaskiel Szmul, 104
Bentkewe [Bendkower?], Syna Szmul, 104
Berber, Mojsze, 27
Bercholc Brothers, 180
Bercholc Family, 108
Bercholc, Chana, 367
Bercholc, Chaskiel, 181, see also Bercholc, Jecheskiel
Bercholc, Dawidke, 181
Bercholc, Ester, 367
Bercholc, Fincia-Laja b. Szotland, 75
Bercholc, Herszel (aka Herszel Shakher), 49, 52, 75, 163, 367
Bercholc, Jankiel, 367
Bercholc, Jecheskiel, 145, see also Bercholc, Chaskiel
Bercholc, Luzer, 363
Bercholc, Michał-Lajb, 52, 75
Bercholc, Mote, 134
Bercholc, Perla, 367
Bercholc, Sura-Jachet, 363
Bercholc, Syna, 49
Bercholc, Szmul, 367
Berg, Abe, 277
Berg, Abraham b. Nisenberg, 366
Berg, Chaim-Icek b. Nisenberg, 378
Berg, Fajga (Nisenberg), 378
Berg, Jacob David b. Nisenberg, v–vi, xiv–xv, xx, xxiii, 37, 48, 60, 70, 78, 84, 163, 235, 253–54, 257–58, 264–65, 273–284, 286–87, 292–94, 306, 311, 322–25, 333–36
Berg, Jankiel Chaim-Icek's, see Berg, Jacob David
Berg, Jonah b. Nisenberg, 366
Berg, Kasriel b. Nisenberg, 366
Berg, Louis, 284
Berg, Millie, 333
Berger, Icek/Icze-Majer, 56, 68
Berger, Sura, 373
Bergman, Rachel, 275–76, 281
Bergman, Ray, 261, 278, 284
Berholz, see also Bercholc
Berholz, Perla, 367
Berholz, Zalman, 367
Berkowitz, S., 289

INDEX

Berman [from Russia], 34
Berman, Szmul, 124
Bernheim, Henry, 290
Bernholc, Necha m. Szwarc, 399
Beserglik, Mojsze (aka Mojsze Pabianicer), xxiv, 86, 88, 101
Beserglik, Szmul-Lajb (aka Szmul-Lajb Pabianicer), 101
Betcajg, Luzer (aka Luzer Melamed), 85, 101, 164, 377
Betcajg, Szajna-Rywka b. Monat, 377
Bialek, Chana b. Horn, 367
Bialek, Ester, 138
Bialek, Icek, 149, 302
Bialek, Joel, 138
Bialek, Josef, 225
Bialek, Lea'le, 184
Bialek, Naftali ben Jakub, 367
Bialer, Jehuda, 302, 310
Bialer, Judel, 306
Bialer, Szaja-Ber, 134, 137
Bialystoker[?], Moszke, 67
Biebow, Hans, 220
Biedak [Poale Zion leader], 301
Biedak, Mordechai, 139, 160
Biedak, Mordechai Dawid, 29
Bimka, Chaja m. Igielska, 384
Bimka, Icek-Luzer, 384
Blacharz[?], Chaiml, see Fiszer, Chaim and Fiszel, Chaim
Blachowicz, Sarah, 305
Blajman, Basia m. Goldberg, 364
Blajman, Elisha, 364
Blajman, Jehuda, 364
Blajman, Reb Abraham, 364
Blajman, Sylvia b. Keselman, 364
Blankiet, see also Blianket
Blankiet, Syna, 212
Blankiet-Sułkowicz, Abraham, 212
Blas, A., 291
Blat, Berl, 50, 75
Blat, Chaiml, 75
Blat, Icze [Icek], 75
Blat, Many (aka Many Nafthendler), 50, 75
Blat, Mojsze, 50, 75, 316
Blat, Rywen, 28, 75
Blat, Szabtaj, 75
Blecher, Abraham, 304
Blianket, see also Blankiet and Bendkower
Blianket, Jecheskiel Szmul (aka Jecheskiel Szmul Bendkower), 58
Blianket, Syna, 58
Blianket/Klianket, Lajbl, 49
Blianket/Klianket, Syna, 49
Bobes (the tall Bobes) [*shames*], 66, 70
Bobes [gravedigger], 55
Bobes, Abrahamele, 57
Bocian, Abraham-Gerszon, 363
Bocian, Aszer, 181
Bocian, Dawid, 363
Bocian, Szaja, 27
Bojakiewicz, 13
Bonian, Benjamin, 181
Borensztajn, Abraham Szaja Heszl, 72
Borensztajn, Abraham Joszua [rabbi], 50
Borensztajn, Jekutiel Zalman [rabbi], 50, 68, 69, 72, 138, 146–47, 205, 208, 210, 219, 223, 245, 286
Borkowski, Lajbuś (aka Lajbuś Hentshkemakher), 61
Borochov, Ber, 29, 160, 172, 227
Brakash, B., 254
Brandszaft, Genia, 233
Brandszaft, Icek, 373
Brasz[?], Jankiele, 59
Braszes[?], 107
Brilliant, Aron, 57
Broder, Szmul, 146
Broder, Szmul-Zeinwel, 136
Bronowicer, Anszel, 401
Brzeziner[?], Dwojra-Chana m. Pinczewska, 75
Brzeziner[?], Icek, see Szpiro, Icek [rabbi]
Brzeziner[?], Jekiel, see Szpiro, Jankiele/Jekiel
Brzeziner[?], Naftali, 67, 75
Brzeziner[?], Szlama [son of Icek], 67
Brzeziner[?], Szmul, see Pachter, Szmul
Brzeziński, Jukiel, 112
Brzeznicer[?], Ajzykl, see Erlich, Icek-Eliezer
Budkowski, 246
Budnik, Josef, 57
Budnik, Menachem, 37, 45
Budrzewski, 13
Buchner, Mojsze, 397
Buki, 73
Buki, Aron, 134
Buki, Aron-Ber, 379

Buki, [Bajla], 207
Buki, Bajla-Bina b. Lomaniec (Loomanitz), 379
Buki, Josef, 379
Buki, Moniek, 379
Bundkin, N., 157
Bundowski, Izrael, 141
Burakowski, Icek, 367, 404
Burakowski, Mojsze, 404
Burakowski, Szlama, 404
Burokowska, Chajka, 404
Bursztajn, Abraham, 361
Bursztajn, Chaja-Gitla m. Estusz, 361
Bursztajn, Fiszel ben Mojsze-Szmul, 361
Bursztajn, Gitel m. Winter, 376
Bursztajn, Jankiel, 361
Bursztajn, Josef, 361
Bursztajn, Machel, 361
Bursztajn, Mojsze-Szmul, 367
Bursztajn, Mojsze-Szmul ben Dawid, 361
Bursztajn, Mordechai, 361
Bursztajn, Perla-Laja b. Neifeld, 361
Bursztajn, Rywen-Hersz ben Mojsze-Szmul, 361
Bursztajn, Rywka m. Najman, 385
Bursztajn, Szajndla b. Abramowicz, 361
Bursztajn, Walter [Wołek], 361
Bussgang, Fay Vogel, xi, 342
Butkowski, Jakub, 302
Buxbaum, N., 29
Byk[?], Lajbl, see Szajbowicz, Lajbl
Byk[?], Lemel, see Lefkowicz, Lemel
Całek, Josef (aka Josef Soyfer), 54, 90, 136
Całek, Szaja/Szyja, 54, 90
Celcer Brothers, 134
Celcer, Hersz Wolf, 63
Cemak, Emanuel, 164
Chazen[?], Golda, 76
Chazen[?], Mojszl, see Sterns, Mojszl
Chazen[?], Szmul, 69
Chernick, Nathan, 290
Chernick, Roda, v
Chernick, Rudy, 290
Chroziemski Brothers, 55
Ciołek[?], Rywen, see Blat, Rywen
Cohen, Izrael, 251, 253, 257, 263, 272
Cohen, Sam, 249
Cooper, Cywia (Celia), 396
Cuker, Cywia-Necha b. Działoszyńska, 393
Cuker, Gitel, 393
Cuker, Mendele, 393

Cuker, Sura, 393
Cwern, Chanina, 63
Cwerner, Herszel, 175
Cymerman, Jakub, 305
Czumski[?], Abraham, xxiv
Dantsis, Mordechai, 256, 294
Davis Family [friends of I. Kacenelson], 185
Dawidowicz, Jankiel, 29, 173
Dembiński, Mordechai, 371
Diamond, A., 289
Diamond, Abraham, 371
Diamond, Alta-Laja, 371
Diamond, Bajla, 371
Diamond, Chaim-Ber, 371
Diamond, George b. Gerszon Dymant, 249, 250, 291, 369
Diamond, Jack, 289
Diamond, Joan, 371
Diamond, Joseph, v–vi, xv, 235, 254–55, 263, 266–67, 275–76, 278, 281–82, 284–85, 287, 289, 291, 333
Diamont, Leon, 371
Diamont, Paul, 371
Diamont, Pauline, 371
Dimov, Osip, xxv
Długoszewski [editor from Warsaw], 159
Dorfsman, 187
Drengel, Morris, 249, 291
Drucker [attorney], 205
Dwarter, Berl, 69
Dwarter, Izrael [rabbi], 50, 51, 54, 69, 72
Dymant, 13
Dymant Brothers, 134
Dymant Family, 81
Dymant, Abraham, 189, 370, 371
Dymant, Aron-Hersz (Urka), 370
Dymant, Bajla, 371
Dymant, Bela, 370
Dymant, Blume, 370
Dymant, Chaim-Ber, 45, 56, 82
Dymant, Chaiml, 134
Dymant, Chana b. Sperling, 370
Dymant, Eliezer, 370
Dymant, Emanuel, 56, 59
Dymant, Emilia, 370
Dymant, Ester, 371
Dymant, Fiszel, 210, 236
Dymant, Frymet, 371
Dymant, George, 370

INDEX 415

Dymant, Gerszon, see Diamond, George
Dymant, Icek, 204, 206, 208, 236–37
Dymant, Icze Ber, 49, 369
Dymant, Jakub-Dawid, 369–70
Dymant, Jan, 335, 370
Dymant, Jekiel Dawid (aka Jekiel Dawid Dzik), 63
Dymant, Joel, 143
Dymant, Josef, 371
Dymant, Lajbel, 371
Dymant, Majer (aka Olek), 142
Dymant, Majer, 56, 207, 369, 371
Dymant, Małka, 369
Dymant, Mojsze-Icek, 371
Dymant, Mordechai,, 371
Dymant, Mordechai-Icek, 371
Dymant, Mrs., 246
Dymant, Rajzel, 370
Dymant, Ruchele, 187
Dymant, Sonia-Szajndel, 370
Dymant, Stefa, 370
Dymant, Syna, 49
Dymant, Szajndel-Bela, 371
Dymant, Tauba-Ruchel, 369
Dymant, Zelig, 210
Dymov, Osip, 188
Dytman, A., 385
Działoszyńska, Chana (Chana the Lodzerin), 75
Działoszyńska, Cywia-Necha m. Cuker, 393
Działoszyńska, Fajga, 405
Działoszyńska, Fela, 370
Działoszyńska, Małka b. Fuks, 405
Działoszyńska, Sara, 306
Działoszyńska, Tema m. Hamer, 373
Działoszyński, 246
Działoszyński, Aron, 75
Działoszyński, Icze [Icek], 75
Działoszyński, Josel, 75
Działoszyński, Kopel, 405
Działoszyński, Lajbuś-Mendel, 75
Dzialoszynski, Ludwig, 405
Działoszyński, Mojsze, 27, 75
Działoszyńskis of Pabianice, 94
Dzik[?], Jekiel Dawid, see Dymant, Jekiel Dawid
Edelson, Hersz-Icze, 137
Edelstadt [revolutionary poet], 156
Efroimowicz, Aron, 201, 214, 245
Efroimowicz, Blimele, 386
Efroimowicz, Chaim-Majer, 386
Efroimowicz, Dora m. Markus, 386
Efroimowicz, Ester, 386
Efroimowicz, Esterl, 386
Efroimowicz, Marjeml, 386
Efroimowicz, Mindel m. Horn, 386
Efroimowicz, Rywka b. Szotland, 386
Efroimowicz, Rywka, 386
Efroimowicz, Szyfrele, 386
Efroimowicz-Braun, Ruchel, 386
Eksztajn, Ezriel, 236
Eksztajn, Fiszel, 63, 387
Eksztajn, Rajzel m. Lefkowicz, 387
Eksztajn, Zlata, 387
Eksztajn-Czernik, Rhoda, 387
Epsztajn, 187–89
Erich, Hanka, 142
Erlich Family, 48
Erlich, Henryk, 98
Erlich, Icek-Eliezer (aka Ajzyk Brzeznicer), 79
Erlich, Izrael, 79
Erlich, Jechiel, v, xv, 47, 77, 79, 163, 305–6, 308, 310, 327
Erlich, Josef, 306
Erlich, Małka Chana b. Froman, 48, 79, 163
Erlich, Szymsi, 137
Erlich, Szymszon, 44, 69
Erlich, Szymszon Michał, 79
Estusz, Chaja-Gitla b. Bursztajn, 361
Estusz (Winter), Jechiel, 376
Fabisiak, Josef Rywen, 63
Fabisiak, Mordechai Icek, 63
Fadayev, 228
Fajbisiak [*gabbai* of Khevre Kedishe], 208
Fajgenbaum, Icek, 334
Fajn, Cyna-Ruchel, 407
Fajn, Jakub-Szlama (Herszel Litvak's grandson), 407
Fajn, Majer-Wolf, 407
Fajn, Szymon-Josef, 407
Fajn, Tauba-Laja, 407
Fajngold, Ester b. Lipska, 392
Fajngold, Berl [rabbi], 392
Fajnkind Abraham, 392
Fajnkind Herszel, 392
Fajnkind, Berl [rabbi], 146
Farber, Mrs. Ch., 368
Federzajl, 29
Fensterman, Jenta b. Amzel, 362

Fensterman, Mojsze, 362
Fidler, Godel, 163
Fidler, Henoch, 163
Fidler, Isachar, 304
Finger, Hersz, 27, 30
Fiszel, Chaim-Israel (aka Chaiml Blacharz), 387
Fiszer, Abraham-Ber, 387
Fiszer, Chaiml (aka Chaiml Blacharz), 142
Fiszer, Frajdl, 387
Fiszer, Isachar, 302, 304–5
Fiszer, Izrael, 305
Fiszman, Mojsze, 175
Flajszer, Mrs., 390
Flajszer, Phillip, 390
Flam, Chaim, 317
Flam, Mrs, 330
Flamholc, Dwojra, 390
Flamholc, Ester b. Lustig, 380
Flamholc, Jakub, 390
Flamholc, Szmul-Szaja, 390
Fogel, Abraham, 77, 380
Fogel, Abramcze, 387
Fogel, Aron, v, xv, 32, 50, 73, 77, 79, 140, 163, 202, 244, 310–11, 327
Fogel, Bajla (Ajgele), 399
Fogel, Benjamin (aka Benjamin Beker), 77
Fogel, Brucha, 318, 387
Fogel, Chajele b. Kalisz, 396
Fogel, Cwi-Hersz, 399
Fogel, Dan [son of Dan-Aszer], 319
Fogel, Dan-Aszer, 181, 318
Fogel, Dwojra, 387
Fogel, Eliezer-Zev ben Icek, 387
Fogel, Ester-Laja (aka Ester-Lajele the baker), 214, 327
Fogel, Fajgele b. Najman, 79
Fogel, Fulka, 400
Fogel, Herszel, 79
Fogel, Hersz-Wolf, 387
Fogel, Hudes, 380
Fogel, Icek, 318, 387
Fogel, Izaak, 77
Fogel, Jacob, 77, 253, 287, 290
Fogel, Jakub Szlama, 42
Fogel, Josele, 387
Fogel, Krajndel, 400
Fogel, L., 291
Fogel, Melech, 77, 230, 231
Fogel, Mojsze, 36, 77, 305

Fogel, Szaja, 387
Fogel, Szoel, 163
Fox, Abe, 335
Fox, Abraham, 278, 284, 286
Fox, G, 391
Fox, Gussie, 392
Fox, Julius, see Fuks, Jehuda
Fox, Max, 390
Fox, Mollie, 287
Fox, Mrs. Sam, 186
Fox, Sam (aka Syna Fuks), v–vi, xv, 105, 186, 270, 275, 278, 284, 291
Fox, Sam (Syna Tauba's [Tauba's son]), 392
Fox/Fuks, Libcia b. Badower, 363
Frajdenrajch, Ruchel b. Grosman, 368
Frajm, 330
Frajnd, A., 73
Frajnd, Abraham, 26, 27, 38
Frajnd, Gedalia Fiszel (aka Fiszel Ferdinand/Hamid Pasha), 109–12
Frajnd, Gela, 81
Frajnd, Szlama, 109, 111
Frank, Abraham ben Szmul, 387
Frank, Minnie, 262
Frank, Mojsze, 104, 313, 315
Frank, Morris, 286, 306, 335
Frank, Mrs. Minnie, 387
Frankensztajn, 33, 218, 308
Frankensztajn, Dan-Josef, 392
Frankensztajn, Gerszon, 244
Frankensztajn, Mojsze-Icek, 73, 133, 215, 305–6, 310
Frankensztajn, Rywka, 386
Frankensztajn, Sura-Hinda, 392
Frankensztajn, Szlama-Judel, 392
Frankensztajn, Wolf, 386
Frankensztajn-Wołek, 134
Freed, 330
Freifir, Isaac, 394
Frohman, Dwojre-Małka, 390
Frohman, Edzia b. Kujawska, 395
Frohman, Jakub, 390
Frohman, Szulem, 395
Frohman, Szymszon, 390
Frolich, Mollie, 385
Froman Family, 48
Froman, Abraham (aka Abraham Warszawer), 48–49, 79
Froman, Ezriel, 81, 163

Froman, Fiszel, 302
Froman, Icek (aka Icek Ajlszleger), 81
Froman, Icek, 48–49, 54, 79
Froman, Jankiel, 163
Froman, Jekiel, 97
Froman, Małka Chana m. Erlich, 48, 79, 163
Froman, Mojsze, 134, 163
Fryde, Abraham, 391
Fryde, Abraham-Albert, 391
Fryde, Aszer, 63, 392
Fryde, Bajrech, 391
Fryde, Bernard, 330
Fryde, Chana-Anna, 391
Fryde, Daniel, 391
Fryde, Dora, 391
Fryde, Ester, 392
Fryde, Herszel, 391
Fryde, Icek, 391
Fryde, Jonah-Jean, 391
Fryde, Kajla-Ita, 392
Fryde, Klara, 391
Fryde, Małka, 391
Fryde, Mojsze, 134, 391
Fryde, Natan, 391
Fryde, Pauline, 391
Fryde, Perla-Laja m. Hamel, 391
Fryde, Szmul, 391
Frydman, Icek Hersz, 362
Frydman, Mendel, 203
Frydman, Zelig, 181
Frydman, Zysio, 146
Fuchs [Gestapo], 219
Fuchs [Old Fuchs], 82
Fuks, 73
Fuks Family (aka Malarz), 105
Fuks, Abraham, 77, 105, 305, 390
Fuks, Abraham-Judel (aka Watemakher, aka Kolewizner), 390
Fuks, Aron, 390
Fuks, Aron-Icek (Tauba's), 383
Fuks, Chaim-Lajb, 226, 228
Fuks, Chana, 391
Fuks, Ester, 105, 389
Fuks, Ester (aka Dr. Esther Fox), 243
Fuks, Helen, 389
Fuks, Hersz, 389
Fuks, Hersz ben Mojsze-Chaim, 389
Fuks, Herszel, 77, 388
Fuks, Icze [Icek], 77, 105, 388, 391

Fuks, Irena, 389
Fuks, Izak, 405
Fuks, Jachet b. Milsztajn, 383
Fuks, Jehuda (aka Julius Fox), v–vi, 85, 144, 160, 242–44, 270, 275–76, 279, 281, 283, 285, 301, 308, 310, 315, 335, 389
Fuks, Josef-Mendel ben Mojsze-Chaim, 389
Fuks, Judel, see Fuks, Jehuda
Fuks, Krajndel bas Jecheskiel, 389
Fuks, Krajndl m. Lerer, 381
Fuks, Laja, 389
Fuks, Lajbuś, 77, 105, 175, 388
Fuks, Lazar, 226
Fuks, Lipman, 77, 388
Fuks, Majerichie, 77
Fuks, Maks, 391
Fuks, Małka m. Działoszyńska, 405
Fuks, Malya, 76–77
Fuks, Marja/Maryla, 389
Fuks, Marjem bas Josef, 390
Fuks, Masza-Chaja,, 389
Fuks, Max, 405
Fuks, Mendel, 390
Fuks, Mindel, 390
Fuks, Mojsze, 390
Fuks, Mojsze-Chaim ben Szymon, 389
Fuks, Molly, 388
Fuks, Pine (aka Pine Tauba's), 63
Fuks, Pola, 388
Fuks, Rafał, 390
Fuks, Rywka, 391
Fuks, S., 275
Fuks, Syna, 77, 390
Fuks, Szmul, 390
Fuks, Tauba bas Mordechai, 389
Fuks, Tola (Tauba), 389
Fuks, Wolf, 390
Fuksel, Szlama, 34
Funt [the *felczer*], 188
Funt, 73
Funt Family, 81
Funt, Hyman, 253
Furman, Abraham-Aron, 78
Furman, Zalman, 78
Futterliebs [German family], 48
Gajer, Szmul-Mojsze (aka Szmul-Mojsze Litvak) [rabbi], 138, 143
Gamzon, Fannie, 262
Garber, Abraham Icek, 79

Garber, Aron, 81
Garber, Aszer [grandson of Aszerl], 81
Garber, Aszerl, 81
Garber, Dawid Melech, 81
Garber, Dawidl, 81
Garber, Herszel, 81
Garber, Jakub Josef, 79
Garber, Mendel, 81
Garber, Noech, 81
Garber, Regina, 81
Gąsior, Mr., 142
Gelb, Icek, 50
Gelb, Szlama (aka Szlama the lame), 26, 50
Gelb, Szlama, 39, 46, 52
Gelb, Towie Haljas, 52
Gerszeniak, Mojsze, 391
Gerszon, Abrahaml, 362
Gerszon, Chaja b. Amzel, 362
Gerszon, Herszele, 362
Gerszon, Lajbel, 362
Gerszt Brothers, 141
Gerszt, Chaja-Szajndel m. Grynszpan, 369
Gewirc, Arje, 369
Gewirc, Heniek, 369
Gewirc, Naftali, 369
Gewirc, Rajzel, 369
Gewirc, Sura, 369
Gewirc, Szaja, 369
Gewirtz, A., 369
Ginsberg, 189, 246
Ginsberg, Benjamin, 368
Ginsberg, Chana-Rywka bas Mojsze, 368
Ginsberg, Mojsze, 302
Ginsberg, Mojsze-Icek, 29, 322, 324
Ginsberg, Mordechai Wolf, 139–40, 368
Ginsberg, Noemi, 368
Gips, [Abraham's daughter], 189
Gips, A. B., 60
Gips, Abraham, 37, 42, 53, 99, 368
Gips, Jakub-Ber, 37, 226–28, 230–31, 368
Gips, Moris, 368
Gips, Szajndel, 368
Gips-Blumsztajn, Rachela, 368
Glazer, Mr., 142
Glazer[?], Uri, see Szaibowicz, Uri
Glicklich, Daniel, 249
Goldberg, Basia b. Blajman, 364
Goldberg, Blume, 92
Goldberg, Cyril m. Halberszadt, 93, 97, 99

Goldberg, Dobryś, 364
Goldberg, Eli (aka Eli Szajber), 63
Goldberg, Icek, 385
Goldberg, Icze-Mendel, 364
Goldberg, Laja, 92
Goldberg, Mojsze Zyndel, 21, 41, 51, 92–93, 96, 103
Goldberg, Naftali, 364
Goldberg, Perla, 50, 92–93, 96–97, 103
Goldberg, Perla-Ruchel, 385
Goldberg, Towa-Ruchel, 364
Goldberg, Tyla m. Mendlewicz, 59, 93, 97–99, 163
Goldberg, Wowe, 385
Goldberg, Z., 73
Goldberg-Działoszyńska, Sara, 310
Goldfarb Brothers [publishers], 228
Goldkranc, Icek-Lajb ben Jakub-Hersz, 368
Goldkranc, Jakub-Hersz, 317
Goldkranc, Regina, 368
Goldkranc, Rywka b. Wiślicka, 368
Goldkranc, Syna, 36
Goldkranc, Szlama, 368
Goldkrantz, Joseph-Hersz, 274
Goldman, Mojsze, 181
Goldsztajn, Blume m. Halbersztadt, 98, 103
Goldsztajn, Josel, 98
Goldwaser, Chaja-Gitel m. Bekermus, 363
Gombiner[?], Abraham Abele (Abraham Abele Segal) [rabbi], 101
Gomulińska, Cywia, 403
Gomuliński, Lajbel, 403
Gomuliński, Mojsze, 403
Goodman, Mrs. Bess, 392
Gordin, Aba, 256
Gordin, Jacob, xxv, 188
Gorky, 228
Gostyński, Fiszel, 136
Gostyński, Jancze, 136
Gostyński, Lajb, 136
Gotek[?], Josef, see Krell, Josef
Gotlib Family, 81
Gotlib, Abraham-Jakub, 369
Gotlib, Adele, 60
Gotlib, Benjamin, 369
Gotlib, Chaim, 73
Gotlib, E., 60
Gotlib, Emanuel, 228
Gotlib, Ezriel, 237

INDEX

Gotlib, Frymet, 369
Gotlib, H.B., 73
Gotlib, Jechiel Mojsze, 21, 56, 73, 75, 78, 82, 369
Gotlib, Lajbl, 56
Gotlib, Leon, 369
Gotlib, Rechel m. Herszenberg, 78
Gotlib, Rywka, 369
Gotlib, Surele, 187
Gotlib, Szymon, 56
Gotlieb, Abraham-Jacob, 335
Gracz, 76
Gracz [had counting house], 56
Grajcer, Godel, 63
Green, Joseph b. Grynberg, 189
Green, Masha, 262, 275, 279
Green, William/Willie (Vevche), 253, 266, 276, 278, 286, 291
Gribs, Morris, 289
Groman, Aszer'l, 56
Grosman, Abraham-Izrael, 369
Grosman, Abraham Szaja, 80, 163
Grosman, Aszer, 296, 368
Grosman, Balcia, 368
Grosman, Cywia, 368
Grosman, David, 80, 335, 367
Grosman, Dawid-Melech, 368
Grosman, Emanuel, 56
Grosman, Emanuel-Ajzyk, 80
Grosman, Emanuel-Ajzyk ben Abraham-Szaja, 367
Grosman, Ester-Chana, 369
Grosman, Ester-Chana bas Jechiel-Chaim, 367
Grosman, Hersz, 80
Grosman, Icze [Icek], 80
Grosman, Jeremia, 80
Grosman, Josef, 169
Grosman, Laja, 368
Grosman, Ruchel, 368
Grosman, Ruchel m. Frajdenrajch, 368
Grosman, Rywka, 280
Grosman, Wolf, 368
Gross, Abraham, 406
Gross, Emanuel, 406
Gross, Rywka, 406
Grubsztajn [publisher], 228
Grundsztajn, Chaja, 369
Grundsztajn, Chana, 369
Grundsztajn, Hersz-Icze, 369
Grundsztajn, Jerachmiel, 369
Grundsztajn, Jochwet, 369
Grundsztajn, Lajbuś, 369
Grundsztajn, Rywka b. Manis, 367
Grynbaum, Aron, 36
Grynbaum, Charles, 369
Grynbaum, Gertrude, 369
Grynbaum, Icek, 100
Grynbaum, Jekiele (aka Jekiele Kishkemacher), 144
Grynbaum, Josef-Zanwel (aka Zhirardover), 369
Grynbaum, Judel, 144
Grynbaum, Laja, 369
Grynberg, Josef (aka Joseph Green), 189
Grynberg, Mojsze-Icek, 306
Grynfeld, Chaim-Icek, 52, 69, 75, 98, 175, 176, 178, 302, 305
Grynfeld, Ruchel b. Nisenberg, 366
Grynfeld, Sura-Bluma b. Szotland, 74
Grynholc, Fajga b. Szotland, 369
Grynholc, Josef, 369
Grynholc, M., 369
Grynszpan, Abraham, 208
Grynszpan, Chaja-Szajndel b. Gerszt, 369
Grynszpan, Chajkel, 133–34, 206
Grynszpan, Herszel, 369
Grynszpan, Pejsach, 27, 82
Grynszpan, Szymon-Josef, 369
Gukman, Maks, 368
Gukman, Tema, 368
Gurt, Berl, 78
Gurt, Ester b. Herszenberg, 78
Gutentag, Yontov [rabbi], 146–47
Gutkind, 304
Gutkind, Abraham-Icek [rabbi], 51, 81, 136, 146–47
Gutkind, Dawid, 368
Gutkind, Emanuel (Maks), 368
Gutkind, Icze, 368
Gutkind, Icze-Majer, 81
Gutkind, Maks, 368
Gutkind, Menachem, 315
Gutkind, Mojsze-Majer, 68, 81, 136
Gutkind, Monisz/Manny, v, xv, 304, 326
Gutkind, Nachman, 51–52, 56, 69, 98–99, 163, 175, 304, 306, 326
Gutkind, Róża, 368
Gutkind, Sura [dark-haired], 68, 81, 136
Gutsztadt [had printing shop], 134

Ha'am, Ahad (Asher Ginsberg), 295
Haber, Esther, 290
Haber, J., 290
Hajker, Mojsze-Kalman, 163
Hajnsdorf, Mojszel, 100
Halberstam, Chaim, 94
Halberstam, Wowe [Vove], 69
Halbersztadt Family, 92
Halbersztadt, Abraham-Icze, 103
Halbersztadt, Aron, 93–94, 97–99, 102
Halbersztadt, Blume b. Goldsztajn, 98, 103
Halbersztadt, Chaim-Szlama, 98
Halbersztadt, Cyril b. Goldberg, 93, 97, 99
Halbersztadt, Dawid-Lajb, 41, 98, 103
Halbersztadt, Genendel, 95, 97, 103
Halbersztadt, Gucia b. Herszenberg, 98, 103
Halbersztadt, Małka, 98
Halbersztadt, Melech, 93–95, 97, 103
Halbersztadt, Mojsze, 103
Halbersztadt, Pinkus-Elimelech, 103
Halbersztadt, Ratkel, 103
Halbersztadt, Sura, 103
Halbersztadt, Szyfra-Golda/Szyfkele m. Mendlewicz, 98–99, 103
Halbersztadt, Tyla (Tola) m. Weksler, 103
Halbersztadt, Wolf, 98–99, 103
Halewi, Azriel, 49
Halewi, Elke b. Szpiro (later m. Sapir), 49
Halewi, Jechiel Majer [rabbi], 74
Hamel, Fani, 391
Hamel, Henri, 391
Hamel, Marguerite, 391
Hamel, Mordechai, 391
Hamel, Perla-Laja b. Fryde, 391
Hamel, Rosette, 391
Hamer, 75, 189
Hamer, Abraham, 373
Hamer, Dawid, 177, 374
Hamer, Dwojra, 374
Hamer, Gołda, 373
Hamer, Icek, 374
Hamer, Jenta, 374
Hamer, Lajbuś, 374
Hamer, Małka, 374
Hamer, Mojsze, 373–74
Hamer, Mojsze Ber, 175
Hamer, Mrs., 160
Hamer, Pinkus, 374
Hamer, Rywka, 374
Hamer, Tema b. Działoszyńska, 373
Hamer, Zelda-Perla, 374
Hamid Pasha, see Frajnd, Gedalia Fiszel
Hamid, Sultan Abdul, 109
Hanower, Dawid, 163
Hanower, Mendel, 163
Har-Jaffe, Mojsze b. Szajnberg, v, xv, 244, 277, 282, 288, 301–2, 304–6, 308, 310–311, 326, 403
Har-Jaffe/Szajnberg, Cypora, 310, 403
Hasid[?], Mojsze Dawid, 61
Hasid[?], Szlama (aka the big Szlama), 163
Hauser, Louis/Louie (Luzer), v– vi, xv, 263, 268–69, 275–76, 278, 282
Hauser, Ruth, v–vi, 260–61, 277–78, 284, 287
Hauser, Sara, 258
Hauzer, 220
Hauzer, Aba, 372
Hauzer, Aron, 372
Hauzer, Chaim, 372
Hauzer, Eliasz, 372
Hauzer, Frajdl, 372
Hauzer, Gołda, 372
Hauzer, Jechiel, 372
Hauzer, Jochwet, 372
Hauzer, Josef, 374
Hauzer, Juliet, 374
Hauzer, Laja, 372
Hauzer, Louis, 372
Hauzer, Majer, 372
Hauzer, Majer ben Szaja, 372
Hauzer, Pejsach ben Szaja, 372
Hauzer, Róża, 372
Hauzer, Ruchel, 372
Hauzer, Rywen, 372
Hauzer, Sala, 372
Hauzer, Szaja, 372
Hauzer, Wolf ben Szaja, 372
Hauzner, Zelig, 28
Hayman, Anna, 261
Hayvens[?] Family, 105
Hemlin, Isaac, 281, 333
Hendler-Gociał, Rywka, 236
Hendricks, Morris/Moishe, 275, 278, 281
Hendrik, Jechiel, 239, 374
Hendrik, Rhoda m. Karpatkin, xxv, 238, 374
Hendrykowska, Helen bas Lajbele, 374
Hendrykowski, Eli, 239
Hendrykowski, Jechiel, xxv

INDEX

Hendrykowski, L., 80
Hendrykowski, Lajbele, xxv, 59, 78, 163, 239, 374
Hentshke-makher[?], Lajbuś, see Borkowski, Lajbuś
Hercberg, Gerszon, 374
Hercberg, Gitel, 374
Hercberg, Leon, 374
Hercke, Icze [Icek] Ber, 74
Hercke, Josele, 74, 163
Hercke, Mojsze Aron, 74
Hercke, Wolf, 74
Herszberg, Icek, 306
Herszberg, Jankiel, 56
Herszenberg, Abraham, 302
Herszenberg, Benjamin, 406
Herszenberg, Benjamin (aka Benjamin Melamed), 89–90, 136
Herszenberg, Benjamin-Icek, 78
Herszenberg, Cudek, 99
Herszenberg, Dawid, 374
Herszenberg, Eliezer, 78
Herszenberg, Ester m. Gurt, 78
Herszenberg, Fajgele, 374
Herszenberg, Gucia m. Halbersztadt, 98, 103
Herszenberg, Icek, 302
Herszenberg, Jakub, 138
Herszenberg, Jakub ben Josef-Efroim, 374
Herszenberg, Jechiel-Mechel, 374
Herszenberg, Jechiel-Michał, 305
Herszenberg, Jekiel, 78, 91
Herszenberg, Josef Efroim (aka Josef Machel's), 34, 78, 99
Herszenberg, Kajla-Rywa m. Ledershniter, 78
Herszenberg, Laja m. Ikka, 78
Herszenberg, Machel, 78
Herszenberg, Melech, v–vi, xv, 89, 189, 406
Herszenberg, Mojsze-Szyja, 98
Herszenberg, Nute, 99
Herszenberg, Perla, 78
Herszenberg, Rechel b. Gotlib, 78
Herszenberg, Ruchel (aka Aunt Ruchel), 78, 91
Herszenberg, Ruchel, 374
Herszenberg, Sara, 374, 406
Herszenberg, Sura b. Joskowicz, 78, 90
Herszenberg, Szmul, 78
Herszfinger, Chaja, 373
Herzl, Dr. Theodore, 35, 79
Hillel, Jacob, 249, 291

Himelfarb, Herszel, 161
Hirsch, Leah b. Krawiecka, 406
Hirsch, Melech, see Herszenberg, Melech
Hirschbein, Perec, 188, 256
Hirszenberg, Samuel, 98
Hoffman, Roza, 402
Hochspiegel, Abraham Mojsze (the yellow Abraham Mojsze), 45–46, 61, 63
Holc, Majer, 246
Holcberg Family, 48
Holcberg, Aron (the *shoykhet*), 48, 50
Holcberg, Fiszel, 50
Holcberg, Hillel (the *shames*), 48, 50, 69, 72
Holcberg, Jojne, 50
Holcberg, Laja m. Rozenblum, 50
Holcberg, Perla b. Szpiro, 50
Holcberg, Szlama, 52
Holcberg, Szmul Hillel, 52
Holcberg, Szyfra, 50
Homel, 330
Horn, 14, 330
Horn, Blume, 82, 328
Horn, Chana m. Bialek, 367
Horn, Ester, 386
Horn, Gecel, 380
Horn, Lemel, 82, 244, 277, 279, 302, 305–6, 308, 310–11, 328
Horn, Louis/Louie (Luzer), 82, 253, 261, 263, 267, 275–78, 281–82, 284–86, 306
Horn, Majer, 14, 45, 82
Horn, Mindel b. Efroimowicz, 386
Horn, Mojsze ben Fiszel, 386
Horn, Morris, 330
Horn, Rywka b. Lustig, 380
Horn-Kaufman, Penina, 308
Horowitz, M., 291
Hoyker[?], Baruch, 106
Hoyker[?], Kalman [the hunchback], 46, 56–58
Hurgin, Dr. Pinchas, 279
Hyman, Sam, 258, 263, 268, 275, 278, 281
Ibanez, Blasco, 228
Igielska, Chaja b. Bimka, 384
Igielska, Chawciele, 384
Igielska, Hudes m. Pluśnik, 384
Igielska, Surecia m. Najman, 384
Igielska, Topcia b. Klajnman, 384
Igielski, Abraham-Lajb ben Berl, 384
Igielski, Berl, 384
Igielski, Chaim, 302

Igielski, Dan-Aszer ben Abraham-Lajb, 384
Igielski, Henry ben Abraham-Lajb, 384
Ikka Brothers, 155
Ikka, Ajzykl, 362
Ikka, Aron, 368
Ikka, Chana, 396, 405
Ikka, Dawid, 21, 135
Ikka, Fela, 362
Ikka, Fiszke, 205–10, 214–15, 219, 236
Ikka, Helen m. Orensztajn, 362
Ikka, Henoch Meilich, 61
Ikka, Hudesa, 405
Ikka, Icek ben Izrael Gerszon, 368
Ikka, Jechiel-Majer, 405
Ikka, Jojne, 362
Ikka, Laja, 368
Ikka, Laja b. Herszenberg, 78
Ikka, Leon-Lajbuś ben Mojsze Zyndel, 405
Ikka, Mania, 396, 405
Ikka, Matel, 405
Ikka, Mojsze Zyndel, 396, 405
Ikka, Mordechai, 21, 50, 78
Ikka, Pesa b. Zylberberg, 362
Ikka, Róża, 362
Ikka, Sonia, 362
Ikka, Sura, 396, 405
Ikka, Szaja, 405
Ikka, Szyja, 99
Ikka, Szlama Josef, 33
Ikka, Trajna, 362
Ikka, Wolf, 61, 405
Ikka, Zev, 405
Ikka-Fuksel, Szlama-Josel, 99
Imber, P., 284
Irlicht, Dr., 204–5, 245
Irlicht, Mrs., 246
Isz, Mrs., 187–88
Jablonka, Regina b. Rozenberg, 401
Jabotinsky, Ze'ev, 295
Jakubowicz, 141
Jakubowicz [attorney], 205, 245
Jakubowicz, Abraham, 34, 75, 380
Jakubowicz, Brucha, 135
Jakubowicz, Bruchecia m. Szydłowska, 75
Jakubowicz, Chaim-Dawid, 380
Jakubowicz, Chana, 380
Jakubowicz, Dawid, 164
Jakubowicz, Herszel (aka Herszel from Wały), 34, 36
Jakubowicz, Josef, 380
Jakubowicz, Lajzer, 30
Jakubowicz, Mme., 380
Jakubowicz, Perec, 34, 56, 68, 75, 82, 132, 136
Jakubowicz, Pincia, 75, 132, 136, 139
Jakubowicz, Pinkus, 34
Jakubowicz, Szmul, 380
Jakubowicz, Szymon, 34, 46, 75
Jaloff, Edward, 290
Jamalut, 76
Janasowicz, Icchak (aka Yitzhak/Isaac Janasowicz), 24, 165
Janower, Chanina, 136, 163, 246
Janowska-Ardenbaum, Gitel, 310
Jarnower, Berysz, 37
Jaskółka[?] Family, 105
Jelski, Dr., 175, 176
Jerozolimski, Lajbel, 181
Joab, Ester-Gitel m. Pawe, 392
Jokisz [Kotzker Hasid], 67
Jokisz, Szaja, 67
Joskowicz, Sura m. Herszenberg, m. Perlmuter, 78, 90
Jubiler, Abraham-Pejsach, 58, 73, 80, 136–137, 163
Jubiler, Chana-Golda b. Żychlińska, 58, 73, 163
Jud, Nachum, 198
Jurkiewicz, Dawid and Ester-Małka (Mania), 396
Kacenelson, Icchak, xxiv, 183–6, 227
Kacyzne, Alter, 54
Kaczka, Dawid-Mendel, 394
Kaczka, Fiszele, 394
Kaczka, Marjem-Hinda, 394
Kaczka, Surele, 394
Kahan, Lazar, 227
Kahn, Izrael, 109
Kalish, Charlie, 287, 335
Kalish, Helen, 258, 262
Kalish, Max, 287, 335
Kalisz, Abraham-Josef, 394
Kalisz, Chaja, 394
Kalisz, Chajele m. Fogel, 396
Kalisz, Leon, 394
Kalisz, Mojsze, 394
Kalisz, Mojsze-Lajb (aka Mojsze Moc [strong]), 63, 396
Kalisz, Rajzel-Laja, 396

INDEX

Kalisz, Szlama Lajb (aka Szlama Lajb Krulik), 63
Kalisz, Urka, 394
Kalman, Mojsze, 135
Kalmus, Abraham, 396
Kalmus, Chaim-Lajb, 396
Kalmus, Mojsze, 50, 140
Kalmus, Sura-Ester, 396
Kaluszyner[?], Abraham [*melamed*], xxiv, 87
Kapelusz, Hessa, 402
Kaplan, B., 256
Kaplan, Benjamin, 283
Karger, Hersz-Lajb, 369
Karger, Icek-Mendel, 369
Karger, Szajndel, 369
Karpatkin, Rhoda b. Hendrik, xxv, 238, 374
Kashamakher[?], Abraham, 74
Kashamakher[?], Aron, 74
Kashamakher[?], Chaiml, 74
Kashamakher[?], Chana, 74
Kashamakher[?], Dobryś, 74
Kashamakher[?], Lajb [son of Izrael], 59
Kashamakher[?], Syna, 74
Katsev[?], Hercke, 53
Katsev[?], Szymon, 57
Katzenelson, Yitzhak, see Kacenelson, Icchak
Kaufman, Berta, 290
Kaufman, Dawid, 163
Kaziv, 330
Kazman, Mojsze, 396
Kejzman, 73
Kejzman, Abraham-Mordechai, 396
Kejzman, Aron, 402
Kejzman, Aszer, 402
Kejzman, Becalel, 396
Kejzman, Chana, 396
Kejzman, Dina, 396
Kejzman, Eliasz, 396
Kejzman, Herszel, 396
Kejzman, Masza, 396
Kejzman, Natan, 402
Kejzman, Perla, 396
Kejzman, Rajza, 396, 402
Kejzman, Regina, 396
Kejzman, Rywka, 396
Kejzman, Sura, 396
Kejzman, Szaja, 396
Kejzman, Szmul-Aron, 396
Kejzman, Szyfra, 396
Kejzman, Szymon-Josef, 396
Kempner, 189
Kersz, Icek, 37
Kersztajn, Gołda, 399
Keselman, Sylvia m. Blajman, 364
Kesler, H., 291
Kirszbaum, Dawid, 380
Kirszbaum, Sara, 380
Kishkemacher[?], Jekiele, see Grynbaum, Jekiele
Kiszenower, Aron, 76
Klajnbaum, 219
Klajnhaus, Dr., 205, 245
Klajnman, Topcia m. Igielska, 384
Klajn-Zelig, M., 377
Kleinert [medical practitioner], 207
Kleinert, Fiszel, 145
Klezmer[?], Dawid Hersz, 81
Klezmer[?], Fiszele, 81
Klianket [Blianket?], Lajbl, 49
Klianket [Blianket?], Syna, 49
Klinger, Chaim-Dawid, 163
Knox, Izrael (aka Dr. E. Naks), 256
Kohn, Frymet, 362
Kohn, Herszele, 362
Kohn, Mendel, 362
Kohn, Szmul, 362
Kochberg, Abraham, 66
Kochberg, Aron-Lajb, 66
Kochberg, Aszer-Zelig, 66
Kochberg, Hersz-Mendel, 66
Kochberg, Icek-Majer, 66
Kochberg, Ita, 66
Kochberg, Jakub-Szlama, 66
Kochberg, Jerachmiel, 66
Kochberg, Rutcia, 66
Kochberg, Sura, 66
Kochberg, Syma [daughter of Herszel Litvak], 66
Kochberg, Szmul-Dawid, 66
Kochman, Mordechai, 52, 140, 143, 301
Kolabik[?], Szymon, see Nowak, Szymon
Kolewiziner, Syna, 49
Kolwizner, Jecheskiel, 163
Kon, Frajdel, 381
Kon, Hersz-Lajb, 381
Kon, Jechiel, 381
Kon, Jochwet, 381

Kon, Małka, 381
Kon, Necha, 381
Kon, Pinchasl, 381
Kon, Szaja-Awigdor, 381
Kon, Szlama ben Szaja-Awigdor, 381
Kop[?], Mendel [*melamed*], 88
Kopel, Mojsze, 49, 61, 105–6, 135, 181
Kopel, Syna, 49
Kopler [head of Jewish public school], 142
Kopmann, Manen, 213, 219, 223
Kordelas, Jankiel, 57, 81
Korekh[?], Abraham, see Rozen, Abraham
Korekh[?], Herszel, see Rozen, Herszel
Korekh[?], Syna, 49
Korman, Dr., 143
Kornblum Brothers, 145
Kornblum, Chemia, 396
Kornblum, Gołda, 396
Kornblum, Herszel, 396
Kornblum, Izrael, 181, 306
Kornblum, Szyja, 181
Kornblum, Josef, 396
Kornblum, Josef Aszer, 81, 396
Kornblum, Morris, 396
Kornblum, Pesa, 396
Kornblum, Sura, 396
Kornblum, Szyja, 396
Korolenki, 223
Korpel, Mojsze, 26
Kosher[?], Ruwen [rabbi], 123, 125
Kossuth, Lajos, 110
Kotsker, Chaim-Lajbele, 51
Kotsker, Chaiml [rabbi], 226
Kowalska, Masza, 385
Kowalska, Sura, 396
Kowalski, Isaac, 385
Kowalski, Mojsze, 396
Koyke[?], Elija Mojsze [gravedigger], 55
Kozak, Majer, 27
Koznakov, General, 46
Krakowiak, Lajzer, 368
Krakowiak, Pesa bas Izrael-Gerszon, 368
Kranc, Herszel, 42
Krasowska, Alina, 389
Krasowska, Nata, 389
Krasowski, Dr. Władysław, 389
Kraushorn, Fiszel, 387
Kraushorn, Laja, 387
Kraushorn, Mojsze-Jehuda, 387

Kraushorn, Raszka, 394
Krauze, Gerszon, 140, 368
Krauze, Hersz, 49
Krauze, Syna, 49
Krawiecka, Chana Chaja, 39, 57, 406
Krawiecka, Leah m. Hirsch, 406
Krawiecki, Szymon, 44, 57, 406
Krawiecki, Tobiasz, 236
Krawiecki, Tuwia, 145
Krell, Josef (aka Josef Gotek), 61
Krengel, Morris, 249, 271
Krengel, Stach [Stanisław], 145, 180–81
Kriger, Izrael, 111
Krok, Abraham, 317
Krongold, Jehuda, 69
Krongold, Szmule, 69
Krongold, Szymon, 306
Krongrad, 244
Krongrad, Eliezer (aka the ample Eliezer), 138
Krongrad, Fiszel, 77, 244
Krongrad, Jakub-Hersz, 77
Krongrad, Jehuda, 77, 134, 137
Krongrad, Mrs., 244
Krongrad, Sura m. Maliniak, 77
Krongrad, Szymele, 52, 77, 138, 163
Krongrad, Szymon, 56, 175, 302
Krongrad, Tojwen Luzer, 77
Krulik[?], Szlama Lajb, see Kalisz, Szlama Lajb
Kujawska, Bronia, 395
Kujawska, Brucha, 395
Kujawska, Dwojre-Laja, 374
Kujawska, Edzia m. Frohman, 395
Kujawska, Jochwet, 395
Kujawska, Perla-Pola, 395
Kujawska, Rywka, 395
Kujawski, 60, 142, 330
Kujawski, Abraham-Josef, 374
Kujawski, Anszel, 395
Kujawski, Aron, see Kuyawsky, Aaron
Kujawski, Bernard, v, 335
Kujawski, Chaim-Hersz, 374
Kujawski, Dan-Aszer (aka Dan-Aszer Beker), 77, 246, 374
Kujawski, Eliasz-Eli, 395
Kujawski, Mojsze, 395
Kujawski, Symche-Binem, 77
Kujawski, Szlama, 395
Kujawski, see also Kuyawsky

INDEX

Kuker[?], Mojszele, see Rozenberg, Mojsze
Kutner[?], 215
Kutner[?], Jehoszele [rabbi], see Trunk, Izrael Jehoszua
Kuyawsky, Aaron (Kujawski, Aron), 77, 251, 253, 255, 257, 263, 291
Kuyawsky, Abraham, 272
Lachman [school director], 144
Lachman Brothers, 335, 380
Lachman, Berl, 138
Lachman, Blume, 103
Lachman, Herszel, 52, 73–74, 138, 163, 326, 380
Lachman, Mark, 74
Lachman, Mordechai, 74
Lachman, Ralph (Jerachmiel), 74
Lachman, Sam (Szulem), 74
Lachman, Steve, 74
Lachman, Szymon, 335
Lachowska (Milsztajn), Chajka, 379
Lachowski (Milsztajn), Abraham, 379
Lajfer, Joel, 105
Landau, 134
Landau, Icek, 90
Landsbergers [rich family in Tomaszów], 89
Lange, Chana, 385
Laska, Małka Ruchel, 379
Lasker, Fiszel (aka Fiszel Shoykhet), 137, 319
Lasky, Meyer, 275, 279
Lasky, Renee, 262, 275, 279
Lax, Jack, 290
Łęczycka, Chana, 380
Łęczycka, Chana-Laja, 379
Łęczycka, Marjem, 320
Łęczycki, 136, 304
Łęczycki, Dawid, see Lencicki, David
Łęczycki, Eliasz, 58
Łęczycki, Icek Majer, 36, 58
Łęczycki, Mojsze, 380
Łęczycki, Mordechai (aka Mordechai Pakel), 52
Łęczycki, Mordechai, 379
Łęczycki, Nachman, 37
Łęczycki, Natan, 36, 61, 134, 137, 320
Łęczyńcka, Mindel, 400
Łęczyńcki, Chaim-Symcha, 400
Lederman, Herszel, 163
Ledershniter[?], Eliezer, 54
Ledershniter[?], Hersz/Herszel, 69, 78, 99
Ledershniter[?], Kajla-Rywa b. Herszenberg, 78
Lefkowicz, Abraham, 380
Lefkowicz, Dawid, 380, 387
Lefkowicz, Ester-Małka, 380
Lefkowicz, Fiszel, 380
Lefkowicz, Lajzer, 380
Lefkowicz, Lemel (aka Lemel Byk), 59, 104
Lefkowicz, Lemel, 380
Lefkowicz, Perla, 380
Lefkowicz, Rajzel b. Eksztajn, 387
Lefkowicz, Ruchel, 380
Lefkowitz, Rose, 262
Lehrer, Lajbuś, 256, 292, 333
Lehrer, Mary, 261
Lehrer, Mrs., 333
Lechtreger, Aron, 14
Lechtreger, Icze, 145
Lechtreger, Judke, 173
Lechtreger, Motel (the short one), 187
Lechtreger, Motel (the tall one), 187
Leivick, H., 256
Lencicki, Chajce, 320
Lencicki, David b. Łęczycki, v, xiv–xv, 61, 320–21
Lenga, Henie, 380
Lenga, K., 380
Lenga, Szulem, 380
Lerer, Abraham ben Symcha, 381
Lerer, Aron ben Szlama, 381
Lerer, Cypa m. Richter, 381
Lerer, Frajdel, 381
Lerer, Hinda, 381
Lerer, Chaiml, 381
Lerer, Chaim-Wolf ben Mojsze, 381
Lerer, Izrael-Icek, 381
Lerer, Izraelik, 381
Lerer, Jakub-Hersz, 381
Lerer, Krajndl b. Fuks, 381
Lerer, Mania, 381
Lerer, Mojsze, 381
Lerer, Szaja, 57
Lerer, Szaja-Awigdor, 381
Lerer, Szlama, 381
Lerer, Szulem, 72, 381
Lerer, Szulem ben Izrael-Icek, 381
Lerer, Wolf, 381
Lerer-Singer, Małka, 381
Lerer-Szajbowicz, Sara, 381

Levy, Sarah, 262
Lewandowski [Firemen's Hall caretaker], 188
Lewi, Azriel, 49
Lewi, Issachar, 49
Lewin, Icze Majer, 146
Liberman, Hersz, 163
Liberman, Mendel, 163
Liebeskind [printer], 231
Lichtel[?], Lajbel, see Rozenblat, Lajbel
Lichtensztajn, Chaim, 406
Lichtreger, Hinda bas Abraham-Nachum, 379
Lichtreger, Icek, 379
Lipman, Chanina, 68
Lipska, Ester m. Fajngold, 392
Lipski, N., 392
Lipszyc, Cwi Dov, 318
Lipszyc, Mina, 318
Liskiewiczer, A, 61
Litvak[?], Cyna-Ruchel, 170
Litvak[?], Cywia, 170
Litvak[?], Herszel, xxiv, 66, 86, 169–70, 407
Litvak[?], Hersz-Chaim, 170
Litvak[?], Isroelik, 170
Litvak[?], Jakub-Icek, 170
Litvak[?], Josef-Henoch, 170–71
Litvak[?], Sima, 170
Litvak[?], Sura-Chana, 170
Litvak[?], Szmul-Mojsze, see Gajer, Szmul-Mojsze [rabbi]
Litvak[?], Tema, 169–70
Litwin, Szulem, 177
Lodzer[?], Josel, 106
Loew, 29
Lomaniec/Loomanitz, Bajla-Bina m. Buki, 379
Loomanitz, Benny, 253–54, 263
Loomanitz, Ester-Fajga, 379
Lukekhbeker[?], Josef, 82
Lustig, 27
Lustig, Alter, 380
Lustig, Anczel, 181, 380
Lustig, Bela m, Szyf, 380
Lustig, Ester m. Flamholc, 380
Lustig, Ruchel-Liba, 380
Lustig, Rywka m. Horn, 380
Lustig, Szaja, 380
Lustig, Wolf, 380
Lutomski [German], 213
Magnes, 33
Mahler, Dr. Rafał, 29

Majerholc, Bluma, 405
Majerholc, Fajga, 382
Majerholc, Szaja, 405
Majerowicz (aka Sosek), 140
Majerowicz, Abraham (aka Abraham Sosek), 104–6
Majerowicz, Berysz (aka Berysz Sosek), 104
Majerowicz, Perel, 140
Majranc, Hinda m. Mendlewicz, 101
Majranc, Jehunsen, 101
Malamut, Chajka, 187
Malarz[?], see Fuks
Malech[?], Jecheskiel [went to Israel], 73
Maliniak, Bruche, 77
Maliniak, Chajele, 77
Maliniak, Chawecia, 77
Maliniak, Fajgele, 77
Maliniak, Fishel/Fiszel, v–vi, xv, 77, 131, 146, 235, 269–70, 275–76, 278, 280–81, 283–87, 302, 310, 315, 333, 335
Maliniak, Icek, 77
Maliniak, Josel, 77
Maliniak, Josel Szulem's, 137
Maliniak, Rajze, 135
Maliniak, Sam, 275
Maliniak, Sura b. Krongold, 77
Maliniak, Symele, 77
Maliniak, Szlama, 77
Maliniak, Szulem (aka Szulem Waynshenker), 76, 132
Maliniak, Wowcie [Vovche], 77
Mandel, Icze, 181
Mandel, Icze-Ber, 163, 382
Mandel, Ita, 382
Mandel, Szymon, 140
Manhajm, Gela b. Szotland, 403
Manis, Rywka m. Grundsztajn, 367
Map, Eliezer, 49
Map, Syna, 49
Markowicz Family, 306
Markowicz-Erlich, Bluma, 310
Markus, Dora b. Efroimowicz, 386
Maroko, Jakub, 237
Martov, L., 29
Meisel, N., 256
Meisels, Eliahu Chaim [rabbi of Łódź], 49, 228
Melamed[?], Abraham Mojsze, xxiv, 54, 84
Melamed[?], Benjamin, see Herszenberg, Benjamin

INDEX

Melamed[?], Chaim Mojsze [rabbi], 54
Melamed[?], Dawid, 53
Melamed[?], Eliezer, 54
Melamed[?], Gimpele, xxiv, 37, 86, 101
Melamed[?], Henoch, xxiv
Melamed[?], Henoch [brother of Icze-Majer Melamed], 86
Melamed[?], Icek-Mendel, 101
Melamed[?], Icze-Majer, xxiv, 86
Melamed[?], Jankiele [rabbi] (aka the blind Jankiele), xxiv, 53–54, 82, 84
Melamed[?], Jeremia (aka the *vzvodny*), 101
Melamed[?], Josef, 54
Melamed[?], Libele (*rebetsn*) [wife of Jankiel Melamed], 53
Melamed[?], Luzer, see Betcajg, Luzer
Melamed[?], Majer, see Rozen, Majer
Melamed[?], Nechemia (aka the *zvorny*), 54, 143
Melamed[?], Pinkus [rabbi] (aka Pinyele), 54
Melamed[?], Szlama Perec, 54, 85
Melamed[?], Szmul Mojsze, 54, 101
Melamed[?], The Glowner [from Głowno], 87
Melamed[?], The Lutomiersker [from Lutomiersk], 87
Melekh, Eliezer, 49
Melekh, Syna, 49
Meler, Judel, 80
Mendlewicz, 304
Mendlewicz Family, 92
Mendlewicz, Abraham-Chaim, 101–3
Mendlewicz, Aron, v, 36, 42, 92, 101, 103, 306, 310–11, 325
Mendlewicz, Aron-Lajb, 99–100
Mendlewicz, Fajwel-Majer, 57, 69, 92, 98–99, 103
Mendlewicz, Heniek, 100
Mendlewicz, Herszel (aka Herszel Mojsze Zyndel's), 93–96, 98–99, 102, 163
Mendlewicz, Herszele [gdson of Herszel], 102
Mendlewicz, Hinda b. Majranc, 101
Mendlewicz, Icze [Icek], 98–100, 103
Mendlewicz, Mojsze, 100
Mendlewicz, Mojsze-Mordechai, 101–2, 382
Mendlewicz, Perla b. Temkin, 100
Mendlewicz, Pinkus, 100, 103
Mendlewicz, S., 315
Mendlewicz, Szyfra-Golda/Szyfkele b. Halbersztadt, 98–99, 103
Mendlewicz, Taubcia b. Nowomiast, 102

Mendlewicz, Taubcia b. Wolman, 100, 103
Mendlewicz, Tyla b. Goldberg, 59, 93, 97–99, 163
Mer-Goldkranc, Mrs. Guta, 244
Mickiewicz, Adam, 110
Michrowska, Chaja, 317
Michrowska, Chana, 368
Michrowska, Laja, 368
Michrowska, Masza, 368
Michrowski, Abraham, 274, 317
Michrowski, Dawid Mendel, 56, 368
Michrowski, Elimelech, 306, 317
Miler, Dawid and Jehudit, 402
Miller, Abe, 257
Miller, B., 289
Miller, Chanka, 382
Miller, Eli Ber, 63
Miller, Hetty, 290
Miller, Majer, 382
Milner, Elka, 66
Milstein, Sam, 279
Milsztajn, Cywia, 383
Milsztajn, Cywka m. Zylberberg, 383
Milsztajn, Chaim ben Abraham, 383
Milsztajn, Henri, 383
Milsztajn, Izrael, 383
Milsztajn, Jacques, 383
Milsztajn, Jachet m. Fuks, 383
Milsztajn, Josef ben Chaim, 383
Milsztajn, Małka, 383
Milsztajn, see Lachowski
Milsztajn, Cywka m. Zylberberg, 407
Minkoff, N. B., 256
Mirkin [established modern kheyder], 42–43
Mitelsztajn, 246
Mitelsztajn, Fiszel, 141, 302
Mizes [Fraulein], 207
Mizes, Perec, 82
Młynarzewska, Perla-Rywka (Polja), 396
Młynarzewski, Abraham, 396
Młynarzewski, Herszel, 108
Moc[?], Mojsze, see Kalisz, Mojsze-Lajb
Monat, Szajna-Rywka m. Betcajg, 377
Mosel, Herr [Mr.], 334
Moskowicz, Izak, 405
Moskwer[?] [accessories store], 77
Moskwer[?], Chanele, 77
Moszkowicz, Sara, 382, 405
Moyfes[?], Eliezer, 57

Mshumak[?], see Winter, Emanuel
Muraczewski, Andrzej, 158–59
Mydlak, Fajgele (aka Fajga the water carrier), 55, 215, 220
Mydlak, Icze/Iczele, 55, 156, 215
Nafthendler[?], Many, see Blat, Many
Najman, 14
Najman, A, 244
Najman, Abraham, 384
Najman, Aron, 385
Najman, Aszer, 385
Najman, Bela m. Pilichowska, 385
Najman, Brucha, 385, 407
Najman, Chaim, 385
Najman, Chaim-Jehuda, 385
Najman, Chaskiel, 79, 137, 150, 407, see also Jecheskiel Najman
Najman, Chawcia, 384
Najman, Elimelech (aka Elimelech Jecheskiel Roda Laja's), 54
Najman, Fajgele m. Fogel, 79
Najman, Fiszel, 385
Najman, Gołda-Kajla, 385
Najman, Hendel, 385
Najman, Izrael, 385
Najman, Izraelik, 385
Najman, Jecheskiel, 385, see also Chaskiel Najman
Najman, Jecheskiel (aka Jecheskiel Roda Laja's), 42, 52
Najman, Jecheskiel (aka Jecheskiel Shenker), 52, 163
Najman, Jojne, 385
Najman, Lajbel/Lajbuśl (aka Lajbel/Lajbuśl Shenker), 54, 163
Najman, M, 73
Najman, Mordechai, 385
Najman, Perla (Percia), 385
Najman, Pinkus, 385
Najman, Polia, 385
Najman, Rajzel, 385
Najman, Roda Laja, 52, 54
Najman, Ruta Laja, 79
Najman, Rywa (aka Kashemakher), 386
Najman, Rywka b. Bursztajn, 385
Najman, Surecia b. Igielska, 384
Najman, Syna (aka Kashemakher), 386
Naks, Dr. E. (aka Izrael Knox), 256
Neifeld, Mojsze-Zev, 361

Neifeld, Perla-Laja m. Bursztajn, 361
Newman, Charlie, 289, 385, 407
Newman, Ester bas Majer, 386
Newman, Harry, 290, 385
Newman, Isidor, 386
Newman, Machel, 385, 407
Newman, Sam, 249, 291
Newman, Willi, v
Newman, Wolf, 385, 407
Niedźwiedź, Wacław, 139, 162
Niewiadowicz, Aron, 376
Niewiadowicz, Chanele, 376
Niewiadowicz, Ester-Laja, 376
Niewiadowicz, Fajga, 376
Niewiadowicz, Fajwisz, 376
Niewiadowicz, Fiszel, 376
Niewiadowicz, Herszel, 376
Niewiadowicz, Josel, 376
Niewiadowicz, Róża, 376
Niewodowicz, Ezekiel, 28
Niger, S., 256
Nikolajewski, 76
Ninenbergs [German family], 48
Nirenberg, Jakub, 30
Nisenberg (Berg), Abraham, 366
Nisenberg (Berg), Fajga, 378
Nisenberg (Berg), Jonah, 366
Nisenberg (Berg), Kasriel, 366
Nisenberg, Chaim-Icek (aka Chaim-Icek Ajnbinder), xxiii, 37, 48, 60, 69, 78, 163, 336–37, 365, 378
Nisenberg, Chajela b. Szotland, 75, 336
Nisenberg, Fajgele bas Kasriel, 365
Nisenberg, Gitel m. Rozenblum, 365
Nisenberg, Issachar, 60
Nisenberg, Izrael (the yellow Izrael), 336
Nisenberg, Jakub Dawid, see Berg, Jacob David
Nisenberg, Marjem b. Szotland, 365
Nisenberg, Ruchel m. Grynfeld, 366
Nisenberg, Rywka m. Tajtelbaum, 365
Nisenhaus, Kuna, 389
Nisenhaus, Michał ben Rywen, 389
Nisenhaus, Rywen ben Michał, 389
Nordau, Max, 295
Nowak, Ab., 385
Nowak, Arcie ben Zalman, 384
Nowak, Bajla-Chana bas Motel, 385
Nowak, Chaim-Nuchem ben Zalman, 384

INDEX

Nowak, Chana bas Zalman, 384
Nowak, Cwi-Jehuda ben Szmul Dawid, 391
Nowak, Fajgele, 385
Nowak, Gela-Fajga bas Szmul-Dawid, 391
Nowak, Hersz, 385
Nowak, Herszel, 382
Nowak, Ita-Małka, 385
Nowak, Josele, 384
Nowak, Laja m. Tajfel, 385
Nowak, Lajele, 384
Nowak, Matel b. Pakula, 384
Nowak, Mordechai, 385
Nowak, Morton, 382
Nowak, Naftali ben Zalman, 384
Nowak, Nachum, 181
Nowak, Rajzel b. Szydłowska, 384
Nowak, Szmul-Dawid, 385
Nowak, Szymon, 385
Nowak, Szymon (aka Szymon Kolabik), 52
Nowak, Zalman (Prusak), 384
Nowomiast, Mojsze, 102
Nowomiast, Taubcia m. Mendlewicz, 102
Nubiński, Arje, 175
Nusbaum, Maks, 386
Opatowski, Abraham, 27, 30, 222, 246
Opoczyński, Abraham Jonas, 63
Opolian, Eliezer (aka the fat Luzer), 164
Opolion, Mojsze-Josel, 138
Oratowski, Fajga, 368
Oratowski, Lemel, 368
Orenstein, Mark, xxv
Orensztajn, Helen b. Ikka, 362
Pabianicer[?], Mojsze, see Beserglik, Mojsze
Pabianicer[?], Szlama, 69
Pabianicer[?], Szmul-Lajb, see Beserglik, Szmul-Lajb
Pachczer [Pachciarz?], 201
Pachter, Szmul (aka Szmul Brzeziner), 124
Paja, Abraham, 169
Pajczer, Danielekhl, 50
Pajger[?], Aron, see Waldman, Aron
Pakel[?], Mordechai, see Łęczycki, Mordechai
Paker, Eliezer, 57
Pakrels, Abraham, 63
Pakula, Gussie, 261, 275, 279
Pakula, Jakub, 384
Pakula, Matel m. Nowak, 384

Pakull, Anna, 262
Parzęczewski, Pincia-Noech, 136
Parzęczewski, Pinkus, 143
Pas, Josef, 237
Pat, Dr. Emanuel, 256
Pat, Jacob, xx
Pawe, Ester-Gitel b. Joab, 392
Pawe, Josef, 392
Pawe, Szlama-Jakub ben Abraham, 392
Peizer, Toviah, 251, 253, 255, 257, 291
Pereira, Rabbi [chief rabbi of Holland], 334
Peretz, I. L., 70
Perlmuter, Abraham Cwi [rabbi], 72, 78, 91, 99
Perlmuter, Arje Dawid, 10, 35, 41, 60, 68, 72, 78, 136, 173
Perlmuter, Eliezer, 42
Perlmuter, Izraelik, 54
Perlmuter, Mojsze Eliezer, 35–36
Perlmuter, Seweryn, 207, 219
Perlmuter, Sura (Herszenberg) b. Joskowicz, 78
Peters, Harry b. Piotrkowski, 81, 271, 275, 279
Pieczana [Russian policeman], 45, 55
Pilater, Abraham, 391
Pilater, Ajdel, 391
Pilater, Becalel, 391
Pilater, Chaim, 391
Pilater, Emanuel ben Chaim, 391
Pilater, Ester, 391
Pilater, Gołda bas Jakub-Szlama, 391
Pilater, Henoch, 391
Pilater, Hinda bas Hersz, 391
Pilater, Mariem, 391
Pilater, Matel-Fajga, 391
Pilater, Perla bas Cwi-Mendel, 391
Pilater, Rywka b. Rymer, 391
Pilater, Rywka bas Abraham, 391
Pilater, Towa, 391
Pilichowska, Bela b. Najman, 385
Pilichowska, Natalia, 389
Pilichowski, M., 385
Pilichowski, Ryś [Ryszard], 389
Pilichowski, Sławek, 389
Pilichowski, Stach [Stanisław], 389
Pinczewska, Dwojra-Chana b. Brzeziner, 75
Pinczewska, Fajga, 75
Pinczewska, Perla-Laja, 380
Pinczewski Brothers, 325
Pinczewski, Henoch, 75, 137
Pinczewski, Hersz Mendel, 34, 56, 75, 163

Pinczewski, Lajbuś-Mendel, 136
Pinczewski, Naftali, 75
Pinczewski, S., 67
Pinczewski, Szlama, v, xv, 75, 279, 325
Piotrkowska (Peters), Sura-Ita, 395
Piotrkowska, Cywia, 393
Piotrkowska, Rechel, 393
Piotrkowska, Ruchel, 393
Piotrkowski, Abraham-Nachum, 81
Piotrkowski, B., 393
Piotrkowski, Benisz, 145
Piotrkowski, Hersz, see Peters, Harry
Piotrkowski, M., 289
Piotrkowski, Perec, 61, 393
Piotrkowski, Pinchas-Hersz, 393
Piotrkowski, Tuwia, 81
Platau, Dr. [in Warsaw], 97
Pluśnik, Hudes b. Igielska, 384
Pluśnik, Szajele, 384
Pluśnik, Zalman, 384
Polański, 43
Polewinczyk, Abraham, 104
Poliwoda, Abraham-Elije, 393
Poliwoda, Chana-Kajla, 393
Poliwoda, David, v, xv, 302, 304–5, 310, 311, 315, 326, 393
Poliwoda, Laja, 393
Poliwoda, Majer, 63
Poliwoda, Zebul, 306
Poliwoda, Zelda-Ruchel, 393
Potasiewicz, Ita-Małka b. Szeps, 134
Potasiewicz, Jakub, 134–35
Poznańska, Gela, 393
Poznański, 239
Poznański, Icze, 157
Poznański, Majer, 393
Pozner, Phillip, 393
Princ, Henoch, 163
Pruszyński, 302
Psilke [*shames*], 70
Pytel, Chaim Ber, 63
Rabinowicz, Szmul, 61, 63
Raczkowski, 76
Radoszycer, Natan, 63
Radoszycki, I. H, 185
Rajchman, Eliezer (the ample Luzer), 61
Rajchman, Menachem, 302
Rajchman, Mendel, 306
Rakhmones, Szymon bal, 47, 48

Ranis, Chaja-Sura, 66
Raszewski, 33, 73, 237
Raszewski, Małka-Rajza, 397
Raszewski, Mojsze, 134, 210
Raszewski, Mojsze ben Nisen, 397
Rechseit, Hyman, 249–50
Rechtzeit, Jack, 145
Richter [Gestapo], 220
Richter, Aszer, 381
Richter, Chaim, 363, 381
Richter, Cypa b. Lerer, 381
Richter, Fela b. Baron, 363
Richter, Izraelik, 381
Richter, Mania, 381
Richter, Nachman, 381
Ringelblum, 29
Ringort, Chana b. Rozen, 399
Rogodziński, Josel (aka Josel Warszawer), 58
Rochwerg, 73
Rochwerg, Jekiel, 139
Rochwerg, Jankiel [rabbi], 53
Rose, Malka b. Rozenblum, 187, 189
Rosen, see Rozen
Rosenfeld, Morris [poet], 156
Rosman, Abraham Icek, 252
Rosman, Icek, 253
Rosman, M., 252
Rotholc, Mrs. S, 378
Rotholc, S., 378
Rotman, Gitel, 366
Rotman, Icek, 366
Rotman, Marjem b. Rozenblum, 366
Rotter, L., 386
Rotter, Mrs. L., 386
Rozen, 13
Rozen, Aba Hersz, 51
Rozen, Abraham, 385
Rozen, Abraham (aka Abraham Korekh), xxiv, 75
Rozen, Basia, 172
Rozen, Chana m. Ringort, 399
Rozen, Cypa (the Gerer *rebbe*'s daughter), 399
Rozen, Eliezer-Mendel, 137
Rozen, Ester, 399
Rozen, Fajga, 399
Rozen, Fela, 385
Rozen, Herszel (aka Herszel Korekh), xxiv, 33, 52, 56, 75
Rozen, Itka, 399

Rozen, Josef, 29
Rozen, Luzer-Mendel ben Majer, 399
Rozen, Majer, 399
Rozen, Majer (aka Majer Melamed), 137, 143
Rozen, Małka, 399
Rozen, Mira, 221
Rozen, Rywka b. Szwarc, 399
Rozen, Sura-Laja, 399
Rozen, Syna (aka Syna Naczelnik), 172
Rozen, Szaja, 399
Rozen, Tyla, 51
Rozen, Yekl (aka Yekl Tyla Aba Hersz's), 51
Rozenberg [nurse], 207
Rozenberg [paint & kerosene], 163
Rozenberg, A., 73, 276
Rozenberg, Abraham, v–vi, xv, 79, 82, 144, 148, 179, 275, 279, 281–82, 285, 333, 399
Rozenberg, Aron Kalman's, 163
Rozenberg, Aron, 82, 173
Rozenberg, Aszer ben Mojsze, 368
Rozenberg, Chana, 400–401
Rozenberg, Chana-Jochwet b. Wolrajch, 401
Rozenberg, Chanina ben Kalman, 400
Rozenberg, D., 244
Rozenberg, David, 305
Rozenberg, Dwojra, 399
Rozenberg, Dwojra (aka the Elijeta), 79, 397
Rozenberg, Eliasz-Chaim, 399
Rozenberg, Elija, 397
Rozenberg, Elija (aka Elija Cypora-Ruchel's), 79, 163
Rozenberg, Ester bas Mojsze, 368
Rozenberg, Ester, 400
Rozenberg, Feivel, 79, 163, 257, 272–73, 275, 278, 291, 399
Rozenberg, Henie, 401
Rozenberg, Icze (aka Icze Mojszele Kuker's), 52
Rozenberg, Izrael, 228
Rozenberg, Jakub, 244
Rozenberg, Josef, 82, 401
Rozenberg, Josef ben Kalman, 401
Rozenberg, Josel (the blind Michał's), 52
Rozenberg, Kalman, 82, 163
Rozenberg, Laja, 401
Rozenberg, M, 291, 400
Rozenberg, Mania-Róża bas Mojsze, 368
Rozenberg, Mariem, 401
Rozenberg, Menachem Mendel, 400
Rozenberg, Michał, 79, 397
Rozenberg, Michał (the blind Michał), 52
Rozenberg, Mindel, 400
Rozenberg, Mojsze, 82, 368
Rozenberg, Mojsze (aka Mojszele Kuker), 52
Rozenberg, Mojsze (Kalmus), 134
Rozenberg, Mojsze-Icek, 400
Rozenberg, Pawa, 401
Rozenberg, Ruchel, 400
Rozenberg, Sura, 400
Rozenberg, Sura-Frajdel bas Aszer, 368
Rozenberg, Zelda, 399
Rozenberg-Jablonka, Regina, 401
Rozenblat, Benjamin, 399
Rozenblat, Chawa, 399
Rozenblat, Izzy, 400
Rozenblat, J., 289
Rozenblat, Lajbel (aka Lajbel Lichtel), 63
Rozenblat, M., 399
Rozenblat, Szaja, 399
Rozenblum [professor], 142
Rozenblum, A., vi
Rozenblum, Abraham-Dawid, 365
Rozenblum, Adela, 228
Rozenblum, Anna, 335, 398
Rozenblum, Arje, 365
Rozenblum, Bencion, 365
Rozenblum, Berysz, 163
Rozenblum, Chaim Rafał, 140, 246, 398
Rozenblum, Chaja, 398
Rozenblum, Chajele, 365
Rozenblum, Dwojra, 398
Rozenblum, Fela, 366
Rozenblum, Gitel b. Nisenberg, 365
Rozenblum, Gołda, 365
Rozenblum, Herszel, 246
Rozenblum, Herszel ben Chaim-Jona, 398
Rozenblum, Hersz-Iser, 36–37, 171–72
Rozenblum, Iser, 155
Rozenblum, Isidor, 335
Rozenblum, Izzy (Icek), 398
Rozenblum, J., 275, 279
Rozenblum, Jakub Eli, 36
Rozenblum, Jechiel, 365
Rozenblum, Jonah, 398
Rozenblum, Laja b. Holcberg, 50
Rozenblum, Lajb (aka Lajb Lekhernejer [buttonhole maker]), 397
Rozenblum, Lajzer, 365–66

Rozenblum, Lajzer ben Chaim-Jona, 398
Rozenblum, Lyuba b. Szotenberg, 173
Rozenblum, Majer, 155, 171–73, 189
Rozenblum, Małka, 398
Rozenblum, Małka (aka Malka Rose), 187, 189
Rozenblum, Manuele, 365
Rozenblum, Marjem, 365
Rozenblum, Marjem m. Rotman, 366
Rozenblum, Mendel Majer, 50
Rozenblum, Mojsze, 365
Rozenblum, Mojsze-Jojne, 36, 171–72
Rozenblum, Rachel, 261
Rozenblum, Różka, 365
Rozenblum, Sura-Gitel, 366
Rozenblum, Symcha, 398
Rozenblum, Szaja, 302
Rozenblum, Szaja (aka Szaja Zeygermacher), 141
Rozenblum, Szymon, 398
Rozenblum, Trajna bas Lajzer Chaim-Jona, 398
Rozenblum, Velvel/Welwel, 169, 184, 189, 254
Rozenblum, Zlata-Laja, 365–66
Rozenfeld, Alter, 251–53, 255, 257, 275, 278, 284, 286, 291
Rozenfeld, Willie, 275, 279
Rozenkranc, Szmul, 181
Rozenkrantz, Izrael, 249
Rozenkrantz, J. H., 291
Rozenstrauch, 14
Rozenstrauch, Dwojra m. Benkel, 376
Rozenstrauch, Hil, 14
Rozenstrauch, M., 28
Rozman, A., 291
Rozner, B., 400
Rozner, Josef ben Aba-Hersz, 400
Rozner, Tyle bas Rafał, 400
Rubin, Dawid, 397
Rubin, Izrael, 228
Rubin, Mojsze, 73, 400
Rubin, Szprynca, 400
Rubinstein, Kive, 249
Rubinstein, S., 289
Rudnicki, Henie, 390
Rudnicki, Szlama-Hersz, 390
Rumkowski, Chaim, 221–22
Rymer, Rywka m. Pilater, 391
Sanberg, Louis, v
Sapir, Elke b. Szpiro (Halewi), 49
Sapir, Syna [rabbi], 49, 112

Schilsky, see also Silski
Schilsky, Izzy, 275, 279
Schilsky, Molly, 262
Schiper, Dr. Icchak [Ignacy], 20
Schulsinger, Nathan, 402
Schwartz, S., 278
Schwartz, Szlama, 275, 287, 335
Segal, Abraham Abele (aka Abraham Abele Gombiner) [rabbi], 101
Segal, Herbert, 290
Segal, Max, v
Segal, Menachem Mendel HaCohen [rabbi], 165
Segal, Shirley, 386
Segalowicz, Zusman, 70, 341
Seikin, Dr., 256
Selin, Aaron, 79, 266, 269, 275, 279, 291
Sender, 208
Sender, Lajbl, 27
Shaibowicz, see also Szajbowicz
Shaibowicz (Shaw), Joseph, v–vi, xv, 3, 118, 273, 275
Shakher[?], Herszel, see Bercholc, Herszel
Shames[?], Hillel, see Holcberg, Hillel
Shapiro, Esther, 262
Shefner, B., 256
Shein, M. [Manager of International in Canada], 283
Shenker[?], Jecheskiel, see Najman, Jecheskiel
Shenker[?], Lajbel/Lajbuśl, see Najman, Lajbel/Lajbuśl
Sher, M., 291
Shirhamayles[?], xxiii, 58–59
Shoykhet[?], Dawid Hersz, 69
Shoykhet[?], Fiszel, 72, 136, 143
Shoykhet[?], Fiszel, see Lasker, Fiszel
Shoykhet[?], Fiszel, see Żychliński, Fiszel
Shulsinger Brothers, v
Shuster[?], Aron, see Aronowicz, Abraham
Shuster[?], Majerke, 54
Shuster[?], Mojsze, see Aronowicz, Mojsze
Shuster[?], Srulke/Izrael, see Sułkowicz, Izrael
Shveyger[?], Fajgele, 107
Shveyger[?], Menes, 107
Sieradzka, Frajdel, 407
Sieradzki, Berysz, 407
Sieradzki, Lajb, 29, 173
Sieradzki, Wolf, 407

Silski, Mirel, 68
Silski, Szlama, 35, 43, 59, 60, 68, 72, 76, 98
Silverstein, J., 291
Singer, J. J., 20
Singer, Małka b. Lerer, 381
Sirota, Gerszon, 155
Sklita, Benjamin Ze'ev Benedict [rabbi], 334
Skurnik, Fajga, 386
Snyder, E., 279
Snyder, Manny, 275, 291
Sobovinsky, Katie, 258
Sobowinsky, David-Lajb, 386
Sobowinsky, Fajga-Brucha, 386
Sobowinsky, S., v–vi
Sobowinsky, Sol, 386
Sochaczewski, Judel (aka Judel the water carrier), 215, 220, 225
Sorkin, 112
Sosek[?], see Majerowicz
Soyfer[?], Dawidl, 54
Soyfer[?], Josef, see Całek, Josef
Soyfer[?], Juda/Judel, 54, 82, 138
Spektor, Elchanon [rabbi of Kowno], 49
Sperling, Chana m. Dymant, 370
Spiegel [teacher], 142–43, 301
Srocker, Herszel, 163
Śrubka, Mindel b. Wajnberg, 375
Stajn, Aneta, 187
Stal Family, 404
Stal, Abraham, 404
Stal, Brajna, 404
Stal, Jechiel, 404
Stal, Mojsze-Dawid, 404
Stal, Mojsze-Josef, 367, 404
Stark, 208, 209
Staszewer, Jankiel, 56
Stawian, 61
Stein, S, 367
Stein, Sam, 290
Sterns, Mojszl (aka Mojszl Chazen), 61, 72, 81, 138, 155
Stodółkiewicz, Dr., 10, 169
Strykower[?], Fiszele, see Szpiro, Fiszele
Strykower[?], Wolf [rabbi], 125
Strykower[?], Szlama, 43
Strykowski, Herr [Mr.], 334
Strzyszewski, Herszel, 46
Strzyzewski, Jankiel, 54
Sułkowicz, 18, 73, 218

Sułkowicz Brothers, 82, 134
Sułkowicz Family, 212
Sułkowicz, Aba-Hersz, 76
Sułkowicz, Bronia, 244
Sułkowicz, Chaja, 378
Sułkowicz, Chana, 310
Sułkowicz, Chanele, 76
Sułkowicz, Dawid, 76, 144
Sułkowicz, Ester, 144
Sułkowicz, Frajda, 244
Sułkowicz, I., 244
Sułkowicz, Izrael, 82
Sułkowicz, Izrael (aka Srulke/Izrael Shuster), 76
Sułkowicz, Izrael Dawid, 246
Sułkowicz, Jakub, 175, 208
Sułkowicz, Jojne, 76
Sułkowicz, Jukiel, 76, 246
Sułkowicz, Majer., 311
Sułkowicz, Mrs, 244
Sułkowicz, Rywcia, 246
Sułkowicz, Rywka, 259
Sułkowicz, S., 60, 73, 244
Sułkowicz, Szmul, 76, 305–8, 305, 310
Summer, Nachum/Nathan, v–vi, xv, 190, 249, 257, 263, 275, 279, 294–95
Światłowski Brothers, 141
Światłowski, Benjamin, 136
Światłowski, Mojsze, 75
Swinto [Gestapo], 220
Syngalowski, 187
Szaferman, Berl, 63
Szafman, A., 73
Szafman, Abraham, 137, 204, 206, 236
Szafman, Ester, 66
Szaibowicz, Joseph, 211
Szajber[?], Eli, see Goldberg, Eli
Szajbowicz, see also Shaibowicz
Szajbowicz, Basia, 402
Szajbowicz, Gabriel, 402
Szajbowicz, Gecel, 402
Szajbowicz, Josef, 140, 402
Szajbowicz, Josef Baruch, 29
Szajbowicz, Josele, 402
Szajbowicz, Lajbel ben Gecel, 402
Szajbowicz, Lajbl (aka Lajbl Byk), 27
Szajbowicz, Mendel, 402
Szajbowicz, Monisz, 140, 402
Szajbowicz, Pesa, 402

Szajbowicz, Ruchele, 402
Szajbowicz, Rywele bas Jankiel, 402
Szajbowicz, Sara b. Lerer, 381
Szajbowicz, Szulem, 402
Szajbowicz, Uri (aka Uri Glazer), 26
Szajnbach, Z., 244
Szajnberg, Josef, 305, 403
Szajnberg, Mojsze, see Har-Jaffee, Mojsze
Szajnberg, Mrs., 244
Szajnberg, Nechemia, 237, 403
Szajnberg, Rywka, 403
Szaldajewska, Gucia b. Wajnberg, 375
Szary, Emanuel, 341
Szechtman, 76
Szeps, Eliezer, 49, 79
Szeps, Ita-Małka m. Potasiewicz, 134
Szeps, Josef, 79
Szeps, Luzer, 77
Szeps, Mrs. Luzer, 77
Szeps, Syna, 49
Szeps, Wolf, 77, 79, 134, 163
Szmulewicz, Herszel, 27
Szmytke [Shabes *goy*], 51
Sznajder, Kozele, 32
Szotenberg, 136, 213
Szotenberg [innkeeper], 183
Szotenberg, Dawid, 145, 180–81
Szotenberg, Icze-Ber, 82
Szotenberg, Lyuba m. Rozenblum, 173
Szotenberg, Mojsze Aron, 14, 17–18, 38, 45, 56, 58, 82, 105, 173
Szotland Family, 304
Szotland, A. Z, 403
Szotland, Abraham-Machel, 75
Szotland, Chajela m. Nisenberg, 75, 336
Szotland, Dawid-Lajb, 75, 403
Szotland, Dwojra-Laja, 75
Szotland, Efroim, 75
Szotland, Ester, 75
Szotland, Fajga/Fajgele, 75
Szotland, Fajga m. Grynholc, 369
Szotland, Fincia-Laja m. Bercholc, 75
Szotland, Fiszel, 74
Szotland, Frymet, 75
Szotland, Gela m. Manhajm, 403
Szotland, Gila, 75
Szotland, Icek, 74–75, 336
Szotland, Josef, 74
Szotland, Marjem, 75

Szotland, Marjem m. Nisenberg, 365
Szotland, Mojsze, 75
Szotland, Mojszele, 188
Szotland, Chaim [rabbi], 334
Szotland, Rywa, 75
Szotland, Rywka m. Efroimowicz, 386
Szotland, Sura-Bluma m. Grynfeld, 74
Szperling, Aba, 376
Szperling, Mojsze-Dawid, 376
Szpicer, Majer Bunim, 57
Szpiro, Elke m. Halewi, m. Sapir, 49
Szpiro, Icek [rabbi] (aka Icek Brzeziner), 67, 123, 125
Szpiro, Fiszele [rabbi] (aka Fiszele Strykower), 23, 25, 47–48, 50, 79, 123–25, 327
Szpiro, Jankiele/Jekiel (aka Jekiel Brzeziner), 48, 79, 123, 125
Szpiro, Jeszajele, 125
Szpiro, Josef Jehuda/Lajb [rabbi], 47, 123
Szpiro, Laja, 47
Szpiro, Mojsze, 48–49, 79
Szpiro, Perla m. Holcberg, 50
Szpiro, Szymon Josef, 48, 50
Szufleder, Mordcha, 205
Szufleder, Szlama [rabbi], 51
Szulc Brothers, 141
Szulc, Fiszel, 137
Szulc, Lipman, 137, 246
Szulzinger, 60, 73
Szulzinger, Abraham-Icek, 402
Szulzinger, Ala, 402
Szulzinger, Bajla, Aszer, 402
Szulzinger, Chaim Baruch, 36, 72, 140, 246, 402
Szulzinger, Dawid Hersz, 72
Szulzinger, Dawid-Hersz (aka the tall *shoykhet*), 402
Szulzinger, Dina, 402
Szulzinger, Małka, 402
Szulzinger, Resza, 402
Szulzinger, Symcha, 402
Szulzinger, Szlama, 72
Szulzinger, Szlama (*shoykhet*), 402
Szwab, Jecheskiel, 79
Szwab, Mojsze Aron, 79
Szwajcer, Berysz, 378
Szwajcer, Rywkele m. Tuszyńska, 378
Szwarc, Aron, 404
Szwarc, Bina-Laja, 404

INDEX

Szwarc, Bluma, 404
Szwarc, Chaim-Icek, 366
Szwarc, Dawid, 404
Szwarc, Frajda, 404
Szwarc, Icek, 404
Szwarc, Jecheskiel ben Mojsze, 391
Szwarc, Josef, 366
Szwarc, Majer, 27
Szwarc, Majer Ber, 181
Szwarc, Marjem, 366
Szwarc, Mojsze, 399, 404
Szwarc, Necha b. Bernholc, 399
Szwarc, Rywka m. Rozen, 399
Szwarc, Sura b. Tajtelbaum, 366
Szwarc, Szlama, 404
Szwarcpelc, Szlama, 132
Szydłowska, Bruchecia b. Jakubowicz, 75
Szydłowska, Rajzel m. Nowak, 384
Szydłowski, Mojsze, 75
Szyf, Bela b. Lustig, 380
Szyftman, Lajbel, 181
Szyldwach, Ruchel, 402
Szymkowicz, Dawid, 246
Szymonowicz (Aron Aszer's), 56
Tabak[?], Luzer, 87
Tajczer, Rywka, 234
Tajerman, Mojsze [rabbi], 163
Tajfel, Laja b. Nowak, 385
Tajfel, Szlama, 385
Tajtelbaum, Herszel (aka Herszel Ajnbinder), 365–66
Tajtelbaum, Rywka b. Nisenberg, 365
Tajtelbaum, Sura m. Szwarc, 366
Tandejter, Zachariasz, 80, 91, 134
Tanenbaum, Fannie, 261, 275, 279, 281, 284
Teitelbaum, Szyja, 143
Temkin, Michał, 100
Temkin, Perla m. Mendlewicz, 100
Tenenbaum, Henry, 389
Tenenbaum, Mietek, 389
Tenenbaum, Ruth, 389
Tobiasz, Dawidl, 361
Tobiasz, Jankiel, 361
Tobiasz, Mechele (Marcel), 361
Tobiasz, Perla b. Abramowicz, 361
Toping, A., 291
Topolewicz, Abraham, 210, 382
Topolewicz, Chana, 382
Tornhajm, Mojszele, 52
Trunk, Izrael Jehoszua [rabbi] (aka Jehoszele Kutner), 101
Tryber, Izrael, 145, 236
Tryber, Mojsze Josel, 63
Tsanin, M. [journalist], 283, 287, 307
Tshes?, Abraham Mojsze, 59
Tushinsky, Fela, v
Tushinsky, Max (aka Max Tyson), 189, 275–76, 279, 378
Tuszyńska [nurse], 207
Tuszyńska, Chaja, 382
Tuszyńska, Dora, 378
Tuszyńska, Fajgele, 378
Tuszyńska, Fela, 382
Tuszyńska, Frajda, 378
Tuszyńska, Pola, 378
Tuszyńska, Regina, 378
Tuszyńska, Rywka-Laja, 379
Tuszyńska, Sura-Ita, 378
Tuszyńska-Szwajcer, Rywkele, 378
Tuszyńska-Topolewicz, Hendel, 382
Tuszyński, 104, 134, 218
Tuszyński, Abraham, 378
Tuszyński, Abramele, 59, 78
Tuszyński, Chaim Fiszel, 378
Tuszyński, Dawid, 218
Tuszyński, Devi [Parisian artist], 59
Tuszyński, Eli-Nisen, 379
Tuszyński, Fredzia, 378
Tuszyński, Hersz, 378
Tuszyński, Herszel, 378
Tuszyński, Icek (aka the deaf Icek), 59
Tuszyński, Icek, 56, 59, 378
Tuszyński, Izy, 378
Tuszyński, Jechiel Majer, 378
Tuszyński, Jerachmiel, 58–59
Tuszyński, Josef, 382
Tuszyński, Melech, 378
Tuszyński, Mojsze-Izrael, 382
Tuszyński, Syna, 379
Tuszyński, Szlama-Szymon, 382
Tuszyński, Szymon, 378
Tuszyński, Szymszon, 59, 378
Tuszyński, Tewel, 378
Tuszyński, Urcie [Uryn], 382
Tuszyński, Welwel, 378
Tuszyński, Zajnwel, 378
Tyson, Max, see Tushinsky, Max
Tyson, Mrs. Max, 378

Urbach, 220
Wagmajster, Joel, 97
Wachler [played bass fiddle], 57
Wajnberg, Abraham, 368
Wajnberg, Mania, 367
Wajnberg, Róża, 368
Wajnberg, Zyse, 367
Wajnberg-Szaldajewska, Gucia, 375
Wajnberg-Śrubka, Mindel, 375
Wajnberg-Zygmuntowicz, Gencia, 375
Wajnkranc (Bakel), Majer, 375
Wajnkranc, Chana, 375
Wajnkranc, Fania, 369
Wajnkranc, Hercke, 369
Wajnkranc, Mindel-Fajgel, 369
Wajnkranc, Naftali, 375
Wajsberg, Regina, 142
Wald, Abraham-Eliasz, 375
Wald, Arje, 319
Wald, Cyrel, 375
Wald, Dawid, 57
Wald, Hencia, 375
Wald, Jacob Leib, 253, 263
Wald, Jakub, 319
Wald, Natan, 46, 63, 375
Wald, Sonia, 375
Wald, Szymszon, 375
Waldman, 60
Waldman, Aron (aka Aron Pajger), 61
Waldman, Chana, 375
Waldman, Chuna, 306
Waldman, G., 320
Waldman, Gedalja, 244, 302, 304, 310
Waldman, Menachem, 375
Waldman, Perele b. Windheim, 375
Waldman, Pesa, 375
Waldman, Szmul, 375
Waldman-Łęczyska, Chana, 310
Walter, W., 289
Warhaft, Dr. Stanisław, 204–6, 223–24, 237, 260
Warhaft, Mrs. Stanisław, 237
Warshavsky, Mark [writer of "Oyfn Pripetchik"], 76
Warszajnlich, 176
Warszawer[?], Abraham, see Froman, Abraham
Warszawer[?], Josel, see Rogodziński, Josel
Warszawski, Izrael Mojsze, 33

Wasilkowski, 34
Wasserman, Mrs., 297
Watemakher[?], Aba-Hersz, 80
Watemakher[?], Luzer, 143
Waynshenker[?], Szulem, see Maliniak, Szulem
Web, S. [Łódź Social and Cultural Association], 238
Weinberg, Hershka, 249
Weinrib, Sally, 385
Weksler, Tyla (Tola) b. Halbersztadt, 103
Wika, Fiszele, 57
Windheim, Perele m. Waldman, 375
Winer, Dora b. Zagon, 223
Winter, 13
Winter, Emanuel, 61
Winter, Ester, 29, 160, 388
Winter, Gitel b. Bursztajn, 376
Winter, Jechiel Estusz, 376
Winter, Lajbuś-Mendel, 56, 376
Winter, M., 335, 376
Winter, Mordechai, 18, 26, 39–40, 46, 63, 105–6, 135, 208
Winter, Mrs. M, 376
Winter, Roman, 56, 82
Winter, Szulem, 77
Wiślicka, Marjem bas Aszer, 368
Wiślicka, Rywka m. Goldkranc, 368
Wiślicki, Dawid, 368
Wolborsky, Jack, 249
Wolf, Natan, 139
Wolfschmidt [German], 183, 213
Wolkoff, Maks, 406
Wołkowska, Matel, 406
Wołkowski, Abraham, 406
Wolman [pharmacist], 35
Wolman, Jachet, 393
Wolman, Jecheskiel-Dawid, 393
Wolman, Mrs., 35
Wolman, Szoel, 100
Wolman, Taubcia m. Mendlewicz, 100, 103
Wolman-Jankielewicz, 163
Wolrajch- Rozenberg, Chana-Jochwet, 401
Wyrobnik[?], Fajwel, 59
Yak[?], Mendel [father of Mojsze Yak], 52
Yak[?], Mojsze, 52
Yezhover[?], Mendel [*melamed*], 88
Young, Mr. and Mrs. A., 396
Zadoks, Herr [Mr.], 334

Zadów, Berl, 52
Zadów, Jankiele, 52
Zagon, Alter, 42
Zagon, Dora m. Winer, 223
Zagon, Jasza/Jakub, 204, 206–8, 219, 224
Zagon, Szyja, 205
Zagon, Lajzer, 205
Zagon, Perec, 244
Zagon, W., 73
Zagon, Wolf, 140, 306, 310
Zahavi, Josef b. Złotnicki, 304, 305
Zajde, Jankiel (aka Jankiel Zapałki/Zapałki-makher), 61, 63
Zajdenberg, 330
Zajdenberg, Simon, 331
Zajdman, Dawid ben Chaim, 377
Zajdman, Dina, 377
Zapałki/Zapałki-makher[?], Jankiel, see Zajde, Jankiel
Zeifert [Gestapo], 221
Zelig, Binem, 377
Zelig, Ester, 377
Zelig, Mojsze-Pinkus, 56, 139, 146, 377
Zelig, Sara, 377
Zelwiański, 187
Zerubawel, 29
Zeygermacher[?], Szaja, see Rozenblum, Szaja
Zgiwer, Chaiml, 63
Zigman, Celia, 290
Zigman, S., 393
Zigman, Sam, 289–290
Zimmerman, Sasha, 256, 276, 283
Zimnawoda, Karolina, 405
Zimnawoda, Róża, 405
Złotnicki, Josef (Zahavi), 304
Złotnicki, Mojsze, 36
Zomb, Mendel, 59
Zwerin, Anna, 262
Zycher, Dawid, 244, 305–6
Zycher, Mrs., 244

Żydek, Welwel, 163, 393
Zygmunt, Jankiel-Mojsze, 140
Zygmunt, Mojsze, 246
Zygmuntowicz Brothers, 180
Zygmuntowicz, Bela, 187
Zygmuntowicz, Emanuel, 14, 17–18, 38, 46, 56, 82, 105
Zygmuntowicz, Gencia b. Wajnberg, 375
Zygmuntowicz, Janek, 145, 181
Zygmuntowicz, Moniek, 145, 181
Żychlińska, Chana-Golda m. Jubiler, 58, 73, 163
Żychlińska, Fajgele, 75
Żychlińska, Masza, 167
Żychlińska, Ruchel, 74
Żychliński, Chaim, 74, 377
Żychliński, Fiszel, 74
Żychliński, Fiszel (aka Fiszel Shoykhet), 58
Żychliński, Frankel, 377
Żychliński, Icze, 377
Żychliński, Jume, 74
Żychliński, Lajbele, 36, 43, 49, 75, 163
Żychliński, Lajbele [son of Fiszel], 58
Żychliński, Lazar, 74
Żychliński, Luzer, 377
Żychliński, Syna, 43, 49, 74
Żychliński (Frankel), Syna, 377
Żychliński, Szmul, 74
Zylberberg, Abraham-Michal, 383, 407
Zylberberg, Cywka b. Milsztajn, 383, 407
Zylberberg, Gitele, 383, 407
Zylberberg, Mordechai, 383, 407
Zylberberg, Pesa m. Ikka, 362
Zylberberg, Szulem, 383, 407
Zylbercan, Abraham, 302
Zylberman, Syna, 181
Zylbersztajn, Josel, 246
Zylberwaser, Chana b. Amzel, 362
Zysholc, Mrs. S., 374
Zysholc, S., 374
Zyskind, Josef, 246

www.ingramcontent.com/pod-product-compliance
Lightning Source LLC
Chambersburg PA
CBHW082002150426
42814CB00005BA/198